Wisconsin Folklore

Wisconsin Folklore

Edited by
James P. Leary

THE UNIVERSITY OF WISCONSIN PRESS

The University of Wisconsin Press
2537 Daniels Street
Madison, Wisconsin 53718

3 Henrietta Street
London WC2E 8LU, England

1   3   5   4   2

Printed in the United States of America

Library of Congress Cataloging-in-Publication Data
Leary, James P.
Wisconsin folklore / edited by James P. Leary.
560 pp.   cm.
Includes bibliographical references and index.
ISBN 0-299-16030-0 (cloth: alk. paper).
ISBN 0-299-16034-3 (pbk.: alk. paper)
1. Folklore—Wisconsin.   2. Wisconsin—Social life and customs.
I. Title.
GR110.W5L43   1998
398.2'09775—dc21   98-16371

For Janet

CONTENTS

Part Two. Storytelling

Part Three. Music, Song, and Dance

Part Four. Beliefs and Customs

Part Five. Material Traditions and Folklife

In 1846, two years before Wisconsin became a state, the English scholar William J. Thoms coined the word "folklore." A partisan in the romantic and nationalist movements that swept Europe in the mid-nineteenth century, Thoms was fascinated by the sayings, stories, music, songs, beliefs, customs, and crafts practiced by English peasants. He felt, as did the Brothers Grimm in Germany, that intellectuals and artists need no longer look for inspiration beyond the medieval "dark ages" to the "classical" cultures of Greece and Rome; rather they could find more appropriate and immediate stimulation in the traditions of their own humble peasants. Thoms and others like him also recognized that folklore was far more than mere raw material awaiting transformation by an educated elite, it was valuable in its own right not only for its aesthetic qualities but also because it expressed the experiences, the attitudes, the "soul" of a given nation's ordinary people.

More than 150 years later, on the occasion of Wisconsin's sesquicentennial, my own interests and motives as the compiler of an anthology of Wisconsin's folklore differ little from William J. Thoms and the Grimms. To be sure, like most contemporary folklorists, my notion of "folk" extends far beyond peasants, my sense of "tradition" embraces change as much as continuity, and my all-inclusive concept of just who constitutes a place's "people" counters perversely narrow interpretations that have justified potato famines, pogroms, holocausts, and ethnic cleansings.

But I am very much a hardcore cheesehead. I was born and raised in Wisconsin and, for me, it is the center of the world. I don't mean this in a narrow chauvinistic sense. I believe that every place is, for its particular people, the center of the world, and that no place is inherently better than any other place. But Wisconsin is my center, my place, and, echoing America's southern regionalists, Wisconsin is where "I'll take my stand."

I was born in 1950 and raised in Rice Lake, where my parents had built a home at the city's edge, between a woods, a swamp, and two lakes—a few hundred yards from the site of an old trading post where Frenchman August Carot swapped goods for pelts harvested by local Ojibwe. Our near neighbors were German, Bohemian, Norwegian, French Canadian, and Irish. Mostly Catholics and Lutherans, they were dairy farmers, loggers, woodworkers, gunsmiths, factory hands, and resort owners; some ran trap lines for beaver and muskrat, hunted ducks and deer, and fished year round; some picked mushrooms, gardened, and tapped sugar maples.

As a kid I hunted and fished, skated and skied, worked on haying crews and peeled bark with a spud in the pulpwoods. I heard jokes about Ole and Lena performed in lilting dialect by wool-clad former lumberjacks whose cheeks bulged with "snoose." I sampled the Tschernachs' homemade sauerkraut and sniffed the lutefisk for sale in Gammelgard's Grocery. I ate aged Swiss from Hilfiker's cheese factory that was so sharp it made my mouth itch, and I sneaked into Broome's Club 48 for a draft of Breunig's Lager Beer. I played "Dirty Clubs" in Mike Gesicki's basement, danced the polka at Sokup's Tavern, and listened to WJMC radio when you could still hear the Erik Berg Band broadcast Scandinavian music "live" under the sponsorship of the Indianhead Rendering Plant.

All this and more marked me with what scholars call a particular worldview, *weltanschauung,* or *mentalitie.* At sixteen I went off to Australia as an exchange student, and then to school and work in Indiana, Ireland, North Carolina, Washington, D.C., and Kentucky. I came to think critically; to view my home territory from the inside and the outside; to evaluate, to compare, to contrast. But I had never really left home.

In 1970, as a junior in college, I learned that one could study folklore as an academic discipline. Four years later—after earning a B.A. in English Literature from Notre Dame and an M.A. in Folklore from the University of North Carolina— I found myself pursuing a Ph.D. in Folklore and American Studies at Indiana University. There I listened and looked, mostly in vain, for comprehensive accounts of the rich folklore I had encountered while growing up in Wisconsin and the surrounding Upper Midwest. Disappointed but determined, I began combing libraries, archives, and bookstores; seeking out some of the writers whose works I found; carrying a tape recorder to interview my old neighbors about their cultural traditions; and discovering with delight that a handful of others were doing the same thing.

This anthology invites readers to share my sense of discovery and delight, to glimpse Wisconsin's diverse folk cultural traditions, and to meet their practitioners and chroniclers. Choosing what to include, however, has not been easy. I have done my best to rely on the twin criteria of readability and representation.

Regarding readability, the essays that follow are chiefly descriptive, although more than a few are suffused with theoretical sophistication. Some include highly technical passages concerning, for example, construction techniques for drums and boats, dance steps, and the nuances of vocal performance. But all of the essays avoid the excessive academic jargon that occasionally masquerades as learned discourse.

Representation is a trickier matter. Every individual's experience with folklore will vary, and one person's experiences can never be conveyed entirely to another through any medium. But we do what we can. I chose the essays here primarily because they present the full range of the state's most prevalent and distinctive traditions, past and present. I have also tried to offer a fair reflection of the folklore bound up with Wisconsin's evolving ethnic and occupational cultures; its men and its women; its geographical subregions; its urban, small town, and rural settings. The particular authors, from 1884 through 1998, likewise are anthropologists, ethnomusicologists, folklorists, historians, journalists, museologists, ordinary citizens moved to reminisce, sociologists, students satisfying term paper requirements, and writers of fiction—all of whose work accurately spans the varied prose styles and perspectives applied to Wisconsin's folklore. Since folklorists, predictably, have written the most about the state's folklore, their work is included to a greater extent, and it is cast not only in the format of polished articles but also in the modes of exhibit text, fieldwork report, and edited interview transcription that exemplify current public folklore practice.

The essays are clustered with regard to the forms or genres of folklore, partly because the plethora of Wisconsin's cultural groups would have made any other arrangement unwieldy, but mostly because, through juxtaposition, I hope readers will apprehend both the distinctions and the parallels between, for example, Algonquian and German place names, or Norwegian fiddlers and Hmong *qeej* players. Beyond selecting and arranging the essays, I have preceded each with commentary that combines personal observations, supplemental references, biographical information, and remarks on their various historical, theoretical, and institutional contexts.

This anthology has been a long time coming and I am happy to acknowledge many debts. In the spring of 1975, the late John Meggers extended me the opportunity to teach Folklore of Wisconsin at Rice Lake's University of Wisconsin–Barron County campus, over which he presided as dean. Full of enthusiasm and trepidation, I persuaded Warren Roberts, in whose Indiana Folklore course I was enrolled at the time, to allow me to compile an annotated bibliography of Wisconsin folklore. Many of the articles I located that semester have found their way into this anthology.

Since then I have been able to pursue my interests in Wisconsin's folklore with the support and inspiration of many individuals and institutions. The latter include, among others, the Cedarburg Cultural Center, the Chippewa Valley Museum, Folklore Village Farm, the Hocak Wazijaci Language and Culture Program, the John Michael Kohler Arts Center, the National Endowment for the Arts, Northland College, the Smithsonian Institution, the State Historical Society of Wisconsin, the Wisconsin Arts Board, the Wisconsin Folk Museum, the Wisconsin Humanities Council, and especially the Folklore Program at the University of Wisconsin–Madison, where I have been employed intermittently since 1984.

Within those organizations and elsewhere, fellow scholars and enthusiasts have generously shared their insights and excitement with me. I cannot hope to mention them all, but those who come to mind most often include: Lisa Akey, Arnie Alanen, Terese Allen, Lois Anderson, Bob Andresen, Jim Bailey, Tom Barden, Phil Bohlman, Bruce Bollerud, Metin Ekici, Ken Funmaker, Sr., Matt Gallman, Robert Gard, Janet Gilmore, Michelle Greendeer, Victor Greene, Gina Grumke, Jack Holzheuter, Niels Ingwersen, Lewis Koch, Jack Kugelmass, Marina Lachecki, Geri Laudati, Nancy Lurie, Richard March, Phil Martin, Tom Martin-Erickson, Marjorie McClellan, Susan McLeod, Doug Miller, Roger Mitchell, Juha Niemela, Ruth Olson, Emily Osborn, Tim Pfaff, Anne Pryor, V. Narayana Rao, Judy Rose, Harold Scheub, Joanne

Stuttgen, Steve Sundell, George Talbot, Randy Tallmadge, Bob Teske, Bill Tishler, Tom Vennum, Mark Wagler, Walker Wyman, Phillip Zarrilli, and Mary Zwolinski.

I might never have compiled this anthology, however, had it not been for Mary Elizabeth Braun of the University of Wisconsin Press who encouraged me to produce a manuscript. Once underway, John Solon offered invaluable service as he scanned some of the lengthier essays into a computer, and Rosemarie Lester enlightened me regarding the spelling and meaning of Wisconsin German expressions. The generous and perceptive criticisms of Jan Harold Brunvand and Tom Vennum, who carefully read my work in progress, have immeasurably improved its final rendition.

My mom, Patricia Berigan Leary, died in 1992. She and my dad, Warren Leary, fostered my passion for cultural expressions and helped me see them in my own backyard.

Janet Gilmore, fellow folklorist and partner in life, has been my best friend and critic as we have traversed the state that I love almost as much as she does her native Oregon. I dedicate this book to her.

Wisconsin Folklore

Introduction: On Wisconsin Folklore

James P. Leary

The notion of Wisconsin folklore begs consideration of the palpable yet elusive nature of Wisconsin itself. Wisconsin, the word, is an anglicized spelling of a French version of one or several native expressions variously attributed to the Ho-Chunk, the Menominee, and the Mesquakie (Vogel 1965). Wisconsin, the place, emerged as a descriptive phrase for an indefinite area, gained physical and political dimension with its designation as a territory in 1836, then saw its boundaries shift and shrink prior to statehood in 1848.

Wisconsin—as not just a word, place, or political entity but as an idea—has long resonated with people and with culture, with folk and with lore. And Wisconsin folklore, like Wisconsin's people, is unarguably heterogenous, diverse, pluralistic. Yet it is also creolized, hybridized, amalgamated—contributing to a north coast cultural booyah, a hearty one-pot meal of varied origins, that is every bit as grand as the chowder, gumbo, or salsa of more celebrated American regions.

Peoples, Words, and Foods

Recent national surveys tell us that Wisconsin, "America's Dairyland," leads the nation in cheese and milk production. Wisconsin has the highest incidence of obesity of any state, it leads the country in per capita brandy consumption, and is consistently among the leaders in beer consumption. Some observers have linked these facts to the state's northern and central European heritage (Vogeler 1986: 9–15). In 1890, Wisconsin ranked first among states east of the Mississippi in its percentage of foreign-born residents; and those residents were overwhelmingly northern and central European (Rippley 1985: 43). In 1980, when the United States census gave people the option of indicating a specific ancestry, 91 percent of the people in Wisconsin cited particular nationalities. Only North Dakota, Minnesota, and Hawaii had higher proportions of respondents.

Wisconsinites are clearly conscious of their own and others' ethnicity. When I first entered grade school in the mid-1950s one of the first questions I recall hearing was "what nationality are you?" By that time I was quite aware that I was Irish and, having listened to my dad, I could already match my neighbors' surnames with their ethnicity: Uchytil was Bohemian, Gagner was French Canadian, Rogowski was Polish, DeGidio was Italian, Eidsmoe was Norwegian, Ahonen was Finnish, Lawton was English, Destache was Belgian, Ivanauskas was Lithuanian, Schaubschlager was German, and Bandli was Swiss.

Roaming the grocery store with my mother I often overheard locals ordering jars of *sill* (Norwegian for pickled herring), or commenting on their taste for *schmierkäse* (German for cottage cheese—sometimes spelled "smearcase" on handwritten store signs). When gathered with my buddies on the grade school playground, I delighted in singing "Ninety-nine Bottles of Beer on the Wall" and, eventually, "In Heaven There is No Beer." I subsequently learned parts of the latter song in its original German, and I have since heard it sung by Wisconsinites in Walloon French and Norwegian.

I considered this diversity normal until I went to school outside the state and was told that the names of my schoolmates back home were "weird," that some of my expressions were "foreign," that not every kid sang songs about beer, and that I "talked funny."

In the early 1920s, Konrad Bercovici toured ethnic enclaves in the United States, compiling material for a book chronicling the adaptation of various immigrant groups to rural American life. Bercovici must have consulted the work of George W. Hill, a professor at the University of Wisconsin, who compiled ethnic maps based on state census data:

The state of Wisconsin, upon which the countries are marked in different color to denote the various foreign populations, makes that state look like a colored checker-board. There is not a single nation on earth that is not represented. The names of some of the towns and townships convey the information that the whole world is represented in Wisconsin. There is a Geneva, a Denmark, a Kaukauna, a Casanovia. There are names of French origin as well as German, Scandinavian, and many other nationalities, all within the bounds of the state of Wisconsin. . . . No other State has been populated so rapidly by foreign population as Wisconsin. One can literally pass through Wisconsin with any language one happens to possess, sure in advance of finding someone to speak to. (Bercovici 1925: 35)

Fifty years later, when my Oregonian wife, Janet Gilmore, first visited Wisconsin, she had the impression that most of the people she met spoke English as a second language.

Linguists with an interest in dialect have commented on the influence of various "foreign" tongues, particularly German, on variants of Midwestern English spoken in Wisconsin. The English "th" sound is typically reduced to "t" or replaced by "d" among older speakers of German, Scandinavian, Finnish, Slavic, and Italian ancestry who prefer "dis," "dat," "dem," "dese," and "dose" to their Standard American English counterparts. The German and Scandinavian *ja*, sometimes spelled as "ya" or "yah," is the standard Wisconsin equivalent of "yes." The German preposition *bei*, meaning "at," is often rendered "by" by Wisconsin speakers who reckon "by Joe's dey say t'ings are pretty busy yet," or "you can get a good deal by Shopko."

I.1. A "brat fry" in Sheboygan celebrates the German culinary heritage of America's "wurst city," 1950s. Wisconsin Folk Museum Collection, courtesy Mead Public Library, Sheboygan.

Likewise a child who is sick or who is not permitted to visit a friend's house might be told, "You stay to home," from the German *zu haus.* The German intensifier *einmal* or simply *mal*—which literally means "once" but actually signifies "why don't you"—is frequently incorporated into Wisconsin English in expressions like "come over once," or "get me a beer once." Meanwhile, in Milwaukee especially, the Yankee contraction "ain't" is combined with a German dialect rendering of *nicht* (not) as *ne* to make "aina" or "enna"—an expression understood to mean "isn't that true?" For example, "The Brewers are pretty lousy this year, aina?"

While Germanisms flavor Wisconsin talk, German drink and food have become statewide fare. Milwaukee, once dubbed the "German Athens," has also been known as "Beer City" in recognition of the economic rise of such late-nineteenth-century German *braumeisters* as Blatz, Miller, Pabst, and Schlitz. Meanwhile, the *bratwurst,* often served on a bed of sauerkraut and slathered with spicy mustard, is essential at summer cookouts and, in the "lake-to-lake" region (between Lakes Winnebago and Michigan), is the centerpiece of community fundraisers known as "brat frys" (Fig. I.1). "Sheboygan brats" are prized well beyond their home base, but they are especially appreciated in the greater Sheboygan area. Heather Teske, a friend and formerly an elementary school teacher near Sheboygan, was drilling her students with rhyming words that incorporate short "a" and end in "at." When presented with a "c," the class chimed "cat," when presented with an "r," they responded "rat," and so on with "p," "m," "fl," and "sl." When the kids came to "br," however, they abandoned the short "a" synonym for an unruly child to pronounce "brat" as if it were an abbreviation of *bratwurst*—"braht."

Wisconsin is also the state with the largest tribal variety of Woodland Indians, and it claims a greater population of native peoples than any state east of the Mississippi. Scores of American Indian names have been attached to Wisconsin's counties (Outagamie, Waushara, Kewaunee), cities (Menomonie, Oconomowoc, Waunakee), rural hamlets (Ogema, Tuscobia, Wabeno), and lakes (Windigo, Winnebago, Mendota). Outsiders commonly mispronounce these names and regard them as peculiar, but they are simply "everyday" words in Wisconsin that everybody knows and knows how to say.

An awareness of ethnic pluralism and a tendency to speak English laced with native and immigrant contributions both clearly characterize the cultural experience of Wisconsinites. Not surprisingly, there are numerous other examples of folklore that the state's residents hold in common. Most, for example, have participated in or been affected by the state's love affair with the Green Bay Packers; most have heard or told snippets about the legendary Ed Gein, perhaps Wisconsin's most famous criminal; most have a rich array of verbal, customary, and material responses to winter; and most have encountered sometimes heated expressions of rivalry between Wisconsin and neighboring states.

Packermania

Formed in 1918, the Green Bay Packers are one of the National Football League's oldest franchises. What's more, the team is owned by the community rather than some wealthy individual, situated in the NFL's smallest city, and named for humble meat packers. The Packers' antiquity, local base, and small town, even rural, working-class associations—not to mention their periodic success—have won them an extraordinarily loyal following throughout Wisconsin. Their 1996 championship season and victory in the 1997 Super Bowl, for example, were accompanied by a flurry of verbal, customary, and material folklore, which was linked in turn to ongoing traditions within the state.

One of the first jokes I recall hearing, in the mid-1950s, linked Lena, the heroine of countless Scandinavian dialect jokes, with the Green Bay Packers—and, by extension, allied the team with ethnic Wisconsin. In the mid-1990s, Lena's paramour Ole and his sidekick Sven figured in another joke I heard (and told) frequently:

Ole and Sven died in a boating accident on Green Bay and found themselves in hell. The devil had lots more friends in Chicago than in "God's Country," so he decided to really make them suffer. He turned the heat way up.

Ole was really sweating, but he turned to Sven and said, "Yah know, dis ain't so bad. It's yust like cutting first crop hay in Wisconsin in June."

The Devil didn't like that, so he cranked the heat up as far as it could go. Now Ole was really sweating and getting red in the face, but he turned to Sven and said, "Yah, dis is hot, but it ain't so bad. Yust like da hay mow back in Wisconsin in August."

The Devil was furious. He figured if he couldn't roast them, he could freeze them. Pretty soon it was fifty below. Ole was just blue, but he got really excited: "Sven! Sven! Da Packers are gonna vin da Super Bowl!"

Perhaps too esoteric for outsiders, the punchline referred back to the Packers' fabled victory over the Dallas Cowboys on the "frozen tundra" of Green Bay's Lambeau Field in 1967's "Ice Bowl." It also made contemporary reference to the Packers' inability to beat Dallas in big games during the 1990s.

The "Packerization" of stock ethnic characters in a familiar afterlife setting was paralleled in 1996 by a makeover of the Lord's Prayer that circulated via photocopiers, faxes, and the Internet. "Our Favre" beseeched the Packers' quarterback, Brett Favre, to lead the team to the Super Bowl in New Orleans:

Our Favre, who art in Lambeau, hallowed be thy arm. Thy Bowl will come, it will be won, in New Orleans as it is in Lambeau. Give us this Sunday our weekly win, and give us many touchdown passes. But do not let others pass against us. Lead us not into frustration, but deliver us to Bourbon Street. For thine is the MVP, the best in the NFC, and the glory of the cheeseheads, now and forever. Go get 'em.

Nor is the religious association with the Packers anything new. During the team's "glory days" in the 1960s, the priests in my hometown invariably hurried the last service on "Packer Sundays" and instructed churchgoers to drive safely as they left for their television sets. The introduction of Saturday evening masses in the 1970s quickly became very popular during the football season.

Magical beliefs or superstitions likewise cluster around Packer games, as they do around any significantly regarded yet unpredictable activity. Nicole Zimmer, a student in my fall 1996 American Folklore course at the University of Wisconsin–Madison, reported that her friend, Phillip Van Heiden of Chippewa Falls, wears a Packer jersey in the belief that it will affect the team's performance:

He told me a story that supported his claim that it is a lucky shirt. When he went back home to Chippewa Falls for a weekend last year, his mom washed the jersey on Saturday. When the Packers played the next day, they lost. Phil attributes this to having the luck "washed out" of his shirt. A similar event happened this year when his mom washed the jersey, and instead of losing, the Packers played poorly during the first half until "I got the luck back in the shirt," says Phil. The Packers went on to win the game. Because of this, he or his mom only wash the shirt about once a football season.

Countless other Packer fans similarly attempt to ensure their heroes' triumph by engaging in recurrent actions or donning special regalia in colors ranging from the team's green and gold to the fluorescent orange that doubles as deer hunting garb.

The State Ghoul

The perverse autumnal deeds of Ed Gein, a Plainfield bachelor farmer, are nearly as memorable in Wisconsin as those of Packer quarterbacks Bart Starr and Brett Favre. Gein is notorious for murdering two women in 1957, one of whom he gutted and butchered like a deer. A subsequent investigation of the killer's home revealed that he had regularly robbed women's graves and, relying on the tanning and taxidermic skills of many an "up north" woodsman, had turned their body parts into assorted furniture, articles of clothing, and displays. In his monograph on Gein, folklorist Roger Mitchell of Eau Claire observes that lore concerning Gein "seems to bring out the worst in Wisconsinites and residents in nearby Minnesota." Mitchell's data, drawn from ninety-two informants in sixty-six Wisconsin communities, includes numerous crude jokes and rhymes about Gein—many of which remain in circulation. Among them:

Why was Ed Gein expelled from school? He was such a cut up.

• • •

Didn't you hear? Gein was released from Waupun and they got him a job . . . but he got to moonlighting and they sent him back to Waupun. . . . They caught him selling arms to the Arabs.

• • •

> An old man from Plainfield named Ed
> Never took a woman to bed.
> When he wanted a little,
> He cut out the middle,
> And hung the rest in a shed. (Mitchell 1979: 50)

Far from wishing to forget about Gein, some Wisconsinites take a perverse pleasure in noting that a fiend from their state partially inspired motion pictures such as *Psycho* and *The Texas Chainsaw Massacre*. Indeed, a friend of mine who has Wisconsin roots but lives in Washington, D.C., made a point of buying books on Gein for friends in the nation's capitol—much in the way that Floridians might dole out a case of grapefruit or Kentuckians might bestow a flask of bourbon.

The Long Winter

While Gein's deviance may coax macabre associations with the late autumn deer hunt, winter brings out other lore among Wisconsinites. In a place where it is proverbial to complain that the year typically consists of "nine months of winter and three months late in the fall," people are especially adept at artful talk about the coldest season. Some refer ironically to Milwaukee as "the Riviera of the Arctic Circle," while others inversely praise the south shore of Lake Superior with phrases like "it's colder by the lake." When sleet, then snow, falls, cars churn the stuff into "slush" that often clings to their frames in stalactite-like "snirts" (mixtures of snow and dirt). "Glare ice" on the highway can become dangerous "black ice"; meanwhile the first ice that "makes" on lakes is "glassy" until covered with a flat crust of "pancake ice" which, as spring approaches, becomes "rotten ice," "grey ice," or "honeycombed ice."

Habitues of Rice Lake's Buckhorn Tavern told me when I was a kid that the tunnels in decaying ice indicated the work of ice worms. I put enough credence in the legend to look for them when I rowed along a narrow channel of mostly frozen Lake Montanis during "break up" (melting) time. Otto Rindlisbacher (1895–1975), the original proprietor of the Buckhorn Tavern in Rice Lake and an accomplished taxidermist, festooned his walls with actual stuffed animals, as well as taxidermic hoaxes like the shovel-tailed snowsnake and the fur herring. The former, fitted with red glass eyes and painted a lurid green, was obviously carved from wood, but the herring, an actual fish with a pelt jacket, was more convincing. A mock scientific newspaper article vouched for its authenticity.

While legendary and tall-tale accounts associated with winter circulate widely in Wisconsin, they are not as common as true stories on recurrent themes. Over the years I have built up my own repertoire of personal stories regarding the biggest snowfall, or the coldest day, or the most treacherous driving, or the most consecutive days of shoveling I have ever experienced during a Wisconsin winter. Driving stories, in particular, branch into numerous subcategories: marathon journeys alone in a blizzard, narrow escapes on the ice, accidents, and encounters with snow banks. Nearly everyone who has ventured out between October and April can tell a few such winter stories—often amid the seasonal gatherings held to stave off "cabin fever."

Winter games and activities, many of them traditional, have long been an antidote to said fever. I learned very early, like my dad and my daughter, to lie on my back, flailing arms and legs, to form "snow angels." Soon I was chasing and being chased along pie-shaped paths trampled in the snow for a backyard game of "fox and geese." The school playground was the site for "king of the hill," enjoyed atop mounds of plowed snow. Bundled in our winter clothing, we boys also tackled one another amidst "pom pom pullaway," and strafed each other with snowballs. We built snow figures and structures when the snow was "packy."

When we were daring enough and the roads were slick, we tried "skitching" (skiing and hitching) by hanging on to a truck's back bumper. Like our parents and grandparents, we skated on the lake and on flooded lots, enjoying games like "tag," "crack the whip," and modified versions of hockey. Whereas some of our elders had fashioned skis from barrel staves, ours were store-bought; but like them we "panked" the snow to build small jumps. And when we were old enough to drive, we were foolish enough to fashion "doughnuts" by turning sharply and accelerating on snow-covered parking lots. Another of our tricks involved tying a toboggan to a car's back bumper and then dragging it and a rider over a frozen lake.

Frozen lakes were also the site for "hard water fishing." Small "shanty towns" still form each winter on Lower Rice Lake within sight of where I grew up. Most are and always have been homemade: cobbled from scrap lumber, paneling, and sheet metal; often fitted out with a window and a wood stove; some are of flat-roofed squarish design, others gabled rectangles resembling the old "two-holer" outhouses. Ice fishermen nowadays often buy their jig poles and tip-ups (set lines with flags that pop up when a fish bites); they favor manufactured ice augurs; and they haul their

I.2. A bait shop, woodpile, and snowmobile offer a typical "up north" still life. Bayfield County, 1989. Photo: James P. Leary.

gear on molded plastic sleds. Not so long ago, however, no such equipment could be bought. Dedicated ice fishermen like Bob Egan of Monona, John Feavel of Neenah, Dale Schuebel of Rice Lake, and many others fashioned their jigs from sawed-off broom handles and the arms of their tip-ups from umbrella spokes. They formed fishing holes with chisels made by welding axes or other toolbits to automobile drive shafts, and crafted wooden sleds to suit their ice fishing needs. Some sleds held a thermos of coffee or hot chocolate. But winter is likewise a time when many in Wisconsin swallow schnapps, egg nog, glugg, a Tom and Jerry, a hot toddy, or hot buttered rum. Certain taverns specialize in these old favorites and some even invent new drinks in honor of winter.

Images and Borders

Those who wander in search of winter drinks from Hurley, Wisconsin, into Ironwood, Michigan, or from Superior, Wisconsin, to Duluth, Minnesota, may notice little change when crossing the border. One common joke I have heard over the years involves a fellow who moves one summer from Ironwood to Hurley. Old friends ask him how he likes the change? "Oh fine," he says, "and I'll be especially glad in six months—I won't have to go through those cold Michigan winters anymore." (Ironwood and Hurley are adjacent border towns beset by exactly the same winter weather—fierce cold compounded with immense "lake effect" snowfalls.) The point of this joke, of course, is that there is little difference between northern Wisconsin and the Upper Peninsula of Michigan.

Perhaps one of the most effective ways of gauging the degree to which people of a given state have a sense of shared culture is to elicit attitudes about their state vis-à-vis neighboring states. While residents of the East and West Coasts may hold the parochial view that all Midwesterners are the same, those who live in the region are sharply aware of what links them with and separates them from their neighbors. Minnesotans, for example, delight in referring to Iowa as "Baja Minnesota," and they exchange numerous jokes about the supposed rusticity of Iowans: Q: Why do the football teams play on natural turf in Iowa? A: So the cheerleaders can graze at halftime. Iowans, meanwhile, joke that the secession of its southern counties to join Missouri would raise the IQs of both states.

Wisconsinites, for the most part, make few distinctions between themselves and dwellers in the Upper Peninsula of Michigan. The "U.P." was part of the old Wisconsin Territory until the 1830s, when it was ceded to lower Michigan in compensation for the loss of the "Toledo Strip" to Ohio. It was also effectively isolated from lower Michigan until the Mackinac Bridge was completed in 1959. Moreover, the U.P.'s native and immigrant peoples, its environmental features, and its logging, mining, commercial fishing, and tourism industries coincide with those of northern Wisconsin. Dwellers in the western Upper Peninsula especially often look to Wisconsin for employment, goods, and entertainment, emigrating to Milwaukee in search of jobs, traveling to Green Bay to shop, and tuning in the Packers and Brewers as often as Detroit's athletic Lions and Tigers. As Conga Se Menne, an inimitable Finnish reggae band from Marquette, put it:

> When they score touchdown or field goal,
> We shout out hooray.
> We go Green Bay, to watch the Packers play.

The lyrics to "We Go Green Bay" go on to mention "Yoopers," the jocular designation for residents of the U.P., as well as their attraction to Shopko, a regional discount department store (Conga Se Menne 1994). Commercial advertisers, not surprisingly, also acknowledge cross-state symbiosis. In the early 1990s, a television come-on for the Ford Motor Company offered a map of Wisconsin and the Upper Peninsula, while jingle singers crooned: "There're two special places to be: here in Wisconsin, and the wild U.P."

Perhaps because the border with Iowa is so small, because it joins sparsely populated rural areas of each state, and because it is not crossed by major transportation routes, Wisconsinites pay little attention to Iowans, with the annual exception of college football games between the Wisconsin Badgers and the Iowa Hawkeyes. Hardcore Wisconsin fans have had a particular antipathy toward Iowa coach Hayden Fry—most obviously because of his aggressive manner, but perhaps more so because he speaks an alien southern dialect that renders Wisconsin as "Wesconsin," and the fact that, until the arrival of UW coach Barry Alvarez, he had been successful at recruiting fine Wisconsin players to "turn" on their home state.

Wisconsin and Minnesota—which share, among other things, borders, climate, a progressive political tradition, and an abundance of citizens with Scandinavian and German heritage—enjoy a sense of cultural similarity. There are, however, rivalries and occasional frictions. To cite just one example, Minnesotans, as their license plates tell us, are justifiably proud of having "ten thousand lakes" that team with game fish. Wisconsinites, however, may wonder what's the big deal: after all, Wisconsin has nearly fifteen thousand lakes. Avid fishers also debate which state has the "best" fishing, often conceding that Minnesota boasts better walleye lakes, while fishing for muskellunge is unparalleled in Wisconsin. Interstate debates also center around which state produces the best fishers. In the late 1980s Governors Tommy Thompson of Wisconsin and Rudy Perpich of Minnesota made a symbolic attempt to settle the matter with a fishing contest along the border—on Lake Pepin. Nothing was resolved: one caught the most fish, the other caught the biggest.

Residents of northwestern Wisconsin are occasionally rankled by media bombardment from Minneapolis-St. Paul, the Twin Cities, about the prowess of football's Vikings and baseball's Twins. My dad, Warren Leary of Rice Lake, a diehard Packer and Brewer fan, refers to these Minnesota teams as the "Viqueens" and the "Twinkies." The Twin Cities area likewise sends thousands of tourists and summer cabin-dwellers into nearby Wisconsin, a very few of whom annoy the locals with manners which are, or are perceived as, loutish—prompting jokes like this one that made Rice Lake's coffee klatch rounds in 1995: Q: What's the difference between a cheesehead and a blockhead? A: The St. Croix River.

Wisconsin vitriol for outsiders, however, is chiefly reserved for Illinoisans and especially for those from Chicago. These sentiments are sometimes returned. A student in one of my Folklore of Wisconsin classes, Glenn Tacke, interviewed fourteen residents of the two states regarding "The Wisconsin/Illinois Rivalry." Since Tacke had lived in both southern Wisconsin and northern Illinois, he also drew upon his own experience.

High school friends from Illinois often jeered, "All there is in Wisconsin is beer and cheese and brats—why do you want to go there?" Dave Gray, of Crystal Lake, Illinois, exclaimed, "Those hillbillies, they don't know anything. 'Cheesehead' fits them perfectly."

Hillbillies? Cheeseheads? Whence these names?

"Hillbilly," applied early in this century to southern Appalachian mountaineers, has become a generic term throughout the United States. On the one hand, it may be used pejoratively by outsiders to suggest rustic dolts. But insiders, the "hillbillies" themselves, sometimes use the word to express satisfaction in their "backward," yet fiercely independent, ways. I have heard folks in northern Wisconsin, for example, refer to themselves rather proudly as hillbillies. A contingent from Jump River, in northwestern Taylor County, participates regularly in summer parades decked out as classic jug-toting ragged hillbillies in a rattletrap car. Names like "jackpine savages," suggesting wild dwellers of the northern pinery, and "stump jumpers," referring to the difficulties of farmers on logged-off or "cutover" acreage (for an explanation of the term "cutover," see chapter 10, Roger Mitchell's "Farm

Talk from Marathon County," p. 93), are likewise declarations of independence when used by insiders and terms of ridicule when flung by outsiders.

"Cheesehead" is similarly double-edged. Wisconsin cheese is known throughout the country. Billboards across Wisconsin, and particularly along the southern border with Illinois, tout the cheese, which tourists purchase from specialty shops. In the mid-1980s, when designs were submitted to replace the state's butter-colored license plates, then governor Tony Earl parodied New Hampshire's "Live Free or Die" motto to suggest that Wisconsin's might be "Eat Cheese or Die." Meanwhile, diehard fans of the Green Bay Packers and Milwaukee Brewers began appearing at games wearing on their heads cardboard triangles that were painted to resemble wedges of Swiss cheese. Mass-produced wedges of molded plastic soon lined retail shelves. Such regalia sparked a goofy pride in Wisconsin's chief export and its agrarian tradition. But the wedges have also exposed cheeseheads to taunts that they are rubes with brains of curdled milk.

That these taunts have come most frequently from Illinois is hardly surprising. Wisconsin resorts have attracted Illinois residents in considerable numbers since the 1920s. The bulk of the tourists have come from the greater Chicago area and have typically patronized summer playgrounds all over the state of Wisconsin: Lake Geneva, the Wisconsin Dells, Door County, and the Minocqua-Woodruff area. Accustomed to a fast-paced urban lifestyle, some Chicagoans seek respite in the slower, rural rhythms of Wisconsin. Perhaps a few mistake their neighbors' style as a sign of stupidity.

Wisconsinites, for their part, have mixed feelings about tourism. While some welcome the economic benefits of out-of-state visitors, others fear the consequences of excessive development by and for outsiders. Hence such terms of mild hostility as "Illinoyance," "Illinoitian," "flatlander," "berry picker," and "FIB." "Illinoyance" melds annoyance with Illinois. "Illinotian," like "martian," suggests visitors from another planet. "Flatlander," a counter to "hillbilly," refers to the flat prairies that occupy most of Illinois. "Berry picker" is a generic name for a tourist in northeastern Wisconsin; Pat Johnson, whom Glenn Tacke interviewed, attributes this term to the fact that bears often cross over into another bear's territory to eat berries. He adds that, in areas like Minocqua and Tomahawk, people from Illinois "just come up here to fish or boat for a week and then leave, they don't need to live with the litter or polluted lakes like we do." Finally, "FIB" stands for "fucking Illinois bastard." "FIP" (fucking Illinois person) and "FISH" (fucking Illinois shithead) have also entered the language of interstate rivalry.

The "fish" sobriquet is reminiscent of "sucker," the common term for an Illinoisan among Wisconsin residents of the early nineteenth century. Adele Gratiot, who settled in Lafayette County in 1827, offered an explanation in her memoirs that might well fit the current seasonal visitations of tourists from the Land of Lincoln:

Every spring, when the grass was high enough to afford pastures for their teams, large numbers would come and do all the heavy hauling during the summer, over beautiful prairies furnishing all they could desire. But at first frost they would all disappear not to return until the next spring. Their habits of migration being exactly timed with that of a fish called the "sucker," which abounded in all the creeks and rivers, caused the people of the upper settlements to give that name to those of the lower [i.e. Illinois] counties. (Draper 1883–1885, quoted in Bicha 1992–1993: 123)

In contrast to fair-weather "suckers," Wisconsin's hardier "Badgers" endured whatever the climate offered.

While much of the jousting between Wisconsinites and Illinoisans exists informally on the folk level, some of it has been spurred by advertising agencies, corporations, municipalities, and the press. In late 1989, for example, Appleton's Fox Valley Chamber of Commerce issued a postcard, "Street Art," that juxtaposed urban Chicago with the "tranquility of Wisconsin." The card's Chicago side offered a chalkline around a homicide victim, while the Wisconsin side displayed a hopscotch course. Some Chicagoans sent the card to the late *Chicago Tribune* columnist Mike Royko. Royko cited the card as a "cheap shot" about a serious problem, then went on to malign natives of the Badger State as "cheeseheads . . . content to chomp on bratwurst," and as deer-hunting, red-flannel-wearing, cow-kissing farm folk. The Associated Press picked up the "story" and it ran in various regional newspapers, including Madison's *Capital Times* where the February 2, 1990, headline read: "Hot Air Heats Up Badger War With Windy City." (As an etymological aside, I might add that the Second City's association with wind invariably reminds me that the name Chicago closely resembles *zhigaag*, an Algonquian word for skunk.)

While Mike Royko's stereotypical portrait was delivered tongue in cheek, and while it hardly describes the cultural variety found within Wisconsin, it does comment on some cultural facts about the state. Considered as a whole, Wisconsin *is* different from its neighbors, and especially from its Chicago neighbors.

Because of the cultural heritage of its people and the nature of its environment, Wisconsin folklore expresses an appreciation for ethnic pluralism, a fascination with the pleasures and horrors of small-town life, a gritty affection for the rigors of winter, and a rustic, egalitarian *joie de vive* which, however unsophisticated, remains a source of genuine pride.

The Study of Wisconsin Folklore

While verbal, musical, customary, and material folklore have been sustained vigorously by the many who have called Wisconsin home, that folklore's study has depended upon a few. The American Folklore Society, at the time of its formation in 1889, had but three Wisconsin members: Alice C. Chapman of Milwaukee, William F. Allen of the University of Wisconsin, and Ruben Gold Thwaites of the State Historical Society of Wisconsin (Camp 1989: 10). Five years later Gardner P. Stickney of Milwaukee grumbled that "The American Folklore Society . . . is at present but feebly represented in Wisconsin" (Anonymous 1894: 162).

The twentieth century, however, would tell a different story as the study of Wisconsin's diverse folklore has been undertaken by an array of scholars. Some have worked independently, but most have had the support of such organizations as the

University of Wisconsin, the State Historical Society of Wisconsin, the Milwaukee Public Museum, the Smithsonian Institution, the Library of Congress, and an assortment of public arts and humanities agencies. United in their passion for documenting folklore, they have differed in focus and purpose to include: literary scholars with an appreciation of oral traditions, anthropologists and historians of museological bent; performers and writers of populist inclination; and ethnomusicologists, historic preservationists, and folklorists with a commitment to public culture.

Out of the Ivory Tower

In 1919 Franz Rickaby traveled northern Wisconsin in search of narrative folksongs or ballads sung by the region's woods workers. Born in 1889 and raised in Springfield, Illinois, Rickaby distinguished himself as a poet and musician prior to earning an M.A. in English Literature from Harvard University in 1917. At the time Harvard was the center of American folksong scholarship. It was there that Francis James Child, an admirer of the Brothers Grimm, had compiled *The English and Scottish Popular Ballads* (1882–1898), a five-volume concordance of 305 ballad "types" or recurrent plots from the isle of Britain. An "armchair scholar" who worked only with Old World manuscript collections, Child nonetheless inspired a succession of genteel yet determined academic heirs to set down folksongs from the lips of their North American singers.

One of them, the Texan John Lomax, published *Cowboy Songs and Other Frontier Ballads* in 1910. Franz Rickaby was likewise fascinated by the frontier, in his case America's "Old Northwest," the "lumberjack frontier" of Michigan, Wisconsin, and Minnesota. Here he believed the isolated, dangerous, and demanding work of loggers would, as had been the case with cowboys, generate comic, heroic, and tragic ballads of the sort that flourished along the contested borderland of England and Scotland. Rickaby's *Ballads and Songs of the Shanty-Boy* (1926), published a year after his premature death from heart failure, was the nation's first full treatment of lumber camp folksongs (Greene 1968; Leary 1996). In addition to including texts, tunes, and annotations for such classic ballads as "The Jam on Gerry's Rock" and "The Little Brown Bulls," *Ballads and Songs of the Shanty-Boy* revealed the powerful influence of Irish *ceilidh* traditions on lumber camp performance, while sketching the biography of Wausau's William N. "Billy" Allen—a timber cruiser and logger poet whose "Driving Saw Logs on the Plover," "On the Banks of the Little Eau Pleine," and "Shanty Boy on the Big Eau Claire" were widely sung throughout upper Midwestern lumber camps (Laws 1964: 147–48, 152, 261).

The preoccupation of Franz Rickaby with what he called a "cultural frontier" was sparked not only by Francis James Child, but also by Frederick Jackson Turner, the University of Wisconsin historian whose "frontier thesis," propounded in a series of essays beginning in 1893, conjoined the American character with the westward pursuit of land. Curiously, while Rickaby found Wisconsin's "cultural frontier" epitomized in the folk ballads of William N. Allen, Frederick Jackson Turner drew fundamental inspiration from another William Allen—William F. Allen, one of Wisconsin's trio of charter members of the American Folklore Society.

William Francis Allen (1830–1889) was born in Northborough, Massachusetts, to an extended family of farmers, Unitarians, and abolitionists. Musically adept and an 1851 Harvard graduate in history and philology, Allen journeyed to the Sea Islands of South Carolina in November 1863 to teach newly freed slaves in a school sponsored by the Educational Commission for Freedmen (Epstein 1977: 304–10). There he became fascinated with the songs of former slaves and, in collaboration with Charles Pickard Ware and Lucy McKim Garrison, published *Slave Songs of the United States* (1867)—the first serious study of African American music and the work that launched the acceptance of "Negro spirituals" into America's musical canon. A member of the University of Wisconsin's faculty from 1868 until his death, William F. Allen undertook no more folklore research. Yet his folkloristic foray beyond the ivory tower imbued him with what was at the time "the heretical doctrine that scholars should use every possible tool in their quest for truth." Frederick Jackson Turner regarded Allen as the seminal influence on his own work, remarking: "I have never, in Johns Hopkins or elsewhere, ever seen his equal as a scholar" (Billington 1973: 36, 31).

The frontier, folklore, and woods workers likewise combined to fascinate K. Bernice Stewart and Homer A. Watt, respectively an undergraduate student and an English instructor at the University of Wisconsin. In 1916 Stewart and Watt coauthored the first scholarly assessment of the legendary timber giant Paul Bunyan (reprinted in this anthology, pp. 139–48). And like Rickaby and Turner, they drew inspiration from a mentor of interdisciplinary mien, Arthur Beatty.

Beatty (1869–1943) was an Ontario native who heard the tall tales of woods workers while growing up. Having just earned his Ph.D. from Columbia University, Beatty joined the English faculty at the University of Wisconsin in 1898. Primarily a specialist on the English romantic poets, and William Wordsworth in particular, Beatty was at Columbia during the early tenure of Franz Boas, the father of modern anthropology and the editor of the *Journal of American Folklore* from 1908 to 1924. Sojourning in anthropological fashion beyond the literary scholar's ivory tower, Beatty contributed articles that included Anglo-Celtic folk ballads sung in Wisconsin to the *Journal of American Folklore* in 1907 and 1909.

As a teacher, Arthur Beatty exerted a significant influence not only on Stewart and Watt, but also on Stith Thompson, the most internationally respected folklorist of this century, the eventual founder of the Folklore Institute at Indiana University, and the author of such essential works of folktale scholarship as *The Types of the Folktale* (with Antti Aarne, 1928), *Tales of the North American Indians* (1929), *The Motif Index of Folk Literature* (1932–1936), and *The Folktale* (1946). Under Beatty's tutelage, Stith Thompson completed his undergraduate degree in English at the University of Wisconsin in 1909, undertook his first comparative folklore research on the recurrent narrative forms (or "types") and the smaller plot elements (or "motifs") of folksongs and folktales, and delved into the folklore of American Indians. Until his death, Arthur Beatty "remained an advisor to Thompson" (Martin ca. 1977: 4; see also Thompson 1996: 35–39, 89).

Relics of Vanishing Cultures

Arthur Beatty's interest in the oral traditions of American Indians, unusual for a literary scholar of his generation, is perhaps attributable to his Ontario upbringing, Columbia training, and professional life in Wisconsin at a time when the state's richly diverse native cultures were undergoing scrutiny by a succession of anthropologists.

J. E. Fletcher's "Manners and Customs of the Winnebago" (1854) is perhaps the first work focused exclusively on the folklore of any of Wisconsin's Woodland Indian peoples—although one might make an argument for the editor of the work in which Fletcher's essay appears, Henry Rowe Schoolcraft. Schoolcraft (1793–1864) was an Indian agent at Sault Sainte Marie, Michigan, who married into a métis (mixed Indian and European) family from whom he gained a remarkable understanding of Ojibwe cultural traditions. His *Algic Researches: Indian Tales and Legends* (1839), chiefly concerning Ojibwe storytelling, was the first full study of American Indian folklore. It includes many narratives still told among Wisconsin's Ojibwe peoples (in this anthology, see "Wenabozho and the Birds" from the telling of Dee Bainbridge, pp. 126–27).

Like Henry Rowe Schoolcraft, the first anthropologists to document the folklore of Wisconsin's native peoples were employed or sponsored by the federal government, particularly by the Smithsonian Institution's Bureau of American Ethnology established by Major John Wesley Powell, an erstwhile natural scientist, in 1880 (Feintuch 1988: 251–52). The Bureau's workers largely subscribed to notions of cultural evolution derived from Charles Darwin's concepts of natural selection: "simple," "primitive" cultures were slowly but surely "vanishing" before the advance of more "complex" and "civilized" Euro-American culture. It was the duty of the anthropologist, therefore, to salvage what cultural relics still remained. This mission included not only the representative documentation—through writing, still photography, sound recording, and film—of an array of traditional verbal, musical, customary, and material traditions, but also the physical procurement of artifacts. Nor was the Smithsonian Institution, the "nation's museum," alone in its acquisitive zeal. Museums of natural history—whose purview included both the natural world and indigenous cultures—proliferated and competed throughout the United States, rivaled of course, by private collectors and dealers.

Notions of their inevitable disappearance to the contrary, Wisconsin's Ho-Chunk, Menominee, Ojibwe, Oneida, Potawatomi, and Stockbridge-Munsee cultures—as complex and civilized as any other—have persisted, albeit through many changes, along their own evolutionary lines. Yet despite premature, wrongheaded, ethnocentric notions about native cultures, the pioneering anthropologists investigating Wisconsin's Woodland Indian folklore succeeded in documenting an abundance of significant traditions. And indeed most were attracted to their work less for its relationship to an abstract theory than for its immediate testimony to the variety, dignity, and artistry of the human experience.

The cavalcade of anthropologists concerned with the folklore of Wisconsin's

Woodland Indians from the end of the nineteenth century through roughly the first half of the twentieth begins with Walter J. Hoffman, who from 1888 to 1891 published five articles in the fledgling *American Anthropologist,* and for the Smithsonian's Bureau of American Ethnology concerning the religious practices, games, and mythology of Ojibwe and Menominee peoples. Thereafter such researchers as Victor Barnouw, Samuel A. Barrett, Frances Densmore, Albert Jenks, William Jones, Truman Michelson, Paul Radin, Robert Ritzenthaler, Alanson Skinner, and Huron Smith—affiliated variously with the American Museum of Natural History, the Bureau of American Ethnology, and the Milwaukee Public Museum—chronicled everything from wild ricing customs and technology (Jenks 1902) to the building of birchbark canoes (Ritzenthaler 1950), from ceremonial dances (Barrett 1911) to place names and their narratives (Skinner 1919).

Frances Densmore (1867–1957) was arguably the most continuously active, prolific, and versatile anthropological chronicler of Wisconsin's American Indian peoples. Born in Red Wing, Minnesota, Densmore displayed an early aptitude for music, earning a degree in the subject from Oberlin College. In 1892 she heard a lecture by John Comfort Fillmore of Wisconsin's Ripon College on American Indian Music (regarding Fillmore, see Clements 1986: 217–18). And soon after, she met Alice Fletcher, author of *A Study of Omaha Indian Music* (1893), who would make pioneering sound recordings of Omaha singers from 1895 to 1897 (Lee and La Vigna 1985). Inspired by Fillmore and Fletcher, Frances Densmore turned her attention to the Woodland Indians of the Upper Midwest.

She began dubiously with a series of public performances consisting, in the manner of the era's genteel composers, of native music arranged for the piano. These parlor exercises were soon abandoned along with, eventually, the evolutionary theories of her anthropological predecessors. By 1901, Frances Densmore had commenced fieldwork with the Upper Midwest's Ojibwe singers, and in 1907 she began an affiliation with the Smithsonian's Bureau of American Ethnology that would last until her death. Notwithstanding this association, Frances Densmore's work "became increasingly independent" in the estimation of American folklore scholarship's leading historian, W. K. McNeil:

Her notes clearly indicate that the people she interviewed in her fieldwork were every bit as exciting to her as their music. Densmore considered herself to be a musical archeologist, digging up the songs of yesterday but, unlike some collectors with similar aims, avoiding hasty work and a sense of urgency that might antagonize informants. She preferred showing respect for these people as individuals, an attitude that helped developed a relaxed relationship with those from whom she collected. (McNeil 1996: 200; see also Vennum 1973)

The legacy of Frances Densmore regarding Wisconsin's Woodland Indian peoples includes published monographs on *Chippewa Music* (1910, 1913) and *Menominee Music* (1932); an unpublished book on *Winnebago Music* (1940); two documentary sound recordings produced by the Archive of American Folksong in the Library of Congress, *Songs of the Chippewas* (L22) and *Songs of the Menominee, Mandan and Hidatsa* (L33); hundreds of sound recordings and ethnographic photographs housed at the Library of Congress; and the first comprehensive study of *Chippewa Customs* (1929).

The Art of the People

A woman in a male-dominated profession, an erstwhile practitioner of western art music whose energies turned to "primitive" performance, and a tireless field researcher who almost singlehandedly captured the music of Wisconsin's first peoples amidst radical cultural changes, Frances Densmore was also the precursor of Helene Stratman-Thomas who, like Densmore, was supported by a federal agency, the Archive of American Folksong of the Library of Congress.

Stratman-Thomas (1896–1973) was born in Dodgeville, in southwestern Wisconsin. Although a German grandfather and nearby Cornish neighbors sang folksongs and Welsh hymns reverberated from a nearby church, her musical training was chiefly institutional and refined. She received bachelor's and master's degrees in music from the University of Wisconsin, then joined the faculty, where she taught courses and conducted the women's chorus. In 1939 Professor Leland Coon of the University's music department sought funding from the Library of Congress to document the state's folk music, ultimately tendering the project to Helene Stratman-Thomas. Neither folk nor folklorist, she warmed to the task.

State and federally sponsored folksong collecting flourished as never before just prior to World War II as fieldworkers labored for the Farm Security Administration, the Works Progress Administration, and the Library of Congress. Guided by tenets of populism and pluralism, these agencies and their workers extended previous documentary emphases on rural English-speaking blacks and whites to include peoples whose first tongue was "foreign" (Hickerson 1982). And so in the summers of 1940, 1941, and 1946, Helene Stratman-Thomas and a shifting trio of recording engineers visited forty-one counties in Wisconsin where more than 150 individual and group performers—representing over thirty Euro-, Native, and African American traditions in nearly as many languages—regaled them with over seven hundred secular songs, sacred hymns, and instrumental dance tunes (Stratman-Thomas 1948; Peters 1977). Her efforts placed Wisconsin alongside California, Florida, Michigan, and Texas as the first states to document a broad range of non-Anglophone musical traditions (fig. I.3).

Historic within the national context of folksong collection, Stratman-Thomas's work was also propitious with regard to Wisconsin's cultural evolution. The state was not yet a century old in 1941. There were many still-active singers and musicians whose traditions were rooted in Woodland Indian ways of life, in European village celebrations, in lumber camp entertainments, and in the festivities of preindustrialized and small-town existence. At the same time, private and public schooling in music, printed song books, phonograph records, radios, and "opera houses" hosting traveling professionals were engendering vernacular syntheses of folk and popular musical cultures.

I.3. Pioneering field researcher Helene Stratman-Thomas with traditional singer Harry Dyer, a former logger and Mississippi riverman, Madison, 1941. State Historical Society of Wisconsin, WHi (S75) 9.

Buoyed by ideological currents, federal dollars, and a wealth of musical performers, Stratman-Thomas was also aided by technological advances. By 1940, reliable cars, improved roads, rural electrification, and newly available, bulky-yet-portable recording equipment made it possible to capture music almost anywhere. We do not know if Helene Stratman-Thomas intended to survey Wisconsin systematically, but with the exception of Milwaukee (where she recorded just one singer despite the abundant presence of traditional musical cultures that persist today) and the extreme northeast (where Iron County's curiously neglected Gogebic Range continues to sustain diverse folk musical traditions), her forays extended from Superior to Kenosha, from Platteville to Rhinelander, and to numerous points between (Leary 1987).

The efforts of Helene Stratman-Thomas, undertaken within the national context of Franklin D. Roosevelt's New Deal, also coincided with her own university's embrace of the "Wisconsin Idea," an activist philosophy characterized by a commitment to public service and by the notion that "the boundaries of the University are the boundaries of the state" (Stark 1995). Most commonly associated with scientific, agrarian, economic, and public policy endeavors, the Wisconsin Idea has been applied as well to cultural matters.

In 1934, for example, University of Wisconsin Agriculture and Rural Sociology faculty worked with Slovak immigrant farmers in the community of Moquah, in Ashland County.

Professor G. Humphrey . . . was often a speaker and cattle judge during the Moquah Guernsey Fair Days, held yearly usually August 15 at Moquah. It was Profesor Humphrey that acquainted the Department of Rural Sociology at Madison of the customs of the Slovak people at Moquah. As a result the Department of Rural Sociology sent Miss Amy Gessner to Moquah to acquaint herself with the people, and asked them to put on a program for her. A program of Slovak dances and songs were held in the school house basement. The music was provided by Mr. Philip Johanik, Jr, who played his accordion, and Rudy and Paul Letko played home made drums. This program was so successful that Professor A. F. Wileden of the Department of Rural Sociology requested a program for himself and two other members of the department. Receiving much encouragement the group decided to organize. (Novak 1966: 29; Leary 1981)

Soon the Slovaks were performing throughout northern Wisconsin at Civilian Conservation Corps camps, county fairs, community picnics, and for school children (fig. I.4). And although this group disbanded in 1940, the children, grandchildren, and great-grandchildren of its members have participated in similar Slovak dance groups through to the 1990s. By not only offering scientific and technical assistance, but also encouraging Moquah's Slovak Americans to perform and display aspects of their folk culture, Professors Humphrey, Wileden, and Miss Gessner conjoined the Wisconsin Idea with the "Settlement House" movement established by Jane Addams. Intended to help newcomers adapt to American life, Addams's movement also stressed that the retention and public presentation of folk costumes, music, and dance might simultaneously promote immigrants' morale while encouraging their neighbors' tolerance (Addams 1981; Lloyd 1997).

Humanists and artists were the most active of the University of Wisconsin's

I.4. The Moquah Slovak Dancers in heirloom immigrant clothing typical of the Carpathian Mountains: the women arrayed in lace caps, bodices, and aprons, the men in woolen vests and pants. Bayfield County, mid-1930s. Courtesy Jerry Novak.

faculty in bringing Addams's notions and the Wisconsin Idea to bear upon the state's folk cultures. Prominent among them were: John Steuart Curry and Aaron Bohrod, who encouraged rural people to portray their occupational and ethnic cultures through painting and carving (Barton 1948); the Norwegian linguist Einar Haugen, who broadcast programs on Scandinavian and Scandinavian American folklore over Wisconsin Public Radio; and the dramatist, novelist, and storyteller Robert E. Gard.

A native Kansan, Gard (1910–1992) came to the University of Wisconsin in 1945 after stints directing the New York State Playwriting Project (1938–1943) and the Alberta (Canada) Folklore and Local History Project (1943–1945). Robert Gard was deeply influenced by Frederick H. Koch, founder of the Carolina Playmakers and "the major figure in American folk drama in the 1920s" (Glassberg 1990: 242; quoted in Lloyd 1997). Koch was in turn inspired by the Irish Dramatic Movement wherein Lady Gregory, John Millington Synge, William Butler Yeats, and other romantic nationalists drew upon the folklore of Irish peasants to create a literature that they hoped would convey the spirit and the art of the people. Robert Gard attempted the same for the people of Wisconsin:

Gard, both in his own writing and in his conception of theater, was a regionalist, a believer that persons could create valid and significant art by describing experiences that were unique to the area in which they lived. He turned first to developing playwrights. One of his methods was to present a weekly radio program, "Wisconsin Yarns," in which he communicated Wisconsin folk material that could be used by playwrights. (Stark 1995: 155)

One such playwright was David C. Peterson, Gard's colleague within the University of Wisconsin's Department of Continuing Education in the Arts. From the 1960s until his retirement in 1994, Peterson wrote and produced dozens of regionally based plays incorporating the folklore of Wisconsin's farmers, loggers, Great Lakes sailors, Woodland Indians, European ethnics, and African Americans. As for Robert Gard, he wrote, coauthored, compiled, or contributed to some forty books, including several directly concerning the folklore of Wisconsin: *Down in the Valley* (1971); *The Romance of Wisconsin Place Names* (1968); *The Trail of the Serpent: The Fox River Valley Lore and Legend* (1973); and *Wisconsin Lore* (1962).

Yet unlike Helene Stratman-Thomas, who carefully recorded the *individual voices* of Wisconsin's traditional musicians, Robert Gard most often invoked the state's folk raconteurs in *his own* voice, an Anglo-Kansan drawl. Indeed he was prone to "folksy up" or even invent the actual speech of Wisconsin talkers, whatever their dialects, until it conformed with the sort of homogenized aw-shucks inflections expected of generic rural Midwesterners within American popular culture. One rural storyteller Gard had met, Dale Muller of La Farge, put it this way: "Bob Gard came around here. And I've seen his books. Everybody sounds the same. They all sound like they've got a straw hanging out of their mouth" (Wagler 1997). Robert Gard was hardly unique in his methods. Like many fellow champions of the art of the people—indeed, like most writers who have sought to popularize folklore amongst as broad an audience as possible—Robert Gard purported to deliver the real stuff of folklore, when in fact it often served as raw material to be made over in his own romantic compositions. Such criticisms notwithstanding, it is important to remember that Robert Gard's chief motive was not to document regional folklore, but to stimulate a region's people to write—and in that regard he succeeded admirably.

Toward Cultural Democracy

Robert Gard's regionalist notion that we might find the universal in the local, that we might view the world in our own backyards, has been vigorously endorsed in recent decades by an array of scholars with a common interest in Wisconsin's rich folklore. Sometimes toiling together, often in conjunction with various state, federal, and private nonprofit organizations, they include dedicated amateurs, historic preservationists, ethnomusicologists, and folklorists. Evidence of their work suffuses this anthology. And like Robert Gard, one among many regionally based populist writers and dramatists, today's chroniclers of and advocates for Wisconsin's folklore have all been partisans in a larger cultural movement spawned by the dream of a truly inclusive "Great Society" that came swirling out of the 1960s.

A "public folklore" movement has emerged in America, and in Wisconsin, over the past quarter century (Baron and Spitzer 1992; Feintuch 1988). The Folklore Institute initiated in 1948 at Indiana University by Wisconsin alumnus Stith Thompson was flourishing by the 1970s, as were academic folklore programs in a handful of other universities. Schooled in intellectual inquiry, their students were also moved by social activism, by the desire to increase and apply their knowledge, to scrutinize and to serve. During that decade the Smithsonian Institution's fledgling Office of Folklife Programs and Cultural Studies came of age through the production, amidst the nation's 1976 bicentennial, of a twelve-week "Festival of American Folklife"—a massive accomplishment staged appropriately on Washington, D.C.'s, Mall and realized through the hired labor of scores of young folklore graduate students and hundreds of traditional artists and musicians from every part of the country. The mid-1970s likewise saw the creation of the American Folklife Center in the Library of Congress. Since its inception, the Center has succeeded not only in the expansion and increased accessibility of the Library's Archive of American Folksong, but also in working with the Department of the Interior, the National Park Service especially, to ensure that the conservation of America's heritage includes those cultural resources, both tangible and intangible, residing in the folklore of our nation's varied peoples. Since the late 1970s the National Endowment for the Arts (NEA), and to a lesser extent the National Endowment for the Humanities, have also fostered the documentation, preservation, practice, and public presentation of folklore, especially through the NEA's Folk Arts Program. Under the leadership of Bess Lomax Hawes, the Folk Arts Program has made grant funds available to establish parallel programs in every state. State folk arts programs in turn undertook projects and offered grants to encourage further grassroots recognition of America's varied folklore.

So it was that in Wisconsin, Philip Martin and Lewis Koch acquired federal and state grants in the late 1970s to record and photograph old-time Norwegian fiddlers, to launch a spate of media productions, and eventually to found, in Martin's case, the Wisconsin Folk Museum. So it was that William Tishler and Arnold Alanen of the University of Wisconsin's Department of Landscape Architecture, and Alan Pape of the Wisconsin Ethnic Settlement Trail (WEST), have been able to undertake the documentation and preservation of Wisconsin's ethnic folk architecture in local communities, historic districts, state and national parks, and through the State Historical Society's Old World Wisconsin—an outdoor museum of ethnic farmsteads that rivals the great folk museums established in Europe in the nineteenth century. Wisconsin's currently active public folklore veterans also include: Thomas Vennum Jr., senior ethnomusicologist for the Smithsonian Institution's Office of Folklife Programs and Cultural Studies, whose research among Woodland Indians, especially the Ojibwe, has resulted in books, sound recordings, and films chronicling powwows, drum making, wild ricing, and canoe building; Richard March, traditional and ethnic arts coordinator for the Wisconsin Arts Board, who created an apprenticeship program for traditional artists, helped broaden the audience for regional folk music through the "Down Home Dairyland" program on Wisconsin Public Radio, and oversaw the staging of Wisconsin's 1998 sesquicentennial folklife festival; Janet Gilmore, an independent folklorist and former curator of the Wisconsin Folk Museum, whose painstaking investigations of women's handiwork traditions and of the folklife of commercial fishers have resulted in exhibits, publications, and media productions; and Robert T. Teske, director of the Cedarburg Cultural Center, who has produced a quartet of traveling folk art exhibits and corresponding catalogs, most recently *Wisconsin Folk Art: A Sesquicentennial Celebration* (1998).

My own life and work have been bound with all of these people and with the full range of public folklore institutions. In June, 1975, as a young graduate student in folklore at Indiana University, I sought advice from Robert Gard prior to teaching a short course in Wisconsin Folklore at the University of Wisconsin's two-year campus in my hometown, Rice Lake. Later that summer, while photographing log buildings in Wisconsin's cutover, I met Bill Tishler and Arnie Alanen, who were conducting a survey of rural architecture from a base near Drummond. In 1976, Tom Vennum and I both worked for the Smithsonian Institution's summer-long bicentennial Festival of American Folklife, and our fieldwork excursions in northern Wisconsin have overlapped ever since. That fall Richard March—then likewise an Indiana folklore graduate student—and I gathered information on Wisconsin's ethnic communties for the Center for Twentieth-Century Studies at the University of Wisconsin–Milwaukee—the first of our many, mostly folk-music-related collaborations including the coproduction of more than 150 "Down Home Dairyland" radio programs. From 1980 to 1981, Janet Gilmore and I lived in Washburn, on Chequamegon Bay, where, thanks to a grant from the Folk Arts Program of the National Endowment for the Arts, I recorded the music and life histories of ethnic groups in the Lake Superior region. Janet meanwhile augmented her knowledge of Pacific Northwest commercial fishers with the practices of those working the Great Lakes. In 1985 I worked with Phil Martin and Lewis Koch on the first of many collaborative projects, this one concerning Wisconsin's German music. Three years later Janet and I would rent an office from Martin in Mount Horeb's Wisconsin Folk Museum, and we remained affiliated with that organization, acquiring grants and producing exhibits, until its demise in 1995. Since 1986, when Milwaukeean Bob Teske returned to Wisconsin after service with the NEA's Folk Arts Program, Janet and I have done research and written essays for a succession of "Teske-produced" folk art exhibits. I have also had the good fortune to teach "Folklore of Wisconsin" and other courses at the University of Wisconsin–Madison, since the Folklore Program's inception in 1984.

With the current generation of Wisconsin folklore scholars, I share a commitment to cultural democracy, to the conviction that we cannot understand the full range of Wisconsin's cultural life without recognizing that Ho-Chunk and lumber camp storytellers must be celebrated alongside such Wisconsin novelists as Edna Ferber, Zona Gale, Hamlin Garland, and Glenway Wescott; that the floral designs of Ojibwe beadworkers and Norwegian *rosemalers* yield as much in their own way as the images of Georgia O'Keeffe; that powwow drums and polka bands say more about who we are than symphonies and that the builders of Belgian bake ovens, Finnish log houses, German bank barns, and Polish shrines should be no less known than the visionary architect Frank Lloyd Wright. Indeed our ongoing research, publications, and especially our public programs concerning Wisconsin's diverse folk cultural traditions contend that folklore, beyond its "raw" utility for "fine" artists, eloquently articulates the experience and aspirations of paradoxically ordinary yet extraordinary people, and that it more than merits consideration in its own right.

I.5. James P. Leary interviews concertinist Bob Mathiowetz in the basement "music room" of his Ashland home, 1990. Photo: Don Albrecht, Wisconsin Folk Museum Collection.

Charles Edward Brown

Certainly Charles Brown recognized the intrinsic worth of Wisconsin's varied folklore. Pioneer, participant, and prophet, Brown contributed to or anticipated every phase of the study of Wisconsin folklore.

Charles Edward Brown (1872–1946) was born in Milwaukee. As a young man, he worked with American Indian collections at the Milwaukee Public Museum, then served as a curator of ethnology within the larger Louisiana Purchase Exposition in St. Louis, where he mingled with the era's distinguished anthropologists and archeologists. Brown was a founder and the secretary of the Wisconsin Archeological Society from 1903 to 1940, and served likewise as editor of *The Wisconsin Archeologist*. In 1908 he became director of the Wisconsin State Historical Museum, a post he held until retirement in 1944. Charles Brown was also named to the University of Wisconsin faculty in 1915 and taught courses in anthropology and museum administration (Halpert 1985).

Brown fixed his earliest efforts on creating "a statewide interest in the collection and preservation of Wisconsin folklore" at 1910, when he instituted a series of summer session programs on the University of Wisconsin's campus. Brown's first folklore publication concerned the legend of Paul Bunyan (Brown 1922). From 1922 through 1945, Brown authored some thirty Wisconsin-related pamphlets on topics ranging from lumber camp narratives to settlers' yarns, the legends of ghosts and monsters, the mythology of Woodland Indians, and the lore of flora and fauna. Brown also published occasional articles on Wisconsin folklore in the *Hoosier Folklore Bulletin* and *The Wisconsin Archeologist*, a publication that included numerous folklore entries under Brown's editorship.

From 1935 to 1938, Brown was instrumental in establishing a Wisconsin Folklore Project, based at the State Historical Museum, but largely funded by Roosevelt's WPA. Dorothy Moulding Miller (whom Brown eventually married) directed the Project, which supported clerical staff and several field researchers who investigated the folklore of ethnic and occupational cultures. During that period Charles Brown also assisted the National Folk Festival—America's still vibrant and oldest multicultural folk festival—in the inclusion of such traditional Wisconsin performers as Rice Lake's Otto Rindlisbacher and the Wisconsin Lumberjacks; Ho-Chunk singers and dancers; a troupe of Swiss yodelers and musicians from New Glarus and Monroe; a quartet of Norwegians from McFarland who played the *psalmodikon* (a plucked one-string instrument originally used to accompany hymns); Oconto French Canadian singer Mary Agnes Starr; and Milwaukee's Mazur Polish Dancers.

In 1939 Brown and Miller formed the Wisconsin Folklore Society which, besides issuing the couple's pamphlets, sought to foster a larger understanding of Wisconsin folklore by offering courses to summer school students at the University of Wisconsin. Brown also organized "sunset folklore meetings" on the terrace of the University's Memorial Union. Those gathered included Einar Haugen, the era's foremost authority in the realm of Scandinavian American Studies, the distinguished dialect scholar Frederic G. Cassidy (see chapter 9, "Apple-Picking Terms from Wisconsin," pp. 85–88), and Helene Stratman-Thomas from the University's School of Music. More than forty years would pass before a similar resurgence of folklore scholarship would occur at the University of Wisconsin.

It is hard to imagine a more dedicated and productive life in the service of Wisconsin's folklore than that of Charles Edward Brown. Yet as a graduate student, seeking to understand the study of Wisconsin folklore I once dismissed the few fragments of Brown's career I had then glimpsed through publications and papers lodged in the State Historical Society of Wisconsin. With youthful ignorance I held Brown to scholarly standards not established until after his death. My published annotations of his pamphlets, including *Bluenose Brainard Stories* (1943), even criticized Brown for offering "literary versions of presumably oral tales," for eliminating bawdy elements, for not revealing the sources from whom he acquired the tales, and for revealing nothing about the contexts in which they were originally told (Leary 1982: 57–59).

Fortunately, Herbert Halpert, a distinguished folklorist and someone who knew Brown slightly in the 1930s, chided me gently:

We must bear in mind that the modern stress on presenting context, on giving the storyteller's exact words . . . , and today's freedom to publish the obscene and scatological are largely post–World War II phenomena. Brown's texts, though obviously not in the language of the storytellers, are quite straightforward and not over-embellished. His small collections provide us with welcome evidence of the existence of certain story traditions that might otherwise have been lost. To protest that he failed to use currently approved folklore methods is unhistorical. (Halpert 1985: 56–57)

Hence I offer this history of the study of Wisconsin folklore, as well as the annotations which accompany this anthology's entries, in atonement and as a tribute to the life and work of Charles Edward Brown. Without his visionary efforts we would know far less.

Sources

Addams, Jane. 1981. *Twenty Years at Hull House.* New York: New American Library.

Anonymous. 1894. "Wisconsin Branch." *Journal of American Folklore* 7:25, 162.

Baron, Robert, and Nicholas R. Spitzer. 1992. *Public Folklore.* Washington, D.C.: Smithsonian Institution Press.

Barrett, Samuel A. 1911. "The Dream Dance of the Chippewa and Menominee Indians of Northern Wisconsin." *Bulletin of the Public Museum of the City of Milwaukee* 1:251–406.

Barton, John Rector. 1948. *Rural Artists of Wisconsin.* Madison: University of Wisconsin Press.

Beatty, Arthur. 1907. "Some New Ballad Variants." *Journal of American Folklore* 20:77, 154–56.

Beatty, Arthur. 1909. "Some Ballad Variants and Songs." *Journal of American Folklore* 22:83, 63–71.

Bercovici, Konrad. 1925. *On New Shores.* New York and London: The Century Company.

Bicha, Karel D. 1992–1993. "From Where Come the Badgers?" *Wisconsin Magazine of History* 76:2 (Winter): 121–31.

Billington, Ray Allen. 1973. *Frederick Jackson Turner: Historian, Scholar, Teacher.* New York: Oxford University Press.

Brown, Charles E. 1922. *American Folk Lore: Paul Bunyan.* Madison: State Historical Society of Wisconsin.

Brown, Charles E. 1943. *Bluenose Brainard Stories: Log Cabin Tales From the Chippewa Valley in the Wisconsin North Woods.* Madison: Wisconsin Folklore Society.

Brown, Charles E. 1943. "Wisconsin Folklore Society." *Journal of American Folklore* 56:221, 190–91.

Camp, Charles, ed. 1989. "Members of the American Folklore Society, 1989." In *Time and Temperature: A Centennial Publication of the American Folklore Society.* Washington, D.C.: The American Folklore Society.

Clements, William. 1986. *Native American Folklore in Nineteenth Century Periodicals.* Athens, Ohio: Ohio University Press.

Conga Se Menne. 1994. *Finnish Reggae and Other Sauna Beats.* Conga Records. CD recording, CR94–1CD.

Draper, Lyman C., ed. 1883–1885. "Adele De P. Gratiot's Narrative." *Wisconsin Historical Collections* 10:268.

Feintuch, Burt, ed. 1988. *The Conservation of Culture: Folklorists and the Public Sector.* Lexington: University Press of Kentucky.

Fletcher, Alice. 1893. *A Study of Omaha Indian Music.* Cambridge, Mass.: Archaeological and Ethnological Papers of the Peabody Museum, vol. 1, no. 5.

Fletcher, J. E. 1854. "Manners and Customs of the Winnebagoes." In *Information Respecting the History, Condition, and Prospects of the Indian Tribes in the United States,* vol. 4, ed. Henry R. Schoolcraft. Philadelphia: Lippencott, Grambo, and Co., 51–59.

Glassberg, David. 1990. *American Historical Pageantry: The Uses of Tradition in the Early Twentieth Century.* Chapel Hill: University of North Carolina Press.

Greene, Daniel W. 1968. " 'Fiddle and I': The Story of Franz Rickaby." *Journal of American Folklore* 81:322, 316–36.

Halpert, Herbert. 1985. "A Note On Charles E. Brown and Wisconsin Folklore." *Midwestern Journal of Language and Folklore* 11:1, 54–59.

Hickerson, Joseph. 1982. "Early Field Recordings of Ethnic Music." In *Ethnic Recordings in America,* ed. Judith McCulloh. Washington, D.C.: Library of Congress, 67–83.

Hoffman, Walter J. 1888. "Pictography and Shamanistic Rites of the Ojibwas." *American Anthropologist* 1, 209–29.

Hoffman, Walter J. 1889. "Notes on Ojibwa Folklore." *American Anthropologist* 2, 215–23.

Hoffman, Walter J. 1890. "The Mythology of the Menomini Indians." *American Anthropologist* 3, 243–58.

Hoffman, Walter J. 1890. "Remarks on Ojibwa Ball Play." *American Anthropologist* 3, 133–35.

Hoffman, Walter J. 1891. "The Midewiwin or 'Grand Medicine Society' of the Ojibwa." *Seventh Annual Report of the Bureau of American Ethnology, 1885–1886.* Washington, D.C.: Smithsonian Institution. 143–300.

Jenks, Albert E. 1902. "The Wild-Rice Gatherers of the Upper Lakes: A Study in American Primitive Economics." *Nineteenth Annual Report of the Bureau of American Ethnology, 1900.* Washington, D.C.: Smithsonian Institution. Part 2, 1013–1137.

Laws, G. Malcolm. 1964. *Native American Balladry.* Philadelphia: American Folklore Society.

Leary, James P. 1981. "The Musical Traditions of Moquah's Slovaks." *North Country Folk* 1:4, 4–8.

Leary, James P. 1982. "An Annotated Bibliography of Wisconsin Folklore." *Midwestern Journal of Language and Folklore* 8:1, 52–81.

Leary, James P. 1987. *The Wisconsin Patchwork: A Companion to the Radio Programs Based on the Field Recordings of Helene Stratman-Thomas.* Madison: University of Wisconsin, Department of Continuing Education in the Arts.

Leary, James P. 1996. "Franz Rickaby." In *American Folklore: An Encyclopedia,* ed. Jan Harold Brunvand. New York: Garland. 625.

Lee, Dorothy Sara, and Maria La Vigna. 1985. *Omaha Indian Music: Historical Recordings from the Fletcher/La Flesche Collection.* Washington, D.C.: American Folklife Center, Library of Congress. LP recording and booklet, AFC L71.

Lloyd, Timothy. 1996. "Whole Work, Whole Play, Whole People: Folklore and Social Therapeutics in 1920s and 1930s America." *Journal of American Folklore* 110:437, 239–59.

Martin, Peggy. [ca. 1977]. *Stith Thompson: His Life and His Role in Folklore Scholarship.* Bloomington: Folklore Publications Group, Indiana University. Monograph Series, vol. 2.

McNeil, W. K. 1996. "Frances Densmore." In *American Folklore: An Encyclopedia,* ed. Jan Harold Brunvand. New York: Garland. 200.

Mitchell, Roger. 1979. "The Press, Rumor, and Legend Formation." *Midwestern Journal of Language and Folklore* 5:1–2. Special issue.

Novak, Jerry. 1966. *The History of the Moquah Area.* Ashland, Wisc.: Northland College Press.

Peters, Harry. 1977. *Folksongs Out of Wisconsin.* Madison: State Historical Society of Wisconsin.

Rickaby, Franz. 1926. *Ballads and Songs of the Shanty-Boy.* Cambridge, Mass: Harvard University Press.

Rippley, LaVern J. 1985. *The Immigrant Experience in Wisconsin.* Boston: Twayne.

Ritzenthaler, Robert. 1950. "Building a Chippewa Indian Birchbark Canoe." *Bulletin of the Public Museum of the City of Milwaukee* 9:2, 1–47.

Schoolcraft, Henry Rowe. 1839. *Algic Researches: Indian Tales and Legends.* New York: Harper and Brothers; reprinted with an introduction by W. K. McNeil in 1992. Baltimore: The Clearfield Company.

Skinner, Alanson. 1919. "Some Menomini Place Names in Wisconsin." *The Wisconsin Archeologist* 18:3.

Stark, Jack. 1995. "The Wisconsin Idea: The University's Service to the State." In *Wisconsin Blue Book 1995–1996,* compiled by the Wisconsin Legislative Reference Bureau. Madison: State of Wisconsin. 100–179.

Stratman-Thomas, Helene. 1948. "Folk Music in Wisconsin." *Badger Folklore* 1:1.

Thompson, Stith. 1996. *A Folklorist's Progress: Reflections of a Scholar's Life.* Bloomington, Ind: Folklore Institute.

Vennum, Thomas Jr. 1973. Introduction to the reprint of Frances Densmore, *Chippewa Music.* Minneapolis: Ross & Haines. i–xii.

Vogel, Virgil. 1965. "Wisconsin's Name: A Linguistic Puzzle." *Wisconsin Magazine of History* 48, 181–86.

Vogeler, Ingolf. 1986. *Wisconsin: A Geography.* Boulder, Colo: Westview Press.

Wagler, Mark. 1997. Personal communication regarding his field research with LaFarge, Wisconsin storyteller Dale Muller in 1985.

Terms and Talk

1

The Significance of Manitowoc

E. P. Wheeler

Place names—their origins, their meanings, their stories—fall prey to "progress" as surely as the land. In an era when emergency 911 systems have stimulated the conversion of local road names into numbers, only the elderly and the antiquarian may recall or care that West 18th Street was once the "Swamp Road"—especially since the swamp has been drained and filled. Many place names once invoked by Wisconsin's Woodland Indian peoples have vanished altogether before the onslaught of armies, settlers, and entrepreneurs eager to mark the land with words that celebrate themselves, the old worlds they've left and those they imagine: Dodgeville, Fort Atkinson, Weyerhaeuser; Bangor, Pulaski, Rhinelander; Arcadia, Mount Horeb, Richland Center. Yet some native names linger, particularly when rendered official through incorporation and canonized by mapmakers. Peculiar to European Americans, they inspire speculations both wise and otherwise.

Oconomowoc, for example, has been linked jocularly with a new "settler" driving out an elderly original inhabitant. Exhausted, the "old Indian" drops in his tracks, exclaiming in pidgin dialect, "I can no mo' walk" (see my *Midwestern Folk Humor* [Little Rock: August House, 1991], 64, 233). The name Sheboygan is likewise associated facetiously with a "chief" who, like French Canadians attempting English, switches gender pronouns. Hoping for a daughter after many sons, he learns his wife has delivered yet another boy: "Ugh. She boy 'gain" (Leary 1991: 63–64, 233). Ignorance and invention in wit's guise were paralleled more seriously in the 1920s when the *Wisconsin Magazine of History* included a regular "Question Box" feature in which "experts" solved or pondered historical riddles submitted by readers. Consider E. P. Wheeler's representative conjectures regarding Manitowoc's translation as "spirit timber." While Wheeler's condescending and pejorative use of "heathen" is a fine example of western Christian bias masked as intellectual objectivity, his notion that native peoples would not likely mix *manito* with Catholicism is apt. After all, Wisconsin's Algonquian-speaking Menominee, Ojibwe, and Potawatomi peoples generally referred to Franco-Americans as *wemitigoozhi*, "those who thrust crossed sticks in your face," an obvious satirical reference to the religious zeal of those in black robes.

Subsequent investigators of Wisconsin's Indian place names have offered alternative explanations of Manitowoc. Robert E. Gard and L. G. Sorden's *The Romance of Wisconsin Place Names* (Spring Green, Wisc.: Wisconsin House, 1969) draws upon Manitowoc area correspondents to state that "The first white men thought the Indians called the place where they speared whitefish at the mouth of the river *Munedowk,* but the accepted phonetic spelling became Manitowoc. In the Indian language it meant 'spirit land' or 'river of bad spirits' and also 'devil's den.'" Virgil Vogel's far better informed *Indian Names on Wisconsin's Map* (Madison: University of Wisconsin Press, 1991) dismisses demonic references in support of a contention—made in 1856 by Augustin Grignon, a French-Menominee trader—that Manitowoc is a Menominee name meaning the (presumably wooded) "home or place of the spirits." Finally, Wheeler's reference to a "totem pole" likely describes an upright column of less than six feet inscribed with a single clan animal; it should not be confused with the elaborate multi-clan totem poles common in the Pacific Northwest.

Reprinted from *Wisconsin Magazine of History* 4 (1920–1921): 106–7.

1.1. Several versions of this 1907 postcard circulated in Wisconsin, depicting the still current and facetious Sheboygan place-name legend wherein a Woodland Indian father, hopeful of a first daughter instead of yet another son, ruefully switches gender pronouns: "She boy again." State Historical Society of Wisconsin, WHi (X3) 51648.

Urgent business matters have interfered with a prompt reply to your inquiry made in your last communication. You will remember it related to the question as to whether or not the name Manitowoc could have been derived from a cross set upon the shore near by, by the early Catholic missionaries.

This derivation of the name I consider as improbable. My reasons for this opinion are as follows:

First. The name given by the Algonquin languages to the cross has been one which designated it as a cross-stick. The Indian word spelled in the English orthography is *"Ah-zih-day-yah-tig."* I never knew the cross to be called by any other name than the one given. It has in it an implied feeling of contempt, as our word "stick" designates a diminutive and comparatively worthless article. The ending *"woc"* in the word Manitowoc involves the meaning of wood as timber or forest and so means a great deal more than a stick. If the cross had given name to the place, it would probably have been a word something like *"Ah-ziu-day-yah-tig-gong,"* meaning place of the cross.

Second. I have never known of any case where the Indians gave a name to a place because of its cross, this notwithstanding the Catholic missionaries have such landmarks almost everywhere in their exploring expeditions. There was one at Madeline Island. There was another at Sault Ste. Marie. On the Pacific slope, almost every Mission Station was dedicated by the erection of a cross.

Of course, it might be said that while later usage among the Indians after the name of the cross had become established might have made it impossible for the Indians to call it a "spirit timber," which Manitowoc means, yet in the first instance, the Indians finding a symbol strange and weird, someway connected with the idea of God, might have called it as given. But I think the objection can fairly be raised to this assumption which will be my third reason: that the heathen opposition to the white man's religion would be stronger to start with than it became afterwards. Therefore, the improbability of the Medicine Lodge of heathenism allowing its own sacred name of Manitou to be applied to the cross is still more so.

It is a singular fact that notwithstanding the triumphs of Christianity among the Indian peoples, the original name of cross-stick obtains in their language. I think the theory that the name Manitowoc either refers to a totem pole erected by a clan of the Medicine Lodge, or that it is derived from a grove made sacred by certain forms of worship in the woods gives origin to the name. So I would conclude that Manitowoc comes either from a totem pole or from a grove used for certain Medicine Lodge ceremonies.

2

Names in the Welsh Settlement

Charles T. Roberts

The Welsh immigrated to southern Wisconsin in the early 1840s. Around Rewey—along the Peca-tonica River in Iowa and Lafayette Counties—they were farmers, lead miners, and fervent devotees of Congregational, Presbyterian, Methodist, and Baptist churches. This account, set down by Charles Roberts in the early 1940s, concerns the Rewey "Welsh Settlement" in the late nineteenth century and makes prominent mention of the Congregational church "Bryn Zion," the Calvinistic Methodist "Rock Church," and the Presbyterian "Carmel" and "Peniel" churches. *Bryn* means "hill" in Welsh, while Peniel, the name of the angel with whom the biblical Jacob wrestled, is a common one for Welsh Presbyterian churches, among them the Peniel church in Winnebago County, south of Oshkosh.

Roberts also lauds his community's "good singers," a claim that is made repeatedly about Wisconsin's Welsh, invariably with reference to church choirs (e.g. Phillips G. Davies, *Welsh in Wisconsin* [Madison: State Historical Society of Wisconsin, 1982], 3, 18–19; Fred Holmes, *Old World Wisconsin* [Eau Claire, Wisc.: E. M. Hale, 1944], 197–210; and Helene Stratman-Thomas in Harry Peters, ed. and compiler, *Folksongs Out of Wisconsin* [Madison: State Historical Society of Wisconsin, 1977], 24). When Charles Roberts was a young man, William R. Jones was the "song-master" at the Peniel Church, leading the congregation's singing of hymns in four-part har-mony. At the close of the twentieth century the longstanding interdenominational Welsh song fest, or *Gymanfa Ganu,* remains a significant institution among Wisconsin's Welsh, drawing partici-pants from Rewey's Peniel to the Peniel Church in Winnebago County, and to the Cambria, Nee-nah, Oshkosh, Redgranite, and Wild Rose communities where they continue to sing hymns in Welsh and English.

Local historian Melva Knebel aptly preceded Roberts' account with an explanation of the many nicknames required in the Rewey Welsh community where so many people shared both surnames and given names, and where a Davies might marry a Davies, a Hughes a Hughes, a Jones a Jones, with none related to the other. One William Jones, who hailed from Cottage Inn, was called "Bill Cottage." Another William Jones was called "Bill the Mason" in association with his craft. And two Richard Jones of differing heights were dubbed "Big Dick" and "Little Dick." Married women's nicknames combined their first names with their husbands': Maggie Hughes was "Maggie Jim," Elizabeth James was "Lizzie Sam," while John Jones' wife Elizabeth was "Lizzie Jack." Welsh names were also given to Rewey farms and, in the case of two men named John Davis, farm names were invoked to distinguish one as "Davis *Glyn*" and the other as "Davis *Tenona.*"

The same Welsh names proliferated elsewhere in Wisconsin, as did nicknaming tactics. In the early 1940s Fred Holmes traveled to Cambria to locate John Jones, a prominent practitioner of Welsh traditions. There were thirty Joneses in the community, three of whom were Johns:

2.1. John Williams leading Welsh singers at a *Gymanfa Ganu* in the Peniel Church near Pickett, Winnebago County, 1946. State Historical Society of Wisconsin, WHi (X3) 38843.

"Did you ever hear him called John Jones-*Tannyralt?*" inquired the cheesemaker, endeavouring to assist me. Upon my increasing bewilderment, he asked if I knew whether Mr. Jones lived on the brow of a hill. All the time the mystery was deepening for me.

"I think you must want to see John E. Jones-Tannyralt," he added. "I will give you directions to his farm."

"But, I want to visit John Jones, not John Jones-Tannyralt," I protested.

"'Tannyralt' is just a handle on the Jones name for distinction," he interposed, drawing a road map for me to follow.

The map took Holmes where he wished to go. And after John and Annamary Jones had enjoyed a laugh over their visitor's confusion, Mrs. Jones explained:

Almost every farm has a Welsh name. . . . Because our farm is under the slope of the hill, it has always been called "Tannyralt," which is the Welsh descriptive word for that location. And, so that our checks at the bank are properly charged, since there are so many Joneses, we use the farm name also in the signature. Not far from here are other farms with significant names: *Coed Mawr* (the big woods); *Tred Dolphin* (a village in *Wales*); *Ty Bricks* (the brick house); "Snowden" (the highest mountain in Wales); *Vron Haelog* (sunny slope) and *Tany-bwlch* (brow of a hill). (Holmes 1944: 202–3)

Phillips Davies similarly enumerates the use of farm names near Columbus to distinguish between "the several John Joneses or David Williamses in the settlement." The farm names attached to surnames included *"Pen y Daith* (End of the Journey), *Bryn Mawr* (Big Hill), *Ty Hen* (Old House), *Y Plas* (The Manor), *Ty'n-y-Coed* (House in the Wood), and such place names as *Hendref* and *Bryn Hafod."* The Columbus area's Welsh also appended occupational names, such as John Owens the Church, for a deacon, as distinct from John Owens the Singer (Davies 1982: 33).

Reprinted from *In the Shadows of the Mines: The Village of Rewey, Wisconsin 1880–1980* (Rewey, Wisc.: The History Committee, 1980), 30–31.

The Account of Charles Roberts

I will now start this history from the northeast side where William O. and Joseph Powell land and homestead were. Traveling west David M. Thomas farm, then Walter Powell and John Lewis and Benjamin Gibbon farm and homestead. Then the David D. Davies farm and homestead (called the *Glyn*), next Thomas Thomas and Reese Davis farm and homestead, then Robert J. Hughes farm and homestead on west side of settlement, all of these on north of Country Trunk A.

Start now on the east side, Peter Powell farm and resident [*sic*], then the Baptist Church built in the year 1864 located on the John J. Davies land known as "Hyde Park," the James Davis land then, John W. Jones land then John Lewis homestead and James Williams farm and Griffith Roberts land. Then Mrs. John Phillips home then, John Owens homestead, the William Thomas, then Bob R. Hughes on west side.

No. 8 Schoolhouse on east side of the Welsh Settlement, Robert Hughes farm coming west then the David Griffith farm and William Jones (Cottage), then William Jones (Mason) then Hugh Jones Sr. (*Telog*), then John W. Jones then the Bryn Zion Church, Congregational demonination, built in the year 1871. The William Owen and John Morgan home and Peter Jones and Edward Williams and Richard Humphrey farm and homestead, then start on the east side, Reese Harris farm (Pen Bank). Then the Welsh flour mill on the Pecatonica River for water power, ground with stone burs [*sic*] on Benjamin Williams land then Thomas Davies and John E. Jones (Mason) then the Old Hendra land and James Phillips and Ebenezer Davis farm and homestead and No. 9 Schoolhouse and Moses Jones farm. Now the Peniel and Carmel parsonage, then Thomas H. Jones then Peniel Church built on land homesteaded by John P. Jones (Cabin). The old Davies homestead about the center of the Welsh Settlement, the David C. Davies farm then the Rock Church built the year 1854 now where Carmel Church was built in 1852. Then William Phillips (*Gloque*) [i.e. "quarry"] and David P. Jones (farm *Luide*) then William D. Jones and John Owens.

Then starting on east side of old Hendrea and next James Phillips (*Glaspunt*). Then Eben Davis home, the Moses Jones homestead about the center of the Welsh Settlement. Most of the Welsh families came, they settled around these parts and it became quite a large settlement as they built churches and schoolhouses. It was noted for the fine church sermons and Sunday schools and the singing, as the Welsh were noted as good singers. Then start at the east side, John P. Jones (Cabin) then Peniel Cemetery then John H. Jones and Griff Roberts, then at east side Elias Williams and Michael James and Henry Harris, then Thomas Jones (*Carnaven*), the Noah Thomas farm and Jericho No. 7 schoolhouse, Owen Hughes and John W. Thomas Sr. and John W. Davis (*Tenona*) then William D. Roberts (4 crossing). Then start at east side David J. Jones (*Dufrin*) then Edward Jones (Big Ned).

Then William P. Roberts land and homestead bought in the year 1864, now owned by Charles T. Roberts now where Dewey Roberts lives, one of the grandsons.

The Welsh Settlement is located in Iowa County on the southwest side next to Lafayette County and some of the Settlement is in Lafayette County. I was born on the home farm in Lafayette County, son of William P. and Ann Roberts, Welsh parents both from Angel Shier [*sic*], North Wales, coming to America when very young, and married in America. There are not any of the first settlers here now and they did not leave any written history so I have done what I know about it now. . . . I was born April 21, 1870 and lived here all the time. So, you will excuse my poor writing by an old man.

3

German Nicknames of Places in Early Dodge County

C. H. Bachhuber

Dodge County has been, since the 1830s, among the most German areas of America's most German state. In a county where German was actively spoken on the streets through the 1930s, where children were educated in German parochial schools, where occasional church services are still conducted in German, and where such German names as Herman, Huilsburg, and Leipsig festoon the official map, the unofficial presence of German nicknames for places does not surprise.

C. H. Bachhuber, likely a native Dodge County German, was living in West Allis when he became one of many "locals" with whom the State Historical Society of Wisconsin's Charles Edward Brown corresponded regarding Wisconsin's folklore. (Lester Seifert mentions a Bachhuber's Saloon in Mayville as an important nineteenth-century Dodge County institution in "Some German Contributions to Wisconsin Life," *Yearbook of German-American Studies* 18 [1983]: 173–83.) Between 1935 and 1944, Bachhuber also supplied Charles Brown with manuscripts on "Bavarian Rhymes," "Bavarian Proverbs," and "English Words in General Use in the Bavarian Settlement of Town LeRoy, Dodge County, in 1890."

Bachhuber's report of belittled Bavarians begs further comment. The widely held rotund, leather-panted, beer-swilling, sausage-chomping, tuba-blowing, polka-dancing German stereotype derives from Bavaria—that old Catholic, alpine, southern German kingdom whose capital is Munich, home of the world's most famous tavern, the Hofbrau Haus, and hearth of annual Oktoberfest revels. Yet Dodge County's German population hails overwhelmingly from the more austere Lutheran regions of north Germany. These *Plattdeutschers,* or "low Germans," from Brandenburg, Pomerania, and Prussia were joined by a small but significant contingent of "Forty-Eighters," or "Latin Farmers," urban intellectual refugees following the failed liberal revolution of 1848. Both parties tended to regard themselves as superior to Bavarians, whom they often viewed as rustic clodhoppers. Indeed I encountered this attitude as recently as 1986, while doing intensive field research on German music in Dodge County, when a Bavarian Catholic farmer and concertina player complained of haughty treatment from his neighbors.

Reprinted from a report of March 20, 1944, submitted to Charles E. Brown; Brown papers, box 7, folder 9 in the Archives of the State Historical Society of Wisconsin; box 7 also holds the additional Bachhuber manuscripts.

Probably the most famous nickname in Dodge County was that given to Old Lomira. This is the original village, and is located on the Fond du Lac-Milwaukee Trail, now Highway 41. It is said that a certain jolly tavern keeper greeted every guest with a lusty "*Schenk' ir*'." This is Bavarian for "*Schenke irn,*" fill the glass. Thus this name was applied to the village far and wide. It is pronounced shĭń gē.

3.1. This tall-tale postcard, ca. 1910, is possibly by Alfred Stanley Johnson of nearby Waupun, whose work is enshrined in the Waupun Heritage Museum. At the time, Watertown, in Dodge County, was known for "Watertown Stuffed Geese" and sometimes referred to as "Goosetown." Wisconsin Folk Museum Collection, courtesy Watertown Historical Society.

Please don't ask me to vouch for the truth of the foregoing explanation of this name.

In the northwest corner of Town Lomira there is a locality known as Pontsville (the "o" very short). The story is that a certain farmer of that section was blessed with an immense paunch, [in] German—*panz,* and the whole section of the town came to be called Pontsville (Panzville).

This explanation appears to be true.

Along the northeast portion of Horicon Marsh there is a section known as Smud's Point, locally Schmud's Point. It is said that several Bavarian immigrants, who were unusually filthy, had located there. The German word for dirt or filth is *schmutz*—and the place was called Schmutz Point, corrupted into Schmud's Point.

I doubt the correctness of this explanation. It may well represent the efforts of the German immigrants to read some meaning into the name. However, I recall a few residents of that locality who would have qualified as to *schmutz.*

4

Deutsche Sprichwörter: German Sayings in Milwaukee

Louis Pierron

Prior to the mass popularity of the self-help industry, with its plethora of dull phrases about role models, mentors, parenting, self-esteem, and safety, caring elders placed greater reliance on sharing proverbs: wise, witty, poetic, sometimes acerbic pronouncements that, as folklorist Roger Abrahams elegantly suggested, offered "traditional solutions to traditional problems." As a kid in the 1950s and 1960s I heard plenty from my dad, Warren Leary. Perhaps his favorite was "the old dog for the hard road," reserved for those not infrequent occasions when my "old man" demonstrated that his sagacity and stamina exceeded mine.

Louis Pierron was raised in a German-speaking Milwaukee neighborhood in the last quarter of the nineteenth century where he heard the seventy-seven proverbs or *sprichwörter* that fall below, although he tells us little about who used them, when, where, or why. Of his ancestry, Pierron had this to say in 1936 when he wrote to Charles E. Brown of the State Historical Society of Wisconsin:

> Grandmother on father's side came from Bavaria in 1838 direct to Milwaukee. She was Katherine Arnold, first employed as housemaid of the later Governor Harrison Ludington; shortly thereafter marrying Louis Pierron, a trader, who in the fire of 1843 lost his all to the extent of $500 in a small store he then conducted. He came from Alsace-Lorraine. He died in 1853 when my dad, William Pierron, was but four years of age. My mother, from Mainz, was born in 1853 and came over in 1855, her mother being a Hessian. *Der Toepfer* was the stepfather who took the reins of the Pierron clan before and after the Civil War.

Unfortunately, Pierron's correspondence tells nothing about himself, although it was written on the 1936 stationery of Milwaukee's "North Side Cycling Club," an athletic organization that lists Pierron as a director. Judging from the surnames of other officers listed on the letterhead (Aussem, Koehn, Warnken, Jaeger, Stenzel, Mueller, Runkel), the club was an aggregation of fitness-minded German American males. Perhaps some of them contributed to Pierron's list?

A smattering of Pierron's proverbs have English counterparts and persist to the present (numbers 16, 28, 32, 38, 41, 53, 60, 63, 75), but we know little about the extent to which many others have been used, especially those with esoteric rural and ethnic content. In October 1997, Elizabeth Wagner—a student in my Folklore of Wisconsin class who had grown up in the heavily German community of Glen Haven, in Grant County—read Pierron's manuscript and observed:

> There are a couple that my parents seemed to use frequently when I was a young adult. I can hear my father's intonation and see the slight curl on his upper lip when he would say, "Self-praise stinks!" . . . My mother, on numerous occasions, such as relating neighborhood events or family relationships, will state, "What one doesn't know, doesn't hurt them." . . . One of my peers, Bonnie, comes from a Germanic heritage in Kiel, in the eastern side of Wisconsin.

She remembers her grandparents talking negatively of red-haired people, which relates to another of the sayings, "Red hair and *ärlen* wood do not grow on good soil."

(For another dozen German proverbs from Milwaukee, see Albertine Schuttler's contribution to Robert E. Gard and L. G. Sorden's *Wisconsin Lore* [Spring Green, Wisc: Wisconsin House, 1962], 316–18.)

Reprinted from a report, January, 1936, submitted to Charles E. Brown; Brown papers, box 7, in the Archives of the State Historical Society of Wisconsin.

Spelling and capitalization have been regularized and some editorial emendations have been made.

1. *Hoffen und Harren*
   macht manchen zum Narren.
   (Hoping and waiting make a fool of many.)

2. *Wer den Pfennig nicht ehrt,*
   ist des Thalers nicht wert.
   (Who does not honor the penny is not worth the dollar.)

3. *Ein blindes Huhn find et auch ein Korn.*
   (A blind chicken also finds a kernel of grain.)

4. *Rothe Haare—Ärlenholz*
   wachsen auf keinem guten Boden.
   (Red hair and alder wood do not grow on good soil.)

5. *Jedem Narren gefällt seine Kappe.*
   (Every fool likes his cap.)

6. *Wer den Schaden hat braucht*
   für den Spott nicht zu sorgen.
   (The laugh is always on the losers.)

7. *Not kennt kein Gebot.*
   (Need knows no law.)

8. *Hochmut muss Not leiden.*
   (Pride must suffer need.)

9. [Es ist] *Sist nichts so fein gesponnen*
   es kommt doch endlich in die Sonne.
   (Nothing is spun so fine that will not come to light.)

10. *Wie der Herr so ist Gescherr.*
    (As the master is, so is his household.)

11. *Der Krug geht so lange zum Brunnen bis er bricht.*
    (The jug goes to the water until it breaks.)

12. *Der Schuster hat immer die schlechtesten Stiefel.*
    (The shoemaker always has the worst boots.)

13. *Du must in sauern Apfel beissen.*
    (You must bite into a sour apple.)

14. *Muss ist eine harte Nuss.*
    (Must is a hard nut.)

15. *Du bist ein Hanswurst.*
    (You are a Hans sausage—i.e., a fool.)

16. *Eine Hand wäscht die andere.*
    (One hand washes the other.)

17. *Herren Gunst und Lärchengesang,*
    Tönt sehr schoen, doch wahrt nicht lang.
    (Honors and lark's songs sound very nice, but do not last long.)

18. *In der Not frisst selbst der Teufel fliegen.*
    (In distress even the devil flees.)

19. *Unrecht gut gedeihet nicht gut.*
    (Injustice won't last.)

20. *Friede ernährt, Unfriede verzehrt.*
    (Peace nourishes, unrest destroys.)

21. *Neue Besen kehren gut.*
    (New brooms sweep clean.)

22. *Des Menschen Wille ist sein Himmelreich.*
    (A man's will is his kingdom of heaven.)

23. *Fremdes Lob klingt, Eigenlob stinkt.*
    (Praise from others rings, self praise stinks.)

24. *Der Kuckuck ruft sein eigenen Namen.*
    (The cuckoo calls his own name.)

25. *Man soll den Tag nicht vor dem Abend loben.*
    (Don't praise the day before the evening.)

26. *Was Hänschen nicht lernt, lernt Hans nimmermehr.*
    (What little Hans does not learn, Hans never will.)

27. *Mit dem Hut in der Hand,*
    kommt man durch das ganze Land.
    (Good deportment will carry one through the entire land.)

28. *Was man nicht weiss*
    macht man nicht heiss.
    (What one doesn't know won't hurt one.)

29. *Aller Anfang ist schwer.*
    (All beginnings are difficult.)

30. *Morgenstund hat Gold im Mund.*
    (The morning hour has gold in its mouth.)

31. *Der Geiz ist die Wurzel allen Übel.*
    (Stinginess is the root of all evil.)

32. *Was du nicht willst dass man dir tut,*
    das füge auch keinem andern zu.
    (Do unto others as you would have others do unto you.)

33. *Vögel die früh morgens singen,*
    frisst am Abend leicht die Katz.
    (Birds which sing early in the mornings are easily eaten in the evening by the cat.)

34. *Eines Mannes Rede ist keine Rede,*
    man soll sie hören, alle beide.
    (Always hear both sides of a story.)

35. *Mitgefangen, mitgehangen.*
    (Caught with wrongdoers, hanged with them.)

36. *Wie man in den Wald hinein ruft,*
    so schallts wieder heraus.
    (As one calls in the woods, so it also echoes back.)

37. *Eine Krähe hackt den andern*
    das Auge nicht aus.
    (One crow does not pick another crow's eyes.)

38. *Schuette das Kind nicht mit dem Bade aus.*
    (Don't throw the baby out with the bath water.)

39. *Die Nürnberger hängen keinen;*
    sie hätten ihn denn zuvor.
    (The Nürnbergers do not hang a man before they have him.)

40. *Was mehr wert is wi' ne Laus*
    sollst du mitnehmen nach Haus.
    (Be content with even small gifts.)

41. *Den fröhlichen Geber hat Gott lieb.*
    (God loves a cheerful giver.)

42. *Wo Tauben sind, fliegen Tauben zu.*
    (Pigeons fly to where pigeons are.)

43. *Der Sperling in der Hand ist besser als zehn Tauben auf dem Dache.*
    (A sparrow in the hand is better than ten pigeons on the roof.)

44. *Wo Frösche sind, gibt es auch Störche.*
    (Where there are frogs, there are also storks.)

45. *Für das Gewesene gibt der Jude nichts.*
    (The Jew cares nothing for what has passed.)

46. *Unkraut vergeht nicht, es schlägt lieber doppelt aus.*
    (Weeds do not perish, they double in growth.)

47. *Ein Unglueck kommt selten allein.*
    (Misfortunes seldom come singly.)

48. *Das arme Tier gejungt.*
    (The poor have many offspring.)

49. *Freunde in der Not, gehen tausend auf eine Lot.*
    (Friends in need would fit a thousand on a plumb bob.)

50. *Den kann auch loben in allen Wirthshausern, ohne Bier.*
    (He can be praised in all taverns, without beer.)

51. *Viele Kunden sind des Herren Tod.*
    (Many customers are the merchant's death.)

52. *Selbst ist der Mann.*
    (A man is what he is.)

53. *Wer selbst im Glashaus sitzt soll andere nicht mit Steinen bewerfen.*
    (He who sits in a glass house must not throw stones at others.)

54. *Fishfangen und Vogelstellen verderben manchen guten Gesellen.*
    (Many a good soul is ruined by levity.) [Literally: Catching fish and hunting birds ruins a good person.]

55. *Der Horcher an der Wand hört seine eigene Schand.*
    (The listener at the wall hears his own shame.)

56. *Ein Narr kann viele Narren machen.*
    (One fool can make many.)

57. *Geteiltes Leid ist halbes Leid,*
    geteilte Freude, doppelte Freude.
    (Shared sorrow is half sorrow, shared joy is doubled joy.)

58. *Schuster bleib bei deinen Leisten.*
    (Shoemaker, stick to your last [talents].)

59. *Wenn man den Wolf nennt, kommt er gerennt.*
(Mention the wolf and he comes running.)

60. *Irren ist menschlich.*
(To err is human.)

61. *Morgen, morgen nur nicht heute*
sagen alle faulen Leute.
(Tomorrow, tomorrow, not today, say all lazy people.)

62. *Wer einmal lügt dem glaubt man nicht*
und wenn er auch die Wahrheit spricht.
(Who once lies is never believed.)

63. *Verschiebe nicht zum andern Tag*
was Heute du verrichten magst.
(Postpone not until tomorrow what can be done today.)

64. *Hoffnung liehst nicht Schaden werden.*
(Hope buoys up sorrow.)

65. *Mit der Zeit pflückt man Rosen.*
(In the course of time one picks roses.)

66. *Spare in der Zeit, so hast du in der Not.*
(Save in time and have in time of need.)

67. *Ein jeder kehr vor seiner Türe findet Not genug dafür.*
(Mind your own business.)

68. *Kommt man über den Hund,*
kommt man über den Schwanz.
(If one gets over the dog, one can get over his tail.)

69. *Der Wolf nimmt auch gezählte Schafe.*
(The wolf also takes counted sheep.)

70. *Vorsicht is die Mutter der Weisheit.*
(Foresight is the mother of wisdom.)

71. *Wenn zwei sich streiten,*
freut sich der Dritte.
(When two quarrel, a third is pleased.)

72. *Man ist immer klüger wenn man vom Rathaus kommt.*
(One is always cleverer when one comes from the court house.)

73. *Gefundenes vertrohten ist so gut wie gestohlen.*
(Failing to return lost property is as good as stealing.)

74. *Der Hehler ist so gut wie der Stehler.*
(The holder is as good as the thief.)

75. *Wie sich einer bettet, so schläft er.*
    (As one makes his bed so will he sleep.)

76. *Ein jeder muss sich nach der Decke strecken.*
    (Everyone must stretch himself according to the length of the cover.)

77. *Wer sich nicht nach der Decke streckt,*
    dem bleiben die Beine unbedeckt.
    (Who does not stretch himself according to the length of the cover will have uncovered feet.)

5

Milwaukee Talk

The Grenadiers

German-inflected talk has become part of the regional vernacular in Milwaukee and throughout much of eastern and central Wisconsin. Paralleling the celebration of Scandinavian dialect by Minnesota's filmmaking Coen brothers, of *Fargo* fame, and radio monologist Garrison Keillor, such diverse Wisconsin musicians as avant-rocker Sigmund Snopek and Two Happy Cowboys from Wisconsin (Rob Johnson and Rick Murphy) have toasted Beer Town's talkers with numbers like "Aina Hey" and "Howe's Bayou" (i.e. How's by You?); see Snopek, *WisconsInsane* (Dali Records DLP 20010, 1987); and the Two Happy Cowboys from Wisconsin's eponymous compact disk (Waubesa Ranch Records, 1993). Meanwhile the *Milwaukee Journal* was chronicling that city's Teutonic phraseology well before University of Wisconsin linguist Jurgen Eichoff began his scholarly investigations—as summarized in "German in Wisconsin" (in *The German Language in America,* ed. Glenn C. Gilbert [Austin: University of Texas Press, 1971], 43–57).

In 1951 the *Milwaukee Journal* published *Milwaukee Talk,* a pamphlet that was soon promoted by staff writer Don Trenary. His "Such Talk You Hear By Milwaukee," published in the paper's "Sunday Section" on August 25, 1951, asserted that "The rigid rules of grammar and syntax are warped in backyard conversations but a living, colorful speech is created." Trenary continued: "In Milwaukee, the common tongue is flavored by the fading Germanicism that casts its warm patina over the bustling city. Sometimes it makes itself evident in a strong contraction, like the colloquial 'spade's ace' for the more watery 'ace of spades.' Sometimes it is an explosive interjection, like the most useful 'enna?'" *Milwaukee Talk* had its origins in the popular Heinie and His Grenadiers radio program on the *Journal's* WTMJ station. Heinie, a radio character created and performed by Milwaukee-born announcer Jack Bundy, held forth from 1932 until 1964, with a hiatus during World War II. Bundy's Heinie specialized "in Deutsch brand corn freely seasoned by outrageous accents that listeners seemed to relish" (Jay Joslyn, "Heinie Regroups His Grenadiers," *Milwaukee Journal,* November 26, 1965). For their part, the Grenadiers were a tight German band that made the first of several 78 rpm recordings for Decca in 1939. The Heinie and His Grenadiers broadcasts enjoyed an extraordinary following throughout southeastern Wisconsin. Following an on-air discussion of Milwaukee's "colorful folk talk," listeners sent in 2,117 letters that offered their favorite Milwaukeeisms and formed the basis for *Milwaukee Talk.*

Reprinted from the pamphlet *Milwaukee Talk* (Milwaukee: *Milwaukee Journal,* 1951). Copyright © 1998 Journal Sentinel, Inc., reproduced with permission.

Introduction

There was a time, as everyone knows, when Milwaukee was known as a German community and that it was just that, no one can deny.

5.1. A signed photograph by Jack Bundy, a.k.a. "Heinie," in his Grenadiers regalia and invoking the German dialect greeting with which he commenced his program on Milwaukee's WTMJ radio, late 1930s. Wisconsin Music Archives, University of Wisconsin.

The years have changed this situation just as they have changed many other things so that today Milwaukee is very similar to our other great American metropolitan centers.

There lingers on, however, a link between today and yesterday in some of the colorful expressions which at one time represented true English translations from the German and later other tongues. These unusual twists to the English language afford all of us a good many chuckles.

We decided to prod the memories of Milwaukeeans and see how many typical expressions of this earlier era could be brought to life. A contest staged on the Grenadiers program brought in thousands of entries, some of them so typical and so humorous that it was decided to publish them in a booklet. Thus *Milwaukee Talk* came into being.

> *Remember, dear reader, this book's just for fun*
> *'Cause folks in Milwaukee—down to the last one—*
> *Get a kick out of living—and relish each bit—*
> *So read on and enjoy what our list'ners have "rit"!*
> The Grenadiers, "The Band of a Million Friends"

A Two-Oven Smile and Such a Clear Picture, Too

Two women talking on the corner of West Wisconsin Avenue and North Fourth Street:
"Gee, Mary, a lot of things have happened since I saw you last."
"Yeah, Gretchen? F'r instance."
"I've had all my teeth out, and an electric stove and a television set put in."

Diagnosis: Winter Thickness

"Stanley, come broom off the snow. The sidewalk is getting thick."

I'm From Milwaukee, and It Doesn't Show—Much

A Milwaukee area farmer phoning-in a classified newspaper ad:
"Just put what I told you. Vun day about a week ago last munt I heard me a noise in the middle of the pack yard that did not jused to be. I jumped mit the bed out, and ran mit the door off, and der I found my pig grey mare tied loose and running mit the stable off. Whoever prings him pack pays $5.00 reward."

And Never the Swain Shall Meet

One gay blade to another sharpie:
"I asked Grace to steady go, but she already was a-wenting."

Bag of My Heart, I Love You

A woman in a dime store:
"Put me in a sack for five cents of kiss candy."

Where's the Pane?

Mother talking to her boy:
"Johnny! Make that window shut. It pulls me in the neck!"

Doggone!

"Tie the dog loose, and shut the gate open. Let him run the alley out until the kids from school come home."

Milkman, Shush Those Bottles

Heard across the back fence at North Forty-seventh and Keefe:
"Last night I was on a party, and in the morning when I stood up, was I already yet tired."

Downtown and Back on One Ticket

A lady requesting a bus transfer at Capitol Drive and 41st Street:
"Punch me long, mister, I'm going by City Hall."

Tempus, Fooey!

The Irish, too, take their turn at twisting the tail of the English language. Listen as Pat talks to his foreman in a paint factory:
"Mr. Putnall, today I've been here 16 years."
"Well, Pat, that's a long time."
"No, time doesn't seem when it's gone once in awhile as long as it really is, does it!"

Crazy Rhythm

One teen to another down by where the street car the corner bends:
"Let's go down by the Eagles where they got two musics and dance like mad."

Weather Forecast: Beware of Low Hanging Muscular Cumulus Formations

Locust Street mother to her son:
"Come from out the yard in. I tink a tunder shower is pulling up."

Since She Took Sicken, Tanta Tain't Tickin'

Oklahoma Avenue spinster telling her neighbor about a sick aunt:
"She's pretty worse. I guess she won't make it much longer yet. Ain'na?"

Mice-Self?

Mrs. Schmidt calling to woman downstairs:
"You know, I killed the little mouse in my kitchen this morning all by myself."
"Oh, Johanna, don't get so excited. In my front hall, I killed myself two once."

Sow Big

Overheard in a dress shop:
"The size I don't know, but try it on I will even if it ain't for me, but my sister, Hanna. We are both the same fat."

Medical School Was Never Like This

Mama on the porch telling Junior what to do:
"Ride up town the bus. Then go by the butcher shop and pick up for me my pigs' feet and your papa's brains, and don't forget the cat's liver."

In Wisconsin . . . Cannibals?

A call heard over the back fence:
"Willy, come in once and eat yourself. Ma is on the table and Pa's half ett already."

Grounds for Something

"Grease yourself a piece of bread and I'll put you on a hamburger."

A Home Is Every Man's Ghoul

A Mitchell Street man was trying to explain to one from down by Kinnickinnic, just where he resided:

"I live by the cemetery where they bury the funerals."

Bat Your Life

A night at Borchert Field (where the Brewers play ball) produced this:

"C'mon, let's go. Hit it once a coupla times."

They Never Forget a Face

"You come me so close, but know you I can't."

What? No Brains?

"My boy, August . . . all what comes in his head is fishing tackle and worms."

I'll Pass

"Why don't you hello me when you know me so easy?"

Toupee or Not Toupee

On returning from the beauty parlor one afternoon Mrs. Schulz was greeted by her neighbor, Mrs. Finkelmeister, with the statement:

"Oh, Mrs. Schulz, how nice ain'na, you had your hairs made."

The Hole Story

Stonemason instructing his apprentice while constructing a wall:

"Dese stones are too close apart. Dey should be furder togedder."

Slow Burn

"Don't nervous me, I get easy mad."

A Delicatess'

The butcher had just finished waiting on a woman for whom he sliced eight pieces of baked ham. The next customer up said to him:

"Slice me too eight times like you did the other lady."

Lost and Bound

"Here I sit my heart tied in knots on Two Street and Mitchell with a switch-ticket [streetcar transfer] in my hand not knowing which way should I."

An Onion Tip

One Milwaukee hausfrau was visiting another as the story goes. She felt called upon to make a comment on the salad she was served.

"For why you always everytime putting in so much onion, you know always it comes me up so much. Always I like it more without."

He's His Own Grandpa

"Our baby was Monday one year; our pa is going to be next week."

Fall In

New recruits were lining up at a meeting of one of the components of Wisconsin's Thirty-second Division. One raw was heard to say to a not quite so raw:

"Stanley, Stanley. I don't know where I should stood."

"You stood where you are, Auggy, and don't move a step."

Butter Ball

"I get so easy warm; so dance me loose."

Some People Say Swell

"Is that neat ever, hey!"

The Once Over Lightly

One school girl to another down by Eleventh and Mitchell where the street car bends:
"Come around by my house yet before the movie and whistle me out so my pa knows who I hang by."

Sauce for the News

A newspaper boy collecting from an elderly man:
"Vat you vant?"
"I came to collect for the paper."
"Oh, so you come to collect. Vell, you go by the bushes in and look for the money. Dat's vere my paper I find."

What About the Stares

Instructions to a small boy:
"With the hose take the broom and wash down the front porch, and be careful. Don't splash up your Sunday pants."

Powder Room Palaver

"Rosie, borrow me your looker. I bet my lips are all. Everytime I eat or drink, so quick I gotta fix 'em, yet."

Opportunity Knocks Itself Out

"He told me for a job, and I asked him no, but if he would come last week sometime, I would look and find nothing."

Oh, for a Quiet Riot

"Don't holler me so loud at. You ain't so good like you think you look it."

Dr. Kipen's Daily Dosin

"Sometimes I don't feel so good, but then on the radio comes Milwaukee Talk, and I so much have to laugh all the time. I think already yet feel me much better."

A Noose Neck

Two ladies were talking on the telephone when a knock came at one's door. She said:
"Hang once, I hear someone at the door."
Returning later she immediately queried:
"Are you still hanging?"

Double Nagative

"My wife she no like that night working business, but if she was like she ain't, I would quick took the job."

Tension on the Old Camp Ground

Two cub scout packs arguing over a camp-site:
"If you don't like us here, go there where we ain't, and forever don't come back."

Milwaukee, the Tanning Center

It is not said:
"Be a good little boy, Louie, or you will get a spanking."
In Milwaukee 'tis spoken:
"I'll give you such a one that you'll have it."

Papa's the Limit

"Run me up the shade and look for me outside if worms are getting papa for fishing."

Monday Blues, or She Hung One On

"All morning I'm hanging outside 'til it starts to rain yet, then I'm having to hang myself the rest of the day in the basement. Am I tired."

He's Never Seen a Collection Basket

"In church I always sit in the last pew so I can get quick out."

And Never the Brain Shall Heat

"Between the ears you've got ice in the head. You don't know nothing and you always will."

Time for Bed, Lamb

Mama at dusk:
"Mar-ry! Mar-ry! Come vunce right away qvick in da house. Papa he vistled da back vindow oudt tree times already. You vant him he should come oudt?"

Duty and the Beach

Picture the waves tumbling up onto the sand at Bradford Beach on a hot July afternoon as a father explains the responsibilities of a lifeguard:
"See that man, son. He's a swim-saver. After people are drowned in the water, he saves them."

Fry This One

"From the refrigerator get the eggs out and I will fry you."

Short But Suite

"I'm glad the concert lasted so early."

In the Sill of the Night

"Thank you for the invite. If we do come it will be in the night late; so we will rap you by your front windows if we can't wake you up by the door."

Oh What a Face Had Mary

"She was the kind you liked better the more you saw her less."

Fifth Floor . . . Notions

It happened in a department store elevator. One clerk was amazed to see another going up:
"Bertha! It's you. I thought you were on your off."
"Oh, no, Frieda, my off is all already."

A Case of Pillow Palaver

Mother telling visiting nurse about her daughter:
"She always dreams loud. She did that from little up."

No Inning or Outing

"They called off the ball game and picnic because it gives something down like a drizzle out."

Cause for Deferment

Father to the draft board:
"You think my son don't want in the army . . . when you know how he snores. He sleeps open his mouth and makes noise so much the whole barracks all time wakes up."

Looking in on Lily

This is the way a woman at the Washington park bandshell explained to a friend that she had purchased a ticket for the Pons concert but stood outside of the fence enclosure to hear Miss Heidt:
"I saw Lily Pons on the inside, and Winifred Heidt on the outside."

No Chattanooga Chew-Chew

Mrs. Splitstoessen hollering to her neighbor:
"Hoo-hoo! Mrs. Hansmann! What you never heard yet. On scrubbing this morning I lost my teeth!"
"Lost your teeth?"
"Ya, and what is so bad, it should happen right in front of my vacation yet."

Oh, You Keats

I give to you a violet
In token of I'm glad we met.
I hope we may already yet
Once more again together get.

And Sit in the Shade?

"It's warm in here. Why don't you run up the window?"

Music Maestro Flees

Hans and Fritz met on the street one Sunday morning. Said Hans:
"Did you go to the party?"
Replied Fritz: "Oh sure. You should of was there once. Did we have glad! Two musics was blowing."

From Bed to Curse

"You should have heard me cuss. When I stood up this morning and looked in the clock's face, it was already later than what it should have been."

An Alarming Situation

Mama Talking:
"Johnny, go let the dog out once, but don't let him bark the neighbors up. They're already to bed sometimes early."

Parting Is Such Sweet Confusion

Pretty young high school thing telling her girl friend:
"I gott clean my hairs. They're so greasy. And then I'm gonna bend them square, side by each on the wireless so they blouse nice."

Son-Rise Serenade

Papa rousing his sleepy offspring:

"Hans, stand up! Don't sleep off your head. It's already five after the clock, and you fishing wanted to go."

What! No Sugared Saucer!

Hubby home from the plant:

"I'm not too hungry, dear. I'll just have a coffee cup and a bread slice."

6

Ten Thousand Swedes:
Reflections on a Folklore Motif

Peter Munch

Rhymed ethnic taunts have long been part of everyday banter in culturally diverse Wisconsin. Columbia County Yankees razzed their "foreign" neighbors with "the Irish and the Dutch, they don't amount to much," while Catholic Celts in working-class Ashland heckled their Slavic co-religionists with "Irish, Irish, ring the bell/Polack, Polack go to hell." Initially intended cruelly, such gibes also engineered intimacy. In a region where "everybody's ethnic," where Old Stock and "100 percent" Americans have never been able completely to control the sociopolitical order, a relative egalitarianism prevails wherein the good-natured exchange of taunts becomes a means by which combatants reveal their cultural differences and common humanity.

In Rice Lake, during the 1950s, I learned all about the lone Norwegian that shamed ten thousand Swedes—just as my dad had learned in the 1920s. That we were Celts not Scandinavians hardly mattered. Rice Lake was, after all, amid that belt of Norwegian settlement that dominates western Wisconsin. Authentic "Norskie" dialect could be overheard in stores and on the streets, while it was rendered more theatrically over WCCO radio, which beamed Charlie Boone and Roger Erickson's broad accents all the way from Minneapolis. Just as we cheerfully admitted we were "micks," "harps," "Paddies," and "fisheaters," we knew that Swedes and Norwegians alike might be teased as "herring chokers," "Scandihoovians," "snoose chewers," and "square-heads." We also knew that Swedes and Norwegians were rivals who, while less bloodthirsty than in years past, still relished taunting one another.

Peter Munch, a Norwegian sociologist who taught for many years at Southern Illinois University, may well have encountered the "ten thousand Swedes" taunt while doing fieldwork in Wisconsin in the early 1950s (see his "Segregation and Assimilation of Norwegian Settlements in Wisconsin," *Norwegian-American Studies and Records* 18 [1954]: 102–40). His examination of this "folklore motif" reveals both its Old World roots and its New World provenance—although he does not suggest the likely contribution of the Sons of Norway fraternal lodges to the sustenance of stories surrounding the "Ten Thousand Swedes" rhyme. The ballads "Peter Todenskjold" and "Sinklars-Visen" both appear, in Norwegian and English, in the widely circulating *Sons of Norway Song Book* (Minneapolis: The Supreme Lodge of the Sons of Norway, 1958). I bought my copy in the early 1990s in Mount Horeb, Wisconsin.

Reprinted from *Midwest Folklore* 10:2 (1960): 61–69.

In an interesting report on Norwegian American folklore in the Indiana University Archives (Brunvand 1957), reference is made to a saying which, I believe, is well-known (and cherished!) by all Norwegians in the New World:

Ten thousand Swedes
ran through the weeds
—chased by one Norwegian!

The popularity of this little mock rhyme is significant in itself and reveals something about the good-natured rivalry between Swedes and Norwegians that still persists in many parts of the United States. The saying is easily classified with numerous jests and anecdotes boasting the Norwegians at the expense of the Swedes, such as the story about the Norwegian who was mistaken for a Swede because he had just gotten out of the hospital after a long illness.

A connection is seen between this motif and seven versions of a tale, also found in the Indiana University Archives, about a victory for a small group of Norwegians against heavy odds, which appears to have reference to an episode in the so-called Kalmar War (1611–1613) between Denmark-Norway and Sweden (Brunvand 1957: 225–28). During this war a party of Scottish mercenaries, hired by the Swedish king Gustav Adolf, attempted to march from Romsdal, on the west coast of Norway, to the Swedish border but were attacked and defeated by Norwegian peasants at Kringen in Gudbrandsdal on the 26th of August, 1612. This is the so-called "Sinclair campaign," tales of which remained a living oral tradition among the local population up to the present time. Toward the end of the 19th century, tales and fragments relating to the Sinclair campaign were collected from the various localities of Romsdal and the Upper Gudbrandsdal region by a local teacher, who put them together into a *soge* (Austid 1899; Krag 1838; Christiansen and Liestöl 1931).

The tales of the Sinclair campaign are well known in Norway even outside of Gudbrandsdal, particularly from the popular "Sinclair Ballad," written by the folk poet Edvard Storm (1749–1794), a minister's son born and raised in Vaga, not far from Kringen. The ballad was very popular during the latter part of the 19th century and found its way into several popular song collections published during this period: *Den nyeste Visebog for Hvermand* (1901) and Karl Seip's *En liten visebok for hjemmet*, both standard equipment in homes and schools in Norway around the turn of the century. The Sinclair Ballad still holds its own as one of the standard popular songs in Norway as evidenced by its inclusion, in abbreviated form (and with an English translation by W. S. Walker), in a more recent collection of Norwegian popular songs and music, *Norway Sings* (1950). It is hardly an exaggeration to state that the Sinclair Ballad is, even today, known and sung all over Norway.

It is evident that the Sinclair tales are known among Norwegians in America as well, although they are hardly as widespread and popular as they are in Norway. Three of the seven victory tales reported from the Indiana University Archives are clearly referable to the incident in the Kalmar War. The three versions were collected in Minnesota in 1947. It is also obvious that an important source of this tradition even in America is Edvard Storm's Sinclair Ballad.

According to one of the local tales, Sinclair went on shore on a small island on the coast of Norway and there received a threatening warning from a woman: "Wait

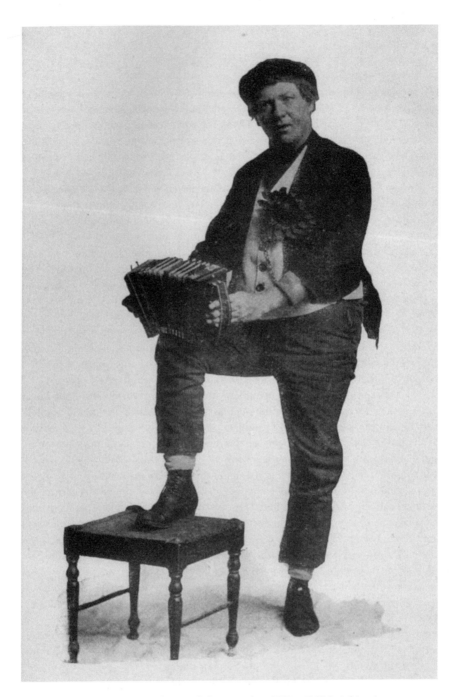

6.1. Eau Claire Scandinavian dialect comedian, William F. Kirk, in his guise of the "Norsk Nightengale," ca. 1905. Wisconsin Folk Museum Collection.

till you meet the valley people," she said, "then you'll get to bow your neck and kiss the turf!" Sinclair swore that when he had conquered the country he would return and "chop her to pieces" (Austlid 1899: 17). In the ballad, the woman has become a mermaid (Norwegian: *havfrue*), and so also in the two Minnesota versions including this motif, one of them quoting directly from the ballad (Brunvand 1959).

Version A—"from an elderly couple visiting the United States":

The Swedes paid a large sum of money to a Scottish nobleman to outfit a ship and attack Norway from the west . . . As Sir Sinclair crossed the North Sea, a mermaid arose out of the water and said, "If you see the coast of Norway, you will never return alive."

Version B—"from a retired Norwegian-American pastor":

The *havfrue* was a kind of sea-hag that came up to the surface and foretold events. When the Scotch conquered Sinclair and he came to Norway to fight for the money paid by the Scotch government, the *frue* warned him: "If you come to Norway, I tell you the truth, you'll never come back alive."

Sinclair answered: "You evil troll, always you prophesy disaster. If I ever catch you, I'll chop you to pieces."

The *havfrue's* prophesy came true. Sinclair did not come back.

For a comparison, I would like to quote three stanzas from the ballad:

> 3. Maanen skinner om Natten bleg,
>   De Vover saa sagtelig trille;
>   En havfrue op af Vandet steeg,
>   Hun spaaede Herr Zinklar ilde.
> 4. "Ven om, vend om, du Skotske Mand,
>   Det gielder dit Liv saa fage!
>   Kommer du til Norrig, jeg sieger for sand,
>   Ret aldrig du kommer tilbage."
> 5. "Leed er din Sang, du giftige Trold!
>   Altidens du spaaer om Ulykker.
>   Fanger jeg dig engang i min Vold,
>   Jeg lader dig hugge i Stykker."

There is also evidence of a direct connection of the Minnesota versions with the oral tradition as known in Norway. Versions A and C make reference to the prominent figure *Pillar-Guri*, a young girl who, according to the local tradition, warned the peasants by blowing her *prillar-horn* from a vantage point across the valley as the Scotchmen approached. Other versions of the name are *Pilar-Guri, Prillar-Guri*, and *Pella-Guri*. The form most commonly found in Norway is *Pillar-Guri*, although originally it was probably *Prillar-Guri*. The girl obviously got her nickname from her skill in blowing the *prillarhorn*, a musical instrument made from a goat's horn.

One of the Minnesota versions makes her the "leader" of the Norwegians. Version A:

. . . As [Sir Sinclair] sailed into the fjord, an old woman living in the mountains named Pella Guri sounded the alarm. The women, children, and the old men gathered for the defense of their land. They cut huge quantities of timber and fastened them at a strategic place on the mountain where it juts out over the fjord. When the ships passed that point, the timber was released, and the Scotch fleet was destroyed.

Version C:

When Norway and England were at war, Saint Sinclair, a warrior from England, together with a crew, became the victim of the tricky Norwegians whose leader was the prominent character Pilar Guri. A band of Norwegians who hid in the mountains loosened the rocks around them. Sinclair and his crew were in the boat below. When she blew her horn, the English warriors were covered with the stones.

The Pillar-Guri motif, which looms large in the oral tradition in Norway, is not mentioned in Storm's ballad, at least not in the versions found in the popular song collections. On the other hand, the Minnesota versions show certain deviations from the Norwegian tradition which may possibly be regarded as "generalizations" of a tale that has been removed from its locale and cultural milieu. For one thing, the name of the locality, Kringen where the battle was fought, has dropped out, although this is a firmly established element in the Norwegian tradition. Versions A and C have the Scottish fleet destroyed even before the men got on shore. More pertinent to the question of a possible connection between the Sinclair tales and the mock rhyme about the 10,000 Swedes is the fact that two of the Minnesota versions apparently have forgotten that the Swedes were involved at all. Version B makes Sinclair a mercenary of the "Scotch government," and version C has Norway and England at war and makes Sinclair "a warrior from England." It is characteristic that the one version (A) which does recognize the role of the Swedes in the affair was collected "from an elderly couple visiting the United States," obviously from Norway.

Nevertheless, the three versions of the "victory legend" that we have considered so far are easily identified as variants of the Sinclair tale. All of them contain specific elements which are characteristic of this tale alone, such as particularly the identity of the villain (Sinclair) and of the heroine (Pillar-Guri), as well as the general course of action.

The four remaining versions reported from the Indiana collection are of a more general nature. There is nothing in these versions to identify them with a particular historical event, and the action is rendered in general terms of standard folklore motifs. Most specific are versions E and G. Version E relates an encounter of "twenty Vikings" with "the entire Scottish army" and could be regarded as a corrupt variant of the Sinclair tale if it were not for the fact that it tells an entirely different story:

Many years ago there were twenty Vikings who were in danger of running headlong into the entire Scottish army. The leader of the Vikings saw only one chance for the small group of men. He told his men to gather all of the kegs of beer that they could find and place them in a circle. When the Scottish army approached, they saw the kegs of beer and stopped to quench their thirst. After a time, the Scotchmen became inebriated. The Viking leader told his men to march around the circle of Scotchmen. The men of the Scottish army, owing to the fact that they could not see well, thought they were surrounded and surrendered to the twenty Vikings.

The Swedes are the enemies in version G, which places the episode in the 19th century and attributes it to an imaginary Norwegian war of independence against Sweden:

From the war in which the Norwegians won their independence from Sweden in the 1800s, comes this story. The Swedes were in a castle and outnumbered the oncoming Norwegians five to one. The Norwegians, however, strung their men out and marched around and around the castle and scared the Swedes into thinking they were outnumbered terrifically; hence the Swedes surrendered.

The leading motif in both these versions is capture by deception, making the enemy think he is outnumbered by having the soldiers march in a circle. In Norwegian tradition, this motif is particularly associated with the conquest in 1719 of the Swedish fortress Karlsten, near Marstrand in Bohuslan, by Peder Wessel Tordenskiold, Norwegian-Danish naval hero of the Great Nordic War (1700–1720). This tradition gave rise to the phrase "Tordenskiold's soldiers," used in Norway even today in reference to any bluff involving numbers. Version G in the Indiana collection could be a vague recollection of that story. But the motif is too common in warfare traditions to be really descriptive of any particular legend. The two remaining versions of a "victory legend" in the Indiana collection, D and F, are the only ones that tell about the encounter of one Norwegian with a number of Swedes (in version D, 10,000 of them). These are also the only two versions which have been explicitly associated with the "10,000 Swedes" rhyme by the informants themselves. Also, they are the most general of all the versions with no indication of time, place, the identity of the actors, or any of those specific traits which are usually characteristic of the truly historical folktale.

Version D was collected in Michigan in 1950 from a boy who had it from his Swedish father:

The Swedes and the Norwegians were fighting. 10,000 Swedes were in a valley surrounded by mountains with only one pass in which they could enter or leave. One Norwegian put on a robe, which gave him supernatural looks, and came running down from the mountains. All the Swedes began to run and they left the valley. We say, "10,000 Swedes were chased through the weeds by one Norwegian."

Version F was told in 1952 by a Norwegian student at Michigan State University:

When the Swedish troops were in Norway and marching through a mountain pass, a Norwegian soldier saw them from above and by throwing rocks and boulders down on them he wiped them out, either killing or trapping all of them. This led to the phrase, "10,000 Swedes chased out of the weeds by one Norwegian."

Although version F vaguely suggests the Battle of Kringen, it is hard to see any traditional connection between these anecdotes and either the Sinclair tale or the tale about Tordenskiold's soldiers. I strongly suspect that these versions have gener-

ated from the rhyme, having possibly been made up even by the informants themselves in order to "explain" the rhyme, applying well known folklore motifs such as
the rock pile (possibly by a vague recollection of the Sinclair tale) and the magic
robe. This is quite conceivable, especially if the untrained student collectors have
given the slightest indication that such an "explanation" might be of interest. Seen
on this background, it is not very likely that the "10,000 Swedes" motif or its various
expressions, either the mock rhyme itself or any of the related "Swede stories," have
been derived from the Sinclair tale or any other victory legend from Norway. This,
however, does not mean that there is no relationship between them. It might be
useful in this connection to distinguish between "content" and "form" of a tradition,
or to use Opler's distinction between culture "themes" and their "expressions." According to this view, every culture is characterized by certain general ideas or "values" (themes), declared or implied, which become manifest in specific patterns of
behavior, attitude, or thought, described as their expressions.

With regard to the delight that Norwegians in America appear to take in deriding the Swedes more than any other group, it is obvious that this is a theme which
has been transplanted from the Old World. During about four centuries of Danish
rule, with numerous wars between Denmark-Norway and Sweden, the Norwegians
had become conditioned to think of "the Swede" as the traditional enemy. And when
Norway was finally ceded from Denmark and united with Sweden under one king in
1814, the traditional military strife was soon to be replaced by a no less bitter political opposition to Swedish supremacy, which eventually culminated in the dissolu-
tion of the union in 1905.

Particularly to the Norwegians of the late 19th century was this a vital concern
because it was felt that the national identity of the Norwegian people was not fully
recognized by the world, especially in relation to the Swedes. And so the negative
side of this strong sense of national identity was directed particularly against the
neighbor to the east.

Important—although by no means the most important—expression of this
theme were found in tales about greatness in warfare. Folk tradition in Norway even
during the 19th century was rich in tales about the alleged atrocities of Swedish
troops campaigning in Norway during the "Danish period," as well as about heroic
and clever deeds accomplished by Norwegians in the many encounters with the
Swedes. This is the background for the popularity of the Sinclair tale, the tale about
Tordenskiold's soldiers, and hundreds of similar legends. It is quite obvious that this
theme was retained and cultivated by the Norwegians who migrated to America during the second half of the 19th century. The Norwegian settlers in the Middle West
had a strong feeling of national identity as Norwegians and took a live and active
interest in Norway's strivings for political recognition and sovereignty over against
[vis-à-vis] Sweden. It may be significant that the peaks of Norwegian migration to
America in the 1860s and the 1880s coincided with periods in which the political
tension between the two countries was particularly high. And, apparently, the feelings were re-enforced as Norwegians and Swedes settled down side by side, increasing the frequency of contact. Besides, there was the constant need to point out and

emphasize one's national identity over against [to] other Americans who were wont to lump Danes, Norwegians, and Swedes together as "Scandinavians," a habit which annoyed the Scandinavians no end, especially the Norwegians, whose strivings for recognition of their national identity in the Old World had been strong and recent. In this way, the negative attitude of Norwegians toward the Swedes was even transmitted to the following generations, and there are indications that the rivalry between these two closely related nationality groups has persisted more vigorously in the United States than in Scandinavia itself.

At the same time, the rivalry between the two groups had to find new and different forms of expression. Military achievements of the one group over the other were hardly meaningful any more in the new situation, and emphasis on this motif was not even proper in relation to the general values, or leading themes, of the American frontier. But a milder form of expression of group differentiation, not entirely unfamiliar to the immigrant, was offered by the culture of the frontier in the deriding joke, which differs from the traditional folklore by being obviously made up, with no pretention of relating to actual events. If we look upon the "10,000 Swedes" motif in this light, it may explain the fact that most of the jests and anecdotes of this category are definitely American in their setting and obviously were created in America. The fact that the mock rhyme itself is built around an all English rhyme Swedes-weeds (which would be lost in translation), points in the same direction. To my knowledge, none of these jests and anecdotes have counterparts in Norway. I cannot even recall ever having heard any of these "Swede stories" told in the Norwegian language; they always seem to be given in English, even if a switch in language would be involved. In the bilingual situation of the Norwegian settlements in the Middle West, for example, jests and jokes were seldom translated from the one language to the other. When this was done in order to accommodate an occasional monolingual listener, there was always a feeling that the joke lost its point.

All this may serve as an indication that these anecdotes and jests including the mock rhyme about the ten thousand Swedes running through the weeds chased by one Norwegian have not been derived from tales or legends transmitted from Norway. [Indeed] Mr. Brunvand has kindly drawn my attention to the similarity between the "10,000 Swedes" rhyme and a line in "The Battle of the Boyne Water," a ditty recorded by Bayard from Fayette County, Pennsylvania in 1943 (Bayard 1949: 47–48):

> Fierce and long the battle raged,
> Till, crushed by the fearful slaughter,
> Ten thousand micks got killed with picks
> At the battle of Boyne Waters.

Bayard's text is a "burlesqued and garbled fragment of the stirring Anglo-Irish piece 'The Boyne Water,'" which refers to the defeat of James II at the Battle of the Boyne in 1690. Apparently, the Pennsylvania ditty served a social function similar to that of the "10,000 Swedes" rhyme, boasting one group over another—in this case the English over the Irish. Bayard reported that one had only to sing this fragment "to bring on a small riot if any Irishmen were within earshot." Similarly, in Melbourne and Sydney, "children used to gather round convent schools on the anniversary of the Battle of the Boyne, chanting

> The Irishmen ran down the hill,
> The Englishmen ran after,
> And mony a Pat got a bullet in his back
> At the Battle of Boy'an Wather.
> Up to me knees in shandygaff,
> Up to me knees in slauther,
> Up to me knees in Irish blood
> At the Battle of Boy'an Wather. (Opie 1959: 343)

In these cases, the partisan ditty does show a direct line of tradition from a specific historical event in the Old World.

As shown above, I cannot see a similar connection for the 10,000 Swedes rhyme. However, from South Bend, Indiana, comes this little ditty delivered in a mock-Scandinavian accent (courtesy of Mr. Frank Hoffman, Indiana University, who collected the rhyme, and communicated to me by Mr. Brunvand):

> Ten thousand Swedes went through the weeds
> In the Battle of Copenhagen;
> Ten thousand Jews jumped out of their shoes,
> They smelt them frying bacon.

The "Battle of Copenhagen" may refer to the naval battle between the English and the Dano-Norwegian fleets in the harbor of Copenhagen on the 2nd of April 1801, or to the bombardment and conquest of Copenhagen by the English, September 2–5, 1807 (usually the former). In neither case were the Swedes involved, and the connection of the 10,000 Swedes rhyme with this battle is obviously secondary. It may possibly have come about through a diffusion of form from the Battle of the Boyne ditty.

Such related English language rhymes lend credence to the argument that the rhyme and stories regarding 10,000 Swedes probably sprang up in the mixed ethnic milieu of the American Middle West. Their main function seems to have been to boast the Norwegians and deride the Swedes in the eyes of Americans, thereby emphasizing a social differentiation, often ignored by outsiders, but of the greatest importance to the Norwegians.

Such partisan rhymes and ditties are quite commonly associated with social differentiations in many different cultures—the oldest known example may be found in Genesis 49. They offer a clear illustration of the role of folklore in an almost subliminal system of social control: "collective representations." Ideas and values, as well as the "proper" attitudes to them, are transmitted and reinforced from generation to generation by means of catching phrases, which seemingly have an entirely different function but become popular to the extent that they do express an important cultural theme. In our case, we are concerned with one of the most important themes in any culture, that of collective identity.

Sources

Austlid, Andreas. 1899. *Sinklar-Soga.* Oslo, Norway.

Bayard, Samuel Preston. 1949. "The British Folk Tradition," in *Pennsylvania Songs and Legends,* ed. George Korson. Philadelphia.

Brunvand, Jan. 1957. "Norwegian-American Folklore in the Indiana University Archives." *Midwest Folklore* 8. Pp. 221–28.

Christiansen, Reidar Th., and Knut Liestol. 1931. "Norsk Folkesegner," in *Folksagner and Folksagor,* vol. IXB of *Nordisk Kultur,* ed. C.W. von Sydow. Stockholm, Oslo, and Copenhagen. Pp. 161–80.

Den nyest Visebog for Hvermond. 1901. Norway: 4th edition.

Krag, P.S. 1838. *Sagn samlede i Gudbrandsdalen om Slaget ved Kringlen.* Kristiana, Norway.

Norway Sings. 1950. Oslo: Norsk Musikforlag.

Opie, Iona and Peter. 1959. *Lore and Language of Schoolchildren.* Oxford, England: Oxford University Press.

Opler, Morris Edward. 1945. "Themes as Dynamic Forces in Culture." *American Journal of Sociology* 61. Pp. 198–206.

Seip, Karl. 1923. *En liten visebok for hjemmet.* Norway.

7

Characters on the Chippewa Waters

Gregg Montgomery

Dangerous occupations breed characters and characters are known by nicknames. Indeed the acquisition of a moniker often indicates a worker's shift in status from callow outsider to full-fledged veteran.

The Chippewa Valley was the heart of Wisconsin's "pinery," with lumber camps, river drives, boom operations, and sawmills dominating the region's economy from the 1840s through the early decades of the twentieth century. The era's noted woods workers—whether Anglo-Canadian or Yankee, whether French, Irish, métis, or Norwegian—commonly acquired nicknames indicative of their brawling, profane, hard-drinking, boastful, relentless, tough, and dexterous natures.

Gregg Montgomery's vivid survey of the Chippewa Valley's characters, their nicknames, and their stories was compiled in the 1930s when she served as a field researcher for the Wisconsin Folklore Project, a federally funded program of the Roosevelt administration that was directed by Charles E. Brown of the State Historical Society of Wisconsin. In a letter of April 13, 1937, written from Chippewa Falls, Montgomery mentioned Louis Blanchard, "the lumberjack with the French-Canadian dialect," and Dave Goulet, who had carved "a miniature lumbercamp." Montgomery then offered an inventory of the folklore she had documented: "lumberjack songs (I haven't the music), games, jokes played on novices, stories of characters on the Chippewa River and its tributaries, stories of French Canadian "Pea Soupers" of this community, and the process of logging from the time the camp is built through the cutting, skidding, and delivering to the landing; the interesting and colorful drive down the river in the spring; rafting and floating the lumber down the Mississippi to its final destination." (See also chapter 38, "Woods Customs", pp. 373–74.) Montgomery's correspondence and the records of the Wisconsin Folklore Project are held in the archives of the State Historical Society of Wisconsin.

At least one "character" described below by Montgomery, "Whitewater Ole" Horne, remained prominent well after his death on a river drive in 1905. Sixty-two years later, nonagenarian Fred Mero Hunter recalled "Whitewater Ole" as "the man who was supposed to be able to get on a log and ride it anywhere, over the rapids or through the sluiceway on a dam." (For the transcription of an interview with Hunter conducted by Robert B. Krueger, see *Historical Collections of Washburn County*, vol. 1, ed. E. Ward Winton and Kay Brown [Shell Lake, Wisc.: Washburn County Historical Society, 1980], 101.) According to Malcolm Rosholt, Ole Horne, an immigrant from Norway, had "married only a short time before tragedy took his life at Little Falls," along with ten other men working to loosen a log jam. William Hoyer, a former river driver, told Rosholt that several of the drowned drivers were farmers who lived along the Chippewa River: "When the body of one of them accidentally drifted ashore near his own farm, and when Whitewater Ole drifted all the way to Chippewa Falls where he lived, a legend grew that the men all drifted ashore next to their own place 'as if they were going home.'" (See Malcolm Rosholt, *Lumbermen on the Chippewa* [Rosholt, Wisc.: Rosholt House, 1982], 195–98.)

7.1. Loggers in their bateaux on the Chippewa River drive, near the mouth of Paint Creek, ca. 1900. State Historical Society of Wisconsin, WHi (X3) 14967.

Reprinted from the papers of the Wisconsin Folklore Project, under the federal auspices of the Works Progress Administration, ca. 1937—a microfilm copy of which is held by the State Historical Society of Wisconsin, reel P84–2055.

Peg Leg Pat McCann

In 1876 a railroad with the wood burning variety of locomotive was completed between Eau Claire and Chippewa Falls. To celebrate the event, the city of Chippewa Falls held a pageant and a general celebration. A parade was one of the features of the day and to add to the fun and hilarity, Peg Leg Pat McCann's leg was sawed off in front of the First National Bank, amid screams of pain from Pat, and fainting and screams of fright from the women.

Those who were not well acquainted with Peg Leg Pat did not know that he had lost a leg during the Civil War and went about with a substitute. For the parade his wooden leg was removed and a round piece of wood the shape of a leg fastened in its place. As the float in which Pat was riding stopped in front of the bank, he was held, struggling, to a table by several husky lumberjacks, while the leg was being sawed off. To add a touch of gore, gruesomeness and reality to the operation, a can of red paint was used as an excellent substitute for blood.

Big Mouth Jack

Big Mouth Jack was a notoriously bad man on the Chippewa River, whose only asset was his skill in chopping down trees. His talent for felling trees with an ax was unequalled. But Big Mouth Jack was heartily hated by every lumberjack because of his abusiveness and loud mouth.

One time he took a train to Phillips to work in the woods. The night he arrived he had supper at the hotel and in his traditional manner began publicly abusing the waitress. The proprietor knew the futility of reasoning with the bad man, so he didn't try—he shot him instead.

Nobody mourned over the death of Big Mouth Jack and he was dragged to the edge of town and buried in a shallow grave. Several days after the shooting a lumberjack passed the new grave and noticed it had been disturbed. He went into town and returned with a few men and dug up the body. They found the head had been severed and was no place to be found.

The general belief was that some doctors had heard of the murder, and knowing the man's reputation for queerness and meanness, had taken the head for a post mortem examination.

The Widow Quimby

The Widow Quimby was so called because he was minus a leg. During the old lumberjack days Quimby bought a circus tent and set it up as a hotel. He installed a kitchen and bunks to accommodate 75 or 80 men. The tent was kept warm in the winter by being banked heavily with snow.

Tote team drivers, scalers and lumberjacks going to and from camp made this hotel their stopping place and with this exploit Widow Quimby became rich.

Jack-the-Tar-the-Frog-Eater

Jack-the-Tar-the-frog-eater was so called because he would eat frogs and minnows alive; some were pretty big, too. A doctor had told him this practice would ward off consumption.

He was a former sailor on Lake Superior, who turned lumberjack. One night in the spring of 1893, about a mile from Fifield, one Ed Laloch lay in his bunk sick and groaning with pain. A bully in camp started using abusive language against him for making too much noise and keeping others awake. Jack-the-Tar reprimanded the bully for picking on the sick man, and in return was given a sassy reply. The fight was on. In the struggle that followed, Case bit the Tar in the thumb. The Tar said, "So that's the way you want to fight? I'll show you how to bite." He bit the tormentor on the upper lip until it was hanging by nothing more than a piece of skin. That ended the fight.

Jack-the-Tar was always a hard fighter, but never bothered anyone if they left him alone. He met his death in a fight at Duluth when some Italians stabbed him to death.

Patty-the-Pig

Patty-the-Pig was an Irish driver who was always drunk; he never sobered up from the time he came off the drive until his stake was gone.

One time he came into a saloon as drunk as a lord and with only a quarter left out of his season's earnings. He put the twenty-five cents on the counter and said, "By Jasus, what's the use to be down-hearted when twenty-five cents worth of licker will make you rich and happy."

Black Joe, Bald-Headed Joe, and Joe-Come-Lately

The above names were used to distinguish three Joes in one camp. Many nicknames got their start in just such a way.

Sliver McCraw

Sliver McCraw was a Canadian who drove logs on the Flambeau for several years. Finally he went back to Canada to visit his folks. He was pretty well "lickered up" by the time he got home and anxious to demonstrate his skill as a logger to his family. On the river he was known as a "white-water man"—one who can drive logs skillfully over rough waters and dangerous falls.

He took his family out to the wood pile in the back yard, grabbed a stick to use as a peavy and started making the wood fly. He kept getting more excited and shouted to his mother, "This is a center (jam), mother, and a bad one."

The Clam River Bear

Alfred Doucette with the rest of the crew was one time laid up because of a head wind that kept blowing the logs upstream so the boys couldn't pole them to the dam. Things were dull for the lumberjacks so they went over to Clam Falls for a little fun. Soon they were all teed up and the Bear got a little unruly and noisy. Some of the boys slipped down and got the village marshall who put him in jail for disturbing the peace. The place was only eight feet in diameter and had a little window about eight inches square with iron bars across it. The Bear was mad and used considerable bad language on a representative of the law. Finally he got his back to the wall and said, "I'll tip this damn jail over, I'm the Clam River Bear."

His fine was $5, so the boys, after having their fun, passed the hat, paid the fine and took the Bear home. From that time on he was known as the Clam River Bear.

Tough Blanchard

When Blanchard was a small boy he had great endurance. He was never sick, never tired, never cold, so his father dubbed him "Tough" and he was known everywhere by that name.

In the year 1899 Tough was on a drive down the north fork of the Clam River. While the boys were in camp one night they spied an eagle's nest high up in a pine tree on the bank. The tree was a Norway pine and about 90 feet tall. The fellows thought if they could only get the eaglets they could sell them and have some fun that night. Windy Martin volunteered to climb the tree, so two of the boys went into town and borrowed a pair of telephone man's spikes.

Windy climbed about 20 feet and got scared of the high wind. He made a bet with Tough Blanchard that he couldn't make the climb. Tough put on the spikes and shinnied up to the eagle's nest. The old eagles, resenting his interference, attacked him, clawing and biting him terrifically. He knew he could never get down with both birds so he threw one out of the nest and immediately the old ones swooped down to save it. In the meantime he grabbed the other one and came down the tree as fast as he could. The eaglet that had been thrown from the nest broke its leg when it fell, but even so the two eaglets brought $25 at Clam Falls, and Tough, the brave, never accepted any more bets to rob eagle nests.

Old Sittin' Bull

Jack Whidden, known in old logging days as "Old Sittin' Bull," was one of the most prominent loggers on the Chippewa in his day. He was the head man for the Chippewa Log and Boom Company on the south fork of the Flambeau River. He was excellent driver and a fine dam builder.

Jack Pearl, Jack Whidden, and Fred Leonard

No three men were better known to the old lumberjack and river driver than Jack Pearl, Jack Whidden, and Fred Leonard. Jack Pearl had charge of the drive on the east fork of the Chippewa and every spring with a rollicking daredevil crew of 100 or more men would drive from Glidden near the headwaters down through lakes and cataracts to the main river where Fred Leonard, who had charge of the drive on the west fork, would take them down the river to the flowage of Little Falls dam where the village of Holcombe now stands. Jack Whidden, known as "Old Sittin' Bull," had charge of the Flambeau River Drive. This crew under the supervision of Whidden was considered to be just the best crew of drivers obtainable, and they had to be to drive down that turbulent stream through miles of wilderness down to where the Flambeau poured into the lordly Chippewa at the Flambeau Farm.

Big Wanigan Tom

"Big Wanigan Tom" Murphy got his name from being the most skillful man on the river in handling wanigans over falls. [Note: Wanigans were barge-mounted cookshacks used to feed workers on spring log drives.]

Check Stiles

"Check" Stiles ran a logging camp in the north woods and also a livery stable on East Spring Street in Chippewa Falls. When a livery customer got ready to settle his bill, Stiles would always say, "Check to me." This saying became so much a part of him that he began to be known as "Check."

One time Check was getting together his crews to go into the woods and had all but his ox teamster. In those days any man who was at all desirable could get a job with no trouble at all. A stranger came to Stiles and asked for a job. He was asked, "Can you drive cattle?" The applicant replied that he could. Check said, "All right, follow me."

They went to Pat Tierney's saloon on East Central Street where there was a formidable collection of goad sticks that had been left at various times by teamsters who made their exit in no condition to remember their profession.

Check asked Pat for the use of one of the sticks and then said to his prospective employee, "Now I will take this chair and it will be the nigh ox, and I will be the off ox. Now let's see if you are an ox teamster."

The cattle driver waved the goad stick and shouted, "Come here, haw!" Check and the chair went in the opposite direction. The driver again waved his goad and yelled, "Come here, haw!" but the would-be ox team continued in the wrong direction. Calling "Come here, haw!" once more he resorted to the old tactics of the ox teamster and gored Check. With a yell of pain Stiles got up and said, "You are hired and I will treat the house."

Ox Bow Hickey

Ox Bow Hickey was so called because his back was stooped. He was a "river pig" (driver). When he left the river he sold hospital tickets to the lumberjacks.

Bulldog Mason

Bulldog Mason was known along the banks of the river and in the lumber camps as a fighter who was "hard to lick."

Whitewater Ole

He got his name from his skill of running the rapids. The whiter the water, the better he liked it. One of his pet expression was, "I lost my yacket on the yam of de yump."

Whitewater Ole was drowned at the time of the tragedy near Holcombe on July 7, when thirteen men were drowned breaking up a jam.

The Rooney Boys

Pete, Jim, Bartley and Mike Rooney had the reputation of being able to ride anything heavy enough to float. During the '80s and '90s Pete was considered the best man on logs on the Chippewa River. He met and defeated all competition.

Tricky Mickey Rooney

Mike Rooney, better known as "Tricky Mickey," was one of four lumberjack brothers. He was the lightest on his feet of the four and an old saying around Chippewa Falls of his skill in riding logs was, "He could ride a bubble on the water if it were necessary."

Jake and John Pusel

While the Rooneys were considered the best men on logs, Jake and John Pusel were considered the best sawyers on the Chippewa waters. The boys spent their Christmas holidays in Chippewa Falls; a week or so before the holidays they would speed up and fall enough timber to keep the skidding crew busy until after their return.

Tanner Josie

Bill Josie, better known as "Tanner," was known by every lumberjack on the Chippewa Waters. It was an understood fact that during the winter Bill would visit every camp in the pineries. A good singer and storyteller, he was always welcome at the camp, especially by the lumberjacks who knew the monotony of camp life would be changed when he made his visit.

Pete Jack Bell

Roaring Jack Bell, also known as "The Iron Man," was one of the most eccentric and well loved characters on the Chippewa Falls. Born in Worcester County, Maine, in 1841, he began his lumberjack career at the age of fourteen years.

In the year 1881 he came to Chippewa Falls and spent most of the remainder of his life in that vicinity, logging on the Chippewa River.

Bell was easily distinguished because of his outlandish dress. His hair was long and on rare occasions he wore a Stetson hat, but usually he wore nothing on his head. His shirt and jacket were always open at the neck, winter and summer; he wore knee boots and generally one pant leg tucked in and the other hanging out. Then sometimes he would refuse to wear the customary driving boots and wore only rubbers and quite often one of those would be missing. He seldom wore an overcoat nor mittens. In build he was a raw-boned six footer with an unusually wrinkled face. He was called "Roaring Jack" because he had a loud and blustering character.

When Bell came west he worked for the Shaw Lumber Company of Eau Claire for two years, landing logs on the Holcombe flowage. Next he took a contract with the Mississippi River Lumber Company of St. Louis. For this concern he logged twenty-two years on Mud Brook, twenty miles north of Chippewa Falls. At this time he also ran a camp on Clam River, later selling out.

Bell was one of the greatest loggers and dam builders on the Chippewa waters. He drove his men to the limit, but never expected of them what he was unable to do himself. He was a courageous leader, working his men from 4 A.M. to 10 P.M. which were the hours he kept. Unmindful of time, he swore and cursed his men, at the same time working beside them at the hardest tasks. He seemed immune to cold weather. If one of his men seemed to be suffering from cold, he would rub snow on his bare chest to set himself as an example of hardiness.

If logs should be hung up on a sand bar during the spring drive, Roaring Jack would lead his men into the icy water, shouting, "Jump into her boys, it won't burn you."

Sometimes on the drive he would step into mud up to his hips—he would become angry and his standard safety valve was, "Get them logs rolling or I'll kill every damn 'mushrat' on Mud Brook."

Jack Bell was a man of varied activities; he logged, drove team, ran camps, and drove logs down the river. But his greatest achievements were the dams he built, which were the best in logging country.

8

The Brewing Industry

Charles E. Brown

From the mid-nineteenth through the early twentieth centuries, hardly a town in Wisconsin lacked a brewery. In the 1870s the destruction of Windy City breweries by the Chicago Fire, the proliferation of reliable railroads, and new refrigerator cars combined to vault Milwaukee into prominence as "Beer City" (see Jerry Apps, *Breweries of Wisconsin* [Madison: University of Wisconsin Press, 1992]).

No wonder musicians as diverse as Cleveland's Polka King Frankie Yankovic and Louisiana's rockabilly piano pounder Jerry Lee Lewis invoked Brew Town through such national hits as "Milwaukee Polka" and "What Made Milwaukee Famous (Made a Loser Out of Me)," respectively. True to his Slovenian roots and "happy music" genre, Yankovic emphasized beer as an elixir of conviviality:

> Beer from Milwaukee,
> The finest beer in town,
> Makes me so talky.
> Drink it down, drink it down, drink it down!

In contrast to Yankovic, the southern Anglo-Celtic honky-tonk pianist Lewis imagined himself a lost soul on the wrong side of a moral line dividing teetotalling Christians from the devil's beer-sucking disciples.

Charles E. Brown's occupational glossary, drawn from Milwaukee brewery workers in 1938, not only illustrates the specialized equipment and corresponding speech that the work demanded, but also reveals the strong presence of German-speaking workers and German American customs. Still, it begs as many questions as it answers: for example, how and from whom did Brown gather this list? How were these words used at work, and why was profanity "noticeably absent"? Not even a foreman screaming "*Gott in Himmel!*" if some *Dummkopf* let a bunch of kegs fall off the beerwagon?

During the same period Brown also compiled a glossary of occupational speech used by workers in Wisconsin foundries and machine shops. Both lists formed part of the Wisconsin Folklore Project, which Brown initiated. Within the evolution of folklore scholarship, such lists of texts and lore resemble the species of animals and plants and specimens of rocks gathered by biologists and geologists: useful as inventories, for structural examination, and as the basis for typological classifications, but only hinting at the dynamics of either biological or cultural spheres.

Reprinted from the papers of the Wisconsin Folklore Project, under the federal auspices of the Works Progress Administration, 1938—a microfilm copy of which is held by the State Historical Society of Wisconsin, reel P84–2053.

Touring In Milwaukee

8.1. A Milwaukee German amid his city's beer, cheese, pretzels, and sausage
in this comic postcard, ca. 1900. Wisconsin Folk Museum Collection.

The brewing industry is a key industry in Wisconsin. The actual brewing of beer now employs few people in proportion to other industries. The bulk of employees are to be found in the bottling department which is quite separate from the brewing process.

Employees in the brewing process are mostly German and in many cases German is still the only spoken language.

Profanity is noticeably absent among brewery workers. Among workers in the bottling department the conveyor system (endless chain) together with the noise make much conversation impossible.

ausbrenner	Device to get rid of old pitch in kegs before adding new pitch.
beaudelot	Copper pipes for cooling beer with beer running outside pipes, copper at top, stainless steel at bottom.
beer schiessen	Beer time for workers.
can packer	Puts bottles in cases or cartons.
carousel	Conveyor.
case-in man	Puts bottles in cases or cartons.

case unloader	Empties cases or cartons and removes cancelled stamps.
cellar men	Men who work in the cellar.
clutch man	Works on washing machine.
cooker	Man or machine boiling percentage of rice or corn grits (rice or grits mash).
cooperage	Term applied to the wooden keg beer (in some cases to any keg, metal or wood).
depitching	Process of removing old pitch.
dumper	Empties cases or cartons and removes cancelled stamps.
enclosed coolers	Double pipe with wort [fermented beer mash] running inside water and ammonia outside.
fass	Removal of beer from fermentation.
filter man	Takes beer from storage tank and filters it.
filter mass	Cotton asbestos pulp used to filter beer before shipping.
flat beer	Beer having no gas [carbonation].
graining out	Taking a spent grain out of lauter tub.
high kraussen	When foam on beer resembles cauliflower.
Irish moss	Used to clarify beer.
Kaiser's geburtstag	Payday (literally "Kaiser's birthday").
kuehl schift	Cooling unit for wort.
Kuesel guhr filter	Uses diatomaceous earth.
lauter tun or lauter tub	Where wort is separated from spent grain.
leaker	Leaking barrel of beer.
mal zeit	Meal time.

malt mill	Cracks malt kernels so that starch can be reached.
mash cooker, mash tub, mash tun	Introduction and mashing in of grain.
morgen or morgens	Typical form of address regardless of time of day or night.
pfanf	Pipe to create back pressure on grains.
pitch yard	Room where pitch applied to kegs, comes from fact that years ago kegs and casks were taken out into a yard and pitch applied by hand.
preheater	Device to get rid of pitch before adding new pitch.
racker	Man operating racking machine.
racking room	Where kegs are filled.
rice cooker	Machine boiling percentage of rice or corn grits.
ruh cellar	Room in which beer ages in tanks not under pressure.
sal tag	Payday (literally "salt day").
schiess eins	Shoot one, drawing a glass of beer and shooting it along the bar to the person ordering it, quite an art to do this without losing any beer.
schlaucker	Man handling hose and emptying tanks.
set-across man	Puts filled cases or cartons on conveyor.
set-in man	Puts bottles in pasteurizer.
settling tubs	Where fermentation is started.
shooting a well	Dropping dynamite and blasting.
skids	Rods on which kegs are rolled.
sorter	Sorts empty bottles.
soaker	Machine where dirty bottles are washed in a solution.

sparging	Adding water to mash to dissolve extract from grains.
spritzing	Splashing.
starting tanks	Where fermentation is started.
steamer man	Checks quantity of caustic in solution and temperature of pasteurizer.
sternewirt	Brewery bar where beer is dispensed free.
stieffel wichsen	Transfer beer from one department to another (literally, "to wax shoes").
take-out man	Takes bottles out of pasteurizer.
throw-down man	Puts empty cases or cartons on chute.
throw-on man	Puts empty cases on conveyor.
trub	Precipitation of aluminoids and sludge from wort.
tuer zu	A typical sign equivalent to "shut the door."
wort cooler	Equipment to cool hot wort to fermentation temperature.
wrench immer aufhängen	A typical sign combining English and German [meaning, "always hang up your wrench"].

9

Apple-Picking Terms from Wisconsin

Frederic G. Cassidy

Thanks in part to the efforts of the University of Wisconsin's Extension system, apple production was established in the state early in the twentieth century. The apple industry persists in the hill country of western Wisconsin, from whence these terms derive, as well on the Bayfield Peninsula that juts into Lake Superior.

Frederic Cassidy's elegantly written study provides both a solid glossary and a step-by-step elaboration of the apple-picking process in the 1940s. Would that similar studies had been conducted for Wisconsin's other specialized, agrarian industries centered on, for example, cranberries, ginseng, and sphagnum moss. (For a glimpse of tobacco talk in the 1980s, see chapter 47, "Tobacco Growing in Southwestern Wisconsin: Ethnicity in a Traditional Labor Practice," pp. 76–85.)

Now a professor emeritus at the University of Wisconsin–Madison, Frederic Cassidy was active in the Wisconsin Folklore Society of the 1930s, as well as the short-lived Badger Folklore Society that formed during Wisconsin's 1948 centennial. In 1947 he published *The Place Names of Dane County, Wisconsin* (Greensboro, N.C.: American Dialect Society), a model study that includes a dozen place names associated with local legends.

Long an advocate of the importance of fieldwork and tape-recorded interviews as the primary methods for understanding the nature of dialect, Frederic Cassidy became the director of the American Dialect Society's ambitious dictionary project in 1962. Drawing upon his understanding that "the numerous local differences in Wisconsin speech could be correlated with settlement history and other social factors," Cassidy oversaw the development of questionnaires eventually employed by field workers to document dialect throughout the United States. The result is the massive, comprehensive, and still-in-process *Dictionary of American Regional English,* the third volume of which was published in 1996, with at least two volumes to come. For an account of this project's genesis and methods, see its introduction (*Dictionary of American Regional English,* vol. I, Frederic G. Cassidy, chief editor [Cambridge, Mass.: Harvard University Press, 1985]).

Reprinted from *American Speech* 18 (1943):74–76.

On the bluffs above Gays Mills, in the Kickapoo Valley in western Wisconsin, is an apple orchard region of about 1,200 acres which produces annually about 350,000 bushels. The fruit is picked mostly by men from nearby farms, and packed by their wives and daughters. Some outsiders there are (as I was), but not enough to affect local usage. Following is a list of words which I found in use in Kickapoo orchards this year (1942) by apple-pickers and -packers. The picker first puts on a

PICKING-SACK or -BAG, which straps over the soulders and across the back. It is of canvas, the top held open and reinforced with metal to the shape of a kidney, the

9.1. Sorting apples in the Kickapoo valley, late 1940s. Photo: John Newhouse,
State Historical Society of Wisconsin, WHi (N48) 13049.

concave part of which fits against the picker's stomach. The bottom is open, but the picker folds it back on itself and clips it to the face of the sack, and the weight of the apples keeps it folded. When it is full, he unclips it and lets it unfold, and the apples roll out below. One orchard uses instead a small

PAIL or BUCKET, which hooks on to the front of the harness. Early in the season when only part of the apples are ripe, the trees are picked for

SIZE AND COLOR, which means that only those that have

HALF COLOR (are 50% red) or more, and are no smaller than a certain size (according to the variety of the apple being picked) are taken. At this time, each picker carries a

SIZE RING of sturdy metal, and picks only such apples as will not pass through it. A picker may

BOTTOM a tree (picking everything he can reach standing on the ground), or

TOP it, taking off the highest ones. But when the season is advanced and all or nearly all the apples on a tree are ripe, he

STRIPS or CLEANS it, taking everything. This he likes best, as he can go fast and make most money. He does not like to pick

STRAYS (trees planted among those of a different variety, usually replacing others that died) because they are scattered throughout the orchards, and he spends his time dragging his ladder about instead of picking. With each crew of pickers is an

ORCHARD BOSS, who does not pick but assigns the trees, sees that supplies are brought (crates, baskets, drinking water, etc.), and that the picking is steady and careful. The picker must not pinch, scratch, or bruise the apples, and must leave no

SPURS on them (the small bit of twig just above the stem). What he picks will later be sorted by the packers into

FIRSTS (the best of all) and

SECONDS (those with small blemishes, worm holes, etc.); but these are never mixed with those picked up off the ground. The latter are officially known as

WINDFALLS (though the wind has not always been to blame), and colloquially as

FALLS, DROPS, or (once gathered) PICK-UPS. The picker empties his sack into a wooden

CRATE which holds about a bushel, and the full crates are taken to the packing shed on a

WHOOPEE (TRUCK), a wondrous contraption made by taking the body off an old Ford or Chevrolet, and substituting a flat wooden platform directly on the chassis. The whoopee holds about twenty crates, and, with the aid of chains, makes its way up hill and down, throughout the orchard, without the benefit of roads. Taking in the apples on the whoopee is called

SKIDDING them, probably an inherited term, for when the slopes are too steep or the ground too wet even for the whoopee, a

SKID is used—an affair like a stoneboat, drawn by a cateripllar tractor. Once the apples have been picked, they must go to the

(PACKING) SHED, a large, barn-like building, sometimes with a refrigerator room attached. The sorting and packing are mostly done by hand, though at the height of the season some orchards use

SORTING MACHINES. The packers stand at

PACKING TABLES (one orchard puts these right out among the trees). The whole process of packing is done upside down, the apples being all in place before the basket is put on over them. The packer begins by placing on her table a

FACER, a sort of metal basin with a vertical flange of the same diameter as the top of a bushel basket. Into this are put carefully the apples which will appear on top when the customer sees the basket. These are, of course, the best looking, and are also called

FACERS. Just before they are put in, the metal facer is lined with a

COLLAR, the festooned bit of green or purple paper that edges the top of a full bushel. The facer apples hold this in place; then on top of them is scattered a handful of

CONFETTI, or thin strips of colored tissue paper. Next, the

TUB is put in place. This is of galvanized metal, the size and shape of a bushel basket, but open at both ends; it is lined with a paper

LINER, and both are fit over the flange and rest on the metal facer. Into this form the rest of the apples are put, and when it is full the tub is removed, leaving the apples held in place by the liner. Over this is inverted the

BASKET, and the packer's job is done. The whole bushel is now turned right side up by a lad called the

BASKET TURNER, or, where machinery is used for this purpose, it is done on a

MULE. In any case, the basket turner must now press down the apples well, take off the facer, place a circular

PADDING of paper over the apples to protect them, then put on the

LID, and the basket is ready for shipping.

10

Farm Talk from Marathon County

Roger Mitchell

For more than a century Wisconsin's farm population has declined steadily, with one "farm crisis" succeeding another. Those family farmers who persist have typically relied not only on their own skill and hard work, but also on the assistance of neighbors, grandparents, parents, and siblings. The participation of farmers in a multifaceted and multigenerational community is particularly evident in the rich and, to outsiders, often esoteric quality of their occupational speech. Roger Mitchell's elaboration of vocabulary, proverbs, and expressions of belief is exemplary of the kind of talk a careful listener might hear amidst Wisconsin farmers over the varied course of a typical year—which is exactly how these terms were collected.

From 1979 to 1982, Roger Mitchell—recipient of a Ph.D. in Folklore from Indiana University and a professor at the University of Wisconsin–Eau Claire—traveled to Easton, in Marathon County, during summer vacations, weekends, and school vacations to work and hang out on the Thorpe family farm. The result was a full-length study following the outline advanced in Mitchell's introduction:

> I will tie the Thorpe family's traditions to those historical currents which initiated that great transfer of a large portion of Norway's poor to the New World with its beckoning empty land. From these beginnings will follow the generation by generation development of what is today the Emery Thorpe dairy farm, concluding with the great-grandsons of the original immigrants, Karl and Anne. In the process of lining out the several lives of hard work that culminated in this one family farm, I will take care to present those traditional complexes of farming practices, technology, and attitudes that make Karl's great-grandsons willing and able to invest their lives in the continuation of the Thorpe dairy farm. (13)

The "Farm Talk" reprinted here formed the appendices to Mitchell's larger study. Much of it was set down "on the job" as, amid various activities, he kept pen and notebook in a pocket to record an emergent word or phrase and its meaning:

> This is a body of tradition not easily come by. There is little of the comfortable sitting down with some elderly informant, tape recorder on the ready, and probing his fond memories of things long gone. Instead, it calls for observation and participation, with much information collected within the ordinary ebb and flow of everyday affairs. It demands large segments of time, for the tempo of the farm changes from season to season. Spring planting, summer haying and silo filling, fall harvesting of grains and straw for bedding, and the long winter's milking and caring for the animals while in the barn: each of these periods has its own finite characteristics. (10)

10.1. Charlie Kubista brings in the hay, with pitchforks aligned in traditional parallel fashion, rural Sarona, mid-1930s. Wisconsin Folk Museum Collection, courtesy of Rose Kubista Tomesh.

Mitchell's willingness to experience each period stemmed in part from his similar roots on a dairy farm in wooded northern Maine during the 1930s and 1940s—a place where, as in Wisconsin, farmers have also been loggers, hunters, trappers, fishermen, carpenters, and mechanics.

Consequently, the farm talk reprinted here is accompanied by indications of the presence, divergence, or total absence of a given Wisconsin expression in Maine. Likewise Mitchell was well aware that the "wisdom" of proverbs and the "truth" of folk beliefs tend, for those who use them, to cluster variously along continua of acceptance and rejection, seriousness and jocularity. As he put it, the Wisconsin dairy farmer

> does not wait for the oak leaves to attain the size of a squirrel's foot before he plants his corn. As soon as the soil dries out enough to get on it with his heavy machinery he begins to put in his crops. Nor does he hold back from mowing hay when he notices the family dog eating grass, although a local saying has it this is a sure sign of rain. He pays much more attention to radio and television weather forecasts, even though he realizes that the weatherman, too, is often wrong. Why then have I heard so many bits of lore referring to old ideas about animal behavior, health, bad luck, and weather in time spent on the Thorpe farm? (9)

The answers—for there is no single answer—range from the desire to control, if only through imagination, forces that are perpetually beyond control; to romantic nostalgia for old ways and their practitioners; to the entertainment value of some topic that "makes for good conversation anyway."

Reprinted from Roger E. Mitchell, *From Fathers to Sons: A Wisconsin Family Farm,* a special issue of *Midwestern Journal of Language and Folklore* 10:1–2 (1984):146–67, appendices 1–3.

Part I: Selected Vocabulary

This listing of words and phrases is not meant to be comprehensive. I have not included many words which are common to dairy farming on the national level and would appear to be part of the national vocabulary or at least no farther from the average reader than a standard dictionary. I have not attempted to search out any particular word or expression but rather recorded this vocabulary as it appeared in day-to-day activities. A number of terms included are from an earlier period of time, when the Maine or Wisconsin farmer worked at least part-time in the woods and with horses.

Using Karl Thorpe and others of the original settlers as the first generation, his children as the second generation, grandchildren as the third and great-grandchildren as the fourth, I will indicate those words of phrases that are not used by all three surviving generations (2nd, 3rd, 4th). Those common to both Maine and Wisconsin will be in upper case. Some of the words or phrases included are probably local and not widely used. If Maine has an alternative word or phrase I will include it in the definition. By "Maine" I am referring to my home area in Northern Maine.

Aiming fluid. Any of the inexpensive, strong wine brought to hunting shack by members of the hunting gang. 4th.

ARTIFICIAL BREEDING. The bull semen is brought to the farm by the technician who breeds the cow via a hypodermic syringe and a tube.

Back-shooting. When a deer which is being driven doubles back on the drivers and is shot.

Balloon barn. Barn with an arched roof.

BARK PEELER. A dull cant hook (or peavey) that does not get a solid hold on a log slips and tears the bark.

Barn floor. The space between two mows that allows tractors or horses to pull in their loads. Used as an extra hay mow or machine storage today.

Barn hill. The stone ramp going up to the barn floor.

Beggies. A variety of turnip the rutabaga, earlier raised for cow feed, and a favorite vegetable.

Bird boards. Thin throw-away slabs removed from logs in the sawing process. So called because the children use them to make bird houses.

Bird hawk. Any of several species of small hawk. Maine: Chicken hawk.

The Block. A section of land with roads completely around it. To the Thorpes the particular section which includes the Emery Thorpe farm.

Borrow. Used as a substitute for "loan." "He borrowed me his tractor."

Breaking plow. A heavy one-share plow used to plow up virgin land after it has been cleared of trees and stumps.

Breed back. To have a milking cow bred again usually a couple or three months after she has had a calf.

Brush fence. A crude fence made of piled brush and trees. 2nd, 3rd. Maine: Hedge fence. Thus the Maine saying "Ugly as a hedge."

Bull cook. Assistant cook in a lumbering camp. 2nd.

Bull gear. First gear in a tractor. See "creeper gear." Maine: Bull low.

Bull over. If a cow has been bred back and does not become pregnant she is said to have "bulled over." Maine: "Bulling" means "in heat."

BUNGED-UP. To be used up, not able to do anything. In wide usage in Maine. 2nd generation in Wisconsin.

BUNK. The heavy crosspiece on lumbering sleds (sleighs, bobsleds) on which the logs rested. 2nd, 3rd.

BUZZ ON. "To have a buzz on." Drunk. 2nd, 3rd.

Cant hook. Wooden handled tool with a pivoting hook for rolling logs. A similar tool with a heavy metal spike in the end is used in Maine and called a peavey or cant dog.

CARRIERS. The heavy timbers that support the floor joists as they pass from wall to wall.

Casein. The phosphoprotein in milk which forms the basic protein in cheese when curdled by rennet. Can also be used in the manufacture of plastic-like material glue and coldwater paint. Made from the whey as a by-product.

CAST HER WITHERS. For a cow to expel her uterus in the birthing process. Maine: To cast her wethers. 2nd, 3rd. Younger farmers use the technical term learned from veterinarian: prolapsed uterus.

CATCH. When a cow becomes pregnant after breeding she is said to have caught.

Catfaces. A scar on the side of a tree where the tree has not healed well from an injury.

CHICKEN COOP. In Maine called the hen house. In Maine, the coop is a small structure, often for one hen and her chicks.

Chip rocks. Fieldstone consisting of chunks of broken granite, large and small. Also called "sliver rock."

Chopper box. A high-sided wagon into which green hay is blown from the silage chopper. It has also an unloading device powered by the tractor's power take-off, which feeds the silage into the silo filler.

CLEAN. For a cow to expel her afterbirth.

CLEANINGS. The afterbirth.

CLEAR CUT. Removing all trees from a selected area.

CLEARING. The first small fields cleared from the woods by the original settlers. 2nd. General usage in Maine.

CLOSE TO THE AXE. To be running low on firewood. Maine: Close to the saw.

COBBLESTONES. Round, water-worn stones.

Colored cows. Guernseys and Jerseys. Popular breeds before quantity of milk became more important than butterfat [content].

COMING IN. Due to have a calf. "A cow came in today."

COMPANY MACHINE. A piece of machinery owned in company with others.

COOKIE. A woods cook's helper. 2nd. General usage in Maine.

Cooning apples. Stealing apples.

CORD WOOD. Firewood cut in four foot lengths for sale, usually as furnace fuel. 2nd, 3rd. General usage in Maine.

CORNER BINDS. Short chains used to bind the two outside on the bottom layer to a sleigh. 2nd, 3rd.

COW JOCKEYS. Traveling cattle buyers. 4th.

Cow poke. A metal collar with spurs top and bottom, and put around a cow's neck to keep her from pushing her head out through the fence.

Creeper gear. First gear in truck of tractor. Maine: Bull low or the amen hole.

Crotch. A crude sled made from a tree crotch and used to move logs from the woods to the pile. It could also have a body, one end of which dragged on the ground, for use in hauling hemlock bark. 2nd.

CULBERT. Culvert. 2nd. General usage in Maine.

Cutover. Forest land in Northern Wisconsin after timber companies had removed all the marketable timber. Often further damaged by forest fires.

Cutter. A small sled once used for transporting people. In Maine called a sleigh or pung. See "sleigh." 2nd, 3rd.

DEAD HEAD. A large rock just below the surface, struck when plowing. 3rd.

Death Row. The portion of the barn where culled cows are tied, waiting for the truck that will haul them away. 4th.

Deck. Logs piled on skids, the deck. On the Thorpe farm logs stacked at the mill, ready for sawing. Piling them thusly is decking them.

DINNER. The farmer's noon meal. A lunch is a snack. See "supper."

DISK. A harrow with cutting disks used to break up sods in newly plowed fields.

Down Cow Company. Companies that specialize in buying sick, dying, and dead cows. The prices are low.

Dozy. Rotten trees. Maine: Doty.

Drag. A harrow used for leveling out plowed and disked fields preparatory to planting. Maine: Spring tooth harrow.

DRAG. A log of wood cut for firewood. 3rd.

DRAG SAW. A crosscut saw, often powered by a gas engine, used to saw large logs into firewood. 2nd, 3rd.

Dry Pile. To stack newly sawed lumber with narrow sticks between layers to facilitate its drying. Maine: Sticking.

Dump planks. Narrow planks laid on a wagon for picking rocks. The rocks are dumped by tilting the planks one by one.

DUNG. In Maine a word that can be used in polite company in such compounds as "dung fork," "dung spreader," and "dung heap." ("A rooster is king on his own dung heap.") Considered coarse in Easton, Wisconsin.

Easton Tail-Walk. To reduce a cow's tendency to kick or to encourage her to go by forcing her tail up at the base. I have never seen this done in Maine. 4th.

EDGING. To run boards through the sawing process to remove bark from the edges and square up the timber.

Elm. Rock elm, a favorite for barn timbers, being long and straight. Also called "bastard elm."

EVENER. Wooden bar which pivots on a pin and to the ends of which the whiffle trees are hooked. It allows the teamster to adjust the rigging to throw the greater part of the load on the stronger horse. 2nd, 3rd.

Eye-ball, eye-balling. To judge the alignment of timbers and buildings, to sight by eye without the use of instruments.

Farmer's haircut. A closely trimmed cut which leaves a band of light skin contrasting with the tanned portions of neck and face, especially above the ears. 4th.

Feed alley. The space in front of the cows where they are fed.

FOOL KILLERS. Dead limbs that can become dislodged when a tree is cut and cause fatal injuries to a careless sawyer. 2nd, 3rd. General usage in Maine.

FOOTINGS. The broad, often metal reinforced, layer of concrete on which the basement wall is placed.

FREE MARTIN. A sterile heifer, this caused by the heifer having been born in company with a bull. The male's hormones cause the female reproductive organs to develop improperly. 2nd, 3rd.

GARGET. Thick, clotted milk caused by mastitis. 2nd, 3rd. General usage in Maine.

GIRT. A heavy, horizontal plank running from post to post in a barn, to which the boards are nailed and which provides rigidity. For example: "The mow is filled to the first girt." 2nd, 3rd. General usage in Maine.

GOOD CATCH. When the grass germinates well.

GO-ROUND. A session or encounter, verbal or physical.

Grade entry. A house door level with the ground, off to one side or in the back, used by the family when coming in from work. Keeps dirt out of the parlor, etc.

Granny hole. First gear. See "creeper gear."

Green chop. To machine chop young oats and grass into moveable feeder wagons, to provide a high protein supplement, especially for milking cows in summer pastures.

GUMMING OUT. To deepen the grooves between the teeth on a saw after the teeth have worn too short for good cutting.

Hammered up. Drunk. 3rd, 4th.

Hammering. Swedging a saw. To put set in the teeth of a saw by broadening the points by "hammering" them.

Hand pike. A short, stout pole used to pry logs. Maine: Hand spike.

Hatch around. Hustle around. 4th.

HAYBINE. A combination machine which both cuts and crimps hay causing it to dry faster than if just cut. From "combine."

Haylage. Green, chopped hay, partially dried and stored in a silo from "silage."

HAYWIRE OUTFIT. A farm or outfit where things are not properly repaired, but "Just wired together." From the use of haywire for temporary repairs.

HEAD CHEESE. A highly spiced sausage-like food made from the pig's head and put in broad pans rather than in sausage casings.

HEAVES. A lung disease common among horses and aggravated by hot humid weather and dusty hay.

HEMLOCK. A preferred timber for building barns, being highly resistant to rot. In Maine, spruce is the favored barn timber.

HEMLOCK BARK. Peeled off in four foot lengths and [once] sold to tanneries because of its high tannic acid content. No longer done. 2nd.

HIP ROOF. A rural term for a gambrel roof.

Hog's back. A sharp ridge found in glaciated terrain. Maine: Horse back.

Hot deck. A temporary pile of logs. Maine: Hot yard. 2nd.

Hung-up. Trees that get caught in other trees instead of falling when cut. Maine: Lodged.

Illegal hay. Hay put in the mows before being properly dried. 4th.

Ironwood. Strong heavy tree valued for whiffletrees and handles. Maine: Hornbeam.

JAMMER. Log jammer. A device using pulleys or, today, hydraulic power for loading logs. The one using pulleys and horsepower was called "parbuckle" in Maine.

Jig fish. To fish with a hand-held line. Called "hand line" in Maine. "To jig" means "to snag" fish in Maine.

Jim pole. A pole rigged up with a pulley for getting timbers of other heavy objects in place.

Johnson bar. Floor shifting lever on a truck.

Jumper bull. A young bull of no particular heritage pastured with heifers to get them with calf for the first time. Maine: Settler or dunghill bull.

Kiln wood. Wood of not very high quality, once cut and sold to brickyards for firing the brick kiln. 2nd.

KINGPIN. The heavy iron pin that passes through the bunk and holds it to the sleighs. 2nd, 3rd.

Klub. A blood sausage formed into a loaf rather than put into a casing.

LAND POOR. Owning more land than can be profitably worked.

Lefsa. A potato pancake. Norwegian.

Lines. Maine: reins. 2nd, 3rd.

Loafing barn. A low, sheet metal and pole structure, open on one side, usually to the south. Used to house heifers, save barn space, and reduce daily chores.

LODGED HAY. Hay that has been pressed to the ground by wind and rain, making it hard to mow. See "hung-up."

LOG. Used to separate the cutting of timber from the cutting of pulp. "To go logging."

Lutefisk. Dried and salted cod that has been soaked in fresh water, put through a mild lye solution, steamed or boiled, and eaten with melted butter. Norwegian, from "lye" and "fish."

MAKING SAG. The filling out of a cow's udders as she approaches the delivery of a calf. With heifers a sure sign that they are with calf.

Making wood. Cutting the winter's supply of firewood. Maine: Cutting wood.

Manure boat. A homemade, sled-like conveyance used to haul away the manure in the winter. It was brought into the barn with horse or tractor, loaded, taken out to the fields, and spread.

Maple. Hard maple. The sugar maple. Maine: Rock maple. Used as barn timbers. Soft maple: a second grade tree. Maine: White maple.

Matting. The final working over of cheese solids after the whey has been recovered. 2nd, 3rd.

MILK PAIL. The tinned or stainless steel pail used to handle milk, as distinguished from the common galvanized pail used to feed.

Mortgage raisers. Pigs raised as a secondary source of income. 2nd, 3rd.

Mortgaging a buck. To have a preliminary drink from the wine bought to celebrate the shooting of a buck. 4th.

MOW. That portion of the barn used for hay and straw, as compared to the barn floor. Also called in Maine "bay," as in "two-bay barn."

Mud. Mortar, as used for building walls and chimneys.

Mud hock. A wooden tray for carrying or holding mortar. A hod.

NECK YOKE. A yoke which holds up the pole on horse-drawn machinery and is fastened to the horses' collars. 2nd, 3rd.

New breaking. Newly cleared land ready for planting. Maine: New land.

Nigger heads. Large, round, water-worn stones.

NO-SEE-UMS. Midges, gnats. 2nd. General usage in Maine.

Notch. The cut made in the front of the tree, preparatory to sawing it down. Maine: Undercut.

NUBBINS. Small, not well-filled-out corn cobs. 2nd, 3rd. General usage in Maine.

Nurse crop. A crop such as alfalfa planted with oats. It will mature the second year.

Oak. Red oak. Considered a top grade hardwood timber. White oak. Strong, tough wood favored for use as handles, wagon poles, whiffletrees, etc. Black oak. A scruffy, second class oak. Oak does not grow in Northern Maine.

Old Stump Blower. Strong white port wine, bought for hunting to celebrate the shooting of a buck. 4th.

ON RUBBER. "To put on rubber," describes the shiftover from metal-wheeled machines to rubber tires, when the original steel wheels were replaced with rubber.

Open up. To split the bark on a tree, preparatory to removing its bark with a bark spud. Maine: Splitting.

OVERALL JACKET. Denim jacket. 2nd, 3rd.

OVERALL TROUSERS. Jeans. 2nd, 3rd.

PEAVEY. Similar to a cant hook but with a strong metal spike in the end. Also called in Maine "cant dog." 2nd. General usage in Maine.

PIKEMEN. Also polemen. Used long poles tipped with metal pikes, and guided logs on river drives. 2nd.

Pole saw. An engine-powered circle saw used for cutting logs and small trees into firewood. Maine: Circular saw.

Pole wood. Limbs and small trees cut for firewood. Maine: Circular wood.

POPPLE. The poplar tree. The major pulpwood tree in Wisconsin. Two kinds, "green" and "yellow," so-called from the color of the bark.

PULPWOOD. In Wisconsin mostly poplar and cut in 100″ lengths. In Maine, mostly balsam fir and spruce, cut in 40″ lengths.

Pump house. Houses the pump by pond, spring or well. Maine: Well house.

PURLINE PLATE. The timber which supports the rafters at a point between the eaves and the peak.

PURLINE POST. The upright timber that supports the purline plate and thus governs the height of a roof in a gambrel-roofed barn.

Rakings. That hay left scattered on the field by the loaders, and reraked so as not to lose any hay. Maine: Scatterings. No longer done. 2nd, 3rd.

Rampike. A standing, dead tree trunk. Maine: Stub.

RAVES. The U-shaped metal strap that holds the crossbar in place on a sleigh runner. 2nd, 3rd.

Raw Fries. Potatoes peeled and fried, especially when there are no cold boiled potatoes for hash. Maine: Fried potatoes.

Rennet. An enzyme that curdles milk, traditionally prepared from animal stomachs. Used in the cheese-making process.

RING. To cut around a hemlock tree trunk at 4 foot intervals in order to remove the bark for sale to tanneries. 2nd, 3rd.

River hogs. Men who took the rafts of lumber down the river. 2nd.

Rocking chair rack. A large set of horns on a buck deer. Not many of this size are shot.

ROLLING HITCH. To so hook a chain of skidding tongs that the log will roll and free itself from obstructions when the horses begin to pull. 2nd, 3rd.

Run. The distance between the runners on a sleigh, its width. "An eight foot run." 2nd, 3rd.

RUNS. Diarrhea, animals or humans.

SCALE RULE. The calibrated rule by which one calculates the board feet in a log.

SCHOOLMARM. A crotched tree. 3rd. General usage in Maine.

Scrubs. Cows of no particular ancestry, such as were common at the turn of the century. Maine: Dunghill breeds.

Second crop. The second cutting of hay, which has more leaves and higher protein rating. Maine: After grass, and used for pasture.

SECOND GROWTH. Trees that have grown up after the virgin timber has been cut.

Self-binder. A reaper that both reaps and ties the grain into bundles, 2nd, 3rd. Maine: Reaper.

SELL ON STUMP. To sell one's timber to someone else who does the actual cutting. Maine: To sell stumpage.

SETTLE. To get a cow with calf.

SHAKY HEMLOCK. Trees whose growth layers have separated, causing splits in the lumber sawed from such logs ("shaky lumber").

SHARP SHOD. When the calks on a horse's shoes have been drawn out to points to prevent slipping on ice. 2nd, 3rd.

Shearings. Timberland that has been clean-cut, with everything cut. Maine: A chopping.

Sheeny man. Horse and cow dealer. Rag buyer. "A pretty sharp dealer."

Sheeting. The boards or plywood covering the outside walls of a building. Perhaps from "sheathing," as in "sheathing paper."

Shined up. Somewhat intoxicated.

SHIPPING FEVER. Severe diarrhea in cows. So called because it is common in newly purchased animals. Maine: Referred to respiratory infections common in horses just shipped in from the West.

Short jeans. Jeans (overall pants) as compared to overalls. 3rd.

Shypoke. The bittern. Maine: Shitpoke.

Silo corn. Corn planted to fill the silo or to green chop. Maine: Fodder corn.

Skidding. The pulling of logs out of the woods. Maine: Twitching.

Skidding tongs. Heavy tongs used for skidding, instead of a chain.

Slab Wood. Slabs sawed into firewood. Maine: 16" pieces of logs split into slabs for use in cookstoves.

SLABS. The sides that are sawed off a log to square it when sawing out lumber.

SLASHINGS. Wisconsin: the same as shearings. Maine: the debris left after logging or pulping a timber lot.

Sleigh. Double sleds used for hauling logs. Maine: Bobsleds.

Slippers. The floor joists. Maine: Stringers. Perhaps from "sleepers."

Slippery Jims. A sweet cucumber pickle, consisting of peeled, ripe cucumbers.

Sliver rock. Chunks of broken granite. See "chip rocks."

Slusher. Twin-handled earth-moving scoop, pulled by horses. Maine: Scraper. 2nd, 3rd.

Smart weed. A hot-tasting weed.

Smoke wood. Basswood. Doesn't burn well. Light, poor quality lumber or wood from the basswood tree.

SMUDGE. A small, smoky fire to keep away biting insects. 2nd. General usage in Maine.

Snake, snaking. Pulling logs out of the woods.

SNAP A CHALK LINE. After rubbing a [string or wire] line with chalk and extending it between two points, to snap it against the surface to provide a straight line.

Snat. Snathe. The handle of a scythe. 2nd, 3rd.

Sooner hound. A poor hunting dog. "Sooner lie down than hunt." 4th.

Spiking. Putting bundles of grain into the threshing machine. Maine: Feeding.

SPILES. The hollow tubes, wooden or metal, put in the hole bored in a sugar maple for the sap to run through. Maine: taps.

SPUD. A metal tool used for prying the bark off trees. A bark spud.

Spud man. He who debarks a tree. Maine: The spudder.

Squirts. Severe diarrhea in calves.

Stab churn. Plunger churn. 2nd, 3rd.

STAGS. Boots with the tops cut off, or shortened trousers.

Stake out. To tie an animal on a chain so it can graze. Maine: tethering.

Stay lathe. Boards nailed to hold timbers temporarily in place on a construction job. Maine: brace.

Stepping Off. To estimate length by counting one's steps. Maine: Pacing off.

STONE DRAG. A conveyance made of planks for hauling off big stones. In Maine, such stones are called "drag rocks."

Stone fence. Fieldstones piled along property llnes so as to form a fence. Maine: Stone wall.

Straight on for coons. A dog that will run only coons, will not be sidetracked by deer or rabbits. 4th.

Striping. Smoothing the mortar between concrete blocks with a bent ½"pipe.

SULKY PLOW. A plow having wheels and a seat for the driver. 2nd, 3rd.

SUPPER. The evening meal. Dinner is the noon meal. Lunch is a snack.

Swamp. A low, wet part of a farm. In Maine, a swamp is in the woods. In a field or pasture, wetland is a "swale."

Swamp auger. A mythical, mole-like creature. In the old days, a mythical tool that greenhorns were sent in search of.

SWAMPER. One who cleared brush and trees from logging roads. 2nd.

Swamp grass. A coarse, wild grass found in wet areas. Maine: swale grass.

Swamp hook. Hook on the end of a chain, used to load logs or pull them out of mud and snow.

Sway bars. Two poles that connected the two sleighs used in logging.

Swede saw. The bucksaw. Maine: Frenchman's fiddle.

Swedge. See "Hammering."

Swing man. The man on a sawing crew who carries out two tasks: helps roll the logs on the carriage and also aids in carrying away the newly sawn lumber.

Sy. The scythe.

Tail sawyer. He who carries away and piles the newly sawn lumber.

TAP. To bore a hole in sugar maples to accomodate the tap (spile); or to make an incision in a cow that is bloated, in order to let out the accumulated gas.

Talk like a sausage. To talk wildly, without common sense. B.S.

Third eye. To shoot a sick animal. "Give it a third eye." 4th.

Three banger. A cow giving milk from only three quarters. Related to "two banger," a two cylinder engine.

Three bottom woman. Strong and of substantial size. Related to "three bottom plow," one with three shares.

Threshing rig. Threshing machine.

Throw a calf. Freshen, give birth.

TIMBER CRUISER (or land-looker). One who surveys a wood lot for its timber potential.

TOE NAIL. To nail in at angles, such as in a wall joist.

TOPS. The remnants of a logging operation, but not clear cut.

Top shelf. First class.

TOTE ROADS. Roads for "toting" supplies in to a woods camp. 2nd.

TRACE CHAINS. The chains running from the whiffletrees and attached to the horse's harness. 2nd, 3rd.

Tree bind. A log that because of its growth pattern will tighten up and "bind" the saw.

TROTS. Diarrhea, of both animals or humans. Also called in Maine "backdoor" trots," from "back house" or "privy."

Turn around. A road or driveway with a circle or cleared area for turning at the end. Maine: "round turn."

UP NORTH. The northern part of the state. In Maine also called "Up River."

WASHBOARDING. When a road gets out of shape and forms wave-like ridges across it.

Water out. To de-salt meat by soaking it in fresh water. Maine: freshen out.

WHIFFLETREES. Singletrees. The pivoting wooden bars forming part of a machine, to which the horse is attached by its trace chains.

Whistle trousers. Corduroy knickers. Made a noise as the wearer walked. 3rd.

WING SHOULDERS. A cow that stands with her shoulder blades turned out from her body. Often caused by bad legs or ankles.

WOODBOX. "In the woodbox." Sick. Maine: Sick abed in the woodbox.

Wood butcher. The woods camp carpenter. 2nd.

WRAPPER CHAIN. The chain bound around a load of logs. 2nd, 3rd. Maine: wrapping chain.

WRECKING BAR. A carpenter's tool for pulling spikes and prying timbers. In Maine also called "pinch bar" and "spike puller."

Yellow dog weather. Pleasant weather that causes boys especially to feel lazy. To have the "yellow dogs."

YOUNG STOCK. More commonly called "heifers" in Easton.

Part II: Proverbs and Proverbial Phrases

Those proverbial expressions which are also used in Maine are marked with an asterisk (*). Annotations are added where deemed necessary for fuller understanding, along with those Maine expressions that appear to be variants on the same theme. The arrangement is alphabetical by key words.

Ankle deep. To be involved to the point of being unable to make a change. Maine: "Up to my knees."

*Barbwire. The cow "can go through four strands of barbwire without touching a strand." Said of animals that constantly get out of the pasture.

Beans. "Not worth a row of beans." Maine: "Not worth a hill of beans."

*Blood. "Like getting blood out of a turnip." Won't pay debts.

Bricks. "A few bricks short of a load." Somewhat retarded.

*Bright-eyed and bushy-tailed. Full of pep and ready to go.

*Bull. "Couldn't hit a bull's ass with a barn shovel." Poor marksman.

Chest high by the Fourth of July. The hoped-for progress of the corn crop.

Closer than a sailor's haircut. Cutting hay so as to leave a very short stubble.

*Colder than a witch's elbow. Cleaned up from the "witch's teat" commonly heard in Maine.

*Cost all outdoors. Expensive.

Devil stands ready. He takes advantage of carelessness.

*Dog. "Every dog has its day." In Maine the saying continues: "and every bitch two afternoons."

*Dog. "If you kick a dog enough, he'll bite."

Eat. "They'll eat anything that won't eat them first." Strong appetites.

Father. "A father and his son ought to live at least a forty apart."

Gall. Salesmen "have the gall of a scalded cat." Maine: "the gall of a government mule."

Goldenrod. "When the goldenrod is yellow and the oats are brown, it's time to harvest."

Half an inch. "Half an inch is a lot if it's on the end of your nose." Used in reference to the care necessary in carpenter work.

*Hay. "If you can't hay, you might as well go fishing." That is take some time off.

*Haying on the halves. To do a poor job of mowing, leaving a lot of hay standing or mauled down.

*Hide mistakes. "A good carpenter can hide his mistakes."

*Hindsight is 20-20.

Hot to Trot. Ready to go, often used unfavorably of women.

Idle hands are the Devil's tools.

Idleness is the Devil's workshop.

Last dog. "To stay until the last dog is hung." To remain to the end of activities. Maine: "To stay until the last gun is fired."

*Make do, wear it out, or do without.

*Nail. "Couldn't nail a nail." Not handy with tools.

Old. Too soon old and too late smart.

Pick dry. "You can't pick a field dry." In stony land, you can never get them all.

Plate. "It's on Joe's plate." It is his fault.

*Rain. "The more rain, the more rest." In Maine, often followed with "Another day in the hay." That is, to sleep in the haymow.

Ready to Hoe. To be ready to go to work.

Resting. "Do it while you're resting." Do it in your spare time.

*Rot-rust. "They'll rot out before they wear out." In Maine, more often "rust out" instead of "rot out." Said of farmers' leaving machines outdoors.

*Setting hen. "Couldn't pull a setting hen (or cluck) off her nest." In reference to a poor team of horses or a small tractor.

*Shake a stick at. "Come tax time there were more poor teams than you could shake a stick at." Large numbers.

*Shirt sleeves. "From shirt sleeves to shirt sleeves in three generations." The heirs fail to maintain the prosperous business developed by the grandfather.

Shoot snipes. "Might as well go West and shoot snipes." To be engaged in useless activity.

Signs. "All signs fail in dry weather." Humorous comment relating to weather omens.

*Sing a different tune. "He sang a different tune when his kids started doing the things he used to do."

*Sit on your thumb. To have no chair in which to sit.

Snuff. "Giving a Dane a chew of snuff is like giving him a nickel." He takes half the box (from when snuff was a dime a box).

Spend money. "He spends money like it was coming out of a well." Maine: "Go through money like water."

*Stay with. "Fried potatoes stay with a man." Nourishing.

*Step. "One step forward and two backwards." Poor management.

Strainer pad. "That town is the strainer pad of Wisconsin." It catches all the human rubbish.

*Streak. "He was going like a streak of grease."

*Strong back. "Farming calls for a strong back and a weak mind."

Sweating like a butcher. Maine: "Sweating like a steer (or horse)." Perspire heavily.

*Tail. "To have the world by the tail with a downhill start." To be in control.

*Thick as hair on a dog's back.

Thick lips. "To go around with thick lips." Dejected.

*Three men and a horse. A job demanding great strength.

Town. "Just like in town." Things going smoothly and well.

Two friends. "Going on his two friends." Walking. Maine: "Shank's mares."

Two hands while learning. Said of a learning carpenter if he grips his hammer with two hands.

Ugly. "He's so ugly the Devil doesn't want him." That is, he won't die.

Ugly. "He looks as if he'd been beaten with an ugly stick." Unattractive.

*Up. "No way to go but up." Standard comment after the ground floor has been completed on a new house.

*Useless. "As useless as teats on a boar hog."

Vas a wagon. What a car.

Walk. "Walk like a side rake." Walk crookedly.

*Waste not, want not.

*White around the gills. Pale, as when frightened or sick.

*Woodbox. "In the woodbox." Sick. In Maine: "Sick abed in the woodbox." Sometimes added: "And soaking your feet in a basket of chips."

Part III: Omens, Beliefs, and Folk Medicine

Most of this material was presented in a humorous context. In a few cases, it was pointed out that some people still believed or practiced the custom. An asterisk (*) will indicate that a few people still show a degree of faith in the validity of the statement. Double asterisks (**) designate beliefs common to both Maine and Wisconsin.

**Animal fur. When a coon's (or squirrel's) fur is thick, it will be a cold winter.

**Arthritis. A copper wire around one wrist and the opposite ankle helps. It establishes a current.

**Beavers. If a beaver's feed pile is large, it will be a long, hard winter.

Blessing. If you eat without asking the blessing, you will have the heartburn.

Blessing. If there are less than five things on the table, you don't have to ask the blessing.

*Bloat. A piece of wood tied cross-ways in a cow's mouth will make her chew on the stick and expel gas from her stomach.

Burnt toast. It will give a person a good singing voice.

*Calves. Calves will choke if allowed to drink from a pail sitting on the floor. It should be held up.

**Cards. Playing cards are associated with the Devil.

Carrots. Eating carrots causes curly hair. Maine: Causes good eyesight.

*Castration. Bulls should be castrated during the full moon, or they might bleed to death.

Cat. Cat washing herself with her leg in the air means guests are coming.

**Cats. Cats will steal a baby's breath, causing it to choke.

*Chickens. If their bones are red, it will be an easy winter. White bones, a hard winter. Maine: A lot of gristle on the tip of the breastbone means a rainy season.

*Colored cows. The golden color of Guernsey milk is related to the red in their hair and hide.

Comet. Halley's Comet was believed to be a sign the world was going to come to an end.

Concrete. Wash your hands before the job is done and the concrete will crack.

*Cow cleanings. If a cow eats her cleanings, she will choke. (Cows will eat the afterbirth if not prevented from doing so.)

**Cuds. If a cow loses her cud, she will become ill. Cure: get her another one from another cow. Maine: make her one.

Cricket. To step on a cricket brings rain. Maine: To step on a spider causes rain.

**Dandelions. If you blow away all the fluffy seeds from a dandelion blossom in one breath and make a wish, it will be granted.

Deer. Deer coming out of the woods during the day means rain is on the way.

**Dogs. Dogs eating grass, it's going to rain.

*Dogs. Dogs (and cats) eat grass to make them vomit and so clean out their stomachs.

Easter Water. A bucket filled before daylight on Easter morning can be kept all year and won't become stagnant. Wash in it any time during the year and it will make you healthy.

*Electricity. The current will seep from high voltage lines and harm people and animals who pass below.

**Fire. Play in fire, wet the bed.

**Fish. Fish is brain food. It'll make you smart.

Gophers. Striped gophers can dodge a .22 bullet.

**Heifers. Heifers born in company with a bull can't have calves.

Last Days of a Month. The last three days predict the weather for the first fifteen days of the next month. Rain on the 29th, rain on the first to the fifth; sunny on the 30th, sunny on the sixth to the tenth; cold on the 31st, cold from the 11th to the 15th.

Milk fever. Can be treated by pumping air into the cow's udders.

Oak leaves. When they are the size of a squirrel's foot, it's time to plant corn. Maine: When poplar leaves are the size of a mouse's ear, it's time to plant potatoes.

Pepper. Eating pepper makes hair grow on your chest. Maine: Molasses will make hair grow on your chest.

**Porcupines. It's against the law to kill them, for they are the only animal a lost man can get without a gun.

Potatoes. Should not be planted until the wild plum trees blossom.

**Rabbits. Should not be eaten. They cause a disease.

Red sky. "Red sky on Friday night, rain before Monday."

**Rooster eggs. Tiny eggs with no yolks are rooster eggs.

**Smoke. If smoke curls to the ground, it will rain.

**Snakes. Kill a snake but it won't die until sundown.

Snakes. Dead snakes call other snakes.

**Snakes. A mother snake will swallow her young in time of danger.

*Spleens. Red pig spleens predict a warm winter; long spleens mean a long winter; short thick spleens short winter.

**Stutter. Tickle a baby's feet and he'll become a stutterer.

**Styes. "Pee in the ditch, get a stye in your eye." Maine: "Pee in the middle of the road get a stye in your eye."

Sunday. Don't whistle on Sunday. It will call the Devil.

Sunday. Whittle on Sunday and chips will burn in the palm of your hand in hell.

Sunday. A general prohibition on unnecessary activities including sewing and knitting. In Maine: "Come the Day of Judgment, every stitch sewn on Sunday will have to be picked out with your nose."

Tamarack. When the tamarack needles turn brown, cold weather is coming.

Throat. For a sore throat use lard or skunk oil.

Throat. For a sore throat, rub on Vicks and then wrap a dirty woolen sock around your neck.

Toothache. Heat a piece of haywire and jam it into the cavity.

**Toothache. Pack the cavity with ground cloves.

Turtles. Turtles will not die until sundown. See Snake.

Warts. You can catch warts from milking cows that have warts. **To get rid of warts, pull them out by the roots. Tie a knot around a wart, bury the knotted string in the basement. When the string rots, the wart will disappear. Bury it on the full moon. Sell the wart to somebody for a nickel. **To cure a wart, touch it with the juice from milkweed or dandelion.

**Water witching. Ground water occurs in veins and some people have the gift of finding it by using a forked stick, a switch, or wire. Maine: a forked stick.

Water witching. This power is a gift from God. But for it to work people must have faith in it.

**Wedding ring. It is bad luck for your marriage to take your wedding ring off.

**Worms. If you eat too much sweet stuff, you'll have worms.

11

Application to Live in Northern Wisconsin (North of Highway 29)

Anonymous

Highway 29 runs from east to west, linking Green Bay, Wausau, the Chippewa Falls/Eau Claire area, Menomonie, and River Falls, while neatly separating Wisconsin's northern region from the south. Above this line lakes, woods, and log trucks proliferate. It's the home of self-described "jack-pine savages," and the place where I grew up.

In 1960 the hometown Rice Lake Warriors basketball team made it to the state tournament in Madison. That was before the present system of four divisions based on relative population, and schools competed with one another irrespective of size. Eau Claire Memorial's "Old Abes" were the perennial "up north" entry, so little-known Rice Lake was greeted by downstate papers and rival players as a collection of rubes, hicks, and honyocks (immigrant German or Slavic farmers). Perhaps intimidated, Rice Lake was quickly eliminated. But the team was back in the tournament the next year. My dad, Warren Leary, publisher of the *Rice Lake Chronotype*, smarted over negative stereotypes. Rather than tout sophistication (and risk more ridicule), he began to write about Rice Lake's team as the boys from "Woodpecker Point"—a local nickname for the city's rustic extreme west side where his pals Bob and Dix Sandburg had lived in the 1930s. By swapping Rice Lake for Woodpecker Point, an in-your-face boondocks byword, my dad pointed out, as much with a grin as a sneer, "Yeah, we're from up in the woods, what's it to ya?" Rice Lake went on to trounce a pair of downstate teams before losing in the finals to Milwaukee Lincoln in overtime on, of course, a disputed, last-second basket. In the aftermath, ardent fans like Alphonse Liedl could be seen around town garbed in jackets outfitted with Wisconsin maps across their backs. Woodpecker Point appeared alongside a star in the northwestern quadrant normally occupied by Rice Lake.

The "Application to Live in Northern Wisconsin" plays similarly with both insiders' and outsiders' stereotypes of the people living above Highway 29. The collective image of an insular, inbred, male-dominated, outdoorsy, gearhead culture of sex-crazed, drunken Packer fans is wildly exaggerated, yet built around a core of truth. "Up north" natives recognize the absurdity of confusing image with reality, but many delight in the image—partly because they enjoy poking fun at themselves, partly because it allows them on occasion to play the wise fool, to act the country bumpkin when patronized by tourists and government officials who assume the role of "Arkansas travelers."

Not surprisingly, the up north stereotype shares much with popular images of others living in such rustic American margins as the Ozarks and the southern Appalachians. Indeed, an "Application to Be a Hillbilly" precedes this northern Wisconsin version, as indicated by the residual presence of southern "redneck" elements: the Confederate flag, "Dixie," Elvis veneration, incest, Jack Daniels, and references to parents as Mamma and Daddy. And just as southern musicians have long made comic use of the hillbilly persona, so too do up north musicians—most notably Da Yoopers from the old Wisconsin Territory in Ishpeming, Michigan, and Bananas at Large, whose "Da Turdy Point Buck" situates the quintessential up north rustic in a deer camp.

11.1. In the early 1990s Larry Peterson and Rob Mitchell drew some local criticism when they launched Spooner's "Jackpine Savage Days." For Peterson, however, the festival was both a tongue-in-cheeky recognition of "north woods" stereotypes and a means to make light of them. Logo courtesy of Spooner Area Chamber of Commerce.

The application's form and medium merit final comments. Nowadays even backwoods dwellers are confronted with a flurry of forms and a continuous barrage of electronic communiqués. Hence this phony application parodies the questionnaires we are too often forced to fill out, and its transmission is not by word-of-mouth, but via the copier, the fax machine, and the Internet. Reprinted from the anonymous document circulating on the Internet, March 17, 1995.

NAME: _____

NICKNAME: _____ CB HANDLE: _____

NECK SHADE: ____ Light Red ____ Bright Red ____ Dark Red

NUMBER OF TEETH EXPOSED IN FULL GRIN: Upper: ____ Lower: ____

LENGTH OF RIGHT LEG: _____ LENGTH OF LEFT LEG: _____

DADDY (if unknown list three suspects):_____

_____

MAMMA:_____

CAN YOU BEAT YOUR WIFE AT ARM WRESTLING:_____

ARE YOU MARRIED TO ANY OF THE FOLLOWING:

____ Sister ____ Cousin ____ Cousin's sister ____ Sister's cousin

DATE/LOCATION OF YOUR LAST SIGHTING OF ELVIS: _____

MOBILE HOME COLOR:

____ Two-tone, brown and white   ____ Two-tone, pink and white

____ Faded green   ____ Baby-shit yellow

____ Don't remember what it was before it all peeled off

MAKE AND MODEL OF PICKUP TRUCK: _____

TIRE SIZE: ____   NUMBER OF BEER CANS ON FLOOR OF PICKUP: _____

TRUCK EQUIPPED WITH:

____ Gun rack   ____ Mud flaps   ____ Camper top   ____ Air horn

____ American flag   ____ 4-Wheel drive ____ 8-track   ____ CB

____ Fuzzbuster   ____ Roll bar   ____ Mud tires   ____ Rust

____ Load of wood   ____ Dents   ____ Confederate flag

____ Deer repelling whistles   ____ Deer poaching spotlights

____ Neon colored wiper arms, license plate frames, radio antenna, and netting across back of truck box

____ Empty Coke bottle for collecting tobacco juice whenever it's too cold to open a window to spit

____ Playboy emblem air freshener hanging from rear view mirror

____ Pine tree air freshener hanging from rear view mirror

____ Woman's garter hanging from rear view mirror

____ Horn that plays 26 different tunes, including "Dixie"

BUMPER STICKERS:

____ Honk If You're Horny   ____ Fuck 'em Bucky!

____ Almost Heaven—Hayward   ____ Where da Hell's Rhinelander?

____ Ducks Unlimited   ____ DNR—Damn Near Russia

____ I'm the NRA   ____ Flush Illinois

____ Tommy Bartlett Water Show   ____ Eat Cheese or Die

____ Nuke the Gay Whales for Jesus   ____ Coke is It!

____ Women—You Can't Live With 'em, and You Can't Shoot 'em

____ The Pack is Back

DO YOU OWN ANY SHOES, not counting boots? _____

PRIMARY SOURCE OF INCOME:

____ Welfare   ____ Burglary   ____ The J-word

____ Unemployment compensation   ____ Drug sales   ____ Poaching

____ Workman's compensation   ____ Recycling your empty beer cans

FAVORITE PANTS: ____ Bib overalls   ____ Polyester, with snags

FAVORITE MUSIC: ____ Country   ____ Western   ____ Country Western

____ Anything played on an accordion

____ Anything a person sings through their nose

THINGS IN YOUR FRONT YARD:

____ Various kitchen appliances   ____ Assorted vehicles on blocks

____ Piles of split firewood   ____ Dismantled snowmobiles

____ Bathtub grotto   ____ Horseshoes mounds

____ Dog run—with all the grass worn down to rock hard dirt

_____ Deer hanging from tree limb—in season

_____ Deer hanging from tree limb—out of season

_____ Wood cut-out of bent over old lady

FAVORITE MEAL:

_____ Anything fried in lard   _____ Brats and Pabst Blue Ribbon

_____ Pickled pig's feet   _____ Venison and Pabst Blue Ribbon

_____ Pickled eggs   _____ Cheese curds and Pabst Blue Ribbon

_____ Beef jerky   _____ Twinkies and Pabst Blue Ribbon

_____ Green bean, mushroom soup, and tater tots Casserole

FAVORITE RECREATION:

_____ Deer huntin'   _____ Deer huntin' while drinkin'

_____ Snowmobilin'   _____ Snowmobilin' while drinkin'

_____ Fishin' with live bait   _____ Fishin' with live bait while drinkin'

_____ Watchin' Green Acres reruns _____ Watchin' Green Acres reruns while

_____ Drillin' the old lady   drinkin'

_____ Cruisin' the streets for wimmin' and tryin' to entice 'em into my truck by
  makin' crude animal noises and suggestive tongue gestures

FAVORITE WEAPON:

_____ .357 magnum _____ .30–06 _____ Morning breath _____ Ice auger

_____ Chain saw _____ Tire iron _____ Forehead _____ Wife

FAVORITE ODOR:

_____ Wet dog   _____ Diesel fuel _____ Pabst Blue Ribbon

_____ Minnow bucket _____ Frying spam _____ Old canvas

_____ Hoppe's No. 9 Powder Solvent _____ The girl across the road

_____ Any paper mill on a hot August day _____ Any scent emanating from a body

FAVORITE CAP EMBLEM:

_____ Budweiser _____ Bearwiz Beer _____ Stihl _____ Old Fart

_____ Point Beer _____ Old Style _____ John Deere _____ 4 × 4

_____ Pabst Beer _____ Jack Daniels _____ Skoal _____ Remington

_____ Kill 'em all and let God sort 'em out

FAVORITE READING MATERIAL:

_____ Fishing Facts _____ American Rifleman _____ Soldier of Fortune

_____ Enquirer   _____ TV Guide   _____ Beer bottle labels

_____ Polka Digest _____ Welfare Application _____ Watchtower

_____ Hustler (just for the articles)

_____ Sports Illustrated (swimsuit edition only)

FAVORITE TAVERN NAME:

_____ Dew Drop Inn   _____ Whygoby Inn

_____ County Line Tavern   _____ Lake (insert name of lake) Tavern

_____ (Name) and (Name)'s Bar _____ Pine (view, wood, etc.) Tavern

_____ Open   _____ Club (insert highway number)

FAVORITE WAY TO GREET SOMEONE:

_____ Ya, hey.

_____ Good mornin' der!

___ Dem Packers is playin' like a buncha old women.

___ Dem Brewers is playin' like a buncha old women.

___ Dem Badgers is playin' like a buncha old women.

___ Dem Bucks is playin' like a buncha old women.

___ Dey should just let dem Indians spear dose idiots at da DNR!

___ Dey should take dat whole buncha dem Madison liberals and queers and line 'em up and shoot 'em!

___ Wanna see da new tatto I got da odder day?

FAVORITE VEHICLE:

___ 1967 Ford Galaxy ___ International Scout

___ Anything you can take the bumpers off and jack the body up four feet above road level

FARTHEST AWAY MEMORABLE EVENT YOU'VE EVER ATTENDED:

___ Minocqua Moose Call Madness Competition

___ Antigo Tater Trot Carnival

___ Gleason Grouse Mating Gala

___ Ringle Roundhouse Right Beer Tent Brawl

___ Herbster Jaycees Seagull Doo-Doo Days

___ Lake Tomahawk Outboard Motor Repairs Finals

___ Ogema Crew Cut Championships

___ Spread Eagle Proctologist Probe For Gold Weekend

___ Chetek Carp Queen Beauty Contest and Carp Cuisine Cookoff

___ Eagle River Shout-Off For The Deal (held the week after the annual Snowmobile Derby)

___ Phelps Early Spring Indian Walleye Spearing Festival

___ Parrish Cafe Grease Lover's Jamboree and Porta-Potty Exhibit

___ Hamburg Monthly Deer Poach and Warden Shoot

___ Glidden Annual Chipmunk Roundup and Polka Fest

FAVORITE SONG OF ALL TIME:

___ Lucille

___ Theme from Beverly Hillbillies

___ Theme from Green Acres

___ Red Neck, White Sox, and Blue Ribbon Beer

___ She Got The Gold Mine and I Got The Shaft

___ Take This Job and Shove It

___ Anything lip-synched by the stripper at the Boom Bay Bar

Your X (a signature will do): _____

PART TWO

Storytelling

12

Turtle Trying to Get Credit
(A Tale)

Paul Radin

The traditions of Wisconsin's Winnebago (or, as they are now known, Ho-Chunk) people tell them they have always been here. Certainly they occupied villages throughout southern Wisconsin— particularly along the Black, Fox, Rock, and Wisconsin River valleys—at the time of European contact. In the nineteenth century, the United States government forced the Winnebago to move successively to reservations in Minnesota, South Dakota, and Nebraska. Many people, however, resisted forced relocation and hid out in Wisconsin, while others relocated to western reservations, only to return later. Eventually the Wisconsin Winnebago won federal recognition. Nowadays they have no central reservation, but are variously settled around such communities as Baraboo, Black River Falls, La Crosse, Neillsville, Tomah, Wisconsin Dells, Wisconsin Rapids, and Wittenburg.

Perhaps because of the hardships endured, Wisconsin's Ho-Chunk people have sustained their cultural traditions to a high degree. In the early 1990s they established the Hocak Wazijaci Language and Culture Program, under the leadership of Kenneth Funmaker, Sr., primarily to maintain the language, but also to accumulate, archive, and conserve documentary materials on the Ho-Chunk people—including materials produced by Paul Radin.

A pioneering anthropologist, Paul Radin (1883–1959) was a student of Franz Boas at Columbia University before devoting much of his professional life to Winnebago culture. His many publications include three classic works: *The Autobiography of a Winnebago Indian* (Berkeley: University of California Press, Publications in American Archeology and Ethnology, vol. 16, no. 7, 1920); *The Winnebago Tribe* (Washington, D.C.: Smithsonian Institution, Annual Report of the Bureau of American Ethnology, vol. 37, 1923); and *The Trickster: A Study in American Indian Mythology* (New York: Philosophical Library, 1956).

The story offered here originally appeared with three others as appendices to Radin's "Literary Aspects of Winnebago Mythology." Radin, however, conducted most of his fieldwork with Ho-Chunk converts to the Native American Church. Because their new religion no longer bound them to keeping sacred stories secret, they departed radically from traditional practices by offering them to an outsider. Hence I am unwilling to reproduce myths or *waika* (literally "what is old"). Such stories belong to their respective clans and medicine lodges, Ho-Chunk institutions that are very much intact. Rather, I offer "Turtle Trying to Get Credit," a humorous post-contact story about a popular trickster figure. As Paul Radin states:

> It is palpably a modern production. It is in brief the story of a man with a bad reputation who tries to get credit from a merchant in order to buy food for his family. After he has been rebuffed a number of times, a kindhearted merchant takes pity on him because of the poverty of his family. In return he goes hunting and returns with canoes full of the finest furs for his benefactor. This hero, however, is Trickster, and all the characteristics that are associated with him in the Trickster cycle are found here. He is untrustworthy, boastful and a gambler. As in the cycle, so here also there are humorous touches. Trickster is of course a hero of "myth." Nevertheless the Winnebago follow a commonsense classification and call this story a "tale."

Just as contemporary Ojibwe storytellers continue to involve the mythological trickster Wenabozho in new tales, Radin's Ho-Chunk "raconteur-authors use the figures of the older mythology in the modern tales," involving in this instance Frenchmen, guns, liquor, and the fur trade.

Reprinted by permission of the American Folklore Society from "Literary Aspects of Winnebago Mythology," *Journal of American Folklore* 39:151 (1926):18–52. Not for further reproduction.

There was a village in which a chief lived. Turtle lived there too. The village was situated near a large river.

One day they said to each other, "Look, the traders are coming." They were the Frenchmen. Finally the traders landed and settled in houses along the edge of the water down the stream. A large number of Indians immediately surrounded these houses. They were dressed in their best, with white and black wampums around their necks. Many of the women also wore earrings. The men were painted in various colors.

Everyone went there except Turtle. One day he said, "Younger brothers, the Indians are getting credit and we also ought to be able to get some. However, I thought it would be better to wait till all the others are gone. They need clothing, and we do not need such things the others are able to get credit, I shall surely be able to do the same because all the traders are my friends." Thus he spoke to his younger brothers.

Beside Turtle there were present the Soft-Shelled Turtle, Keka, and the Little Red Turtle. All these latter were unmarried. The Turtle himself, however, had a wife. He lived in a long lodge with two fireplaces. When he was ready to go he said, "Now then it is about time for us to go and get credit, for even these womanly fellows are getting it. Now I am going to talk to my friends."

When they got to the first trader, Turtle said, "This is my intimate friend, but let us go a little farther." When he came to another trader, he said the same thing, and thus they went from trader to trader until they came to the last man. There Turtle stopped and said, "Here we shall enter, for this man is a friend of mine." As soon as they had entered the trader came up to him and shook hands with him. "Second-Born (Soft-Shell Turtle), you try to get credit first." Then he asked the trader (for credit) but he was unsuccessful and so were the others. "Turtle cannot do it," said the trader, "I was forbidden to do it when I started out. They told me that you are not to be trusted because you never repay what you borrow. They told me that you are lazy, that you don't even try to go out hunting and that you gamble and lie with women and go on the warpath. Because you always do these things, I am forbidden to give you any credit. If you were to cheat me it would go hard with me because this is all the money I have. I cannot give you any credit. The other people have lots of money and perhaps they might help you out."

Then they went away and came to the trader nearest to this one. Turtle had said that this one never refused him but when the Second-Born went up to him and asked him for credit he refused just as the other one had done. All four turtles pleaded with him a long time but he absolutely refused. "Turtle," said this trader, "we are

12.1. Ho-Chunk singers with bone whistle and hand drum, Wisconsin Dells, 1946.
State Historical Society of Wisconsin, WHi (S75)28.

115

not going to buy any scalps." So again they failed. In like manner Turtle went to all the traders but they all refused.

"Younger brothers, you may all go home to your sisters-in-law. I will return later as I want to finish some interpreting for which I was engaged, and besides, I want to have a good long talk with the traders." So they all went home and he remained behind. There he stayed four days and nights without anything to eat. There were some young men drinking but they always avoided him because they said that he would arrest them.

All that was left for Turtle to do was to sleep at night near the camp fires of the traders.

Turtle went around, hungry, dusty, his lips parched. The trader to whom he had gone first, seeing him in this plight took pity on him and called him to his store and said, "Turtle, come here." Then he gave him some crackers, a can of fish and a piece of cheese. "Turtle, when I looked at you this morning I took pity on you and I am going to give you a little credit and if you don't pay me I am willing to stand the consequences. This store is mine anyway. I know that giving you credit will be the same as throwing money away because you are noted for your worthlessness. That is the reason I was told to refuse you any credit. As soon as you get through eating, you may go after your wife and brothers and bring them here."

As soon as Turtle had finished eating, he went after his wife and his brothers. "Now then I have come after you. We are going to get credit. Those womanly fellows were the ones that had forbidden the traders to give me any credit, but now I have fixed them up. They told things that were not true about me, but that too I have fixed up. Now, they are all after me so that I might ask them for credit, but I dislike them so that we will go clear to the end of the road where we went the first time."

When they got to the end of the road Turtle said, "Second-Born, you may go in first and get what you want." So he went in and bought the following things: a blanket and some yellow-edged broadcloth for leggings; armlets and small buckles for his front hair braids; a pair of boots that reached up to his knees so that he could wear them when he went out wading to set traps or when he went hunting; some steel traps, and a gun. All these things he bought. Then Turtle told the Third-Born to go in and get what he wanted and he bought the same things as the first one. As soon as he was through, Turtle sent the Fourth-Born into the store. He bought the same things that his two elder brothers had bought with the exception that he took a short gun instead of a long one. "Aha!" said Turtle when he saw his youngest brother coming out of the store with a short gun, "I always said that the youngest took most after me. All the others have bought guns entirely too long. With the gun you have bought, however you can sit in a pit and load and thus you can fight." "Say, Turtle [the trader said], there you are at it again. That is why people speak so badly of you. You know that your brothers are not getting these guns for the warpath. But I knew that you were not a person to be trusted and I knew that everything I trusted you with meant an absolute loss to me."

By this time all Turtle's younger brothers had finished their trading. Then Turtle said to his wife, "Old woman, you may go in now and get whatever you think necessary, and after you have finished I will go in and get what I need." So the woman went in and bought kettles, dishes, knives and some shot and powder. Then Turtle went in and got a small handaxe, four quarts of whiskey, etc. When he was all finished he told the trader that he was through and started home. When he got home, he immediately began to gamble and continued it for many days. It was the fall of the year and some people had already left the village. Soon, others went and before long only a very few were left. With these few he used to gamble. He lost everything, even the things that his younger brothers had bought for themselves. Soon everyone was gone and they remained there alone. Then Turtle's younger brothers said, "I wonder why our elder brother is doing this. He ought to be out hustling for himself. I suppose he is going to stay here permanently. It is on account of these actions that the trader said those ugly things about him."

The next morning the Second-Born said, "Older brother, all the people have moved to the best hunting places. Why are we still here? Thus we were asking one another. So we decided that we should go somewhere." Thus spoke the Soft-Shelled Turtle. "Oh my younger brother, you are right. That is what we also said last night. Your sister-in-law and I, long ago, when we were first married, hunted in a place where there were many animals with furs. There we ought to go, we said. However we were afraid that the other people might follow us, so we stayed here purposely so that we might go alone after the rest had left. It is not good to hunt with other people because they always rush forward in order to get ahead of you. So it is best to hunt alone and that is why I am doing this," Turtle said. "If they followed us and prevented us from hunting in the way we like best we would not be able to kill anything. So tomorrow we shall move," he said.

In the meantime the traders were telling Turtle's creditor that Turtle was still around. "You see," they said to him, "what Turtle is doing and that is why we were told not to give him any credit. All the things with which you trusted him he lost shortly after in gambling, as well as the things belonging to his younger brothers." Thus they spoke. "I don't care. They were all my things and I did it because I took pity on him. I did it without expecting anything back." Thus spoke the trader.

The Turtle moved very early the next morning and the Soft-shelled Turtle sat at the head of the canoe while Keka sat behind at the rudder. As son as they had started Turtle said, "Younger brother, Second-Born, as soon as we get to the place I will give you warning because it is at a point where the creek empties into this water and is not noticeable. We will have to watch very closely for it is generally obstructed by young willows. As soon as one gets up the creek as far as that, the water becomes very deep. However up a little ways farther it becomes a regular creek. When your sister-in-law and I first got married I did my hunting here, and there used to be many furred animals, bear and deer. The creek was full of game in those days and the game must be even more abundant now for that was a long time ago. If they have been breeding ever since, there must be very many animals now." Thus he spoke. The woman said the same thing. "Oh, when we were very young, your older brother hunted here. At that time he was not much more than a boy." Then the Turtle spoke, "Now then, you must watch very closely as the place must be pretty near here. It is impossible to find it sometimes because often there are no signs of a creek. That is why they never hunt here. The water comes into it in a slightly different manner. That is the only way one can tell whether one has reached it." Then the Soft-Shelled Turtle said, "Well, older brother, here is just such a place as you have described. Here the water seems to come in a sort of rushing way." This must be it, younger brother. Do not break any willows for if we are discovered the animals will be scared away from us in the hurry of other people to get as many animals as they can."

They cleared away the willows carefully as they went through and they bent them back after they had passed. In this way there was no trace that anyone had passed through. After they had gone up stream a little way, sure enough the water became deeper. "Older brother, here the water is deeper," said the Soft-Shelled Turtle. "Yes, I told you that it used to be that way. It will get wider still as we go farther on and finally it will become a chain of lakes. When we reach that place we will strike our camp. In olden times it was a good camping place." Just as he had said, the creek began to get wider and soon they saw a beaver feeding on the shore. There were also otters there. "Older brother, I am going to shoot one." Turtle, however, forbade him. "Don't do it, you will make them wild. Just leave them alone."

The game became more plentiful as they went along and the stream of water became wider. It was now evening. "Second-Born", said Turtle, "Shoot one of the larger ones so that we may eat it when we arrive. This shooting will not make them wild, especially if you draw your gun back immediately, for this will muffle the report. That is what I used to do when I wished to kill secretly." So the Second-Born shot one of the animals and, sure enough, the report of the gun was not very loud. Then they put the animal into the canoe, and the Turtle said, "Second-Born, get out and walk. After a while you will come to the timber-wood. Go towards it. That is where we used to live. It is a grove of red-oak, and around the edge there used to be a growth of brush. Those you may use as frames for your furs. Have a fire ready."

At that place, therefore, he went ashore and they went on without him. Finally they heard the report of his gun. "Ah, he must have done that to a third-born (bear)," said the Turtle. Finally they arrived at the place Turtle meant; they got out and walked. It was just as he had said. The timber-wood was very thick and around the edge there was some brush. When they got to this place they found the Soft-Shelled Turtle building a fire already. He had a bear lying near him. Then immediately they built a lodge and the young men got ready to hunt. Turtle then said to them, "Younger brothers, when the animals become wild it is impossible to kill many of them, so don't do it now. Besides the furs are not good yet. Come, help me camp so that your sister-in-law may make some soup for you." So then they all helped in the making of the lodge. They wanted to go hunting right away but he would not let them. They therefore attended to the animals—the beavers and bears that they had already killed.

When they had finished their lodge, Turtle said, "My younger brothers, tomorrow morning we will get the materials for the frames on which we are to place the furs we obtain; go hunt, therefore, for the necessary wood." After a while he continued and said, "Do not hunt (game) right away for the animals are likely to get wild if you hunt them too soon. Let us therefore settle down here for a while and not hunt until they get used to us, and then we will be able to kill them in great numbers. It is just because the people kill them too soon that I dislike to go hunting with them." Thus he spoke. In the morning they cut the frames for the furs, but the younger brothers said to one another, "We are tired of making these frames. Why don't we go out hunting? What is the sense of cutting these frames if we don't kill any game?" Then Turtle said to them, "My younger brothers, you don't know anything about hunting if you are so desirous of hunting right away. Remember also, before letting your frames freeze, that you must dry them, because that always makes the furs look better and permits the frames to be used over and over again. If the frames are not dried before they are allowed to get frozen they become very brittle." Turtle's younger brothers were very tired of making frames, however, and wanted to go hunting immediately. Then Turtle spoke to them again and said, "My younger brothers, go out and get what we call a carry-all. This we generally make either of bark or simply of a piece of wood, and in that we can afterwards carry the furs which will be too heavy to carry on our backs." So they made a carry-all for themselves.

Thus they lived, only killing animals for food when their supply was exhausted. Turtle spoke to them again, "Younger brothers, as soon as it gets cold, let us make some racks for our furs. Otherwise the mice will gnaw holes in them." So they made some racks, intending to make more as soon as these were loaded with furs.

All winter they waited for the animals to get used to them and only shot animals when they needed them for food. The snow was now very deep and it was cold and the waters were all frozen hard. "Well," said Turtle, "my younger brothers, let us begin to hunt. When the weather is like this, the animals don't pay much attention to themselves." The younger brothers dreaded to go out at that season but he told them to get their carry-alls ready and start with him. The first thing they came across was a beaver house. Turtle cut this open and went in and killed all the beavers who were there. Then he killed as many otters as he came across. It was very easy for there was no place to which they could run. His younger brothers were using their carry-alls to good purpose and brought home many animals. It was a very high pile of furs that they were able to stack up when they came home. At night Turtle and his wife would attend to the dressing of the skins. In the morning, when the young men were up, they saw all the furs hanging on the racks. In this manner they continued, day after day, until their material for frames was exhausted. "Do you now see why I wanted you to make frames? But you paid no attention to me and got tired too soon. Now we shall have to hunt and get material for our frames at the same time. This is a nuisance." He tried to use the sticks that had been used before but they were all frozen and brittle, as the young men had not permitted them to dry first. However he found a few that had been dried and these he could use again. Then the furs were tied in bundles and placed on the racks and before long the racks were all covered. Finally they had gone over the entire hunting ground. The racks were overloaded so they roasted as much meat as they could. The young men continued hunting and were very successful. They killed many badgers and coyotes and skinned them and placed the furs on frames. It was now spring and most of the people had returned to the village. Turtle, however, was nowhere to be seen. Everyone knew of everybody else's where abouts; but of Turtle they knew nothing. "He must be killed," they said.

As they were thus hunting, Turtle said to his wife one day, "Old woman, I am going over to the village to see the people, for they must all be home by this time, and I will try to borrow my friend's boat if I can. Pack the worst furs for me." So they packed the coyote and badger skins for him and he started out. He got to the village at night. "Ho! ho! my friend, I have come back," he shouted. "Ah, it is good," said his friend, "for they were saying that you had been killed." Then the trader gave him some food. When Turtle had finished his meal, he said to the trader, "My friend, I have brought over a few furs for you. They are just outside your door." He went out, and sure enough there he found some furs. He thanked Turtle. "Really, my friend, it is good," he said. "I did not expect this, for I just wanted to get rid of the things and so I let you have them on credit. Indeed, it is good." "My friend, I have only brought you the poorest furs I had. I have been hunting for you all winter and I will bring you the others if you will let me have your boat. I will start early tomorrow morning and fetch you the other furs." "It is good, but I will send my servants along with you so you need not work. Now then, my friend, you must be tired, here therefore is something for you to drink." Then he gave him four quarts of whiskey.

All night Turtle drank and in the morning when the trader got up he gave him some more. Then he sent his servants along with many presents so that if Turtle was really telling the truth they could give them to him. Two servants went along and early in the morning they started. The Turtle did not even have to do the rowing but instead drank all the time. When they got to the creek he told them it was over yonder, "The road will be full of broken sticks," he told them. After a while they got out of the boat and walked on foot. Turtle had to be led by the two servants because he was too drunk to walk. When they got there, the food was just cooking and the servants ate with the others. Then the servants carried the furs to the boat on long sticks that they had prepared. They loaded on the boat all the furs that Turtle and his companions had obtained. Four days it took them to carry the furs to the boat, so many were piled up. Then when they were ready to start home, they put new clothes on Turtle; a black coat, what they called a king's coat, one with a red breast. Then they put a large quantity of wampum, and four silver medals around his neck. They decorated him with armlets, bracelets and yarn-belts which they tied around his head. Finally they gave him four quarts of whiskey, and in this manner they came back. They wouldn't let him do the slightest work and they treated him like a king.

About noon the boat appeared some distance from the village. "Well," said the Indians, "it must be some trader's boat." But when they could see the occupants they recognized Turtle. "Why, Turtle is in the boat," they said. He had the king's clothes on and he was drunk and was being held up by the servants. "Ho! ho! it is Turtle. He has brought back very many furs," the Indians said and stood on the beach waiting for him. "Look, he has done a good season's work." At the house of his friend he brought his boat to the shore. The trader was very much surprised. Then the other traders said, "Turtle, let us buy some of the furs from you. "They do not belong to me. They belong to my friend." "Turtle, they are worth much more than all the stores here. Indeed they are worth a great deal more. Your friend hasn't got anything. He can't buy all those things." "Nevertheless, I will not sell any of them to any of you because they belong to him, for it was for him that I hunted. I tried to get credit from you but you would not give me any, and you would not trust me. This man was the only one who would give me credit, so therefore I determined to go out hunting for him and get him furs. They belong to him." He refused to talk to them any more. "My friend," said the trader to Turtle, "this entire store I give to you and I will go to my home in the morning as the boat is already loaded. The servants will watch the boat during the night as someone might want to steal something. All the whiskey in the store belongs to you too." The next morning the trader went home and Turtle remained in possession of the store.

13

Ojibwe Stories from Northern Wisconsin

The most populous of Wisconsin's native peoples, the Ojibwe (or Chippewa) occupy six reservations in the northern part of the state: Bad River, Lac Courte Oreilles, Lac du Flambeau, Mole Lake, Red Cliff, and St. Croix. At the time of European contact, they were situated near Sault Sainte Marie, at the western edge of the Upper Peninsula of Michigan, and moved west with the fur trade. Henry Rowe Schoolcraft, an Indian agent, was the first to report on Ojibwe storytelling traditions in 1839. Since then Ojibwe traditional tales have been documented by many anthropologists, folklorists, and interested parties.

The following sketches of two storytellers and their repertoires illustrate the ongoing dynamic between continuity and change in contemporary Ojibwe oral tradition. Ancient mythological stories of the trickster and culture hero Wenabozho persist, as do local legends based upon long-standing beliefs. Yet these stories have been updated in accordance with their tellers' experiences. And they are likewise matched by European folktales and Christian devil legends, albeit made over as Ojibwe stories set in trading posts, lumber camps, and dance halls.

I interviewed Dee Bainbridge in July 1996 in connection with fieldwork for Wisconsin's 1998 sesquicentennial observance. Alissa Matlack interviewed Keith Wilmer in December 1995, as preparation for writing a paper for my course on the folktale at the University of Wisconsin--Madison. The "motifs" mentioned herein constitute the smallest elements of traditional tales that persist in tradition, and the numbers attached to them derive from the classificatory system of the comparative folklorist Stith Thompson (*Motif-Index of Folk Literature* [Bloomington: Indiana University Press, 1955–1958], six volumes).

Dee Bainbridge, Ojibwe Storyteller

Commentary, Transcriptions, and Annotations by James P. Leary

Delores "Dee" Bainbridge was born in 1931 on the Red Cliff Ojibwe Reservation north of Bayfield, Wisconsin. Her mother died when Dee was four and she was brought up by her grandparents, John and Ida Mary. John DePerry was the son of a "half-breed" French Ojibwe fur trader, Michel DePerry (a.k.a. DuPrez), and an Ojibwe mother. John DePerry was trilingual in English, French, and Ojibwe. He had worked in the woods as a lumber camp teamster in his younger days. Ida Mary De-Perry (ca. 1885–1972) was an Ojibwe from the Lac Courte Oreilles Reservation area and the daughter of George Neviaush. As Dee recalled, her grandmother grew up living a traditional life: "If suckers were spawning they would go to that place and

13.1. Dee Bainbridge telling stories in her Ashland home, 1996. Photo: James P. Leary.

harvest. Then for wild rice they'd go to another place and harvest. Then when the berries were ripe they'd go to the berry field. They were pretty nomadic in her earlier years." Arbitrarily named Ida George by the Bureau of Indian Affairs, with her father's "English" first name serving as her surname, she was known as Johnnyqwe when she first settled among the Red Cliff Ojibwe (i.e. "Johnny's woman" from the English name and the Ojibwe suffix *qwe*, indicating a woman's name). At the time, shortly after 1900, she understood very little English, although she came to speak the language gradually.

Growing up in the 1930s and 1940s, Dee became fluent in both Ojibwe and English, while hearing a smattering of French. The family lived three miles from the village of Bayfield and eked out a subsistence existence with "no modern conveniences." They gardened, gathered berries, picked herring from the gill nets of commercial fishers, cut firewood, ran trap lines, set rabbit snares, "bobbed" for whitefish through the ice, caught speckled trout in streams, and sold home brew.

The DePerry place was also one of the gathering places for house parties with square and step dancing to fiddle, accordion, and pump organ:

All the people from around Red Cliff. They'd have it at my grandma's house one night, then maybe in a month at somebody else's house. Different houses. That's how they entertained themselves. Pretty much Indian people from the reservation. . . . And they would bring each something, like a can of milk or a cake. And that was the prizes they played for. It was kind of different . . . A man by the name of Babineau, he was a good jigger. And Joe Wabidosh, he was a good jigger. And even some of the ladies were pretty good. A lady by the name of LaMoureaux, she was a very good jigger.

Dee's grandfather and her Uncle Mike generally played the fiddle at these gatherings.

The DePerry home was likewise a site for storytelling by Dee's uncles Mike DePerry, Fred DePerry, and John Soulier, by a comical fellow known as "Big Louis," and especially by Ida Mary DePerry. Dee's grandmother would seldom tell stories during the day, but in the evening

She would burn tobacco. We had an old iron stove, kitchen stove. This was an offering to the spirits so she wouldn't offend anybody. Then she would burn cedar, which is supposed to take away all the evil spirits. The whole house would be like incense. She did that pretty regularly. They tell us now that we shouldn't talk about Wenabozho unless there's snow on the ground. Otherwise a big frog will jump on your bed and leave welts on your body. Well I said I've violated that, but if a frog jumps in my bed I might kiss him and see if he turns into a prince. But I don't remember that she ever said it was taboo. But I've read that several times since that you shouldn't tell stories in the summer. But some stories that don't pertain to Wenabozho I guess are okay.

While some of the stories swirling around the DePerry home were in English, Dee's grandmother told hers in Ojibwe. Dee absorbed some stories by simply listening, but others were acquired more formally. She recalled that her grandmother "would tell me a story, then ask me to repeat it. That's how I got started."

Dee went through eight grades at the Catholic Mission School at Red Cliff, then attended Bayfield High School. She worked at various jobs, married, raised six children, and provided a home for her grandmother. In the Bainbridge home, Dee and Ida Mary DePerry relied on Ojibwe as a "secret language" when they didn't want the children to understand. Likewise Dee continued to enjoy talking and joking with elders in Ojibwe. In early 1973 she began a twenty-two-year career teaching the Ojibwe language, Indian history, and storytelling at Bayfield High School, where roughly 70 percent of the student body is Ojibwe. About the same time she began teaching Ojibwe at Ashland's Northland College. Beyond telling stories amidst other Ojibwes and within the context of her classes, Dee Bainbridge has performed for various community groups and organizations.

She is equally comfortable telling stories in Ojibwe and in English. Her delivery is stately and sure, accompanied by occasional mimetic gestures, and reliant on subtle vocal shifts that convey character and mood. In the 1990s Dee Bainbridge has been recognized by the local Ojibwe, the Wisconsin Arts Board, and the National Endowment for the Arts for her storytelling.

I first learned of Dee Bainbridge in the early 1980s when I was working on a National Endowment for the Arts (NEA) traditional music project at Northland College where she was teaching Ojibwe. Subsequently I heard of her storytelling from folklorist Richard March of the Wisconsin Arts Board, from Smithsonian Institution ethnomusicologist and seasonal Madeline Island resident Tom Vennum, and from Walt Bressette, a Red Cliff Ojibwe, Bayfield businessman, and political activist. In December 1992, while doing a grant review for the NEA Folk Arts Program, I was able to hear Bainbridge perform, along with Ojibwe storytellers Billy Blackwell from Grand Traverse, Minnesota, and Joe Migwanabe, originally from Manitoulin Island, Ontario, but then residing on the Hannahville Potawatomi Reservation near Escanaba, Michigan. The setting was an evening gathering of mostly Ojibwe high school students in a large wigwam adjacent to Marvin and Diane DeFoe's Bayfield home.

Impressed by Dee Bainbridge's repertoire, traditional performance style, reserved yet friendly personality, and considerable experience as a teacher, I wanted in particular to record her stories in connection with field research undertaken in July 1996 in preparation for Wisconsin's 1998 sesquicentennial celebration. She was very gracious in consenting. The 1996 session took place in the afternoon in the Bainbridge living room where, seated in a comfortable armchair with a boom microphone angled above her, Dee performed her stories and told of her life.

Wenabozho's Beaver Dam

[This etiological or origin legend regarding the formation of Chequamegon Bay also concerns the Ojibwe culture hero and trickster, Wenabozho (a.k.a. Winabijou, Manabozho, Manabus, and Nanabush), who wanders the world having many adventures. The soft dam is constructed of mud in William W. Warren's *History of the Ojibway People* (St. Paul: Minnesota Historical Society, 1984; reprinted from the original 1885 edition), 102. A more expanded version appears, with reference to Warren, in Guy M. Burnham, *The Lake Superior Country in History and Story* (Ashland, Wisc.: Browzer Books, 1975; reprinted from the original 1929 edition), 46–47.]

• • •

Wherever Indian people live there's always stories pertaining to that area. In this part of the country we have the story that's told about the Apostle Islands. They say that when Wenabozho was living in this part of the country then there were no islands in Lake Superior.

One day he saw a big beaver swimming around in the bay—he was over toward Bayfield. Oh, he was really impressed, it was the biggest beaver he had ever seen. He built a dam across the bay to trap that beaver in there. He had his dam built and the beaver was trapped in there, and he was really excited. But lo and behold that beaver broke through and swam out into the lake. Now Wenabozho was so angry that he took what he'd used to build his dam—sticks, rocks, and whatever—and he threw it as the beaver swam away.

And they say that with each handful he created an island. And that's how the Apostle Islands were created. Now in our language—they say what's left of the dam is still visible, that's Long Island—in our language, we say *jagawaamikoong:* that means soft beaver dam.

That's the story that pertains to this area.

Wenabozho and the Birds

[As Dee Bainbridge points out, this old story of the "Hoodwinked Dancers" (motif K826), involving the characteristics of the "hell diver," or grebe, is widely known not only to the Ojibwe—among whom it is told as both an independent story and an episode within a larger mythological story associated with the medicine lodge—but also to native peoples throughout North America. Victor Barnouw, who published a version recorded in 1944 from Tom Badger at Lac du Flambeau, contends persuasively that the story is so widely known because it "is such a good story." See Victor Barnouw, *Wisconsin Chippewa Myths and Tales: And Their Relation to Chippewa Life* (Madison: University of Wisconsin Press, 1977), 26–28. Barnouw reports versions from the Eskimo of Labrador; the Beaver and Chipeweyan of the Mackenzie River district; the Cree, Canadian Ojibwa, Potawatomi, Kickapoo, Menomini, and Fox of the Central Woodlands; the following tribes of the Plains: Southern Ute, Southern Paiute, Comanche, Kiowa, Osage, Arapaho, Gros Ventre, Cheyenne, Omaha, Ponca, Crow, Dakota, Pawnee, Iowa, Blackfoot, Piegan, and Assiniboine; the following northeastern Algonkian tribes: Micmac, Passamadquoddy, and Malecite, Montagnis-Naskapi; the Huron-Wyandot of the Iroquois area; the Cherokee, Caddo, and Creek of the Southeast; and the Jicarilla Apache of the Southwest.

The earliest published Ojibwe version appeared in 1839 in Henry Rowe Schoolcraft's *Algic Researches: Indian Tales and Legends,* reprinted by the Clearfield Company (Baltimore: 1992), 154–55. As Bainbridge mentions, this tale has often been performed by Ojibwes as a story song. Frances Densmore, the pioneering ethnomusicologist, recorded it from Skipping Day at Minnesota's White Earth Reservation in 1907; and linguist John Nichols collected another rendition from seventy-six-year-old James Littlewolf of the Mille Lacs Reservation in 1971. Littlewolf may be heard on a sound recording produced by Thomas Vennum, Jr., *Ojibway Music from Minnesota* (St. Paul: Minnesota Historical Society and the Minnesota State Arts Board, 1989).]

• • •

She [Ida Mary DePerry] told one in particular about [how] Wenabozho was always hungry.

On one occasion he decided to invite all the birds. All the birds would come. The partridges, the pheasants, all the birds. And they all were in a circle there.

And he said, "I have some new songs to sing for you. And," he says, "when you dance now, I want everybody to dance blindfolded."

So they did. All the birds had blindfolds on. They were dancing.

And Wenabozho would say, "Sing loud, sing loud. *Adagook nagamoon, adagook neman.* Dance hard." They were having a good time. They were making different kinds of noises.

One little bird said, "This is strange. I don't know if we should trust Wenabozho. He likes to cheat people." So the bird kind of snuck away his blindfold and took a peek. Here Wenabozho was just grabbing as many birds as he could grab. He was wringing their necks and throwing them in a pile. Just grabbing as many as he could reach. And the little bird yelled, "*Hiyaa Wenabozho, nisigonaan.* Wenabozho is killing us."

And so they all scattered and ran to get away. And the little bird was kind of slow as he ran out. And Wenabozho stepped on him and said, "You will walk this way forever, because you disobeyed and you have to suffer the consequences. And your eyes will be red because you looked, you peeked."

That's why the hell diver has red eyes. And of course you know how ducks walk, like their back is broke. Those are the consequences that he suffered.

You know most of the legends have where you suffer the consequences because you didn't do what you were told. That story is told on all the Ojibwe reservations, and there's some variations. In fact when I heard an old man at Lac Courte Oreilles tell it, he said it like he was pretending to be Wenabozho singing to these birds as they danced.

Smart Pills

[This tale is a fine example of the Euro-Indian exchange that emerged from Wisconsin's fur trade and lumber camp eras. Although "Smart Pills" concerns Wenabozho in this version, it is clearly an ancient European jest wherein an itinerant trickster dupes some higher-up. It appeared as early as 1535 in the English chapbook *Tales and Quicke Answeres, Very Mery, and Pleasant to Rede;* reprinted in *A Hundred Merry Tales, and Other Jestbooks of the Fifteenth and Sixteenth Centuries,* ed. P. M. Zall (Lincoln: University of Nebraska Press, 1963). Dee Bainbridge learned the story from her uncle, Mike DePerry, who heard the story in lumber camps. She used a jar of rabbit droppings as a prop when I first heard her perform it to Ojibwe teenagers in Bayfield in December 1992.]

• • •

And, of course, Wenabozho they said was smart. All the people thought of him as being so smart.

He had some rabbit droppings in his pocket. And the people were asking him all kinds of different questions and he was answering. And they said, "Well how come you're so smart?"

So he reached in his pocket and he took out a handful of rabbit droppings and he showed them. He said, "I take smart pills." He said, "These are smart pills."

The people said, "Ohhh?!?"

He said, "Yes! Smart pills."

So they looked again. They said, "You know, Wenabozho, that looks like rabbit droppings."

And Wenabozho said, "See, you're getting smart already." [Laughs.]

Those are cute.

The Little People

[Stories about "little people" among American Indians are widespread. William Jones and Truman Michelson present several in *Ojibwa Texts* (New York: Publications of the American Ethnological Society, vol. VII, 1919). The small rock masses known as concretions are abundant along the south shore of Lake Superior. In the 1990s, Byron Buckeridge maintains a small concretion museum in his barn situated along Highway 2 between Ashland and Hurley. A sign painted on the barn's gable proclaimed "Nothing Like It In New York!" See also Keith Wilmer's "The Little People," in this chapter.]

• • •

At Waverly Beach, that's out near Odana, we talk about little people. You have leprechauns and gnomes and fairies. The Indian people have their little people too. They're supposed to be little miniature Indian people. They live at Waverly Beach. And during the thunderstorms, when it's lightning and thundering, they're busy making concretions.

I don't know if you know what concretions are? Little round stones. Some are large, some are small. They vary in size. Now to prove they've been on the beach, you walk along you'll find little rock formations that are shaped just like tiny feet. And you find those on Waverly Beach.

They say at one time that was considered a sacred area because the little people lived there. You weren't allowed to cut any trees or do any hunting or desecrate the land in any way.

Now it's a public beach and no longer do the people honor or give respect to that particular area. But concretions are pretty popular. I'm sure you've seen them.

The Windigo

[Stories of windigos—cannibal giants with hearts of ice—have been widespread among Ojibwe peoples in both the United States and Canada. In chapter 5 of his *Wisconsin Chippewa Myths and Tales,* Barnouw presents texts and commentary for seven Windigo stories recorded in the 1940s at Lac Courte Oreilles and Lac du Flambeau.]

• • •

I asked her [Dee's grandmother] one time what a windigo was. She just said a giant. She didn't say a cannibalistic giant. That's what I've read about. She just said a giant, she didn't say much more than that. I don't remember the details, but I remember a story she told.

Everybody was supposed to protect themselves. Maybe the windigo was coming. Some danger was near. And she says that's how—you've seen what hazelnuts look like. That's how they protected themselves. They put the peeling on.

She used another example of some other kind of fruit that disguised itself because the giant was coming. I don't remember the details. I was real little and she didn't tell that as often as the Wenabozho story.

The Lac Courte Oreilles Frog

[This story likely involves an encounter with the larger-than-normal "chief" or leader of the frog people; a figure who takes pity on the starving hunter and assists him with food. The traditional association of two generally simultaneously occuring natural phenomena—the frogs' first chirping and the walleyes' spawning—is a mnemonic technique found in many cultures.]

• • •

Down at Couderay [Lac Courte Oreilles] they have a story called the Lac Courte Oreilles Frog. And they said this man's family was starving and he had gone hunting day after day. Came home and didn't bring any food. And he was getting very despondent. And he was walking. As he was down by the stream he happened to look across it. And there was a big frog sitting there, a giant frog.

So he took his arrow and he aimed. He was just about to shoot the frog, and the frog said, "Wait, wait. *Bekaa, Bekaa* in Indian we say. "Don't shoot me," the frog said. "If you spare my life I will see, I will reward you that you will have plenty to eat."

Well the man didn't know what to think about it. He said [to himself] that frog will make a fine meal for my family. He said [to himself], well how will he reward me? So he was pretty compassionate. He said, "All right then."

Then the frog said, "You listen, you will hear my signal. You will hear the frogs. They will let you know that the food is wherever you want to use it, wherever you take it."

Anyway the man went to bed that night. And toward morning, doggone, he heard the frogs, big bull frogs were croaking, and the little frogs were chirping. He said, "My goodness, I wonder if that's the signal so soon?"

So he went down to the stream where he saw that [frog] and sure enough there the walleye were spawning. He had plenty of fish, he had plenty of food. And they say to this day when you hear the frogs chirping in the spring, you will know the walleye are spawning.

And it's true, that is true.

Big Nose

[The setting is a traditional wake where people gather during the four days when the deceased's soul travels the road to the spirit world.]

• • •

We have a story that's told in Ojibwe. . . . The story goes that one Indian man had died. And all the people came to his house. They were going to sing and they were going to pray and they were going to eat. And they all sat around.

And two ladies were sitting there together. And they were visiting and talking. And then the door opened. And one lady came in. And this one said to the other one, "Oh my, who is that with the big nose?" And that lady [with the big nose] came and sat next to them. She sat there too. They were singing and praying.

Finally one of the ladies there kind of nudged her. "Why don't you help us sing?"

And she said, "No."

And they said, "Why?"

And she said, "My nose is too big."

And that's the end of the story.

Of course Indian people say you should never criticize anyone, or you will have to experience that yourself. [Dee makes this proverbial observation in Ojibwe.] Don't criticize because you will have to experience that same kind of situation.

That's kind of an example of that kind of thing. But it's real comical in Ojibwa because the words sound the same. Like when they say: "Who is that that came in with the big nose?" But when you translate that you lose a lot of the punchline.

Too Sick

[Traditional stories about lazy people are found throughout the world. Hence the proverb: He who does not work does not eat. This story is reminiscent of another often reported in North America wherein a lazy man who is starving refuses a gift of rice or corn because it is not cooked. He starves to death. See Antti Aarne and Stith Thompson, tale Type 1951, Is Wood Split? *The Types of the Folktale* (Helsinki: Suomalainen Tiedeakatemia, 1961), 519.]

• • •

There was another story that she [Ida Mary DePerry] told in Ojibwe, about a young Indian boy. He was sick. She'd tell this in Ojibwe. When they wanted him to haul water or bring in wood, he'd say, "No I can't, I'm too sick."

They'd say, "Bring us some water. We need some water to cook."

He'd say, "No I can't, I'm too sick."

And the old woman who was there said, "What's the matter with you? You're always sick, you're always sick."

"Well," he said, "the same thing that ails my grandfather, that's the same thing that's ailing me."

She said, "Oh you lie. I knew your old grandfather. He starved to death."

That was the story.

It was told in Indian. The words sound comical. But then you translate it.

When I was tired and didn't want to do something, or my grandma would mention that I should do, or suggest, I would say [in Ojibwe, then English] "What ailed my old grandfather, that's the same thing that ails me."

So we used to have fun with those kind of things.

At the Trading Post

[Dee Bainbridge learned this story from her Uncle John Soulier, who worked in lumber camps and trapped. Antti Aarne and Stith Thompson note its diffusion throughout Eurasia and the Americas, and classify the tale as Type 1336A, Man Does Not Recognize Own Reflection in the Water (Mirror) (1961:397). I also recorded the tale in 1977 from Pete Trzebiatowski, a Polish American tavernkeeper, in Stevens Point, Wisconsin. For a fine version from the Ozarks, accompanied by Herbert Halpert's detailed notes on the tale's North American diffusion, see Vance Randolph, *The Talking Turtle* (New York: Columbia University Press, 1957), 197–98.]

• • •

They say during the fur trading days the Indian people trapped the animals and brought them into the fur trading post. And they say this one old fellow always came in with a nice big pack of furs to trade. And as he came in the door there was a big mirror there.

He was really impressed. He looked up and he looked down. And the clerk come by. And he said to the clerk, "Who is that?"

And the clerk said, "That's you, that's your reflection."

He said, "Will I trade my furs and take this home?"

The clerk said, "No, no. That belongs to the American Fur Company. But," he says, "if you go 'round when you're shopping to the back there's little ones, this size, small, you could take and put in your packsack."

The old fellow went along and he was pulling off blankets and wool socks and treats for the kids. And he had his pack practically full and then he came to the mirrors. He thought, "Oh," his wife would be happy to have this. So he took the mirror and he put it in his packsack. Then he got a couple more pairs of socks and filled his packsack right to the top. He used up all the credit he had, so then he went home.

When he got home his wife was angry. She scolded him. "You been gone too long. We need water, we need wood. You'll have to go right away." So he left.

And his packsack was there. So she decided she would unpack. Take everything out of there for him. And she was taking socks out. And she liked the blanket. And then she came to the mirror. She looked at the mirror, she looked and she started to cry. She said to her mother, "Oh look, he found a new woman."

The old grandma come over there and she said, "Let me see." The old grandma took a look, she held the mirror up, and she said, "Don't worry my girl, she's old and she's ugly."

So that was the first story they used to tell.

It Was So Cold

[Fred DePerry's tall tale of winters so hard that the unfreezable freezes is closely related to Type 1889F, Frozen Words (Music) Thaw (Aarne and Thompson 1961:

511). Ernest Baughman cites more than a score of stories from throughout the United States under motif X.1623.3.1*, Flames freeze with unusual results, in his *Type and Motif-Index of the Folktales of England and North America* (The Hague: Mouton, 1966), 567.]

. . .

Of course, they [Dee's uncles] talked about their experiences, not just tales all the time. I had another uncle, Fred. He used to work in Alaska.

He said it was so cold up there you didn't have to blow out the lamp. You just picked up the flame [Dee gestures as if pinching a flame betwixt thumb and index finger] and you put it on the side. [Laughs.]

Real preposterous kind of things.

I Ate So Much Rabbit

[The idea that one acquires the characteristics of an animal from eating it is an old one in many cultures. In the Ozarks during the Great Depression rabbits were sometimes referred to as "Hoover pork." Vance Randolph reports an old woodsman saying, "I et so many rabbits when Hoover was president, that every time a dog barked I run for a holler log!" See his *We Always Lie to Strangers: Tall Tales from the Ozarks* (New York: Columbia University Press, 1951), 262.]

. . .

I would go in the woods when my grandfather cut wood. And we ate a lot of rabbit when I was little. My grandfather would set snares near the woodlot. We would cut wood, then get a rabbit from the snare.

We each got a designated piece of meat. My grandma would get the ribcage. I would get the backbone with the kidneys still attached. My grandfather would get the arms.

I ate so much rabbit, I said, that when the dogs barked I used to run and hide.

That was about the only meat we had access to. And a lot of fish. Once in awhile, when my uncle went hunting, he'd get venison, so we ate venison.

Devil at the Dance Hall

[Legends associating the devil with dancing, revelry and, often, fiddle music have deep European roots. See, for example, "The Demon Dancer" in Reidar Christiansen, *The Migratory Legends* (Helsinki: Suomalainen Tiedeakatemia, 1958), 53; and motif G303.10.4.0.1, "Devil Haunts Dance Halls," (Thompson 1955: vol. 3, 332). The legend presented here is found throughout French Canada and those areas of the northern United States marked by the fur trade, logging camps, and métis culture. Its elements of animal/human mergers and of the summoning of spirits through dancing easily blended with parallel beliefs among native peoples. See, for example, Michael Loukinen's 1991 film, *Medicine Fiddle*, and James P. Leary, "Sawdust and

Devils," in James P. Leary, ed., *Medicine Fiddle: A Discussion Guide* (Marquette: Northern Michigan University/Up North Films, 1992). In a related anecdote, Dee recalls a nun's horrified reaction to her revelation that not only was her favorite instrument the "devil's instrument," but her favorite tune also had demonic associations: "I hadn't heard much music but my grandfather's fiddle. And I said, 'Devil's Dream.' [Laughs.] She was rather shocked . . . 'Devil's Dream' was the only tune name I remember my grandpa could play." For another version, see Keith Wilmer's "The Dancing Devil," in this chapter.]

• • •

That was a story that the grandmas would tell us.

Indian people always like to have these dances. And they said on one occasion a man came in with a long overcoat on. And he was dancing. And as he swung around—"Allemande left and allemande right" they'd say—and, as he swung around, his coat would fly up and they could see his tail.

And another thing they said was, he liked to dance, but he liked the fiddle music too.

So he went on the stage. At one dance he was fiddling, this man. And they said the people were dancing so hard they practically danced their feet off. This man in the black overcoat. Then he says, "Well I'm tired fiddling." So he says to the next fellow, "Come here, you fiddle. I want to dance."

So the man says, "Well, I don't know how to fiddle." And that man in the black coat says, "Yes you do." He gave him the fiddle and, doggone, he could play the fiddle.

But they were always talking about the devil attending their dances.

And I don't know if they originated those stories, or if the nuns originated them to try to scare us. 'Cause you know they thought that dancing was evil and sinful.

Bearwalkers and Fireballs

["Bearwalkers," the shape-shifting sorcerers of Ojibwe tradition, were said to assume the forms of bears and other animals when traveling by night. Sometimes they used magic to harm or kill their enemies, and a flashing light or fireball was often regarded as a sign of their presence. For stories of Ojibwe bearwalkers in northern Wisconsin and the Upper Peninsula of Michigan, see Barnouw, *Wisconsin Chippewa Myths and Tales*, 137–40; Richard M. Dorson, *Bloodstoppers and Bearwalkers: Folk Traditions of the Upper Peninsula* (Cambridge: Harvard University Press, 1952), chapter 2; and Sister M. Carolissa Levi, *Chippewa Indians of Yesterday and Today* (New York: Pageant Press, 1956), chapter 36. See also Keith Wilmer's trio of stories regarding sorcery, in this chapter.]

• • •

I've heard, but just kind of hints about it. I imagine some people had some kind of strange power. If you're involved in a natural setting where your home is a birchbark wigwam, and you eat all the wild food, and you swim in the river, you're part of nature. I think that some of those people acquired a certain power from some kind of animal. And they could do the bearwalk and different other psychic kinds of things.

They talk about fireballs. Indian people who did evil sometimes would send a fireball to somebody's house. And that fireball would leave something bad. They always say that's a bad sign, a bad omen.

I've forgotten a lot of this stuff. We used to ask my grandma. She'd get tired of us asking and say, "Oh, I don't know."

The Stories of Keith Wilmer

Commentary and Transcriptions by Alissa Matlack, Annotations by James P. Leary

Keith Wilmer is a quiet guy. Originally from Ashland, Wisconsin, he lived down the hall from me on the eighth floor of Witte B dormitory at the University of Wisconsin-Madison. Our first conversation started as many do at the beginning of a freshman's first semester. "Hi. Where are you from?" Upon discovering that we lived near each other (I am from Lake Nebagamon), Keith and I immediately started comparing notes. The conversation soon turned to the dominance of one high school football team over the other, since our former schools have a longstanding rivalry and Keith himself had been a team member. Since then Keith and I have had many conversations about home, common acquaintances, and college life. He was, however, a little hesitant about agreeing to be tape recorded for this project; yet his good nature overcame his apprehension and I think he did fine.

We decided to have our discussion in the den, a gathering place for floor residents. The informal setting created a more comfortable atmosphere, since most of our previous conversations had also taken place in this room. Here we were on common ground. Though there were other people in the room, a football game on television ensured privacy by masking the sounds of our conversation. The other occupants of the room were too busy telling their own jokes and stories to pay much attention to us anyway. The background noise that they provided, while making the taped conversation difficult to understand at times, helped alleviate some of the tension.

Even though Keith isn't normally an aggressive speaker, his demeanor was more subdued than usual. I'm not sure if this was due to the types of stories he was about to tell me—most were of a personal nature—or to the content of the stories themselves; most people tend to lower their voices when speaking of the supernatural, perhaps to add gravity to a tale of questionable source. Keith spoke straightforwardly without beating around the bush. With the exception of a few "likes" and "ahhs," he told his stories very coherently. I don't think Keith would normally tell these tales without prompting from an audience; his nature is against it, so he hasn't developed a characteristic style and wasn't skilled at elaboration, usually skipping extraneous details. His stories do, however, show organization. Rarely did Keith have to backtrack to the beginning of an oration to add a pertinent detail that he had neglected to mention the first time through. For my part, I found his stories interesting and entertaining. I tried to ask questions when I didn't understand or wanted specific details. Keith was willing to interact with me, and allowed me to lead him into several discussions with my questions. He had decided what stories he would tell beforehand, so the session did not include any spontaneous recollections, which might also contribute to the subdued atmosphere of our conversation.

Keith learned many of his stories from either his uncles or his father. They would often share these tales while in the woods hunting or fishing, usually if camping. His father is the youngest of twelve brothers to whom Keith refers collectively as "my uncles." All were born on the Bad River Ojibwe Reservation near Ashland, and all live there today. Though many of his uncles traveled when they were young men, family ties are strong bonds, and all the brothers returned to the area in order to help one another and their parents.

The majority of Keith's repertoire is composed of family stories; events that happened to his grandfather, uncles, cousin, or himself. I would guess that he was told most of these tales as a means of establishing a family identity. Though Keith knows many stories involving his grandfather, he remembers little of the medicine man, who died while Keith was young. Though the doctors claimed he died of cancer, Keith believes that the evil spirits that plague powerful medicine men finally overpowered his grandfather.

Many of Keith's stories could also be told to entertain. Each of us has experienced the fun of a marathon storytelling session that gets started when one person says, "Remember the time when . . . ?" Keith likewise related an educational story about a "bad place." This place was characterized by three holes in the ground, bottomless pits. Parents would warn their children not to play in the area of these pits because evil little people would take them away. Keith openly admitted that he didn't believe that such a place even existed, but that adults would often tell about it just to manipulate a child's behavior.

One of the most interesting aspects of Keith's repertoire is the mixing of devil stories, associated with the Christian religion, with more traditional Ojibwe stories involving little people and changelings. As a child, Keith attended a Catholic elementary school. Some of his most vivid memories at this school are of seeing other Indian children punished for speaking their native language or telling traditional stories. Considering the mixed messages that he received throughout his early childhood—practicing Indian culture at home while being told at school that his lifestyle was inferior—the mixed nature of his storytelling repertoire is understandable.

Grandpa and the Changeling

[Within traditional Ojibwe mythology there is perpetual warfare between the higher spirits of the air, particularly the thunderbirds, and the spirits of the underground or underworld—often embodied in snakes, lizards, toads, and frogs. Sometimes referred to as *macimanidog* (evil spirits), these creatures were said to inflict blue choke marks on the throats of people they overheard telling mythological stories concerning them—hence the traditional practice of telling stories in the winter, when such creatures were hibernating. Although occasionally helpful to people, as in Dee Bainbridge's story of the "Lac Courte Oreilles Frog," underworld animals were more commonly the source of sorcerers' medicines (see Barnouw, 132–37; and Levi, chapter 36). As Alissa Matlack points out, Keith Wilmer heard supernatural stories regarding his grandfather within the natural context of hunting camps when darkness and proximity to the site of past occurences heightened his experience.]

• • •

My uncles were telling me one night—my grandpa, him and a couple other guys were hunting. And they were hunting and my grandpa shot at a deer. And he's always been known as a good shot. And so, ya know, he dropped the deer.

They, they went to track the deer—it was at night—they were shining. Ahhhh, they got to where it was and then, they saw a dead, well not a dead frog, but a frog with a hole in it, really.

It was weird 'cause my grandpa's a medicine man. And it was like this changeling or something. Like I guess, well, he stomped on it and started squishing it, trying to kill it. But when he lifted his foot up, like a lizard [it] ran away.

My uncle told me that was a real freaky one for him.

Uncle and the Fireball

[See Dee Bainbridge's "Bearwalkers and Fireballs."]

• • •

My uncle also told me about a time when he was alone, he was hunting and a fireball came up to him. And everyone says, you know, they're like: "It happens in nature." And I don't buy that.

He said, "It's like an eye. They just, like, look at you, see what you're thinking." And they say not to be scared of them: then that's bad, then they can hurt you. He just started telling us about this one night when we were going to go hunting the next day, because he had seen it when he was hunting. He said it was blue and it can be peaceful, but I've heard stories where it chased people. I don't know any specific ones though.

They can be bad, but basically they just check you out.

Grandpa's Night Visitor

[Night is the time when shape-shifting Ojibwe sorcerers pursue their enemies. Note here too the "clip-clopping footsteps," indicative of the Christian devil's cloven hoofs, that recur in the subsequent devil story and demonstrate the fusion of European and American Indian beliefs.]

• • •

Another neat story was—my dad told me about this, so did my uncle, they both told it the same way—since my grandpa was a medicine man, there were all these spirits that were trying to get him. So they lived at the top of a hill and they locked their doors at night.

And one night while they were sleeping, they heard someone open the door and start walking through the house. Kind of clip-clopping footsteps.

Well, my grandpa got up to check and—both doors were locked—and they had this huge dog. And he looked for the dog.

They found him under the heating stove. He had squished under there, he was so scared, and died—because he was so scared. I don't think he cooked to death.

The Dancing Devil

[Keith Wilmer acknowledges this story's antiquity, but updates it by calling the dance a prom. See also Dee Bainbridge's "Devil at the Dance Hall."]

• • •

There's a story that—like a long time ago when they still used horses—that a guy showed up at the prom. He danced with this one girl all night, sweet talking her and whatnot.

And, as they were leaving, everybody kind of noticed that he had hooves for feet. They knew the guy had hooves because they kind of heard the clip-clop as he walked.

They . . . the girl was never seen again after that night.

It was weird. I've heard that one a couple times.

The Little People

[As Alissa Matlack mentions, Keith's parents and uncles invoked the little people to keep curious youngsters from visiting potentially dangerous places. It is likely that they also told legends, akin to Dee Bainbridge's "The Little People," regarding nearby Waverly Beach and the doings of little people. Consequently it is hardly surprising that such creatures would figure in dreams and resultant personal experience stories.]

• • •

The story that's neat was: my cousin used to see little people. He was between seven and fourteen when he was seeing them. He'd wake up in the middle of the night and there'd be an Indian chief on one bedpost and a squaw on the other. And there'd be a bunch of bad ones. These two were good, they protected him. And there'd be a bunch of bad ones on the floor. Trying to take him away.

And my cousin shared a room with his brother and would wake up in the middle of the night. He'd be saying that [he could see the little people].

[And the cousin's brother would say] "Why are you saying that? Shut up and go to sleep." He couldn't see them.

He [Keith's cousin] seen them for the longest time, he always used to see them.

Then one night he didn't see them, but something was wrong. He got up to go to the living room and he seen someone laying on the couch; he thought it was his dad. He said, "Dad, Dad." And the guy stood up. I guess my cousin said he was like eight feet tall, and started walking toward him. The kid took off, and he ran through one of those baby gates. He was like five or six or seven, and he ran through one. He didn't even slow down, he just shot through it and landed on the stairs.

That was weird. His parents never saw the man.

14

Legends of Paul Bunyan, Lumberjack

K. Bernice Stewart and Homer A. Watt

Paul Bunyan is an inescapable presence in contemporary Wisconsin. One can read about his exploits in fourth-grade social studies texts, see his mighty ax at Wisconsin-Minnesota football games, gorge in his restaurants in Minocqua and Wisconsin Dells, pose alongside his statue in Eau Claire, and marvel at the immensity of his underwear in Rhinelander. Bunyan's current association with the bygone days of white pine logging, lumber camps, and river drives is undeniable. But the extent to which Wisconsin's bygone woods workers actually told stories about Paul Bunyan remains a matter of debate.

Bunyan first appeared in print on July 24, 1910, when James McGillivray, a former Michigan lumberjack, strung together a dozen short anecdotes in a story for the *Detroit News-Tribune,* "The Round River Drive." Nearly four years later, on April 25, 1914, Douglas Malloch of Chicago rendered McGillivray's stories into verse for the *American Lumberman* magazine. That same year, W. B. Laughead, who had worked in northern Minnesota's woods from 1900 to 1908, compiled a thirty-two page pamphlet for the Minneapolis-based Red River Lumber Company that intermixed Paul Bunyan stories with advertising copy. Laughead, with a popular audience in mind, went on to revise and expand Bunyan's exploits and by the early 1920s Bunyan had become a national figure, celebrated in mass media and claimed by every logging community in North America (see Daniel G. Hoffman, *Paul Bunyan: Last of the Frontier Demigods* [Philadelphia: Temple University Press, 1952]; and Richard M. Dorson, "Twentieth-Century Comic Demigods," in his *American Folklore* [Chicago: University of Chicago Press, 1959], 214–26).

There is considerable evidence, however, that Wisconsin lumberjacks knew few if any Bunyan stories before that figure's popularization through print in the 1920s. It was not until that decade, for example, that Paul Fournier established the Paul Bunyan Resort in Rice Lake, where the former timber cruiser assumed Bunyan's persona to entertain tourists with tall tales. Subsequently the local bakery sold Paul Bunyan Bread. Nor was Bunyan's ox neglected. On December 16, 1925, the *Rice Lake Chronotype* reported: "The burial place of Babe, the famous blue ox of Paul Bunyan, has been located about a mile west of Turtle Lake by the county highway commissioner, who says the ground is sacred to every loyal lumberjack and can never be disturbed for road building." The Bunyan bandwagon kept rolling thanks to promoters of northwestern Wisconsin's "Indianhead Country," who touted the region's natural beauty and legendary heritage in hopes of luring free-spending visitors.

In a parallel instance, John Emmett Nelligan, following an extended career in logging camps from the Canadian Maritime Provinces to northeastern Wisconsin, published his reminiscences, which included a string of Bunyan stories, as *The Life of a Lumberman* in 1929. Yet the Bunyan material was eliminated when Nelligan's account was serialized in volume 13 of the *Wisconsin Magazine of History.* Why? Editor Joseph Schafer discovered that Nelligan, an accomplished raconteur and a storehouse of vivid woods anecdotes, had in fact never heard any Paul Bunyan stories while working in the woods. Undaunted, Nelligan's collaborator, Charles Sheridan of

Washburn—who had written popular articles about logrolling and would eventually play a key role in Bayfield's boosteristic "Mystic Knights of the Blue Ox"—had lifted Bunyan stories from books in hopes of attracting a wider readership.

Indeed, the only legitimate claim to Bunyan's existence in the narrative repertoires of some Wisconsin lumberjacks was advanced in 1916 by K. Bernice Stewart and Homer A. Watt. A native of Madison who had clearly spent time in the logging country of northern Wisconsin, Bernice Stewart was a student at the University of Wisconsin and a reporter for the campus newspaper, The *Daily Cardinal.* Perhaps her "little collection" of Bunyan tales was prepared for a class offered by Homer A. Watt, a colleague of Arthur Beatty and likely an acquaintance of Charles E. Brown, who was an instructor in English at the University of Wisconsin from 1908 to 1916.

Mistaken in their acceptance of the then current "communal composition" theory that folktales are created mystically by communities rather than by creative individuals, Stewart and Watt nonetheless provide evidence that a few oral tales about Paul Bunyan circulated in Wisconsin lumber camps prior to his mass-media ascension. As Bunyan scholar Daniel G. Hoffman aptly stated, Stewart and Watt's collaboration not only "was Paul Bunyan's introduction to the academic world," but also "is one of the few authentic sources from which students today can estimate the spread of oral tales before widespread printed dissemination" (1952: 5).

Reprinted from *Transactions of the Wisconsin Academy of Sciences, Arts, and Letters* 18 (1916): 639–51.

The following study of lumberjack legends has grown out of a little collection of these tales made in the lumber camps by Miss Stewart, who for years has heard the stories told by the lumberjacks of Wisconsin and Michigan. Recently by corresponding with and interviewing lumbermen and others who are or who have been intimately connected with the lumber camps we have added to the original collection a considerable number of new legends, besides many different versions of stories already in our collection, and a great deal of miscellaneous information about the hero, Paul Bunyan and his blue ox. Some of these stories, as must be expected of any such series, are too coarse for publication. It has seemed to us, however, that for the most part the tales are quite wholesome; perhaps the circumstances under which they were collected have automatically excluded those of the rougher type. We realize, moreover, that our present collection represents only a comparatively small number of these stories; versions which have come to us from Oregon and Washington indicate that the tales are widely spread. We expect to continue our search for Paul Bunyan material, and shall be very glad to receive any information which will assist us. Communications should be addressed to Mr. H. A. Watt, Department of English, New York University, New York.

We wish to acknowledge our indebtedness to Mr. B. R. Taylor, Mr. M. W. Sergeant, and Mr. Harold Stark, students in the University who have recently lived in the lumber districts of northern Wisconsin, and who have heard Paul Bunyan tales from boyhood, to Mr. Douglas Malloch of Chicago for a copy of his poem, The Round River Drive, a metrical version of some of the tales which was published in *The American Lumberman* for April 25, 1914, to the Red River Lumber Company of Minneapolis, Minnesota, and to lumbermen and others who have sent us material from the lumber districts.

The most significant of recent developments in the study of folklore and the

14.1. Paul Bunyan and his ox, Babe, haul the timber in the imaginary Section 37 (there are but 36 sections in a town). State Historical Society of Wisconsin, WHi (X3) 7919.

popular ballad began with the discovery that the making of folktales and communal poetry did not cease entirely with the coming of the printing-press, but that in certain isolated communities unreached by the paralyzing contact of the printed sheet the process of communal composition has gone on, roughly, fragmentarily, perhaps, but nonetheless genuinely. Here in America there is a complete cycle of ballads celebrating the exploits of the outlaw Jesse James; Professor John Lomax has made an extensive collection of cowboy songs; and the isolated mountaineers of Kentucky and Tennessee have many songs and tales, some curiously distorted fragments of old-world ballads, others quite local in subject-matter and tone. The student of folklore has come, in fact, to expect that wherever there is more or less permanent isolation from the outside world of large groups of people engaged in the same occupation or at least having a community of interests, there is almost certain to spring up in time tales peculiar to that community. It is not, accordingly, surprising that such legends exist among the lumbermen of the Great North, among a community shut off from the world for months at a time and bound together by peculiar bonds. It is among these toilers of the forests that the legends of Paul Bunyan have originated: Paul Bunyan, the greatest lumberjack whoever skidded a log, who with the aid of his wonderful blue ox and his crew of hardy lumbermen cleared one hundred million feet of pine from a single forty and performed other feats related about the roaring fires of the lumber shanties. The legends of Paul Bunyan are widely distributed throughout the lumber districts of the North. The tales in our little collection have come from lumbercamps in the Northern Peninsula of Michigan and from the Saginaw Valley in the Southern Peninsula, from Langlade County and from camps along the Flambeau and Wisconsin rivers in Wisconsin, from northern Minnesota and from camps as far west as Oregon, Washington, and British Columbia. It is quite apparent that the lumberjacks in their slow migration westward have carried the tales freely from camp to camp into all of the lumbering states of the North and into the forests of Canada.

The antiquity of the tales is more difficult to determine than the extent of their distribution. It seems certain, however, from the circumstances that they have been passed down from one generation of lumbermen to another for a long period of time, that these stories of Paul Bunyan date well back into the early days of lumbering in Michigan and were carried from Michigan to Wisconsin about the middle of the last century. It seems certain, too, that many of the tales now included in the Bunyan cycle were narrated long before Bunyan became the lumberman hero. Similar tales, lacking, of course, the local color of the Bunyan yarns, are to be found in the extravagant stories of Baron Munchausen and of Rabelais as well as in folktales from more settled parts of the United States of America. An extremely interesting study—so complex, however, that we have not yet completed it—is the tracing of the old world originals of the Bunyan stories to determine just to what extent the American tales are new and to what extent they were brought from France and England by early pioneers.

Whether Paul Bunyan ever lived or is as mythical as Sairey Gamp's Mrs. Harris we have not yet succeeded in definitely finding out. All lumberjacks, of course, believe, or pretend to believe, that he really lived and was the great pioneer in the lumber country; some of the older men even claim to have known him or members of his crew, and in northern Minnesota the supposed location of his grave is actually pointed out. A half-breed lumberman whom Miss Stewart interviewed asserted positively that there was a Paul Bunyan and that the place where he cut his hundred million feet from a single forty is actually on the map. We have found in several localities characters still living about whose prowess as lumbermen exaggerated stories are already being told; it is probable that the tales will continue to be told, with additions, after these local heroes have died. In a similar manner, we believe, did Paul Bunyan come into existence. He was probably some swamper or shacker or lumberjack more skillful and more clever than average, about whose exploits grew a series of stories; after his death his fame probably spread from camp to camp, more tales were added to those told about him, and thus, gradually, he became in time an exaggerated type of the lumberjack, and the hero of more exploits than he could possibly have carried out in his lifetime.

The Bunyan stories are usually told in the evening around the fires in the bunkhouses. The older narrators speak in the French Canadian dialect, and the stories are often full of the technical jargon of the woods. Usually the stories are told to arouse the wonder of the tenderfoot or simply as contributions in a contest in yarning. They are always of a grotesque and fabulous type, and they are all more or less closely related to the exploits of Bunyan and his lumbering crew. "That happened," says the narrator, "the year I went up for Paul Bunyan. Of course you have all heard of Paul." And so the tale begins. It is matched by a bigger yarn, and the series grows. Often the scene of the exploits narrated is quite fictitious, like the Round River, which is in section thirty-seven, or the Big Onion River, three weeks this side of Quebec. Often, too, the lumberjacks will tell of events that they say occurred on another lumbering stream than the one they are working on; thus the men of the Flambeau camps will tell of the deeds of Paul Bunyan on the Wisconsin River or on the Chippewa River. Sometimes the storytellers will take Bunyan abroad and will tell of his doings, for example, among the big trees of Oregon, or they will tell of what happened when Paul was a boy on his father's farm. Usually, however, the tales are supposed to have occurred in the "good" days of lumbering, some forty or fifty years back when the country was new, and in localities not far from the camps in which the yarns are told.

But to our tales. Bunyan was a powerful giant, seven feet tall and with a stride of seven feet. He was famous throughout the lumbering districts for his physical strength and for the ingenuity with which he met difficult situations. He was so powerful that no man could successfully oppose him, and his ability to get drunk was proverbial. So great was his lung capacity that he called his men to dinner by blowing through a hollow tree a blast so strong that it blew down the timber on a tract of sixty acres, and when he spoke, the limbs sometimes fell from the trees. To keep his pipe filled required the entire time of a swamper with a scoop-shovel. In the gentle art of writing Bunyan had, however, no skill. He kept his men's time by cutting notches in a stick of wood, and he ordered supplies for camp by drawing pictures of what he wanted. On one occasion only did his ingenuity fail; he ordered grindstones and got cheeses. "Oh," says Paul, "I forgot to put the holes in my grind-stones."

Bunyan was assisted in his lumbering exploits by a wonderful blue ox, a creature that had the strength of nine horses and that weighed, according to some accounts, five thousand pounds, and according to others, twice that. The ox measured from tip to tip of his horns just seven feet, exactly his master's height. Other accounts declare that the ox was seven feet—or seven ax-handles—between his eyes, and fourteen feet between his horns. Originally he was pure white, but one winter in the woods it snowed blue snow for seven days (that was the winter of the snow-snakes) and Bunyan's ox from lying out in the snow all winter became and remained a brilliant blue. Many of the Bunyan legends are connected with the feats performed by the ox. Bunyan's method of peeling a log was as follows: He would hitch the ox to one end of the log, grasp the bark at the other end with his powerful arms, give a sharp command to the animal, and, presto, out would come the log as clean as a whistle. On one occasion Paul dragged a whole house up a hill with the help of his ox, and then, returning, he dragged the cellar up after the house. Occasionally, as might have been expected from so huge a creature, the ox got into mischief about camp. One night, for example, he broke loose and ate up two hundred feet of towline.

One favorite tale connected with the blue ox is that of the buckskin harness. One day old Forty Jones of Bunyan's crew killed two hundred deer by the simple process of tripping a key-log which supported a pile of logs on a hillside above the place where the animals came to drink. The skins were made into a harness for the blue ox. Some days later while the cook was hauling a log in for firewood, it began to rain, the buckskin began to stretch, and by the time the ox reached camp the log was out of sight around a bend in the road with the tugs stretching back endlessly after it. The cook tied the ox and went to dinner. While he was eating, the sun came out boiling hot, dried the buckskin harness, and hauled the log into camp. Another version of this tale is reported to us by Professor Beatty of the University of Wisconsin, who heard the story when he was a boy in Canada. Whether Professor Beatty's version is simply a detached member of the Bunyan story-cycle or whether, conversely, it existed originally as an independent tale and was later connected with the blue ox, we do not know. The latter explanation seems the probable one.

One tale of the blue ox had best be told in the words of the lumberjack who sent it to a friend of Miss Stewart's, in a letter written with very evident care and with every other word capitalized.

Paul B Driving a large Bunch of logs Down the Wisconsin River When the logs Suddenly Jamed in the Dells. The logs were piled Two Hundred feet high at the head, And were backed up for One mile up river. Paul was at the rear of the Jam with the Blue Oxen And while he was coming to the front the Crew was trying to break the Jam but they couldent Budge it. When Paul Arrived at the Head with the ox he told them to Stand Back. He put the Ox in the old Wisc. in front of the Jam. And then Standing on the Bank Shot the Ox with a 303 Savage Rifle. The Ox thought it was flies And began to Switch his Tail. The tail commenced to go around in a circle And up Stream And do you know That Ox Switching his tail forced that Stream to flow Backwards And Eventually the Jam floated back Also. He took the ox out of the Stream. And let the Stream And logs go on their way.

Most of the exploits of Paul Bunyan center at Round River. Here Bunyan and his crew labored all one winter to clear the pine from a single forty. This was a most peculiar forty in that it was shaped like a pyramid with a heavy timber growth on all sides. The attention of skeptics who refuse to believe in the existence of the pyramid forty is certain to be called by the storyteller to a lumberman with a short leg, a member, the listener is solemnly assured, of Bunyan's crew, who got his short leg from working all winter on one side of the pyramid, and who thus earned the nickname of "Rockin' Horse." From this single forty Bunyan's crew cleared one hundred million feet of pine, and in the spring they started it down the river. Then began the difficulty, for it was not until they had passed their old camp several times that they realized that the river was round and had no outlet whatever. According to another version this logging occurred on a lake with no outlet.

Bunyan's crew was so large that he was obliged to divide the men into three gangs; of these one was always going to work, one was always at work, and the third was always coming home from work. The cooking arrangements for so many men were naturally on an immense scale. Seven men with seven wheelbarrows were kept busy wheeling the prune-stones away from camp. The cookstove was so extensive that three forties had to be cleared bare each week to keep up a fire, and an entire cord of wood was needed to start a blaze. One day as soon as the cook had put a loaf of bread into the oven he started to walk around the stove in order to remove the loaf from the other side, but long before he reached his destination the bread had burned to a crisp. Such loaves were, of course, gigantic—so big, in fact, that after the crew had eaten the insides out of them, the hollow crusts were used for bunkhouses, or, according to a less imaginative account, for bunks. One legend reports that the loaves were not baked in a stove at all but in a ravine or dried riverbed with heat provided by blazing slashings along the sides.

Such a stove as Bunyan's demanded, of course, a pancake griddle of monstrous size. As a matter of fact, Bunyan's cook, Joe Mufferon, used the entire top of the stove for [a] griddle and greased it every morning by strapping hams to the feet of his assistant cooks and obliging them to skate about on it for an hour or so. Of this famous tale there are several versions. According to one the cook mixed his batter in a sort of concrete-mixer on the roof of the cook shanty and spread it upon the stove by means of a connecting hose. A version from Oregon shows the influence of local conditions upon the Bunyan tales; from this version we learn that two hundred Japanese cooks with bacon-rinds or bear-steak strapped to their feet skated upon the stove before the cook spread his batter. In a Minnesota version Bunyan employs his twenty-four daughters for the same menial task. By mistake one day the near-sighted cook put into the batter several fingers of blasting-powder instead of baking-powder, and when the mixture was spread upon the griddle the cookees made a very rapid ascent through the cook shanty roof and never returned to camp.

Paul Bunyan's ingenuity in keeping his men supplied with food and drink appears best in the pea soup lake story, of which there are several versions, and in the wondrous tale of the camp distillery. Near the Round River camp was a hot spring, into which the tote-teamster, returning one day from town with a load of peas, dumped the whole load by accident. Most men would have regarded the peas as a dead loss, but not so Paul. He promptly added the proper amount of pepper and salt to the mixture and had enough hot pea soup to last the crew all winter. When his men were working too far away from camp to return to dinner, he got the soup to them by freezing it upon the ends of sticks and sending it in that shape. According to another version of the pea soup lake story Paul deliberately made the pea soup; he dumped the peas into a small lake and heated the mess by firing the slashings around the shore. In a Wisconsinized version of the Michigan tale the peas have become, for some reason, beans. A much exaggerated version of this story comes from northern Wisconsin. According to this account the tote-teamster was driving across a frozen lake when a sudden thaw overtook him. The teamster saved himself, but the ox was drowned. Bunyan dammed up the lake, fired the slashings around the shore, and then, opening the dam, sluiced down the river to his laboring crew an abundance of excellent hot pea soup with ox-tail flavor.

The legend of the establishment of the camp distillery is one of the most entertaining of the Bunyan tales. Paul had trouble in keeping any liquor in camp because the men sent to town for it drank it all up on the way back. The following is Mr. Douglas Malloch's versified account of how he solved the difficulty:

One day the bull-cook parin' spuds
He hears a sizzlin' in the suds
And finds the peelin's, strange to say,
Are all fermentin' where they lay.
Now Sourface Murphy in
Was standin'. And the face he wore
Convinced the first assistant cook
That Murphy soured 'em with his look
And when he had the peelin's drained
A quart of Irish booze remained.
The bull-cook tells the tale to Paul
And Paul takes Murphy off the haul
And gives him, very willingly
A job as camp distillery.

Some of the tales of the camp exploits concern members of Paul Bunyan's crew rather than the hero himself. One of the men, for example, had two sets of teeth, and, walking in his sleep one night, he encountered the grindstone and chewed it to bits before he was fully aroused to what he was doing. In the adventure of another member of the crew we have the familiar tale of the man who jumped across the river in three jumps. The crew sometimes showed ingenuity on their own account as when they rolled boulders down the steep sides of the pyramid forty, and running after them ground their axes to a razor edge against the revolving stones.

Connected very frequently with the Bunyan tales are accounts of fabulous animals that haunted the camp. There is the bird who lays square eggs so that they will not roll down hill, and hatches them in the snow. Then there is the side-hill dodger, a curious animal naturally adapted to life on a hill by virtue of the circumstance that it has two short legs on the uphill side. Of this creature it is said that by mistake the female dodger once laid her eggs (for the species seems to resemble somewhat the Australian duck-bill) wrong end around, with the terrible result that the little dodgers, hatching out with their short legs down hill, rolled into the river and drowned. The pinnacle grouse are birds with only one wing, adapted by this defect for flight in one direction about the top of a conical hill. There is little doubt that these animal stories existed outside the Bunyan cycle, and are simply appended to the central group of tales.

The story of Bunyan's method of paying off his crew at the end of the season shows the hero's craftiness. Discovering in the spring that he had no money on hand, Bunyan suddenly rushed into camp shouting that they had been cutting government pine and were all to be arrested. Each man thereupon seized what camp property lay nearest his hand and made off, no two men taking the same direction. Thus Bunyan cleared his camp without paying his men a cent for their labor.

Not all of the Bunyan stories are concerned with Bunyan's life in the Round River or the Big Onion camps. There are several accounts of his exploits far from the forests of the north-central states. It is said that when he was once dredging out the Columbia River, he broke the dredge, and, sticking it into his pocket, walked to the nearest blacksmith shop in South Dakota, had it repaired, and returned to the Oregon camp before dark. Besides his blue ox Bunyan had, according to some versions, so many oxen that their yokes, piled up, made twenty cords of wood. One day he drove all of these animals through a hollow tree which had fallen across a great ravine. When he reached the other side, he found that several of the oxen had disappeared, and, returning, he discovered that they had strayed into a hollow limb.

Occasionally one hears some account of Paul Bunyan's boyhood exploits on his father's farm. It is said that on one occasion he and his father went out to gather a huge watermelon which was growing on a sidehill above a railroad track. They carelessly forgot to prop the melon up before they severed the stem with a cross-cut saw, and as a result it broke loose, rolled down hill, burst open on striking the rails, and washed out two hundred feet of track. This tale and similar ones do not seem to belong strictly to the Bunyan cycle, but to be, rather, like the animal fables, mere appendages.

What is there in these exaggerated tales of interest to the student of literature? We believe, first, that, crude as they are, they reveal unmistakable indications of having grown up under the same principles of literary development which produced by a slow process legend-cycles much more romantic and famous. The tendency to group the tales about one hero is universal in legend, as is illustrated by the Arthurian and Robin Hood cycles, and less completely by the folk tales of Rubezahl, the spirit of the Riesengebirge of Germany, Puck, or Robin Goodfellow, and the strong man, Tom Hickathrift, of England. Moreover, like other legend groups, the Bunyan stories tend to be concerned with a single locality, Round River or Big Onion River. Finally, many of the legends are more less closely connected with a single exploit, the clearing of the pyramid forty, in much the same way, to compare the little with the great, that Greek legends center in the Argonautic Expedition and the Trojan War, and Arthurian legends in the search for the Holy Grail.

Of more interest, however, is the remarkable quality of the exaggeration in the Bunyan legends. This quality is worth analysis not only because it shows universal tendencies, but because it is the basis of what has come to be known as American humor. The tendency in all legend is to exaggerate, to make the physical strength or craft of the hero much greater than normal, to make an Ajax or an Odysseus of him. But in classical romance and epic this exaggeration is a thing of slow growth. It happens naturally, through a desire to make the deeds of the hero seem more wonderful, and not deliberately, through a desire to arouse amusement by gross exaggeration; it is an apotheosis, not caricature. The exaggeration in the legends of Paul Bunyan is certainly of a different sort from that in classical legend; it is more Munchausenesque. The teller of the tale of the pea soup lake, and of the camp distillery, and of the great Round River drive has two motives: first, he wishes to excite wonder; second, he wishes to amuse. In their wonder-motive the Bunyan legends belong to that numerous class of travelers' tales typified by the fabulous accounts in Mandeville and Hakluyt, and in the books of other collectors. They are stories designed to be swallowed by camp followers and tenderfeet for the entertainment of hardened dwellers in the woods. In their humor-motive they belong to that large class of stories which depend for their effectiveness not upon true representations of facts but upon gross departures from normal standards. Humor is a difficult thing to define, but one of its important elements is certainly that surprise which comes from the sudden and unanticipated contemplation of an incongruous variation from the normal. Good taste has gradually set limits to what cultivated persons regard as legitimate humor, but the child still laughs at the drunkard and to some the abnormality of insanity is still amusing. Humor has, accordingly, very often taken the form of gross exaggeration or caricature, especially under the spur of a contest in yarning. This type of humor is typically American. It is really only a natural development of the attempt to "boom" new sections of the country by representing conditions as superior to what they actually are. It is but one aspect of the cheerful, rose-colored, but quite distorted optimism which aroused the disgust of Dickens and other Englishmen (see Martin Chuzzlewit) and has earned for Americans among Europeans, whose boom days are over, the name of braggart.

It is this quality of humorous exaggeration, then, and the idea of a contest in lying, which makes the Bunyan legend cycle typically American, or, it might be better to say, typically pioneer, in spirit. And the reader does not have to look far for American parallels. Mark Twain's books are full of tales of the same stamp; Owen Wister's Virginian teems with them; lately in Harry Leon Wilson's Ruggles of Red Gap we again meet this characteristically American type of story. The note is the same throughout—gross caricature in fact and characters to arouse the wonder of the tenderfoot and to amuse the initiated by the mere bigness of the yarn.

The Bunyan cycle of legends certainly contains a great many tales which sound strangely familiar to the person who meets Bunyan for the first time. It is altogether probable, in fact, that a great many of these stories had their origin elsewhere than in the woods and have simply been added to the Bunyan collection. We have been told on good authority that a legendary blue ox exists in a certain mountain district of Tennessee and that in this same district not only the men but even all the animals have short legs to adapt them to hill-climbing. The tale of the man who jumped across the river "in three jumps" is, as has been pointed out, widely distributed. Some of the Bunyan stories, on the other hand, almost certainly originated in the woods. To Professor Cairns of the Department of English at Wisconsin we are indebted for an ingenious explanation of the possible origin of the tale of the pyramid forty and its prodigious supply of timber. In the early days of lumbering in the North more than one man staked out a claim on a single forty and, ignoring section lines, cut "government pine" for miles around, securing, it was humorously reported by those who knew but winked at the robbery, a great deal of timber from one forty. This cutting of government pine appears definitely in at least one Bunyan story, the tale of the method adopted by Bunyan to pay off his crew. Excepting for stories of this sort, however, which seem distinctly confined to the lumber districts, and which would, indeed, have little reason for existing elsewhere, the majority of the Bunyan legends are very likely adaptations of tales which have elsewhere an existence in some form.

15

Ghost Stories
(As Told by Old Settlers)
Thor Helgeson

Wisconsin's European immigrants hailed overwhelmingly from peasant communities animated by the supernatural. Kitchens, barns, crossroads, lakes, rocks, and woods were—especially at night and during seasonal transitions—the territory of ghosts, little people (fairies, leprechauns, *nisse*), giants, and such peculiar beasts as trolls. Sometimes hostile, they were more often simply mischievous and could be appeased with gifts of food or kept at bay with charms. Sorcerers and devils were more problematic. They might make you sick, afflict your animals, or steal your soul.

Those Old World creatures bound to particular places figured mostly in the recollections of Wisconsin's newcomers. The consensus was that they hadn't found passage on trans-Atlantic ships. Ghosts, practitioners of witchcraft, and the devil (a.k.a. the "Black One," "Erik," and *"Hinkarn"*) were far more mobile, however, and localized stories concerning their doings abounded.

Thor Helgeson's "Ghost Stories," originally written in Norwegian, offers a rare glimpse of a supernaturally inclined storytelling session involving immigrants in western Waupaca County in the late nineteenth century. Some of the stories hark back to Norway, while others occur in Wisconsin, sometimes to the tellers themselves. A careful listener and gifted writer, Helgeson conveys a rich sense of the session's participants, its flow, and its inclusion of debates between skeptics and true believers. The stories themselves are alternately hilarious and sobering, and some—like those of Professor Erik and the black book—were widespread among Wisconsin's Germans (see chapter 29, "Faith and Magic," pp. 323–30).

Translator Malcolm Rosholt encountered Thor Helgeson's writings in the 1950s when he began to compile a history of Waupaca County's Scandinavia and Iola Townships, where all four of his great-grandparents had settled. "When I began to work on the Helgeson translation," Rosholt explains in the introduction to his 1985 edition of Helgeson's stories, "children of the pioneers, most of them in their seventies and eighties, told me that Helgeson 'wrote too much about all that drinking and stuff,' or 'he made fun of the pioneers.' But Helgeson, an artist, was unconcerned about his critics. In modern parlance, he 'told it like it is.'"

Einar Haugen, the Norwegian American linguist, had also encountered Helgeson's earthy reputation when visiting Waupaca County in 1942:

> He was the sexton here. He was sexton for a great many years. Now Helgeson was this way that he liked a glass of beer now and then, and when he was in good company, he might sometimes take a tiny drop too many. Then the pastor had heard about this once that he had been at a beer party and was going to give him a reprimand. But he came out with it in so strange a way. He said, "I dreamt that I was in heaven," he said, "and there I went into the house that was prepared for sextons," he said, "and there they were carrying on something awful. They weren't decent at all, and they were loud-mouthed and they had stuff to drink there, and they weren't decent at all." "Is that so," said Helgeson. "Well, I also dreamt," said he, "that I was in heaven, and went into the room that was prepared for the pastors. But there

I didn't find a single pastor" (*The Norwegian Language in America* [Bloomington: Indiana University Press, 1969], 497).

Einar Haugen subsequently fashioned a biography of Helgeson from interviews with old-timers like John Barikmo, the source of the prior anecdote, and researches into the Norwegian American press.

Born September 29, 1842, in the township of Tinn, Norway, the son of a farmer and logger, Thor Helgeson trained to be a teacher before emigrating to America in 1862. After stays of a year each in the Norwegian settlements of Muskego and Koshkonong, he settled in the Portage and Waupaca County area in 1863, where he taught in Lutheran schools and wrote until his death on May 5, 1928.

Besides its account of "Ghost Stories," Helgeson's *Fra Indianernes Lande* is laden with anecdotes and accounts of such customary activities as weddings, Christmas celebrations, husking bees, ladies aid society meetings, and house parties. But supernatural tales were clearly one of the immigrant schoolmaster's passions. Barikmo, a former student, informed Einar Haugen that Helgeson often told his charges "tales of ghosts and trolls from Norway until they were afraid to go to bed." No doubt some were included in *Folksagn og folketro* (Folktales and Folk Beliefs), which Helgeson published in 1923. That same year Waldemar Ager, editor of Eau Claire's Norwegian-language newspaper *Reform*, lauded Helgeson as "the P. C. Asbjörnsen of the Norwegians in America," in reference to a prominent Norwegian folklorist who, with Jörgen Moe, published the classic collection of Norwegian folktales in 1842 (see Einar Haugen, "Thor Helgeson: Schoolmaster and Raconteur," *Norwegian-American Studies* 24 [1970]: 3–27; for an overview of Norwegian legendry and many stories paralleling those Helgeson presents, see Reidar Christiansen, *Folktales of Norway* [Chicago: University of Chicago Press, 1964]).

Reprinted from Thor Helgeson, *From the Indian Land* (Iola, Wisc.: Krause Publications, 1985), 257–60, translated and annotated by Malcolm Rosholt from Helgeson's originals, *Fra Indianernes Lande* (From the Indian Land) (1915), and *Fra Indianernes Lande: Den Anden Samling* (From the Indian Land: A Second Collection) (1917).

I do not recall what occasion brought so many people together at K's (Christian Christianson Thoe), nevertheless, it was a big company. The men talked first about the wind and weather, and then about the wheat crop, wheat prices, stock for butchering and timber dealings. When these topics, which are so interesting to farmers, were exhausted, they gradually began to talk about other events about trolls, elves, fairies and ghosts. Many of the older pioneers still believed in the power of the underground folk and all that was said about them as sure as God's truth. But others believed they were nothing but nonsense. It was the opinion of some people that the progress and education of the 19th century had scared both the trolls and elves so far into the ground that they never dared show themselves again. It was during the period of the lack of enlightenment that people believed these dark spirits had power to rule on earth. Now days it is people, not trolls or goblins who rule the earth.

Our fathers and forefathers, Ola began, have always imagined that these trolls, goblins and other supernatural devilishness actually existed and that people had seen them or others had seen or heard them. As for me I have never seen a troll or a goblin or a ghost, and what's more, I don't believe in them, not a word.

Neither do I, said Gregar (Holla, Jr.). The only ghost I ever saw was something that appeared near Granbera's corners in Scandinavia (in Waupaca County, Wisconsin). There I saw a man clad only in a shirt, glaring at the moon. But even as I stood and watched him, the man turned into a popple stump.

15.1. Trollodin, who dwells behind Mount Horeb's Open House Imports, wanders the "trollway" business district during the village's annual Fall Fest, 1992. Photo: James P. Leary, Wisconsin Folk Museum Collection.

So-o! You don't believe in these underground creatures and ghosts? said Per, who held strong beliefs on the subject.

Perhaps you have seen some of them, said Ola, who was one of the doubters. Well, I haven't seen much, but there are people living here who have both seen and heard such things and they are honest and law-abiding people who neither lie nor cheat, said Per, a bit impatient with the doubter. Tell us then, shouted the others.

That I can, if I want to, said Per, and after he had stuffed his black clay pipe, he began to explain, in confidential tones, all about the ghosts on the Opsal farm in Norway. In Gausdal of Gudbrandsdalen, Per began, there was a place called Opsal farm. Here a terrible commotion once occurred with the ghost and which no one could understand or fathom, because big boulders rolled into the fireplace chimney and both large and small stones came flying in as if they had been thrown through the window panes of the hut. Wood in the fire place was thrown across the floor while pots and pans and such things were scattered into the corners.

There were many explanations given for this strange event and it led to a religious revival in the whole of Gausdal, Per continued. Some said that the mountain trolls were on the loose and some thought that the people living on Opsal had provoked the underground people. Others thought that the Black One himself and his equally black followers were out to do mischief. But what they could not understand was why the devil should pass up the big estates instead of living in a forlorn tenant farmer's house.

The pastor of Gausdal, Andreas Jorgen Fleischer, was called in. Although big and broad as he was, he was no match for the Black One, that's for sure. For by now the Black One had gotten such a foothold in the house that the people had to send word to the pastor in Faaberg to get rid of him. And if the Faaberg pastor couldn't put wings on him, then no one else could, said Fleischer.

Well sir, they sent word to Pastor Rasmus Lygn at Faaberg, a man with a red hand and a red foot. He was not slow in coming and as soon as he arrived in the house, he took a piece of chalk and wrote several doodlings on the wall which neither Fleischer nor anyone else could read. By this device he sent the devil and all his works straight out of the community. And you can be sure they never came back to Opsal again.

Pastor Lygn was just the man to effect this housecleaning. He had studied at the school of magic in Wittenberg, Germany, and could read the Black Book forward and backward. If a student wished to become a pastor of any influence in olden times, he had to matriculate in this school at Wittenberg and take his examination there. There were always 12 students in the school. When they had taken their examination, 11 were permitted to leave, but the twelfth one Professor Erik kept as an assistant. The students drew straws to see who was to become Erik's boy. At the time Pastor Lygn took his examination in black magic, they also drew straws and it fell to Lygn to serve as Erik's boy. But Lygn was on to him, you can bet your boots. He was so learned and experienced in the black arts that he fooled Erik into taking his shadow. People therefore said that the Faaberg pastor didn't have a shadow or second self. But that was not true because I saw very clearly that he cast a shadow both in sunshine and in moonshine. But perhaps he had fooled Erik into getting his shadow back again. Who knows?

Let me see now. How did it go with that man who was standing in his shirt and turned into a popple stump, Gregar?

Well, this story is soon told because it's a short one, said Gregar. Christian, a neighbor boy, was often plagued with colic and one day he was so severely stricken that he lay on the floor and twisted like a snake on an ant hill. A member of his family came to me and asked if I would run down to Granbera's store after a quart of brandy. They had to give Christian something strong, they said, I was young and fleet of foot as a deer and it did not take long before I was at Madam Granbera's. I got the brandy all right and was about to leave except that there were some men in the place who were drinking and telling ghost stories. I had to listen and became so interested that I completely forgot both Christian and his colic. When I saw that the sun was setting, I remembered my errand and galloped back as fast as I could. The road went entirely different at that time as it was laid out along Goat Back Ridge (Gjeiteryggen) and crossed a valley. The moon came up big and beautiful and the tree stumps stood out all around. When I came down in the valley and was about to climb the north hill I saw on top of the hill a man clad only in a shirt. There he stood and twisted this way and that and gazed at the moon. He came at me. A young boy is easily scared and when I recalled all these stories I had just heard about ghosts and other evil powers, I became even more frightened. Hah! I thought Christian is already dead because I did not get the brandy to him in time and now he is out spooking me. The more I looked at the figure, the worse it became. At last I stood on my knees in the middle of the road and read the Lord's Prayer. After that I became a little more daring and went forward, step by step, until I saw what kind of a spook it was—another popple stump! The bark had peeled on one side so that it turned in the moonlight.

When I finally arrived back, Christian had already recovered. The brandy came too late, to be sure, but Christian felt that it could do no harm to "smear" one's insides with a brandy punch just the same. This might even keep the colic from coming back. So he "smeared" himself and gave some to the others.

Matias Bergshaugen continued with the story telling. He was an upright man and no one ever doubted his word on anything.

It happened one fall, Matias began, that I and some other lumberjacks were in the woods building a logging camp. I remember it as well as if it happened today. We finished with the work on Thursday night, and we had just finished our evening meal and were sitting by the stove with our clay pipes and telling stories, when all at once we heard a noise and a rumbling like a strong thunderbolt. We got up from our chairs and rushed out together. Every single window which we had installed that day had fallen out and there they all lay in a row on the ground. It was a cold, star-filled night without a cloud in the sky. There was no thundering. But what was it anyway? Can anyone really tell me?

A deep silence filled the house. No one could answer Matias' question, and the others sat there dumbfounded and speechless.

Per was the first to be heard from. He listened to Bergshaugen's story with attention, just as if he had been listening to a festival sermon.

Many strange things can happen in this sinful world, he said. I remember a story I heard many years ago. Something happened in a small village on the Mississippi River which people are still wondering about. The name of the village was . . . well, I can't think of it now. It's bad when one becomes so forgetful. But it is all the same with the name. At the time this village was established, a prominent family came there and purchased an entire block of land on which a store was built, an extremely handsome brick building. How this family lived and what they lived off no one ever learned for they had nothing to do with other people. But they had everything, you understand, and they remained there many years. But one fine day the entire family left town just as if they had blown away.

After this beautiful building remained empty for many years, it was examined by some folks who wished to live in it. They took it over and shortly later moved out as fast as they moved in. There were so many strange noises and spooking in the building that neither people nor tramps could live there.

But one does not have to travel to the Mississippi to find spooks, said Bergshaugen. You can find them much closer to home. Several miles south of Waupaca there was something like this on a Yankee farm where people were obliged to leave both home and farm. Nobody could live there and the farm has been a wilderness for many years.

Well, now, was it not like that over there by Iver Naes' place? asked one of the others. We don't need to go to Waupaca to hear such stories. There was no doubt some spooking at Naes', I am sure. There, night after night, people saw two men, one big, one small. The big one had on a high hat, or at least it seemed that way because he could make himself big or little according to his wishes. From the high hat came a flame of fire which reached way over to Ovald Person's place. It was, I tell you, a terrible spook.

Now let me tell you another one. It wasn't so free of spooks down there at Hans Jacob Eliason's place in Scandinavia either. One evening in the fall some loafers came to Hans Jacob with a jug of whisky and a deck of cards and they sat down for a game and some heavy drinking. But at the height of the game they heard a rumbling sound which got them to their feet in a jiffy. The card sharks let Hans Jacob keep both the jug and deck of cards and they beat it home as fast as they had learned to run.

One evening Anne Kjendalen, wife of Anders in Scandinavia, came from the village at twilight. Just as she approached the gate into the yard, she saw a big, ugly looking tramp sitting on the fence near the gate post. She jumped, naturally, although she was not so frightened that she could not say "good evening" to him. He did not say a word before he disappeared into the ground.

Now Per took up the story telling. We all know Tobias (Guto of Helvetia Township), he said. That Tobias is a "seer" because he often sees things that others can not see. And he is an upright man who never fools around with nonsense of any kind. One day when Tobias came home from the village it was snowing a little and it became difficult to see even the footprints of others who had gone ahead. When he reached Flaatbakken, he saw a small chap who trotted up the hill, dodging in and out. Tobias thought this was one of Jacob's boys (probably Jacob Fjeldbo) who was lost, and Tobias hurried along to learn what he was up to. But to catch up? That was impossible! The little chap disappeared right in front of Tobias' nose. Tobias then went back to see whether he could pickup his tracks in the snow but found no tracks other than his own big clod hoppers.

Then there was another evening that Tobias had been visiting at Paul Barlundstuen and was on his way home. When he reached the north side of Valbergbakken (Valberg Hill) which lies just north of the farm where old Captain Sivertson once lived, he met Gunnar Valberget in his workaday clothes and ax on his shoulder. Gunnar was dead. He had died suddenly but did not die by his own hand as some have been yacking about.

We have heard the same about Ovald's-Ingeborg (Mrs. Ovald Person) said Matias Bergshaugen, taking up the thread again. She died suddenly and no one knew what she died of. There were lots of questions asked. On one occasion after Ingeborg was put in the ground some people from New Hope came to visit Ovald. On their return home they were crossing Ovaldsbakken where they met Ingeborg right in the middle of the hill. She was in her ordinary house dress just as in life.

A farm in New Hope was also supposed to be spooked. But one man in the township swore that the whole story about ghosts on this farm was just plain nonsense and a story hatched at a coffee clutch [sic]. But he would not deny that there were ghosts in Prestejonbakken (Preacher Jon's Hill) because people had seen a headless man there. But he really could not understand why the spooks should be chasing after Preacher Jon all the time.

It often happens that people frighten themselves, remarked one of the company. It is usually in the evening or during the night that they see spooks. When they see something they can't make out they at once take it for a ghost. They scare themselves, at least for the most part.

The first resident pastor on the Indian Land was Pastor Duus. His wife was named Sophie. I believe that everyone remembers this kind pastor's family, especially Mrs. Duus because she was as kind as the day was long. She died in the Scandinavia parsonage and lies buried in the cemetery there. If I remember correctly, it was the same evening she died that somebody saw a beautiful white ghost in the neighborhood of the parsonage. It flew past the house and toward the cemetery. You can imagine how bug-eyed people became when they saw this beautiful apparition which they took for a good angel sent down to take the kindly Mrs. Duus home.

But this good angel was none other than the pastor's good neighbor, Christian who, in a long, white summer coat, was strolling over to see his old friend Jens Hellom north of the cemetery. You can imagine how Olson laughed and enjoyed himself when he learned that he had been taken for an angel. "Yes, to be sure, they saw a beautiful angel that time," he said.

Many years ago there lived an Englishman over by the range line (Iola-Helvetia) named John Wolf, one of the story tellers related. One evening when he came home from town he found his wife sitting in a corner as confused as a scared chicken.

"What's happened to you and why are you sitting like that?" asked John.

"The devil has been here. I don't dare be alone any more," said the woman.

"Do you want me to believe that? What did he want here? It's some other terrible person you've seen, perhaps an Indian."

"No! Never! The Black One himself has been here," said the woman, sticking to her story.

"What did he look like?"

"Oh, he was so black and ugly I can scarcely describe him," said the woman. "He had feet as big as half that stove there. One head was like a small haycock and when he glared at me, one was bright as a hot ember in his throat because he had only one eye as far as I could see. On his fingers he had long, wide claws which I clearly saw when he warmed his hands over the stove. It was the devil and no one else."

John sat and thought about this for a time and burst into laughter. "Now I know what kind of a man you saw. It was the old girl on the farm north of us. She goes and herds the cattle about the marshes here. When it's as cold as it is today, she puts on all the rags she owns and covers her head with all kinds of scarves. I've seen her several times in that habit and she also has only one eye."

But the woman would not give in. "No sir-e-e! It was the devil," she said. "From now on you will have to remain at home, John, and if you go away, you will have to take me along because it's the man and not the devil who must care for a woman."

Matias Bergshaugen urged the story teller to continue and he began: Ola and Matias Hoyord one time returned from the cedar swamp where they had been making repairs to their shanty, I think. It was winter and uncommonly cold, too. Now Ole had bought himself a newfangled winter cap with a flap which could be lowered over the face against wind and weather. Matias was driving the horses. On the road they met Old Nils who was driving to Benson Corners, too. When Nils could not see Ola's face, which resembled a coal-black dot, he thought at once it was Hinkarn, who was out on the prowl. He glared at the dark figure and drove off the road as far as he could because he did not wish to form any closer liaison with Hinkarn. As soon as he drove past, he lay to the horses and galloped towards Benson Corners. He came into the store almost scared out of his wits and said, "Boy! Today I've really seen an awful sight—something awful, I tell yah!"

"What kind of a sight?" someone asked.

"Believe it or not, if I can understand it myself. Matias Hoyord drove over the devil today because he drove up to a figure with a face as black as a kettle," said Nils.

One winter night, Ola continued, Jens Hellom returned from Scandinavia where he had been on a spree. When he came to the cemetery he saw a black shadow crawling on all fours along the cemetery fence. When Hellom moved, the shadow moved and when Hellom stopped the shadow also stopped. Hellom became frightened, for now he was quite certain that he was being followed by Hinkarn. He started to run but stumbled in a snow bank. The shadow also began to run and ran ahead while Hellom dug himself out of the snow. The scare had a sobering influence on him and when he finally returned home he vowed that he had run a race with that black pig of his.

At this time Hellom had a blacksmith shop and every Sunday night he could be heard puffing and pounding until all hours. Johan Hartvig, his brother-in-law and neighbor, was tired of listening to this everlasting blacksmithing on Sunday. But to talk to Hellom about Sunday as a day of rest was the same as trying to drown a fish. One Sunday evening Hartvig hid himself back of a bush west of the blacksmith shop and threw one snowball after the other at the wall of the shop. This seemed to frighten Hellom as he hurried down to his house as fast as he could and after that day there was no more Sunday blacksmithing. Well, it's true, we hear quite a bit about spooks here in America too, said Ola, but in Norway it was much worse with such foolishness. For there one could find *Jutal* (dwarfs), *Bergtroll*, (mountain trolls), and *Bergkjaerring* (troll women) in every mountain top; *Nisse* (elves) or *Hulder* (hill siren with long, cowlike tail) in every brush; and *Skromt* (spooks) in every other cemetery. But, as I said, I don't believe much in these old stories. If anyone saw anything unnatural, it was either an illusion or the devil himself, for this person could reveal himself in all kinds of shapes. But for the most part people scared themselves. That's what I think.

In Brunkeberg in Telemark one time a wedding was being held on an estate which lay about a forty from the church. Shortly before the bridal couple was to return home, the musician got into an argument with the bridegroom, took his fiddle and left. He was so drunk he did not know where he was going and finally tumbled into the mortuary under the church. There he sat down on a coffin and started to play so hard it could be heard far and wide. Wedding guests and others who went by the church took to their heels because they thought for sure that Erik was playing for the important people laid to rest there. For in olden times it was a fact that prominent people had to be buried under the church floor. They naturally could not sleep together with the peasants and cotters out in the cemetery. That's the way things were then. Some time later these good Brunkebergers discovered that it was their own fiddler who had played for the dead under Brunkeberg's church.

A boy working in Selemdal forest went to town one day, Ola continued. On his way home he caught sight of a big black shadow approaching him as he entered the forest. Everything was so dark he could not see what it was. Without saying a word the shadow threw itself on the sleigh by his side. The boy thought he had Erik himself on board, lay to the horses and drove like the wind to the first farm in Selemdal forest. There the horses stopped dead because they could not run any further. Then the black shadow got off and thanked the boy for the ride. It was only a simple-minded girl who habitually wore many layers of rags and other clothes. She often wandered about the roads catching free rides with anyone going to or from the village.

Well, you can say what you want to, you can't convince me that these mountain trolls don't exist, said Per. I'll tell you a story which I know to be true because honest people have repeated it to me. In Valdris there was once a family who had some of these mountain trolls for neighbors. It happened often that the troll women came to the Valdris woman to borrow this and that which the underground people had use for, and the Valdris family was always in good standing with the trolls and no harm came to them, you understand. These unseen hill trolls helped the family and they enjoyed greater riches year after year.

Later, these Valdris people thought they could do even better for themselves in America, and came over here to settle in a Norwegian community near Manitowoc. When they had lived here a number of years it happened one day that a strange woman came to the door of this particular Valdris family and asked the woman if she might borrow a spinning wheel.

"But where are you from? asked the Valdris woman.

"Oh, that I can tell you. I live over there in the next hill. Don't you recognize me?" said the troll woman, for it was she.

"No," said the Valdris woman.

"We knew each other in Norway quite well, for there we were neighbors and now I am here in America." said the troll woman.

"Yes, it does seem like I've seen you before, but I can't quite recall your name. When did you come?"

"We came to America this spring. We had to leave because when they began to build a new road, there was so much commotion and blasting that the mountain shook. We could not live there any longer, but if you will loan me your spinning wheel, you would be very kind," said the troll woman.

The troll woman took the spinning wheel and also brought it back later. But after that day no one has seen anything of the hill people in the Norwegian settlement near Manitowoc. They are probably all dead.

I thought a troll woman and all these underground creatures could live to a couple hundred years, according to what some people say, said Ola with a wink at the others.

It makes no difference to me what you unbelievers think, said Per. I shall tell you of another incident about the underground people and it makes no difference whether you believe it or not because I know it to be a fact. In Valdris valley in Norway there lived a man called Anders Kjos. When he was about to build a barn on his farm there arose a terrible racket and the higher the building got, the worse the noise got. One morning, just as it was getting light, two beautiful young girls came to Anders and said "You're building a barn but it's in the wrong place, for it stands directly over our house and we have no peace when we eat. If you will build it a few rods farther west, I think they said, you will trouble us no longer, and we will stop troubling you."

The barn was moved and since that day no one has seen any underground people at the Kjos place.

16

Gamroth the Strong

Harriet Pawlowska

Legends celebrating great strength are common in rural and industrial settings and, not surprisingly, they flourish in Wisconsin. Indeed farm and factory hands, particularly when they are members of new immigrant groups at the bottom of the economic ladder, are often stereotyped by outsiders as being "all brawn and no brain," or "strong but stupid," or "having a size 52 shirt and a size 2 hat." But insiders typically regard them as gentle, playful, helpful fellows possessing awesome power.

In the summer of 1975, Jerry Booth of Bruce told me of Sylvester "Syl" Urmanski, part of a contingent of Polish immigrant farmers in western Rusk County, who could easily heft laden oil barrels. Once his grain wagon broke down on a railroad crossing. With a train coming and the horses unable to pull the wagon free, Urmanski put his shoulder to the load and averted disaster. In 1979, while doing fieldwork with traditional musicians in the Ashland area, I met a stout Norwegian guitarist and hymnsinger, George Dybedal, who was reputed to have rigged a special harness that fit around his shoulders and a pony's belly. Standing on his barn's second level, just over the horse stall, he did deep kneebends and hefted the beast from the floor. In 1984, when I taught my Folklore of Wisconsin class for the first time at the University of Wisconsin–Madison, a Milwaukee student told me about "Crusher" Lisowski, a gravel-voiced professional wrestler whom I had admired during my own grappling career. Apparently the Crusher's favorite training method was to get a keg of beer from a neighborhood tavern, toss it on his back, jog to the shores of Lake Michigan, drink the keg, then weave back with the empty.

In the early decades of this century, while growing up in Oconto County, Mary Agnes Starr heard a whole cycle of strongman tales from Claude Nicholas, a former lumberjack. They concerned a French Canadian farmer-logger Louis Cyr: "According to Claude Nicholas and many other lumberjacks and old lumbermen, the name of Paul Bunyan as a Badger state woods hero was unknown in Wisconsin lumber camps prior to the turn of the century. . . . Many an old French-Canadian-American lumberjack who could not recall a single Paul Bunyan tale could go on at length about Louis (Looie) Cyr. They invariably ended with the phrase, 'He didn't know his own strength'" (Mary Agnes Starr, *Pea Soup and Johnny Cake* [Madison: Red Mountain Publishing, 1981], 35).

Albert Gamroth, the Silesian strongman, was similarly acclaimed among fellow Trempealeau County immigrants. The stories of Gamroth were recorded by Harriet Pawlowska. Hailing from Detroit's Polonia, Pawlowska was a student of folklorist Emelyn Gardner at Wayne State University when, from 1939 to 1941, she undertook fieldwork in Hamtrammack that resulted in the finest extant collection of Polish American folksongs, *Merrily We Sing: 105 Polish Folksongs* (Detroit: Wayne State University Press, 1961). From 1946 to 1947, Pawlowska worked on a survey of Polish culture in Trempealeau County under the direction of Edmund Zawacki of the University of Wisconsin's Department of Slavic Languages. Photographs and scores of ethnographic questionnaires from the unpublished survey form part of the archival collections of the State Historical

16.1. Mrs. Thomas Walek at her Friday morning baking with an outdoor oven, or *wielok*, holding fifteen to sixteen two-pound loaves of rye bread ordered by her Polish American neighbors, Independence, 1947. State Historical Society of Wisconsin, Zawacki Collection, (WHi) X3 34457.

Society of Wisconsin, as do copies of sound recordings made for the Archive of American Folk Song at the Library of Congress: AFS recordings 8575–8637, 59 discs containing the speech, traditions, legends, and folksongs of Polish residents of the Town of Independence.
Reprinted from *Badger Folklore* 2:3 (1950): 7–9.

Somewhere along in the early 1850s, a young Silesian serving in the German army heard about the wonders of America. Some of his comrades had received letters from relatives in the new land which told of its unlimited opportunities, and the talk which followed these letters fired the imagination of Albert Bautch, the young Silesian. After he returned to Popielowo, his native village near the Oder River, even the responsibilities of married life could not drive away his restlessness. In 1855, he organized a small group of emigres who were willing to stake their future in America with him as their leader. In this group were his brother-in-law, Jacob Sura, with his wife and children, two fellow villagers and their families, and, of course, his wife and their two children.

A sailing vessel took them across the Atlantic and down the St. Lawrence River. Albert Bautch's descendants could not tell me at which point this band of voyagers boarded a train, which eventually took them to Chicago, but they know of the near tragedy which met the Silesians in that city. It was there that Bautch discovered the loss of a small trunk and with it the address of a Chicago cousin who was to help him get a start in the new land. For the next seven years, Bautch and his group worked their way from Chicago to Milwaukee, then down to New Lisbon in Juneau County, and finally up to Trempealeau County where the group took homesteads near the present site of Independence.

Trempealeau County pleased the Bautches and the Suras, and they wrote glowing accounts of their successes in America to their relatives and friends back in Popielowo, urging them to join the homesteaders. You must believe me when I tell you that our own Missourians have nothing on the Silesians when it comes to demanding proof. After ten years of urging and coaxing, a group of four or five young men, chosen by the villagers for their alertness and wisdom, left Popielowo for Trempealeau County to investigate the merits of the new land. They sent a report of their findings back to the Old Country, and in the next thirty years nearly half of Popielowo and the neighboring village of Siełkowice settled in the area between Arcadia and Independence.

It was in the first wave of this immigration that Albert Gamroth and his brother came to Trempeauleau County. Both Gamroths were men known for their prodigious strength, but it was Albert who left in his wake a series of strongman tales of legendary proportions. He had already established a reputation for his amazing physical strength before coming to America. In the words of one of my informants, it was said of him that "when he served in the German army, he once leaped upon a horse and broke its back with the impact of the weight of his huge form." When working his land in Upper Silesia, he often used his teeth to lift a large bag of grain, and carried it thus for some distance.

In America, his tremendous strength often proved to be a useful gadget to the founders of the new community. "They say, although I never saw it," confessed another of my informants, "that Albert Gamroth carried a granary, $12' \times 16'$, across the road at New City, with the help of another man, probably one of the Bautches." Today, New City is but a fork in the road a mile out of Independence. Its mill is torn down, its tavern and its store were moved to Independence shortly after the latter town was incorporated in 1875. What remains at the crossroads is the farm of Albert Bautch, the leader of the trek from Poielowo, and the founder of the Polish community of Independence. The farm is now operated by the fourth generation of Bautches. But to get back to Gamroth: "They say, although I never saw this, that Gamroth could carry fifteen or sixteen grain sacks tied to his back, from the threshing machine to the granary."

As his reputation spread, there were those who liked to challenge Gamroth. One day he was asked if he could throw some grain onto a threshing machine with his customary ease. "*Cofnijcie sie, chłopcy. Jo wom pokoze*" (Move over boys, I'll show you how it's done, he said). He picked up the ptichfork and lightly flipped an oversize heap of grain *over* the machine. He did this two or three times, looked at his challengers, and walked away.

One day a fellow driving a wagon loaded with bricks became mired badly. Gamroth came up to him, heaved the rear end of the wagon with one shoulder and started the wagon on its way.

A fourteen-year-old lad who listened while his father told me this incident looked at the father scornfully and said, "Ah, that isn't true."

"I didn't see it," explained the father, "but that's what they say."

"It's possible," said the wife, "because he was a mighty fellow, but he never used his strength to hurt anyone. He was slow of movement, and slow of speech, but kind. His bywords were *'Cofnijcie sie, chłopcy'* (Move over, boys) or *'Co chcecie, chłopcy? Jo wom pokoze'* (What do you want, boys? I'll show you how it's done)."

He liked to lift an ox by its tail and swing it around and around. A powerful plaything for a powerful man. During the Christmas season, it was customary to celebrate *Niedzwicdzia* or the Festival of the Bear. A man, dressed in a fur coat and covered with as many trimmings as could be found to further the illusion of the bear, was led through the streets by a group of merrymakers who danced and cavorted about to the music of a group of strolling players. On one such occasion, Gamroth led an ox around instead of the customary bear. When the party came to the door of the tavern, to further the hilarity, he lifted the ox in his arms, and to the amazement of his companions, carried it over the threshold into the tavern where the fun continued.

One day three or four men, who were trying to stand a telephone pole in its assigned place, met with considerable difficulty. Gamroth came by and drawled out in his customary manner, "*A cos to chłopcy chcecie zrobic?* (Well, what do you boys aim to do?) *Cofnijcie sie* (Move over)." He continued to the men, who did not understand his language. Then he picked up the pole and put it in its place without any difficulty.

In America, his feats of wonder included not only lifting, moving, or carrying objects of tremendous size or weight, but also the handling or brushing aside his fellow men as if he were a character of *Jacob's Fairy Tales*. Two men were fighting one day when Gamroth came upon them. He pushed one of them "lightly," when the poor devil fell, insensible, to the ground. "*Jo ino qo loko puknoł a on pod na ziemie,*" he explained, confused. (I only gave him a light poke, and he fell to the ground.) His own strength did not impress him; sometimes it confused him. People say that he was careful about "poking" men after that.

17

George Russell: The Repertoire and Personality of a North Country Storyteller

James P. Leary

As a folklorist who, since the 1970s, has sought regionally distinctive storytellers throughout Wisconsin, I have often been told "You should have heard old so and so, he could tell stories all night." Traditional storytelling is hardly a lost art in contemporary Wisconsin, but stories—even if they are the same stories—do change with time as their tellers update them to fit changing circumstances. In 1980, I wrote: "both George Russell's early life and his repertoire of sayings and stories are integral with the final phase of European immigration, pioneer homesteading, and lumbercamp labor in northern Wisconsin." Old stories by old tellers like Russell offer glimpses of worlds we have lost. I was lucky and privileged to interview him before he died.

A second-generation Irish American whose parents came to Wisconsin by way of Ontario, George Russell was characteristic of those Celts who introduced aspects of the Old World *ceilidh* or house party into the lumber camps and agrarian settlements of northern Wisconsin. Emphasizing some sort of performance by all comers—a joke, a riddle, a song, a tune, a dance, a trick—this form of local wintertime entertainment was particularly strong when Irish commingled with French Canadians who used the word *veillee* for the same basic tradition. In Russell's home community of Dobie, where French and Irish dominated, jokes flew, as did jigs and tunes—thanks to the fiddling of Irishman "Red" Donnelly and Frenchman "Bat" DeMars.

Reprinted, with slight alterations, from *Folklore on Two Continents: Essays in Honor of Linda Degh,* ed. Carl Lindahl and Nikolai Burlakoff (Bloomington, Ind.: Trickster Press, 1980), 354–62.

George Russell entered the world on October 10, 1886, in Dobie, Wisconsin, a pioneer farming community in Barron County's Oak Grove township, five miles northeast of Rice Lake. His father had come there in 1868, paddling up the Red Cedar River from Menomonie to stake a claim, clear the land, and build a hewn log house. Born in Ireland amidst famine, Patrick Russell had traveled with his parents from the old country to Perth, Ontario, at the age of two. Wisconsin's burgeoning post–Civil War timber industry drew the young Irish Canadian southwest to the Chippewa Valley, and a fiancée left behind inspired him to invest his wages in property. Catherine Russell bore eleven children, the family prospered, and the "Russell Place" became a well-established farm.

George grew up helping his mother with household tasks, then moving outdoors to tend crops and livestock with his father and brothers. He attended a one-room school with French Canadian and Bohemian neighbors, and later continued his education at a Minneapolis agricultural college. After a stint in the army during World

War I (he saw no overseas action), George found work with the Canadian-North-western Railroad. The company owned great expanses of virgin woodland and George scaled timber cut by loggers around Rainy Lake on the Minnesota-Ontario border. Footloose, young, with money in his pocket, George wore smart clothes, sprouted a moustache, picnicked with "nice girls," and visited others in "sportin' houses." But in the early 1920s, as logging played out, he ceased his wanderings and returned to Dobie.

Patrick Russell had died, so George commenced farming with his brother Charlie. The Russells raised—"for show, wool, stock, or mutton"—some of the finest sheep in the Upper Midwest. The care of livestock and cropland occupied the remainder of George's working life. In the early 1950s, even after retiring to a small farm east of Rice Lake, he kept sheep, cattle, and chickens, and leased acreage for hay, corn, and oats. In his last years, George spent considerable hours touring the rural countryside and conversing with area farmers: Jerry Booth, his former hired man; Tony Tomesh, who had purchased the original Russell place; men at feed mills and livestock sales. In the fall of 1976 he died.

Curiously, for a man with ten siblings, George had no surviving kin to mourn him. Some of Patrick and Catherine Russell's children died young or saw their own offspring perish; the rest were spinsters, nuns, widowers, or bachelors. For several reasons—a sweetheart's untimely death, an independent streak, the longevity of his mother, and the presence of housekeeping sisters—George never married. George realized that he was the end of the line, and thus made it his final living accomplishment to see that he would be buried along with all the other Russells beneath handsome granite headstones in the family plot at Our Lady of Lourdes Catholic church in Dobie. A tangible, but nonetheless real, memorial to the man lies in the legacy of stories he left behind for old friends to recall, even retell.

As a child in the mid-1950s and early 1960s, I lived an easy walk through the woods from the farmhouse shared by George, Charlie, and their sisters Ann and Sadie. I would often go there after school for cookies and the cool water George took pride in, pumped from the well and cooled in the refrigerator in a cedar pitcher. Other times I encountered George in Rice Lake, his round face aglow, coming out of the American Legion Club or Wolf's Bar. He would always give me some pocket change for "a little treat." In collegiate years, during occasional vacation afternoons with the old man, I learned why my dad affectionately termed George "an old raconteur who likes to paint his nose." Aided by his favorite drink, brandy and Seven-up, we would scan family photographs, drive through familiar territory, visit his friends, or haunt taverns. All the while I would ask questions and George would answer with a constant stream of anecdotes, jokes, and witty observations.

During a pair of too brief visits (24 June and 8 July 1975), I managed to tape thirty-six "items" of verbal art, together with reminiscences on pioneer crafts, customs, and the community of Dobie. Despite my failure to document more than a fragment of George's repertoire, what I did record is valuable for several reasons. The texts he performed for me had been stable items in his repertoire for more than fifty years; that is, each was acquired prior to 1925, in Russell's youth and, espe-

17.1. George Russell in his days as a timber scaler, ca. 1918. Courtesy Jerry Booth.

17.2. George Russell on the Russell family's Lake Montanis
farm, Rice Lake, 1960s. Courtesy Jerry Booth.

cially, during that period of his life when he was a young farmer, a student, a soldier, and a lumberjack—a roving "man of the world" whose occupational endeavours spanned the range of his generation. "Fifty years ago," George reckoned, "I could tell you a lot more stories. I've heard stories traveling on trains. And I heard lumberjack stories, and all sorts of 'em." Indeed both George Russell's early life and his repertoire of sayings and stories are integral with the final phase of European immigration, pioneer homesteading, and lumber camp labor in northern Wisconsin.

The thirty-six traditional performances I recorded from him divide into five overlapping yet distinct categories: there are seven toasts and routines appropriate to male-dominated taverns, six "Irishman" jokes (mostly concerning "Pat and Mike"), eight Scandinavian "dialect stories," five humorous tales about farmers and lumberjacks, ten "true" anecdotes of local characters (which, like their fictional counterparts, concern farmers, ethnics, and woods workers). Russell's preferences correlate well with those of other regional raconteurs in northern Wisconsin, the forests of Minnesota, and Michigan's Upper Peninsula; they too spun yarns of pioneer struggles, farmers, woodsmen, and ethnics (e.g. Dorson 1952; Leary 1991).

Most crucially, I had heard most of George's texts several times, unsolicited, and in a variety of contexts. The man had apparently honed his stock of stories and quips into a manageable number to be performed again and again. But George's repetition was not random; each item skillfully illustrated points, augmented conversations, or dramatized his life. George Russell's calculated use of a self-selected repertoire argues that, beyond their obvious historical and cultural significance, his sayings and narratives carried personal meanings worthy of further explanation.

Given his bachelor status and seasonal occupation, George spent idle time in the company of other males, conversing and sharing a drop. Whether in a tavern or at home, he was a thoroughly sociable man. And whenever I visited him, he always offered a drink, often coupled with "a short little toast." One echoed the speech and economic pursuits of the region's Swiss German cheesemakers: "*Gesundheit!* Eat cheese and make your ass tight." Another placed American tipplers on a world stage:

> Here's to the English that drinks his drink.
> And here's to the German that drinks his drink.
> And here's to the American that drinks up the whole damn business.

A third memorialized a Minneapolis man who murdered his wife's lover early in the twentieth century.

> Here's to Tell that sits in his cell,
> Thinking of the girl he loved so well.
> And he often wonders if they'll take his life
> For killing the man who poonced his wife.
> But still old Tell gets free at last,
> And the first thing he does is look for more ass.

A fourth offered romantic and, likely, carnal devotion.

> To the girl that I love, true and mighty.
> And I long for that night to come;
> With my pajamas next to her nighty.

Mastered to be "pulled" amid a "party of boys," these brief forms not only entertain but invite like responses; they are verbal devices for generating a kind of fellowship and camaraderie George valued. Moreover, these toasts, with their euphonious lilt and occasional philosophizing, touch upon themes—ethnic diversity, rural life, and sexuality—which dominate George Russell's repertoire.

George was highly conscious of ethnicity, both his own and that of his neighbors. Brought up by Irish Catholic parents in a partially Irish community, George always considered himself a son of the "old sod." He would read about the old country and often talked about Ireland's many "saints and scholars." He also derided the English who "treated Ireland cruelly." Witness this tale:

There was an Irishman got on a train. And there happened to be an English lord sitting across from him. The lord was kinda snobby. And he looked out the window and there was an Irish setter going by. So, he said to the Irishman, "There goes one of your relatives." The Irishman looked out and he told the lord, "Bejasus, if he isn't related to both of us."

Beyond evident national pride and scorn for the English, Russell's story presents the Irish as a disenfranchised people who must live by their wits. These sentiments come out more strongly in the following example, with its only slightly veiled references to sabre-rattling by European powers:

There was an Irishman, a Frenchman, and a German. And they wanted to see who had the biggest prick. Frenchman, he had a pretty fair sized one. But the German, he had a great big one. The Irishman had only a little thing, but he said, "Made in Ireland, where there are men, not pricks." (For a parallel version, see Legman 1968: 297.)

While championing his parentage, George was no raving chauvinist. Like other Irish, both in the old country and America, he fancied a good joke on his own people.

Stories and songs of comic Irishmen, often named Pat and Mike, were common in America from the late eighteenth century through the early decades of the twentieth century. Typically these stock characters were none-too-bright immigrants, just off the boat and wandering in search of work, as in this pair of tellings:

Pat and Mike come over to this country, and they were very green. There was a lot of tools they used in the United States they didn't know what they were for. So, they were walking out through the country and there was a father and a son sawing wood with a crosscut saw. And, uh, one'd pull it, the other'd pull it. And Mike thought the old man was trying to take it away from the kid. So, he went over and took it away from the old man and handed it to the boy.

• • •

Mike and Pat come over to this country. And Mike got rutting around. And Pat got a pretty good job where he learned quite a bit about America. And, by God, whatever kind of a deed Mike pulled, they were going to hang him. And they had their trapeze all ready to hang Mike when Pat come along to visit him. And he inquired where Mike was, and they told him: "He's up there on the scaffold." And Pat come along, and he says, "Well, Mike, what're you doing up there?" "Oh," he says, "I make a lot of money doing this. And if you want to make it, I'll exchange places with you." So Pat thought that was all right. So, when they tripped the rope, something didn't work right. So, Pat fell off the scaffold. And he says, "Some damn fool could get his neck broke doing this stunt."

Although George probably learned these classic numskull stories much as he told them, both are more widely known and venerable folktales. The former, known to other Upper Midwestern loggers, has also been attributed to the German and Pennsylvania Dutch trickster, Till Eulenspiegel (Leary 1991: 237); the latter is tale type 1332, "Lazy Numskull Takes Place of Man on Gallows," as classified by Antti Aarne and Stith Thompson in *The Types of the Folktale.*

George Russell's tendency to respect and simultaneously poke fun at his own ethnicity corresponded to his attitudes and actions toward the diverse peoples with whom he lived and worked. His neighbors were "good, they were fine, and we tried to be just the same way." As a young man, George often went to house parties amongst French Canadian families: Crotteaus, Derousseaus, Robarges, and Rouxs. Local Czechs, invariably referred to as Bohemians, picked mushrooms on the Russells' land, and there were Germans just down the road. George went to school, shared labor at threshing time, and picked bluberries with members of all these groups. He told an occasional funny story about them too. One concerned a German or "Dutchman" named Ritz.

Now this farmer Ritz, he had a place near the Mitchell School, where [county roads] V and M meet. And he used to come into town for supplies. And he'd always take a drink, sometimes too many. Next day, he'd be hung over and he wouldn't want to work. It was time for the threshing ring to work on his place. He just sat on the porch and watched. And his excuse would be [here George put on his best German accent], "Da doctor told me to eat vell, sleep vell, do notting."

Beyond Dobie neighbors, George was familiar with Norwegians scattered in agrarian communities throughout Barron County; he also worked in the woods with both Norwegians and Swedes, learning to mimic "their lingo." One of his stories, also told in a very similar version by Rice Lake lumberjack Charles Gaulke, was set at a local dance.

When the lumberjacks came to town in the spring, some of the local girls would have a little party for them. And this one lumberjack went up to a Swedish girl. She wasn't bad looking, but she was big. And shy too. So, he asked her, "Would you like to dance?" She told him, "Whan aye dance so, aye sweat so. When aye sweat so, aye stink so. So, aye don't t'ink so." (See also Legman 1968: 447.)

Like the Irish stories of Pat and Mike, this tale is more playful than deprecating. George enjoyed living amidst the north country's diverse cultures; he worked, socialized, and joked with them all.

Many of George Russell's tales reveal strong feelings concerning other aspects of his rural environment. Continuing his father's occupations as a lumberjack and farmer, George loved the land and the work that went with it. He fondly remembered helping his mother make soap, stacking shocked oats, carrying for animals; and he treasured pictures and ledger books from his days as a timber scaler. But his vision was realistic, not romantic. He also recalled the early deaths of friends, the drunkenness and despondency of a "smart, educated" Irish neighbor and others who "drank up everything they had," and lean times when lightning destroyed the family's investment in lumber (see also Leary 1975).

Through jokes and anecdotes, George leavened with humor the hardships he and his fellows endured. In the summer of 1975, with the help of George's former hired man, Jerry Booth, and his four-wheel-drive truck, we drove on overgrown paths into the Blue Hills: "hardscrabble" country not far from the rocky, stump-laden "cutover" land the Russell family had cleared. We came upon an old caved-in log house and an accompanying farm overgown with aspen and underbrush. Both George and Jerry knew more than a few immigrant would-be farmers who had abandoned the Blue Hills' poor soil and short growing season. Then George recalled the fictive pioneer settler whom a money-seeking preacher approached. As they walked the farm, the preacher remarked "This is a fine house you and the Lord have," followed by similar exclamations regarding the barn, the fields, and the orchard. At litany's end, the settler deadpanned, "Yes, but you should've seen it when the Lord had it alone" (Leary 1978; for comparative versions, see Randolph 1965: #236).

Folklorist Ernest Baughman found three versions of "Hunter mistakes louse on his eyelash for game" extending from New York state through Michigan (1966: 312). George learned his in the lumber camps and, with fellow woodsworkers, made light of filthy conditions.

One evening in the camps this jack lay down after dinner. And he dozed off. But we heard him talking like he was in the woods deer hunting. He was saying, "Where's my gun? There goes another deer, and there's another." And we looked at him. And there were lice running across his eyelids. He thought they were deer.

Another pair of stories—one fictitious, the other true—dealt with the inescapable and prolonged drudgery of farming. Like it or not, there were no total holidays on the farm; animals, especially, demanded year-round care.

There was a Norwegian couple that was always writing on those contests. But they never won anything. So he quit writing but she kept on. And she won. She met her boyfriend and said, "You know, Ole, I've won!" He said, "What did you write on?" "I wrote on Carnation Milk." "Well, what did you write, Lena?" "I wrote:
    'Carnation Milk is the best of all,
    No tits to pull, no shit to haul.' "
(For other versions, see Legman 1975: 369 and Anonymous 1955: 58.)

• • •

Elmer G. that sold out over at Rice Lake. And Anderson, that lived right along side me, he knew Elmer. He said, "You sold out Elmer?" "Oh, I got tired smelling cowshit."

But, unlike Elmer, George never got tired enough of the farm to leave it.

Several of his jokes mildly lampooned those upwardly mobile souls who, especially in the early twentieth century, left the farm seeking urban, professional lives. At the same time, through the experiences of his own sisters—teachers, domestic workers, a nun—he understood the limited opportunities and larger aspirations of rural women. In this story a lumberjack intentionally mistakes the significance of powder on a schoolgirl's face.

Well a homesteader up in northern Minnesota had a pretty good looking daughter. And he was talking to a lumberjack one day, talking about how fast his daughter was advancing in school. And she'd graduated and finished. And the lumberjack said, "Well, I thought she was the cook with all that flour on her face."

The reference to homesteaders in this and the following tale meant much to George, the son of homesteaders who followed in his parents' path.

The settlers built a school house. And the first teacher that they hired that year, there was a homesteader that just didn't think he was good enough teacher. And the other members of the board thought he was all right. And they argued with the fellow that was dissatisfied that he was all right, that it wasn't necessary to look for a new teacher. And the one that was dissatisfied said, "Well, you know, I want my boy to be lawyer." And the other one spoke up and said, "Well, when your boy be lawyer, my bull'll be giving milk."

There may be a trace of envy in these tales, but I doubt it. George had been to school in the big city, he had traveled in the army, but his heart stayed with the land. There was nothing he liked better than exchanging rural lore with neighbors, or patiently enlightening eager but ignorant listeners like myself.

Not surprisingly, George delighted in narratives displaying the country folk's cleverness at the expense of city folk. As a rural, forested area, Russell's Barron County has long been visited seasonally by tourists, fishermen, and hunters. While locals have welcomed their business, they also sometimes have resented intruders, especially those known to put on airs, knock down fences, catch more fish than their limit, and shoot livestock. And even well-liked outsiders have been fair game for pranks and tall tales. Consequently, George Russell relished a widespread story told on local hunting guide Paul Fournier, a retired French Canadian timber cruiser, noted performer of tall tale and "Frenchman" dialect stories, and proprietor of Rice Lake's Paul Bunyan Resort.

One time a fellow from Illinoise come up and Paul was his hunting guide. So in the morning Paul got out of the cabin and decided he'd go out and look over the land. He told the men to pay attention and he'd try to drive some bears back. So, Paul found a bear out in the woods and he got in its way and made it mad. It got to chasing him and he was running toward the cabin. But he fell down and the bear ran right past him and through the cabin door. Paul jumped up, slammed the door, and hollered inside: "Skin that one and I'll be back with another." (For other versions, see Baughman 1966: 403.)

As successful farmers who marketed sheep throughout the Upper Midwest, the Russells had considerable dealings with well-to-do urbanites. Invariably, they held themselves equal to and sometimes better than those they met. George relished the memory of a city girl named Foy. She was a lawyer's daughter and [George's sister] Ann worked for them. Ann took the girl home to the farm country one time. And we were out riding in the buggy. It was the late summertime and we were going through the fields. And Ann said, "Nice country, isn't it?" She said, "Yes, but you can't see over the corn."

George reckoned this "lawyer's daughter," however urbane, was nonetheless ignorant on two counts: she had little conception of what lay beyond the corn, and she did not realize how much of the country's beauty resided precisely in the cornfields surrounding her. The remark became proverbial for George and the Russells. Whenever I displayed similar naiveté, he would slap me on the back and say, "Jim, you're all right, but you can't see over the corn."

As a "man of the world" and a breeder of animals, Russell conveyed in stories not only his regional and occupational consciousness, but also his fascination with sexuality. He told me, in reference to his youth, "I paid my money in sporting houses and went about my business." Once, while working as a timber scaler, he met "an educated half-breed girl" who was waiting for a train in a hotel at South Leech Lake, Minnesota, nearby the Leech Lake Ojibwe Reservation. With unembarrassed fond exuberance, George related how they went upstairs for "a little party"—his generation's euphemism for a sexual tryst. "When she said goodbye, she threw her legs around me and drew me to her." A favorite joke recalls the era.

A schoolteacher come to Rainy Lake. And he got to where he was friendly with a girl who worked at the hotel. So they decided to get married. But they couldn't go anywhere for the honeymoon because he had to teach school and she had to work in the hotel. So they were going to sleep the night there. Now, what this school teacher didn't know was that she'd had relations with some of the men in the town. And that night they decided to take a ladder and lean it up against the window and listen. And the top one would whisper down what was happening. So, he's saying [in a whisper], "Now they're getting into bed." And she told her husband, "You're putting it where no man ever put it before." And the fellow on top whispered, "He's putting it in her asshole." (For other versions, see Hall, 1927: #230; Hoffman 1973: 259; Legman 1968: 483–484; Lockridge 1947: 176; and Randolph 1976: #78.)

Following his roving days, when George was a bachelor in a tight-knit rural community, his sexual encounters were limited to infrequent trips to "sporting houses" and occasional liaisons with "hired girls" and neighbor women. Another of George Russell's jokes chronicles a sexual advance similar to one George confessed to making with a young woman in the barn.

There was a young farmer and he had a girlfriend. And he took her out to show her his farm. And as they walked down through the field there was a cow and her little calf. And they were smelling noses. And he said, "I'd like to do that." She says, "Go ahead, it's your cow." (For other versions, see Legman 1968: 225; and Moulton 1942: 202.)

Beyond romantic forays of his own, George showed great interest in the exploits of his acquaintances. Throughout the 1950s and 1960s he employed young hired men, many of whom spent evening hours parking with girlfriends. Their accounts and George's speculations (he gauged whether or not his employees had been "fooling around" by the redness of their eyes) reminded him of wild oats sown in his own youth. No wonder that, as an old man, he continued to enjoy performing the sexual jokes about Scandinavian "newcomers," Ole and Lena, that had circulated in the Upper Midwest from the time of his youth.

In them Lena, a stock character understood to be an immigrant domestic, enjoys sex just as much as the stolid and foolish Ole (or Lars), typically a lumberjack, farmhand, or laborer. Both are confounded by American ways and their speech is marked by old country inflections.

Well, Ole was going with Lena. And Lena got in trouble. She took Ole to court for rape. And when the judge asked Lena how the condition of things were, she said [in dialect], "Vell, he took so long, so he could. And he put it up to me so far, so he could." And the judge said, "Did you holler, Lena?" "No, Ole had his mout' open, aye t'ought he vas gonna holler."

There was a couple went to the judge to get a marriage license. And since their names were Ole Olson and Lena Olson, the judge asked them if they had any blood relationship. "Yah, vunce in St. Paul and vunce in Minneapolis. Ole couldn't vait." (See also Legman 1968: 164.)

Lars and Lena was having a little party one night. And Lars said, "Do aye hurt you, Lena?" "Oh yah, you hurt me gude." (See also Legman 1968: 705.)

Even in his mid-eighties George was wary of old widow women who wanted to come round and cook meals for him. He figured he might be tempted to "take a little piece" and then they would want to marry him for his money.

Although an occasional seducer, fantasizer, and teller of bawdy stories, George Russell was far from a "dirty old man." His conceptions of women were formed by the male notions of his generation and preserved through his bachelor status. Writing about the culture of Upper Midwestern lumberjacks, folklorist Richard M. Dorson noted that they followed a scrupulous code of behavior. Lusty among "fast women," their manners were exemplary in the company of those "outside the 'profession.'" They loved their mothers, defended their sisters, were gallant and sentimental toward sweethearts (Dorson 1952: 186–96). So it was with George Russell. He never made advances or indiscreet remarks in the presence of "nice girls" or married women; he managed the farm for his mother after Patrick Russell's death, helped support several sisters, and kept treasured mementoes of his lost sweetheart. When he died, the bulk of his estate went to the convent of his late sibling, Sister Lothair. In the words of my parents, George was "an Irish gentleman."

Perhaps because of his Irishry, George enjoyed a humorous quip for its own sake, and many of his true stories were built around the witty or foolish repartee of neighbors. Many concerned some communal work situation of the sort that were recurrent in the first half of his life.

There was one Fourth of July our neighbor, Mr. Hillary Karas, was raising a new barn. And he invited some of the neighbors around to help him that day. My brother Charlie went over.

And, in the evening, Mr. Karas had a keg of beer for them. So, he had a young boy of about nine years old, called Raymond. And the boy was telling them after the bee and the beer they'd had: "We had beer on July." And he meant the Fourth, it was the Fourth of July we raised the barn on. And he said, "We had beer on July."

George also drew upon such sayings as mnemonic devices to aid him in recalling everyday incidents from his past; more subtly, these narratives emphasized the importance Russell placed on sociable talk in all phases of life.

Well, up on the Russell farm we used to cut about fifty cords of wood. And there was a man by the name of John Drost that had the machine that done the cutting. And the discussion come up, when we were cutting, about planting potatoes. What time? With the moon? And everyone had their own ideas about planting potatoes. And Mr. Drost, the sawyer, said, "Well, I'd get up in the morning and plant them."

Or, alternatively, "I'd plant them in the ground."

After performing such a story, George would often repeat the final line several times, savor it, and chuckle. This was especially true of poetic or euphonious comments.

When I was working up on Rainy Lake we stayed at a boarding house. And the food wasn't always so good. So one morning this Irishman put down his plate and spoke to the lady that kept the place. He asked her [George broadened his already noticeable Irish brogue], "Have you got any ham, ma'am?" [Laughter.] Have you got any ham, ma'am! (A variant appears in Ives 1964: 143–45.)

Another time the families belonging to Our Lady of Lourdes parish in Dobie were asked to quarry and haul a certain amount of stone from the nearby Blue Hills for the new church. The work was not easy and was only done in the cold of winter when the heavy stone could be towed across the snow on sleds.

Tom Donnelly and my brother Charlie had quarried up—what they called "quarrying it out and throwing it down." They had more than they needed for their loads. So Pat Haughian come in and he went up and loaded that loose stone on that they had quarried out and pulled down. And Tom said to Pat, "It didn't take you long." "Oh," he said, "there's luck in leisure." This was all quarried out for him. [Laughter.] There's luck in leisure!

Haughian's quick thinking was also lucky. Through it, he turned potential anger into laughter. And, in his telling, George laughed along with Tom and Charlie.

The man's appreciation of wit and humor sustained him throughout a long and sometimes difficult life. While many of his contemporaries fell prey to self pity, loneliness, drink, physical troubles, financial woe, and fear of death, George remained his irrepressible self to the end. Indeed, George Russell's repertoire bespoke a personal philosophy. Forever sociable, delighting in ethnic diversity, a proud defender of rural life, with an eye for the ladies, and a glib phrase on his lips, George always strove to experience his small world fully and to enjoy its every phase.

Not long before he died, I spent a day with him, sharing drinks and stories, visiting his old friend Jerry Booth, roaming the countryside, and devouring what he called "a good steak feed." As we drove home through the darkness, I mentioned what a fine day it had been. Eyes twinkling, he agreed and added, "It's a grand life if you don't weaken."

He never did. And it was.

Sources

Aarne, Antti, and Stith Thompson. 1961. *The Types of the Folktale.* Helsinki: Folklore Fellows.

Anonymous. 1958. *Sexorama.* New York: Derby Press.

Baughman, Ernest. 1966. *Type and Motif Index of the Folktales of England and North America.* The Hague: Mouton.

Dorson, Richard M. 1952. *Bloodstoppers and Bearwalkers.* Cambridge, Massachusetts: Harvard University Press.

Hall, J. Mortimer. 1927. *Anecdota Americana.* Boston: Humphrey Adams.

Hoffman, Frank. 1973. *An Analytical Survey of Anglo-American Traditional Erotica.* Bowling Green, Ohio: The Popular Press.

Ives, Edward D. 1964. *Larry Gorman: The Man Who Made the Songs.* Bloomington: Indiana University Press.

Leary, James P. 1975. "'The Land Won't Burn': An Esoteric American Proverb and Its Significance," *Midwestern Journal of Language and Folklore* 1:1. Pp. 27–32.

Leary, James P. 1978. "More Than Just a Story." *Badger Folklore Society Newsletter* 1:2. Pp. 4–5.

Leary, James P. 1991. *Midwestern Folk Humor.* Little Rock: August House.

Legman, Gershon. 1968. *Rationale of the Dirty Joke.* New York City: Grove Press.

Legman, Gershon. 1975. *No Laughing Matter: Rationale of the Dirty Joke, Second Series.* Wharton, New Jersey: Breaking Point Press.

Lockridge, Norman. 1947. *Waggish Tales of the Czechs.* New York City: The Candide Press.

Moulton, Powers. 1942. *2500 Jokes for All Occasions.* Philadelphia: Circle Books.

Randolph, Vance. 1965. *Hot Springs and Hell.* Hatboro, Pennsylvania: Folklore Associates.

Randolph, Vance. 1976. *Pissing in the Snow.* Urbana: University of Illinois Press.

18

Finnish Folktales

Walter Jackola

Finnish Americans settled in northern Wisconsin and the greater Lake Superior region in the late nineteenth and early twentieth centuries, establishing small farms on cutover acreage, and toiling in the woods, in the mines, and as domestics. They brought with them a rich folk culture that included woodworking and weaving, songs and dance music, and an array of stories ranging from magic tales, to supernatural legends, to jokes regarding fools and tricksters, to anecdotes of local characters. In the 1940s, folklorist Richard Dorson recorded a wealth of Finnish American narratives in towns along the Wisconsin-Michigan border in his *Bloodstoppers and Bearwalkers* (Cambridge, Mass.: Harvard University Press, 1952). Nearly half a century later, I heard dozens of jokes in the same area told in a "Finnglish" dialect about the antics of stock characters with such typical Finnish names as Eino and Toivo, Helvi and Lempi (see my *Midwestern Folk Humor* [Little Rock: August House, 1991]).

The stories given here were set down by Walter Jackola in a trio of letters sent to Charles E. Brown of the State Historical Society of Wisconsin: the first three in August 1933; the next five in June 1935; and the final pair in March 1941. A Finnish American, Jackola was one of many correspondents cultivated by Brown regarding folklore in their respective locales. Besides the manuscripts reproduced here, Walter Jackola also enlighted Brown regarding "Some Wisconsin Finnish and Finn-Swede Superstitions" and "Superstitions Related to Firearms." The former collection hints at a larger complex of supernatural legends—also reported by Dorson from the Upper Peninsula of Michigan—regarding spirits, devils, and sorcerers, or *noitas:*

> An old farmer said that when he moved onto his farm the place was in the hands of very powerful evil spirits. These gave him no rest until he put a pint of whiskey under the floor of his house as a peace offering.
>
> Some people "sold themselves" to the Devil who claimed them just before death. When such men were being transported to the graveyard, their bodies were often too heavy for the horses to draw. Wise men were sure that the Devil and his confederates were tugging at the body and thus retarding the progress of the hearse.
>
> In cemeteries there are a strange people known as "church people." They are usually dressed in white. They were sometimes big, strong spirits but often they were "wizards," little dried-up men. They would pursue certain unfortunate individuals. Not everyone could see them. Sometimes they would be seen away from their natural haunts by certain privileged persons who claimed to have talked with them. These latter were sorcerers—either men or women.

Walter Jackola heard these and other stories told by neighbors in the Finnish enclave of Commonwealth, located in Florence County, Wisconsin, just across the border from the mining community of Iron Mountain, Michigan.

The first story below, regarding St. Peter, is one of many Old World tales regarding the apostle's foibles. Antti Aarne and Stith Thompson's *The Types of the Folktale* (Helsinki: Suomalainen Tiedeakatemig, 1961) grouped most of these under Type 774, Jests about Christ and Peter, but Jackola's story is a version of Type 752B, The Forgotten Wind. The stories of simpletons are likewise well known, with the Finnish Hölmölä paralleling such other imaginary fool towns as the Danish Mols and the English Gotham. More particularly, they are versions of Type 1203A, The Scythe Thought to be Serpent, and Type 1225, The Man Without a Head in the Bear's Den. The first story about Old Henry Viljamaa is, although told as true, likewise an old tale, Type 1313A*, In the Open Grave. Likewise, the story about "Old Paul" contains the widespread motif of mistaking bread dough for brains, rendered most recently in urban legends involving a commercial brand of frozen dough (Jan Harold Brunvand, personal communication with the author, October 1997). The other stories about Old Henry and his fellow settlers are exemplary of the rough-and-tumble lives of immigrant farmers, loggers, and miners in northeastern Wisconsin. The Finnglish dialect is evident in the final line of "Lice Powder."

From correspondence submitted to Charles E. Brown; Brown Papers, box 7, folder 7, in the Archives of the State Historical Society of Wisconsin; Jackola's other manuscripts are also in box 7.

St. Peter as a Farmer

After much missionary work involving a great deal of traveling, St. Peter became tired. He yearned to have a farm of his own, so that he could sit at home in the evenings, and smoke his pipe. So he asked God to give him a farm; but God told him, "You would not make a good farmer, Peter." But Peter envied his friends who sat about in the evenings, telling stories and smoking their pipes.

Finally Peter persuaded God to give him a farm. Peter said, "Just give me lots of wind and sunlight."

Peter's crops grew very well. His grain was just as good as anyone else's. Then, one day, the wind began to blow and blow. It blew so hard that Peter's grain was destroyed.

Next year, Peter said to God, "Give me only plenty of sunlight and rain."

Again Peter's crops thrived marvelously. But just before harvest time came the sun came out, and it shone and shone. Soon Peter's crops shriveled up and died.

Then Peter said the next year, "Give me only rain."

Peter's crops grew well again. But it commenced to rain. It rained so hard that Peter's crops were beaten to the ground.

Now Peter said to God, "You take care of my crops as you see fit. You know what they need to grow successfully."

So Peter's crops grew better than they ever had. He harvested a better yield than any of this friends. And ever since that experience, Peter was a successful farmer, who enjoyed smoking his pipe in the evenings.

This tale comes from the old Finnish Colony in Värmland, Sweden.

Two Tales About the Simpletons

In some parts of Finland, there is a settlement called Hölmölä (which translated means, "the place where simpletons dwell"). These Simpletons are very cautious

18.1. To the west of Florence, and a generation later, Finnish American singer and storyteller Walter Johnson holds one of his record albums, *Oulun Poika Laulaa* (Oulu Boy Sings), outside his home in Oulu Township, Bayfield County, 1979. Photo: James P. Leary.

people, and every thing they do, they first think over very carefully in advance, so that no harm would be wrought by too hasty action. The following two tales are related about them, showing some of their carefully planned out projects.

How the Simpletons Harvested Their Grain

When the Simpletons harvested rye, they needed seven men to do so succesfully. One pressed down a stalk of rye, another held a chunk of wood under it, while still another Simpleton cut the stalk with an ax. Then another (the fourth) carried the stalk to the bundle-tier; the sixth Simpleton carried the bundles to a pile and seventh stacked them.

A man named Matti happened to pass by, and seeing how the Simpletons harvested, was quite amazed. Only a small piece of grainfield had been cut over, although the harvesters worked hard all day. Matti wanted to help the Simpletons, so he went at night with a sickle, and cut all of the remaining grain. Then he left his sickle on top of the last grain stack, and went away to sleep.

When the Simpletons returned the next morning, they saw how all the grain had been cut; and they saw the sickle on top of a grain-stack. They marveled greatly and began to speculate as to who had cut the grain. Finally they all decided that it was the work of some sorceror, who had changed himself into a sickle. It seemed to them that work done so quickly was harmful, and could not be done except by sorcery.

So they decided that the only thing to do was to drown the sickle, so that it could not again spoil the harvest labor of cautious people by its hasty work. But it was not good to touch the sickle, which was such a dangerous instrument; for that reason, they tied a rope to a long pole, and with the aid of a noose, succeeded in snaring the sickle and pulling it down from the grain-stack. Everyone was delighted to see how the sickle had to come along with the pole, although it caught itself on stones and stumps, and fought back as hard as it could. Finally the Simpletons succeeded in getting it to the shore of a lake, and it was lifted into a boat. Then a big stone was tied to the pole with strong ropes. When the middle of the lake was reached, the stone and pole were thrown overboard with a shout of joy. But the sickle caught on the gunwale of the boat; and the weight of the stone was so great that the boat capsized. The Simpletons barely escaped with their lives from the sorceror's last bad action.

The Simpletons' Bear Hunt

The Simpletons once went on a bear hunt. When they found a bear's den, they sat down and ate a hearty meal, then had a lengthy discussion. It was decided that the man named Pekka should go and crawl down into the den, and chase the bear out. For safety's sake a rope was tied to Pekka's leg, so that if danger threatened he had but to kick and he would be pulled out. Pekka crawled in, but as soon as he found the bear, his head was bitten off. He kicked about for a while, and gave up the ghost.

The men outside said, "Now Pekka is kicking—he must not be having a pleasant time down there!" So they hauled him out, and saw that he was headless. Then began another lengthy discussion. Someone said that after all, it was not so sure that Pekka had a head in the first place.

"Not so," said another. "I should know. I saw his whiskers moving when he was eating dinner."

Stories or Anecdotes from the Finns in Commonwealth

All of these stories were told by the individuals concerned, or by their relatives, and there is no breach in propriety in submitting them, as far as those who are directly connected with them are concerned. Several stories are told about "Old Henry" Viljamaa, an early settler who died over twenty years ago.

Resurrection

"Old Henry" was a heavy drinker. One time he was coming homeward from Florence, and being rather unsteady on his feet from the effects of the bottle, he turned into the Commonwealth Cemetery, where he thought he would pass the night until the ground would be more steady under his feet. While staggering about among the gravestones, he suddenly pitched headlong into a newly-dug grave, which was partly filled with water.

Stunned by the fall, Old Henry did not wake up until broad daylight. He looked up at the blue sky overhead and marveled how he lay there on his back in a grave. His fogged mind could not grasp it. Suddenly it occured to him that he must have died, and had been buried, and that this was Resurrection Day. The simple force of this conclusion prompted him to climb up from the grave to see just what it feels like to be resurrected from the dead. He looked about, and there were gravestones and raised mounds all around him; now he began to wonder how he alone had been resurrected. Then, glancing down at his muddy clothes, it occured to him that maybe he had been fooled, for he lacked the white robes necessary to classify him as a saint.

Old Henry's Long Rifle

Old Henry owned a long Winchester rifle which he used to carry with him wherever he went. One day a Florence policeman saw him sleeping alongside of a sidewalk, the long rifle gripped in his hands. Thinking that Old Henry would shoot someone if his rifle was left with him, the policeman picked up the rifle to carry it away; and then laid it down again with a grin. The barrel on the rifle was full of caked mud.

Shooting Deer

Old Henry liked his rifle mainly because it made so much noise. Often, when he was drunk, he would throw open the door of his cabin and shoot at imaginary deer until his gun was empty. Evidently Old Henry did not always need to open the door to see these imaginary deer, for the bullet holes can still be seen in the door, and in the log walls, even near the roof.

No wonder that fishermen made a wide circle around Old Henry's farm on their way to the river. So impressed were they by the stories of Old Henry's spectacular fireworks that none but local settlers dared visit him.

• • •

The next two stories were told by Jack Sironen and "Old Paul" Johnson, respectively, about their own experiences.

The Hayfield

Some time ago Charlie and I (Jack Sironen) went to see "Black Mike," who, as you know, is the overseer of the lands around by the mining company. Charlie and I wanted to rent some hay land from him.

Mike said, "I'll have to call up Mr. Hopkins, the superintendant." So, Mike prepared for the telephone call by first driving his wife and his children, with the dog and the cat, into the woods; then he paced the floor, evidently struggling to think up the right words to say to Mr. Hopkins, the superintendant. Then he rolled up his sleeves, walked over to the telephone, cranked the bell, lifted the receiver off the hook, and said, "Mr. Hopkins, ple-ase!"

All the time he was talking, Charlie and I were lying on the floor beneath the table, holding our breath; and Charlie was so suffocated by the time Mike finished the telephone call that I had to pound him on the back to revive him.

But we got the hayfield.

Old Paul's Story

There comes a time in every man's life when he wants to dispose of his pressing cares. Well, many of us do—by getting drunk. I remember one time when I mixed up some dough for bread and, as is my custom, hung the dough bucket on a hook near the ceiling to rise. Well, I felt a little lonesome, and so I got drunk.

I woke up lying on the floor next to the dough pail. Then I heard someone walking toward the house, so I got up to meet him. When I opened the door, I saw my son, and he looked at me so strangely that I thought he had gone crazy. He stood staring at me. "Why father," he said, "your brains are sticking out of your head!"

I reached up and felt a lump of dough stuck in my hair. Well, to this day, my son claims that the dough looked exactly like a portion of brain; and I guess, that in my case, there isn't enough difference to be worth arguing about.

Lice Powder

A Finnish lumberjack in Northern Wisconsin was bothered by lice, so he decided to buy some lice powder in town. As he knew only a few words of English, he was for a time at a loss to know how to obtain the powder. Finally, when he reached town, he thought of a way.

He found a stray envelope on the street. Into it he placed a louse which he picked from its coat. He walked into a drugstore and carefully shook the louse out of the envelope onto the counter. Pointing to the louse, he said to the clerk: "Givida this falla tinneri." [Give to this fellow a dinner.]

A Fighting Man Can Always Find Weapons

A man who had gained a reputation for being a fierce fighter because he used all manner of weapons was taken to a court in Finland, charged with assaulting another man with some weapon which the court had no knowledge of.

"Where do you always manage to find your weapons?" the judge asked the fighter.

"A fighting man can always find weapons," said the fighter, quoting an old proverb.

The judge smiled and said, "Let us see how you would go about finding weapons for fighting in this court room."

The fighter saw the judge's dog under the table. He grabbed the dog by the tail and hit the judge with the dog.

"Get out of here," said the judge.

19

Woods and Waters

Hunting and fishing have been part of Wisconsin life for centuries. The dwelling places and activities of native peoples revolved around the pursuit of fish and game, and many Indian people continue to hunt deer and capture fish with their ancestors' dedication. European immigrants and their descendants have also found Wisconsin a proverbial land of plenty—a place where former peasants were free to hunt deer in the manner of nobles and kings.

Deer hunting dominates late autumn life in Wisconsin. During my high school years in Rice Lake, the end of football season yielded to the anticipation of deer hunting, at least among "the boys." Talk abounded. When asked "Are you gonna get your deer?," Vic Roux, who lived on a farm northeast of town bordering Swamp Road, replied, with a grin, "It's already hanging on the tree." Listeners were left to figure out whether this was a confident hunter's prediction, or a bold poacher's confession. Dave Saffert was both teased and praised: "buck fever" once kept him from raising his rifle until the deer was almost out of range and he felled it with an admitted "lucky shot." Dan Boe was ill-fated to mistake a cow for a buck: had he not been a basketball star and "city guy" unused to the woods, his manhood would have been seriously questioned.

E. E. LeMasters, a professor of social work at the University of Wisconsin–Madison, encountered a similar hotbed of woods talk in a Middleton tavern frequented by skilled construction workers from the greater Madison area. LeMasters' *Blue-Collar Aristocrats: Life-Styles at a Working-Class Tavern* is also the finest extant study of Wisconsin tavern sociability.

"The Deer and Elk Hunt," the anonymous story that follows, exaggerates and parodies the typical hunter's opening day experience, yet it also echoes more than a few real experiences that form the basis of stories. Perhaps it originated in lower Michigan, where an elk-hunting season has been in place longer than in Wisconsin.

"Hunting and Fishing" by E. E. LeMasters is reprinted from E. E. LeMasters, *Blue-Collar Aristocrats: Life-Styles at a Working-Class Tavern* (Madison: University of Wisconsin Press, 1975), 132–36. (The bracketed text herein is LeMasters'; it has been retained from the original.)

"The Deer and Elk Hunt" is reprinted from a photocopy in circulation, early 1990s.

Hunting and Fishing

E. E. LeMasters

Most of the men at The Oasis love to hunt and fish. When the deer season opens in the fall there is a mass exodus of the customers as the hunters "head north," and the tavern is almost deserted for a week or ten days until the hunters return and

19.1. Les Rondau files a duck decoy while astride a shaving horse
in his garage shop, De Pere, 1986. Photo: James P. Leary.

begin to spin their yarns as to how "I got my buck," or, in some cases, "how I missed my buck."

To me, the deer season (and the stories after) are the climax of the year at The Oasis. [Some industries in this area don't attempt to operate during the deer season, having learned from past years how many men seem to "get sick" that week.] Before the men leave the air is full of stories about guns—new guns, old guns, and "gun swaps."

"I've had that old sonofabitch since 1932 and she shoots as true today as she ever did. I wouldn't sell that bastard for a hundred dollars."

"This guy down at the shop sold me this Remington for forty bucks—said he couldn't hit anything with it. I took it out to the Gun Club and bore sighted it and she shoots perfect. The dumb bastard never had the sight aligned properly!"

"My father used this gun and never missed a buck and by God so far I haven't missed one with it either."

To portray the year-long cycle of the men at The Oasis we propose to follow one man through a typical year. This man may hunt and fish more than the average man at the tavern but he is quite representative of the general attitude that prevails toward hunting and fishing at The Oasis.

Bill is a policeman in the nearby metropolitan community. His occupation influences his hunting in two ways: (1) he is expected to be skilled in the use of firearms, and (2) he can accumulate "time off" and get away from the job whenever the various seasons open.

In the spring Bill waits for the opening of the trout season. He has several favorite spots not over an hour's drive from the tavern, and he fishes these streams methodically. If he catches too many trout for immediate consumption they either go into the family freezer or are given to friends and neighbors.

During the summer Bill fishes several lakes in the area, one of them less than a mile from his house. From these lakes he usually takes "pan fish": perch, blue gills, etc.

But fall is the time of year that Bill loves: rabbits and squirrels, the pheasant season, and then the exciting influx of Canadian geese, the hunter's dream. [Several hundred thousand Canadian geese stop each fall at a huge marsh about an hour's drive from the tavern. Special permits are sold to hunt Canadian geese, and the entire hunt is rigidly supervised by both state and federal officials.] In the fall Bill lives in a sort of fantasy world. You might hear him say something like this: "Took a drive up toward Spring Green yesterday—saw a beautiful male pheasant strutting near the road. When the season opens next week I'm gonna go back up there and we'll see what happens."

You can be sure he has carefully marked the spot and will be back there on opening day.

"Did you get your Canadian geese tag?" I asked him one day.

"You're darned right—I had my check in the mail the first day they were for sale. I wouldn't miss that for anything."

One day he showed us a Canadian goose he had shot. It was, indeed, a beautiful bird. We asked Bill if he had any reluctance or guilt about shooting the goose. "No, I don't," he replied. "The hunting up there is carefully supervised—there are game wardens all over the place. I wouldn't want any part of it if the birds were being massacred or slaughtered, but this is not the case."

Deer season is for Bill the climax of the year, as it is for most of the men at The Oasis. [A family crisis was precipitated at the tavern when a girl scheduled her wedding during the opening week of deer season. At first the father announced that he would not attend the wedding; later on he relented and was present to give the bride away.] He takes a week off for the deer season and has not failed to bag a buck for several years. He always hunts at the same place, with the same group of men.

The annual pilgrimage "up north" never varies. Bill and his hunting companions leave their homes the day before the season opens and arrive at a farm house belonging to a relative of one of the hunters that night. They have a few beers, eat a good meal, and then hold their annual "reunion," reliving the hunts of previous years. [Some deer hunters live in various parts of the state and only see each other at the annual hunt.]

Everybody is up early for the opening of the deer season at daybreak. One year Bill got his buck fifteen minutes after the season opened.

"Well," he told me, "it was the damndest thing you ever heard of. Two years ago I saw a buck at this same spot but he took off before I could get a shot at him.

"So this year I said to myself—do you suppose by any chance that sucker might come back there again?

"Anyhow I found that spot again and had just decided to open my thermos bottle and have a cup of coffee when I looked up and there was this big buck staring right at me, not over fifteen yards away.

"I took one quick look through the sight and hit him right between the eyes—he fell over and hardly took one step. It was the damndest thing that's ever happened to me in all the years I've been hunting."

In a hunting party anybody who gets their buck early in the week spends the rest of the week helping his buddies to get their buck. [In some areas of the state in some years does may also be shot, but the men do not talk about shooting a doe. Only a buck is exciting to hunt.]

On opening day 200,000 or more deer hunters will be in the state forests, and fatal shooting accidents are not rare. [There is another variety of hunting during the deer season: this is called "dear" hunting: Men who don't go north for the deer season but use the week for some extramarital prowling. Some of these men say it beats deer hunting any day.] The men at The Oasis appreciate the chance they take but they feel the excitement of the hunt is worth it. "Christ sake," one man said, "everything worth doing in this world is dangerous—friend of mine fell off a bar stool and broke his back, but that's not going to stop me from having a drink when I feel like it."

At this point another man said: "Why don't they have seat belts on bar stools like they do in cars? Then your friend wouldn't have been hurt."

After deer season, six to eight weeks of wonderful story-telling may be heard at

The Oasis: who got their buck, who didn't, and all the details of how it happened. Sometimes a hunter ran into a bear, or perhaps even shot one, and these stories are always exciting. "I looked up and there was this big black bear looking down at me from the top of this rock. I was debating whether to shoot or get the hell out of there when somebody else shot and the bear took off. We never saw it again."

There are long conversations as to how deer meat should be cooked, whether bear meat is good to eat or not, and who makes the best venison sausage in the area.

When Bill gets home from the hunt he takes his deer to a small butcher shop in a nearby village and has most of the deer meat made into "summer sausage." He once gave me a piece of this, and it was delicious.

Bill carefully preserves the antlers from his bucks and prepares them for mounting: the antlers are sandpapered, varnished, and mounted on attractive wooden plaques. Sometimes he has a metal plate prepared with the year of the hunt engraved on it. These plaques are displayed in various rooms of his home.

With the coming of winter Bill's hunting comes to an end for the year, but he does some ice fishing on the nearby lake "when the mood strikes me."

Bill's wife understands his love for the outdoors and would not think of interfering with his hunting and fishing excursions. She regards him as a good husband and realizes that men can have hobbies that are worse than hunting and fishing.

Some people who don't approve of hunting and fishing regard men like Bill as "ruthless killers" or "despoilers of nature." He does not have this image of himself and does not impress one as cruel and inhuman—in fact, he makes just the opposite impression.

Actually, Bill is a conservationist at heart; he believes in strict regulation of hunting and fishing and abides by the rules established. He sincerely wants to preserve the natural environment for future generations to enjoy as he has enjoyed it.

In defense of deer hunting, Bill points out that under modern game management practices the deer herd in Wisconsin was larger in 1965 than it was in 1920. He sees no reason why fish and other wildlife cannot be protected and preserved by the same methods.

It is a serious mistake to think that Bill merely likes to hunt and fish—he *loves* hunting and fishing. He is an outdoorsman who earns his living in a police patrol car but has never learned to like city life. He is the farm boy who still loves the land. There must be millions like him in America.

The Deer and Elk Hunt

Anonymous

1:00 A.M.—Alarm clock rings.
2:00 A.M.—Hunting partners arrive, drag you out of bed.
2:30 A.M.—Throw everything except the kitchen sink into the pickup.
3:00 A.M.—Leave for the deep woods.

3:15 A.M.—Drive back home and pick up the gun.

3:30 A.M.—Drive like hell to get to the woods before daylight.

4:00 A.M.—Set up camp—forgot the damn tent.

4:30 A.M.—Head into the woods.

6:05 A.M.—See eight deer and elk.

6:06 A.M.—Take aim and squeeze trigger.

6:07 A.M.—CLICK.

6:08 A.M.—Load gun while watching deer and elk go over hill.

8:00 A.M.—Head back to camp.

9:00 A.M.—Still looking for camp.

10:00 A.M.—Realize you don't know where camp is.

    Noon—Fire gun for help. Eat wild berries.

12:15 P.M.—Run out of bullets. Deer and elk come back.

12:20 P.M.—Strange feeling in stomach.

12:30 P.M.—Realize you ate poison berries.

12:45 P.M.—RESCUED!

12:55 P.M.—Rushed to hospital to have stomach pumped.

3:00 P.M.—Arrive back at camp.

3:30 P.M.—Leave camp to kill deer and elk.

4:00 P.M.—Return to camp for bullets, see partner's elk.

4:05 P.M.—Load gun, leave camp again.

5:00 P.M.—Empty gun on squirrel that's bugging you.

6:00 P.M.—Arrive at camp, see deer and elk grazing at camp.

6:01 P.M.—Load gun.

6:02 P.M.—Fire gun.

6:03 P.M.—One dead pickup truck.

6:05 P.M.—Hunting partner returns to camp dragging deer.

6:06 P.M.—Repress strong desire to shoot hunting partner.

6:07 P.M.—Fall into fire.

6:10 P.M.—Change clothes, throw burned ones into fire.

6:15 P.M.—Take pickup, leave partner and his deer and elk in the woods.

6:25 P.M.—Pickup boils over, hole shot in the block.

6:26 P.M.—Start walking.

6:30 P.M.—Stumble and fall, drop gun in mud.

6:35 P.M.—Meet bear.

6:36 P.M.—Take aim.

6:37 P.M.—Fire gun, blow up barrel plugged with mud.

6:38 P.M.—Mess pants.

6:39 P.M.—Climb tree.

9:00 P.M.—Bear departs, wrap gun around tree.

midnight—HOME AT LAST!

    Sunday—Watch football game on TV, slowly tearing up license into little pieces, place in envelope, and mail to game warden, with very clear instructions what he should do with it.

PART THREE

Music, Song, and Dance

20

Menomini Indian Dance Songs in a Changing Culture

Gertrude P. Kurath

The Menominee, or "wild rice people," occupy a small portion of what has always been their northeastern Wisconsin homeland. Yet they harvest timber nowadays to a far greater extent than wild rice, and many other aspects of their culture have changed since the beginnings of European contact.

From the 1920s through the early 1960s Menominee musicians, for example, were as likely to play fiddles, marching band instruments, and guitars as they were the old courting flutes and various drums. The late 1960s and the 1970s, however, saw a revitalization of Menominee traditional music that coincided with the reinstatement of their reservation status. Youngsters like Louis Webster, Myron Pyawasit, and John Teller began seeking out such elders as Nepenanakwat (Summer Cloud) Johnson Awonohopay to learn old songs; and they in turn have attracted musical apprentices. Performing on the powwow circuit, where young enthusiasts can record their performances with hand-held boomboxes, they have also produced cassettes. Among these are Louis Webster, *Woodland Rhapsody* (Sphere C-002); the Smokeytown Singers (led by Myron Pyawasit), *Land of the Menominee* (Sunshine SSCT 4221); and the Summer Cloud Singers (led by John Teller), *Pow Wow Songs of the Menominee* (Woodland Recording WR 1/31/93). These sonic glimpses from the late 1980s and early 1990s reveal an eclectic blend of old Menominee songs, new songs on familiar themes composed in the Menominee language, borrowings from the pan-Indian powwow circuit, traces of fiddle tunes and Christian hymnody, and even a hint of New Age music.

In the mid-1950s, Gertrude Prokosh Kurath documented a similar Menominee amalgam of old traditional dances, ones derived from pan-Indian religious and cultural movements of the late nineteenth and early twentieth centuries, dances stylized for public exhibition to tourists, and dances stemming from that era's powwow innovations. Kurath (1903–1992) earned a B.A. and an M.A. from Bryn Mawr College in the history of art and architecture, but she went on to become her generation's leading scholar of traditional dance in North America, producing important works on African American, southwestern Hispanic, and American Indian dances. Best known for her collaborations with anthropologist William Fenton on the study of Iroquois dance, Kurath also did fieldwork among the Upper Midwest's Menominee, Mesquakie (Fox), Ojibwe, and Ottawa peoples (see Judith Lynne Hanna, "Gertrude Prokosh Kurath," in *American Folklore: An Encyclopedia*, ed. Jan H. Brunvand [New York: Garland, 1996], 429–30).

Reprinted from *Midwest Folklore* 9:1 (1959): 31–38.

The Menomini Indians of northern Wisconsin have remained relatively sedentary in the midst of their roving, shifting neighbors. Their name, "wild rice people," suggests long residence in the country of wild rice. Their culture may thus most closely represent the prototype of Lake Michigan Algonquian culture. Yet in the course of history the Menomini have also shared in the tribulations of their linguistic relatives of Algonquian stock, the neighboring Ojibwe and Potawatomi, the now removed Fox [i.e., Mesquakie]; also to a large extent they were joined in these fates by the Siouan Winnebago [i.e., Ho-Chunk]. The recent changes in their music and dance have been similarly impelled by economic changes and new religious cults since the coming of the White priest, trader and settler.

Yet the Menomini present their special problems and style, compact problems because of the limited geographical expansion, and a simple, fairly consistent style. The musical repertoires can be traced back half a century. The ceremonies and culture can be traced back three centuries. Hence these repertoires and their placement in the cultural setting invite comparative study and temporal retracing in a changing world.

The artistic retracing starts with a series of tape recordings: my own small collection from 1956, George Spindler's from 1952, James Sidney Slotkin's from 1950, all available for study. These were preceded by Frances Densmore's monograph of 1932, based on her recordings of 1928, and by her Library of Congress disk with some of these songs (Densmore 1932 and 1953). For intertribal comparisons there are Ojibwa recordings from Lac du Flambeau, Wisconsin, recent ones by myself and fifty-year old ones by Densmore (1913); there are Fox records from Tama, Iowa, by Martha Huot and myself. For the dance there are scattered printed comments and my observations and motion pictures.

My summary must bypass various important cults such as peyotism, in order to highlight dance activities and associated songs of the conservative Menomini. In the western forests of Shawano reservation the conservatives cling to vestiges of the old ways and keep aloof from the more prosperous Christian elite of Neopit and Keshena villages (Spindler and Goldschmidt 1952).

Religious Songs and Dances

The once important Mitawin society now counts few adherants. The most prominent cults are the Dream or Drum Religion and the Brave or War Dance. The Dream Religion, which is well known in literature, reached the Menomini in 1880 via the Potawatomi (Densmore 1932: 150–83; Keesing 1939: 151, 215–17). It sprang up among the Dakota as a revival in catastrophic times. It had its roots in the Grass Dance, thus ultimately in the Omaha Hethuska. The Brave Dance is probably a revamping of the old Menomini warriors' ceremony, now in the guise of a healing rite (Ritzenthaler 1953). It is prominent throughout Wisconsin and as far west as the Fox of Iowa.

Both are long ceremonies, with series of many songs, some old, some new, some Menomini, some imported from the Dakota and other tribes. Despite tribal differences, all of the songs show the same structure within the present series and between these and older recordings throughout the Middle West and the Great Plains.

Each song contains three phrases, a prelude on the ninth and octave of a te-

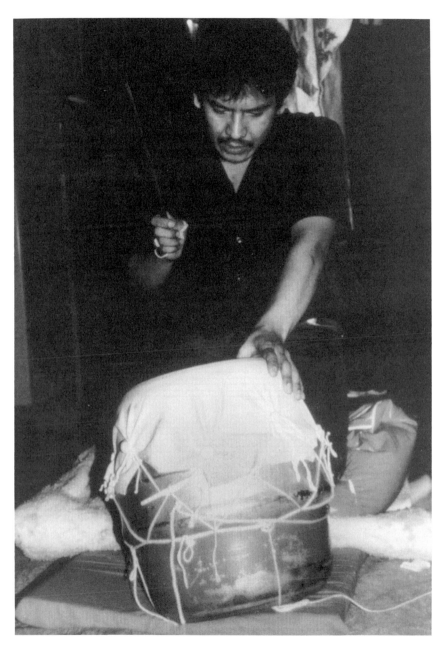

20.1. Jerry Hawpetoss sings with a water drum, fashioned from a beer keg, in the basement of his Keshena home, 1986. Photo: James P. Leary.

20.2. Menomini Songs—Sequential.

tratonic or pentatonic scale, then a central phrase descending in dwindling intervals of fourths and seconds, finally a coda focussed on the second and tonic. The prelude is stated in echo fashion, first by the leader, then by the helpers; the remainder of the song is rendered and repeated by the chorus. The entire form is repeated four times, sometimes with the addition of a "tail," the second and third phrases (Kurath 1956, Side A, Band 2).

The two ritual types are distinguished chiefly by their timing. In Dream Dance the drum beats a strongly accented duple pulse and synchronizes with the isometric melody. In the more rapid Braves Dance the drum syncopates a heterometric melody; its nervousness is intensified by vocal pulsations. [This example is transcribed from Spindler's recording of the Braves Dance.]

These rituals used to contain much dancing with Plains war dance steps by the men, and some female participation in the dancing and singing. Now the Brave

Dance concludes with dancing after a feast, but, according to Slotkin, Dream Dancing has shrunk mostly to shuffling.

Social and Show Dances

The conservative Menomini also engage in Indian social dances and present public shows weekly during the summer months. Under the direction of an acculturated Menomini, John Fossum, they dance and sing with zest all Sunday afternoon at their Peavey Falls dance ground. On Tuesday and Friday nights a contingent of Lac du Flambeau Ojibwe shows.

One category of their secular round dances resembles the ritual songs musically in the structure and pattern of echo and repeats. These rounds are the Squaw Dance, Victory Round, and Fortynine Dance. Their descending, pentatonic melodies conclude with a longer, syncopated postlude on the tonic. Their timing aids identification. Squaw Dance has about the same tempo as Dream Dance, Victory Round is more sedate, and Fortynine is more animated. In the last two the drum beat is trochaic and the melody is often in triplet pulsations and figures.

Choreographically they show more differences. In Squaw Dance the men and women circle in two separate arcs, moving in opposite directions. In Victory Round they intermingle in a closed circle and tromp clockwise to the left, reversing direction toward the end of the song. In Fortynine, couples hold hands in skating position and move clockwise with the so-called Indian two-step. Women often join in the singing.

These male and female groupings reflect the varying antiquity of derivation from the Great Plains. Squaw Dance is an older dance from the Dakota, well established when Densmore visited the Chippewa fifty years ago (1913: 284). Victory Round developed from the Scalp Dance of Oklahoma tribes, probably the Cheyenne (Kurath 1957c), and it had been adopted by the Menomini in 1928 (Densmore 1932: 194). At that time the more recent Fortynine had just arrived from Oklahoma.

Increasingly popular are male war dances with elaborate steps. As the women merely hop up and down, some girls are taking to transvestism to they can join in the fun. Such dances feature in the intertribal war dance contests (Slotkin 1955). They are newer versions of the Grass Dance type, arrived from the Dakota in a second, secular wave. They are accompanied by songs with the same structure and characteristics as Dream Dance, but with bolder intervals and rhythms.

Most of the other show dance songs belong to a different structural type. Each song is in two parts, with two distinctive drum rhythms. The first part undulates downwards between the fifth and tonic of a tritonic or tetratonic scale. The second part repeats one short phrase, focussed around the tonic. Unsually each song recurs only twice (Kurath 1957b).

The Pipe or Calumet Dance is a contest for two males. The men quiver in place during the drum tremolo and gyrate with war dance steps during the duple beat in Dream Dance tempo. The song in the example is the most popular. It has been re-

20.3. Menomini Songs—Binary.

corded also by Slotkin and Spindler among the Menomini, by myself at Lac du Flambeau, and twice at Tama, Iowa. The type has as wide a spread as Grass Dance, but the process took three centuries (Fenton and Kurath 1953: 186–87). Originally it cemented treaties and thereby radiated from the Pawnee and Omaha as far at least as the Iroquois, arriving at the Menomini around 1700.

The next example, though in somewhat slower tempo, has a similar structure and tertial scale. It is known variously as Shawonoga, Southern Dance, Southwind Dance, Shawnee Dance, Corn Dance, and is traced to a southern origin. Early in the century, during visits by Skinner (1913) and Densmore (1932: 51), it served as a healing, condolence, and adoption rite, and was assigned a fairly ripe old age. Densmore tells how the South Manido brought the rite to the Menomini and Ojibwa from the south, and how its sacred character had faded, though not as completely as today. The ritual function has remained intact among some tribes, as the Kansas Potawatomi (Howard n.d.).

Choreographically it differs from Pipe Dance, also from the dance as reported by Densmore. Pairs of men, then of women progress in a clockwise circle. During the tremelo in the first repeat and the slow drum beat in the second repeat they are stationary. During the fast part B they move ahead, the men with war dance steps and the women with a knee-flexing tread similar to the Squaw Dance step.

The Fish Dance has the same binary structure, but several distinctive features. The drum beat is always a slow beat in part A. Second, there are many song repeats. Third, the dancing does not contrast in the two parts. Part B is distinguished from A by the addition of fluttering gestures to the stomp step. Women follow men as in Shawonoga, but in single file.

The scale differs from Shawonoga, in its concentration on the fifth, second, and tonic. In Densmore's older version there was also a fourth (Densmore 1913: 191). The Lac du Flambeau Ojibwe, who learned the dance from the Menomini, substitute a third for the fourth of the scale, but they perform the same motions as the Menomini.

Other animal songs, as recorded in 1928 and 1956, have this same structure and the 54 21 scale, with one exception. Rabbit, Raccoon, Deer Dance appear in shows. They claim great antiquity, and in fact have the same scale and some of the repetitiousness of the oldest songs recorded by Densmore—legends of Manabus, funeral songs, love songs (Densmore 1913: 140–44, 210–12).

Some of these very old songs repeat their one theme in a mildly descending sequence. The Menomini Deer Dance has also been recorded in a variant at Lac du Flambeau by Densmore fifty years ago (1913: 200–201), by myself in 1952. The song has three descending phrases with one melodic interest and a monotone coda. The drum beat resembles that of Dream Dance, but the tempo is slower. The pattern of echo and repeats is lacking. The dance also has no connection with the Plains-derived categories. It is an amusing play between two buck and two doe mimes.

Trends

The oldest surviving songs and dances are connected with animal mime, in keeping with the early animistic religion (Skinner 1913: 10; Kurath 1957). The abandonment of this religion and the secularization of the dances inevitably followed the economic shift to lumbering and modern ways. Continuous waves of outside influences supplied new dances not connected with the hunt. The Calumet Dance arrived during a period of tribal turmoil and concentration near the Menomini, between 1650 and 1700 (Kellogg 1925: 70, 99). Perhaps Shawanoga travelled from more southerly Algonquians at this time and again in the nineteenth century, via the Winnebago. [Indeed] according to Spindler the newer versions of Shawanoga come from the Winnebago. Plains influences brought war and squaw dances and two waves of the Grass Dance, one of them now the predominant cult.

Such influences may have been accepted musically because of trends already present in Menomini songs. The sequential, Plains type was akin to the type represented by the Deer Dance. The binary type, with thematic repetition, was anticipated by some of the older animal dance songs, but it introduced typically southern features as the terminal call.

As to dance affinities, the steps of the newer dances differ from the Woodland trot in the animal dances, but a clockwise circuit links the Plains and Wisconsin tribes. When an exotic dance progressed against the sun, the Menomini reversed it to fit their scheme.

Such voluntary borrowings doubtless introduced songs and dances from adjacent and remote tribes from earliest times and caused no violent adjustments in thought or style. But the changes wrought by the White man caused traumatic shifts (Keesing 1939: 148–243). The hunter turned lumberjack. He introduced Christian ideas into his medicine rites and he had to change the purpose of his rites or secularize them.

Thus the old rites gave way to the Dream religion, which offered a temporary adjustment. It preached tribal solidarity, yet oriented its theology away from nature spirits and towards Christianity.

A new social attitude crept in with new Oklahoma dances. These tend toward sex orientation, in the coupling of boy and girl and in the frequent native or English texts about illicit love. One popular song (not here illustrated) goes, "You can marry sixteen times, but I'll love you just the same." They provide an outlet for a sense of humor which is built into the animal dances.

In the small parcel of primeval forest assigned to the Menomini on their reservation, the conservatives have tried valiantly to preserved their native lore, but with each generation they must yield another notch (Slotkin 1957: 9). Eventually, in the modern life, they will be unable to maintain the songs and dances for the animal spirits either in faith or fun, and will shift entirely to alien forms.

Sources

This article was based on a paper presented to the Society for Ethnomusicology at its annual meeting, December 27, 1957. Kurath's 1956 trip formed part of a field project under a grant from the Michigan Academy of Science, Arts and Letters. Dr. George Spindler's tapes were loaned by the State Historical Society of Wisconsin, Dr. James Slotkin's by personal courtesy. Slotkin's reel of the Dream Society was not on hand for study.

Densmore, Frances. 1913. *Chippewa Music*. Washington, D.C.: Bureau of American Ethnology, Bulletin No. 53.
Densmore, Frances. 1932. *Menominee Music*. Washington, D.C.: Bureau of American Ethnology, Bulletin No. 102.

Densmore, Frances. 1953. *Songs of the Menominee, Mandan, and Hidatsa*. Washington, D.C.: Library of Congress Music Division Recording Laboratory, LP recording L33.

Fenton, William, and Gertrude P. Kurath. 1953. *The Iroquois Eagle Dance*. Washington, D.C.: Bureau of American Ethnology, No. 153.

Howard, James H. n.d. Personal communication.

Keesing, Felix. 1939. *The Menomini Indians of Wisconsin*. Philadelphia: American Philosophical Society, Memoir No. 10.

Kellogg, Louise P. 1925. *The French Regime in Wisconsin and the Northwest*. Madison: State Historical Society of Wisconsin.

Kurath, Gertrude P. 1957a. *Algonquian Ceremonialism and Natural Resources in the Great Lakes* Bangalore: Indian Institute of Culture, Reprint No. 22.

Kurath, Gertrude P. 1957b. "Dance-Music Interdependence," *Ethnomusicology* 10. Pp. 8–11.

Kurath, Gertrude P. 1957c. "Pan-Indianism in Great Lakes Tribal Festivals," *Journal of American Folklore* 70:276. Pp. 179–82.

Kurath, Gertrude P. 1956. *Songs and Dances of Great Lakes Indians*. NYC: Ethnic-Folkways, LP recording 1003.

Ritzenthaler, Robert. 1953. "The Potawatomi Indians of Wisconsin," *Public Museum of the City of Milwaukee Bulletin* 19:3. Pp. 151–56.

Skinner, Alanson. 1913. *Social Life and Ceremonial Bundles of the Menomini Indians*. Anthropological Papers of the American Museum of Natural History 13:1.

Slotkin, James S. 1955. "An Intertribal Dancing Contest," *Journal of American Folklore* 68:268. Pp. 224–28.

Slotkin, James S. 1957. *The Menomini Powwow*. Milwaukee Public Museum Publications in Anthropology, No. 4.

Spindler, George, and Walter Goldschmidt. 1952. "Experimental Design in the Study of Culture Change," *Southwestern Journal of Anthropology* 8:1. Pp. 68–83.

21

The Wanigan Song Book

Isabel J. Ebert

Songs were plentiful in many northern Wisconsin lumber camps during the heyday of white pine logging that extended from the mid-nineteenth century until roughly the time of World War I. Veteran woods workers from Maine and Canada carried a tradition of altering old songs or composing new ones to convey the circumstances of their occupational lives. Some concerned death on the log drive; some chronicled the characters and incidents of a season's labor; while others celebrated skilled competitions.

Franz Rickaby, a young Harvard-trained ballad scholar, provided our finest glimpse of Wisconsin's logging songs when he traveled the northwoods around 1920 to gather lyrics, tunes, and information from singers in Cornell, Eau Claire, Gordon, Ladysmith, Rice Lake, and Wausau. In Wausau Rickaby met William N. "Billy" Allen, a timber cruiser and the composer of three lumber camp ballads that became widespread in oral tradition: "The Banks of the Little Eau Pleine," "Driving Saw Logs on the Plover," and "Shanty Boy on the Big Eau Claire." Born in New Brunswick in 1843, Allen settled in Wausau in 1868. Around that time he began not only to compose "poems," but also to sing them during his frequent visits to lumber camps. (See Rickaby, *Ballads and Songs of the Shanty-Boy* [Cambridge, Mass.: Harvard University Press, 1926].)

Although not a composer of Allen's stature, Emery DeNoyer of Rhinelander, whose story and songs appear below, was perhaps Wisconsin's finest lumber camp singer. His repertoire included not only woods ballads, but sentimental songs and comic ditties in the Irish and "coon song" veins popular in the era's music halls. DeNoyer also played the harmonica and even lugged a record player and a stock of fragile disks to complement his performances in isolated camps.

DeNoyer's chronicler, Isabel Reid Johnson Ebert (1883–1973), was born in Morrisonville and taught there and in various Wisconsin schools. In 1908, she began the first of several teaching stints in Rhinelander. With her husband, Marcus, she founded and directed Minne-Wawa Summer Camp for Girls in 1912, and she was instrumental in starting the area's Northland Historical Society. Isabel Ebert was also active in the maintenance of Rhinelander's logging museum and compiled a list of lumber camp speech, part of which found its way into L. G. Sorden's *Lumberjack Lingo* (Spring Green, Wisc.; Wisconsin House, 1969). Sorden, a longtime Oneida County agent within the University of Wisconsin's Extension system, dedicated his occupational dictionary "To Mrs. Isabel J. Ebert, Lake Tomahawk, Wisconsin. Educator and lifetime historian of northern Wisconsin and coauthor of the original publication of *Loggers' Words of Yesteryears* (1956), and for her assistance in collecting many of these words." Ebert's educator's bent is evident in comparisons she makes between the blind Emery DeNoyer and Homer, while her title, *The Wanigan Song Book,* uses "lingo" to assert the necessity of songs. A "wanigan" is: 1) a lumber camp store; 2) the payroll charges for goods purchased from the camp store; and 3) the cook's raft, which followed the river drive (Sorden 1969: 138).

Thanks to Isabel Ebert's efforts, Emery DeNoyer's Irish-derived "woods style" singing and his harmonica playing were recorded by Helene Stratman-Thomas for the Library of Congress in the

1940s. Readily available performances include: "Shantyman's Life," *Folk Music from Wisconsin* (Library of Congress, AAFS L55); and "The Jam on Gerry's Rock," "The Little Brown Bulls," "Shantyman's Life," "Snow Deer" (harmonica instrumental), and "Tomahawk Hem," *The Wisconsin Patchwork: Recordings from the Helene Stratman-Thomas Collection of Wisconsin Folk Music,* (cassettes produced by Judy Rose, with an accompanying book by James P. Leary [Madison: University of Wisconsin, Continuing Education in the Arts, 1987]).

Reprinted from a mimeographed original published by the Rhinelander Logging Museum, mid-1940s.

The Bard of the Lumber Camps

It is dusk at a logging camp near Rhinelander in the late nineties. The snow is sifting down through the pine needles and settling upon the skidways and the tote roads. Through the growing drifts, a group of tired lumberjacks trudges toward the camp shanties. They are a frowzy crew, unshaven and unshorn, damp with their own perspiration and the snow. But with 3,000,000 feet of lumber logs to get into the rollways before spring breakup, they haven't a minute to waste from daylight until dark. They file wearily into the warm bunk house, to put away their axes and their saws, and to hang up their mittens, their caps, and their mackinaws to dry. Once inside, however, their dejection vanishes. Keen interest takes its place—all because of a lithe young figure they find sitting beside the heater. During the afternoon, Emery DeNoyer, the blind singer of the logging camps, has come in. He turns his sightless eyes toward the door as they enter, eager to catch the sound of a familiar voice or a chance greeting. He is only a young fellow, tall and strapping, not quite twenty years old. Besides being totally blind, he has lost his left arm above the elbow. The men are sorry for him, but they are glad he has come. Tonight they will gather on the "deacon seat" around the roaring heater,

> Load up their pipes and smoke,
> Till everything is blue.

And DeNoyer will sing until,

> At nine o'clock in the evening,
> They to their bunks do go,
> To dream away the lonely hours
> While working in the pines.

He will sing all the popular songs of the day and some new ones they have never heard. He will sing the "Shanty Man's Life," and other camp ballads that are going the rounds. They try to sing these tunes themselves sometimes, but DeNoyer will sing them better, and he will have all the words, while they know only snatches. DeNoyer will sing, too, of home and mother. There is many a lonesome lad among them who would be glad to be away from the hardships the men must accept for the salary which will put them through the lean winters. Home will seem a little nearer as they listen. When he is tired of singing, DeNoyer will get out his "mouth organ" and play it as such an instrument has never been played before,

21.1. Lumber camp singer Emery DeNoyer, Rhinelander, 1941. State Historical Society WHi (S75) 2.

21.2. Fiddlers and cook-shack crew pose in the cook-shack of August Mason's lumber camp against a backdrop of theatrical posters, Brill, 1902. State Historical Society of Wisconsin, WHi (X313) 30497.

So when the cook he calls our 'supper,'
They all arise and go,
For 'taint the style of any o' the boys
To lose his hash, you know

They go out to the cook's shanty with sprightly steps, quite different from the dragging tread that brought them in. They eat silently, as is the custom in the camps, and are soon back again reluctant to miss any of the evening's treat, for DeNoyer will not stay long. Tomorrow, perhaps, he will be on his way again, tramping from camp-to-camp in northern Wisconsin, Michigan, and Minnesota.

This is the scene that unwinds in the listener's mind as the old lumberjacks around Rhinelander tell about Emery DeNoyer's entertainments in the logging camps. They began usually at 6:30. On weekdays they stopped at 9:00 but on Saturday night Emery sang until 11:00 o'clock. If the crew was especially receptive he often kept on until 12:00. Sunday was a holiday; so a Saturday night visit was an especial break for any camp he happened to reach. DeNoyer sang in a naturally placed baritone voice which, they tell me, resembled that of Bing Crosby today. He seemed to get better each year. He picked up new selections as he traveled, so he always brought surprises. He brought the men in the camps the first Victrola playing flat records that was ever heard in Rhinelander. He and his companion, who was usually his brother, carried it about with a few records to play for each part of the program.

"The men went wild over his concerts," a camp superintendant said. "That Victrola went over big. The men paid him real well for his performance too. At the close of each evening somebody'd pass a hat. If a man was out of money, he'd go to the desk and have the boss put in a certain amount for him. This was charged against his wages. It was nothing to see DeNoyer carry away between $35.00 and $50.00 from a camp in one evening.

"We were all glad to see him come. He cheered the men. There was less danger of fights if they were kept amused. When men are worked so hard and such long hours as they were in the logging camps, tempers get on edge easily. Anything that could break the monotony was always welcome and DeNoyer was very popular."

As he tramped through the snow between the camps of three states during the late logging years, Emery DeNoyer unknowingly carried on an ancient tradition. Before history began blind men with sweet voices were walking from settlement to settlement in the classical nations singing at gatherings. They sang hymns to the gods the people worshiped. They sang the praises of the great in death chambers and beside biers. They sang the bravery of a nation's heroes in the banquet halls of their kings. There they also sang stories from their past exploits. In so doing they preserved history before it could be written. Without them much would have been lost.

The best known, but by no means the first of the bards of antiquity, was Homer. He wrote many of the songs of his predecessors and many of his own into stories from the childhood of the Greek nation. We have them in the Iliad and the Odyssey. For centuries, historians believed these romantic tales were entirely fictitious. By following indications in the accounts, however, modern excavators have found the ancient city of Troy. We now accept the two great poems as records of the early history and customs of beginning Mediterranean civilization.

Bards became so popular in ancient times that each tribal leader kept one of his own. The singer entertained the guests in the castle hall and sang praises to his sponsor to keep the subjects always reminded of the greatness of their king. Usually he accompanied his songs on the harp, the lyre, the lute, or the viola. . . . In a modified form the custom has been continued today in the poet laureate of England. He is an outstanding poet paid by the government as a member of the king's court to write poems and odes for state occasions.

Like the bards of old, Emery DeNoyer has had a part in preserving history. Of the many rollicking songs composed by the lumberjacks to entertain their companions around the "deacon seat," few were ever written. The men put them together in their own heads and sang them impromptu when it came their turns to lead the evening's fun. They wrote them down on scraps of paper for the few friends who especially liked them. Most of the old men can remember only the titles and themes now. The three lumberjack ballads that DeNoyer sang, he popularized so thoroughly that they will never be forgotten. The "Log Driving Song," "The Wolf River Shanty Boy Song," and the "Little Brown Bulls," he made traditions of the late logging. They are the three always first mentioned when lumberjack songs are requested.

Besides these, DeNoyer sang one he composed himself. He called it the "Tomahawk River Hymn," but it is really a series of toasts well known to loggers "who camped upon the Tomahawk, where evergreens do grow." The rest of his repertoire consisted of folk songs he learned as he went along, and a long list he commited to memory from phonograph records he could not carry with him. At one time he knew about a hundred songs to choose his programs from. The most popular of the folk songs were the "Irish Jubilee" and the "Three Happy Hunters." Of the record songs two by Bill Murray, "The Good Old Dollar Bill" and "Keep Your Skirts Down, Mary Ann," never failed to bring down the house. Other record songs that took well in the woods were "The Mormon Coon" and the "Rock Candy Mountain" series. "The Birds Sing Sweeter, Lad, at Home," and "There's a Mother Waiting for You at Home" were also popular.

DeNoyer visited logging camps from 1895 until they closed. As they dwindled in number after 1900, slowly up to the time of the World War and then rapidly until they were all gone, he often had open dates. He was forced to find some new way of entertaining and earning. So, he learned to play chord accompaniments on the piano to his best songs. This was an accomplishment to be proud of because he had no left hand. But he managed to play one deep bass note with the stump of his left arm. Then by stretching his right hand to play as heavy a chord as possible in the middle register of the keyboard he got out a full accompaniment. For several years he played thus with an orchestra. The depression put an end to it and for a time he was forgotten. Recently he was remembered in connection with the interest in the history of logging aroused by the logging museum. Since then he has sung for the Oneida County Historical Association and on several club programs. He has also made records for the University of Wisconsin and the Federal Government. People who have heard him marvel at the fine quality of his voice. In spite of the fact that he is well along in his sixties, it is still true and mellow. The comments of his audience if they were translated into the words of Homer might be summed up thus: "Verily, it is a good thing that the lumberjacks had a bard such as this one."

Emery DeNoyer was born at Swamp Creek, Michigan, seventeen miles from Saginaw. He was the youngest of nine children. His father, Alexander DeNoyer, came down from Canada to log in Michigan in 1867. He logged in the Saginaw country for various firms until 1892. By the beginning of the nineties the heaviest logging in the United States was going on along the upper Wisconsin River. There were better wages and more opportunities for employment in any of the towns north of Wausau than there were in northern Michigan where logging was on the wane. Mr. DeNoyer's eldest son had been in Merrill, working as mill wright for the Gilkey-Hanson Lumber Company for several years, and now he found an opening for his father. It was in 1893, during the time his father was in Merrill, that Emery was hurt while hunting with a double-barreled shotgun. The family had remained in Muskegon where they had moved several years earlier until their father could get permanently located. For several weeks the boy's chances to live were very poor. Alexander DeNoyer gave up the job at Merrill and went home to supervise his son's care until he was out out danger. Later he took the lad to Milwaukee and put him in the care of Dr. Joseph Schneider. For a time Emery was at St. Joseph's Hospital. Nothing could be done, however, to restore his sight. The diagnosis was a bitter disappointment to a boy of fourteen, so strong and ambitious. He loved to sing and people liked to hear him, so he spent his idle hours in remembering and practicing the songs he already knew and in learning new ones.

Mr. DeNoyer, Sr., found employment again in Rhinelander with the F. S. Robbins Lumber Company. Rhinelander in 1893 was the booming town in Wisconsin. In every way it had the brightest outlook for the future. The next May he moved his family there. All of the children found work, even Emery. Many camps depended upon Rhinelander for their supplies and so many companies were logging at the same time that they were fairly close together. The men in the camps needed to be entertained and were being visited by salesmen and representatives of charitable organizations. They were liberally rewarding all who bore the rigors of the cold and the hardships of early travel to call upon them. So, just as an experiment at first, Emery and his brother began offering them diversion. They were so successful Emery made camp entertaining his profession.

In 1898 the first Victrola playing flat records came to the north. It was exhibited at the Carlson and Jewett Music Store in Rhinelander. It was one of the first ever made and although it was a small machine it cost $50.00. Alexander DeNoyer recognized its value and bought it immediately for his blind son. The boy and his companion carried the precious machine, knocked down, from camp to camp, often lugging it fifteen or twenty miles each day.

"We didn't mind the walk nor the load," Emery DeNoyer said, "The exercise in the cold was good for us and we had a grand time."

For three years the two men sold hospital insurance for St. Mary's Hospital in Rhinelander as a side issue. All of the hospitals in lumbering districts were selling what they called "hospital tickets" at the time. They entitled their purchasers to a period of free care in case they were ill or injured. Representatives from each hospital were traveling to the camps and telling about the plan.

Mr. DeNoyer still has the Victrola machine. His collection of records, however, were nearly destroyed some years ago by a fire at his home.

"The Jam on Gerry's Rock"

This is the best known of all lumberjack songs sung in the middle west. It was also one of the first written. In some camps it is said to have been sung until it was a bore. In the Rhinelander district, however, it was always popular especially among the river drivers. It was generally known there as the "Log Driving Song."

DeNoyer does not know who wrote it. He learned it in 1892 from "Silver Jack," an elderly man who worked along the Saginaw River. He was a lumberjack of the old type who went into the woods in the fall and stayed all winter. He never changed his clothes until he came down again in the spring.

The ballad tells the story of an actual occurence on the Saginaw River where Gerry's Rock is to be found. Rickaby published it in the "American Song Bag" to a

21.3. "The Jam on Gerry's Rock."

tune containing snatches of the "Wearing of the Green." [Note: Ebert confuses Carl Sandburg's *American Songbag* with Franz Rickaby's *Ballads and Songs of the Shanty Boy.*] The tune printed here is the one DeNoyer learned from "Silver Jack." He believes it to be the one to which it was originally written.

> Come all ye noble shanty boys, wherever you may be,
> Kindly give me your attention, and listen unto me.
> Twas of a bold and hearty crew so noble and so brave,
> While breaking the jam on Gerry's Rock, they met with a watery grave.
>
> Twas on a Sunday morning as you can plainly hear;
> The logs were piled up mountain high, they could not keep them clear,
> "Turn out, turn out," the boss did cry, "Brave hearts avoid a fear,
> And we'll break the jam on Gerry's Rocks and for Riverstown we'll steer."
>
> Some of them were willing while others they held back.
> All for to work on Sunday, they hardly thought it right,
> Till five of those bold Canadians did volunteer to go
> And break the jam on Gerry's Rock with their foreman, young Monro.
>
> They had not rolled off many a log till the foreman he did say,
> "You want to be on your guard, my boys, for the jam will soon give way."

He scarce had spoken that warning when the jam did give and go,
And carried away those five brave men and their foreman young Monro.

When the rest of those bold shanty boys, the sad news they did hear,
In search of their companions to the river they did steer.
There was one fair form among them lay on the banks below
All cut and mangled down the beach, lay the corpse of young Monro.

They drew him from his watery grave, smoothed back his waving hair.
There was one fair form among them, whose cries did split the air.
There was one fair form among them, a girl from Saginaw town,
Whose raving cries did pierce the skies for her true love that was drowned.

They buried him quite decently on the seventeenth of May,
Close in a nook by the river bank beneath a hemlock tree.
And on this tree the words did say, as you can plainly see,
The date, the death, the drowning, of the foreman Young Monro.

Clara was a pretty girl, likewise a raftmate's friend.
Her mother being a widow living by the river's bend,
The wages of her lover the boss to her did pay
And a liberal collection she received from the shanty boys that day.

"The Wolf River Shanty Boy Song"

DeNoyer called his version of this song the "Shanty Man's Life." He learned it in 1904 at a camp in Minnesota on the Cloquet River. The words were slightly different from the ones we are printing. We are indebted for these to Charles Fliegel of Lake Tomahawk who learned them thirty years earlier. The minor tune that DeNoyer sings and the one Fliegel gave, however, are the same. The difference in the words came about, we believe, because the song is so long and it was passed along verbally for so many years before DeNoyer got it.

According to Fliegel the song was written in 1874 by Joe Monahan of Oshkosh. At the time Monahan and his two brothers were running a logging camp up on Lake Norah about two miles west of Eland Junction. Joe made up the song and taught it to the men as part of the evening's entertainment. That winter Fliegel was a member of the crew. He was only a youngster just out of "common school" and this was his first job. He found the work much too hard, so he did not stay long. Long enough, however, to learn the song. He carried it into the railroad camps of the Milwaukee, Lake Shore, and Western where he worked next as a water boy. He sang it until many of the men there learned it also. The other men in the Monahan camp that winter carried it through the camps of three states.

The words have been printed heretofore as they were written down by some of these men. In 1928 the *Milwaukee Journal* printed them as a boy in a camp at Cable, Wisconsin, sent them home in a letter in 1878. A great deal of the song was left out of his version. Fliegel himself could only remember the first eight verses when he was first interviewed. By comparing DeNoyer's version with a copy of the one in the

Come, all you jolt-ly fel-lows and list-ten to my song. It's all a-bout
the pin-ny boys and how they get a-long. They're the jol-liest set of fel-lows
So mer-ry and so fine, they spend the bless-ed win-ter months, In Cut-ting down
the pine.

21.4. "The Wolf River Shanty Boy Song."

Journal, however, he was finally able to reproduce the last six as Joe Monahan composed them. Monahan died a few years after he composed the song. His brothers moved to Rhinelander at the beginning of the boom days, and were well known by all lumbermen and loggers in the north.

> Come all ye jolly shanty boys, I'll sing to you a song,
> It's all about the lumberjacks and how they get along.
> They're a jolly bunch of fellows, so merry and so fine,
> Who spend the pleasant winters in cutting down the pine.
>
> Some have left their homes and friends and all they do love dear,
> And into the lonely pine woods their pathways they have steered.
> And into the lonely pine woods all winter to remain
> Awaiting for the springtime to return again.
>
> Springtime will come and glad will be the day.
> Some return to homes and friends while others stray away.
> The farmer and the sailor, likewise mechanics too,
> It takes all kinds of tradesmen to form a lumber crew.
>
> The choppers and the sawyers, they lay the timber low,
> The skidders and the swampers, they haul it to and fro,
> Next come the teamsters before the break of day,
> "Load up your teams, you jolly men, and to the landing haste away."
>
> Noon time rolls round, the foreman loudly calls,
> "Lay down your tools, you jolly boys, and haste to pork and beans."
> We all arrive at the shanty where splashing does begin;
> The rattling of the water pail, and the banging of the tin.

You will hear all the boys say, "Come hurry up, you Bob and Joe,
For you will have to take the pails and for more water go."
In the middle of the splashing the cook "To dinner!" cries.
You will see the boys all run and jump for they hate to lose their pie.

After dinner it is over we to our shanty go,
Load up our pipes and smoke till everything is blue.
"It's time for the woods, my boys," the foreman he does say,
We all get up our hats and caps, to the woods we haste away.

We all go out with cheerful hearts and well-contented minds,
For the wintry winds don't blow so cold among the sheltering pines.
You'll hear the saws and axes ring until the sun goes down,
"Lay down your tools and axes, boys, to the shanty we are bound."

We arrive at the shanty with cold and wet feet,
Pull off our socks and rubbers, for supper we must eat.
When the cook he cries out "Supper!" we'll all arise and go,
For 'taint the style of any boys to lose his hash, you know.

At nine o'clock of an evening we to our bunks do climb
To dream away the lonely hours while working in the pines.
At four o'clock next morning our foreman he does shout,
"Roll out, you lazy shanty boys, it's time that you were out."

The teamsters, they then get up in a frightful, manful way,
"Oh where's my boots, oh where's my socks, my rubbers have gone astray."
The other men they then get up, their packs they cannot find,
They lay it to the teamsters and curse them till they're blind.

Springtime comes round, oh glad will be the day.
"Lay down your tools, my boys, and haste to break away."
Floating ice is over and business now does thrive.
Three hundred able bodied men are wanted on the drive.

With jam pikes and peavies these able men do go,
All up that wild and dreary stream to risk their lives, you know.
On cold and frosty mornings they shiver with the cold;
So much ice upon their jam pikes that scarcely do they hold.

Now, where e'er you hear these verses, believe them to be true,
For if you doubt one word of them, just ask Mike Dolan's crew.
It was in Mike Dolan's shanties where they were sung with glee,
The ending of my song is signed C, D, F, and G.

"The Little Brown Bulls"

This song originated on the Chippewa waters where the contest it describes took place. DeNoyer learned it from Frank Clapper of Merrill. He is not sure who wrote it, but he thinks it was Pat Murphy, a bull puncher and a very good singer from Chippewa Falls.

21.5. "The Little Brown Bulls."

DeNoyer once sang the song in a camp where McCloskey was working. McClos-key told him that several versions were being sung to several different tunes. He was glad to hear DeNoyer sing it as it was first written and as he, himself, thought it should be sung.

McCloskey was a big Scotchman and very popular wherever he worked. His head was almost entirely bald. He claimed to have lost his hair when he was only eighteen years old

> Not a thing on the river McCloskey did fear,
> As he swung his goad stick o'er his big spotted steers.
> They were round, plump and handsome, girded eight foot and three,
> Said McCloskey, the Scotchman, "They're the laddies for me."
>
> Then along came Bull Gordon whose skidding was full,
> And he hollered "Whoa hush" to his little brown bulls.
> Short legged and shaggy, girded six foot and nine.
> "Too light," said McCloskey, "to handle our pine."
>
> "For it's three to the thousand our contract does call,
> Our skidding is good and the timber is tall."
> McCloskey he swore that he'd make the day full,
> And he'd skid three to one of the little brown bulls.
>
> "Oh, ho," said Bull Gordon, "that you cannot do,
> Although your big steers are the pets of the crew.
> I'll tell you, McCloskey, that you'll have your hands full,
> When you skid one more log than my little brown bulls."

So the day was appointed and soon did draw nigh,
For twenty-five dollars their fortunes to try.
All eager and anxious that morning were found;
The judge and the scaler appeared on the ground.

It was just at sundown one foreman did say,
"Turn out, boys, turn out, it's enough for the day.
We scaled and we counted, each man with his team,
And well did we know which ones kicked the beam."

With a whoop and a yell came McCloskey in view
With his big spotted steers, the pets of the crew,
He said, "Chew your cuds, boys, and keep your mouths full,
For we easy can beat them, the little brown bulls."

Then along came Bull Gordon with his pipe in his jaw,
To his little brown bulls he hollers, "Whoa, haw."
He said, "Chew your cuds, boys, you never need fear;
For we will not be beat by the big spotted steers."

Said McCloskey to Sandy, "We'll take off their skins,
We'll dig them a ditch and we'll tumble them in;
We'll fix them a dish and feed it down hot,
We'll learn them damned Yankees to face the bull seat [bold Scot]."

After supper was over McCloskey appeared
With a belt ready made for his big spotted steers.
To make it he tore up his best mackinaw,
He was bound to conduct it according to law.

Then up stepped the scaler, saying, "Hold, gee, awhile,
Your big spotted steers are behind just one mile.
You've skidded one hundred and ten and no more,
While Bull Gordon has beat you by ten and a score."

The boys then all laughed and McCloskey did swear,
As he pulled out by handfuls his long yellow hair.
He said to Bull Gordon, "My dollars I'll pull,
And you'll take the belt for the little brown bulls."

So here's to Bull Gordon and Sand Berry John,
For the biggest day's work on the Chippewa's done,
So we'll fill up our glasses, boys, fill them up full,
And drink to the health of the little brown bulls.

"The Tomahawk River Hymn"

DeNoyer sang this for a crew working on the Tomahawk River near Goodnow. Mike
Dolan was a popular foreman who ran camps for the O'Day and Daley Lumber Company of Merrill. One of his last camps was on Pine Lake for the Collins Lumber

21.6. "The Tomahawk River Hymn."

Company of Rhinelander. Excepting Dolan, the men mentioned were just ordinary professional lumberjacks from Merrill. Robert Eckeson [Eckerson?] was always a teamster wherever he worked; Mr. Webster, a scaler and top loader; and Marcel Deusette [Doucette?], a landing man. Joseph Stafford worked in a store, but went into the woods occasionally for the winter. Jimmie Robinson, the cook toasted, was known as an unusually good sport. [Note: Ebert unaccountably omits the verse about the teamsters. I include a transcription from the recording DeNoyer made for the Library of Congress on July 26, 1941.]

> Now boys if you will listen to my few lines of care;
> Although we're heart broken, in sorrow we came here.
> We could curse the day that we were ever forced to go
> And camp out on the Tomahawk where evergreens do grow.
>
> It was on the 10th of March, my boys, the weather being fair,
> We'd finished at our shanties and left the skidways bare,
> The logs were on the rollways and now we soon must go
> And camp out on the Tomahawk where evergreens do grow.
>
> It was then we got the order to start without delay
> And haul from Section Seventeen and soon be on our way.
> We pitched our tents that evening while stormy winds did blow,
> To camp out on the Tomahawk where evergreens do grow.
>
> [Oh here's to our jolly teamsters, we will recall a few.
> The first is Robert Eckerson, the playboy of the crew.
> He's never in a hurry, but drives his cattle slow
> And always makes his landing where evergreens do grow.]

The next is our noble scaler whose name to you I'll tell,
His name is Mr. Webster, the jolliest of the crew.
He is seldom in a passion and seldom ever swears;
And he loads and scales and separates and does it on the square.

Here's to our noble landing man, his name is full of fame
We call him Marcel Deusette, from Canada he came.
He landed safe at Merrill without a friend or foe;
And soon struck Mike Dolan's camp where evergreens do grow.

Now here is Joseph Stafford, our noble merchant lad,
Who left behind his sweetheart, it surely made her sad.
She said, "My sweetest Joseph, I hope you will not go
And camp out on the Tomahawk where evergreens do grow."

"Oh, goodbye, my lovely Maggie, I now must go away;
My comrades all are waiting, no longer can I stay.
I will think of you, dear Maggie, wherever I may go.
Yes, even on the Tomahawk where evergreens do grow."

About young Jimmy Rob'son, we'll say a word or two,
He is the only favorite that we've had in the crew.
He is both wise and clever and wherever he may go
He cooks for us poor shanty boys where evergreens do grow.

Spring is now a-coming, the robins soon we'll see.
The small birds seem to sing so sweet in every tree.
And as they fly around us and sing most cheerfully,
It tells to us, poor shanty boys, our time is short to stay.

And when we gain our freedom, it's homeward we will steer;
We will seek the town of Merrill, to all our friends so dear.
And when we strike old Merrill, to all our girls we'll go
And tell them our adventures where evergreens do grow.

"Three Happy Hunters"

A hobo came into the lobby of the Schlitz Hotel in Rhinelander one day and sat down at the piano. He was a dirty unkempt man, but he played some of the latest musical hits and played them well. He also sang this song featuring the ancient disagreement in the British Isles. DeNoyer heard him and was so taken with the song he asked to learn it. The man taught it to him by rote that afternoon.

DeNoyer does not remember the date—only that it was during the time that "Eli Green's Cake Walk" was popular. The dance tune was one that the hobo played particularly well.

Three hunters wenter a-hunting to see what they could find.
They ran across a haystack, and that they left behind.

The Englishman says, "It's a haystack," the Scotchman he says, "Nay."
The Irishman says, "It's a Protestant church with the steeple blowed away."

Then they kept on hunting to see what they could find.
They saw a great big steamboat sailing down the line.
The Englishman says, "It's a steamboat," the Scotchman he says, "Nay."
Pat says, "It's old Ireland, a-floating down the bay."

Then they kept on hunting to see what they could find,
They ran across a porcupine, and that they left behind.
The Englishman says, "It's a porcupine," the Scotchman he says, "Nay."
Pat says, "It's a pin cushion, with the pins the other way."

Then they kept on hunting to see what they could find.
They ran across a monkey and that they left behind.
The Englishman says, "It's a monkey," the Scotchman he says, "Nay."
Pat says, "It's your father with his whiskers blowed away."

Then they kept on hunting to see what they could find.
They ran across a pumpkin and the punk they left behind.
The Englishman says, "It's a pumpkin," the Scotchman he says, "Nay."
Pat says, "It's an orange, from South Americay."

Then they kept on hunting to see what they could find.
They saw a great big new moon, away up in the sky.
The Englishman says, "It's a new moon," the Scotchman he says, "Nay."
Pat says, "It's an electric light, ten thousand miles away."

"Irish Jubilee"

DeNoyer learned this in his childhood. A horse jockey from lower Michigan sang it until he had committed it. It always took well with the lumberjacks.

Just a short time ago, boys, an Irishman named Daugherty
Was elected for senator by a very large majority.
He felt so elated that he went to Dennis O'Cassidy
Who owned a barroom of a very great capacity.

He said to O'Cassidy, "Go over to the brewery
For a thousand kegs of lager beer, and give it to the poor.
Go over to the butcher shop, order up a ton of meat.
Be sure to see that the boys and girls get all they want to eat.

"Send out invitations in twenty different languages.
Don't forget to tell them all to bring along their sandwiches.
Tell that the music will be furnished by O'Rafferty,
Assisted on the bagpipes by Felix McCafferty.

"Whatever the expenses are, remember that I'll put up the ten [tin].
And everyone that doesn't come, be sure and do not let them in."

O'Cassidy at once sent out the invitations,
And everyone that came was a credit to their nations.

Some came on bicycles, for they had not fare to pay;
And those that didn't come at all made up their minds to stay away.
Two by, three by, they marched into the dining hall.
Young men, old men, and girls that wasn't men at all.

Blind men, deaf men, and men that had their teeth in pawn.
Single men, double men, and men that had their glasses on.
Before many minutes every chair was taken.
The front rooms, the mushrooms, were packed to suffocation.

When everyone was seated, they started to lay out the feast.
O'Cassidy says, "Rise up and give us a cake of yeast."
He then says, "As manager we will try and fill the chair."
And they all sat down and looked at their bill of fare.

There were pigs heads, gold fish, mocking birds, and ostriches;
Ice cream, cold cream, vaseline, and sandwiches;
Blue fish, green fish, fish hooks, and partridges;
Fish balls, snow balls, cannon balls, and cartridges.

We ate oatmeal until we could hardly stir about.
Catsup, hurry up, sweet kraut and sauerkraut.
Pressed beef, naked beef, and beef with its dresses on.
Soda crackers, fire crackers, limburger cheese with tresses on.

Beef steak, mistake was down upon the bill of fare;
Roast ribs and spare ribs, and ribs that we couldn't spare.
Reindeer, snow deer, dear me, and antelope.
The women ate muskmelons until the men said, "They canteloupe."

Smoked herring, red herring from old Aaron Bologan,
Fruit cake, sausages a half a mile,
Hot corn, corn salve and honeycomb.
Red bird, read books, sea bass and sea foam.

Baked liver, fried liver, Carter's little liver pills.
Everyone was wondering who was going to pay the bills.
For dessert we had toothpicks, ice picks, and skipping ropes,
And washed them all down with a big piece of barber soap.

We ate everything upon the bill of fare,
And looked on the other side to see if any more was there.
Then the band played hornpipes, gas pipes and Irish reels,
And we danced to the music of the wind that shakes the barley field.

Old piper, he played old tunes, spittoons so very fine,
The piper Hudson, he came in and handed us all a glass of wine.
We pelted the floor till we could be heard for miles around,
And Gallagher was in the air, his feet were never on the ground.

The finest lot of dances you ever set your eyes upon,
And them that couldn't dance was dancing with their slippers on.
They danced jig steps, door steps, and highland flings,
When Murphy took his knife out and tried to cut a pigeon's wing.

When the dancing was over O'Cassidy then told them all
To join hands and sing in this good old chorus.
"Should auld acquaintances be forgot, wherever you may be,
Just think of the good old times we had at the Irish Jubilee."

"The Good Old Dollar Bill"

They are telling of old Glory
Now in pictures, songs, and stories,
And they say it is the emblem of the land,
"It's a grand old flag," they holler,
But the real flag is the dollar.
I've been up against it once and understand.
We respect the flag and love it
But a dollar floats above it.
When you've got one, no one ever treats you mean,
Money talks but seldom tattles,
And in all life's weary battles
It is the only flag of truth, the old long green.

Chorus: Praise the stars and stripes forever,
        And the old red, white and blue,
        Rave about the flag of freedom
        And, oh "Hail Columbia" too.
        Sing the praises of Old Glory
        But I've been through the mill
        And a real star spangled banner
        Is a good old dollar bill.

With a dollar you feel cheery
And the girls they'll call you "dearie,"
They'll smile on you and never, never chaff.
They'll be true blue while you blow it,
You've been there and ought to know it.
When it's gone instead of smiles you get the laugh.
When you're flush your friends are sunny,
Life is peaches, cream and honey.
They will welcome you no matter where you go.
When you're down and out in sorrow,
From a friend you try to borrow,
He won't even lend an ear to hear your tale of woe.

Repeat Chorus

217

"The Mormon Coon"

A coon named Abraham left town one day,
Nobody knew just where he went away,
Until a friend of his received a note,
It came from Abe and this is what he wrote:
"I'm out in Utah in the Mormon land,
I'm going to stay because I'm living grand.
I used to rave about a single life,
Now every day I get a brand new wife."

Chorus: "I got a big brunette, I got a blond to get,
I've got them short, fat, thin, and tall.
I've got a Cuban gal, and a Zulu gal,
That come in bunches when I call.
I got a homely few, I got 'em pretty too.
I got 'em black as octoroons.
I can spare you six or eight, or I can ship them by freight,
For I am the Mormon coon."

"The Birds Sing Sweeter, Lad, at Home"

When but a lad of tender years my dear old dimpled dad,
This maxim would impress upon my mind:
"Remember, Joe, where e'er you go you'll never know the joy
You found with loving kindred left behind.
Strange sights will greet your searchings, strange companions take your hand.
You may wander through the world, my boy, and roam.
Bright birds of every plumage will attract and steal your gaze,
And you'll find the birds sing sweeter, lad, at home."

Chorus: "In every foreign clime
Keep this motto in your mind,
Admire if you will each silvery tone;
And be not led astray
By the birds so very gay,
And you'll find the birds sing sweeter, lad, at home."

Though many years have passed away, my memory still retains
The tender thoughtful words my father said.
He's sleeping now behind the church, and mother, too, is there.
The sweet old birds they loved sing overhead.
No welcome voice is preaching to the one who went away.
When strolling back, the place now looks forlorn.
There were birds of every color, but my dear old dad was right
When he said, "The birds sing sweeter, lad, at home."

Repeat Chorus

22

Kentucky Folksong
in Northern Wisconsin

Asher E. Treat

Eastern Kentucky has long been venerated as a hearth of ancient English folk culture in America. And while that image has often been exaggerated and distorted, there is little doubt that the region's mountain people sustained a repertoire of stanzaic narrative folksongs, or ballads, with deep Old World roots. In the late nineteenth century, some eastern Kentucky families left coal camps and hard times in southern Appalachia for the only slightly better circumstances of northern Wisconsin's lumber camps and cutover farms. Not surprisingly, their numbers included such fine traditional singers as Pearl Jacobs Borusky and her mother, Ollie Jacobs.

In the 1930s the Jacobs family's songs were set down by Asher Treat from nearby Antigo. The singing family's most recent chronicler, folklorist Joanne Stuttgen, offers background:

> In 1925, Paul Jacobs graduated with honors from Antigo High School, and soon after he died. Some time later his classmate, Asher Treat, and his mother, Mrs. A. R. Treat, paid a visit of sympathy to the Jacobs home, where Asher Treat heard the Jacobs women—Paul's mother Ollie and his sisters Pearl and Maud—singing traditional English and Scottish ballads. Treat was a musical man, an amateur French horn player with an interest in regional traditional music partially influenced by Cecil Sharp's recently published compilation, *English Folk-Songs from the Southern Appalachians* (1932). ("Kentucky Folksong in Northern Wisconsin: Evolution of the Folksong Tradition in Four Generations of Jacobs Women," *Southern Folklore* 48 [1991]: 276)

Treat's account, partially reprinted here, inspired subsequent attention from folklorists.

In 1940 and again in 1941, Helene Stratman-Thomas recorded the Jacobs singers for the Library of Congress. Her journal entry for August 30, 1940, states that "Mr. Treat's mother, Mrs. A. R. Treat, drove into the country some distance to bring Mrs. Pearl Jacobs Borusky to the Treat home so that we could have electricity for recording. Mrs. Borusky had an endless repertoire of lovely old English ballads which she had learned from her father and mother. We recorded eighteen of Mrs. Borusky's songs in one afternoon." Stratman-Thomas's journal, along with texts and tunes from the Jacobs family, appears in *Folk Songs out of Wisconsin*, ed. Harry B. Peters (Madison: State Historical Society of Wisconsin, 1977). Their singing has also been released on sound recordings issued by the Library of Congress. Pearl Jacobs Borusky sings "The Rich Old Farmer" on *Anglo-American Ballads* (AAFS L1); "I'll Sell My Hat, I'll Sell My Coat" and "Once I Courted a Charming Beauty Bright" on *Folk Music From Wisconsin* (AAFS L55); and "Well Met, My Old True Love" on *Child Ballads Traditional in the United States II* (AAFS L58). Ollie Jacobs sings "A Ship Set Sail for North America" on the *Child Ballads* recording, as well. Besides influencing Helene Stratman-Thomas, Asher Treat's work was also known to Sidney Robertson, who recorded songs in 1937 for the Library of Congress from such "Kentucks" in the Crandon area as Jack Bailey,

Harry Fannin, Bud Faulkner, Clyde Spencer, and Mrs. and Mrs. Charles Spencer (see Brett Topping, "The Sidney Robertson Cowell Collection," *Folklife Center News* 3:3 [1980]: 4–5, 8).

Reprinted by permission of the American Folklore Society in an abridged form from *Journal of American Folklore* 52:203, (1939):1–50. Not for further reproduction.

It is not a long time since the loggers left northern Wisconsin, but it will be a long time before they come again. Drive eastward or northward from the town of Antigo and you may see why. Stump-studded, brush-choked acres line the road for miles on either side. They stretch far back among the rough little hills until interrupted perhaps by a clear creek, a peat bog, a spring-fed lake, an abandoned railroad, or a paved highway to the resort region farther north.

There is some second growth hardwood, much poplar and birch, which helps to preserve the water level and serves as shelter for small game, occasional wolves, foxes, deer, and bear. Where the land has been partially cleared, you may see a plentiful scattering of glacier-borne rocks; but the soil, even when freed of stumps and stones, is not very fertile. The natural obstacles to cultivation, the shortness of the growing season, and the severity of the winters combine to discourage any but the most stubborn attempts at farming.

The lumber companies, however, with these worthless and tax-encumbered wastes on their hands, told quite a different story to their prospective buyers. Many poor immigrants parted with a lifetime's savings, only to find themselves stranded in a god-forsaken wilderness where they faced the choice of starving to death or making the land support them.

Some of the victims were Polish and Bohemian peasants; some were native Americans in more or less distant parts of the country. Ten or twelve years before the turn of the century a stream of migrants began to flow northward from eastern Kentucky. Most of them came from Powell, Wolf, and Breathitt Counties, some from Elliott and Carter, and a few from Rowan and Greenup. By 1903 or 1904 there were well-established colonies of these people in the Wisconsin backwoods, and the flow of newcomers had just about ceased. A virtual island of mountain culture had been formed, with a population in Forest and Langlade Counties of perhaps two hundred families.

"Kentucks," they were called. Some, perhaps most, were like my friends the Jacobses: honest, diligent, of high native intelligence, and with the most engaging qualities of hospitality, gentleness, good humor, and inborn dignity. Others were shiftless, quarrelsome, lawless, and highly resistant to any modifying influences. The term "Kentuck" is not always a complimentary one as it is heard in the mouths of the Wisconsin farmers and villagers of other than Kentucky ancestry.

Perhaps their tenacity to their southern way of living contributed to the cultural isolation of these people. They had known backwoods life before. They knew how to hunt, fish, cut timber, and scratch the cheap land enough to raise a little corn, a few hills of beans, and maybe some potatoes. But a certain uneasiness and distrust toward them was often manifested by their northern neighbors. Their names, their speech, their manners, their cookery—many things made them seem different from the others; and even now, when many are of the second or third generation of the Wisconsin born, some of those differences persist.

My own early impressions of the Kentucks, which I got as a small boy in the town of Antigo, were mostly from rumors and frequent newspaper stories of shooting or stabbing brawls in the village of Elton, generally involving moonshine liquor in one way or another. Those were Prohibition times, and the newspapers found plenty of copy in the periodic raids on "the Kentucky moonshiners." About their participation in the social life of the areas and settlements in which they lived I have little information. I believe that such participation was limited. Whatever had been their habits in Kentucky, most of the migrants were not regular church-goers in their new environment. Their children went to the local schools, but attendance was often irregular or infrequent.

Assimilation into the general population of the area is already extensive, of course. Intermarriages are common. Intercommunication and access to the larger towns are no longer matters of difficulty. Even the poorer families could not easily dispense with their cars and radios. The neighborliness of the other inhabitants is increasing. There is a county zoning ordinance restricting the future use of the less arable land to forest and recreational purposes. All these things tend to bring the Kentucks out of the "bresh" and into the farm areas and cities. But while the cultural unit is noticeably less compact than it was even a few years ago, there are some localities where things remain pretty much in the same condition as that which characterized the days of the early migration—where the speech, manners, and mode of life are largely transplants from the southern mountains. These remnants are unlikely to survive the older generation by more than a very few years.

The singers of the songs recorded in this collection are all members of one family whose original home was near the town of Grayson, in Carter County, Kentucky. It was there that Madison Green Jacobs married Ollie Jacobs, thus uniting two of the three apparently unrelated Jacobs families who lived in that neighborhood. It was in Carter County, also, that seven of the twelve children were born. In 1906 the family moved to a small farm near the village of Bryant, Wisconsin, about nine miles northeast of Antigo. When most of the children had grown up and moved elsewhere, Mr. and Mrs. Jacobs took another place, also near Bryant, and lived there until Mr. Jacobs died, a few years ago. Mrs. Jacobs is now seventy-six years old. She spends most of her time with her children, five of whom live on farms or in villages within an hour's drive of Bryant, four having children of their own. Mrs. Jacobs is regarded by all her children, and indeed by everyone who knows her, with the greatest respect and affection. Her difficult life and the fortitude with which she has lived it are to be read in every line and contour of her handsome face. She is painfully crippled with arthritis, so that a movement of any kind is often a veritable ordeal for her. Nevertheless, she insists upon taking active and effective part in the housework, and is never known to utter a complaint or to be otherwise than cheerful and lovable.

Pearl Jacobs, now Mrs. Rodney Borusky, is a daughter of Mrs. M. G. Jacobs and the mother of two children. She is tall, thin, and dark, with a high forehead, high

22.1. "Kentuck" ballad singer Mrs. Ollie Jacobs in her rural Langlade County home, 1941. State Historical Society of Wisconsin, WHi (S75) 4.

cheek-bones, large, expressive eyes, and a thin, sensitive mouth. She possesses the same gentle and cheerful dignity which appear in the other members of the family and are reflected in her two children. During the past few years she has learned the importance of collecting and preserving the songs which form so intimate a part of her and her people's experience. She has become accustomed to singing the songs phrase by phrase, so as to make the notation of them easy; and she has gone to much trouble to refresh her own extensive memory by conferring with her relatives and writing down the words to many of the songs in advance of my infrequent collecting trips.

Maud Jacobs, a sister of Pearl, received high school training while still living in Kentucky, and has since then lived for several years in fairly large cities, where she has naturally acquired somewhat more of the urban outlook than have the others. Nevertheless, her memory of the songs is very vivid, so that she has been able to supply words to many verses which her relatives had forgotten. Several of the songs might have escaped notation entirely except for her diligent and continual searching of her memory for them. I am also indebted to her for much of the factual material given above. Although she has sung many of the songs for me, almost all were taken from the singing of Mrs. Jacobs or Pearl.

Others of the brothers and sisters have aided the work by expanding or correcting the material given me by the principal singers. These others are probably no less musical than are Mrs. Jacobs and Pearl, but for one reason or another they have been less accessible to me.

My acquaintance with the Jacobs family goes back to the year 1921, when I entered high school in Antigo as a classmate of Mrs. Jacobs' youngest son, Paul. He and I became friends; but it was not until after his death in 1925 that I came to know the rest of the family. Since that year I have visited them almost every summer, and have learned to have the deepest regard for all of them. The songs have been taken a few at a time since I first heard some of them sung in 1932.

While it might be anticipated that the transplanted musical culture of the Kentucky immigrants would have undergone modification in the new surroundings, and would show the influence of the neighboring groups, it is my impression that this has not happened. I have done a small amount of collecting among other people of the same locality and have found little that I could interpret as evidence of such influence. On the contrary, comparison of certain of these tunes with those collected by Cecil Sharp and others has led me to suspect that in the Wisconsin songs we have material which has been protected from contamination, perhaps to an extent even greater than has the culture of the present day mountain folk themselves. Until the introduction of the radio, there was little opportunity for the Wisconsin Kentuckians to hear singing by others, and it appears unlikely that other versions of the same songs would have been sung by any of the people with whom the migrants came into contact. Mrs. Jacobs and her older children learned the songs while they were still living in Kentucky, and have sung them continuously among themselves ever since.

The singers themselves believe that the songs have undergone no modification. They can distinguish carefully and accurately between their own versions of tunes and texts, and those which they have sometimes heard on the radio. For example, they sang the ballad of Barbara Allen for me on two separate visits, at one time specifying that they were then singing it "the way Bradley (Kincaid) does," and at another time (see No. 19), "the way we hyeard it in Kentucky." [Note: Kentuckian Bradley Kincaid was performing at the time on the "National Barn Dance" broadcast throughout the Midwest on Chicago's WLS radio.] Radio performances have occasionally reminded them of songs which they had temporarily forgotten; but they are not indebted to the radio for any of the tunes or words given here. Almost all of these they regard as of Carter County ancestry. It may be worth noting here that none of Cecil Sharp's collecting was done in Carter County.

The tunes of all of the songs have been transmitted to and among the Jacobses purely by vocal tradition. No member of the family has any knowledge of musical notation. They would have been unable to read the melodies even if they had seen them printed. Mrs. Jacobs, however, reports that her mother possessed a scrapbook containing clippings from country papers in which she found the words of certain verses which she had not previously known or had forgotten. The custom of keeping such scrapbooks was apparently a rather general one. The texts of the ballads would be requested by a reader in one issue of the farm journal, and supplied in a later issue by another reader who happened to remember them. The particular book to which Mrs. Jacobs refers was destroyed by fire many years ago.

So far as I know, the songs were not communicated to the children by any deliberate process of teaching. When asked where a tune has been learned, Pearl usually responds, "O, I hyeard mother sing it." Singing was, and still is, among these people, an almost inevitable though often subconscious accompaniment of housework. On occasions such as funerals, prayer-meetings, or parties it might take on a more deliberate or formal nature; but as is probably the case with musical people generally, scarcely a moment passes during which some tune is not either in the head or on the lips. It was not necessary for the children to "commit" the songs to memory; they learned them without effort, simply by hearing them often. A good thing to see is that Pearl's two children, Claire and James, know a number of the songs and are learning more.

The notation has been done under a variety of circumstances. Some was made at the second Jacobs farm near Bryant. The farm house there was of logs covered with tar paper. There was a single large room, with a loft above which served as a bedroom for those of the family who still lived at home, and with a small alcove at one end where Mrs. Jacobs slept. The large room was the kitchen, dining room, and general family headquarters. A big wood range stood in one corner, supplied with cord wood from a box beneath the south window. Over and around the stove hung long strings of "leatherbreeches"—that is, dried string beans. The furniture included a large folding table, a few chairs, and a long bench.

I would sit on a chair between the wood box and the stove, as far out of the way of cooking operations as good hearing would permit. Five or six people might be busy about the room, mixing biscuits, making gravy, or frying chicken. There was plenty of conversation, and the work of taking dictation was not always easy; but it seemed better not to wait for more favorable circumstances. When a song had been sung once or twice, or through a few verses, I would ask to hear it a little at a time. Mrs. Jacobs soon learned about how much I could conveniently get before it was necessary to interrupt, and from then on she would sing a phrase, or a few notes at a time. While I was busy writing down what I had just heard, she would continue her work and conversation until I asked for more. Then with surprising lack of hesitancy, she would resume singing where she had left off. Repetitions were often necessary, of course, and were always given patiently and carefully. When we had finished I would try the song myself, from my own notation, and would make the necessary changes until the singers and the others would tell me that I had done it all correctly. On a few occasions we were somewhat more business-like about it. In her own house, Pearl would sometimes put aside her work and devote her entire attention to singing and discussing the music.

The visits were often short and generally as much as a year apart. The fund of songs seemed inexhaustible. Some of the tunes were of more interest to me than others, and naturally those were the ones that I wanted first in case any had to be sacrificed for lack of time. In the earlier visits, I took whatever was offered and in whatever order it came. My friends learned before long, however, that I had a preference of some sort. From then on there was no difficulty about postponing a tune in favor of another, if that seemed desirable. Most of the tunes were ultimately recorded, but there are others which remain for future visits.

Once Pearl had started the custom of writing out the words for me in advance, the notation of the tunes progressed much more quickly than it had before. When this had not been done, I occasionally asked to have the words of some of the longer songs recited, in order to save time. The singers complied without apparent difficulty, although they would often sing or hum the air for a few measures as though to refresh their recollection.

Both Mrs. Jacobs and Pearl have a wealth of innate musicianship, wholly uncultivated as it is. They sing accurately with respect to pitch, and generally unmistakably as regards rhythm. The actual pitches at which the songs were sung, were, unfortunately, not noted; but the singers merely chose any convenient starting note, and would occasionally stop and begin over on a new one if the initial choice appeared to be too high or too low. The positions which I have chosen for the tunes have been largely a matter of convenience in avoiding ledger lines, accidentals, and artificial implications as to tonality. The qualities of the singers' voices are not, of course, to be described in words. These people sing as children sing, without effort, and without self-consciousness. No hesitancy is displayed in taking such high tones as occur, for example, in "Tomorrow morn I'm sweet sixteen" (No. 42). The voices are thin and without vibrato, and are unvarying in volume. Ordinarily there is but little accentuation of strong beats, though this is more nearly true of Pearl's singing than her mother's. There is never, of course, any attempt to dramatize a text in any way. Tempi seem to be chosen with considerable latitude. Within limits, one tempo seems as acceptable to the singers as does another. None of the tunes was sung at a really fast rate, and none was dragged.

It is not impossible, of course, that these words described only the performances given for me as an outsider. When by themselves, the Jacobses may unconsciously do things quite differently, and think them still differently. Who does not? Still, none of the family ever gave evidence that the singing of the others was done for me in any manner but that in which they were accustomed to hearing it.

With the accumulation of more and more songs came the problem of how to classify them. One might turn to the singers themselves. How would they group the songs in their own minds? It is unfortunate that the Jacobses have never been asked such a question. I mean to ask them some day; but the question itself may prove to be so artificial a stimulus as to disturb some subconscious classification which already exists for them, and which might be disclosed by careful observation better than by direct inquiry. Obviously the singers or anyone else might form logical groups simply by regarding the songs from the standpoint of their origin: that is, which were learned from whom? Equally rigid categories might be based upon some musical or textual features: which are modal, or which have this or that verse form. That such schemes of classification are useful and interesting is not to be denied; but so far as I am aware, they correspond to nothing explicit in the minds of the Jacobses.

Perhaps a clue to what we are seeking lies in a certain observation which has puzzled me for a long time. That is some of the songs were offered readily, as soon as they came into the singer's head, while others were brought forward a bit apologetically, with perhaps some such remark as, "I didn't think you'd care about having this one." Some surprise might even be shown at my enthusiasm for a tune that had been mentioned in this way, though the surprise never expressed itself more emphatically than by a polite, "Well!" Among such songs were "As I Came Over Yonder's Hill" and "My Old Hen" (Nos. 54 and 55). A few songs although apparently well enough known, were not mentioned until I asked for them specifically, although I cannot believe that this was because of any special reticence with regard to them. These included "What Will I Do with the Baby-Oh" (No. 56), "Going Up Cripple Creek" (No. 50) and "Sally in the Garden" (No. 53).

A judgment on the basis of such scanty information would, of course, be impossible; but it seems worth considering that some of the songs may seem to the Jacobses less dignified than others, less worthy of being recorded and remembered. To ask these people to group the songs in some such way would be certain to embarrass them, and to invite a wholly unnatural response. It would be surprising indeed if some distinction were not made between, say "I Once Knew a Little Girl" (No. 12) and "I Asked That Girl to Marry Me" (No. 11). People far less sensitive than the Jacobses could scarcely go so far astray as to place anything like equal poetical or musical value upon such opposites as these. Nevertheless, the two songs share some common properties: both are sung in the first person; both are accounts of the singer's troubles with women; neither is a dance or a game song, and neither is specially intended for children.

The Songs

[Note: Only a representative selection of the fifty-six songs and tunes set down by Treat are reprinted here. The numbering of songs matches Treat's, with the sequential gaps consequently indicating omissions.]

Forty-nine of the [Jacobses'] songs fall into the category of ballads and "songs of sentiment." Six are probably dance or game songs, and three are songs for children. The songs in each category are arranged alphabetically according to the words of the first line. When they are known to the Jacobses by some title other than the first words, the fact is indicated. In no instance are the words or tunes of any of the songs identical with any published versions which I have seen, and in most cases there is wide disparity. Whenever a song or a fragment of a song has been identified with any of the material collected by Sir Cecil James Sharp, the title is given under which that song appears in Sharp's work, *English Folksongs from the Southern Appalachians* (London, 1932) together with the letter designating the version or versions in Sharp in which the resemblance has been observed.

Ballads and Songs of Sentiment

1. "A Fair Damsel in a Garden"
Sung by Pearl Jacobs Borusky, July 13, 1938; cf. Sharp, "The Broken Token."

1. A fair damsel in a garden,
   A brave young soldier came riding by.
   He drew his reins and thus addressed her,
   "My pretty maid, won't you marry me?"
2. "I have a true-love in the army.
   For seven long years he has been at sea.
   If he remains there seven years longer,
   No man on earth shall marry me."
3. "Perhaps your true love has been drownded.
   Perhaps he's on some battlefield slain.
   Perhaps he's married some fair lady,
   And never will come back again."
4. "O, no, my true-love is not drownded,
   Nor is he on some battlefield slain.
   But if he's married some fair lady,
   I'll love the girl that marries him."

2. "A Farmer Had a Daughter"

Called "The Sweet and Dee" by the Jacobses. Sung by Pearl Jacobs Borusky, July 13, 1938; cf. Sharp, "The Banks of Sweet Dundee."

A farm-er had a daugh-ter Whose beau-ty ne'er was told. Her pa-rents died and left her Five__ hund-red pounds in gold. She lived with her un cle Who__ caused her all her woe, And if you'll but list' to this pret-ty fair miss, I'll prove it all to you.

1. A farmer had a daughter
   Whose beauty ne'er was told.
   Her parents died and left her
   Five hundred pounds in gold.
   She lived with her uncle
   Who caused her all her woe,
   And if you'll but list' to this pretty fair miss,
   I'll prove it all to you.

2. Her uncle had a plow-boy
   That Mary loved so well.
   The way she loved that plow-boy
   No human tongue could tell.
   There was a wealthy squire
   Came Mary for to see,
   But she loved her uncle's plow-boy
   On the banks of the Sweet and Dee.

3. A press-gang came to Willie
   When he was all alone.
   He bravely fought for liberty,
   But they were six to one.
   His blood it flowed in torrents.
   "Pray kill me now" said he,
   "For I'd rather die for Mary
   On the banks of the Sweet and Dee."

4. One day while she was walking,
   Lamenting for her love,
   She spied this wealthy squire

Down in her uncle's grove.
He took a step toward her.
"Stand back, young man!" said she,
"For you've banished the only one I love
On the banks of the Sweet and Dee."

5. He threw his arms around her
And strove to set her down.
She spied a sword and pistol
Beneath his morning gown.
She drew the pistol from its belt,
The sword she used so free.
The pistol fired and the squire fell
On the banks of the Sweet and Dee.

6. Her uncle heard the noise
And hastened to the ground,
Saying, "Now you've killed my squire,
I'll give you your death wound."
"Stand back! Stand back!" said Mary,
"Stand back! Stand back!" said she.
The sword she drew and her uncle slew
On the banks of the Sweet and Dee.

7. A doctor was sent for,
A man of note and skill,
And also a lawyer,
That he might write his will.
He willed his gold to Mary
Who fought so manfully.
Then he closed his eyes no more to rise
On the banks of the Sweet and Dee.

4. "A Ship Set Sail for North America"

Sung by Mrs. M. G. Jacobs, Maud Jacobs, and Pearl Jacobs Borusky, September, 1933; cf. Sharp, "The Golden Vanity."

A ship set sail for North A - mer - i - ca And she
went by the name of "The Turk - ish Re - vil - lee", As she
sails a - long the lone-some low-lands low, As she sails a - long the low-land sea.

1. A ship set sail for North America
   And she went by the name of "The Turkish Revillee,"
   As she sails along the lonesome lowlands low,
   As she sails along the lowland sea.
2. "Captain, O, Captain, O, what will you give me
   If I will overtake 'The Golden Willow Tree,'
   If I'll sink her in the lonesome lowlands low,
   If I'll sink her in the lowland sea?"
3. "I have a house and I have land,
   And I have a daughter that will be at your command
   If you'll sink her in the lonesome lowlands low," etc.
4. "I have a little tool just fitted for the use,
   Boring for salt water, letting in the sluice.
   I'll sink her in the lonesome lowlands low," etc.
5. He fell upon his back and away swam he
   Until he overtaken the "Golden Willow Tree,"
   As she sailed along the lonesome lowlands low, etc.
6. Some with their hats and some with their caps,
   Trying to stop the salt water gaps,
   As she sailed along the lonesome lowlands low, etc.
7. He fell upon his back and away swam he
   Until he overtaken "The Turkish Revillee,"
   As she sailed along the lonesome lowlands low, etc.
8. "Captain, O, Captain, take me on board
   And be to me as good as your word,
   For I've sunk her in the lonesome lowlands low," etc.
9. "Neither will I take you on board,
   Or be to you as good as my word,
   Though you've sunk her in the lonesome lowlands," etc.
10. "If it wasn't for the love I have for your men,
    I'd serve you as I served them,
    I'd sink you in the lonesome lowlands low," etc.

7. "As I Was Walking Through the Grove"

Sung by Pearl Jacobs Borusky, July 13, 1938, and by Maud Jacobs and Mrs. M. G. Jacobs, September 6, 1938; cf. Sharp, "The Lonesome Grove." Pearl had some difficulty in remembering this one, and was not at all sure it would be of interest anyway. She referred to it as a "funeral song," and explained that this term meant it was considered suitable for singing at home funerals. Maud, she said, knew all the words, but had never liked hearing the song sung. The next time I saw Maud Jacobs and her mother, I asked them about it, and readily obtained the remaining words. Maud told of someone who had been so undiscriminating as to sing this song at a prayer meeting, with the result that the congregation was considerably shocked.

1. As I was walking in the grove,
   Sat o'er my head a turtledove.
   For her lost mate began to coo,
   Which made me think of my mate too.

2. O, little bird, you're not alone.
   With you I am constrained to mourn.
   I once, like you, did have a mate,
   But now, like you I mourn my fate

3. (?).* But death, grim death did not stop here.
   I had a babe, to me most dear
   [. . . . .]
   My small loss was her great gain.

4. * Consumption seized her lungs severe
   And preyed upon them one long year.
   Then came grim death at the close of day
   And my dear Mary he did slay.

5. (?). * Then ceased my heart to mourn for Jane
   When my dear Mary she was slain
   [. . . . .]

Last:* I have a hope that cheers my breast
      That my dear Mary she's at rest.
      For while her dying tongue could move
      She prayed the Lord for pardoning love.

*Supplied by Maud Jacobs.

10. "I am a Bo's'n by My Trade"

Sung by Pearl Jacobs Borusky, July 13, 1938. Pearl learned this one from George Brooks, also of Kentucky, who brought it and some other songs to Wisconsin on a visit in about 1909.

1. I am a bo's'n by my trade,
   Jack Williams is my name,
   And by a false alluring girl
   Was brought to grief and shame.
2. I took to robbing night and day,
   Not to obtain or gain.
   Everything I got, I valued not,
   But took to her straightway.
3. Then down to Newgate I was brought,
   With iron chains bound down.
   With glittering chains upon my legs
   They longed to see me on.
4. My trial day came round at last,
   And hanged I was to be.
   It grieved my poor old parents so—
   Think of my miseryl
5. I wrote my love a letter then,
   Some comfort to obtain
   [. . . . .]
6. She wrote me back an answer,
   Saying, "Your company I do not like,
   And as you make your bed, young man
   Upon it you must lie."
7. If ever I get out of this
   One solemn vow I'll make:
   I'll quit all evil practices
   For this false woman's sake.
8. The heavens have proved kind to me,
   As you may plainly see.
   I broke my chains, I scaled the wall,
   And gained my liberty.

11. "I Asked That Girl to Marry Me"

Sung by Pearl Jacobs Borusky, July 15, 1938.

1. I asked that girl to marry me,
   She said, "O, no! I'd rather be free."
2. I asked that girl to be my wife;
   She cut at me with an old case knife.
3. I asked that girl to be my bride;
   She sat right down and cried and cried.
4. And the more she cried, the worse I felt
   Till I thought to my soul my heart would melt.

12. "I Once Knew a Little Girl"

Sung by Mrs. M. G. Jacobs, August, 1935; cf. Sharp, "The Rejected Lover" (B, C, E, F, H, I, J). On September 9, 1937, Pearl sang this song again, including verse five, which was not in Mrs. Jacobs' version. On this occasion a friend of mine was present, whom the Jacobses had not known before. The singing was in no way different from what I have heard on other visits. Songs 3, 19, 39, and 56 were sung under the same circumstances.

1. I once knew a little girl, a charming beauty bright,
   And to make her my wife was my own heart's delight.
   O, was my own heart's delight.
2. I took her by the hand and I led her to the door,
   And I held her in my arms while I asked her once more.
3. She looked up in my eyes with scorn and disdain,
   And the answer that she gave me was, "You can't come again."

4. I stayed away six weeks, which caused her much pain.
   Then she wrote me a letter saying, "Do come again."
5. I answered her letter just for to let her know
   That young men oft-times venture where they ort not to go.
6. Come all you young men and warning take by me:
   Never place your affections on a green growing tree.
7. For the leaves they will wither and the roots they will decay,
   And the beauty of a fair girl will soon fade away.

15. "I Will Not Marry a Farmer"

Sung by Maud Jacobs and Pearl Jacobs Borusky, September 6, 1938; cf. Sharp, "Soldier Boy for Me" (A). Professor Leland Coon of the University of Wisconsin has suggested that No. 55, "My Old Hen's a Good Old Hen," may not be of mountain origin since "section men" were probably not people familiar to the mountain folk. In this connection it is interesting that this song of railroaders was unknown to Mrs. Jacobs.

I will not marry a farmer.
He's always working in the dirt.
But I will marry a railroader
That wears a striped shirt.

A railroader, a railroader,
A railroader for me!
If ever I marry in this wide world,
A railroader's wife I'll be.

There are other verses about the disadvantages of gamblers, etc.

18. "I'll Sell My Hat, I'll Sell My Coat"

Sung by Mrs. M. G. Jacobs, September, 1932; cf. Sharp, "Putman's Hill."

1. I'll sell my hat I'll sell my coat To buy my wife a lit-tle flat boat.
2. I'll sell my pants, I'll sell my vest To get enough money to go out west. And

Down the ri - ver we will float. Come bib-ble in the boo-shy - lo - ree.
there I think I can do the best. Come bib-ble in the boo-shy - lo - ree.

Shool, shool, shool - I - rool, Shool - I - rack - a - shack, shool-a bar - be - cue.

When I saw my sal - ly bab - a - yeel, Come bib-ble in the boo - shy - lo - ree.

   1. I'll sell my hat, I'll sell my coat
    To buy my wife a little flat boat.
    Down the river we will float,
    Come bibble in the booshy loree.
 chorus: Shool, shool, shoolirool,
    School-i-rack-a-shack, shoola barbecue.
    When I saw my sally babayeel,
    Come bibble in the booshy loree.
   2. I'll sell my pants, I'll sell my vest,
    To get enough money to go out west.
    And there I think I can do the best.
    Come bibble in the booshy loree.
 repeat chorus

For the other versions see (1) "Bib-a-lollie-boo," Silvertone record No. 25012-B, sung by Chubby Parker, "Old Time Singin' Acc. by Banjo," Sears Roebuck Company. (2) Lincoln campaign song quoted by Luther A. Huston from Library of Congress collection of campaign song books, in *New York Times* magazine section, Sunday, September 27, 1936.

20. "Last Saturday Night I Entered a House"

Sung by Mrs. M. G. Jacobs, September, 1933. Mrs. Jacobs learned this song from
Walter Justice in Kentucky.

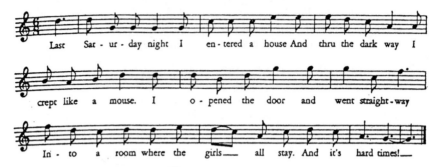

Last Sat - ur - day night I en - tered a house And thru the dark way I
crept like a mouse. I o - pened the door and went straight - way
In - to a room where the girls___ all stay. And it's hard times!___

1. Last Saturday night I entered a house
   And through the dark way I crept like a mouse.
   I opened the door and went straightway
   Into a room where the girls all stay.
   And it's hard times!

2. Such laughing and chatting as we did keep!
   We waked the old widder up out of her sleep,
   And in a few words she did address me,
   "Such an impudent fellow before me I see!"
   And it's hard times!

3. "O, widder, O, widder, you'd better keep cam [calm]
   Until you find out who I am.
   I'm Johnny the Carpenter I go by that name.
   A-courting your daughter, for that purpose I came."
   And it's hard times!

4. "O daughter, O, daughter, O, daughter," said she.
   "To think that my daughter would go before me.
   When I am so old and you are so young.
   You can get sweethearts and I can get none."
   And it's hard times!

5. "O widder, O, widder, O widder at large,
   If you are an old widder you are a great charge.
   O, widder, O, widder, O, widder by name."
   She up with a broomstick and at me she came.
   And it's hard times!

6. Such fighting and scratching! At last I got clear,
   I mounted my horse and for home I did steer,
   The blood running down, my head being sore.
   There stood the old devil with a broom in the door.
   And it's hard times!

7. Come all young men, take warning by me,
   And never a widder's daughter go see.
   For if you do, t'will be your doom.

236

They fight you like Satan and beat you with a broom.
And it's hard times!

21. "My Father Has Often Told Me"

Sung by Pearl Jacobs Borusky, July 13, 1938.

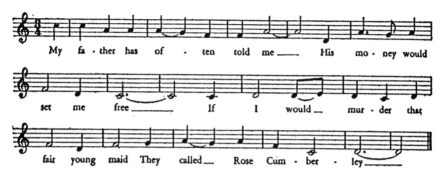

1. My father has often told me
   His money would set me free
   If I would murder that fair young maid
   They called Rose Cumberley.
2. I gave her a bottle of Burgundy wine.
   'Twas not for her to know.
   And there I married that fair young maid
   Down under the banks below.
3. I took out my silver dagger,
   It was my most valuable knife.
   The devil and temptation
   Caused me to take her life.
4. My father sits in his mansion
   With many a tearful sigh,
   Gazing upon the scaffold
   Where his son is condemned to die.

23. "My Father Keeps A Public House"

Sung by Pearl Jacobs Boruskey, July 13, 1938; cf. Sharp, "Edwin in the Lowlands Low." Pearl says that she has heard it sung: "My father keeps a boarding house," but that "public house" is the older version and the one which she heard first. She gives as the title, "Edward Bolds." The E flat was sung a trifle high.

1. My father keeps a public house
   Down by the seaside shore.
   And when you come to stay all night
   He'll meet you at the door.

["Mary's seafaring lover (unapproved by her father) came to stay all night without announcing himself except to Mary"—P.J.B.]

2. "I'll meet you in the morning—
   Don't let you parents know.
   My name it is young Edward Bolds,
   Who plows the lowlands low."

3. Young Mary she lay sleeping.
   She dreamed a frightful dream.
   She dreamed she saw her true-love's blood
   Come flowing in a stream.

4. Then she arose, put on her clothes
   Just at the break of day,
   Saying, "Father where is that young man
   Came here last night to stay?"

5. "His body sleeps within the deep—
   Just where I do not know.
   I sent his body bleeding
   Into the lowlands low."

6. "O, father, cruel father,
   You shall die a public show
   For the murder of young Edward Bolds,
   Who plowed the lowlands low."

29. "O, Mary Dear, Go Ask Your Mother"

Sung by Pearl Jacobs Borusky, July 13, 1938; cf. Sharp, "Awake, Awake," Mrs.
Jacobs says that the verses marked 3 and 4 should come first.

1. "O, Mary dear, go ask your mother
   If you my wedded wife may be.
   And if she says no, come back and tell me
   And it's the last I'll trouble thee."
2. "O, no, I cannot ask my mother,
   For she lies on her bed of rest,
   And in her hands she holds a letter
   That has caused me most of my distress."
3. "O, Mary dear, go ask your father
   If you my wedded wife may be,
   And if he says no, come back and tell me,
   And it's the last time that I'll trouble thee."
4. "O, no, I cannot ask my father
   For he lies on his bed of rest
   And in his hand he holds a dagger
   To kill the one that I love best."

32. "Once I Courted A Charming Beauty Bright"

Sung by Mrs. M. G. Jacobs, September, 1933; cf. Sharp, "The Lover's Lament"
(G. H). Mrs. Jacobs learned this song from Joshua Jacobs in about 1880.

1. Once I courted a charming beauty bright.
   I courted her by day and I courted her by night.
   I courted her for love, and love I did obtain,
   And I'm sure she had no right to complain.
2. She had cruel parents I came for to know
   To gather their daughter and 'way we would go.
   But they put her in confinement and locked her up secure
   And I never, no, never, got sight of my dear.
3. First to the window I thought I would go
   To see if she had forgotten me or no.
   But when she saw me coming she wrung her hands and cried,
   "I never would forget you until the day I died."
4. Then to the war I thought I would go
   To see if I could forget her or no.
   But when I got there, the army shining bright,
   I bore all my troubles to my own heart's delight.
5. Then seven long years I spent in Mexico.
   Then back home I thought I would go.
   But her mother saw me coming and ran to me and cried,
   "My daughter loved you dearly, and for your sake she died."
6. Then I was struck like a man that was slain.
   The tears from my eyes fell like showers of rain.
   Saying, "O, o, this grief I cannot bear.
   My darling's in her silent grave, and soon I shall be there."

34. "One Morning, One Morning, One Morning In Spring"

Sung by Mrs. M. G. Jacobs, July 13, 1938; cf. Sharp, "I'm Going to Get Married Sunday."

One morn - ing, one morn - ing, one morn - ing in spring I
heard a fair dam - sel so gal - lant - ly sing As she sat un - der her
kal - la - ma - king, "Please God, I'll be mar - ried next Sun - day!"

1. One morning, one morning, one morning in spring,
   I heard a fair damsel so gallantly sing
   As she sat under her ka-la-ma-king,
   "Please God, I'll be married next Sunday!"
2. "Fourteen years old is too young to get married.
   A girl of your age is apt to get sorry.

For seven long years I'd have you tarry.
Put off your wedding next Sunday!"
3. "Old man, old man, you talk on a cheap scale.
That's seven long years against my will.
My mind is to marry and I mean to fulfill.
I wish that tomorrow was Sunday.
4. "My shawl and my gown lies under the press.
My love will be here before I can dress
With a bunch of blue ribbons tied around my waist
To make me look neat next Sunday.
5. "Saturday night will be all my care
To feeble (?) my locks and to curl my hair,
And two little maidens to wait on me there
To dress me up neat next Sunday.
6. "Saturday night to dance all around
With a bunch of blue ribbons and new fashioned gown,
Invite all the ladies from Barbersville town
To be at my wedding next Sunday."

42. "Tomorrow Morn I'm Sweet Sixteen"

Sung by Pearl Jacobs Borusky, July 13, 1938; cf. Sharp, "Billy Grimes." The title used by Sharp is also used by the Jacobses. The range of two octaves in this song is noteworthy, as is the horn-like refrain. Both words and melody are very sophisticated for a folksong.

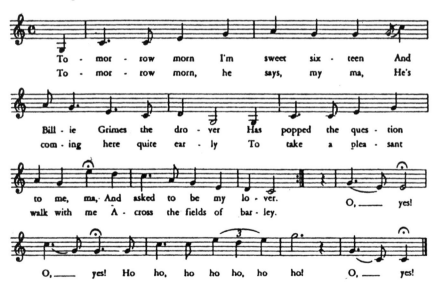

1. "Tomorrow morn I'm sweet sixteen
   And Billie Grimes the drover
   Has popped the question to me, ma,
   And asked to be my lover.
   Tomorrow morn, he says, my ma,
   He's coming here quite early
   To take a pleasant walk with me
   Across the fields of barley."
refrain: O, yes! O, yes!
   Ho ho, ho ho ho, ho ho!
   O, yes!

2. "Now hold your tongue, my daughter dear,
   There is no use in talking!
   You shall not go across the fields
   With Billie Grimes a-walking.
   To think of his presumption, too,
   That dirty, ugly drover!
   I wonder where your pride has gone,
   To think of such a lover!"
   O, no, etc.

3. "Old Grimes is dead, you know, my ma,
   And Billie is so lonely.
   Beside they say, to Grimes' estate
   That Billy is the only
   Surviving heir to all that's left,
   And that, they say, is nearly
   A cool ten-thousand dollars, ma,
   About six hundred yearly."
   O, yes, etc.

4. "My daughter dear, I did not hear
   Your last remark quite clearly.
   Though Billy is a clever lad
   No doubt he loves you dearly.
   Remember then, tomorrow morn
   To be up bright and early,
   To take a pleasant walk with him
   Across the fields of barley."
   O, yes, etc.

47. "Young Johnny He Has Landed"

Sung by Pearl Jacobs Borusky, September 9, 1937; cf. Sharp, "The Green Bed."

1. Young Johnny he has landed,
   He's lately come ashore.
   He's come to the place
   Where he's often been before.
   "O, what's the news, Young Johnny?"
   "O, very bad," said he.
   "I've lost my ship and cargo
   Upon the raging sea."

2. "Go bring you daughter Polly
   And set her down by me.
   We'll drown all melancholy
   And married we will be."
   "My daughter Polly's absent
   And won't be home today,
   And if she were here
   She would not let you stay."

3. He looked upon the young
   And he looked upon the old
   And out in each hand
   He drew a purse of gold.
   . . . .

4. Pretty Polly upstairs,
   Hearing all of this,
   Came tripping down with
   With a sweet smiling face,
   Saying, "Welcome home, Young Johnny,"
   Welcome home from sea!
   My green beds are empty
   And waiting for thee."

5. "Before I'd lay in your beds
    I would lay out in the street,
    For when I had no money
    My lodgings was to seek.
    And now I'll go to the grocery
    And make the dollars whirl,
    Buy a bottle of good brandy
    And chat some pretty girl."

48. "Well Met, Well Met, My Old True Love"

Sung by Mrs. M. G. Jacobs, September, 1933, and again, September 6, 1938; cf.
Sharp, "The Dæmon Lover." Mrs. Jacobs learned this song from her mother.

"Well met, well met, my old true love. Well met, well met," said
he. "I have just re-turned from the salt, salt sea; and 'twas
all for the sake of thee, and 'twas all for the sake of thee.

1. "Well met, well met, my old true love.
    Well met, well met," said he.
    "I have just returned from the salt, salt sea;
    And 'twas all for the sake of thee.
2. "I once could have married a king's daughter fair,
    And she would have married me.
    But I refused that rich crown of gold,
    And it's all for the sake of thee."
3. "If you could have married a king's daughter fair
    I'm sure you're much to blame,
    For I am married to a house carpenter,
    And I think he's a fine young man."
4. "If you'll forsake your house carpenter
    And go along with me,
    I will take you to where the grass grows green
    On the banks of the Sweet Liberty."
5. "If I forsake my house carpenter
    And go along with thee,
    What have you got for my support,
    And to keep me from slavery?"
6. "I have six ships sailing on the sea,
    The seventh one at land,

>   And if you'll come and go with me
>   They shall be at your command."

7. She took her babe into her arms
   And gave it kisses three,
   Saying, "Stay at home, my pretty little babe
   For to keep your father company."

8. She dressed herself in rich array
   To exceed all others in the town,
   And as she walked the streets around
   She shone like a glittering crown.

9. They had not been on board more than two weeks,
   I'm sure it was not three,
   Until she began to weep
   And she wept most bitterly.

10. "Are you weeping for your houses and your land,
    Or are you weeping for your store,
    Or are you weeping for your house carpenter
    You never shall see any more?"

11. "I'm not weeping for my houses nor my land,
    Nor I'm not weeping for my store,
    But I'm weeping for my pretty little babe
    I never shall see any more."

12. They had not been on board more than three weeks,
    It was not four I'm sure,
    Until at length the ship sprung a leak,
    And she sank to arise no more.

13. "A curse, a curse to all sea men!
    A curse to a sailor's life!
    For they have robbed me of my house carpenter
    And taken away my life."

Dance and Game Songs

50. "Goin' Up Cripple Creek"

Sung by Mrs. M. G. Jacobs, September, 1932; cf. Sharp, "Cripple Creek," "Gone to Cripple Creek."

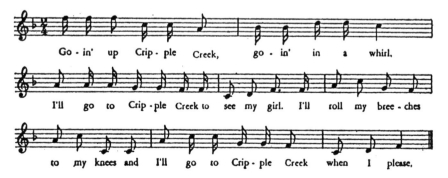

Go-in' up Crip-ple Creek, go-in' in a whirl.
I'll go to Crip-ple Creek to see my girl. I'll roll my bree-ches
to my knees and I'll go to Crip-ple Creek when I please.

1. Goin' up Cripple Creek, goin' in a whirl,
   I'll go to Cripple Creek to see my girl.
   I'll roll my breeches to my knees
   And I'll go to Cripple Creek when I please.
2. Goin' up Cripple Creek, goin' in a run,
   Goin' up Cripple Creek to see my fun!

51. *"King William Was King James's Son"*

Sung by Mrs. M. G. Jacobs, September, 1933; cf. Sharp, "Charlie's Sweet" (D). Mrs. Jacobs described the opposition of her people's sect, The Christian Church, to dancing, and told of this song being used as a substitute at parties. Her mother had been present at such a party when a young couple who had been forbidden to marry were the ones to kneel on the carpet. "You could just see the love in their eyes," she had said. "But it wasn't no use, for her father married her to a nigger-holder" [i.e. a slave owner].

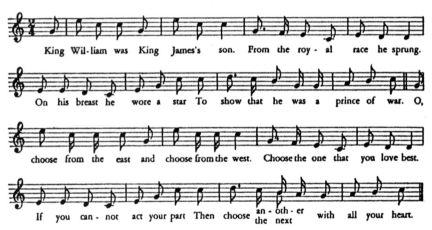

1. King William was King James's son.
   From the royal race he sprang.
   On his breast he wore a star
   To show he was a prince of war.
   refrain: O, choose from the east and choose from the west.
   Choose the one that you love best.
   If you cannot act your part
   Then choose another with all your heart.
2. Down on this carpet you shall kneel
   Sure as the grass grows in the field
   Look at your bride and kiss her sweet
   Rising upon your feet.

53. "Sally In The Garden"

Sung by Mrs. M. G. Jacobs, July 13, 1938; cf. Sharp, "Hog-eyed Man." When I asked Mrs. Jacobs whether she knew "Hog-eyed Man," she fairly rocked with amusement. She hadn't thought of it for years. Nevertheless, she recalled both words and tune instantly. She had never seen the dancing for which the music was intended, for, she said, "You know, I've never been to a dance in my life." Her uncle was a fiddler and used to play and sing this song. The whistling was not an essential part of the performance, but merely a way of communicating to me the wordless part of the tune. I suggested Sharp's words "What are you going to do with your Hogeye," etc. but she said that they were unfamiliar to her. There is a rural community in Arkansas named Hogeye.

Sally in the garden, sifting, sifting,
Sally in the garden, sifting sand.
Sally in the garden, sifting, sifting,
Sue's upstairs with the Hog-eyed man.

Songs for Children

54. "As I Came Over Yonder's Hill"

Sung by Pearl Jacobs Borusky, July 13, 1938. Madison Green Jacobs used to sing a good deal in his youth and middle age. When the youngest son, Paul, was a baby, this was his favorite lullaby. He would often ask his father to "Sing Turkey." When I knew Mr. Jacobs he was already an old man, very hard of hearing, and unable to sing any more.

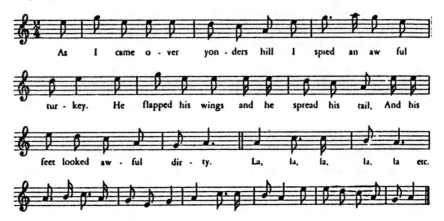

As I came over yonder's hill
I spied an awful turkey.
He flapped his wings and he spread his tail,
And his feet looked awful dirty.
La, la, la, la, la, etc.

55. "My Old Hen's a Good Old Hen"

Sung by Pearl Jacobs Borusky, July 13, 1938. This was another of Madison Green Jacobs' songs. See the note to No. 54 and 15.

My old hen's a good old hen.
She lays eggs for the section men.
Sometimes one, sometimes two,
Sometimes enough for the old damn crew.
Cluck, old hen! Cluck, I tell you!
Cluck, old hen, or I'm a-goin' to sell you.
Cluck, old hen! Cluck, I say!
Cluck, old hen, or I'll give you away.

56. "What Will I Do with the Baby-Oh?"

Sung by Pearl Jacobs Borusky, September 9, 1937; cf. Sharp, "What'll We Do with the Baby." This song had been sung on a previous visit, but was not recorded until the date given. See note to No. 12.

1. What will I do with the baby-oh?
   What will I do with the baby-oh?
   What will I do with the baby-oh?
   When I go down to Jellicoe?
2. Wrap him up in calico
   And take him to his daddy-oh!

23

"The Light Fantastic" in the Central West: Country Dances of Many Nationalities in Wisconsin

Wardon Alan Curtis

Born and raised in Madison, Wardon Alan Curtis received a degree in classics from the University of Wisconsin in 1889, pursued a career in journalism, and eventually settled in Ashland, New Hampshire. Were Curtis writing today, he might be slinging cheeky pseudo-intellectual prose for *Rolling Stone* or, perhaps, forsaking print altogether to foam at the mouth on talk radio or MTV. His account of Wisconsin's dance-hall pluralism, published in a popular national magazine, is pioneering in its focus on the state's non-Anglo European cultures; yet it is chillingly representative of his era's racist anthropological thought, its fascination with environmental determinism, and its faith in assimilation to a purportedly superior Yankee mainstream.

In the late nineteenth century, inspired by Charles Darwin's theories of natural selection, Anglo-American social scientists posited cultural theories espousing that peoples and societies evolved from simple to complex forms. They argued that northern Europeans, challenged by a cold climate, had achieved the height of civilization. Therefore Nordic or Aryan peoples—prominently represented in America by Anglo-Saxons—were, in their estimation, clearly superior. That White Anglo-Saxon Protestant (WASP) supremacy was championed by a Madison Yankee during an era of mass immigration by southern Europeans and Slavs, by Catholics and Jews, is hardly a coincidence.

During the early decades of the twentieth century, for example, prominent Madison intellectuals and civic organizations touted racist evolutionism in the name of progressive politics. Edward A. Ross, a sociologist who joined the University of Wisconsin faculty in 1907, authored *The Old World in the New* (New York: The Century Company, 1914). Maligning Italians as mentally and morally deficient, branding Jews as having "little feeling for the particular," and fretting most about "The Alarming Prospect of Slavic Immigration," Ross's work has been aptly characterized as "a scholarly counterpart to the Ku Klux Klan" (see Harold J. Abrahamson, "Assimilation and Pluralism," in the *Harvard Encyclopedia of American Ethnic Groups,* ed. Stephan Thernstrom [Cambridge, Mass.: Harvard University Press, 1980], 154). Indeed Ross's xenophobia coincided with considerable Ku Klux Klan activity in Wisconsin, particularly with the onset of prohibition and jingoism following World War I. The Klan in Madison worked in coalition with several University of Wisconsin fraternities, the Young Men's Christian Association, and prominent religious and political leaders. United in their notion that "Americanization" meant conformity to Anglo-Prostestantism, they contrived in particular to "clean up" the "Greenbush" neighborhood which, "along with Italians of Sicilian origin . . . was the home of most of Madison's Jews and a high proportion of its small African American population" (Timothy Messer-Kruse, "The Campus Klan of the University of Wisconsin: Tacit and Active Support for the Ku Klux Klan in a Culture of Intolerance," *Wisconsin Magazine of History* 77:1 (1993): 3–38).

Wardon Alan Curtis was but one of many for whom Wisconsin's population harbored potential cultural dangers which, if left unchecked, might mongrelize and debase the American populace. Not only was the state home to various supposedly inferior Indian peoples, but its population swelled with the "lowest" Europeans: Celts, Slavs, and Finns (who were, so went the logic, not true Scandinavians because their language and customs were not "Teutonic"). Moreover, even some of Wisconsin's abundant Germans were southern Germans—deficient, as Curtis put it, "mentally and morally" to northern Germans.

Beyond simple repression—through, for example, Wisconsin Yankee legislators' attempts to outlaw the customs and language of non-Anglo Europeans—the state and nation's concerned WASPs saw two evolutionary solutions to what they perceived as Wisconsin's cultural problem. First, the healthy environment of America's Midwest might, within a generation or two, confer mystical benefits. And second, the proximity of the "foreigners" to upstanding Yankees might instill, to quote Curtis, "the Americanism of Massachusetts [characterized by] the genius of the New England founders of these commonwealths."

Hence Curtis's preoccupation with changes in the ethnic "stock" of succeeding generations; hence also his "ethnological" salvage mission to set down some record of ethnic dance traditions before they succumbed to inevitable oblivion. Of course the theories held by Curtis and his contemporaries (and by too many even today) were dead wrong. Despite the failure of his ideology, Wardon Alan Curtis succeeded in offering worthwhile details on instrumentation, dance repertoire, and customary practices that live on in Wisconsin's contemporary ethnic festival and polka scenes.

Reprinted from *Century* 73 (1907): 570–79.

My very first country dance and my first and last Irish dance, was at the age of eighteen, when, as a college freshman, I was resting from the not too arduous labors of a plain curriculum of the then usual Latin and Greek. One Adolf Baumgartner, having announced a dance, and a raffle for a silver watch, in an old, uninhabited house, I determined to go. Stealing away from my friends, who would not think of taking part in the bucolic Terpsichorean revels of the countryside, I yielded up my quarter and entered the ill-lighted, bare old house. A violin and an accordion were scraping and wheezing away in the corner and a silent mob of young people, with serious and even strained faces, were pounding painfully through a waltz, accenting the first beat of each bar with an extra hard thump of the hard thumps they were dealing the floor. Seeing a small girl of a pleasing rotundity of person in a jersey of an atrocious red and a skirt of an atrocious blue—sitting alone in a corner, I solicited the honor of a dance. Rising with alacrity, she seized me in a tight clutch, and we, too, went whack, whack, whack, whack, whack, whack, for some minutes until a couple, taking in the fact that a stranger was present, stopped, the girl giggling and the boy glowering.

Presently there were several couples giggling and glowering, and my lady broke from me and rushed to a seat, where she hid as much of her face as she could in a very small handkerchief. While I stood lingering near, to comfort and protect her, if need be, a tall young Firbolgian, whose name was appositely Bolger, caromed violently into me, hurled by someone across the room, casting me into a chair, where three more Firbolgians, Gadhaels, or whatever branch of the Celts of Erin they might be, immediately sat superimposed upon my lap, jovially conversing about some person foreign to their social order and an ass, whom I knew to be myself. I could have fought, and entertained the idea. Now some of my ancestors came from Ireland and another lone one from Wales, all before the Revolution, and there is reason to believe that yet others were Highlanders and adherents of the Pretender, for a Scotch name and a devotion to Jacobite songs are not otherwise easily accounted for. So I am not biased when I say that the most numerous branch of the Celtic race, the Irish, does not always fight fair. It is a gallant and brilliant people, handsome and lovable, but I will admit for it that it has faults, and one of its bad and undeniable faults is its habit of fighting any way to win; and though it will not refuse to fight one against three, it will also fight three against one. The three in my lap would all have set upon me had I made a demonstration. I would have been pounded to within an inch of my life; and I had on my good clothes, too, which is ever a hostage of peace. So I smiled, inwardly cursing, dissembled, and, at the first chance, escaped. It was an Irish dance, even though given by Adolf Baumgartner. I have since then eschewed the dances of the Irish, and even those of the Welsh and the Cornishmen, who are scarcely less pugnacious than their kindred across St. George's Channel. I eschewed them not merely because of this experience, but because of the fights which always go on at them; for while the Celts merrily fall upon a stranger, with an inarticulate prayer of thanksgiving to the infernal gods who have provided him, in the dearth of other quarry they will crack one another's skulls. The Kymry are a handsome people to begin with, and there is arsenic in the wells of Wisconsin's lead region, and so the girls of our Welsh-Cornish counties are not only lovely of face, but of brilliant complexions and superb liquid eyes. Would that I might have dances with those Welsh and Irish girls to look back upon, but the cantankerous Celtic men, loaded with usquebaugh and crwrw dha—[whiskey].

I am speaking of Wisconsin, because it happens to be the State where I have pursued my ethnological studies, and because it epitomizes the central West. No other Western State has such a diversity of racial elements. Illinois alone, with its queer colony of Portuguese Protestants at Jacksonville, has an element which Wisconsin has not. None but Wisconsin has Bulgarians and Flemings. It has an Indian population of over eight thousand. It is the greatest Welsh, Cornish, Norwegian, and German State. It has Icelanders with Minnesota; Bohemians with Iowa; and French, Finns, and Hollanders with Michigan. The oldest and only purely Hungarian colony in America is on its soil, and the largest colony of Swiss. It has a native white element as old as the Knickerbockers, and even English-descended families who go back one hundred and fifty years on Wisconsin soil.

Though you may not venture imprudently into a Celtic dance, you may go with impunity where the races are mingled, for a Celt will never hit you so long as a pure Teuton is within reach of his fists. Not so long as there is a German or a Norwegian about will even the most drunken Irishman touch a Yankee. Here is instinct, that ever transcends reason, which at its best is only an artificial and factitious makeshift for instinct—here is instinct declaring the Sassenach next of kin to the Celt. First of all the Celt hits the German; then the Norse, with whom he has some mental traits and even blood in common; then the Sassenach, his half-brother; and finally the Celt: for he must hit somebody.

Let me pause to answer a query that rises in the reader's mind. He has gained the impression that our country dances in the central West are as much occasions of combat as social diversion. There is a good deal of truth in this inference from what I have said: The social entertainment where men do not fight is the last flower of the best of modern civilization. In bucolic communities primitive instincts still rule. In the days of chivalry, all great social gatherings were at once social gatherings and occasions of combat. The tourneys had the element of woman and the element of combat. The noble knights composed madrigals, sang roundelays to the ladies, and cracked one another's heads. In the very lowest estate of savagery, where the man cares not for gold or dominion, he will still fight for woman. The country dance with its usual fight is the legitimate descendant of the old tourney, and the harvest dance at old man Birrenkott's tavern as near an approach to the Field of the Cloth of Gold in essence as we can expect to find in these degenerate days. The country dance that does not count two or three fights is the exception. The sight of woman arouses the immemorial instinct to fight, and emulation, and the desire for renown in her eyes. The excitement of the crowd, the music, and the strong drink add circumstance to instinct.

German dances are like other German things. With all their simple virtues, the German peasantry have few romantic or picturesque qualities. At the German dances, at about the third waltz, you look with suspicion and gathering loathing at the straw-color-haired, round-faced, innocent-eyed girl who, with a curious appoggiatura-like click before each step of the waltz bar, a brief fourth step, an enclitic tap, characteristic of Germans and of no other race, is revolving with you. You smell onions. You lay it to her. You get your nose as far as possible from that glistening straw-colored hair—German straw-colored hair glistens, Norse does not—combed with such painful care, as far as possible from that little, appealing mouth parted in the serious exertion of the dance. But as you pass the stairway, you perceive that it is not the round, good little person you are dancing with who is responsible for the odor of onions. When you think of it, you realize that one small rosebud mouth could not be responsible for all that mighty and "robustious" odor. It floats up the stairway from the banquet-room. It emanates from the viands that constitute "refreshments," a delicate refection of unmentionable sausages, unutterable cheeses, strange pickles, and unholy oniony things of manifold sorts. At the German dances, father, mother, and the more important children attend. The parents sit stolid, the women ever with arms folded, unsmiling, unwinking, while the children make themselves noticeable and notorious. When a couple stops dancing, if they remain on the floor, the man's arm remains about the girl and hers still rests on his shoulder. But if he seats her, he does not sit at her and converse. If he does that, he will set the whole bench of girls giggling. You could walk around the room with your arm about a girl and not embarrass her in the least, but to pay her the unaccustomed attention of talking with her, to show that you believe she has other functions in the world besides being your partner in the dance, working in the field, cooking queer comestibles, with sugar in the beef gravy and salt in cake frosting, embarrasses her and starts her nervous giggles.

Of these Germans, some are dark-haired, olive-cheeked, and some are palest blondes. Some are short and active; some are large, loutish, loosely knit, awkward, their forms and faces alike of an unfinished appearance. You seldom see this unfinished appearance among the Scandinavian- and British-descended people. There are loutish Yankees, Irish, and Norse, but they do not have that curious effect of having been suddenly left by some modeler that is frequent among the Germans.

The lines of the shoulder are poor, the backbone is straight. A lot of these fellows, if they dropped to their hands and knees, would have the straight backbone of an ox. I will not go into the convincing reasons which the late General Francis A. Walker gave to prove his statement that the Swiss, Dutch, Scandinavian, and British peasantry were finer breeds than the peasantry of the rest of Europe. Few of these Germans of the first and second generation are graceful or handsome. Some of the dark South Germans are both, but the North Germans, while superior to the Southerners mentally and morally, are not so personable.

Of all our old immigrant stocks, the German in the raw is the least personable. Nor is he, superstition to the contrary notwithstanding, so big a man as the Yankee or the Irishman. Civil War enlistment statistics proved that our native stock averaged bigger men than any other element. Comparative measurements of Eastern and Western colleges give the effete East the advantage, due, I believe, to the large percentage of Europeans in the Western institutions, inferior in height to the British nationalities. While there are many large and stalwart Germans—probably as many as there are large and stalwart Irish and Yankees—little, short, squatty men are as common among them as they are rare among Norse and Anglo-Celts. Whatever has happened to England in the last forty years, the city-bred German is a smaller man than can be found in any other North European stock in this country. It would seem that the city-bred Englishman to-day is even smaller; but the Yankees did not come from that element, and for two centuries they have lived where there were air and food in abundance. With the third generation the Germans show a change. You can go into an old German town like Watertown, Wisconsin, where the third generation is now to the fore, and actually exclaim at the number of pretty girls you see: the pleasing result of three generations of American life upon the original uncomely material. Faces and forms of men and women have been refined. It is a new race mentally and physically. They are slimmer, cleaner-limbed, much taller. Their backs have a curve un-known to their grandparents, their eyes have a sparkle that never lighted the eyes of that poor peasantry which, until the tramp of the armies of Napoleonic France shook its fetters free, could not leave the soil upon which it was born.

The music at the German country dances is execrable stuff. I maintain the heresy that a German cannot write a good waltz. Physically incapable of translating sinuous, languorous, voluptuous waltz music into other than stiff, jerky, hoppety motion, he cannot in the first place originate music of that sort. His members were not designed to give physical expression to gliding, flowing, melting music; he cannot write it, and his waltzes are all tum, tum, tum, each beat distinct. Germans can beat the world on galops and gavottes, but not on waltzes. The great waltz-writers are Austrians or Slavs, and you never hear any of their music at a German country dance. The waltzes are the work of Berliners, pump-handle things, the same phrase repeated over and over again. They are never lively, nor do they ever have that haunting melancholy characteristic of the perfect waltz, nor that swooning flow where the notes and bars melt liquidly together. There is, indeed, a funny little grouchiness that takes the place of melancholy, a genuine German irritability. This is the music they serve you at a German rural dance. Be they Pommers, Beyers, Badeners, or what not, it is the same music.

In the towns, of course, the music is better. Germans make most of our music in America, and make it far better than British-descended people ever could. The larger orchestras always include many Bohemians, and the Germans tend to be Austrian Germans, who write and play more fiery music than the Germans of Wilhelm's realm. Here is hoping that the domains of the Hapsburgs will never be united with the domains of the Hohenzollerns!

There is far more drinking at German dances than at Irish dances, while at Norse dances there is seldom any at all. But while a drunken Irishman or a drunken Norseman is likely to be even murderous, a drunken German does not usually make much trouble. Beware of the races that drink the burning usquebaugh! But beer is an unwarlike fluid, which lulls the passions of strife to sleep, rather than excites them. It lies too cold in the stomach. Perchance it rises to the head in a fog of vapor that anon descend as maudlin tears; but slumbering wrath and the love of battle it causes to slumber yet the sounder.

You will see more national traits and more interesting ones at a Swiss dance than at a dance of any other nationality, for the Swiss have preserved both their nationality and their customs better than any other race in the West. Until recently they have had very little social intercourse, and intermarried almost not at all with other nationalities. In the case of all other nationalities in the third generation, social relations are very free, and that, of course, means intermarriage and the building of a race which will have no hyphen before "American." Two things are about all that retard amalgamation now—the churches and the fact that nationalities are usually settled in solid bodies both in town and country. But on the border-lines of a row of German townships, meeting rows of Yankee, Irish, and Norse townships, the young people mingle socially. The first intermarriages are of foreigners with Yankees. All inter-marry with Yankees, and have done so for a long time, but the intermarriage of Irish and Germans has only lately begun, and the intermarriage of the two great kindred Teutonic stocks, Germans and Norse, does not take place at all as yet.

At New Glarus, Wisconsin, you find the capital of the largest Swiss colony in the country, which, though it has been somewhat Americanized where its expanding borders impinge upon surrounding Yankees, Norse, and French, in the mother village still remains a bit of Switzerland. The romantic history of this colony and its present aspect, richest of agricultural communities in America, its economic importance in Wisconsin and northern Illinois, founding as it did, the greatest industry of that region, is something which deserves a monograph. He who runs may read, but he who dances cannot write a monograph, and must speak merely of the good Switzers as we behold them at their Kilbi ball.

The Swiss have many dances, but that of Kilbi Monday is the greatest. Kilbi is a Swiss dialectal corruption of Kirch-weihe, or church-hallowing, and is a holiday season observed throughout the Protestant part of German Switzerland, and even in the extreme south of Germany itself. It is in a measure like our Thanksgiving, which is a religious and secular holiday. The last Sunday in September is always Kilbi Sunday. A commemoration sermon is preached in the morning, each family feasts at noon, and then all wait until Monday for the purely secular celebration that would be out of place on Sunday. Just as few towns have a formal celebration of Fourth of

July every year, so Kilbi sometimes goes off with games, processions, and speeches, and sometimes with no other observance than the balls—two or three balls, in fact. The balls are managed for pecuniary profit, and the managers, in order to draw a crowd, provide transportation for all the girls within a radius of several miles. The management which secures the most and the prettiest girls also secures the greatest number of paid admissions from the men. At a Swiss ball it is the correct thing for a man to wear his hat. The Norse, French, and Yankees, who together make up perhaps a fourth of the male dancers, do not follow the custom; but the Switzers speed around in tall, funeral felt hats, the crowns truncated cones, the brims wide and flapping. This hat-wearing has some historical reason in the canton of Glarus, though I could never learn what. In fact, the tenacity with which these Glarners hold to the old cantonal customs is almost equaled by the absence of any knowledge of their origin.

There are many small men among these Swiss. There are also many tall ones, though I fancy the tall ones appear taller by contrast. The French and the Swiss of this region are much alike in appearance, and have many of the same traits. The French are the only people the Swiss cannot buy out. Both are spreading, and the Swiss girls are pretty. They are rustic, but dress with fairly good taste, though the ethnologists say that Alpine people are dowdy. Well, the Swiss girls look well at their parties, anyway. And you may talk to them, though their men do not. The Yankees and the Norse, who come without girls of their own race, talk to the Swiss girls between dances, while the Swiss men retire to the bar-room and pour things into themselves.

Some of these girls are well off. The father of that strapping big girl at the end of the bench is worth eight hundred thousand. That girl I just danced with is the daughter of a half-millionaire. There are twenty more families represented here which range from one hundred thousand up, and all are farmers. But I must note this drawback: Old O has eight hundred thousand dollars, but he has eight daughters and three sons. There is that snapping-eyed, black-haired white skinned T- girl (how the French name got to Glarus, I do not know), the nicest-looking girl in the hall. She would be good-looking in any assemblage, and old T— has one hundred thousand; but he has other treasures as well, and Louise has nine brothers and sisters, and ten goes into one hundred only ten times.

The ball begins at half-past seven, and they are all there at the last dance, which ends at half-past five in the morning. Ten hours of dancing, and such dancing! At intervals the male dancers retire to refresh themselves with intoxicants, but do not give over dancing, keeping an even keel, all awash though they may be. Very curiously, the orchestra is made up of Yankees from Orfordville. The closing bars of each schottische measure (they still polka and schottische in the country) are accompanied by a mighty rataplan of the ample feet of the whole multitude, cheerful, hilarious, exultant, deafening. The Anglo-Saxon musicians play with a verve, dash, fire, that you did not remark up in the townships of the reflective Germans. The music may be ordinary coon-songs of the day, but it is played with an exultant elation, with almost wildness, which, whether it goes from the impetuous musicians to the dancers, or comes from the rushing dancers to the musicians, I cannot tell. At any rate, if you wish to see the old choragic madness as you will see it at no other contemporary occasion, go to a Kilbi ball.

A Norse dance differs so little from a Yankee dance that it is hard to find points of comparison. The Norwegian girls of the present generation and of the better class are very good-looking. They are by no means all blondes. Dark hair, with a glint of gold of the reddish tint of a beam of sinking sun against an eastern hill, is to be found among them. They have fine complexions, with a lovely blending of pink and cream. The beauty of the Norse woman is less likely to be in feature and eyes, as in the case of the Irish and the Welsh, than in her coloring. An amiable, healthy, finely colored face, evidence of good temper lovely in the sight of the ordinary human being. You will not see the handsome Norse girls in the larger towns. There the large number of somewhat bovine girls who come in from the rural districts to enter domestic service lowers the average of Norse good looks and causes an erroneous idea of it to prevail. But if you will go into the Norse villages, neat pretty, bright, the blight of the saloon usually absent, where the old Norse democracy prevails and the young people are all equal socially, where all have received a good education in an English-speaking school, there you will find as good-looking a lot of young people as you can find anywhere.

At a Norse dance the drinking of the German and the Irish dance is absent. Not that Norse do not drink. Their whole history reeks with drink. They were the most terrible fighters and terrible drinkers of antiquity; but in this country Prohibition claims many of them. The moderation of the Germans is impossible to them. When they do drink, they drink to the point of stupor. In their cups they are almost as pugnacious as the Irish, and even more savage. They drink what no other people except Russians drink—pure alcohol. This is not sporadic, but common. And so, knowing that they are prone to excess, they go to the other extreme of shunning liquor entirely.

How the French comport themselves at their balls at Belleville I know not. I have been bidden, but something has always prevented. And I have never seen the Magyars dancing czardas—if they do—at Count Anthony-Haraszthy's old settlement at Prairie du Sac, where the Wisconsin bends westward through its crenelated rampart of towering hills. I have narrowly escaped a Polish dance on the banks of the Fox, and the Indians have dances—not ghost-dances, but regular dances-at Keshena, Lac du Flambeau, and the Apostle Islands, all in Hiawatha's country. The Bohemians of Kewaunee and the Flemings of Green Bay dance, and there are lots of other places where I might study ethnology at country dances but I fear I never shall again. In another generation, if not sooner, it will all be American. With the cessation of immigration to Wisconsin, the link with the Old World has been broken. The old tongues are heard no more. English is fast becoming the language of the churches, last stronghold of foreignism. The paper published in a foreign tongue will soon be a curiousity. The body of the central West will be of all races, but the spirit is and will remain the Americanism of Massachusetts, of fifty years ago. The genius of the New England founders of these commonwealths is still the over-soul of the central West.

24

Hoppwaltzes and Homebrew: Traditional Norwegian American Music from Wisconsin

Philip Martin

"Old-time music." Throughout much of America that phrase is most commonly associated with fiddlers playing the jigs and reels once prevalent at dances in rural New England, amidst the southern Appalachians, and on western ranches. In the Upper Midwest, however, "old-time music" has usually meant polkas, waltzes, and schottisches—and the phrase is a direct translation of the Norwegian *gammaldans*.

In 1926, Henry Ford, fearing the musical influences of African Americans and "foreigners," sponsored a series of "Old-Time Fiddlers' Contests" as quintessentially "American" activities. The cranky industrialist hoped the contests would offer a "wholesome" alternative to what he regarded as the degenerate effects of jazz, thereby bending the musical tastes of Americans in an Anglo-Celtic direction. In some areas of the Upper Midwest, however, contestants for Ford's prizes were almost entirely Norwegian. In Fergus Falls, Minnesota, the top three performers were Norwegians, while the St. Cloud paper proclaimed, "Norwegian Dance Tunes to Be One Feature of Old Time Fiddling Bee." In Albert Lea, Minnesota, enthusiastic applause greeted Botolf Bridley's floral celebration of two Norwegian districts: "Lily of Sogn" and "Lily of Valders." Fiddle Ole was a favorite in Eau Claire, Wisconsin, while the Madison contest was dominated by such Norwegians as Barneveld's E. Pederson, Brooklyn's Ben Gulhaug, Hollandale's Olaf Larson, and Madison's Knute Ellestad (see James P. Leary and Richard March, *Down Home Dairyland: A Listener's Guide* [Madison: University of Wisconsin Extension, 1996], 15).

In the mid-1970s, Philip Martin, a young would-be fiddler, discovered that while Anglo-Celtic performances still dominated the tune books and recordings said to characterize American folk fiddling, there were Norwegian old-time fiddlers aplenty in Wisconsin—yet few of their tunes and little about their lives had been documented. Armed with a tape recorder, and accompanied by photographer Lewis Koch, Martin began to seek out the state's gammaldans fiddlers, their repertoires, their stories. Eventually the Martin-Koch collaboration would produce a slide-tape program and a photo-text exhibit (both called *Kingdom of Fiddlers*), two documentary recordings (*Across the Fields* and *Tunes from the Amerika Trunk*), the booklet which is partially reprinted here, and a book, *Farmhouse Fiddlers: Music and Dance Traditions in the Rural Midwest* (Mount Horeb, Wisc.: Midwest Traditions, 1994).

Philip Martin's initial work was under the aegis of Folklore Village Farm in Dodgeville, Wisconsin, an organization then dedicated to highly romantic and stylized reenactments of Old World folk traditions for purposes of recreation and personal fulfillment. More compelled by the actual New World traditions happening around him, Martin eventually founded the Wisconsin Folk Museum with his wife Jean Johnson in 1986. During its ten-year existence, the Wisconsin Folk Museum produced exhibits, events, sound recordings, and publications concerning the folklore of Wisconsin's many ethnic and occupational cultures. In 1992 Philip Martin left the Folk Museum to found a regional press, Midwest Traditions.

Reprinted in abridged form from *Across the Fields: Traditional Norwegian-American Music from Wisconsin* (Dodgeville, Wisc.: Wisconsin Old Time Music Project, 1982); a version of this article appeared as "Hoppwaltzes and Homebrew" in the folksong revival publication *Sing Out!* 31:3 (1985): 26–34.

In 1979, photographer Lewis Koch and I began a fieldwork project to document traditional Norwegian American fiddle and button accordion music of Wisconsin. Sponsored by the Wisconsin Folklife Center with grants from the Wisconsin Humanities Council and Wisconsin Arts Board, we spent over two years interviewing old-time musicians in their homes. Many of these visits were in the west-central "coulee country" (from the French *couloir*, for steep-walled valley), a hilly region bordered roughly by Eau Claire, La Crosse, and Black River Falls. Seated at kitchen tables and on living room sofas, we were served cup after cup of industrial-strength black coffee, devoured plates of open-faced sandwiches and sandbakkel cookies, and went through reels of tape and rolls of film as these Norwegian-accented farmers told of music in their rural neighborhoods which spanned half a century or more. While we visited, they drew forth well-worn instruments and, often with their wives at piano, played tune after tune from seemingly inexhaustible repertoires.

The music was Norwegian American house party music, which was learned and played at rural dance gatherings in farmhouse kitchens, barns, graneries, tobacco stripping sheds, country schoolhouses and town halls throughout the early decades of this country. Some of the tunes were brought over to the Upper Midwest frontier by the original Norwegian immigrants of the 1840s and 1850s. Other tunes had been composed or adapted, in all likelihood, by the succeeding generations of farmer-fiddlers born in this country. As elsewhere in the United States, the active rural folk tradition consisted primarily of music simply passed on through the aural tradition and never written down. It was learned by ear and played by memory, flowing from one generation to the next.

In a pattern familiar in this century of rapid modernization much of the music was now less frequently in use, and, in some cases, the melodies seemed on their way to oblivion, played by only a few isolated and overlooked elder musicians. The Wisconsin Folklife Center has been working to gain higher recognition of this distinctive music of the Upper Midwest. The region is characterized by a crazy-quilt pattern of 19th and early 20th century ethnic settlement, followed by a continual process of mixing and merging reflective of the neighborly character of rural life in America's northern heartland. As in other parts of the country, we are learning to seek our roots and help support traditional culture in our region.

From Norway to the Upper Midwest

Probably the most fascinating aspect of the Norwegian American music in Wisconsin is its departure from the original Old World Norwegian tunes, techniques, and instrumentation. While there is a lingering Norwegian accent to this music, it has

24.1. The Nyen Brothers Band (Albert, Oscar, Ole, and Helmer, a.k.a. the "Big Four"), Norwegian old-time fiddlers, in the family farmyard at Lakes Coulee, near Blair, ca. 1920. Wisconsin Folk Museum Collection, courtesy of Raymond Nyen.

adapted itself in many ways to the climate and rural lifestyle of the Norwegians in the American Upper Midwest. In the Old World of the 19th century, Norwegian farm families tended to live in small villages or clusters of farmsteads. They preferred not to move far from their place of birth, nor did they stray far from the traditional folk-ways that patterned their lives. Over the course of generations, each small hamlet developed its own dialect of speech, its own variants of music and dance, its own local customs of celebration. While the differences might be slight from one village to the next, from region to region those folkways grew so different as to be mutually foreign. A dancer from the province of Valdres would have had a hard time dancing a springdance to the music of a fiddler from the neighboring province of Telemark.

However, upon immigration to America, these folk patterns, formed by long years of population stability and geographical isolation, began to break down quickly. Early homesteaders did not settle in concentrated villages but spread them-selves across the frontier, seeking out the best tracts of potential farmland with wood and water. These first dwellings could be miles from the nearest neighbors. As more and more immigrants arrived, the early settlers helped the newcomers to raise their cabins, clear land, build barns, and to become acquainted with one another. Gradu-ally, the settlers living within several miles of each other banded together into infor-mal units called neighborhoods. These usually followed the lay of the land, along valleys or ridges, or centered around crossroads or old prairie clearings.

The "work exchange ring" was the main summertime activity of the rural neighborhood. Throughout the warm months of the year neighbors could always be counted on to help out with the chores that were either too big or simply too boring for a single family to manage on its own. These activities ranged from fence mending or chasing down a loose cow, to larger group activities such as quilting, chicken-plucking, and corn-husking, to all-neighborhood gatherings to raise a barn, build a schoolhouse or church, or operate the autumn harvest threshing rig which made its annual rounds of the neighborhood farms.

The wintertime equivalent of the work exchange ring was the series of weekly dance parties held around the neighborhood, hosted in turn by the neighbor families now faced with the isolation of a Wisconsin winter. Beginning in late October with the end of the harvest and continuing until spring planting time, these house parties brought and kept together the same circle of families who worked together the rest of the year. The dancing was approached with an energy similar to that of a threshing bee. Called appropriately "kitchen sweats" or "house parties," the dances took place in parlors, kitchens, downstairs bedrooms—or all of these together—cleared of furniture. Even the heavy cast-iron stove was disconnected and carried out into the yard. Music was provided by a wide range of neighborhood talent from grizzled grandfathers sawing away at fiddles to ma-and-pa family bands, to the visiting hired man who happened to have an old battered accordion tucked away, along with his personal gear, in his quarters. The festivities went long into the night with only occasional pauses for food (the midnight "lunch"), drink ("alcohol punch" or home-made beer), and perhaps a rest break to throw open the doors and let some fresh winter air into the warm household. The dancing continued until the first rays of the rising sun struck the farmhouse windowpanes, signaling an end to the "kitchen sweat." It was time to carry the sleeping children down from the beds upstairs, to hitch up the sleighs, and to return home to do the morning chores.

From Springar to "Skverdans"

In the transition from Old World village culture to the open settlement patterns of the rural Midwest, the Norwegian Americans found themselves exposed to other ethnic groups. Neighborhoods might consist predominantly of Norwegians from one particular area, but there were often Norwegians from other districts of Norway as well. Besides that, occasionally neighborhoods were new homes for other nationalities as well—German, Bohemian, Irish, Swiss, Polish, or resettled "Yankees" from the eastern United States—whose customs differed greatly from the core group of original settlers. But, the neighborly sentiments of the frontier prevailed. The pioneer equality of need and newness encouraged the immigrants to accept and incorporate each other's differences into a workable compromise.

In addition to the sometimes random mixing in neighborhoods, the lumberjack camp of the Wisconsin North Woods as well as other opportunities for seasonal work were arenas for early cross-cultural contact. Norwegian farmers worked with men of many different nationalities, and, while the work was hard, there was occasionally time for recreation. Through these contacts, Norwegian men brought back a wide variety of tunes and dances to their own settlements.

The Norwegian Americans, hard-working and eager to succeed, were not slow to imitate Yankee ways of doing business, farming and politicking. They followed popular styles of dress, quickly discarding the homespun clothes that marked themselves as immigrants. Likewise, they were eager to improve their homes and cultural environment. They purchased pianos and pump organs, and later, wind-up phonographs and radios, bringing the popular music of the day into their parlor.

Though they came from tradition-bound villages, the Norwegians on the frontier were generally willing to try new things that might prove useful or enjoyable. It should be noted that those who immigrated were most often young adults in the prime of life. They were not joined in this country by their elders who would have played a role as guardians of traditional values. Those young people who traveled to America were willing, by choice or by necessity, to face change. Their very decision to leave "the old country" marked them as individuals willing to take risks and abandon old ways for new opportunities.

In the realm of music and dance, first to fall by the wayside in the New World were those village variants most narrowly specific to one particular geographical district in Norway. Dances like the *springdans, gangar, halling,* and *pols* were too complex and over-specialized to fit well in the open, mixed-ethnic environment of the Midwestern settlements. Similarly affected was the eight-stringed Hardanger violin, an unusual Norwegian folk fiddle with a highly-decorated body and neck, and equally ornamented melodies. Its intricacies required long periods of training to master, and its repertoire was tied to those village dances mentioned above. While the Hardanger fiddlers and instruments came to this country in abundance, seldom were their traditions passed on to second and third generations. Player by player, the music and dances faded into the past.

More adaptable to the Midwest were those rhythms common to nearly all Europeans—the waltz, schottische and polka. These melodies continued to flourish and were passed on from fiddler to fiddler. Within the Norwegian American communities, the old-time dances retained their distinctive patterns of bowing and the rhythmic swing that marked their Scandinavian origin.

Yet even these tunes underwent certain unavoidable changes. Norwegian waltzes and schottisches in this country became heavier and more pronounced in rhythm (similar to their Germanic cousins), while the Scandinavian polkas (called "hoppwaltzes" by the Norwegian Americans) came under the influence of American styles of square dance hoedowns and quadrilles. In addition, the instrumentation became Americanized with the inclusion of the ubiquitous parlor piano and the banjo to house party ensembles. Only in a few areas did a more Norwegian sound persist in musical groups of two or three fiddlers playing together—one or two in melody and the others playing a chording accompaniment.

The period of immigration from the mid-1800s to the early 1900s also corresponded with the rising popularity of the one- and two-row button accordion in rural Norway. Many immigrants brought the instrument with them to this country, and the Norwegian American repertoire soon became infused with numerous tunes that reflected the limited key and chord choices of the little "push-pull" squeezebox.

The diversity of music and dance that came with the settlers from remote and isolated regions of Norway continued to exist in memory and occasional use through the end of the 1800s, but in the first part of this century was almost completely replaced by the wealth of schottische, waltz and polka tunes that grew to dominate the Scandinavian American repertoire. Some were standards like "Livet i Finnskogen" (Life in the Finnish Woods), "Lordagsvalsen" (Saturday Night Waltz), and "Johan Pa Snippen," while others less well-known were passed down in local tradition across the Midwest, unnamed and unwritten, to the present.

Norwegian American Music Today

To a modern-day native of Norway familiar with that country's extremely rich regional folk music traditions, the Norwegian American repertoire sounds thoroughly American. The percussive banjos and pianos plunk and pound away, the rhythms are heavily accented, the tunes seemingly simple. Paradoxically, to an American this music sounds Norwegian. The tunes are mostly unknown and have names like "Pete Peterson's Schottische" or "Iver Johnstad's Hoppwaltz." The Norwegian waltzes have a lightness unlike the American old-time waltz. Polkas have an unaccustomed bounciness. And so on.

The music is, in fact, something in between. Its hybrid nature reflects the history, values and special needs of a particular group of people: the Norwegian Americans of the Upper Midwest. For these people, the music is just the right blend. It allows them to be Norwegian in the sense that they recognize through the ethnic elements of the music that they still belong in some way to a Scandinavian culture both ancestral and contemporary. Yet other elements embodied in the traditions of the music allow them to be American, too, with little sense of conflict or separateness.

In a way that only folk music can, the Norwegian American dance tunes carry a host of memories—snow-covered fields outside warm parlors and kitchens filled with families dancing and socializing, blended with the smells of pies baking and coffee brewing, and, through it all, the smooth flow of an old-time hoppwaltz. The music invokes the wholesome atmosphere of Wisconsin rural life in the early part of this century. It was a life of work and hard times but tempered, we should pause to remember, with the joys of friendship, family activities and homemade pleasures.

Though times have changed, these values live on. For some, they live on in the continuation of simple melodies handed down from grandparents to children to grandchildren. This is the musical heritage of the Norwegian Americans in Wisconsin.

A Gallery of Musicians: Past and Present

Spelemann Tomten of Westby

Anton Tomten was born in Biri, Norway, in 1855 and came to Wisconsin in 1868 at age thirteen with his parents to settle in the Westby area. He was married in 1883 and had nine children. Known locally as Spelemann ("Fiddler") Tomten, he was in great demand to play for dances and wedding celebrations all over the area. On occasion he would walk as far as twenty miles in one day to play for an evening dance, returning home the following day.

Many of his children were musical. The two boys, Ingvald and Gilbert, played violin and often accompanied their father at dances, with Ingvald assisting with the melody and Gilbert playing a chording accompaniment or simple harmony. Most of his seven daughters played either piano or guitar, and one daughter, Anna, played violin as well, so there was no lack of music around the hillside farmhome. Since they often played outside on summer evenings, Anton converted a small outbuilding into an ingenious musical instrument by nailing 2×4s on each end and stringing heavy wire across one side. When tuned it could be plucked like an enormous bass fiddle.

Manda Mortenson of Viroqua, one of Anton's granddaughters, recalls hearing the following story that sheds light on the amicable relationship between Anton and the local preacher, Halvor Halvorson.

There was a wedding over by Westby and Grandpa Tomten was on his way there to play for the wedding dance. And he was walking down the street with his fiddle under his arm and he met the minister coming back from the ceremony. And when he saw my grandpa with his fiddle, Reverend Halvorson said, "Well, I've done my part. Now you've got left to do yours."

Randie Severson, Woman Fiddler

Randie Easterson Severson was born 1877 in a log cabin in Pleasant Valley Township near Eleva to parents Ole and Christina, immigrants from the Hardanger area of Norway. She grew up learning to play fiddle along with her two younger brothers, "Colonel" (Cornell) and "Pete" (Peder). The three of them often played for dances in the area, with Colonel generally playing the lead and Pete and Randie playing accompaniment. On occasion, however, Randie played alone for house parties, with only a piano or pump organ backup.

As a young girl she was exceptionally skilled not only with a bow and instrument but also with a needle and thread. At age twelve she was the neighborhood seamstress, and would go from farm to farm sewing everything from men's suits to wedding dresses, for which she received fifty cents a day. When she had saved up enough money she bought herself a "wheel" (a bicycle with a tall front wheel) which she then rode about on her rounds.

In her twenties, she traveled out to North Dakota with her brother Pete to work with the threshing crews, he as a separator man and she as a cook. It was there that she met 6'3" Sam Severson from Fergus Falls, Minnesota, the engineer for the crew. It was a "cook-car romance" and they were married that year, 1903. They returned to Eau Claire to settle down and raise a family.

Randie continued her long playing career in Eau Claire, fiddling for house parties and dances. Her repertoire broadened to include not only Norwegian waltzes, schottisches, mazurkas, and hoppwaltzes, but also multi-ethnic Wisconsin favorites such as the circle two-step, the "Flying Dutchman," "Herr Schmidt," "Coming through the Rye," and square dances.

At age 65 she could still ride a bicycle around the block and dance *springdans* and was playing regularly for senior citizen club dances. At 75 she played violin for her own golden wedding anniversary party. She died six years later, at age 82, in 1959.

Isaac Nelson, Traveling Salesman and Fiddler

Isaac Nelson (ca. 1890–1953) was in the words of one, "a good old scout." A traveling salesman, he peddled his liniments, salves and oil extracts door-to-door in the Blair area, and many recall his friendly personality, and how he liked to sit and visit for hours without worrying about making a sale. He carried his fiddle about with him on his rounds, and it was reported that he would often leave his sales kit neglected on the porch and bring in only his fiddle instead. He also was known to give fiddle lessons to youngsters on his route. Over the years he played for countless community dances at rural schoolhouses and halls in the vicinity, and a number of tunes known in the area are credited to his name, including "Isaac Nelson's Hoppwaltz."

Leonard Finseth

Leonard Finseth (1911–1993) lived most of his life on the family dairy farm north of Mondovi. He got his first fiddle at age 17 from a mail-order catalogue, and soon began an active career playing for dances in the area. As a young man he learned many tunes from Yankee and Scandinavian fiddlers living nearby, including his uncle Ed Quall and Ingvald Syverson, grandson to one of Norway's top fiddlers of the late 1800s. He also picked up tunes from Otto Rindlisbacher, a Swiss tavern owner in Rice Lake, whom Leonard visited frequently for fiddling sessions in the back room of the tavern. Throughout his career Leonard eagerly absorbed tunes from many sources across the Upper Midwest and Norway. He appeared at many regional festivals, as well as twice, in 1974 and 1976, at the Smithsonian Institution's Festival of American Folklife in Washington, D.C.

Ed Stendalen

Ed Stendalen was born November 20, 1915, near Chaseburg. He learned to play the two-row button accordion at age 12, picking up tunes from local musicians, including some handed down from his grandfather, Anton Tomten, one of the premier fiddlers in Westby at the turn of the century. Ed's musical career has consisted mostly of playing for neighborhood house parties, along with a stint in an area dance band, The Wildcats, in the late 1930s. After farming for forty years in Coon Township near Westby, Ed retired and moved into a newly built house on the edge of town. He now plays primarily at home for his own enjoyment, and for that of his grandchildren, who are frequent visitors and avid young dancers. He occasionally gets together with his sister Manda Mortenson, a piano player from nearby Viroqua, and friend Selmer Torger, a fiddler and banjo player, to play for community events in the area.

The Blom Family

LeRoy Blom was born November 13, 1924, and grew up on a farm near Blair. He started his musical career at age five on the harmonica. At age fourteen he took up the mandolin, and shortly thereafter taught himself to play fiddle by "watching a neighbor a lot." He has drawn his extensive repertoire of old-time dance tunes from elder area musicians, including Iver Johnstad, Oscar Nyen, Isaac Nelson, and Reinhard Thurston. He married his wife Marie in 1963, and their children now form the core of their family band, The Scandinavians, which features son Mark (b. 1963) on fiddle, Lisa (b. 1967) on piano and fiddle, Kevin (b. 1969) on fiddle and banjo, and youngest daughter Kari, who at age nine sings a variety of songs from Norwegian ballads to cowboy yodels. The Scandinavians play several times a month for wedding and anniversary dances, showers, ice cream socials, nursing homes, supper clubs, and occasional fiddlers' get-togethers around the region.

Bruce Bollerud

Bruce Bollerud was born in 1934 on a farm two miles east of Hollandale. His first contact with old-time music came from Herman Erickson, a local fiddler who played for house parties and tavern dances. Erickson's band included a violin, banjo, cornet, and bandonion (a large-sized German concertina). Bruce learned to play bandonion when he was ten years old from Blanchardville music store owner Henry "Step-and-a-Half" Hanson. Since joining the musician's union at age sixteen, Bruce has played his bandonion and piano accordion for a number of area dance bands, including Gilbert Prestbroten's Orchestra, Emil Simpson and the Nighthawks, and the Goose Island Ramblers. Currently Bruce works as a special education teacher in Madison, where he continues to play music with his own three-piece dance band, The Good Times Band.

25

Polka Music in a Polka State

James P. Leary

In 1994, the Wisconsin legislature designated the polka as Wisconsin's state dance. It all began when a Madison elementary school teacher and polka enthusiast, Vi Bergum, collaborated with her students on a class project. They approached Senator Gary Drzewiecki, a concertina-playing Polish American from Pulaski representing the greater Green Bay area. The senator drafted a bill, held hearings that were well attended by supporters and the media, and soon the polka shared coveted status with the sugar maple, the robin, and Antigo silt loam as one of the official state symbols.

The essay reprinted here played a small part in the process. In the fall of 1993 the wife of one of Senator Drzewiecki's aides took my Wisconsin Folklore course. She gave a copy of my polka essay, one of the required readings, to her husband, who in turn gave it to the senator. Soon I was asked to offer "expert testimony." I pondered not only the polka's significance in Wisconsin, but also the implications of making it a state-sanctioned dance.

Folklorists have long been committed to the variety of traditional expressions and to the cultures that sustain them. I realized that, because of the state's pluralism, more species of polka music and dance flourish in Wisconsin than anywhere else in the world. Yet polka musicians and dancers have frequently been either ignored altogether by scholars, the mainstream media, cultural institutions, and the would-be hip, or ridiculed by them as foreign, backwards, and square. State recognition, I reasoned, might raise the spirits of polka practitioners while helping polka assume its rightful place alongside other American folk musical traditions.

My resolve to support the polka bill increased when I learned of a counterproposal. For years, square dance supporters have lobbied Congress to make this Anglo-Celtic tradition America's national dance. Their efforts have been opposed consistently by folklorists and ethnomusicologists who have testified that: 1) the square dance is but one of many worthy regional and ethnic dance traditions thriving in America; 2) the square dance has already been America's de facto official dance for more than a century through its adoption by school physical education programs; and 3) legislative sanctioning of the square dance would deny America's cultural diversity while furthering the notion that only Anglo-Celtic folk forms are "American." Undaunted, the square dance faithful have sought to introduce official dance bills in state legislatures throughout the country. Fortunately they did not succeed in Wisconsin, where the importance of the square dance pales beside the polka.

The politics of culture figured similarly in the genesis of my polka essay. In the 1970s, the Folk Arts Program of the National Endowment for the Arts led a movement by federal and state funding organizations to offer grants for the documentation and presentation of America's many folk traditions. The movement's underlying purpose was cultural democracy: to acknowledge, examine, and make better known the traditional artistry of peoples largely neglected by the nation's cultural institutions. And so in 1991, with populist motives and financial support from the National Endowment for the Arts, the Wisconsin Humanities Council, and the Wisconsin Folk Museum, I produced "Polka Music, Polka Culture" as a traveling photo-text exhibit. The whole thing was designed to fit in the back of my station wagon and, departing from the usual places that host exhibits, I took it where polka people might see it: to polka festivals, to dance halls, to ethnic celebrations, and to Art Altenburg's Concertina Bar on Milwaukee's south side.

Nowadays the exhibit remains available through the Wisconsin Humanities Council.

Reprinted from exhibit text for "Polka Music, Polka Culture" and from an accompanying essay, "Polka Music, Ethnic Music" (Mount Horeb, Wisc.: Wisconsin Folk Museum, 1991).

Polka Music, Polka Culture

The polka is to the Upper Midwest what bluegrass is to the upland South, what Cajun music is to southwest Louisiana, what blues is to the Mississipi Delta and Chicago: it is the vernacular music of rural and working class people whose ancestors immigrated from Europe to labor on farms, in lumber camps, and in factories. And like the people, the music has adapted to the New World while retaining elements from the Old World.

The origin of the word "polka" is a matter of debate. Certainly it has been used to describe a Polish woman, just as "polack" (or "polak") has been used to describe a Polish man. Likewise *pulka*, meaning "half" in Czech, may well have evolved into "polka" as a consequence of the the the half-step used in the dance. The polka itself, a couple dance in 2/4 time, emerged around 1820 in a Czech village that was not only near the Polish border, but had been influenced by Germans.

By the 1840s, the polka had spread from Prague throughout Europe to the Americas. Fiddlers played it first, but it was soon oompahed by military brass bands and squeezed from accordions and concertinas. Austrians, Belgians, Czechs, Finns, Germans, Irish, Italians, Norwegians, Poles, Slovaks, Slovenians, Swedes, Swiss and other immigrants brought polka music to Wisconsin and the Upper Midwest in the nineteenth century. They formed brass bands for parades and concerts and fostered solo musicians and small ensembles that played for parties and dances.

Not surprisingly, young folks born in this country learned to play tunes from their immigrant elders. Bruno Synkula of Ashland recalls a neighbor:

I got acquainted with a fellow, he played the accordion. On the way to school I'd see him sitting out on the front porch. He'd be playing that accordion. One day I stopped there after school and asked if I could listen to his music. Then he let me use his accordion, he taught me how to play it-like some of them old time pieces my mother heard in the old country. I used to play them for her and she really enjoyed that. (Ashland, February 23, 1981)

Synkula never "played out" for dances, but plenty of others did.

"Polka bands" past and present favor "polka dancers" with more than just polkas. Their repertoire is likely to include such European couple dances as the waltz, the schottische, the laendler, and sometimes a mazurka or oberek. Revelers in Hungarian or Slovak ethnic communities might, for example, enjoy a czardas. Tom Johanik of Moquah recalls that up through the 1950s his parents' generation "would dance the czardas. Pristashes were pretty good at that. I remember them. They were short and roly-poly. And boy, their feet would *go!* That's a fast dance" (Moquah,

25.1. The Pilsen Band, Kewaunee County's most popular old-time Czech band of the early twentieth century, poses with their wind instruments. They were also known jocularly as the "Pilsen Pissers" because of their fondness for *pivo* (the Czech word for "beer"). *Left to right*, John Jisa, Frank Sladky, Gregory Mhalik, Mike Suess, Joe Altman, Anton Sladky. Courtesy Bill and Rosemary DeBauche.

March 18, 1981). Ethnic Wisconsinites elsewhere enjoyed the Scandinavian hambo, the Polish kujawiak, the German "Herr Schmidt," the Czech "Annie in the Cabbage Patch," and the Slovenian clap-dance.

Informal house parties in both rural and urban neighborhoods—vital through the 1940s and occasional today—were training grounds for young musicians and dancers, places to learn old-time songs, tunes, and steps from performers of the immigrant generation. Vera Dvorak Schultz grew up in an Ashland neighborhood where such gatherings flourished:

During the Depression nobody could afford to hire things done. Eleventh Avenue East was called "Bohemian Boulevard" and everybody would get together and help each other. They would get together on Sunday. The women would fix potato salad, homemade rye bread, dill pickles from the crock. And they'd either lay a sidewalk or dig a basement . . . and then they'd sit around and sing. In our yard we had two big willow trees and this is where they sat. You could hear 'em all over the block. (Washburn, November 5, 1980)

Old-time weddings too have been traditional musical affairs that required marches, bride dances, and songs of admonition and bawdy celebration. Greg Zurawski recalls Portage County weddings:

See, the old Polish style weddings—which had even Czech or German bands playing years ago—you had a two day wedding, sometimes a four day wedding. If you wanted to have a wedding that was out on the farm, there was no problem. All you had to do was have your wedding done at the church, then you come out to the farm home, bride's parents' home. They put up a big tent for the people to dance, put up a big wooden floor. . . . And normally you started Friday night and sometimes you were lucky if you got done Monday night. (Custer, February 26, 1988)

Although altered today, the weddings of Wisconsin's European ethnics remain likely to include dances with the bride, gifts of money, and waltzes and polkas.

In addition to house parties and wedding celebrations, fraternal halls—the insurance societies and lodges formed by particular ethnic groups—were a third early focus for events that included polka music and dancing. One such place, Ashland's "Bohemian Hall," the "jewel of the east side," was built in 1910 for Czech members of the Zapadna Cesko-Bratrska Jednota (Western Fraternal Life Association). Mary Prestil's husband kept the dance floor in top shape: "We had the best dance floor in town at one time. It had to be just so. You couldn't scrub it or anything when my husband was janitor. He'd mix sand with wax, throw it on the floor, and the people would dance over it to take the scuff marks out" (Ashland, October 29, 1980). Since the 1920s, the Poles, Scandinavians, Finns, and others in the community have tested the spring of the old Bohemian Hall's floor.

Stan Stangle joined his father's band to play many a night in the Bohemian Hall. Indeed polka bands are often family bands. The Brueggens of Cashton, the Maroszeks of Pulaski, and the Rubenzers of Chippewa Falls, to name only a few, have spawned numerous bands over the past century. In 1839 Johan Groeschl immigrated from Australia to settle near the eastern shore of Lake Winnebago. Johan was a musician and his son Anton was a bandleader. Syl Groeschl:

My grandfather Anton was considered a fine musician. Years ago the little towns were quite organized. He ran the Charlesburg Community Band. He wrote music for the band—he was more or less a self-taught musician—and he played bass horn. He played violin real well, he played clarinet, and he was a fine concertina player. I can still see him playing that concertina: concertina on his knee, pipe smoke rolling out of his mouth—I can still see him. (Calumetville, August 13, 1985)

Anton's son, Tony, went on to lead a band, and Tony's son, Syl, continues to lead another. Syl Groeschl, who grew up speaking German and playing second trumpet for his dad, still sings the old German songs acquired through oral tradition. He still plays melodies that echoed through eastern Wisconsin a century and a half before.

Besides families, certain Wisconsin communities have spawned a disproportionate number of polka musicians. While Memphis, Tennessee, has nurtured rock and roll and Nashville has its homegrown country pickers, certain Wisconsin communities have been veritable hothouses for polka virtuosi. The squeezebox has long been king in Milwaukee's ethnic European neighborhoods, while a noted Wisconsin Polish song proclaims "Pulaski is a Polka Town." The Lake Michigan shore communities between Manitowoc and Kewaunee—settled in the mid-nineteenth century by Czechs and German-Bohemians from the Old World cradle of polka music—

have produced an astounding number of polka musicians. "Tuba Dan" Jerabek: "There were so many great bands in a small area. When weddings or other dance jobs came along, there was a price war. It was hard for bands to make much trying to play. It's the Bohemians. They all love music and they love to show off. They either played or they wanted to" (Appleton, May 4, 1988). Although Jerabek's observation was made in reference to the 1960s, the truth of it persists.

The proliferation of radio stations in the 1920s inspired many polka bands to seeks sponsors for live programs. Typically introduced by an announcer who likewise read commercials, the bands solicited postcards with requests from enthusiastic fans. Clarence Metzdorf of Juneau had a clever strategy for attracting mail: "We came from Dodge Country over to Poynette to play on WIBU. And we used to ask people to send postcards requesting tunes. We wanted to make a good impression on the manager, so we got all our friends and relations back home to write. Lots of cards came in, but the manager said, 'How come everybody who writes in is from east of Beaver Dam?'" (Burnett, April 17, 1985). Popular radio performers were assured of enthusiastic crowds at dance halls within their station's listening radius. Live shows dwindled in the 1950s, but many bandleaders assumed the role of disc jockey for polka shows that continue today. The emergence of radio stations with specialized formats in the 1980s saw the rise of "polka stations" in Wisconsin. Among them: WAUN of Kewaunee, WTKM of Hartford, and WIBU of Poynette.

By the 1920s Wisconsin bands were likewise beginning to make records. Otto Rindlisbacher and Karl Hoppe of Rice Lake traveled to New York City to record Swiss dance pieces around 1920. Soon after, fledgling Wisconsin record companies, like Port Washington's "Broadway" label, began waxing polka music. Polka sounds have been put out ever since, on formats ranging from 78 rpm to CDs. Leah Bensman McHenry recalls the early 1950s in Sheboygan:

My dad ran an appliance store and he carried records. All the local bands used to come in and ask for polka music. Pretty soon my dad decided to make records. He set up a studio in the back. There was a tavern next door. The bands would come in, have their beer, and make records. I designed some of the record jackets, my mother typed up the names of the tunes. It was a family operation [Polkaland records]. (Mequon, January 8, 1991)

Other noteworthy Wisconsin polka labels include: Milwaukee's "Pfau," Sauk City's "Cuca," Willard's "RY," and Franksville's "HD."

Nowadays, live performances by bands, radio, recordings, and an array of mostly summer "polka festivals" knit together a far-flung community of "polka people" who are fond of proclaiming "polka people are happy people." In the late twentieth century, such polka enthusiasts tend to be rural and working-class folks of varying ages who value their ethnicity and grew up with polka music. Some belong to and wear the regalia of such organized groups as the Polka Lovers Klub of America (PoLKA), the Wisconsin Polka Boosters Association, and a spate of fan clubs devoted to particular bands. They may travel to polka festivals together or even on "polka tours" of the Caribbean and Europe. Many follow the Upper Midwestern polka scene through publications like *Entertainment Bits* or *The Polka*

News. Others affirm their participation in polka culture with an array of buttons and bumperstickers.

Polkas and Ethnic Identity

Outsiders may disparage polka enthusiasts as uniformly fat and jolly folks in short pants and puffy shirts whose bass horns belch "oompah." But insiders can discern variety and sophistication. No two bands are alike. And most shrewdly select names, clothing, album covers, business cards, and logos that present the public with some blend of modern and old time, cosmopolitan and rustic, American and ethnic images.

Ethnicity, however, has been the dominant force in shaping the identity of polka bands. Wisconsin's overall polka culture includes distinct ethnic subcultures. Austrians, Belgians, Croatians, Finns, the Irish, Italians, Mexicans, Norwegians, Swedes, and Swiss have all made contributions. Bohemians (Czechs), Germans, Slovenians, and Poles, however, have done the most to shape Wisconsin's polka music.

Participants in the state's polka scene are uniformly adept at distinguishing one ethnic style from the other. Indeed some will only dance or listen to a single style. And even those open to a variety of polka strains may debate, for example, the relative merits of Polish versus German concertina playing. Supporters and critics aside, each major style has its own particular history, important personalities, and innovations.

Bohemian Brass Bands

Residents of Wisconsin's Bohemian or Czech communities in particular formed bands soon after settlement in the nineteenth century. In the heart of Czech Wisconsin—Manitowoc and Kewaunee Counties—such bands thrived in Stangelville, Pilsen, Maribel, Tisch Mills, Two Creeks, Manitowoc, and Kewaunee. Elsewhere around the state, they flourished in the Czech settlements of Ashland, Haugen, Phillips, and Yuba.

Dominated by brass and reeds, these groups were patterned after European military bands. They led parades on the Fourth of July, played for summer picnics and community dances, and were in demand for both weddings and funerals. For the former, they played festive marches while leading revelers from church to dance hall. For the latter, they favored dirges to accompany the corpse from church to graveyard. Perhaps the musical highpoint of the year was the *Maso Pust* celebration—with costumes, feasting, and two days of dancing—just prior to the solemnity and abstinence of Lent.

By the early twentieth century, however, smaller ethnic dance bands began to play throughout the year. Some old time Bohemian bands—the Straight Eight of Kewaunee, the Bohemian Brass Band of Ashland, the Rott Band of Yuba—persisted until the early 1950s, but they attracted few young players. The new Bohemian bands that began to emerge from the 1920s on retained the bass horn as their "bottom." They also kept trumpets, saxophones, and clarinets that carried the melody. But the upright altos, or "peck horns," and the trombones that contributed rhythm were largely abandoned for a chording piano (or piano accordion) and a set of trap drums.

It was during this period of innovation that Romy Gosz established Wisconsin's most influential Czech or Bohemian sound. Gosz was born in 1910 in Rockwood, Wisconsin, north of Manitowoc. His father, Paul, ran a family band that sometimes doubled as a basketball team, playing for both local sporting events and dances in the early the 1920s. By 1928, Romy had taken over the band, and its seven-piece instrumentation soon became the standard. The Gosz rhythm section featured drums, bass horn, and a piano or a piano accordion, while the "front line" consisted of two reed men, alternating on saxophone and clarinet, and a pair of trumpeters.

Although originally a piano player, Romy Gosz made his name with the trumpet. The Bohemian style is exemplified by slow dance tempos, an emphasis on whole notes, and sophisticated arrangements in which brass and reed instruments alternate phrases. This orderly and "heavy" sound, however, is enlivened by dynamic surges in volume and the slurred tones or "blue notes" associated with jazz. Gosz's trumpet shimmered and shook the stately architecture of old time Czech tunes. Occasional rollicking Czech vocals likewise bent pear-shaped notes off-kilter in keeping with Gosz's bold trumpet lines.

Between 1931 and his death in 1966, Romy Gosz recorded several hundred tunes on such labels as Broadway, Brunswick, Columbia, Decca, King, Mercury, Mono, Okeh, Polkaland, and Vocalion. He also played for countless weddings, picnics, and community dances not only in the greater Manitowoc area, but south to Milwaukee, north to Green Bay and Wausau, and west to Stevens Point. His efforts won him the title "polka king" and coverage in such national magazines as *Time* and *Coronet*. They also inspired numerous musicians to sustain the Gosz sound. Among those playing in the 1990s: Mark Jirkovec, Bob Kuether, Larry Hlinak, the Harold Schultz Orchestra, Tom Siebold and the Brass Buttons, Jerome Wojta and the Two Creeks Farm Hands, and Del Dassow's revived "Romy Gosz Orchestra."

While the vibrato of Gosz's trumpet paralleled the bluesy buzzing of "hot" jazz, the "sweet" blended horn sound established by Wisconsin Czech stylist Lawrence Duchow approached the popular big band music of the 1930s and 1940s. Meanwhile his singers abandoned "foreign" vocals for English.

Duchow, a native of Potter in Calumet County, formed his Red Raven Orchestra in 1932. Over the next twenty years the band barnstormed throughout the Upper Midwest. Their recordings on national labels like Decca and RCA Victor included the "Red Raven Polka" and "Swiss Boy," tunes that have become standards in the polka world. The Duchow band broke up in 1953, but was soon revived as the Red Ravens by Appleton's Jay Wells. Wells and groups like the Lee Rollins Orchestra of Green Bay carry on Duchow's synthesis of Czech music with elements of American pop.

Duchow's flirtations with American pop and the persistence of Romy Gosz's disciples do not, however, comprise the full story of Czech polka music in Wisconsin. Since the 1970s both efforts to recapture ethnic "roots" and cultural exchanges with the old country have fostered new trends. Haugen, Hillsboro, and Phillips, for example, have all instituted summer ethnic festivals to attract outsiders and celebrate their Czech heritage. Each community has also formed a group of "Czech singers," outfitted in costumes, who perform old time favorites in dance tempos to the strains of local musicians.

Some of these local musicians play the button accordion. The button accordion, a sort of bellows-driven harmonica, is limited to a few keys and had been confined to house parties for most of the twentieth century. Its archaism, however, its association with the ethnic past, with memories of grandma or grandpa push-pulling tunes on a winter's night, sparked new interest and Wisconsin Czech groups like Tuba Dan [Jerabek] and the Polkalanders began to work a handful of button accordion tunes into their erstwhile brass and reed repertoire.

The renaissance of the button accordion has also benefited from increased interaction between Czech-American communities. Czech polka enthusiasts nowadays—via radio, travel, or purchased recordings—can enjoy Czech polka bands from Minnesota, Iowa, North Dakota, Nebraska, and Texas. Nebraska bands, in particular, favor the button accordion and have contributed new tunes on the instrument to their ethnic neighbors. The onset of *glasnost* has likewise made it possible for traditional musicians from Czechoslovakia to tour the United States, visiting communities throughout Wisconsin. Performers like the She and He Haugh Band of Hillsboro, and Louie Zdrazil of Antigo, have added tunes from current old-country groups to their playlists.

From Grenadiers to Dutchmen

The evolution of Wisconsin's German polka bands closely parallels that of their Bohemian or Czech counterparts. Indeed in northeastern and west central Wisconsin, many ethnic dance bands have melded German and Czech players and repertoires for more than a century.

Like the Czechs, German immigrants formed community bands that were dominated by brass and reeds but might include an occasional zither or a violin. Summers might find them playing marches, overtures, and patriotic anthems for Sunday afternoon picnics in the park or "beer garden." Formal concerts by the "big band" were often followed by dances as a lesser number of musicians formed a "Little German Band" to play polkas and waltzes.

The Alte Kameraden, to cite a prominent example, fits this pattern. "Old Lutheran" dissenters from Brandenburg and Pomerania settled Ozaukee County's Freistadt in 1839. They formed a band within a decade which has, with a few short gaps, persisted. Still known today as the Alte Kameraden (old comrades), the band, numbering from fifteen to more than twenty members, performs in concert and for parades, but its members have also formed smaller dance ensembles to play for weddings and parties. Similar bands persist in heavily German Dodge, Sheboygan, and Washington Counties.

The numerous taverns, ballrooms, and fraternal lodges established by Germans all demanded dance music, as did weddings. In metropolitan Milwaukee, the "German Athens," a wide variety of musical groups favoring a polka repertoire have flourished since the nineteenth century. They include: Austrian *Schrammel* quartets with their double-necked guitars, violins, and zithers; alpine *ländlerkapelle* with their clarinets, button accordions, *hackbrett* dulcimers, and zithers; concertina clubs with members push-pulling the boxy German squeezebox; and brass and reed ensembles.

The latter included the legendary "Heinie and His Grenadiers." The Grenadiers were led by Jack Bundy, a radio announcer who took on the persona and dialect of "Heinie." Fitted out in quasi-military band uniforms and playing tight arrangements of old German folk tunes, the Grenadiers had an hour-long weekday broadcast on Milwaukee's WTMJ in the 1930s. Beginning with Heinie's "Hello efferybody," the group balanced musical selections with their leader's comic patter and storytelling. The Grenadiers cut four sides for Decca and they also played widely for dances throughout southeastern Wisconsin.

Not surprisingly, World War II made the existence of overtly German bands with militaristic names and garb temporarily unacceptable. The "band with a million friends," however, was reformed after the war, performing on television in 1948 and playing on occasion into the 1960s. Jack Bundy's "Heinie" legacy has continued in the persons of various radio disc jockeys with put-on German dialects.

Ross Gordon assumed the name Uncle Julius while working for Madison's WKOW in the late 1940s. Listeners mistakenly assumed Julius was directing a live band when, prior to spinning a record, he pronounced "Ach so boys, now comes der polka: vun, two, t'ree." He soon formed the Uncle Julius Band and began playing jobs in south-central Wisconsin. And his radio sponsor, Doughboy Feeds, included free dance tickets in their flour. Although neither formed bands, both Fritz the Plumber (Norman Margraff) of Jackson's WYLO and Crazy Otto of Appleton's WRJQ have continued the tradition of German dialect-spouting polka disc jockeys.

The Wisconsin German music that such disc jockeys have played, however, has been made chiefly by musicians from the hinterlands. In the heavily German agricultural counties stretching north and a bit east from Milwaukee (Washington, Ozaukee, Fond du Lac, Sheboygan, Calumet, and Manitowoc), dance bands began forming in the 1920s with an instrumentation similar to that of Romy Gosz. As opposed to Gosz's buzzing musical attack, however, bands led by Shorty Hoffmann, Tony Gosz, Howie Bowe, and Herbie Schneider favored round notes, crisp horns, and foursquare rhythms. They were more likely to play schottisches and an occasional ländler. And they might feature vocals in German or a broad German American dialect. The Groeschl family, for example, inherited a large repertoire of German folksongs, while Howie Bowe's "The Little German Ball" concerned comic doings at "Schultz's beer garden on Saturday night." Today Syl Groeschl of Calumetville and Jerry Schneider of Chilton carry on the old-time German tradition.

The Wisconsin German area extending from Dodge County northeast to Wausau and Merrill in Marathon and Lincoln Counties boasts numerous small ensembles centered around the concertina. Invented by Cal Friedrich Uhlig of Chemnitz, Germany, about 1830, the concertina was brought to the Upper Midwest by immigrants. Its clear tone and easy blending with wind instruments partially accounts for its persistence, but it was also marketed zealously. Perhaps because it allowed a single musician to put out both rhythm and melody, it prospered in a relatively sparsely populated rural area that could not support many large bands.

Irving DeWitz of Hustisford in Dodge County began selling concertinas and giving lessons about 1920 (fig. 25.2). He was aided by Chicago importers, arrangers, and manufacturers (like Henry Silberhorn and Rudy Patek), and by virtuoso concertinists like Milwaukee's Peters Brothers, who barnstormed through rural Wisconsin. DeWitz's students eventually numbered more than five hundred, many of whom went on to promote the concertina. The late Pat Watters of Mosinee and Dan Gruetzmacher of Wausau have played a similar role.

The final major strain of Wisconsin German polka music draws inspiration from Minnesota. From the 1920s through the 1950s bands from New Ulm, Minnesota, exerted a tremendous influence on polka musicians throughout the Upper Midwest. "Whoopee John" Wilfahrt, Harold Loeffelmacher and the Six Fat Dutchmen, Fezz Fritsche and the Goose Town Band, Babe Wagner, and Elmer Scheid and his Hoolerie Band reached Wisconsin musicians through radio broadcasts, recordings, and tours. Their "Dutchman" style, as it came to be known, featured a tuba that abandoned staid oompahing to romp and take leads, a sophisticated blending of brass and reeds, and a concertina that offered improvised solos. Wisconsin bands soon emerged with names like Bobby Art and the Wisconsin Dutchmen (Elkhart Lake), Ray Dorschner and the Rainbow Valley Dutchmen (Menasha), and Whoopee Norm Edlebeck and the Dairyland Dutchmen (Wausaukee).

By the 1970s, economic factors pared most Dutchman bands from seven or more pieces down to six or fewer. Bands began to favor "concertina oompah," as the concertina player, once part of a balanced ensemble, moved to the fore. The innovations of Syl Liebl eased the transition. Born in 1914 in New Ulm, Minnesota, Liebl moved to Coon Valley near La Crosse in the 1930s. While leading the Jolly Swiss Boys, he developed a style that emphasized sixteenth notes, triplets, and trills or "warbles" created by rapid finger movement on two notes.

Although Liebl has retired from playing with a band, his recordings remain popular, as do numerous youthful concertinists who have extended his innovations: Brian Brueggen of Brian and the Mississippi Valley Dutchmen (Cashton), Gary Brueggen of the Ridgeland Dutchmen (Cashton), Karl Hartwich of Karl and the Country Dutchmen (Trempealeau), and Kevin Liss of the New Jolly Swiss Boys (Coon Valley).

25.2. German concertina player and teacher Irving DeWitz, with his daughter
Lucille, Hustisford, 1929. Wisconsin Folk Museum Collection, courtesy Irving DeWitz.

Slovenian Squeezeboxes

Like the "concertina oompah" phase of the Dutchman style, the Slovenian polka sound emphasizes skill with a squeezebox. Slovenians began arriving in Wisconsin in the 1880s and 1890s, settling initially in the Walker's Point area on Milwaukee's south side and in working-class suburbs like West Allis. Between 1908 and 1915, largely through the efforts of Ignac Cesnik, a land agent, Slovenians established farms on logged-off acreage in the Willard area of Clark County.

A few brought Lubas button accordions from the old country, while most retained a rich tradition of songs. A reminiscence by Frank and Angela Auman in *Spominska Zgodovina*/Historical Memories (Willard, Wisc.: Slovenska Druzba, 1987), describes the typical house parties of immigrants and their offspring in Willard:

They gathered together and had parties in each other's homes. There was home brew and homemade wine, the ladies made *potica* (rolled walnut bread) and homemade doughnuts, there was boiled ham and homemade sausage. An old button key accordion was played by Frank Jr.—all the young people danced all night long, but the older folks first got to dancing after the wine and brew started working. The hard times were all forgotten, at least for the time being.

Meanwhile, in urban Milwaukee, tavernkeepers like Joseph Bashell were playing the button box for fellow Slovenians who worked in mills and tanneries.

In the late 1920s and through the 1930s, the second generation of Wisconsin Slovenian musicians was exposed to recordings by the Hoyer Trio. Based in Cleveland, the largest Slovenian American settlement, the Hoyers featured a four-string banjo that chunked out rhythm, and two button accordions: while one handled the basic melody, the other embroidered it with rapid staccato runs. Milwaukean Louie Bashell, especially, drew upon the Hoyers' sound and developed his own style.

Bashell was born in the Walker's Point neighborhood in 1914. By age seven he was playing button accordion for guests at his father's tavern. He took up the more versatile piano accordion in his teens, eventually forming a dance band with twin piano accordions, four-string banjo, string bass, and drums. Bashell's first recordings came in the late 1940s on Milwaukee's Pfau label, and he eventually recorded for Mercury and RCA-Victor. His signature tune, "Silk Umbrella Polka," based on an old Slovenian folk song, "Zidana Marela," has become a standard in the repertoire of polka bands nationally.

Bashell's initial popularity coincided with the emergence of "America's Polka King," Frankie Yankovic. Yankovic was raised in the heart of Cleveland's Slovenian community. Drawing upon the Hoyers and favoring an instrumentation similar to Bashell's, Yankovic specialized in changing "foreign" lyrics to English and adapting Country tunes to polka tempos. His "Blue Skirt Waltz," based on an old Czech tune, and "Just Because," a made-over "hillbilly" number, sold millions nationally. Perhaps because of the presence of Slovenians in Milwaukee, because of the success of local musicians like Bashell, and because of the abundance of prominent accordion manufacturers and teachers in the city, Yankovic won his "Polka King" title at a "battle of the bands" in Milwaukee in 1948. He has enjoyed an enthusiastic following there ever since.

Current Milwaukee area bands led by Barbara Flanum, Joey Klass, Grant Kozera, Bill Savatski, and Jeff Winard champion the Slovenian sound established by Yankovic and other Cleveland bands. Yet each has contributed innovations. All have composed new tunes, some substitute a rasping saxophone for a second accordion, while others incorporate Swiss and Austrian melodies into their repertoires.

Verne Meisner is the elder statesman and the most prominent of Wisconsin's Slovenian style musicians. Born in Milwaukee in 1938, Meisner acquired an accordion at eleven and started a band a year later. Since his first recording in 1957, he has made fifteen LPs. While Meisner's efforts match up with the best work of Cleveland bands, the recordings of his son Steve and a cousin, Gordon Hartmann, have pushed the music in new directions. Aided by electronic modifications of the accordion, both have injected their Slovenian sound with elements of jazz, pop, and rock. Hartmann's 1989 *Polkaholic* album received a Grammy nomination, while his latest, *Polkafriendzy,* has a punkish ring.

While the Meisners and Hartmann push forward, other Wisconsin Slovenian musicians look to the past. The old diatonic button accordion, put away since the innovations of Yankovic, was vigorously revived in the 1970s as Slovenians, like so many other ethnics, sought their roots. "Button box clubs" emerged featuring from half a dozen to a score of button accordionists—many of them brandishing Melodija accordions from Ljubljana, Yugoslavia. Whereas the old Lubas and Mervar button accordions of the immigrant generation had idiosyncratic tunings, Melodijas are tuned to a standard concert pitch that permits ensemble playing. Groups like the Milwaukee area's Badger Button Box Club have further stimulated their chosen instrument's popularity by hosting touring Slovenian virtuosos like Lojse Slak.

Nor has the button box failed to influence Wisconsin's modern Slovenian bands. Willard's Richie Yurkovich, a follower of piano accordionist Verne Meisner, has mastered the button accordion and regularly plays sets on it for dances; *Nuttin' But Button* is one of his most recent recordings. A part-time farmer and professional musician, Yurkovich also runs his own studio and RY label (fig. 25.3). His clientele includes polka bands in many styles, but especially Slovenian bands from northern Wisconsin, Minnesota's Iron Range, and the Upper Peninsula of Michigan.

From Polish Weddings to Push

The Poles who settled Milwaukee, Oconto, Portage, Rusk, and Trempealeau Counties in the nineteenth and early twentieth centuries were chiefly peasants from Poznan, Kaszubia, Silesia, and Galicia. They included fiddlers and clarinetists steeped in the old *wiejska* or village style of rural Poland that typically combined a lead violin or clarinet with harmony violins and a bowed cello for polkas, waltzes, obereks, mazurkas, krakowiaks, and kujawiaks. They also numbered players of such

25.3. Richie Yurkovich in the basement studio of his rural Willard home, 1987.
His RY label features many Upper Midwestern polka bands, especially those
favoring the Slovenian style. Photo: James P. Leary.

newer folk instruments as the button accordion and concertina. These musicians entertained at house parties, at harvest dances, and especially at weddings.

Old-country Polish weddings were rich pageants of fancy dress, feasts, music, and dance that might extend for three days. And so they remained through the first few generations of immigrants. Dick Rodziczak (now Dick Rodgers) of Pulaski recalls that in the 1930s his violinist father played marches to lead the wedding couple to and from the church. Then the elder Rodiziczak would join with a concertinist to play all afternoon, into the night, and, with a little rest, throughout the next day.

The loose improvisatory feel and syncopation of the old Polish style can be heard on twenty-six sides recorded by Milwaukee's Sosnowski Trio for the Mermaid and Columbia labels in the late 1920s. Little is known about the group beyond their names: Jozef Sosnowski, accordion; Stanislaw Kozera, violin; and John Baczkowski, clarinet.

By the late 1930s, however, those Wisconsin Polish musicians venturing beyond the house party were generally swayed either by American pop music, or by influential polka bands from the other three major ethnic styles. Milwaukee's Frank and Max Kucynski were the sons of a violinist and concertina player who entertained at many Polish weddings. They changed their surnames to King after another pop musician of Polish origin, Wayne King. Frank or "Pee Wee" King, a piano accordionist, went on to lead the Golden West Cowboys, broadcast on Nashville's "Grand

Ole Opry," and record such national hits as "Tennessee Waltz." Max King, meanwhile, stuck to the concertina, but specialized in both Western swing and jazz.

Meanwhile, other Milwaukeans of Polish extraction have taken on the Slovenian style so popular in that city. Among them are Don Gralak, Grant Kozera, and Al Roberts (Al Gostomski). In Stevens Point, where Minnesota Dutchman bands made regular appearances, Poles like Ray Chojnacki, Ray Konkol, and Dominic Slusarski have all led German Bohemian bands. Dick Rodgers of Pulaski was likewise inspired by Bohemian stalwarts Lawrence Duchow and Romy Gosz. These "converts" nonetheless retained elements of their elders' Polish repertoire and "feel."

In the early 1950s that feel was sparked with a vengeance by Chicago's Li'l Wally Jagiello. An upstart teenager, Jagiello drew upon older strains of village music still present among the Second City's working-class Poles. With his loose phrasing, slow tempos, reedy concertina, emotional vocals, and disdain for written arrangements, Jagiello energized young Polish Americans. Norm Dombrowski of Stevens Point compared Jagiello to rock 'n' roll's Little Richard and Elvis Presley. And soon Dombrowski and a clutch of young Portage County Poles were playing and singing the same way. They went on to form groups like the "Happy Notes" and the "Kaszuba Aces."

While Jagiello was working his magic, concertinist Alvin Styczynski had already begun to put out a rough but soulful Polish sound. Styczysnki, who grew up on a Pulaski farm, formed the "Jolly Trio" in 1952 and went on to record a string of albums in the 1960s on the Cuca label. One of them featured "Pulaski is a Polka Town," a celebratory pronouncement that remains true at the onset of the 1990s. Although it is a settlement of less than two thousand people, Pulaski boasts an extraordinary number of active polka performers: Gary Gracyalny, the Maroszek Brothers, the Polish Sweethearts, Polkatown Sound, the Polkcadets, Polka Dimension, Chad Przybylski, Dick Rodgers, Steve Rodgers, and Mike Ryba & Changing Times.

Many of these bands have been further influenced by an evolved Polish polka style that whirled out of the Windy City in the 1970s: "Dyno," or "Push." Building upon Jagiello's feeling for heartfelt vocals and relaxed tempos, the new style augmented the concertina with two trumpets that punched out melody, stressed complex electric bass patterns, introduced a piano accordion playing a repetitive "bellow shake," and approached the volume of rock. These exuberant additions and the hot doubletime dancing of the "polka hop" have inspired many young Polish Americans to follow the polka scene.

They Still Polka

In 1907, at the beginning of the twentieth century, Wardon Alan Curtis entertained sophisticated readers of *Century* magazine with a blithe account of "'The Light Fantastic' in the Central West: Country Dances of Many Nationalities in Wisconsin."

While other popular writers of the day were fascinated by the archaic African steps of former slaves in New Orleans, or the quaint "Kentucky running square dances" of Appalachian mountaineers, or the mysterious crown dances of the Zuni, Curtis visited the taverns and halls of Wisconsin's ethnic communities to report with scarcely concealed amazement that dancers "still polka . . . in the country."

Perhaps remarkably, the descendants of those whom Curtis witnessed have carried on their traditions—not by slavishly imitating their elders, but by synthesizing their past with their present, by reinventing polka music and culture to suit each succeeding generation. And so they not only dance on at the twentieth century's end, but they give every sign of continuing beyond the year 2000.

26

Black Gospel Music in Milwaukee

Peter Roller

Black gospel music thrives in such southern Wisconsin cities as Janesville, Kenosha, Madison, Racine, and especially Milwaukee, where African Americans, present since the nineteenth century, have settled in increasing numbers since the 1940s. Hailing from the rural South and from Chicago, they sustain a wide variety of religious performance styles. Yet the vibrant Milwaukee gospel scene has been little studied in comparison with that of such other midwestern cities as Chicago and Detroit. As such, Peter Roller's survey is particularly welcome.

A member of the music faculty at Milwaukee's Alverno College, Peter Roller was trained in folklore and ethnomusicology at Indiana University and at the University of Wisconsin. Since the 1980s he has conducted research on various African American musical traditions for the Florida Folklife Program and the Michigan Traditional Arts Program. Roller is also an accomplished guitarist who toured with the roots rock band Paul Cebar and the Milwaukeeans, and he has provided musical backup for a Milwaukee black gospel group, The Masonic Wonders.

Roller's survey, conducted in the summer of 1996, is the culmination of a fifteen-day research contract with the Wisconsin Arts Board in preparation for the 1998 Festival of Wisconsin Folklife, part of the state's sesquicentennial festivities. Since 1967, when the Smithsonian Institution began the Festival of American Folklife, folklorists have been active in festival production. The process typically begins with field research—interviews, photography, the accumulation of sound recordings—and culminates in a report like Roller's, which introduces a cultural group and its traditions, profiles current practitioners, and then makes recommendations about who might work best in a festival setting. Since arts boards and other public cultural institutions are also clearinghouses for many artistic, civic, and educational organizations in search of "multicultural" performers for their events, field reports like Roller's contribute to a data base that can result in increased work for the performers listed and, ideally, broader understanding of their traditions within the larger society. Reports like Roller's contribute ultimately to the historical record: the Wisconsin Sesquicentennial Folklife Survey materials have become part of the archival collections of the State Historical Society of Wisconsin.

Reprinted in abridged form from a field report produced for the Wisconsin Arts Board's Wisconsin Sesquicentennial Celebration Folklife Survey, 1996.

Southeastern Wisconsin has a significant African American population centered in Milwaukee that maintains vibrant musical traditions. The greatest volume of musical performance is devoted to black gospel music, which is heard weekly in church services, programs held by local groups, and large public concerts. Milwaukee is also home to a number of working blues, R & B, jazz, and rap musicians, but their

26.1. The Happy Harmonizers, a family gospel quartet (*Left to right,* Ardella Herron, Geneva Herron, Shirley Herron, Bertha McMillan), Milwaukee, early 1980s. Wisconsin Folk Museum Collection.

performances are not as regular nor as vital to the African American community as is the outpouring of gospel music. I have, consequently, focused the first phase of my research on the Milwaukee gospel music scene.

African Americans have migrated to the Milwaukee area since the mid-1800s because of the city's opportunities for work and due to the state's progressive politics regarding racial issues. Wisconsin was the only state in the union to openly defy the Fugitive Slave Act and it became a refuge for runaway slaves (Benson 1996). Other signs of Wisconsin's positive social and political climate for blacks are the 1895 state legislature bill that allowed African Americans to go into any public facility (countering federal "separate but equal" laws) and the fact that black workers were supported by organized labor, starting with the 1897 organization of the Shoe Artist Association in Milwaukee to protect the rights of African American shoe shiners (Benson 1996). By the 1930s, second- and third-generation black families in Milwaukee had established the part of the city west of the Milwaukee River and north of downtown as a bustling neighborhood dominated by African Americans and Jews. The Northern Migration of blacks from the Deep South states of Arkansas, Mississippi, Tennessee and Alabama that occurred after World War II gradually turned the North Side of Milwaukee into the majority African American community that it is today.

With the growth of the black community in Milwaukee came churches, both large and small, and the musical traditions that are at the heart of African American religious practices (fig. 26.2). Today in Milwaukee, every Baptist, African Methodist

26.2. Church of God in Christ, a "holiness" church on North Eighth Street, Milwaukee, 1930s. State Historical Society of Wisconsin, WHi (X3) 51499.

Episcopal, Church of God in Christ or Pentecostal church has one or more gospel choirs; with the current trend favoring mass choirs of fifteen to forty people that feature both males and females as well as ages ranging from children to seniors. An ensemble such as the Metropolitan Missionary Baptist Church Mass Choir of Milwaukee has some thirty singers, with ages ranging from five years old to sixty, and a driving band featuring keyboard, bass and drums. All of their vocal numbers are tightly arranged and kept on track by a choir leader who foregoes the timekeeping patterns of the classical conductor for enthusiastic arm motions and emotive facial gestures to cue the rhythmic intricacies of the music. In addition to mass choirs, many Milwaukee churches maintain choirs related to particular groups: youth choir, adult choir, male or female chorus.

The black churches of Milwaukee provide the context for more musical activities than just the performances of their home choirs. Any weekend throughout the year one can find gospel concerts and programs being hosted by North Side churches. The **concerts** usually feature a group that is known nationally on the gospel music circuit, such as The Christianaires of Suntag, Mississippi, combined with two or three local groups who precede the headliners. While gospel **programs** are usually centered on the anniversary of the founding of a local group and they typically feature numerous regional gospel groups who are friendly with the honorees, singing on both Saturday and Sunday evening in a host church. The gospel program tradition in Milwaukee is a longtime format for enjoying local black gospel talent combined with evangelical preaching and congregational singing. It provides a natural circuit for groups to maintain their performing skills while attendees receive uplifting Christian entertainment, within the sanctity of a church. As an M.C. at a gospel program stated at the start of a Saturday night performance, "They say Saturday is the Devil's night, with people running around and getting in all kinds of trouble; we here are gonna make it the Lord's night."

The predominant type of group to perform at Milwaukee programs, as well as at concerts, is the gospel quartet. Though their style is descended from the period in the 1920s and 1930s when groups of four sang a capella gospel in close harmony, quartets at current Milwaukee programs have anywhere from three to six singers as well as backup bands. In my brief survey of Milwaukee's gospel music, I have identified twenty quartets actively performing. The programs that I have attended have usually featured six to ten quartets, with a solo singer or the host church's choir providing the only change from this musical format. **Open** gospel programs allow for any group to show up and draw a number to find out when they will perform, whereas most anniversary programs have a more formal order of groups: local quartets, solo singers or church choirs make up the first half of the program, each expected to sing only two numbers (an "A and B Selection"), while designated "honoree" quartets (usually including out-of-town guests) make up the second half of the program and sing "Selections" that can be from two to five songs. Printed programs are often made up for anniversary programs and state the groups expected to participate and their place in the line-up.

Gospel programs in Milwaukee have a fascinating structure—based upon their dual function as performance venue for groups and religious service—that is as important a tradition as is the quartet music frequently heard in them. Every program has a designated M.C. who is both an evangelist, giving impromptu sermonettes, and a host who announces each group. M.C.s are often female, reflecting the majority female audience that I have observed at black gospel programs in Milwaukee. The M.C. guides participants at gospel programs through an established series of phases that unfold over the course of a three- to four-hour event: Devotion (opening prayer and scripture reading led by a deacon, congregational singing of hymns and spirituals); A and B Selections by local gospel groups; Invitation to Christ (minister preaches and invites attendees to come forward and commit themselves to Christ); Offering (collection of donations from groups and attendees run by designated host group); Selections by honoree groups; and Benediction (closing remarks and prayer by minister from the host church). This basic structure is consistent from program to program, though the length of each event is determined by the number of groups participating and the intensity of the preaching and musical performance. If a group's singing catches the spirit of the congregation, that one selection can grow into a twenty-minute vehicle for improvisatory singing by the lead vocalist performed over call and response background harmonies and a driving groove provided by the band.

Despite being hosted by a church of a particular denomination, gospel programs have an ecumenical spirit—with people from all denominations and walks of life welcomed to participate. Attendees exhibit the characteristics of African American religious tradition by standing, swaying, gesturing, and calling out in response to fervent preaching or inspired singing. In many ways, the gospel program is an updated descendant of the earliest "bush arbor" praise meetings enacted by slaves, where singing of spirituals, reciting of scripture and personal testimony were shared in changing locations but on a regular basis. The long meter hymns that are commonly sung during a program's Devotion, for example, go directly back to the hymn singing of slaves—where a leader delivered a line of text and then the congregation slowly sang that line, giving each word numerous melismatic twists and turns. Likewise the close interplay that occurs between attendees and performers at gospel programs reinforces what Maultsby calls "performer and audience as a single unit," a quality that she finds links African American and West African music traditions (Maultsby 1990). For both the gospel program and the praise meeting, the location (or particular denomination) is not as important as is the characteristic blend of preaching and singing that has energized the spirit of African American communities for generations.

While I have focused on black gospel music in Milwaukee and the importance of gospel programs in that community, numerous other secular and sacred music styles exist for consideration. Milwaukee is a significant hub in the national jazz music scene, with African American artists like saxophonist Frank Morgan moving between local gigs and wider touring. A number of blues and soul groups with black lead singers and interracial back-up bands perform in a culturally mixed circuit that finds them at times in North Side clubs playing for black audiences and at others in the racially mixed context of city festivals or East Side bars. Young hip-hop performers create raps about life in Milwaukee's central city and are increasingly putting out their own recordings to serve a regional audience. Younger African Americans are also energizing gospel music, with rap-style lead vocals and hip-hop inspired playing by back-up bands making inroads into local gospel performance. The Milwaukee audience for gospel music has "skewed younger." As record store owner and gospel D.J. Andrew Taylor states: "Once upon a time it was an older audience, but now we get everyone between young and old" (Tianen 1996). Milwaukee's African American music scene offers a rich array of styles and traditions to explore.

Artist Profiles
Gospel Quartets and Groups

The Edifying Luckett Echoes, contact: Matthew Luckett
Gospel quartet with backing band, made up of brothers Matthew, Leroy, Delon, Jerry, and Avery Luckett with singer Bennie Meeks. They sing original gospel songs written by group members in a R & B flavored style.
Cassette: *The Edifying Luckett Echoes*

The Gill Singers, contact: Thermond Gill
Gospel quartet with two brothers and two sisters as singers and a backing band of drums, bass, keyboard, and guitar. The group was started by their father, Rev. Clayton Gill, and they have been singing together for 36 years. Repertoire is a mixture of originals and traditional gospel songs, with both males and females taking lead vocals.
Cassette: *Old Soldier*

The Gospel Melodies, contact: Mary Johnson
Quartet with women singers, age 30–65 years old, who have been singing together in Milwaukee for 18 years. Male guitarist in his fifties sometimes sings and is joined in the band by a drummer, bass player and guitarist—all of whom are teenagers. They perform traditional gospel songs, often in an up-tempo shouting style.

The Gospel Trumpets, contact: Dale Brown
Male quartet who have been singing in Milwaukee for 48 years. They employ different lead singers whose styles range from a ballad-like version of "Mine Eyes Have Seen the Glory" to gruffly sung traditional gospel shouts.

The Harris Crusaders, contact: Terry Harris
Gospel group with three singers, guitar, bass, synthesizer and drums. Modern funk arrangement of songs with heavy bass, strong improvisatory lead vocals by Terry Harris.

The Hughes Singers, contact: Edda Mae Jackson
The four sisters who sing in this group learned their repertoire from their mother, who was a group member until her death. They sing in the quartet style of the 1940s and 1950s, when voices and a strummed guitar made up the typical group. Their songs include early spirituals like "It's Me Lord, Standing in the Need of Prayer."

The Long Way 'Round, contact: Edward Montgomery
Quartet of men in their 50s and 60s who sing gospel in a smooth, jazz harmony style (ala pop songsters the Ink Spots) to backing tapes.
Cassette: *The Shortest Route to Good Gospel*

The Masonic Wonders, contact: James Mitchell
Gospel quartet drawing on six male singers, ages 45 to 70. Interracial backing band consisting of guitars, bass and drums. Group was formed in 1956 by lead singer Charles McCullum with other members of a Milwaukee Masonic Lodge. Group performs wide range of styles from the sanctified shouts that Charles McCullum learned growing up in Mississippi to country-flavored gospel songs.
Compact Disc: *Higher in the Lord*

The New Vocalaires
Male quartet with bass player who sings lead vocals, plus drums and guitar. The group sings traditional gospel songs in a dramatic manner, with much movement by the lead singer.

O. W. Griffin and the Exalters, contact: O. W. Griffin
Gospel group with four female and two male singers, back-up band. Original gospel songs played in a 1970s soul style. Lead vocals mostly by female group members.
Cassette: *Stretched Out*

The Queens of Harmony, contact: Jesse McCullum
Female a capella quartet with women in their 50s and 60s. They sing spirituals and gospel songs in the original style, with rhythmic chanting in harmony by back-up singers supporting the lead vocal. The group has been singing together in Milwaukee for 28 years.

The Roberson Brothers
Modern-sounding gospel quartet with backing band, built around three Roberson Brothers and singer Ron Staples. Their music is heavy on synthesizers, but covers traditional songs, including "Remember Me," "Come By Here," and "Put Your Hand in the Hand."
Cassette: *Come By Here Lord*

Choirs

Rev. R. J. Burt and the Greater New Birth Mass Choir, contact: Rev. Burt
Mixed-gender choir with 50 singers, ages from teenage to 40s. Back-up band includes organ, synthesizer, guitar, bass and drums. This choir sings intricate arrangements of both contemporary songs and longtime gospel standards like "Jesus is on the Mainline."
Cassette: *Greater New Birth Choir "LIVE" From the Sanctuary*

Guiding Light Missionary Baptist Church Mass Choir, contact: Tonda LaYa Brooks
Mixed-gender choir with 25 voices, age 10 through 20s. Back-up band with drums, bass, organ and synthesizer. This energetic young choir sings very syncopated, sometimes hip-hop flavored, music with lead singer (often Tonda Brooks) always driving the song's concluding section with improvised singing.

Metropolitan Missionary Baptist Church Mass Choir, contact: Dr. Robert Wells
This mixed-gender choir has approximately 30 young people, age 5 through 20s, with a back-up band including keyboard, bass and drums. It allows its youngest members to play in the band and to take on the role of solo singer against the choir's back-up.

Sources

Benson, Clayborn. 1996. "Blacks Found the State a Good Place to Grow." *The Milwaukee Journal Sentinel* (June).

Maultsby, Portia. 1990. "Africanisms in African-American Music." In *Africanisms in American Culture*, ed. Joseph Holloway. Bloomington: Indiana University Press.

Tianen, Dave. 1996. "In the Spirit: Milwaukee Opening Hearts, Souls to Growing Power of Gospel Music." *The Milwaukee Journal Sentinel* (April).

27

Joua Bee Xiong, Hmong Musician

Transcribed and Edited by James P. Leary

Hmong people from mountainous northern Laos began making their way to Wisconsin in the mid-1970s. Recruited during the Vietnam War by America's Central Intelligence Agency (CIA) to harry the North Vietnamese along the Ho Chi Minh Trail, the Hmong also battled the communist Pathet Lao at home. Eventually their villages were overrun. Those who survived sought refuge in camps across the Mekong River in Thailand where they hoped for emigration to America. Now, in the late 1990s, more than thirty thousand Hmong people live in various cities across the state of Wisconsin. Maintaining many aspects of their traditional culture, they have adapted others to their life in the New World.

Hmong women, for example, sustain an ancient tradition of intricate needlework called *paj ntaub* (pronounced "pandau"). Involving tiny hand stitches, embroidery, reverse applique, and a range of geometric symbols, paj ntaub adorns Hmong clothing, as well as the baby carriers and funeral coats essential to rites of passage. In Thailand's refugee camps, however, American social workers, anticipating the adjustments immigration would require, coaxed Hmong women to produce handwork they might sell in the United States. One result was the production of "story cloths," embroidered representations of traditional Hmong life in Laos, of the horrors of war, and of Hmong resettlement in America. Hmong women have also begun to make embroidered stuffed animals, Christmas tree skirts, and even western-style quilts (see *Hmong Art: Tradition and Change,* ed. Joanne Cubbs [Sheboygan: John Michael Kohler Arts Center, 1986]).

Soldiers, farmers, and hunters in Southeast Asia, Hmong men have often found the economic transition to American life difficult. Likewise, their traditional music has undergone many transformations. The Hmong language is tonal, with the same units of sound carrying different meanings depending on their pitch and stress. The tones of spoken Hmong can be replicated on instruments and, consequently, much of Hmong music is best understood as a mode of ritual speech. At the same time it is a poetic speech characterized by recurrent phrases and verse structures. Still practiced within the ancient contexts of New Year's celebrations and funerals, it is no longer an integral part of courtship. Indeed, some active musicians raised the old way perform most frequently to curious cultural outsiders—to not only their new American neighbors but also their own children and grandchildren, who have become westernized and Christianized. Not surprisingly, veteran Hmong musicians now compose songs that lament the world they have lost, while exhorting their descendants to remember their heritage (see Amy Catlin, "The Hmong and Their Music . . . A Critique of Pure Speech," in Cubbs 1986, 11–18).

The following account of Joua Bee Xiong's life and music is derived from field research I undertook for the Chippewa Valley Museum. In an exemplary project, the museum collaborated with members of Eau Claire's Hmong community and its branch of the Hmong Mutual Assistance Association to produce an exhibit, numerous events, and a publication concerning the experiences of the Hmong people who settled in Wisconsin's Chippewa Valley (see Tim Pfaff, *Hmong in America: Journey from a Secret War* [Eau Claire, Wisc.: Chippewa Valley Museum, 1995]). In

1996 Joua Bee Xiong was elected to Eau Claire's city council, the first in his community to hold such an office.

From a tape-recorded interview conducted for the Chippewa Valley Museum, Eau Claire, Wisc., December 1992.

From Laos to Wisconsin

I was born in Laos in a village in the province of Xieng Khouang. I was born around 1961, but the date is not certain. My father was a soldier. I had eight brothers and one sister.

After the Vietnam War, in 1975, the American CIA withdrew from Laos. The communist Pathet Lao took over and they said we, the Hmong people, were the eyes and arms and ears of the American CIA. They tried to kill us, and made it very difficult for us to live there. My family went to hide in the forest. We carried guns, grenades, ammunition—we hid in tunnels or in the forest. We ran out of arms, we totally lost our village. We were in the high mountains of Laos.

In April 1978 they took our village. Most people died, some of us survived. We walked to Thailand with other families, about three thousand people fighting and walking. It took about two and a half months to get to the Mekong River. We had to fight at the river several times and to get around an electric fence. Our family split up.

I sneaked across the border to the river. I told my parents I would try to return with a boat to take them to Thailand. I had to cross the Mekong with two others by floating and swimming with a [bouyant] bamboo pipe. They did not know how to swim, so they were just hanging on. I was their motor. The Mekong was about a mile and a half wide. Water buffaloes looked smaller than chickens on the other side.

Once I got across regulations prevented me from going back. I had to stay there a couple weeks. Then I asked a relative to help me go back to find my parents, my brothers and sister. Lots of Hmong people were still on the Laotian side. They had run out of food. They ate any leaves or anything that was soft enough to chew. Some had gone back to the mountains, some had surrendered. I could not find my parents. They had tried to wait a week or so, but I couldn't come. I walked nearly half way back to the mountains trying to find them, but I could not. I went back to Thailand. Three weeks later my parents and brothers were pretty lucky. They found boats and were able to cross.

Once we were in the camps we only stayed about six months, then I came to Philadelphia in July 1979 with a brother and uncle. My parents came soon after. We were in the city, in a black area. We only knew a few words of English: "Hi," "How are you?," "Good morning." Some black people in school were not very friendly. They thought I was Chinese and, like the people on television, could do kung fu. I got in several fights, one time almost to the death. It was kind of scary.

A few months later my parents came to settle in Chicago, so I telephoned them and moved there. I lived with my parents a few months. There the situation was not much better than Philadelphia. We didn't have good education. We got in touch with

27.1. Joua Bee Xiong plays the qeej in the library of the Chippewa
Valley Museum, Eau Claire, 1992. Photo: James P. Leary.

Kai Moua in Eau Claire. I think he was the first Hmong person to come to Eau Claire. He told us it was a small town with good education. We moved to Eau Claire in August 1980. I went to Memorial High School. I started in tenth grade. It was very difficult at first. I knew math but no English. My past experience as a soldier and a farmer gave me no skills to get by in the U.S.A. My background was nothing.

After high school, I studied computer languages at Chippewa Valley Technical School. After graduating, I worked six months for the Hmong Mutual Assistance Association, then decided I needed more education. So I went back to college and I graduated with a criminal justice major and joined the Eau Claire Police Reserve for four years. Right now I am working with Eau Claire County Human Services Employment and Training Program.

First I worked with Southeast Asian refugee peoples. After one year I changed to doing the same work for the Caucasians. I have been doing that for four years now. My case load is almost two hundred people. I try to help them go back to school, to find child care, to find jobs if they are job ready. Most of my case load is divorced women.

I am the first person to work for my family. I came here single, but now I have a wife and seven children. I bought a home for myself and I have several duplexes for rent. I am proud of these accomplishments.

Learning the Qeej

When I was thirteen or fourteen I began to learn music from my relatives in the village. I worked in the fields in the day. Some days I had to go and fight to protect the village. At night I learned to play. My cousin bought me a *qeej* [pronounced "kheng"], and he said: "Right now, younger brother, we don't have school. So it's very important that you learn this, to help the community." Right then I realized that maybe it would be important for me to learn. One of my masters was Kao Neng Xiong, the other was Kao Yia Xiong. They had no school education, but they knew lots about the Hmong culture and Hmong music. I helped them work during the day and I learned music during the night. I stayed with them until one or two in the morning.

The oldest brother of one of my masters knew how to make the qeej. I saw him make them. It is made of small bamboo. You have to dry the bamboo eight months to a year. You choose the hardest part for the sound cavity, cut it into a rounded shape with a knife. We don't have sandpaper, but we have a leaf that's pretty close. He took that leaf and sanded the bamboo. After he got it like that, then he split the round piece in half and hollowed it out and made cuts so that bamboo tubes could be passed through the sound cavity. The holes had to be measured carefully so that the bamboo fit tightly. The bamboo tubes are fitted with copper reeds that have been pounded many times—it's a free-reed instrument. The halves of the sound cavity are held together with a skein of bark, although tape is often used in the United States. In Laos beeswax was used to seal around the sound cavity if the maker had not fitted the bamboo tightly enough through the holes. The bamboo and reeds passing through the sound cavity are of different sizes to produce different tones, yet you try to keep the tone the same from one qeej to another so that various instruments will have the same sound. The finished instruments may have decorative beads and straps—just something pretty, something to hang it on.

Learning the qeej was the most difficult learning experience I ever had. We did not learn notes. The masters just said, "Follow the sounds." The master played and I listened and watched his fingers. Then I would try, and if I didn't do it I would try and try again until I could match the master's sounds. After two years I had learned just enough to help at funerals, but I was not yet a master. Two years are not enough to learn Hmong music, but I learned quite a bit during the six months in the refugee camps, especially helping elders at funerals. You could hear the qeej all the time in the camps.

Funerals

When my masters were young, there were competitions at the funeral where one player challenged another to see who could follow the other's steps or tactics. Cows and water buffaloes were killed at funerals, there was lots of meat. If a rival qeej player won a funeral competition, they got the largest share of payment in meat. People are not doing that any more. People were mad at each other, so they stopped doing that. And when some Hmong became Christians, they stopped these old traditions.

All the people in the village came to see the funerals during a particular day. The villagers bring food and money and come with another qeej player. The player inside at the funeral has to come outside and welcome the people and the other player and invite the latter inside to play. The players dance and play while this is going on. Many years ago when the outside player came there was a competition between the outside and the inside player over payment for the funeral. Nowadays the outside player plays a few songs and then sets his instrument aside.

In traditional customs, when a person died, they washed the body, dressed it in new clothes, and put it in the living room. The qeej player had to play a certain song. The Hmong people believe that if you die, your body is dead but your spirit is still alive. You need to go back to where you originally came from. You need to become a human being again, or whatever God plans you to become again. We have this song that indicates: right now you've died, but we need to direct your spirit back, step by step. When an elder dies—every village or town or province where he lived before—we take his spirit back to appreciate the town where he lived, the wood he burned, the water he used, to appreciate all those things before he can go to another village. We go from village to village, until we get to the village where he was born.

The Hmong people, when they are first born, have what we call the "baby shirt." It's not really a shirt, it's the placenta. We usually bury that in the house. [In Hmong culture the boy's placenta is buried near the center post of the house, the girl's is buried under the bed.] The qeej master has to take the spirit to get their shirt back to go back to where they came from. We hope they can be a good human being again, not an animal. Because if you become an animal, people will eat you. If you become a stone or a tree, you never will be able to talk. You need to become a human being again. The song that guides the spirit back takes three to five hours.

After that song, we have another song that goes step by step. You direct the spirit back to from where they came. The master has to play the first two important songs. Then after that anyone who knows how to play can help them. After the first two songs you can play the happy songs or the sad songs or what we call "foster songs" for people without parents, or widow songs, or songs for various meals: breakfast song, lunch song, dinner song. We believe that the person's dead, but the spirit is still around. We invite the spirit to have breakfast with us during the breakfast time, and the same for other meals. We do these steps until they are done and the family is happy and feels it's okay to bury the body. Then we have a couple of very important songs at the end when the body is moved outside. Then the family can take the body to bury.

The same songs and basic structure is used for funerals. But additional songs can be added, so the lengths of funerals vary depending upon the age, wealth, number of relatives, and so on of the deceased. Before you put the people in the coffin, we need to have another song that this is your horse and you need to ride your horse back to the spirit world. Whenever people want to kill any animals at the funerals, and dedicate it to that person, we need to play a song. We tell the dead spirit that this cow or pig is from your parents, or your brother, or your cousin, or your sister, or your daughter-in-law. Certain animals represent certain things. The cow represents the umbrella that protects the spirit on its journey—if it's sunshiney and very hot, you can use the umbrella to protect you; or if it's raining, you can use the umbrella too. The chicken will protect the spirit from being scared. The chicken also knows directions. When the spirit goes back to his great-grandparents, the chicken lets him know whether or not the spirit is being received by other spirits that are actually their relatives or bad spirits bent upon deception. Your relatives' spirits are not very nice to you, but the other spirits say, "Oh, how nice you are coming. Come to live with us." Your chicken knows that, so you have to follow your chickens.

There are dangers to the deceased spirit and to the qeej player during the funeral. At the last step, if you don't hide yourself from the bad spirits, they can follow you. They can get your spirit. Then you can sicken and die. We are careful to turn our back. We tell the bad spirits, if they ask the dead person's spirit about the qeej player who guides them, "His eye is so big and his ear is an elephant's ear. He came today, but he went back yesterday. He came on the air, but he went back under the ground." You say this to confuse the bad spirits. They don't know how to follow you. The dead person is also given a crossbow and a gun to scare the bad spirits. And the chicken guides him too.

One song is about the chicken. The Hmong people believe that at an early age there were nine suns and moons, but someone killed eight of them. The remaining sun and moon were very scared to come out in the world. The chicken, the rooster,

27.2. Hmong shaman Neng Lor Lee with traditional swords and head cloth against the backdrop of a home altar to the spirits, Eau Claire, 1992. Photo: James P. Leary.

is the only animal who knows when the sun will come out, and so he crows about three times to tell the sun to rise. The chicken is very important. No other animal has this power. The sun is so happy—in an early era the chicken had no corn—so the sun gave the chicken corn.

After a year the spirit is invited back again by the qeej player and the drummer. We say to the spirit, you have been gone from your family about a year, and now we invite you back. This is the last time that the spirit and the family can enjoy one another. We have all the songs and steps again.

When I say songs, no one sings during the funerals. The instrument sings. What the qeej plays is not music but actual words. I can say, "You are now dead, but I direct you to know whenever you hear insects, you are not hearing insects but your family crying; whenever you hear a big rain, those are their tears." We can tell those words on our instruments. You have to memorize those. You play for three, four days, you have to memorize all those and play them. But the memory is not in my brain, but in my fingers. When I know the family and the song, my fingers remember how to play.

If you don't know enough, those Hmong elderly usually discourage you. All the elderly, or the master qeej players sit around. They pretend they are sleeping, but their ear is listening to you. I learned that. They don't tell you in front, but they tell other people. They say, "Oh, this guy is good!" They say, "Oh, he doesn't know anything about it. How come he's doing that? We don't need his help." You don't want your parents, or your clan, or you to lose face. You need to, out in public, make sure you know most everything. Very occasionally they give you a drink, or they say, "You did a good job." That is the Hmong culture.

While the playing is going on during the long funerals, some relatives prepare food for many visitors. Some keep records of who helps with money or makes donations. Some play cards and tell stories about many things. They make the house warm, they make some fun and some noise so the family doesn't think about the dead person all the time. But the qeej players and the drummer have to play all the time.

The Qeej in a New Country

If people are Christians, they do exactly what other American Christians do. They just go and sing a song. They have a short service, the body is buried, and people go home. But it's not as valuable as the old tradition. If the people are Christians, they're not as appreciative of people who bring money or bring some food. In our tradition, if someone brings money or food, we have to say thank you and there is a bond.

Those Christians feel they are not bound by any people or thing in the world except God. So they don't observe traditions. Even if I give them a fifty dollar donation, they say, "Thank you." That's all. They don't say, "Right now you help me, next time I will help you. I will remember all the things you did to help me." And we can cry too. Those are the last moments and we can be there twenty-four hours. But the Christians, that's different. You can only be there a couple hours, or six hours for singing a song and a family get-together. It's completely different.

We play traditional funerals with the qeej in Eau Claire, twenty-four hours, up to two or three days. We cannot stay three or four weeks here, because it is very difficult for us to reserve the funeral home for that long. And with the Hmong people, if more than one person dies, we cannot have their funeral together, unless they are the same families. We don't want the spirits confused. If two people die at the same time, we will do the funerals in different places. In this country we have to be very careful. In Eau Claire we make arrangements with the funeral director to be there twenty-four hours so that no other body is in the same room during the ceremonies. It was very difficult at first for the funeral directors to understand. But after a few funerals, they learned that it was important to our culture and they gave us a time. And no matter how much they charge, we will be willing to pay because we believe that is the last moment that person can be with us. We have to help the families get it [the spirit] over [to the other world].

Back in Laos, we say the coffin is a horse so the spirit can ride back. But in this country we might say that the coffin is an airplane—because when we came here we rode in an airplane. We tell the spirit that you need to ride an airplane back. Back in Laos, even now, we guide their spirits back to China [from whence the Hmong originally came]. There's lots of insects and there are very cold mountains, so we still make new shoes for them to wear. We still give them to the dead body and sing a song telling them that you have to keep this. And if you are in a cold area, you need to put these shoes on. If you observe dangerous insects, you need to put these shoes on. And if you meet some enemy, you use your gun or your crossbow.

We never play songs to guide the spirits back unless it's a funeral. If you play the song for someone who is alive, that person may sicken and die. There are some songs that are for fun and there is a New Year's song to send the old year away and welcome the new year.

There are also competitions for qeej players [in Minneapolis, for example]. They advertise for everyone who wants to compete with the qeej and they have certain rules for what you have to know and play. Those who come can come from any state or county. Those who register play. There are ten to fifteen judges who know how the instrument is played. Those competitions are not for the songs, they're for the dances. What you play is not words that people understand, just music: "ding, ding, ding, ding, ding." While playing you do difficult steps, leaps, and tumbles.

When I first learned the dances, I had to do them with bare hands first, without any instrument. Roll over, up and down. My master just gave me a piece of wood to start. The real instrument was very expensive—in Laos, we had to pay one or two silver bars. A wife costs only four silver bars. If you broke one of the pieces, you had to take it to a qeej maker to replace, and he charged you much money too. There are not many people who know how to make the qeej. During that time I broke my instrument and I had to walk two days to where someone was who could fix it. I never broke one again.

In 1985 I won a competition in Minneapolis-St. Paul. Just a few years ago I traveled to China where he I met qeej players. Because I have been making so many presentations, I have been playing a lot. Now I believe I am one of the best players in the world.

When I came to this country my parents-in-law were Christians. I stayed with my parents-in-law about a year, and I lost lots of my culture. At that time I struggled a lot to learn English, and I lost lots of my Hmong culture. But now I am glad I can keep some of it. I am still trying to learn some of it. I believe that the qeej is a symbol of the Hmong people. There is nothing like that instrument, in the world, that belongs to other people.

Now I play at the New Year's celebrations and at the funerals, and the elders are really happy. They say I am the best person to dance and play. So I keep playing. When I first came here, I did not play much at funerals, but did make a lot of presentations at churches and schools or at museums—if anyone is interested in Hmong culture and music, then I am willing to take my time to play for them.

When I do these culture shows, I usually tell people how important the qeej is. I tell them when I play it, how I play it, why I play it. Then after that I can play a few songs, a sad song or a happy song that I dance with. Most of what people like about it is the dance part. Sometimes I got paid for the gas money, most of the time I didn't get paid. But I'm willing to put my efforts to explaining my culture in this new world. We are human beings and we have some important things to let other people know.

Songs of Courtship, War, and Cultural Change

At age thirteen to fifteen in the village I began to play other instruments. These were for fun, for dating. The more you know these instruments, the better the girls will like you. Even if you are not very handsome, you can do well by playing well. If you are very good at it, they love to listen to you. And then they miss you and they invite you to come back. Lots of girl friends.

Another reason to play is that a few of the other instruments you can use to protect yourself. If I go from one village to another, I need to play as I walk outside. It can let the parents or other people know that I'm not a soldier—because the war was going on—I'm not a dangerous animal—because we have tigers and lots of other things. A tiger can come and grab a pig. Everyone carried guns. So I played for protection, to let innocent people know you are not there for crime, not a soldier, not an animal—so people don't shoot at you.

The *ncas* is a very small instrument [a pointed tongue of thin metal, similar to the "Jew's Harp," connected by a string to its tubular case]. You can carry it in your pocket all the time. I heard some people saying that this is an instrument for killing other people too, but I've never known of anybody doing that. It's very sharp metal. You carry it in your pocket in a case with a long string. When somebody tries to fight with you or kill you, you can flick so the metal goes through people's bodies or eyes. But since I play this instrument I haven't heard or seen anything like that. Maybe in the early days in China?

When I have the long string and short string, it's when I play to my girlfriends at night. The instrument is not loud, so it must be played at a quiet time. You play love songs on the instrument and you can express things on the instruments that you could not say in ordinary language. You tell her that you like her, that you love her, that she's so beautiful. The Hmong women are very bashful. But anything you say through the instruments, you will not offend them. I have one with a long string and a short string. If I don't like the girl so much, I might use the long string. If she wants to answer me back, she can play inside and I can play outside. Back in Laos the boyfriend usually stands outside the house. You give her the instrument. After she plays, you can pull it back. If you like her, then you can give her the whole thing. She may keep it, and if she keeps it you may want to go back. This ncas is from China. I'll play something on it.

> Dear lover, how can you be so beautiful?
> If you don't mind, can you be my lover forever?

This ncas is from Laos. Because it's bigger, it's a little louder and lower than the one from China. This next song will say:

> I am not so handsome and am very poor,
> But will you marry a poor person who really loves you?
> How will you feel if we get married
> And only have water to drink in the house?

Then she can answer me back and I'll see what she says.

I don't know how to make flutes. I bought them from Hmong people. They are many different kinds. [Various Hmong flutes are generally made of bamboo; the *lub raj nplaim,* or free-reed pipe, includes a brass reed and a gourd resonator; the *lub raj plum liv,* or fipple flute, resembles a recorder with its sharp-edged ventral hole fostering a whistling sound.] This one has a cover where the air can go through. By our tradition, it's safer to play this one. In Laos there are many spirits in the mountains. If you play this, the girl spirits like you too and can make you sick. So I was told by my grandfather that it's safer to play this. They hear and they come through the flute, but they cannot see your mouth and come in to make you sick.

The flute is useful for courting girlfriends and expressing feelings of love and affection. You can tell your stories with a flute. You can say sweet words with a flute. You can make the person happy, make them fall in love with you. I noticed that when I first observed my wife, she kind of liked me too, but not so much. When I sang a very good love song at her house, she fell in love with me. She really liked my song.

I went to her house. I respected her parents and said, "I want to talk to your daughter tonight." This is in America. In Laos, you are outside and your girlfriend is inside. In America I go and asked her parents. And we spent maybe two hours together. She asked me to sing her a song. My song was really meaningful:

> If I get you I will take care of you.
> If there is heavy work I will do it.
> I will love you for ever.

Those songs are poems. They're very good. If I'm not handsome and she didn't like me much, she looked at me differently than before. Here's another song for a girlfriend.

> How come you were born so pretty?
> What kind of food did your parents eat
> That you were born so pretty?
> I'm short and not so handsome,
> But I like you very much.
> My parents say that if you become their daughter-in-law
> They will love you forever.
> Ask your parents to let us marry.

There is another song about a girlfriend and a boyfriend. The boy is going to school and she stays at the house. She has to wait for her boyfriend to come back. The more she waits for him, the better he can study. But if he knows she has another boyfriend, maybe he will be frustrated and he can't study. He can even get sick. This song is one I sing at educational conferences. I can play another one, it's pretty much from this country:

> When I go to school,
> There is nobody to support me.
> I have to struggle by myself and suffer.
> When school is through,
> I have to pay off debts.

One reason why I play is, whenever I get stressed or real lonesome, I can play and speak it through the music. And after I've been playing it through, I feel much better—better than if I had gone to a counselor. It helps. Even if you are very sad, after you play this you feel a little bit better.

> To be a human being is very difficult
> Without your parents.
> When you're a child,
> Your parents love you the most.
> When your parents leave the world
> You have no others who will love you
> As much as your parents.

My brothers play in a Hmong rock band. They would like to do a concert in collaboration with me sometime. They are very good at rock music, but they don't know anything about the old traditional Hmong music. But that's okay, because now-adays young Hmong people are interested in that. They never take any classes or learn from other people. They listen and play at the house by themselves. They have been playing since about 1984. They play some traditional love songs, sad songs, and any songs to make other people become a good human.

One of my daughters plays the American violin, another plays the "American" flute. They don't play the Hmong flute. But I am teaching my two young boys to play the qeej and to dance. They are very good at it. They love to learn it.

PART FOUR

Beliefs and Customs

28

John Mink, Ojibwe Informant

Joseph B. Casagrande

Traditional beliefs, customs, and other forms of folklore are rooted in distinctive ways of life and they are best understood within the contexts of particular individuals' lives. Joseph Casagrande's portrait of John Mink richly exemplifies the traditional way of life of a remarkable person who sustained his people's culture as the world changed around him. Medicine man, hunter, storyteller, staunch traditionalist, John Mink was, for the Lac Courte Oreilles Ojibwe, both a link to the past and an inspiration for such future elders as John Stone, James "Pipe" Moustache, Bill Bineshi Baker, Bill Sutton, and Edward Benton Banai.

Mink's biographer, Joseph B. Casagrande, taught anthropology at Queens College, the State University of New York at Rochester, American University, and for the Social Science Research Council in New York City. His fieldwork among the Comanche, the Ojibwe, and the Navajo resulted in linguistic and ethnographic studies.

Casagrande's account of John Mink derives from six months of fieldwork in the summer and early fall of 1941, with support from the Department of Anthropology of Columbia University. During this period he was accompanied by Robert E. Ritzenthaler of the Milwaukee Public Museum. Meanwhile, other anthropologists, including Victor Barnouw and Ernestine Friedl, were conducting fieldwork to the east among Wisconsin's Lac du Flambeau Ojibwe. Barnouw would eventually publish five of Mink's traditional narratives—about Wenabozho, *windigos*, and sorcerors—in *Wisconsin Chippewa Myths and Tales: And Their Relation to Chippewa Life* (Madison: University of Wisconsin Press, 1977).

From a late-twentieth-century perspective, a few of Casagrande's remarks seem dated, condescending, even offensive. Contrary to his observations, Ojibwe culture is not "vanishing" but vigorously evolving. Casagrande's admittedly involuntary first impression of Mink as resembling an "orang-utan, the old man of the forest" nonetheless contributes to a long history of western intellectuals ethnocentrically comparing tribal peoples with animals. (For a particular summary of human-orangutan equations, see Patricia A. Turner, *I Heard it Through the Grapevine: Rumor in African-American Culture* [Berkeley: University of California Press, 1993], 231.) Likewise, the offhanded characterization of Mink's vanity in wishing to have his photograph taken while dressed in his best might just as easily be made about the anthropologist himself. I am reminded of the portrait of Casagrande, dressed in professional finery on the occasion of his ascent to the presidency of the American Anthropological Association, that hangs in that organization's board room in Arlington, Virginia.

These criticisms aside, Joseph Casagrande was clearly moved by his encounter with John Mink, recognizing in him a common humanity and a forceful personality that would be remarkable in any culture. When Casagrande subsequently revised his 1955 portrait of John Mink (*In the Company of Man: Twenty Portraits by Anthropologists,* ed. Joseph B. Casagrande [New York: Harper and Brothers, 1960]), he offered this appreciation:

John Mink was something of an anachronism. Born in the middle of the last century when the old Ojibwa life still flourished, he escaped the dilemma of younger men whose heritage was a moribund culture and who had no pride in the past and little hope for the future. He took what he pleased of things the white man had to offer—a gun, clothes, whiskey—but beyond such furnishings and what he knew of the rowdy company of the lumber camps he had few contacts with white culture. Nor did he want more. His faith in Ojibwa ways held firm, and he lived out a full life secure in a tradition he had mastered and found satisfying. This sense of integrity and a certain dignity of character are the qualities I remember best in John Mink. To me he seemed a truly exceptional man, one who in another time and place might even have achieved greatness. But he was probably no more exceptional than many another unsung tribal elder. Through his eyes I glimpsed another way of life that he saw whole. I am grateful to him for this, and for his friendship. (467–88)

Reprinted from *The Wisconsin Archeologist* 36:4 (1955): 106–28.

John Mink lived out his ninety-odd years in the relative obscurity of Lac Courte Oreilles Indian Reservation in northern Wisconsin. When he died a decade ago, few outside the pale of this "cultural fence" noted his passing; and few within it were left to mourn, for the old man had neither close kin nor progeny. No editorials were written to memorialize his death, no epitaph was carved on his gravestone, and he left no monument. Like countless others before him whose lives were lived outside the mainstream of history, he slipped unobtrusively into eternity.

Yet John Mink's death was more than the end of a man. He was one of the last of a lingering handful who followed a style of life ancient among the primitive hunting peoples of both the Old World and the New. As the spiritual leader of a small group of "pagans," themselves a minority group in the more acculturated Christian majority, he was well versed in the traditions and customs of Ojibwe life and no one was a wiser judge of men and their motives. Thus, his passing was not only the end of a life, but marked the end of a way of life as well. Many who were close to him must have sensed this dual loss—and the bell has also tolled for us—but they are unlettered and mute. It is for them, and out of my own affection and respect for his memory that I wish to give John Mink brief respite from oblivion and such small taste of immortality as there may be in print.

The anthropologist who would study a preliterate people relies on both his own observations of customary behavior and on the oral statements of informants, for here the memories of men must serve as their archives and their books. However, if he is studying a vanishing culture such as that of the Ojibwe, observations of most aboriginal practices will be denied to him, and he must depend in large measure on the recollections of the very old. Unhappily, wisdom is not so constant a companion of the aged as is senility, and in the relatively small communities with which the anthropologist deals there will usually be few persons of advanced years both temperamentally and intellectually suited to the informant's role and who also understand the anthropologist's purpose and are sympathetic with it. Since anthropological fieldwork is in essence a collaborative enterprise, its successful outcome depends not only upon the anthropologist's own skills but also upon the quality of his informants. Thus, the availability and choice of informants is crucial, and upon

28.1. John Mink, draped with an elaborately beaded bandolier bag and clutching a traditional war club, poses outside his home for Joseph Casagrande, Lac Courte Oreilles, 1941. Milwaukee Public Museum, 5747.

arrival at Lac Court Oreilles our first task was to determine who among the 1700 Ojibwe residing on the Reservation seemed best qualified for the role.

From the testimony of all of whom we inquired, Indian and White alike, it soon became evident that John Mink might be the paragon we sought. Some called him medicine-man, priest, friend; others called him sorcerer, pagan, scoundrel. Some regarded him with awe, others with disdain, but all agreed that his knowledge of the old days was unsurpassed. He was very old, we were told, somewhat infirm, and spoke no English, and he lived alone near the Couderay River in a house that he had occupied for more than half a century.

We found his weathered cabin on the southern slope of a small hill overlooking the river and followed the well-worn path that led to the door. A hoarsely shouted, *"Boju!"* [the customary Ojibwe greeting, borrowed from the French, *bonjour*] came in response to our knock and, somewhat apprehensively, we entered the single, barely furnished room. John Mink had another visitor, his good and trusted friend Prosper Guibord, who on this first of many occasions acted as interpreter and who in this capacity was to become an essential third party to our future conversations. Prosper had brought the Old Man a meal of wild rice and venison which he had finished eating, and when we arrived the two men were smoking *kinnikinnick,* a native tobacco made of toasted bark scrapings, whose fragrant smoke filled the room.

The size of the Old Man's reputation had ill-prepared us for his physical appearance. His large, almost massive head with its mat of unkempt grey hair dwarfed his stocky body and enfeebled legs which he supported with a walking-stick that lay propped against the couch on which he sat. His gnarled hand clutched a pipe, like a root growing around a stone. Squinting at us out of rheumy eyes, slack mouth held open to reveal a few stumps of teeth and head cocked slightly to one side as he listened, one had the impression that all sensory avenues had been dulled by his great age. His clothing—a worn wool shirt, faded outsize overalls and tennis shoes—lent him an almost pathetic air . . . like, I thought—and the image couldn't be repressed—that of an orang-utan, the old man of the forest, appearing at a carnival.

Through the good offices of Prosper, we presented the Old Man with a package of tobacco and explained the purpose of our call. In reply John Mink said that he was old and his life was drawing to a close but that he had lived long and remembered much and would tell us what he could. He added that he was often lonely and would welcome our visits and said that it would make his heart glad to talk of these things. Even on brief acquaintance it was apparent that in Prosper Guibord, a man in his mid-sixties, of half French American and half Indian descent, and equally fluent in English and Ojibwe, we had found an ideal interpreter. We arranged to hire Prosper, who had no other regular employment, and left with plans to meet at the Old Man's house early the next morning.

I was born in the time of ripening strawberries when my people were camped near Rice Lake. My mother's mother helped at my birth and after I was cleaned up my father killed a deer for a feast. I remember being tied up on my cradleboard and watching the bright charms that hung from the hood. My mother put my umbilical cord in a little black bag and hung it from the hood. There were strings of colored beads and muskellunge vertebrae hanging there too.

I remember the taste of my mother's milk. It tasted rich and good like bear fat and I remember crying for the breast. When I was able to eat wild rice and venison and blueberries, I stopped nursing. Later when my parents saw that I was healthy and living good my father gave a feast for my godparents. My mother's father, a speaker of the tribe, gave me the name *Shoniagizik* (Sky Luminary).

When I got off the cradleboard, I got my first moccasins and they had holes cut in the soles to help me walk. I was small and frisky and everyone liked me and laughed at me. My first toys were a little toboggan and a little bow and arrow. I killed squirrels and chipmunks with it and once I killed a partridge that was drumming. The arrow hit him right under the wing and he went straight up in the air and came down with his wings fluttering. My parents gave a big feast when I killed the partridge and the men told about their fasting and their dreams so that I would become strong and a good hunter. There was a big feast too when I killed my first deer with a musket. In those days there was lots of game and I remember the great flocks of passenger pigeons so thick they darkened the sky.

I fasted all the time when I was young. In the early morning I would paint my face with charcoal and go off into the woods without eating. The spirits came to me in my dreams as I fasted and gave me the power to kill game and to cure people. They taught me songs and how to suck the disease from sick people and make medicines.

Thus began our colloquy and an almost daily association that lasted throughout the summer and early fall. We quickly became adjusted to Prosper's part in our conversations, even to the point of becoming forgetful of the fact that he was a necessary medium of communication between us. Prosper's habitual deference to the Old Man, his own keen interest in following the trend of the discussion, and his tact and natural reticence combined to serve him well in the rather anonymous role of interpreter.

By design we had suggested that the Old Man begin by telling us his autobiography. Few devices are better calculated either to put an informant at his ease or to uncover leads that might be followed in subsequent sessions. Moreover, the telling of one's life story is akin to what the psychologist calls a projective test, and through it insights can be gained into both the personality of the man and the nature of his culture.

After a break for lunch the Old Man continued his story in the afternoon with an account of his marriages:

The government used to make payments to us up at La Pointe. That's where I met my first wife. We saw each other and wanted to lie together. We just went to live with her folks for awhile and later we made our own wigwam. We were happy together, but she died in childbirth after we had been married five years. I mourned for her and when I ate I put food in a dish for her and I got clothes and other things for her and kept them tied up in a bundle.

After a year I took the bundle and dish to her folks. They had a feast and gave the bundle of clothes to the guests. Then everyone helped wash and dress me. They combed my hair too and painted my face red and blue. My wife's folks wanted to get another girl for me. She was my wife's cousin, but I didn't want her and refused. When I was young all the women liked me because I worked hard and was a good hunter, but I loved my first wife and even now I feel sad when I think about her.

I was single two years before I married again, and it was then that I began to listen to the old men and learn from them. She was from the whooping crane totem and had been married before and had two girls and a boy. We lived together about ten years and had four children, but they all died when they were infants. Then I was single two years before I was married again. She was married before too and began courting me even before my wife died. We had two children, a boy and a girl, but they died when they were very young. We lived together for a long time, more than thirty years, and then I was single for three years before I was married again. My last wife's name was "Little Girl," and she belonged to the whooping crane totem too. We lived together for ten years and then she died. That was ten years ago.

"That's all the wives I have under the ground," the Old Man said. "They are all buried down there by the river. That's why I don't want to leave this place." Then he lay back on his bed and closed his eyes.

Like many another of his advanced age, the Old Man's memory had a vagrant quality. Incidents of his middle and later years were blurred in outline and events were telescoped so that it was often difficult to disentangle their chronology. One was never sure, for example, which wife was number three and which number four. But he had an almost startling ability to recall happenings of his youth. Narratives of hunting expeditions and various incidents of his early life were described in vivid evocative detail. One had the impression that he was recounting reminiscences that had been cast repeatedly into consciousness during his lonely hours and worked upon his memory as the sea works on a piece of driftwood. He had, moreover, a seemingly endless repertoire of tales, and an encyclopedic knowledge of intricate ceremonial and other lore that, unanchored to time, could be summoned at will from this vast sea of memory.

In the days that followed we came also to appreciate other facets of his intellect, which in its vigor seemed incongruously housed in his old body. He was quick to grasp the point of any question. He had, in fact, answers for which we had no questions, and his own observations of Ojibwe customs revealed a subtle analytical habit of thought that made them as precise as those of any anthropologist.

One day shortly after our first meeting we discovered that Prosper had arrived at the cabin well before us and that he had deloused the Old Man and his bedding, washed and changed his clothes, and attended to his bath. To all of these ministrations, John Mink had yielded without protest, but having suffered himself to be bathed, changed and deloused and made thereby presentable to a wider public, he insisted that we take his picture. He rummaged through the large trunk that served him as both chest and closet and, decked out in all the regalia that could be mustered, posed happily for us outside his door. Such is vanity.

In a small and simply organized society such as that of the Ojibwe, there are few offices that correspond to the professions of large and complex civilized societies. Among these are the roles of the shaman or medicine-man and the religious leader, both of which the Old Man occupied, and which in Ojibwe society as in many other groups provided the only socially sanctioned outlet for one of intellectual bent.

As the days passed and the Old Man's trust in us grew, his early reluctance to talk about religion, medicines and other esoteric subjects diminished so that by summer's end our conversations ranged quite freely across the whole of Ojibwe culture. Nevertheless, when discussing these touchy matters, he was sometimes uneasy lest he be accused of perfidy; nor did he fail to offer tobacco to the supernaturals before broaching sacred themes.

John Mink was a master of most of the healing arts. He was physician, obstetrician, pharmacologist, psychiatrist, homeopath, bonesetter and blood-letter all in one. He had amputated gangrenous fingers and had tried his hand at other minor surgery. The treatment the Old Man used varied according to the nature and sources of the illness which in the more difficult cases he determined with the aid of his spirit helpers. There were many, both pagan and Christian, who sought his services for which he received modest payment in the form of gifts of food, clothing, money or tobacco.

His knowledge of blood-letting and authority to practice it had come through a dream in which a giant horse-fly and mosquito had appeared to him. These benevolent insect powers had taught him how the veins coursed through the body, where they should be tapped for various ailments, and the techniques to use. Before treating a patient he would seek their guidance in both the diagnosis and cure of the complaint. He treated either by cupping or by opening a vein by tapping it with a sharp instrument. In the former method he used a hollow cow horn which was applied to the punctured skin and the blood induced to flow by sucking through a small aperture at the tip of the horn. Others, he said, bled a patient by pricking the skin with the sharp-toothed jaw of a garfish.

As an adjunct to other treatment and to ward off further misfortune, the Old Man often recommended that the patient erect an "offering tree" in propitiation of the supernaturals. For this a straight tree ten or more feet in height was felled. Then, stripped of its lower branches but with the topmost boughs left intact, the tree was erected in front of the patient's house and clothes hung from the tuft of the branches.

The Old Man had wide knowledge of an extensive native pharmacopoeia. He had medicines to cure gonorrhea, to stanch bleeding, to reduce a fever and to ease colic. Diuretics, physics, poultices and tonics were in his repertoire, and he had prescriptions to stop menstruation or to start it and to induce the flow of milk in a new mother. His favorite medicine was one that he had learned from his paternal grandfather and was used to bring on labor. The expectant mother drank the potion from a birchbark vessel on the inside of which the image of a snake was etched with the head at the place on the rim from which the woman drank. As the liquid drained, the figure of the snake was revealed and the child thereby frightened from its mother's womb.

Although much of his pharmaceutical knowledge had been taught him by older relatives, John Mink had paid substantial fees to other native doctors for many of his medicines and he had learned others as part of his instruction in the Medicine Lodge Society.

Some of his medicines were compounded of numerous plants and other ingredients, animal, vegetable and mineral, including such substances as pulverized beaver testicles, cloves, bear fat, moss from a turtle's back and Epsom salts. Other recipes called for rare or exotic plants which were traded from tribe to tribe and hand to hand from places as distant as South Dakota and Canada.

Bundles of dried medicinal plants were stored in the rafters of the Old Man's house and he kept others preserved in cans and jars. Outside his door he cultivated a garden of the more common medicinal herbs. Scarcely a tree or plant grew for which the Old Man did not know a variety of medicinal uses and in instructing me in their indentification, I was carefully admonished to place an offering of tobacco beside the tree or bush or in the root-hole of the plant where, he said, a blind toad always crouched.

He prescribed sweat baths in the pungent steam of resinous evergreens as a remedy for such ailments as rheumatism and bronchial infections. Sweat-lodges were built for the purpose and steam made by throwing a brew of evergreens and other medicinal substances over hot rocks. Steam baths, he said, were also taken in a kind of purification ritual by persons who had handled a corpse and by hunters to rid themselves of tell-tale body odors. The Old Man recalled one occasion when he made sweat lodge for a party of ten men. They had been having poor luck, but the day after taking a bath each killed a deer and one man shot a bear.

One morning on arriving at the cabin we found the Old Man missing and discovered him in the woods nearby steaming his rheumatic legs under a blanket which he had thrown over a small structure of boughs. He explained that he had been troubled by his legs ever since he had years ago accidentally stepped over a discarded menstrual napkin. A woman's menstrual blood was regarded as a highly dangerous substance. It sickened or killed the tiny spirits that dwelt in one's limbs, he said, and cited instances where inadvertant contact with it had led to paralysis or other crippling affliction. Women are careless these days, John Mink said, and young girls are no longer taught the proper menstrual taboos. He told how his first wife used to eat out of her own special dishes when she was menstruating and wouldn't let him come near her, and how when it was over she would walk up to him and kiss him.

By far the most dramatic and powerful therapy practiced by the old man was that performed in a shamanistic seance during which he magically sucked the disease substance out of a patient. He had rarely performed such cures in recent years, but he assured us that he was quite willing to have us witness a demonstration of his art. Prosper, who had not been feeling well of late, avowed that he had been wanting the Old Man to treat him and, his reluctance to ask for this favor dispelled by the Old Man's willingness to undertake a cure, happily volunteered to be his patient. We agreed to act as Prosper's sponsors by providing the necessary payment for the Old Man's services and arrangements were made to hold the curing ceremony on the following evening.

We gathered at the Old Man's cabin shortly after dusk. Besides the principals and us as observers, the company included a drummer, Andrew Q., Mary Marten and the latter's daughter, Alice W., and granddaughter, a child of ten. After we had all assembled the windows were covered to exclude both prying eyes and the last light of day. Andrew, acting as the old man's assistant, tightly closed the door after he had made a brief tour of the premises to see that there were no dogs about whose barking would frighten away the spirit helpers. We spectators sat in a semi-circle around the supine form of Prosper, our faces illumined by the uncertain yellow light of a guttering candle. The Old Man, his figure grotesquely silhouetted, stood opposite us. Prosper lay motionless before him on a blanket, eyes closed and arms extended at his sides. His gifts to the Old Man, a pair of tennis shoes and a package of tobacco, were displayed for all to see. Two finger-length tubes made from the polished leg bones of a deer were put in a shallow pie tin filled with salt water, placed on the floor at Prosper's side and covered with a red bandana.

The scene thus set, the Old Man began the ceremony with a recitation of his fasting experience. He told how in a dream on the fifth night of his fast he was led to a conjuror's hut by a flock of wild geese. Inside the swaying hut, which he entered through a hole at the top, were a spike-buck and six spirits. Later, her approach heralded by the sound of singing and laughter, these six were joined by a beautiful lady in a long dress whose home is behind the sun. These were the ones, he said, who taught him how to cure people and told him the songs to sing in summoning help.

His recitation finished, he took up his rattle (a quart oil can filled with buckshot), and accompanied by Andrew on the tambourine drum, began to sing. After singing a cycle of songs to call his spirit helpers, the Old Man dropped to his knees at Prosper's side and shook the rattle over him and also around his own body. Then, as the drumming continued, he put one of the bone tubes in his mouth and, after a brief pause, swallowed it, shuddering and jerking his body as if the spirits entered it. Still kneeling, the Old Man regurgitated the tube and, bending close, sucked through it several times in the region of Prosper's lower abdomen. After each sucking he blew through the tube into the pan of salt water. Finally, obviously winded by his exertions, he spat out the tube. The drumming abruptly stopped and Andrew helped the Old Man to his feet.

The Old Man sang another song after a brief interlude and began a second series of suckings. This time he succeeded in extracting a small piece of whitish substance which was passed around in the pie tin for inspection before Andrew disposed of it. The Old Man said that he had gotten only part of the disease, but added that he believed he could get the rest of it the following evening when he would use a stronger spirit.

Prosper, his face flushed, arose somewhat giddily from the floor and made a ribald quip. The hushed, intense atmosphere was immediately dissipated, a lamp was lit and a bantering conversation began. Old Mary Marten, a giantess among women and to whom John Mink stood in a joking relationship, invited the Old Man to go for a walk in the woods. With elaborate thanks for the compliment, he declined saying that he had never known a mole successfully to have sexual intercourse with a mountain. In this light mood the women then served a meal of wild rice and sweet buns which they had brought with them. The food eaten, the Old Man sang four more songs, whooping after each, which he said he did to frighten away the disease. The evening's ceremonies thus concluded, we disbanded at midnight.

We reassembled the following evening at the same hour and with some modifications the ceremony of the previous night was repeated. Prosper, averring that he had slept well for the first time in ages, resumed his position on the floor, this time stripped to the waist. His gifts to the Old Man were a pair of gloves and two packages of tobacco.

For the evening's second course of treatments, the Old Man asked Alice to put the tube in his mouth and gave Mary the rattle to shake. He did this, he said, because two female spirits were helping him tonight. After sucking a couple of times he asked Andrew to get a larger bone which was secreted under the bed. He swallowed the tube, alarming us all by momentarily gagging on it, then regurgitated it and sucked again near Prosper's navel. On the first attempt he sucked out several pieces of the same white stuff and announced that he had now gotten it all.

The Old Man said that Prosper had been sorcerized by a woman, immediately identified by Prosper as a former mistress with whom he had lived at Chief Lake for two years and subsequently deserted. Prosper said that he could feel the bone go right through him and that he could also feel the place in his right abdomen from which the disease had been removed. He thanked the Old Man for saving his life, adding that he was sure the disease would shortly have killed him, for the woman had never forgiven him.

For John Mink the line between the natural and the supernatural was thinly drawn. His world was filled with an infinite array of spirits and forces that could influence the affairs of men. Nor was man conceived as a creature apart from nature. For the Ojibwe, as for many hunting peoples, animals and men are akin and the differences between them lay chiefly in outward form. Animals are motivated as men are motivated, live in societies as men live, act as men act and their fates are intertwined. Thus, the Old Man told how when a bear was killed its four paws and head were placed in position on a rush mat and a feast given. The head was decorated with ribbons, beadwork or baby's clothes and food and tobacco placed nearby; speeches were made to the bear's spirit so that it would return to the village of bears and persuade other bears to allow themselves to be killed.

The Old Man believed in charms and portents, in sorcery and transformations, and in the power for both good and evil of those who had fasted and dreamed. There were those, he said (and he was one of them), who could make the skins of loons come alive and cry out in order to foretell the future. He told how Old Man Skunk, now long dead, used a downy woodpecker skin that would move its head and make a tapping sound, and how for evil ends he would use the skin of an owl. And John Mink had often seen the "shaking" conjuror perform, but although he possessed the power and know how to construct the conjuror's hut, he had never practiced the art out of fear of its possible bad consequences.

The Old Man claimed he had never used his power for evil purposes, but there were many on the reservation who swore that they had been sorcerized by him and laid all their misfortunes at his door. Few doubted his powers and most were prepared to lend some degree of credence to the rumors that circulated about him. Even his staunchest friends, Prosper among them, regarded him with a kind of wary ambivalence compounded of both fear and deep respect. In passing it may be noted that the primitive intellectual's special knowledge, like that of his spiritual brother in Western society, is often suspect.

The second office held by John Mink was that of a ceremonial leader in both the Medicine Lodge Society or *midewewin* and in the Drum Dance a quasi-social society centering about a number of highly decorated sacred drums. Although ultimately derived from the Dakota Sioux, the Drum Dance was introduced to the Reservation by a band of Minnesota Ojibwe in the 1870s. John Mink was present on this historic occasion and in the capacity of "runner" participated in the first ceremony held at Lac Courte Oreilles. He supplied a full account of the Drum Dance, its membership, observances and history, including that of an heretical episode when one Steve Grover erected a cross on the dancing grounds and, wearing a vest on the back of which a red cross was embroidered, gave speeches that strongly smacked of Catholic doctrine.

As the foremost priest in the Medicine Lodge Society, the principal ceremonial complex of the Wisconsin Ojibwe, the Old Man had in his custody a birchbark scroll some six feet long on which pictographs and other mnemonic devices were engraved in four panels. Each panel represented the ceremony and related lore to be learned by candidates for the four degrees in the Mide Society, which in the order taken are symbolized by ornamented pouches made from the skins of the otter, raven, fox and bear or other animals of related species. Every spring and fall week-long ceremonies are held at the *mide* grounds, culminating in a colorful and elaborate two-day public ceremony in the Medicine Lodge itself, a long, open structure made of arched poles and dedicated with cedar and pine boughs.

That autumn the ceremonies were held in early October and the Old Man took his usual active part in them. Each morning we drove him to the ceremonial grounds where his days were given to the instruction and catechization of the six initiates. His evenings and a few afternoons were spent in consultation and celebration with other priests and elder members of the society in one or another of the wigwams temporarily erected on the grounds.

One of these councils to which we were admitted was held in Whiskey John Moustache's wigwam. Here we joined John Mink, three other priests, their "runners" and two of the candidates for degrees. The latters' initiation gifts, consisting of several galvanized tin pails and a dozen blankets each, were in two piles beside which drums were placed. A number of medicine pouches hung from the wigwam frame. After presents of tobacco and food were passed out, the Old Man gave a speech asking the spirits to take pity on those present. As he spoke the others shouted, "Ho! ho!", in approbation. Then he took up his big rattle and sang, accompanied by the other priest who shook smaller rattles and Whiskey John who beat a water drum. A brief consultation was then held to decide who should be invited to a later gathering and the "runners" were dispatched with invitation-sticks made of ornamented porcupine quills that had been dyed red. These were collected at the door as each of the twelve newly invited guests entered. Another meal, consisting of baked beans, bologna, raisin pie, cake, and doughnuts, was laid and after it was eaten John Mink arose and gave a lengthy speech admonishing those present to follow the old ways.

We were then asked to leave and the entrance to the wigwam was closed. Long into the night the sounds of speech-making, singing and drumming could be heard issuing from this and other wigwams where the celebrants were gathered.

Preparations finally completed and the Medicine Lodge freshly repaired and decorated, the public ceremonies began on the morning of the seventh day. The American flag was raised. A black mongrel dog was taken off into the woods by one of the runners, killed and its body dragged into the Lodge. The initiates and Society members, dressed in their brightest clothes and carrying their medicine pouches in one hand and buckets of food in the other, lined up at the north entrance. After an opening song, they began to file clockwise slowly around the Lodge. Thus commenced the long and elaborate ceremony. Among its features were the magical "shooting" of the participants with *migis,* the variously colored cowrie shells contained in the pouches, and the ceremonial eating of the dog which, cleaned and singed, had been boiled in an iron camp kettle. It required a strong stomach to taste of the coarse meat, permeated as it was by the smell of burnt hair. Dog was eaten, we were told, so that the human beings who ate it would become as faithful to the supernaturals as a dog is to its master.

The ceremony lasted until sundown of the second day and the Old Man was the last to leave the Lodge. As we drove him home, he complained in a strangely querulous voice that it had gone off too slowly and that too many unnecessary things had been done. He said that he was very tired and didn't think he would last out the winter—and he told Prosper to see that he was buried with his medicine pouch and beadwork bandelier.

As shaman and ceremonial leader, John Mink's services were in demand at every crisis in the life cycle from birth to death, and many were the petitioners who came to his door. He had ushered many children into the world, and had named and been godfather to scores more. One of his boasts was that he had been godfather to child, parent, and grandparent in a single family. He had taken part in numerous mourning feasts and he had been summoned many times by a runner bearing a gift of tobacco to officiate at a funeral.

Others came to him as a kind of confessor or to ask his advice on matters both trivial and momentous. Once when we were engrossed in a discussion of some moot point of custom, we were interrupted by a man who brought the paws and meat of a bear he had just killed. Not knowing the proper ceremony, nor yet willing to risk its omission, he came to ask the Old Man to smoke a pipe with him and to say a few words in celebration of the occasion.

As he was wont to do when queried about a particular observance, the Old Man recounted a personal experience by way of illustration, punctuating his account with brief asides when he touched upon points where custom varied. Thus he described his role on the occasion of the recent death of Mrs. P:

On his arrival in mid-afternoon at the house of the deceased, the Old Man spoke few words of condolence to the bereaved. Then he was handed his pipe and after he had taken a few puffs he sang a song, accompanying himself on a tambourine drum. Since the deceased had not requested a particular person to wash and dress her the

Old Man appointed a woman to take charge of these preparations. The men retired while the corpse was washed, dressed in her best clothes, and a blue circle painted on each cheek. Mrs. P's body was then placed on a rude catafalque of planks, covered with a sheet and her medicine pouch placed on her chest.

After the body was laid out, the Old Man began to sing, but he was interrupted by a group of Holy Rollers from the Whitefish settlement who asked permission to sing a few hymns and said they would stay only a short while. However, they stayed on and began to preach about being saved. The Old Man explained that the Holy Rollers were outsiders, but added that Mrs. P.'s husband and three of her daughters were Catholics, although one daughter by a prior marriage was also a pagan.

After the Holy Rollers finally left, the Old Man resumed his singing and preaching. Meanwhile the women bustled around preparing the food that people had brought to the wake. Before the feast was begun the Old Man presented a bowl of food to the corpse, telling her to eat so that she would be strong for the long journey to the village of the dead. Then he gave the bowl of food to one of the women to eat. The Old Man added that it made him mad because he always had to make this speech and no one else would learn it or had gumption enough to get up and speak.

On the second day the body was placed in a ready made coffin that was supplied by the government. The coffin was carried out of the house through a window, placed in a hearse by the pallbearers, and then taken to the cemetery at Cable for burial. The Old Man explained that a corpse was always removed through a window, or in former days carried out through the back of the wigwam, lest another soon be stricken and die.

After the coffin was lowered into the grave, the Old Man spoke to the corpse about the journey she would take to the land of the dead. He admonished her not to look back, but to go right on and to be careful to leave offerings of tobacco and to obey the injunctions of the spirits she would meet along the way. He told her that on the fourth day she would come to a river spanned by what appeared to be a log, but which in reality was a huge snake. Similarly, what appeared to be a clump of red willows growing alongside the river would actually be a wigwam. The bridge, he told her, is guarded by two gaunt dogs and attended by two old women in whose custody the journey would be completed. After the Old Man finished his oration, the grave was filled and a wood marker on which of the symbol of the deceased's totem was painted upside down was placed at the west end.

The old man strongly disapproved of the changes, such as the practice of holding wakes, tossing a handful of earth on the coffin, or burial in distant places, that had been introduced in the mortuary customs. In the old days, John Mink said, the dead were buried close by in graves lined with birchbark and food was regularly placed at the entrance of the grave houses erected over them. No longer, he said, are poles put up in front of the graves from which passers-by might take the gifts of clothing and necklaces hung there and wear them in honor of the deceased. Nowadays, he said, the dead are neglected and disowned.

The Old Man often expressed a strong craving for the native Ojibwe foods and after a long denial would eat ravenously of such delicacies as fresh-killed venison, bear fat or wild rice. Although frequently in precarious supply, there was variety in the native larder and John Mink described the seasonal round of the food quest with obvious relish. He told in full detail how wild rice, the staple food, was harvested, winnowed and threshed, how in early spring the hard maples were tapped, the sap boiled down and cakes of maple sugar made in birchbark or clam shell molds, and how blueberries were gathered, dried and stored in bark containers.

Hunting and fishing were year-round activities of the men and although deer, bear and muskellunge were prime objects of the chase, lesser game were also prized. Porcupine, rabbit, partridge and smoked black suckers were counted by the Old Man as especially valued foods.

He described how in early April when the black suckers were running up cold streams and their flesh was white and firm they were caught by hand or in a variety of simple traps. Gutted and their heads and tails cut off, they were smoked and stored in bales and the Old Man recalled roasting them in hot coals and eating them as a kind of snack when he was a boy. And he told how the men would joke and the women giggle as they sat on logs alongside a weir and caught the suckers as they swam up onto a rack of poles.

Ice-fishing in the winter, however, was a solitary pursuit. A hole would be cut in the ice over a bar in five to ten feet of water, the Old Man said, and a blanket draped over the fisherman's head and shoulders and tightly secured so that no light would be let in. A weighted decoy in the form of a frog or minnow was bobbed from a short handle and a spear with tines of native copper held ready. When a fish approached the fisherman let the spear slide slowly down into the water until it was about a foot away and then the fish was deftly jabbed. The fish quickly froze solid, the Old Man said, and he would carry them home like a bundle of firewood.

For the hunting peoples of the northern latitudes starvation is a lurking threat that rides the winter blizzards and the biting cold. Stories of cannibalism were related by the Ojibwe and half-believed, for here was a theme, like those of classic drama, fascinating in its horrible possibility.

Thus John Mink told many tales about the *windigo*, legendary cannibalistic monster that stalked the woods in the lean winter months, in whom these fears were joined and given mythological expression:

One winter morning the people noticed that the kettle hanging over the fire began to swing back and forth, and they were scared because they knew a *windigo* was coming. Everyone trembled with fear and no one was brave or strong enough to challenge the *windigo*. Finally they sent for a wise old woman who lived with her little granddaughter at the edge of the village, but the old woman said she was powerless to do anything. The little girl asked what was the matter and they told her that they were all going to die.

Then the little girl asked for two sticks of peeled sumac as long as her arms and took them off home with her while all the others huddled together in one place. That night it turned so bitter cold that the people's bones came near to cracking open. Early next morning the little girl told her grandmother to melt a kettle of tallow over the fire. Meanwhile it turned colder and colder and then the people looked and there was a *windigo* as tall as a white pine tree coming over the hill. Trees cracked open and the river froze solid when he passed by.

The little girl went out to meet him with a sumac stick held in each hand. Her two dogs went on ahead and quickly killed the *windigo*'s dog, but he kept coming closer. The little girl got bigger and bigger as he approached until when they met she was as big as the *windigo* himself. She knocked him down with one sumac stick and crushed his skull in with the other—they had both turned into copper. After the girl killed the *windigo*, she gulped down the hot tallow and then got smaller and smaller until she was herself again. The people rushed over to the dead *windigo* and began to chop him up. He was made of ice, but in the center was the body of a man with his skull crushed in. The people were all very happy and gave the little girl everything she wanted.

That summer we listened to the Old Man tell many tales, including myths of *Wenabojo*, the mischievous and comic culture hero, whom the Ojibwe affectionately called, "nephew." One long tale of *Wenabojo*, two days in the telling, embodied the Noah-like Ojibwe story of the flood and re-creation of the earth wherein after loon, otter and beaver had failed, muskrat succeeded in diving to the bottom of the deep and all enveloping sea and coming up with a pawful of mud from which *Wenabojo*, with the help of all the animals and birds, refashioned the earth. The tale was told with a true story-teller's art that not even translation or our meager knowledge of the language could mask. The Old Man gave all the characters their separate voices, enlivened the tale with interjections, songs, and animal cries, and punctuated it with pauses and dramatic gestures.

Although too young to be himself a participant, the Old Man related many stories, too, of the war between the Ojibwe and the Woodland Dakota Sioux. As a boy he had been present at the "Chief Dances" that were held at both the departure and return of a war party. At these dances he had seen impaled on sticks the bloody trophy heads of the Sioux that had been slain, and he had listened to the returned warriors who, their faces still painted and wearing only a breech-clout and an eagle feather in their hair, described their exploits to the last grisly detail.

By mid-autumn we had spent many days and hours with the Old Man and had covered virtually every aspect of Ojibwe life. The intricacies of kinship and social organization, prime anthropological topics, received particular attention. Using sticks for males and stones for females, we made diagrams in the sand to represent the relationships between various kin. The Old Man supplied the appropriate kinship terms and described the behavior that customarily obtained between persons in specific relationships. In an account spiced with numerous anecdotes, he described the horseplay and broad joking that went on between brothers- and sisters-in-law, and the warm relationships that held between grandparents and grandchild, and between a man and his sister's son. He listed the various *dodems*, the loosely organized patrilines to which the Ojibwe owed allegiance—catfish, wolf, lynx, bear, marten, deer, eagle, sturgeon, bullhead, whooping crane, loon, and the one to which John Mink belonged, *nibanabe*, a creature half human, half fish. If a person's totem or totem animal were insulted, the Old Man said, he would give a feast to which the offender and his totem-mates would be invited and good-naturedly forced to drink huge quantities of whiskey and gorge themselves with food.

He described the old Ojibwe arts and crafts which only a few still practiced, explaining how a birchbark canoe was constructed, how a bow was made and how the arrows were shaped, pointed and fletched, how glue was made from the swim bladder of a sturgeon, and how a lacrosse club was fashioned. He described, too, the bitterly contested day-long lacrosse games that used to be played and on which huge amounts of various personal effects were bet.

The Old Man was familiar as well with the handicrafts that were the women's special province. He told how deer hides were fleshed, soaked in a solution of deer brains, then stretched, scraped again, and after they were dried and white as snow, formed into a closed cylinder and smoked over a smudge pot. He described how the women made rush mats, how they would weave into beautiful colored patterns dyed porcupine quills that had been flattened by pulling them through their clenched teeth, and how they would bite designs into small squares of birchbark.

"That's how things used to be," John Mink said. "The women were proud in the old days. They looked good in their braids and long dresses and they worked hard. Now they are lazy and dress in rags. There was always food in my wigwam then and I had many things. Now I live alone in a cold and empty house. The men no longer believe in anything. It is as though they were lost at a fork in the road and don't know which way to take. There is no one left here to take my place."

I last saw John Mink when we stopped by his cabin on the grey November morning we left the Reservation. He greeted us with a shout, little ponderous jig and flourish of his stick that had become a joke between us. A pot of cold rice on which he had breakfasted stood on the stove. We sat with him to smoke a pipeful of tobacco and talked for a while in the pidgin of Ojibwe, English and exaggerated pantomime that we had jointly contrived. But even had Prosper been with us, there would have been no words with which to say "good bye." When we got up to go the Old Man came outside with us and watched as we walked down the path, his stick raised high in a gesture of farewell. Then as we faded from his dim sight, he turned and slowly went back into his house.

29

Faith and Magic

Magico-religious practices were once extremely widespread among Wisconsin's European ethnic peoples, nor have they subsided entirely. Such Catholic communities as Dickeyville, Forestville, Holy Hill, Loretto, Necedah, Rudolph, St. Joseph's Ridge, and Sinsinawa Mound, for example, include remarkable shrines and grottos, most of which are associated by the faithful with ongoing miraculous cures. (See Lisa Stone and Jim Zanzi, *Sacred Spaces and Other Places: A Guide to Grottos and Sculptural Environments in the Upper Midwest* [Chicago: The School of the Art Institute of Chicago Press, 1993]; and "Religious Folk Traditions," in Anne Pryor's unpublished Wisconsin Sesquicentennial Folklife Survey report, 1996, 10–26.) Before the spread of doctors, veterinarians, and scientific education into rural areas, former old-country peasants and their offspring frequently relied on a combination of home remedies, prayer, and sorcery to heal themselves and their livestock. Sometimes their curative measures counteracted the malignant efforts of a neighbor.

In 1985 I interviewed Rosemary Korger Menard regarding her Bohemian grandparents, the Radas, who lived in rural Tilden, north of Chippewa Falls. Around 1900 old Mrs. Rubenzer, a "Magyar gypsy," was known locally as *die alte hex* (the old witch). According to family tradition, she would hex a Rada cow while standing on a hill, then offer Grandfather Rada a low price for his sick animal. Rather than sell, he paid Mrs. Rubenzer to cure the cow. She would talk to it soothingly, then pet it and the cow would be fine. The Radas always suspected she rubbed the cow's muzzle with some concoction. (Tape-recorded interview with Rosemary Korger Menard at the home of her sister, Agatha Watson, Rice Lake, May 11, 1985.)

The trio of accounts reprinted here, all from German Americans, extend from the final decades of the nineteenth century to the 1930s. Leone Fischer Griesemer's "Hexing" concerns the experiences of her parents, Otto and Ella Mittelstadt Fischer, in the heavily German Mayville area of Dodge County. Mrs. Griesemer's mother (1872–1963) was also a fine singer; she contributed more German songs than anyone else to the recordings of Wisconsin folk music made for the Library of Congress by Helene Stratman-Thomas in the 1940s. The Fischer family's reminiscences about the "black books" of Moses parallel those of Wisconsin Norwegians as reported by Thor Helgeson (see chapter 15, "Ghost Stories," pp. 149, 152; see also "The Sixth and Seventh Books of Moses," in Thomas R. Brendle and William S. Troxell, *Pennsylvania German Folk Tales, Legends, Once-upon-a-Time Stories, Maxims, and Sayings* [Norristown, Pa.: Pennsylvania German Folklore Society, vol. L, 1944]).

Alice Ottow and Bill Brandt, whose respective accounts follow Leone Fischer Griesemer's, were both students at the University of Wisconsin in the early 1950s. Besides the books of Moses and Christian prayers, their essays invoke the common magical practice of "transference" from the afflicted to some external object, and they also concern widespread folk practices of "wart doctoring" and bloodstopping (see Wayland D. Hand, *Magical Medicine: The Folkloric Component of Medicine in the Folk Belief, Custom, and Ritual of the Peoples of Europe and America*

[Berkeley: University of California Press, 1980]; and Richard M. Dorson, *Bloodstoppers and Bear-walkers* [Cambridge, Mass: Harvard University Press, 1952], 150–65).

"Hexing" by Leone F. Griesemer is reprinted from *Mama and Papa: A Personal Account of the Lives of Two German Immigrant Families in the Rural Wisconsin of 1869–1963* (self-published, 1988), 51–53.

"Sorcery" by Alice Ottow is reprinted from a student paper written for an anthropology course at the University of Wisconsin, January 15, 1952; Badger Folklore Society Papers, box 2, folder N–S in the Archives of the State Historical Society of Wisconsin.

"Faith Healing Can and Does Work" by Bill Brandt is reprinted from a student paper written for an anthropology course at the University of Wisconsin, January 15, 1952; Badger Folklore Society Papers, box 2, folder C–J in the Archives of the State Historical Society of Wisconsin.

Hexing

Leone F. Griesemer

"Hexing" was one of the dreaded witch practices and very real to the early settlers, feared by young and old alike. It was believed to be those who owned the *Seventh Book of Moses* (the five accepted books are Genesis, Exodus, Leviticus, Numbers, and Deuteronomy) could perform the acts or miracles attributed to Moses. This *Seventh Book* reputedly contained the secrets of Moses' miraculous powers of defense against the enemies of the Hebrew nation.

Mayville's first introduction to this book was supposed to have come through a pair of Chicago circuit doctors, advertising their periodic visits to villagers and town folk all along the railroad route in the *Dodge County Banner and Pioneer,* offering miraculous medical cures during the close of the nineteenth century.

A distracted local farmer, who was continually losing all his cattle and nearing bankruptcy, came to Papa with his tale of woe.

"Otto, what should I do? The veterinarian doesn't understand it either!"

"Maybe John, the trouble is in your head—a disease, I mean. I tell you what, I'll give you a heifer with calf, and a real young calf besides, and see if you can start a new herd, away from your barn. Maybe a few other neighbors will give you some too. None of us have much, but that's what neighbors are for. Now, John, chin up and we'll see what can be done. Don't lose hope."

Soon thereafter John reported the loss of the new herd as well. Mama joined the discussion and said, "How about those doctors from Chicago?" And she hurried over to the latest *Pioneer* for John to look over.

John took her advice and, after relating his story, the Chicago doctors determined (so the story goes) the case to be a "hexing" problem which could be counteracted only by the same methods. So they recommended John borrow some money (the reputed price was $100) and buy a book they could obtain for him.

"Anything! I'll do anything!" said John desperately. When the coveted book was delivered, the doctors admonished John, "But this book must definitely be used with faith and prayer." (Mama's comment at this point generally was, "That, of course, was the secret.") "And don't speak of this to anybody."

See
back of picture
for information

29.1. Ella Mittelstadt Fischer, flanked by her daughters Edna and Leone,
on Mother's Day, Mayville, 1950. Wisconsin Folk Museum Collection.

The story goes on to say that John and his family evidently studied the book with meticulous care and finally thought they had found the passage that fit their case, and by it took away the curse. For, "John had no more trouble after that."

"Really?" chorused the young Fischers.

"Well, so they say," shrugged Mama.

"Mama, do you know who else ever had such a book? Tell us, please!"

Mama laughed, "Oh ja, there was one in Fussville and in Lannon, too, they say. Anyway, everybody was terribly afraid of these people."

"Afraid, I don't get it? If the book helped?"

"Ja." And Mama sighed heavily, "But the books they say were very dangerous in the wrong hands."

"Oh, how do you mean?"

"Well," then hastily, "now mind you I'm not saying I believed this, or ever read one of the books—I would have been afraid too—but people said those two men used the book to read the plagues and curses Moses used against the enemies of the chosen people. The men at Lannon and Fussville were supposed to have studied Moses' directions, or whatever you call it, power maybe. Well, anyway, people said the men would behex anyone whom they had a grudge against. Those people would stay behexed until that book owner died!"

"How terrible! Couldn't you have him arrested?"

"Goodness no! No, they'd be afraid of being behexed all over again. And the judge as well. Oh no, kinder, everyone nicely left that kind alone. You can be sure of that."

"Golly the whole thing sounds awfully stupid."

"Oh, I suppose it was, but then—well, when one thinks of all Moses did to get rid of the wilderness enemies."

"Yes, but wasn't there anything that could stop men like that?"

"Well yes, that is, now that I'm older I don't know how much of those stories were imagination, but I do know that one man couldn't keep his pants up, no matter what he did. And another man couldn't keep any skin on his arms. Well then they called their priest, Father Schaff, from Fussville to, well, take it away, because they said he had a book too. Everybody loved Father Schaff, both Protestant and Catholic, for he would come wherever he was called to get rid of any curse put on them. He was wonderful!"

"Golly Mama. It all sounds so spooky and, but somehow I like to hear more. Do you know any other stories about this Father Schaff?"

"Well yes, I can remember they said that Mr. Witte was bewitched by Mr. Meister when Witte sold Meister a poor team of horses that he pretended were good by telling Meister, 'You don't have to keep them if you're not satisfied.' When Meister got home, he discovered one to be blind and the other one was spavined. So he took them back the next morning, but Witte laughed and said, 'They're your horses. If you don't like them, sell them—like I did.' Well Meister was mad enough to kill Witte (who weighed 270 pounds), so he said to the big man, 'I can't lick you Witte, but you just bet your life I'll get even with you.' And it seems he did, for it took no time and Witte was down to 78 pounds and no doctor could help him. Everyone said that Witte knew he was bewitched and the worry made him just waste away, until they called in Father Schaff who took it away. I often wondered how Witte felt then."

(Personally, I often wondered whether there really ever was a *Seventh Book of Moses* and whether I would have dared to read it, if I found one.)

Sorcery

Alice Ottow

Both my maternal and paternal grandparents came from Germany around 1870 to the United States where they settled in opposite corners of Wisconsin. Although they did not know each other until about 1910, the two families had many common beliefs and superstitions. Both of my grandfathers practiced the curing of illnesses by supernatural means.

My maternal grandfather, Grandpa Boldt, supposedly had the power to cure the sick of almost any disease. Although my mother did not remember exactly how he did it, she does remember certain facts. He had a book which told how to work these cures which he consulted in case of illness. It was important to read it backwards to thwart evil powers. Evidently my grandpa was called many times by neighbors, particularly to help persons with severely bleeding wounds. After he said certain prayers, ending with the Lord's Prayer, the bleeding would miraculously stop. These cures were not effective through our Christian God, but supposedly were accomplished with the help of the devil. Even to this day my mother believes that grandpa perhaps was possessed by a devil and that he was actually able to perform these feats.

My father has told me similar stories about his father's work in sorcery. Grandpa Ottow did not use a book, but had learned his art from his father. His procedure was similar to Grandpa Boldt's, for he also said certain prayers and ended with the Lord's Prayer. My father remembers that one of their neighbors accidently fed some boiling food to their pigs. The pigs became violent with pain, and unless something had been done immediately they would have died. Grandpa was called and, after he recited the correct words over the pigs, they ceased their raging and became normal. Another time my aunt received severe wounds when a horse kicked her. She was bleeding profusely and it was feared she would bleed to death. Again Grandpa used his powers, and my aunt's wounds stopped bleeding and healed quickly.

Although Mother and Father both believe in the sorcery of their fathers, they have different attitudes toward it. Mother thinks it was against the Christian religion and blames misfortune and suffering in the family upon it. She has told me that she fears her father was connected with the devil and that he himself may have feared some consequences; because for a number of years before his death he refused to perform any more cures. The last request Mother can remember he was asked was when someone asked for Grandpa's help and he brought out his book and gave it to them saying, "it's all in here, do it yourself."

On the other hand my father cannot see anything wrong with the practices or anything in them which is in opposition to the Christian religion. He feels that these men were gifted by God and that their works had nothing to do with the devil.

My sisters, brothers, cousins, and I have listened to all this superstitious talk by the older generation, but . . . we don't believe it because we haven't lived with it. Perhaps if my father or uncles practiced sorcery I would believe it too, but the techniques and knowledge are buried with my grandfathers. Another factor which I think has planted unbelief is our modern education which leads us to be skeptical of things unscientific.

While my grandfathers were performers of these deeds and their children firm believers in them, my generation only knows about them, and I'm sure that to my children they will be just fantastic stories—if indeed they hear about them at all.

Faith Healing Can and Does Work
Bill Brandt

Of the many different aspects of a society's folklore, one of the most interesting is the superstitious beliefs of the different groups of people. To many societies the mere mention of belief in the supernatural is just cause for laughter but to others, who have been brought up believing in mystic rites, it is a very real and serious thing. In our own state of Wisconsin we can find many of these latter groups, one of which is located in Appleton, a community of 38,000 residents. Appleton is a typical modern American city, which has been principally settled by German immigrants. Although I was born and raised in a strictly German environment by German immigrant parents, I was never fully aware until just recently of the part superstition played in the lives of many of these German immigrants.

One evening during the recent Christmas holidays, my father and I were discussing this superstitious aspect of his native culture. Many of the stories which he related I found hard to believe, but I could tell by the manner in which he spoke that they were true. It is my opinion that when a person has been brought up from early childhood believing that certain supernatural feats are possible and has on occasion seen feats performed with complete success attributed to this supernatural power, that he would readily believe in this power. Such was my father's case.

One of the things we discussed a great deal was the faith healer. Faith healers were old men or women who always read the Bible and from it and through visions supposedly learned the cures for sickness and deformity. They enacted these cures either by prayer or by having the person upon whom the cure was to be performed carry out certain instructions. A cure in this manner is entirely possible in my estimation if the person to be cured has faith that the cure will work. It is my opinion that faith healers work their magic much the same as the Indian shamans, especially in the case of minor illnesses. They work on a superstitious person's mind, making him believe that by doing certain things he will be cured. It is very probable that when a person has in his mind the belief that he will be made well he will recover more quickly from his illness. Modern medical science actually supports this theory to a certain degree.

My father related several incidents to me in which faith healers were supposed to have used their mystic powers to cure deformities. To my surprise one of the incidents supposedly happened to me when I was eight years old. According to my father I had several large warts on my fingers which nobody had ever paid any attention to. One day an old neighbor woman, who was visiting my mother, noticed the warts on my fingers. She told me if I wanted to get rid of them I was to go outside after dark of the same day, which was the time the moon would "take off." By "taking off," she apparently meant the moon was starting out on a new phase. I was to take a stone from the earth and cross it three times over the warts in the name of the Father, Son, and Holy Ghost. Then I was to replace the stone exactly as I had picked it up and not say anything about what I had done to anyone. By the time the moon had gone through a complete phase to where it would again be "taking off" my warts would be gone. According to my parents my warts mysteriously disappeared about a month after the old woman's visit.

Another incident similar to the one just related happened to my father when he was eighteen. At the time he had an extremely poor complexion, which bothered him a great deal. One day his father took him to an old hermit who lived in a shack on the edge of my grandfather's farm. When they arrived at the hermit's shack they found him in a typical faith healer's pastime, reading the Bible. His instructions to my father were to take a handkerchief, and on a night when there was a full moon, go to the village cemetery. There he was to take the handkerchief and in the same manner as I had done with the stone, pass it over his face three times in the name of the Godhead. Following this he was to walk into the cemetery through the front gate, go straight through the cemetery, dropping the handkerchief on one of the graves, and leave the cemetery by the back gate. Under no condition was he to look back over the way he had come. According to the belief in this rite a spirit of one of the dead would touch the handkerchief and thereby counteract the affliction. Within a month after this incident my father had a clear complexion, and to this day he has never had another single blemish on his complexion.

Both of these incidents have dealt with carrying out certain instructions. Included in these was always the crossing of the disfigurement three times in the name of the Father, Son, and Holy Ghost. However no prayer had been offered in either case unless the faith healer had offered one privately. This is explained by the fact that the healing was to be done on a disfigurement and not on an ordinary illness. If a person was ill the faith healer would always pray over the person and never perform any rite or ceremony. Invariably within a few hours or days after such a prayer the sick person would be well.

Shortly after my mother gave birth to my older brother she contracted a virus which caused hard pus lumps to form on her body. These lumps pained constantly and, because my mother was not quite sold on faith healing as my father, a doctor was called. There was nothing the doctor could do for her that would immediately relieve the pain. Finally my father summoned a friend of his who practiced faith healing. He prayed over my mother for one hour and then left without saying a word to anyone. Within a few hours the pain left my mother and two days later she was completely recovered.

A few months after the incident just related my father's hand and arm began to swell up. He had been working outside in the open and because it was the middle of winter and a very cold day he thought he had frozen his hand and arm. A neighbor insisted that he go to the doctor, who diagnosed the case exactly as my father himself had. The doctor gave him instruction as to how he should treat the limb and then sent him home. That night his arm began to pain him so much that he went to see the same faith healer who had cured my mother. Once again a prayer was said, only this time for a much longer period of time. My father said that after awhile he could actually feel the pain leave his arm as the faith healer prayed. By the next morning his arm was completely normal.

These incidents which I have just related may seem highly improbable to most people but as I have already mentioned, to someone who has been brought up to believe in such happenings, they are not only probable but they actually take place.

30

The "Plaster Doctor" of Somerset

James Taylor Dunn

Most traditional healers in Wisconsin have practiced their arts within small circles and without widespread publicity. Not so with John Till: having traveled from his native Austria to the lumber camps of northwestern Wisconsin, Till drew on Old World folk medical treatments to attract thousands of patients among the region's working-class immigrants. Like Euro-American folk healers generally, and like his teachers—a "healing blacksmith" and a pious hermit—Till invoked divine powers, asked that people pay only what they could, and dressed plainly. His preferences for going barefoot and wearing gold earrings in the manner of alpine men contributed further to an otherworldly air. Till's financial success and his reduction of a once larger curative repertoire to a single "secret plaster salve"—akin to the "snake oil" of frontier charlatans and the pharmaceutical industry's "wonder drugs"—resulted in attacks from the medical and legal establishments, scrutiny by journalists, the composition of popular songs, and considerable storytelling and debate among supporters and skeptics.

James Taylor Dunn, born in 1912, grew up on the Minnesota side of the St. Croix Valley and eventually served as chief librarian of the Minnesota Historical Society. Dunn's contribution to the "Rivers of America" series—*The St. Croix: Midwest Border River* (New York: Holt, Rinehart and Winston, 1965)—includes accounts of Kickapoo Indian Medicine shows; Dr. McBride, "the self-styled 'King of Pain'"; and John Till in a chapter on "Quacks and Quackery." The expanded overview of Till's career presented here draws upon newspaper sources supplemented by interviews Dunn conducted in the mid-1950s with "the plaster doctor's son, John W. Till" and others, most of whom hailed from Somerset, the French Canadian settlement on the Wisconsin side of the St. Croix River Valley, where Till enjoyed his greatest popularity.

On May 11, 1985, I also interviewed John Till's son, John W. Till of rural Cumberland, in connection with the Wisconsin Folklife Center's German Music Project. Like his father who, in addition to "doctoring," was the leader of an old-time dance band, the younger Till, raised both in Wisconsin and in central Europe, was a fine traditional musician. He played the Austrian double-necked *schrammel* guitar, yodeled, and led a family band, The Singing Tills, that was recorded in 1975 for the Smithsonian Institution's Office of Folklife Programs. Inevitably John W. Till told me about his famous father, including a few facts not mentioned by Dunn: the elder Till was seven years old when injured by a horse and wagon; and he spent twenty-one years with his blacksmith-herbalist mentor before emigrating to Wisconsin, where a brother was living.

Reprinted from the *Wisconsin Magazine of History* 39:4 (Summer 1956): 245–50.

Throughout the fall of 1905, people around Somerset talked of little else but the "miracle cure" of Meline Cloutier, the wife of a farmer living near this Wisconsin village. Mrs. Cloutier had suffered from an infected cheek which many villagers considered serious enough to threaten her life. It was suggested that a woodsman who lived not far from Turtle Lake and practiced medicine on the side could save the suffering woman. Her husband, Octave Cloutier, was told that this man used a healing oil which had performed miracles. In hope that the "Quick Healer" might relieve his wife, Cloutier traveled to the northern Wisconsin village of Turtle Lake and returned home accompanied by a man whose name was soon destined to become a household word throughout the St. Croix Valley. The amazing career of John Till, the "Plaster Doctor of Somerset," was launched when he successfully treated Mrs. Cloutier with his secret plaster salve.

Till was born on August 11, 1870, in the poor mountain village of Einsiedel, Austria (now *Mnísek nad Hnilcom* in Russian-held Czechoslovakia). His shoemaker father had a large family, and could not afford doctor's fees when young John broke both legs and crushed seven ribs in a hay wagon accident. Instead, he was taken to a healing blacksmith (*Kurschmied*) who treated him as best he could, but left the boy with a twisted, deformed leg. When he grew older, Till became a blacksmith and interested himself in the folk cures employed by the *Kurschmied* who had learned herb doctoring from a hermit monk. Till was told, for example, that the best cure for a rattlesnake bite was to eat the snake's skin; that sour red wine boiled with nettles and honey would stop a lung hemorrhage.

At the age of twenty-eight, determined to "get ahead," the shoemaker's son left his native Austria for a better life in America. In 1898 he entered the United States through Canada and a number of years later located at the Turtle Lake lumber camp where he was "discovered" by Octave Cloutier in 1905.

After Mrs. Cloutier's quick recovery, the services of John Till, the "Wonder Healer," became very much in demand. With Cloutier acting as his manager, Till at first traveled from Turtle Lake to Somerset once every three weeks for a short visit. At the Cloutier farmhouse about a mile south of Somerset, he treated all comers with his secret plaster salve and a burning plaster. The salve, which was said to contain a mysterious ingredient known as "4X," was applied to open wounds; and the plaster, composed largely of Croton oil and kerosene, was used for all other afflictions. Such was the demand for these cure-alls that within a few months Till left Turtle Lake and moved in with the Cloutiers. To accommodate the increasing stream of patients, a wing was added to the farmhouse and the "Plaster Industry" had begun in earnest.

From Hudson and New Richmond, and from such Minnesota towns as Marine, Taylors Falls, and Stillwater, strings of teams were constantly Somerset-bound bringing customers by the thousands to what one reporter called "that Eldorado of supposed health" (Stillwater *Messenger*, August 3, 1907). From other points in Wisconsin and Minnesota, railroads carried patients who hoped that perhaps the "Plaster Doctor of Somerset" could cure them. On and on came the believers, suffering from palsy, paralysis, rheumatism, locomotor ataxia, cancer, appendicitis, dyspepsia, blindness, varicose veins, in fact "all the diseases not contagious that man is heir to" (Hudson *Star Times*, December 6, 1907).

Beginning at six in the morning and working through ten o'clock at night, "Plaster John," as he was nicknamed, treated all who sought him. After the patients were seated on the dozen backless kitchen chairs he would go down the row carefully feeling their jugular veins with his unwashed fingers. Till claimed that this method enabled him to diagnose the diseases of his patients. He would then lay bare the sufferer's back and apply his remedy, the plaster concoction, smearing it from the shoulder blades to the base of the spine and using the same sponge for everyone. The plaster was put on in three different strengths: mild, strong, and, if a matter of life or death, "horse treatment." Farmer Cloutier (or "Clootsie" as he was called) followed immediately behind the "doctor," sewing cotton batting on the patients' inner garments to keep the clothes from chafing the tender flesh. After a warning from Till not to expose themselves to cold and rain and to wash their hands only in warm water, thus avoiding extreme suffering or even death, the "squad" of twelve patients was then dismissed and another took its place. A reporter from the Hudson *Star Times* observed that "each contributed as much as he deemed fit, none less than a dollar, which sums were carelessly thrown into the treasury box to the rear of the thrifty and industrious operator who appeared not to give it a thought" (December 6, 1907).

One of the many St. Croix Valley newspaper reporters sent to cover the Till enterprise asked the "wizard of fly-blister" if he could watch.

"For vot purpose? You have nottings de matter mit you."

"Nothing but a severe attack of curiosity," was the answer.

"I'm too busy to help you satisfy dat!" replied Till (Hudson *Star-Times,* December 6, 1907).

Till usually dressed in a plain woolen shirt, collarless and open at the neck. His trousers, held up by oil-stained galluses, were so greasy and dirty that one observer thought "a coal heaver would have blushed in them." His bare feet (for he infrequently wore shoes) appeared not to have been washed in years. Two small gold rings adorned his pierced ears; he seldom shaved, and never cleaned his yellow, snuff-stained teeth. "John is neat—not gaudy," was a differing opinion.

Till's only answer to such statements on his appearance was: "Remember, Christ who owns the whole world was dressed poorly" (Stillwater *Gazette,* September 5, 1906).

And so they came, "squad" after "squad," sometimes as many as 150 a day, dropping their silver dollars into the bucket. It was estimated that Till's income frequently amounted to $20 an hour, and that in one season he made as much as $80,000. Every two weeks he would load his well-filled money boxes on a wagon and truck them into New Richmond where the banker's daughter helped count the coins. Mrs. Grace Thomas recalls that Till deposited on average $3,000 every two weeks. Cloutier's share of Till's earnings was a straight 50 cents per visitor.

Over in Knapp, Wisconsin, Samuel Tufts published a song in 1907 called "John Till of Somerset." Its ten stanzas tell the story of a trip to Somerset, what the "doctor" did, and how the plaster treatment turned out. The first verse begins:

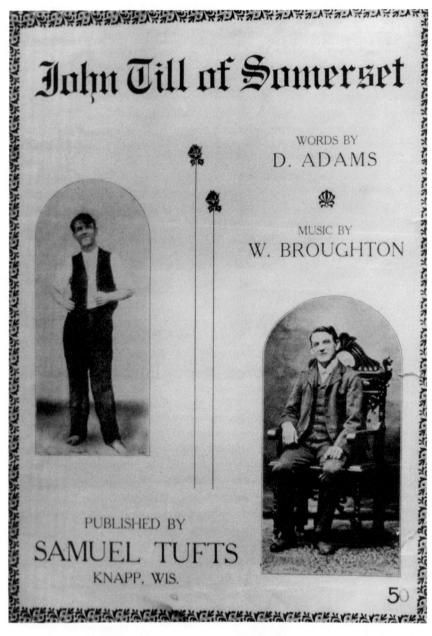

30.1. The sheet music for Samuel Tuft's 1907 ballad of John Till, on display at the home of John W. Till, 1986. Photo: James P. Leary.

We took a trip to Somerset not very long ago,
On the borders of Wisconsin where the Apple River flows.
Our health it was so poorly that we thought that we would try
That Doctor there at Somerset, for he was all the cry.

The "barefoot physician" was not the only one to make money from his enterprise. Hank Farmer, Stillwater's liveryman, had to double the number of hacks crossing the St. Croix River bound for "Plasterville." To accommodate the hundreds of passengers arriving daily by railway sixteen carriages, each capable of holding six persons, plied constantly that four miles between the Wisconsin Central depot at Somerset and Dr. Till's office; and just as many carriages were making two round trips a day from New Richmond. Hotels in Stillwater and Hudson were booked solid, and bars at Somerset grossed as much as $100 a day at a time when a beer cost a nickel and whisky was 15 cents a shot. One farmer, making the best of the housing shortage, spread clean hay on the floors of his two-story barn and did a "thriving business" charging 35 cents for sleeping accomodations, bedclothing not furnished. Hotels, restaurants, saloons, and livery stables raked in large profits, thanks to the plaster doctor, and the little town of Somerset was in a constant "whirl of excitement" (Stillwater *Messenger*, March 14, 1908). Some people, like the cigar maker in Dassel, Wisconsin, "scented easier money" and set themselves up in competition to Till. A Dr. Johnson entered this specialized business in Somerset, but no one seemed able to rival the Till-Cloutier combination.

During Till's almost four years of "doctoring" at the Cloutier farm the Stillwater *Gazette* charged that several deaths were "due directly or indirectly to Till's diabolical and fiendish treatment" (October 30, 1907). These claims, however, were never substantiated and the Hudson *Star-Times* countered: "It is more likely that such unfortunate people were beyond human aid when they went to him for treatment" (December 6, 1907).

Tall stories magnifying the effectiveness of the plaster circulated in the Somerset area. It was said that the plaster was used to cement back on a dog's severed tail and that in ten days the tail was healed and its wag restored. Another hound's tail was chopped off, so the story went, but when the animal ran off yelping, the owner took the remaining piece to Till who used double-strength plaster (the "horse-treatment"?) and grew on a brand new dog.

As was to be expected, Till was a number of times arrested and brought to trial for practicing without a license, but the State Medical Board could not persuade any jury to convict the man. After one of the trials in Hudson, the county seat, "Doctor" Till on his return to Somerset was met at some distance from the village by a great throng of celebrants headed by a brass band. They escorted him triumphantly to his office and that night there was a joyful demonstration of welcome with 1,300 new patients clamoring for consultation. "In the long run," as the Hudson newspaper summed it up, "Till is liable to have many more friends than the . . . [medical] board which is frantically determined to ding away at the legislature until they have made it a felony to take a dose of catnip tea or onion syrup without their prescription" (*Star-Times*, December 6, 1907).

Twice during those years at Somerset, Till visited his native Austria. On the second trip, in 1908, he took members of the Cloutier family with him. While they were gone, Somerset made great plans for their September homecoming. Some tradesmen even went into debt on home and village improvements, expecting to recover their investments when Till got back and money again flowed freely. Amiable Cloutier tied up $3,500 in a new hotel. A big reception for the returning travelers was planned at storekeeper Henry A. LaGrandeur's home. The renowned "doctor" was to be conveyed from the railway station in one of Hank Farmer's best coaches pulled by eight white horses and preceded by a band. There would be feasting and dancing in the streets (Stillwater *Messenger,* September 19, 1908).

But all these plans were upset by a sudden and unexplained rift between Till and the Cloutiers. Exactly what happened is not clear. On arriving at Ellis Island, Till was temporarily detained because of his crippled leg. Many felt the Cloutier family to have been responsible and said that they had deserted their benefactor in his hour of need. Thus it was that instead of returning to the scene of his former triumphs, Till went to the home of a sister in Almena near Turtle Lake. He adamantly refused to listen to the beggings and pleadings of the citizens of Somerset and never went back there.

Without such a careful manager as Octave Cloutier, Till was too easy going, too vain and credulous a mark for swindlers, to succeed alone. He joined forces with his sister, Bertha Stoeberl, at Almena, but they soon fell into disagreement over the division of the "take," and quickly parted company. To make matters worse, Bertha persuaded two of Till's assistants to desert him and join her, since she had tasted success as an independent healer and established her own plaster clinic. Till moved on to New Richmond in 1909 and operated in various locations there until 1916. In spite of continued success, life was no calmer in his new spot. If it wasn't a fight with his associates the Kindervaters or the McDonald's over the profits from another of the "doctor's" money-making projects, the Till Bus Line Company, it was with someone else.

During this time, on one of his frequent trips back to the old country, he married Hedwig Steiner of Freudenthal, Austria. By 1917 the family, with their small four year old son, was living at Turtle Lake. In 1919, doubtless anticipating his "retirement," he had bought a sizeable estate in Dittersdorf, Austria. The Tills' last plaster shop in this country was at North Hudson where early in 1920 they paid $5,000 for Mrs. Jean Jefferson Penfield's private Galahad School for Boys on the shores of Lake St. Croix. There they opened the Till Institute with a *bona fide* but alcoholic M.D. as "Medical Director."

Throughout the post-Somerset years, the plaster king was constantly plagued by law suits and damage claims, varying in amount from $100 to $120,600. The state authorities continued after him. There were numerous private suits by people like Pat Sullivan from Milwaukee who claimed to have lost the sight of one eye because of the plaster treatment. Most of the time, however, the newspapers would merely state: "There have been so many cases of horrible suffering occasioned by visits to Till that we are ashamed to chronicle them" (Stillwater *Daily Gazette,* September 30, 1907). So far as is known, no death was ever legally found to have come about as a result of Till's treatments. He lost money which he invested in the Honduras Development Company, and he came to feel that everyone was out for a share of his coin. Being hauled into court became a common occurrence and he soon regarded it as part of the day's work. Perhaps he sometimes longed for those almost carefree days at Somerset, and the honest business head of Octave Cloutier.

The State Medical Board, long hindered by the fact that Till never posed as a doctor nor charged for prescriptions, finally made an old conviction stick. Several years earlier, while still at Turtle Lake, Till had been found guilty of practicing medicine without a permit. The case was appealed several times, but when the court upheld the conviction, Till in November, 1920, was taken from Hudson and placed behind bars at the Barron County jail. A condition for his release ten months later was that he, his family, and what money he had left should go back to Europe. One area newspaper predicted that Till would soon be sponging the spine of the Khedive of Egypt, or "sewing cotton batting on the undergarments of the Sultan of Turkey . . . Perhaps he goes to cleanse his one and ever ready sponge in the waters of the River Jordan." The Tills sailed on March 12, 1922, apparently unwept and completely unnoticed by all of the St. Croix Valley newspapers that had given him so much free advertising during the years of his plaster doctoring. "Till has promised to leave the country," reported the Hudson *Star-Observer,* "which is something to be grateful for . . ." (November 25, 1921).

What were the reasons for John Till's popularity? Why did so many thousands storm his door demanding the magic plaster and salve? Why do stories of miraculous cures effected by this wonder healer still circulate in the St. Croix Valley? Perhaps the explanation lies in the relative isolation of the farming community and its lack of competent medical assistance. In their overwhelming desire for freedom from pain, these people were easy prey for all the quacks and charlatans who made their fortunes from patent medicine and cure-all nostrums.

Dr. Justus Ohage, as former St. Paul health commissioner, testified at one of Till's 1912 trials. He gave perhaps the best explanation:

If a man suffering from stomach trouble applied to Till for treatment, he became absorbed in the condition of his blistered back and so forgot, by simple psychological process, all about his stomach disturbance. There is just where the success of this man Till lies. When people go over there, as so many thousands do, they can't all be fools! Some of the people are suffering from stomach trouble and when Till afflicts them and gives them sore backs, they can't think of anything else for two months. They are so happy when their backs are healed that they do not think of their stomach troubles. (Hudson *Star-Observer,* November 25, 1921; Hudson *Star-Times,* December 6, 1907)

F. M. Welsh, editor of the Stillwater *Messenger,* spoke for many of Till's satisfied patients when he said that the plaster doctor's word could be relied upon:

He benefitted the health of thousands . . . whether or not there was anything supernatural in this or not, we do not presume to say. Whether people simply imagine Till has cured them, it is still a fact that a great many people claim Till cured them . . . The independent American invalid will have his way in spite of all arbitrary and futile prosecution. (March 9, 1912)

Twenty-four years later, having lost most of his possessions first to the Germans and then the Communists during and after World War II, Till quietly returned to the United State which had granted him American citizenship at Hudson back in March, 1910 (Hudson *Star-Observer,* March 31, 1910). Less than a year after that while visiting friends at Kiel, Wisconsin, he died of a heart attack July 14, 1947.

Over the years, the salve and plaster which Meline Cloutier once brewed have not been forgotten. Many in the country bordering the St. Croix River continue to have complete faith in this wonder medicine and in the miraculous cures of the "Plaster Doctor of Somerset."

31

"Jecz Cha Nacha!": You Are Invited to a Polish Wedding in Wisconsin

Rena J. Grubb

Polish weddings in Wisconsin are justly famous as extended festivities involving the surrounding community. Early in this century local women did all the cooking; the engaged couple delivered wedding invitations personally; musicians escorted the wedding party to the church, then from the church to the dance hall; men paid for dances with the bride by hurling silver dollars onto a plate; women removed the bride's veil, then gave her an apron and a broom while singing ancient songs about the travails of married life; free beer flowed; and the wedding dance proper was followed by the *poprawiny,* a final day-after celebration.

Malcolm Rosholt offers a vivid account of pre–World War I Polish weddings in his history of Portage County, *Our County, Our Story* (Stevens Point, Wisc.: Portage County Board of Supervisors, 1959), 135–37. Adopting a different spelling from that of Rena J. Grubb's title, Rosholt describes the bride's father's crucial role:

> The featured event was the bridal dance, a custom brought over from Poland. Usually reserved for the evening, it began when the father of the bride announced *"Jeszce nasza"* (pronounced yesh-che-nashah!) meaning "Yes sir, she's still ours!" The musicians and guests were expected to echo the same phrase whereupon the men formed a circle around the bride and began to exchange dances. The father stood among the guests and everyone who wished to dance with the bride was expected to throw a dollar against a dinner plate on the table so that it would ring or even break the plate. Each partner was expected to dance only once or twice around the ring and in this manner the young bride was whirled round and round in great humor. The music was furnished by a fiddler or two who played the same tune over and over until it rang in one's ears for days.

The silver dollars from the plates were collected by the father and given to the bride in lieu of a dowry.

Customs have changed over the years, but traditional elements persist. In the late twentieth century many young couples in heavily Polish Portage County, for example, set their date in accordance with the availability of a contingent of older Polish ladies who prepare a wedding feast that must include such ethnic delicacies as *kielbase* (Polish sausage), *kapusta* (sauerkraut), and *pierogi* (a stuffed dough, akin to ravioli, that is parboiled then fried). Couples also hire bands, like Norm Dombrowski and the Happy Notes, that can play Polish dance tunes as well as orchestrate the grand march and the bride's dance. Enormous guest lists include much of the surrounding community. Those invited give cash as often as any other gift and are recompensed with music, food, plenty of beer, shots of brandy, and soft drinks.

The article reprinted here describes a wedding that might have happened during the 1920s in Armstrong Creek, Three Lakes, Weyerhaeuser, or some other northern Wisconsin community settled by Poles in the late nineteenth or early twentieth centuries. With the state's pinery nearly depleted, lumber companies, railroads, local boosters, and speculators sought new settlers to farm the cutover and placed glowing articles in ethnic newspapers. The newcomers were often recent immigrants of peasant backgrounds who sought a healthier alternative to laboring in Mesabi Range mines, Chicago slaughterhouses, Milwaukee tanneries, or Pittsburgh steel mills. Optimistic Finns and a plethora of Slavs—Carpatho-Ruthenians, Croatians, Czechs, Slovaks, Slovenians, Ukrainians, and especially Poles—purchased acreage sight unseen, only to be met with brush, stumps, rocks, swamps, thin soil, and a short growing season. Accounts from individual Czech, Slovak, Slovenian, and Polish families, for example, abound in such community publications as Jerry Novak's *The History of the Moquah Area* (Ashland, Wisc.: Northland College Press, 1966); Terese Trojak and Toni Rohrig's *Phillips Czechoslovakian Community* (Park Falls, Wisc. F. A. Weber & Sons, 1991); the Slovenska Druzba Committee's Spominska Zgodovina/*Historical Memories* (Willard, Wisc.: Slovenska Druzba, 1987); and the Weyerhaeuser Centennial Committee's *Weyerhaeuser: Area Centennial Family Album* (Weyerhaeuser, Wisc.: Centennial Committee, 1984).

The struggles of cutover farmers account for the dark tone underlying Rena J. Grubb's finely detailed sketch of an otherwise joyous Polish wedding. She likewise mentions religious rifts within Wisconsin's Polish community. Some immigrants resented the influence of the Catholic church on so many aspects of their lives, while other Polish Catholics resented the domination of the German and Irish clergy who controlled diocesan structures. The latter faction believed they ought not "Americanize" but instead establish a New World "Polonia"—an ideal ethnic Catholic society of the sort denied in the old country by the partitioning of Poland among Austria, Germany, and Russia. Such dissenters formed a Polish National Church, often in bitter rivalry with the American Catholic Church. (For a fictionalized treatment of ideological conflict based on occurrences in the Berlin, Wisconsin, area, see Wanda Luzenska Kubiak, *Polonaise Nevermore* [New York: Vantage Press, 1962].)

The Wisconsin Magazine, the source of Grubb's article, was published for only a few years in the late 1920s. Aimed at tourists and locals, laden with advertisements touting the state's industry and natural beauty, it included numerous articles on the culture of Wisconsin's native peoples, European ethnics, and loggers.

Reprinted from *The Wisconsin Magazine* (October 1927):13, 24.

"*Jecz cha nacha!*" with ringing clearness sounded the old father's cry above the sharp staccato music played by a hunchback, grey-haired violinist, a sallow-faced blond with an impressively large accordion, and a very solid brown-faced drummer. Through the crowd of laughing, determined dancers one could watch the old father and mother dance with an accuracy and vivacity that made the dance—simple, queer Polish dance that it was—a dance of fascinating strength and elemental beauty.

"*Jecz cha nacha!*" (Yes sir! She is still ours!) again the father's voice rang out above the clamor. That day had been his daughter's wedding day; the bridal dance had ended; the general wedding dance was at its height; until the last guest had departed and the music had ceased, the daughter was still his, but after that—no more. He was stooped and marked by his struggle to wring a scanty living from the wild northern Wisconsin land. His leathery complexion strangely blended with his brown suit and hat, and his wife, even more marked by the life of an immigrant settler, was as swarthy of complexion as he. Around and around, spinning like a top, with dizzy speed, they danced the polka. The men who had probably learned to dance in Poland clicked their heels in unison with the accent of the music; the younger dancers could not or did not. "*Jecz cha nacha!*" and the dark eyes of the father snapped with joy—the only sign of emotion his face expressed.

The barn, which was the wedding dance hall, was lighted by kerosene lamps hung high from the rafters; many red, white, and blue streamers of crepe paper were wound in and out among the post and rafters; and the floor itself, was scrubbed and planed—in some places where it was not hidden by the black shadows of the rafters and posts it fairly gleamed in the lamplight. A plank bench was built around the floor and, opposite the huge haymow doors, a platform for the orchestra had been erected. Perhaps it was the faint suggestion of Chopin's Mazurka; or of Schwarenka's Polish Dances; something in the brisk melody with its emphatic One! two, three, One! two, three echoed the land of the Poles, the land of Reymont, the land whose people were held for generations as serfs of foreigners but now were enjoying the still novel freedom of their adopted country. The simple tune of one oft repeated selection was somewhat as follows:

31.1. Music from a Polish wedding.

Twenty-five or thirty years before the immigrants had purchased the wild cut-over land from the lumber companies, and with nothing but indomitable will and a capacity for ceaseless toil, they had developed the country. Poor farmers they still are; many of them are heavily in debt, but for all our judgments, they are now lords instead of peasants. Instead of four acres in Poland, they may own forty or eighty in America, and even the poorest of them rejoices in his new freedom. The weddings in this community, more frequent in recent years because those of the first generation are old enough to marry, are the means of giving them their one opportunity to celebrate.

The bridal dance had begun at nine o'clock and had ended near midnight. The bridal dance takes the place of our custom of giving wedding presents. A large circle is made by the wedding guests. On the inside of the circle, the father of the bride stands with a plate, and the bride, in wedding dress and veil just as she appeared at the church ceremony before breakfast, stands within the circle. The first man to put a dollar or more on the plate has the first dance around the circle. Unless, as he returns to the starting place near the father, and there deposits another bill, his turn ends and the next man who contributes begins his dance with the bride. This continues for hours, and the money given to the bride frequently totals as much as seven hundred dollars. If a silver dollar is thrown with enough force to break the plate, he who throws it may have two dances with the bride. Always, above the excitement, the old father shouts, "*Jecz cha nacha!*" The bridal dance ends when the gifts cease, or when the bride becomes fatigued. Then the old Polish grandmothers take off the bride's veil, and like our bridal bouquet, a pin or a bit of lace is tossed to the guests.

A Polish wedding in northern Wisconsin begins early in the morning with the church ceremony and does not cease until the wedding cake is cut after the dance.

This is usually near dawn of the next day. The preparation for the wedding begins days in advance because dinner must be served to all the hundreds of guests, and nothing is ever scanty. Hundreds of chickens, a number of hogs, and other animals are killed, cooked, and carved; cookies, pies, cakes, bread, and biscuits are baked for the occasion. Hospitality, joy, and an abundance of food and drinks must characterize every wedding regardless of the cost. At one corner of the barn a small bar is built, and a genial Pole serves all comers at all hours.

After the bride returns from her rest following the strenuous bridal dance, she sits with her husband near the orchestra to receive the best wishes and the greetings of the guests as they depart. Many of the more religous aspects of a Polish wedding have been lost or disregarded by the younger generation. The procession to the church, the many family blessings, the prenuptial rites are generally omitted, but all the feasting and gayety remain. In Poland, where the church dominates all life, this would have been impossible.

Perhaps this difference in religious expression is most clearly demonstrated by the religious situation in the very community of which this wedding was chosen as typical. A small Polish church was built. In spite of Russian domination which prohibited freedom of religion, of speech, and of press among the Poles, they have clung to their old traditions for centuries. Thus it is that the Polish immigrants built their own Polish church with its three altars. But, with the freedom in America, a new sect sprang up under the leadership of a farmer immigrant who had a meagre education. Each Sunday he and those who compose his congregation meet at one of the homes and he translates and explains a few verses of the Bible. Whatever sincerity may have prompted the origin of the sect seems now to be offset by the intolerance of the sect toward the little community church. During a pretty spring religious festival which was observed by a procession and songs outside the church, one of the dissenters exploded several charges of dynamite within sufficient distance of the church to ruin the procession by noise and flying dirt. On Sundays, a tussle between a dissenter and a Catholic in front of the church in the wet clay road is a frequent occurrence.

One wonders how the younger generation is affected by this life of transition. The families are very large—twelve or more children, seldom less. Not one of the hundreds of children reared in this community ever attended the small high school in the nearby village. They were needed on the farm; their country schooling was eked out between harvesting and sowing: work, work, work in order to live. Pleasures were few. After they become of age many of them desert the farm for factory life in Milwaukee and Chicago. One can hardly blame them for leaving, yet it is a tragedy to see the aged parents worn out by toil, left alone on a farm which is too often heavily mortgaged. There can be little family loyalty where the pleasures of home life are necessarily sacrificed to toil and struggle in order to live.

This is but a scanty picture of the life in a Polish farming community; few generalizations can be drawn from it. This trenchant truth, however, persists. From places like this come the strong-faced, hard-working young Americans who man our industries; their ideas of America are formed back in the immigrant community. The immigrant community needs help.

32

The Wisconsin Oneida Wake

Robert Ritzenthaler

Rites of passage involving birth and death retain extraordinary significance among many of Wisconsin's American Indians. Babies may receive an "English name" at birth, but their "Indian name," often bestowed by an elder, comes later. Cradle boards remain in wide use among the Ho-Chunk, while Ojibwe babies may play with and be protected by a "dream catcher." Some Ojibwe, Menominee, and Potawatomi youngsters also wear a pair of "baby moccasins"—duly marred by a small hole so that the baby's pure yet vulnerable spirit might not be lured away before its time by affectionate deceased relatives.

New moccasins are required for the four-day journey to the spirit world. In 1995, while doing fieldwork for the Wisconsin Folk Museum, I interviewed moccasin makers Margaret Hart, Jerry Hawpetoss, and Josephine Daniels. Each was on call to make funeral moccasins for their respective St. Croix Ojibwe, Menominee, and Forest County Potawatomi peoples. The moccasins did not have to be smoke-cured or decorated with beads (as was generally done otherwise), and no payment was expected for them, but they were necessary. No Indian person could be expected to enter the ancestors' otherworld wearing "white man's shoes."

The article offered here concerns funeral customs practiced by Wisconsin's Oneida people. Based on observations made in the 1940s, the article reveals the survival and modification of ancient traditions alongside more recently introduced practices. More specifically, Robert Ritzenthaler juxtaposes old Iroquoian ideas with the Christian hymns acquired by the Oneida from Episcopalian and Methodist sources. In the late twentieth century, Christian hymns sung in Oneida still figure importantly in traditional funerals (see Terence J. O'Grady, "The Singing Societies of Oneida," *American Music* 9:1 (1991): 67–91).

Born in Milwaukee, Robert Ritzenthaler received a degree in anthropology from the University of Wisconsin before earning a Ph.D. from Columbia University. From 1938 through the 1970s, Ritzenthaler was Curator of Anthropology at the Milwaukee Public Museum. He also edited *The Wisconsin Archeologist*. In addition to the Oneida, Ritzenthaler did fieldwork with Wisconsin's Ojibwe and Potawatomi peoples. He coauthored, with Pat Ritzenthaler, an overview of precontact "Death, Burial, and Mourning" customs in *The Woodland Indians of the Western Great Lakes* (New York: The Natural History Press, 1970), 41–45. (For a historical description of Ho-Chunk burial customs as practiced within the Thunderbird, Bear, and Buffalo Clans, see Paul Radin, "Burial and Funeral Customs," in his *The Winnebago Tribe* [Lincoln: University of Nebraska Press, 1990], 92–107.)

Reprinted from *The Wisconsin Archeologist* 22:2 (1941): 1–2.

Eight miles out of Green Bay, Wisconsin, there is a community of about 1,500 Oneida Indians. Formerly one of the five tribes of the League of the Iroquois, they

32.1. Moccasins-in-progress, with trillium and fiddle-head fern beadwork,
rest on the kitchen table of Josephine Daniels, a Forest County Potawatomi, 1994.
Photo: James P. Leary, Wisconsin Folk Museum Collection.

migrated from New York to Wisconsin in 1822 under the leadership of Eleazer Williams, and were subsequently granted 65,000 acres of land near Green Bay which became known as the Duck Creek reservation. They brought with them a body of beliefs and customs, their own language, fragments of their old social and political organization, and the white man's religion. For a while they existed as a cultural island, but with the increasing settlement of the whites about them and the ensuing social and economic contact came a gradual loss of their old culture until today only a few fragments remain.

One of the most interesting survivals is the Oneida wake. It is based on the old Iroquoian idea that when a person died, his body must be guarded for three nights by friends and relatives so that witches would not steal "bits of flesh and fingers." This custom still prevails, but the body is now guarded for only two nights. The following is a description of a modern wake.

When a person dies, his embalmed body is placed in his home, and that night friends and relatives gather at the house. Upon entering the house, one is led to the body and after taking a look, is shown to a seat. The people sit around in silence, broken only by the frequent singing of hymns, mostly in Indian. At sporadic intervals friends or relatives will be called upon to deliver short eulogies, and a hymn is usually sung first to give the person time to organize his remarks. Around midnight a lunch is served with food brought by the friends and relatives. People come and go throughout the evening, but the closer relatives maintain watch until three or four in the morning for two nights. The third day the body is given a Christian burial in one of the church graveyards.

Ten days after the death a feast is given to which the immediate relatives are invited, and they bring various foods which the deceased used to like. The feast starts the spirit on its heavenward journey. If the feast is not given it is believed the spirit will stay on earth and bother people. The wake seemed to me to be the most impressive and beautiful ceremony in the present possession of the Oneidas.

33

Julebukk

On August 22, 1942, the linguist Einar Haugen posed an important question to a seventy-two-year-old woman in the Wisconsin Norwegian stronghold of Coon Valley: "*Julebukk?*" Her answer was immediate: "Oh yes, they still do that in some places. It used to be great fun in the old days, for there were only the young people of the neighborhood . . ." (translated from the Norwegian in Haugen, *The Norwegian Language in America* [Bloomington: Indiana University Press, 1969], 511–12). Variously spelled and variously translated as "Christmas mummery," "Christmas fooling," "Christmas ghosting," and "ragamuffining," Julebukk literally means "Christmas goat," in reference to bestial spirits said to roam the wintry Norwegian night playing tricks on country folk. In former times, Norwegian youngsters, donning masks suggestive of mischievous animals, visited neighbors between December 26 and the Epiphany. Barging into homes to demand food and drink, they enjoyed their hosts' efforts to guess who they were (see Kathleen Stokker, "Julebukk: The Norwegian Art of Christmas Fooling," *The Sons of Norway Viking* [December 1990]:10–13).

The custom was practiced widely among Wisconsin's rural Norwegians through the 1950s, and longer in some areas. Writing in 1976, Trempealeau County farmer-author Dave Woods recalled: "Twenty years ago, everyone knew about Jule Bokking, or Christmas Fooling . . . Grandma used to tell about Jule Bokking in a horsedrawn sleigh. Pa tells about doing the same in a Model "A" coupe, the rumble seat packed sardine-style with merrymakers. And of course everyone tells about getting to Tollefson's just in time to help with morning milking" (Dave Woods, *Wisconsin Life Trip* [Whitehall, Wisc.: Dan Camp Press], 56).

I first heard of julebukking in the late 1960s when sisters Esther and Ruth Frederickson, who worked for my dad in Rice Lake, offered seasonal reminiscences with treats of *fattigmann* ("poor man's" cookies) and *krumkake* (thin waffles rolled into cones). A decade later, Phil Martin encountered numerous julebukking stories from Norwegian fiddlers in Stoughton and Blair (see *Across the Fields: Traditional Norwegian-American Music from Wisconsin* [Dodgeville, Wisc.: Folklore Village Farm, 1982], 31). The tradition has also been reported from Waupaca County Norwegians and, as "*Joulu-Pukki*," from Finnish settlers in Clark County (see Alfred O. Erickson, "Scandinavia, Wisconsin," *Norwegian-American Studies and Records* 15 [1949]:185–209; and Vieno Keskimaki, "How They Celebrated Christmas: The Finns," *Wisconsin Tales and Trails* 4:4 [1963]: 20–23).

The proliferation of Julebukk observances in Wisconsin prompted historian Jane Marie Pederson to count it as one of those "aspects of the Old World culture [that] were sustained longer in the rural communities of the Midwest than in Norway itself, including the retention of particular regional language dialects, peasant crafts . . . and festivities like the charivari and jule bokking ('Christmas fooling')" (*Between Memory and Reality: Family and Community in Rural Wisconsin, 1870–1970* [Madison: University of Wisconsin Press, 1992], 226). Despite its diffusion, the affectionate memories it commands, its status as a relic of Old World culture, and its significance as a feature of Norwegian American identity, julebukking in Wisconsin has not been studied fully. The trio of student essays offered here enlarges our understanding.

All three essays are reprinted from student papers written for an anthropology course at the University of Wisconsin, January 1952; Badger Folklore Society Papers, box 2, in the Archives of the State Historical Society of Wisconsin.

Christmas at Grandmother's

Ken Silver

When mother was a child, around the turn of the century, every Christmas was cele-brated in the same fashion throughout the community. On Christmas Eve the tree had to be trimmed and all work completed before the evening meal could be eaten. It was a cheering thought to realize that every member of the community was eating the same food that was being eaten in the old country. It reminded the elderly people of their youth in Norway. Lutefisk, lefse, and spare ribs were always the main course, with breme, goat cheese, pickled herring, sour milk and flat bread, potata coka, romegrought, and tyte behr as trimmings.

Grandmother would always have the work of preparations and Grandfather would direct the family party after dinner. Grandmother bought and prepared the food, bought gifts, knitted each child a warm pair of mittens, and helped the children decorate the tree. The smallest children always strung popcorn and bright buttons. The older children made tinsel angels and wrapped packages with bright colored paper and cloth. The top of the tree was always crowned not with a star, but with a tinsel angel—that is, a picture of an angel pasted on a card and decked with tinsel. Among other ornaments were the candle holders, which were spring clips that clamped to the tree branch. While the candles were lit, because of fire hazards, each child was assigned to watch a particular one.

After dinner "Pa" took over the ceremonies. He would begin with a prayer, light the candles, then read from the Bible, after which he led in the singing of familiar Christmas carols—all in Norwegian. The oldest child passed out the presents as the candles were extinguished.

Among the customs of that community was the storekeepers' responsibility for those families too unfortunate to celebrate Christmas. My mother's family was the happy recipient of this kindness when Grandfather's leg was broken. Another cus-tom was to feed the livestock or "barn people" abundantly on Christmas Eve before touching their own meal. One belief about these "barn people" was that, for a few minutes around midnight on Christmas Eve, they could talk like human beings.

Between Christmas and New Year's the children would make masks of paper, paint, and charcoal and go from farm to farm yelling "Julebuk! Julebuk!" They would be welcomed into the house where their identity was guessed. When they were through eating at one farm they would proceed to the next, whooping and yell-ing up the country roads.

33.1. *Julebukkers*, or "Christmas foolers" (*Left to right*, Charlotte and Lars Iverson, Grace and Ordy Iverson, Marge and Ralph Stuart, Brad and Barb Barum, Elaine and Ray Jensen, and Newt and Phyllis Duncan) don motley garb before setting out in cars to visit rural neighbors, Elk Mound, 1960s. Courtesy of Phyllis Duncan and Heather Kolstad Davis.

On New Year's Eve a family party would be held and the popcorn balls taken off and eaten. The strung popcorn, being dusty by now, was given to the birds on the next day. On the second of January, every family took down its tree.

Yule Buk

Howard Halvorson

Once popular in southern Wisconsin, the Norwegian Christmas custom of Yule Buk is now gradually fading out. Perhaps the best way to describe this unusual custom is to compare it to our present-day celebration of Halloween. The participants in Yule Buk, or "Christmas fooling," usually dress up in zany costumes or old clothes and go from farm to farm doing pranks such as we do on Halloween. Yule Buk was originated in Norway and brought to the United States by immigrants. Because there was such a heavy settlement of Norwegians near Stoughton, it was natural that this custom should take hold there.

The only people who celebrate the custom of Yule Buk are the farmers, and it is now carried on only in a few isolated sections near Stoughton. These people dress up and start to make the rounds of the neighboring farms. When they arrive at a farm they usually do a few tricks, often a little destructive, and then go into the farmhouse. Various entertaining acts such as playing instruments or singing are performed by the "Christmas fools." The people of the homes then provide a lunch for everyone and plenty to drink. If several couples happen to come together at the same farmhouse, they naturally roll up the rug, bring out the drinks, and the inevitable result is an all-night party. This sort of thing goes on every night between Christmas Day and New Year's Day. It seems quite likely that nearly every "fool" acquires a hangover before New Year's Eve comes around.

Many people may think that it is unusual for the Norwegian people to have such a riotous custom during the Christmas season. A closer look at the way these people live can give a better insight into this question. Most of the farmers in this area, especially near the beginning of the century, lived on large farms that were widely separated. Because these people were immigrants who were working very hard to get established in their new homes, there was very little time or opportunity for entertainment. Therefore, it seems quite appropriate that during the Christmas season, when there is not as much work to be done as usual, that people should enjoy this chance for visiting and for some entertainment. With the introduction of modern farming methods and the general urbanization of this area, the custom of Yule Buk is rapidly fading away. Many of the old-timers, however, will always remember Yule Buk as a colorful part of Norwegian life in Wisconsin.

Christmas Customs in and around Oregon, Wisconsin
Byron D. Wechter

The Christmas customs of my home town, Oregon, Wisconsin, are similar to those of most midwestern communities of the same size. Oregon is a village of approximately fifteen hundred inhabitants located nine miles south of Madison, where many Oregonians have their source of livelihood. Thus one might presume that the customs of Oregon differ little from those of Madison.

I am going to state my observances of the Christmas seasons of two different periods and try to find some differences in the two. As for my suitability as an observer, I have now lived in Oregon for a period of four and one-half years consecutively, having previously lived here for a four-year period in the late 1930s and early 1940s. My remembrances of the Christmas customs of the first period . . . are rather vague, but I have supplemented them by asking questions.

[In the late 1930s] the town had few fancy decorations. The village square was decorated by hanging outdoor lights on a few pine trees that grew there and by putting a wreath on the monument to Oregon war dead. The village businessmen put up small decorations on the fronts of their establishments. The townspeople themselves had . . . a gaily decorated tree in the front window.

The churches played an important part in the Christmas celebrations of this time. The children of the various churches always gave a Christmas program for their parents. After the program, presents were exchanged and a Santa Claus came in and passed out candy, fruits, and nuts to the children. It was a custom for groups to go out caroling at Christmas time—sometimes organized church groups, but more often than not they were just groups of citizens with a good dose of holiday spirit. It was a custom for people who wanted carolers to come to their houses to put lighted candles in a front window as a signal for the singers to stop.

Christmas decorations in the home were not elaborate. There was the yule tree, a holly wreath on the front door, and possibly a few springs of mistletoe hung about the house. Few people had more elaborate decorations than these.

An old Scandinavian custom in the area, observed during the holidays, was called *Juleboking*, meaning "yule fooling." People dressed in crazy costumes, generally the men as women and the women as men. They visited their friends and went through a silly dance routine. Then they expected to be invited into the house and given food and drink. If they were not treated they were likely to pull some prank or practical joke. Sometimes these jokes weren't so funny, especially when the revelers had had more drinks than food. This custom was supposed to run from Christmas to New Year's.

Christmas has become much more commercialized in the post-war years. Manufacturers have realized this and are endeavouring to put more and more articles on sale during the Christmas period. Stores begin advertising months before Christmas and usually have their displays up by the latter part of November. It seems to me that everyone is trying to get into the act and make as much money as possible.

The present decorating of the village of Oregon has changed immensely. The number of trees in the village square has been increased. They are all decorated, along with a huge master tree which is placed in the center of the square. The businessmen of Oregon have purchased long strings of lights which are strung high across the business district. Across the center of the town is hung a huge sign reading, "MERRY CHRISTMAS AND A HAPPY NEW YEAR." One of these signs is also hung at the entrance to the south end of the town. It is put up by a small group of people who have their businesses there. A new custom was started three years ago when the Oregon businessmen offered prizes for the persons having the best outdoor displays. During the first few years the project was largely unsuccessful because there were not enough people taking part, but this last year the project was very successful. Almost everyone in town put up some sort of display and the judges had difficulty for the first time in picking the winners. The businessmen have also sponsored several things that have led to their material gain. They have a Santa Claus come into town on Saturdays who doles out candy and nuts to the younger children. Since Oregon is in the center of a farming area, this practice draws in farmers by the droves because it is the only chance to let their children see Santa Claus. They also have a loudspeaker system set up in the downtown area which plays Christmas carols during business hours.

The churches in town still follow much the same practice as before. They still have the custom of drawing names and exchanging gifts after a program several days before Christmas. The Youth Fellowships of the various churches now carry on the majority of the caroling. They go out and sing at old folks homes, homes of old church members, and at the homes of those who have sickness in the family.

The sending of Christmas cards has grown tremendously in volume during the past few years. In the past people sent cards only to their best friends. Now cards are sent to everyone you know, no matter how slight the friendship is. I can remember when we thought fifty cards were a great deal to receive at Christmas time. Now we think nothing of receiving several hundred. Everyone tries to make displays out of the cards they receive. In our home we string a wire across a double doorway and staple cards onto that. We also suspend ribbons down the sides of the doorway and staple cards onto the ribbon.

Decorations inside the house are also more elaborate nowadays. The Christmas tree hasn't changed much except in price, although there are now many different types of lights that one can use in decorating the tree. Most homes have nativity scenes on tables or some other Christmasy decorations about the house.

The custom of Juleboking is still carried out, but not quite as extensively as in the past. An interesting sidelight on this practice occurred recently when two young men from Oregon held up a tavern near Brooklyn. The proprietor thought they were two people out Juleboking and tried to pull a mask off one of the two. The bandit stepped back and tried to fire the gun he was holding, but evidently it wasn't loaded, which was fortunate for both him and the proprietor.

34

The Yuba, Wisconsin, Masopust Festival

Thomas E. Barden

In the 1850s, Czechs settled along the lower Wisconsin River Valley and to the north around the current Richland County communities of Yuba and Hillsboro. Mostly Catholic and farmers, they brought with them a rich tradition of seasonal religious practices, including Masopust. Like the better known Mardi Gras, Masopust is a pre-Lenten or Shrove Tuesday celebration, a final occasion to eat, drink, and dance before the solemnity of Ash Wednesday and the six-week fast preceding Easter. Part of a liturgy that emphasized sorrow and sacrifice, Lent also coincided with the final throes of winter, a time when fasting would extend a farm family's dwindling food supplies.

Lent's significance has lessened in Wisconsin with the corresponding diminishment of ethnic agrarian religious communities. As a student at St. Joseph's Catholic School in Rice Lake from 1956 to 1964, I gave up treats between meals and not only attended daily mass but also mid-afternoon stations of the cross. In a darkened church, where black cloth covered statues, we meditated on the sufferings of Christ, breathed air thick with incense, heard the blunt tones of wooden clappers rather than pealing bells, and sang mournful Latin verses like "*Stabat mater dolorosa* . . ." In the surrounding hinterlands, and elsewhere throughout Wisconsin's Catholic communities, neither weddings, nor tavern dances, nor any kind of celebration occurred—with the exception of the observance of St. Patrick's Day. No wonder Wisconsin's Czechs enjoyed pre-Lenten masquerading and the chance to consume platefuls of *kolacky* (pastries filled with apples, poppy seeds, and/or prunes), just as Wisconsin's German and Polish Catholics have celebrated Shrove Tuesday with masking, dancing, and the devouring of doughnut-like *fastnacht küchli*, and *paczski*.

Thomas E. Barden offers a thoughtful glimpse of dramatic changes in Masopust that parallel the alteration of Yuba's once-agrarian Czech Catholic way of life. The transformation of Masopust into a largely small-town, secular, generically American tavern dance held on a weekend instead of a Tuesday has not, however, marked the end of overtly Czech events in the Yuba area. Nowadays, in keeping with the New World tradition of summer festivals, the community hosts Cesky Den (Czech Day), a two-day event that includes Czech polka bands, a Czech singing group, and ethnic foods. In contrast to Masopust, where local customs might baffle and even terrify outsiders, Cesky Den is widely promoted and accompanied by a printed program that conveys the community's ethnic heritage to tourists and local youngsters.

Although born in Richmond, Virginia, Thomas Barden was a summer resident and active researcher in southwestern Wisconsin in the 1970s and 1980s. Barden earned a Ph.D. in English, with a concentration in folklore, from the University of Virginia and teaches at the University of Toledo. His study of Norwegian tobacco culture also appears in this anthology, pp. 476–85.

Reprinted from *Midwestern Journal of Language and Folklore* 8:1 (1982): 48–51.

About twenty-five years ago a man and his family were driving through southwest Wisconsin in February. They stopped at a filling station in the small town of Yuba to get gas. The man went to the wash room, and when he returned he found a group of people at his car putting burnt cork black-face on his wife and son. Not knowing what was going on, he pulled out his pistol to defend his loved ones. After extensive discussion his assailants explained that they didn't mean the travelers any harm. It was just something they did in Yuba, they said, during the *Masopust*. They invited the travelers to come and see. They did. And they've been coming back in February ever since.

What they had stumbled onto was a traditional Czechoslovakian shrovetide festival which has been maintained in Yuba since the first Bohemian immigrants arrived in the area in the 1860s. The word *masopust* means "abstain from meat," or "meat, go away." According to Zdenek Salzmann and Vladimir Scheufer's monograph *Komarov: A Czech Farming Village* (New York: Holt, Rinehart, and Winston, 1974), Masopust was a festival of long standing in rural villages of Czechoslovakia, where the accompanying dances were held in taverns or inns. In Yuba the festival took place in private homes until a tavern was constructed in 1876. After this, it reverted to a public setting. In 1915 it was moved to the newly constructed Yuba Opera House, where it has continued ever since.

The data presented here come from three sources: 1) The Salzmann and Scheufer monograph description of the Masopust in Czechoslovakia, as it was in the past and as it has changed over time, 2) the description of the festival as it used to be in Yuba as described by various townspeople, and 3) observation of the Yuba festival made by the writer and Emily Osborn while doing field work in the Ocooch Mountains region in February of 1980.

The occasion of the Masopust is the onset of Lent, the Catholic Church's designated period of fasting and abstention for forty days before Easter. There is no public dancing or celebration during this period, and in both the old and new country up until recently even weddings were forbidden. So the Monday and Tuesday before Ash Wednesday (the beginning of Lent) serves as a last chance for the community to celebrate and indulge. In this way Masopust is similar to the New Orleans custom of *Mardi Gras*, or Fat Tuesday.

In the Bohemian village of Komarov, Masopust began on Sunday after Mass. The youth of the village would go from house to house collecting contributions for the band, which accompanied them. There were served beer and traditional shrovetide foods, including *kolachki* (prune cakes) and fried bread. This procession included several masked figures, often a bear, a stereotypical Jew, an old woman with a basket on her back with an old man in it, and several runners, or clowns, who ran around the edge of the group to keep it in order. The band began in the afternoon. People danced through the night on Sunday, again Monday evening until morning, and on Tuesday evening until midnight. The Tuesday night dance was dedicated to the farmers and farm wives. Carnival season was buried amid joking and teasing at midnight on the eve of Ash Wednesday. It was generally represented by a fat man, with the ceremony mocking a church funeral service. This feature of Masopust shows striking similarities to the Hungarian shrovetide practice known as "Burying the Fiddle," in which a double bass, draped in black and representing "good times," is buried in a mock church service. In a Cleveland, Ohio, version I have seen performed at St. Margaret's in the West Cleveland Hungarian community, called Buckeye Road, the mock priest uses a toilet plunger as a wand and says "Hockus Pockus" as a parody of Latin. In Komarov the practice of having one night of Masopust include a masquerade procession died out toward the end of the last century, and attempts to revive the custom have been largely unsuccessful.

In Yuba, the tradition of masquerade has faded as well, but not died out entirely. In 1980 there were approximately twelve masqueraders in a crowd of over 500 in the Yuba Opera House. Mrs. Marci Levy, the keeper of Adolph's Tavern (downstairs) and the Opera House (upstairs) told us that this feature of the festival has been on the decline since Masopust changed from Monday and Tuesday to the weekend. "There's not so much emphasis on the costumes anymore. It used to be almost everybody, the young ones at least, would dress up the first night. Now they don't bother," Mrs. Levy stated.

Each informant we spoke to concerning Masopust noted how the festival has changed. Mrs. Tina Rott, who is 94 and the wife of an original member of the Yuba Band, and her nephew, Mr. Lyle Tiedrich, also placed the demise of the masquerade at 1956, when the two-day dance (the English name for Masopust) moved from its church calendar dates to the standard American weekend. In 1980 they still conducted the procession to judge the best costume, even though there were only six couples participating, and a prize was still awarded.

Among other features of the old which are no longer current in 1980 are two of special interest. One is the tradition of face blackening with burnt cork mentioned above. This practice parodies the Ash Wednesday service, in which the priest places a small cross on the forehead of each celebrant of the Mass. "People would get their good clothes messed up and ruined, and if somebody didn't want it done, they'd do it anyhow. So that would lead to fights," says Mrs. Levy. This practice also stopped in 1956.

That year may constitute such a watershed in the life of the festival because of the death of Mrs. Levy's father, Robert Novy, who according to Mrs. Levy, "was a great hand at keeping up tradition." When Novy died Mrs. Levy took over the tavern and got responsibility for the Masopust along with it. At this point traditional aspects of the festival began to drop away. The maintenance of Czech identity in the new world was important to Novy, and the force of his personality was a factor in keeping the festival's ethnic features alive.

The other important traditional feature now discontinued in Yuba is the house-to-house visiting, which was so conspicuous in the old country practice. When the festival was still held according to the church calendar, and when there were "fewer outsiders," this visiting was central to the festival. Mrs. Rott recalled,

Some of the men would dress as women, you know. They took the horses and sleds and went around to the farmers, and they'd stop at a farm, and they'd come in and start to play. And the women would have to dance with them, see? Then when they got through, they'd want some money or some food, or they'd take oats so they could sell it and have some money just to have a good time.

Curiously, this happened on Wednesday, after Lent started. Special food was prepared. "Oh, we'd bake all day on Wednesday because we'd be expecting the crowd to come. We'd make kolachki, you know, *rohliki*, things like that." Other Bohemian delicacies such as sweet and sour cabbage, and caraway ribs were served at this time as well. Lyle Tiedrich said *shuleke soup* was common during Masopust too. "It's Norwegian, not Czech," he said, "but you know there are a lot of Bowegians in the area."

All the changes in the Yuba Masopust point in the direction of eliminating features which distinguish it as an ethnic event. From the description in [Komarov], we can see that the Yuba festival was originally more or less identical with the old world one and stayed that way until Novy's death. After that, the changes began which made the 1980 two-day dance almost indistinguishable from any Saturday night dance that might be held in any small town in the Ocooch region.

There has been no self-conscious reformulating of Masopust into a "revival" event, a "folk festival" which would accentuate its ethnic features. What has occurred instead is a set of adjustments. There is an assimilation into a framework from the cultural mainstream (the move from Monday and Tuesday to the weekend). There is a deletion of features which are perceived as troublesome or "a bother." Significantly these are the ethnic ones.

What is interesting is how much these features remain alive in the minds of the participants and were referred to throughout the 1980 enactment. In these memory referents there was also a significant amount of concern for the reasons behind this "dehassleization" syndrome. The story of the travelers in the region which began this report was told widely during the 1980 Masopust and clearly seems to express the tensions which developed when "outsiders" came into contact with Masopust's traditional features.

The Yuba festival has reached a critical point as a community event. The traditional features are still in the shared possession of the group, if only in memory. As more time passes with these features submerged, the danger of Masopust losing its integrity as an ethnic festival increases. If it is to continue with its traditional features all intact, it is likely it will have to make the transition to a "revival" event, one in which the traditional features are enumerated and insisted upon.

35

Dyngus

Anne Pellowski

Dyngus, or "Switching Day," is an ancient rural Polish custom practiced by youngsters on Easter Monday and Tuesday. Its origin is said to recall the crowd that gathered around the tomb of the risen Christ. When guards could not command people to disperse, they used switches, then water. Dyngus was widely practiced by Wisconsin's Polish Americans and other Slavs well into the 1940s, with the boys taking the initiative on Mondays and the girls on Tuesdays (see Fred L. Holmes, *Old World Wisconsin: Around Europe in the Badger State* [Eau Claire, Wisc.: E. M. Hale, 1944], 352).

On June 13, 1978, Florence Trzebiatowski, who grew up in rural Portage County, told me about her experiences as a girl in the 1910s:

> Monday was for boys, Tuesday was for girls. Early in the morning. Some farmers had a lot of eggs, other farmers just had a few hens. You'd have a big basket, you'd go to the neighbors. Usually boys did that. Girls didn't feel too much like doing it. But the boys—if there was two, three girls there, each one would have to give them a dozen of eggs, otherwise he'd beat her to dickens with this whip [generally a willow switch]. . . . The parents would let them in. That was tradition. And sometimes the boys would come home with twenty dozen of eggs. . . . Well, they didn't really whip to hurt. You'd hide yourself under the bed, in the closet, up in the attic, to hide away from them. Sometimes they didn't find you. When we heard the guys coming, we would sure enough shoot out of bed . . . but they knew that we were in the house. And sometimes they'd just tear the house upside down to find you.

While going along with the practice, Florence's parents remained watchful. Her dad once told a wagonload of seven boys who knocked at the farmhouse door, "No, that's too many. Only three of you can go in."

Anne Pellowski, whose account from the 1930s appears here, grew up on a farm near Pine Creek, in Trempealeau County, where her grandparents had settled with other Kashubian Poles in the nineteenth century. When she was young the Pellowski children practiced Dyngus mostly within the family circle. Now retired and living in Winona, Minnesota, Anne Pellowski earned degrees from the College of St. Teresa in Winona, Minnesota, and from Columbia University. She eventually served as the Director of the Information Center on Children's Cultures, part of the United Nations' Committee for UNICEF in New York City.

An active storyteller, Anne Pellowski is also the author of a series of reminiscent novels concerning not only her own girlhood experiences, but also those of young women in every generation of her extended Polish American family. In the manner of folklorists and oral historians, Pellowski interviewed numerous family members, friends, and neighbors; she also consulted field recordings of her relatives and other locals made in the 1940s by Harriet Pawlowska for the Library of Congress (see the introduction to chapter 16, "Gamroth the Strong," p. 159). Her charmingly written books are remarkable for their details of everyday life, and provide our finest glimpse of evolving Polish American culture in Wisconsin. Long out of print, they are currently being reissued by St. Mary's Press of Winona, Minnesota. For a justly appreciative assessment of Pellowski's writings, see Thomas J. Napierkowski, "Anne Pellowski: A Voice for Polonia," *Polish-American Studies* 52:2 (1985): 89–97.

Reprinted from Anne Pellowski, *Stairstep Farm: Anna Rose's Story* (New York: Philomel Books, 1981), 102–9.

On Thursday of Holy Week, the week before Easter, they washed clothes and curtains and sheets and towels and rugs. On Good Friday, before going to church, they cleaned the house from top to bottom and put the clean rugs on the floor, the curtains on the windows, and the sheets on the bed. On Saturday, Mama baked all day. By late afternoon, the pantry shelves were filled with fresh loaves of bread, snails, and square, plump doughnuts. Mama called the doughnuts *ponchki.* Anna Rose could never decide which tasted better: the cinnamon and raisin flavored snails with the vanilla frosting, or the *ponchki* with their crispy outer crust covered with sugar.

On Saturday evening, Mama brought out as many old cups and jars as she could find. She poured in hot water until each cup or jar was half full; then she added drops of food coloring. There were only four colors in the bottles: red, yellow, blue, and green. But Mama knew how to mix red and yellow to make orange. With red and blue drops she made violet. To make brown, she put in drops of red and yellow and blue. Finally, she placed a large bowl of hard-boiled eggs in the center of the table.

Each of the children could dye four or five eggs, choosing any color combinations they wished. Angie made swirls and patterns by dipping only part of an egg in at one time. When she took them out and dried them on an old rag, they looked like pastel candies of pale pink, blue, yellow, green, and lilac. Millie did the opposite. She let her eggs stay in a long time and when they were ready, each was a deep, vibrant color.

After they had completed dyeing the eggs, they placed them in their Easter baskets and left them in the center of the table. During the night the Easter Bunny would put so many candy eggs in each basket, the real eggs would be almost covered up.

Lawrence watched as the others dyed their eggs and prepared their baskets. He did not color a single egg.

"Aren't you going to color any Easter eggs?" Anna Rose asked him.

"I don't need to. I know a better way to get them," Lawrence answered.

"The Easter Bunny won't bring you any candy," teased Mama.

"Oh, I don't care. I'll manage to get some, you'll see." Lawrence smiled and seemed unconcerned.

The next morning, when they came down to breakfast, the Easter baskets were full to the top with candy eggs. There were chocolate eggs and marshmallow eggs and jelly bean eggs. Propped in the middle of each basket was a small chocolate rabbit. Only Lawrence had no basket. Off to the side was a lone chocolate rabbit. That was all the candy he got. Anna Rose and Millie felt sorry for him.

35.1. Easter eggs decorated in the Polish American "drop-pull" wax-resist style
by Helen Wieczorak Boyer, Portage County, 1986. Photo: James P. Leary.

"Here, you can have one of my marshmallow eggs and one of my chocolate eggs," offered Anna Rose. Millie gave him a marshmallow egg and a handful of jelly beans.

"That's nice of you, but you really don't have to worry about me," insisted Lawrence. "I still intend to get my share of candy." But he did not refuse the offerings of his sisters. He ate them up as soon as they had returned from church.

The girls and Francis nibbled at their candies on and off all day. They each cracked a real egg and ate it with salt and pepper. By evening, their baskets were still more than half full. The candy and eggs would last them all week.

Early on Monday morning, Anna Rose heard Angie and Millie get up. There were morning chores to do, even though they did not have to go to school.

"Eeeek! Help!" Shrieks and hollers came from the other side of the house, near the kitchen door. Anna Rose jumped out of bed and went to the window. She could not see a thing but she could hear Angie and Millie yelling and yelping. She could also hear Lawrence calling out something, but it was impossible to make out the words.

Quickly Anna Rose got dressed and ran down the stairs. Mama was seated at the kitchen table, smiling and sipping her coffee.

"What is going on?" asked Anna Rose.

In answer, the door burst open and Angie and Millie ran in. They were dripping wet. Anna Rose looked out the window at the bright sunshine.

"How did you get so wet if it is not raining?" she asked.

Both Angie and Millie were giggling so hard they could not answer. At last Angie spoke.

"It is showering outside."

Once more Anna Rose looked out the window. All she could see was blue sky and bright sunshine.

"There is not a drop of a shower in sight," she insisted.

"If you don't believe us, go outside and see," Millie said, wiping her hair with a towel.

Anna Rose marched to the kitchen door, opened it, and stepped outside onto the short sidewalk that led to the woodpile and gate. She had not gone more than three steps when a shower of water swooshed over her head. It dripped onto her face and down her body. Lawrence's voice called out from behind the woodpile:

Dyngus, Dyngus, po dwa jaja!
Nie chc chleba tylko jaja!
Dingus, Dingus, for two eggs!
Don't give me bread, only eggs!

Lawrence stepped out with the hose in one hand and a switch of willow branches in the other. He swatted her with the branches and continued to sprinkle her as she tried to run away. She squealed and yelled: "Turn it off!"

"Promise to give me two eggs."

"I promise!" screamed Anna Rose. The water was cold and tingly. As soon as Lawrence turned it off, Anna Rose went back into the kitchen to dry off.

"So that is how Lawrence is getting his Easter candy," she said.

"You did not remember about *Dyngus* Monday," laughed Mama, "because the last time Lawrence did that, you were only three years old."

"What is *Dyngus?*" asked Anna Rose.

"It's just a custom we have from the old country," explained Mama. "On Easter Monday the boys give the girls a switching and a sprinkling of water and in exchange they want eggs or candies."

When Mary Elizabeth and Janie got up, Lawrence did the same thing to them. He only gave them a light spanking and a quick sprinkling, so as not to scare them, but he insisted they each give him two candy eggs from their baskets. They did not like it, but Mama agreed those were the rules. By the end of the day he had eaten eight candy eggs and four colored eggs.

"That's not fair," cried Angie. "Now he got more than any of us."

"Aren't you forgetting about tomorrow?" Mama reminded her that Easter Tuesday was the day for girls to play *Dyngus* on the boys.

"But how can we get back any eggs? He ate them already," complained Millie.

"Never mind that," Angie dismissed the complaint with a wave of her hand. "We still have pretty many jelly beans and eggs. The important thing is to give him a good soaking and a switching."

"I think you will have a hard time catching him," chuckled Mama. "He will be on the lookout for you all day."

That evening Anne Rose huddled in bed next to Angie and Millie. In whispers, they made their plans for the next day.

"Are you sure you can keep after Lawrence while we make our preparations?" Angie asked Anna Rose.

"I know just what to do," she assured her sisters.

On Tuesday morning, Lawrence got up very early. He was out of the house before any of his sisters were awake. In the barn he knew he was safe because Pa would not let them fool around while they were near the cows.

"Bring me a hunk of bread and jam," he said to Francis. "I don't trust those girls to let me in for breakfast without getting a sprinkle." Francis brought him two thick slices of bread with jam between them.

All morning, Lawrence worked in the barn, cleaning out the gutters and the stanchions. He shoveled the manure out the back door, into the manure spreader. Once or twice he came to the front door and peeked out. He could see Anna Rose standing there, holding a sprinkling can.

Close to noon, Lawrence began to get really hungry.

"Aw, c'mon," he called. "Let me go by!"

"I'm not leaving here until you leave the barn," Anna Rose informed him.

"We'll see about that," Lawrence laughed in reply. He went to the back barn door, stepped out, and slowly walked to the lower corner. Peering around it, he could see that the front door to the house was unguarded.

"I can run faster than any of them," he said to himself. "I'll go in that door." He raced toward it, opened it quickly, and entered the house.

"Ha! Ha! You didn't get me," crowed Lawrence gleefully, when he saw Angie and Millie setting the table. They just smiled back at him.

Anna Rose came in the door. She was smiling smugly.

"Aren't you mad I snuck by you?" asked Lawrence.

Anna Rose did not answer. She just kept on smiling as if she had a secret. Angie and Millie were also silent.

Lawrence was puzzled. His sisters seemed so confident. He had better watch more carefully than ever.

They laughed and joked at the dinner table. When they were finished, Angie moved over toward the kitchen door.

"Oh, no you don't," cried Lawrence as he ran for the door ahead of her. "I'm going out first." Lawrence turned the knob and pulled the door open. In the same moment, Angie stooped and pulled a string lying loose at the left edge of the door sill.

Splash! Lawrence stepped out into a torrent of water. The pail that Angie and Millie had rigged up over the kitchen door emptied out completely, right over his head. Millie ran to get the willow switches they had prepared and began to switch Lawrence on his legs and backside.

"Tee, hee! We fooled you!" Anna Rose cackled and danced with merriment. "We wanted you to come in the front door. Angie said you would, if I could stand at the front barn door all morning with a sprinkler, and I did. We didn't want you to see the pail."

Lawrence came back into the kitchen, shaking his head to get the water out of his eyes. As he reached for the roller towel, he could hear the kitchen exploding with hilarity.

"Serves you right," Daddy said cheerfully. "Don't try to get the better of these girls. They are too smart. And besides, you're outnumbered."

36

Belgians Bring Along Their Customs

Math S. Tlachac

In 1853, nine families of Walloon Belgian farmers left the province of Brabant to settle in Wisconsin. They were bound for Sheboygan County, a German and Dutch stronghold, but soon traveled to the hinterlands around Green Bay where their dialect was more compatible with that city's large French-speaking population. More than fifteen thousand Belgians emigrated to the region in the next decade, resulting in what remains America's largest rural Belgian enclave.

The essay included here first appeared in a series published by the *Algoma Record-Herald* in 1974, shortly after author Math Tlachac's death. His ten articles were gathered soon after into a forty-page pamphlet by the area's Belgian American Club. As his Czech surname suggests, Math S. Tlachac is of "Bohemian and Belgian" parentage, a common blend in the Brown, Door, and Kewaunee tricounty area where Czech and Walloon Catholics continue to intermarry and share interests in old-time ethnic traditions. In 1944, Fred L. Holmes wrote of the similarities between the two groups and even included an extended description of Bohemian traditions in a chapter called "Belgian Dust Dancers Celebrate" (*Old World Wisconsin: Around Europe in the Badger State* [Eau Claire, Wisc.: E. M. Hale, 1944], 352).

Of the customs sketched by Tlachac, Belgians and Bohemians alike continue to practice the *kermiss* (literally, "church mass") tradition of celebratory fund-raising, which has parallels in autumn church dinners and bazaars throughout Wisconsin. Both groups likewise participated in religious processions through the rural countryside, especially when fields and seeds were blessed prior to planting. And both groups erected wayside shrines, although the Belgian chapels were far more elaborate and numerous (see William G. Laatsch and Charles F. Calkins, "The Belgian Roadside Chapels of Wisconsin's Door Peninsula," *Journal of Cultural Geography* 7:1 [1986]:116–28).

The distinctively Belgian cuisine Tlachac describes remains part of the area's home and church supper fare, and it is central to the annual mid-July Belgian Days festival held in Brussels. "Belgian pies," however, are no longer baked in outdoor ovens, and the Czech polka has succeeded the Belgian quadrille. Fortunately, various researchers, in addition to Tlachac, have documented these bygone traditions. Cultural geographers Charles F. Calkins and William G. Laatsch, the latter a faculty member at the University of Wisconsin–Green Bay, coauthored "The Belgian Outdoor Ovens of Northeastern Wisconsin," *Pioneer America Society Transactions* 2 (1979). In the 1940s, Helene Stratman-Thomas recorded Walloon singer Alfred Vandertie and fiddler Emil Boulanger for the Library of Congress, while in the 1970s Françoise Lempeurer of Belgian national radio recorded Wisconsin Walloon musicians for a record album (see *The Wisconsin Patchwork: Recordings from the Helene Stratman-Thomas Collection of Wisconsin Folk Music*, cassettes produced by Judy Rose, with an accompanying book by James P. Leary [Madison: University of Wisconsin, Continuing Education in the Arts, 1987]; and *Les Wallons d'Amerique* [Wisconsin], *Anthology of Walloon Folklore, Volume 7* [Belgium: Centre D'Action Culturelle De La Communaute D'Expression Francaise, ca. 1977].)

Reprinted from Math S. Tlachac, *The History of the Belgian Settlements in Door, Kewaunee, and Brown Counties* (Brussels, Wisc.: Belgian-American Club, 1974), 34–37.

When the Belgian immigrants came to this country, they brought with them several customs which had been celebrated each year in their mother country for over a hundred years. The Belgians are a congenial people and like to take part in frivolous as well as religious activities. Foremost and perhaps the most popular one was the Belgian *kermiss*. After the harvesting was completed, it was customary for the people in Belgium to attend Mass to give thanks to the Lord for a bountiful harvest. This was followed by feasting and dancing. Some of the Belgians are musically talented and in most every community where a *kermiss* was observed a local band was formed to play at dances. The *kermiss* usually lasted three days.

By 1858 some of the Belgian immigrants had been in the United States for five years. Many were lonesome and homesick for their native land. Thus far there had been hard work, poverty and privation in the New World. Something was needed to lift the sagging spirits of many when young broad-shouldered Amia Champaign, also a Belgian immigrant, had the answer. Said Champaign, "Why don't we have a *kermiss?*" He passed along his idea which received favorable approval by his countrymen. "It is the thing we need," said many Belgians. "We have had good crops and we should thank the Lord for them."

The succeeding days were busy ones in the new, sparsely settled communities. In every home preparations for the event were made. Old trunks were dragged out from under puncheon floors or lifted down from the loft and there was a feverish overhauling of their contents to see if they contained any bits of finery for the coming event. Leather shoes, long set aside for special occasions, were re-oiled and made flexible. Fresh evergreen boughs were cut and brought to replace the ones that served in lieu of a mattress. Earthen floors were newly sanded and there were long pilgrimages made to Dyckesville and Green Bay for supplies to replenish the larders.

Then came the baking which in the early days was done in outdoor ovens. As many as three dozen Belgian pies could be baked at one time. The Belgian pie! What would the kermiss be without the famous delicacy, the crust of which was made of dough, spread over with prunes or apples and topped with homemade cottage cheese? So tasty it was that one bite invited another. Some families baked as many as a hundred pies which were set on an improvised table in the cellar where it was cool and damp, to keep the pies soft and mellow. The Belgian women were experts in the art of baked goods, and the brown crusted loaves of bread which came out of those outdoor ovens were light as a feather.

But the Belgian pie was only a part of the Sunday dinner menu. There was the famous "chicken boyoo"—a thick soup which was very tasty and appetizing. In addition there was *trippe*, sort of a sausage made out of the choicest lean pork from a recently butchered hog. Cooked cabbage with various spiced seasonings were included in the trippe ingredients. There also was *jut*, a dish made with cooked cab-

36.1. Dorothy Massart prepares raisin, apple, and prune "Belgian pies" in the kitchen of her rural Rosiere home, 1993. Photo: James P. Leary, courtesy Cedarburg Cultural Center.

bage and potatoes well mashed and seasoned with salt and other ingredients such as butter or cream. Some housewives included *kaset* in the menu, which is home-made cottage cheese, pressed into balls the size of an orange, seasoned with salt and pepper, then put into crocks to cure out until it could be spread on bread like butter. Some of the men made homemade beer out of barley and wild hops, found growing in the locality.

At last the day came when the first Belgian kermiss would be held in America. It was in the year 1858, and it was held in Rosiere on the third Sunday of September, the same day a similar event was taking place in a community called Rosiere in their native home of Belgium. Father Daems came from Bay Settlement to say the Mass in Rosiere. The church was well attended by people who came for the Mass and to partake of a sumptuous dinner prepared by housewives in each home.

The Belgians enjoyed the inspiring sermon by Father Daems, who spoke their native language. After the Mass was over and as people were leaving the church, they were met by the local band consisting of Joseph Lumaye, who played the cornet, Carl Masey, who played the slide trombone; Norbert Mignon, violin, Theophile Le-Botte, clarinet, Frank LeGreve, bass drum. The band members were specially dressed for the occasion and striking out a tune they marched, preceded by a flag bearer, to an improvised hall.

Halfway to the hall the procession halted for a dance on the earthen road. This was called "the dance in the dust," and after several such dances, the band escorted the dancers to the hall. All afternoon and into the wee hours of the morning there was merrymaking and festivities. There were waltzes, two-steps and quadrilles. Such dances as tango or fox-trots were unheard of.

Usually after a quadrille, the caller would shout out, "All promenade to the bar." However, women did not enter a saloon in those days since it was beneath their dignity. If a woman wanted a glass of the amber-colored liquid, it was brought to her by her dancing partner, and with him, she drank it out-of-doors.

But dancing was not all the frolicking which took place at a kermiss. There were all kinds of games of skill, such as trying to catch a greased pig. If anyone could catch the hog, he could claim it. There was a greased pole which some tried to climb, usually in failure. There were foot races and wrestling matches. In some instances a live goose was buried, leaving the head and neck protruding. Then a blind-folded person was given a scythe and if he could decapitate the goose, the goose was his. This cruel form was soon abolished.

A lunch wagon was on hand, where for five cents one could purchase a piece of baloney between two crackers or slices of bread. Usually the piece of baloney was cut from the link at an angle to make it look larger than it actually was.

The next day was Monday, a day reserved for the "old folks" who in the evening came to the old folks' dance. In spite of difficult manual labor on the farm, it was surprising how people in their 70s and even 80s could swing around dancing waltzes or two-steps. So uniform did they keep in step that the lanterns hung up from the rafters of the hall swung up and down in unison.

As the Belgian communities developed and new church congregations were forming, more kermisses were held. The first one after harvesting was completed was held in Grandlez, now called Lincoln. It was followed by kermisses in Brussels, Namur, Rosiere, Champion, Dyckesville, San Sauveur, Tonet, Thiry Daems, and Misere. By the time the last kermiss was held in November, the ground was already frozen or sometimes covered by snow.

Such were the Belgian kermisses which continued every year from 1858, simultaneously with those held in Belgium in localities of the same name. These kermisses among the Belgian settlement in the United States continued on until the First World War, when they slowly died out and are to the present generation only a memory.

Another beautiful custom brought along by the Belgians was the procession held each year on Ascension Day. The procession was usually called the Rogation Procession, so-called because people walking in procession were supposed to sing litanies of special supplication. First came the cross bearer in surplice and cassock, carrying the cross. Then followed little girls attired in white, carrying baskets of flowers which they strewed along the procession route. The priest followed attired in sacerdotal robes of dignity, carrying the Blessed Sacrament, and overhead was the canopy carried by four men. Following the priest came the women of the parish praying the rosary in unison and they in turn were followed by the men.

The procession marched along the highway to the nearest wayside chapel or shrine where Benediction was said, after which the procession returned to the church. The coming of the automobile made highway travel dangerous and such processions were discontinued and held on church grounds or within the church.

The first Sunday of Lent was usually a significant one to the Belgians. Another custom brought with them to America was that of carrying straw to an open field, making a pile and then lighting it when darkness came. The fire was supposed to ward off the demon and to remind people that the season of Lent had arrived, when personal sacrifices and fasting were good for the soul. Like other customs, this one, too, has passed away and is no longer remembered by the present young Belgian generation.

When a Belgian was elected to some office, a maypole was erected in his honor by his neighbors. A tall balsam was cut, the bark was peeled, leaving a top of branches to which were tied colored strips of cotton ribbons. The elected official then furnished the crowd assembled with a keg of beer in appreciation of the honor bestowed upon him. Sometimes the local school teacher was so honored with a maypole planted near the schoolhouse in which he was teaching, and this also cost him the price of a keg of beer. Likewise, this custom has passed away.

37

The Swiss Colony at New Glarus (excerpt)

John Luchsinger

In 1845, Nicholas Duerst, a forty-eight-year-old judge, and Fridolin Streiff, twenty-eight and a blacksmith, left the Swiss community of Glarus in search of a site for "New Glarus" across the Atlantic. Upon their recommendation, 140 emigrants followed the next year to found what persists as the most prominent Swiss settlement not only in Wisconsin but in the United States. They soon established a Swiss Reformed Church, made first of logs, then later, in 1858, of stone. John Etter, the congregation's minister from 1859 until 1896, wrote of the white, yellow, and blue houses nestled within the green forests surrounding New Glarus: "In their midst on a small hill the beautiful new stone church with its cupola tower presents a lovely picture, especially at sunset when the cattle come home with their musical bells tinkling in the breeze" (quoted in Millard Tschudy, *New Glarus: Mirror of Switzerland* [Monroe, Wisc.: The Monroe Evening Times, 1965], 19). The church likewise had a bell, and its prominent tolling mingled with the ringing bells of dairy cows on surrounding hillsides—much as had been the case back home in Switzerland.

In the late twentieth century, when many congregations have altered or vanished as a result of population shifts, mergers, the spread of new faiths, or the decline of old ones, it is easy to forget that for much of Wisconsin's history its churches have been ethnic churches—and that those churches have been hubs for an ethnic community's activities, both sacred and secular. Thus John Luchsinger writes not only of weekly services, baptisms, and weddings within New Glarus's Swiss Reformed Church, but also of the rowdy *kilbi*, or "church hallowing" celebration. Akin to the Belgian kermiss the New Glarus kilbi attracted not only local Swiss but also curious French, Irish, Norwegians, and Yankees from surrounding settlements—including, in 1907, Wardon Alan Curtis, whose description appears in chapter 23, "'The Light Fantastic' in the Central West," pp. 256–58.

By the mid-1960s, the kilbi festivity had become "relatively mild, revolving about the Sunday church observance" (Tschudy 1965:19). The decline of kilbi, with its Swiss Reformed connections, coincided with the rise of secular events, nurtured by the New Glarus Chamber of Commerce. Perhaps best known for the Wilhelm Tell drama its citizens have staged in German and English since 1938, New Glarus bills itself "America's Little Switzerland" and attracts thousands of tourists with a succession of ethnic festivals from January through October.

Perhaps John Luchsinger foresaw such a future? His essay, published in 1879 by the State Historical Society of Wisconsin, was clearly intended to inform outsiders, and Yankees especially, about the Swiss. Hence his mention of Swiss celebrating the Fourth of July "with American fervor" and his enthusiasm for "American youth from a distance, who have learned to share" in Swiss festivities. Born in Glarus, Switzerland, on June 29, 1839, John Luchsinger was brought by his parents to the United States in 1845. The family settled first in Syracuse, New York, and then in Philadelphia before arriving in New Glarus in 1856. The Wisconsin Swiss colony's most prominent early chronicler, Luchsinger served as Green County's treasurer and in the Wisconsin legislature; he was also on the board of the State Historical Society of Wisconsin.

Reprinted from "The Swiss Colony at New Glarus," *Collections of the State Historical Society of Wisconsin,* ed. Lyman C. Draper (Madison: State Historical Society of Wisconsin, 1879), 411–45; subsequently published in *History of Green County,* ed. C. W. Butterfield (Springfield, Ill.: Union Publishing, 1884), 635–37.

As it may be interesting to others to know how the services are conducted, the following order on Sundays will give a proper idea: At about 9 o'clock the first bell is rung, not tolled, as in many other churches; and between the first ringing and 10 o'clock, the worshipers begin to come in, taking seats where they please, except that the sexes sit separately on either side of the church. At 10 o'clock both bells are rung, which is the signal that the minister has started from his house, about eighty rods away; the ringing continues until he enters the building, when the people rise as he enters, and remain standing until he reads prayers, and announces the text, and also during the singing, which is led by a good choir of male voices, accompanied by an organ. After the sermon is over, prayers are again read, followed by singing and the benediction. Then follows the singular custom of the female part of the congregation leaving the church first, the bells ringing the while, and the men standing; and not until the last skirt has passed the door, does the male part follow, led by the pastor.

The origin of this custom, according to tradition, is as follows: some 500 years ago, the Austrians being at war with the Swiss, attempted to surprise the town of Nafels, in Glarus; or, as other traditions have it, a battle occurred between the combatants in the neighboring canton of Grisons or Graubunden. In either case, the circumstances were the same—the people were at church—whether Sunday or holiday is not recorded; but a woman leaving church during service discovered the enemy, and gave the alarm; and, it is related, that the women on that day did valorous service, rolling and throwing rocks upon the enemy, and aiding in great measure to gain a decisive victory over their old enemy the Austrians. Since that time, tradition says, the right and honor are accorded to the female worshipers in all the churches of the canton of Glarus, to leave the church first, the men standing in deference while they pass out. The custom is rigidly, and without exception, kept up here, no matter what the occasion for meeting and worship.

Weddings are for the most part solemnized by the ministers; seldom by a justice of the peace. Tuesdays and Thursdays are the only days on which a Swiss will be married; the latter is the favorite day. The other days of the week are not regarded as fortunate; Wednesday is especially considered the most unlucky. Persons about to enter matrimony, sometime before the ceremony takes place, go together to the houses of those whom they wish to invite as guests to the wedding, and verbally request their presence. Wedding feasts are of late mostly arranged at a hotel; but formerly at the home of the groom or bride. After being pronounced man and wife, at the church or in the minister's house, the couple, with the invited guests, partake of the wedding dinner, after which dancing is indulged in till a late hour. Before and after the marriage ceremony, the lads and young men salute the bridal party with a profuse discharging of fire-arms. The more noise, the greater the honor. Very rarely

37.1. Swiss Americans hoist old-country banners during a horseback parade through the streets of New Glarus, ca. 1890. Wisconsin Folk Museum Collection, courtesy New Glarus Historical Society.

do the Swiss here intermarry with the people of other nationalities; almost without exception, they marry among their own country folks.

The baptism of infants is another occasion for a feast. Children are usually christened when less than three months old; and the ceremony takes place in the church, except in a few instances, a godfather and godmother invariably witnessing the baptism at the altar. According to church rules, parents are not permitted to act as sponsors. If parents are church members, no fee is required for weddings, baptisms or funeral services; otherwise a fee is collected, which is paid into the church fund, and not as a perquisite to the preacher, as in other societies.

When a person dies, the relatives, friends, and countrymen are notified by messengers of the time of death and burial; and the accompanying of the dead to their last resting place is a duty which is faithfully fulfilled, over 150 teams being often seen at a funeral. The church bells are made to do duty on all of these occasions. A couple of bell-tolls give notice to the sponsors that the minister is at the altar, ready to proceed with the baptism. On account of baptisms being always performed at the close of the regular services, the godmother and child remain in some convenient dwelling near the church, until summoned by the bell. This is so arranged that the congregation may not be disturbed by any fretfulness on the part of the infant, to whom no doubt the services would often become as tedious as they sometimes do to older children, not only in this, but in numerous other churches.

At weddings they ring a merry peal; and at funerals the bells are tolled until the coffin is lowered into the grave. They are also rung twice each day, as is the custom in Switzerland, at 11 A.M., and at dusk every evening, for five minutes each time; and at midnight of the 31st of December they are rung a whole hour, to welcome in the New Year.

Kilbi, as it is termed here—a corruption of *Kirchweihe*, or church hallowing— is the holiday of all days. The 4th of July is celebrated with American fervor; but Kilbi is a blending of all holidays into one. This day occurs on the last Sunday of September of each year; and, as its name denotes, is strictly a religious festival, being the anniversary of the dedication of the church. On that day the pastor, at the close of the services, dedicates the building anew; and this is as far as religious observances are kept. In the afternoon, target-shooting and dancing are moderately indulged in; but Monday is the great day. Strangers come from a distance, and neighbors and friends meet, and renew friendships, over loaded tables and foaming glasses. The youth, and in fact almost everybody, repair to the village; and music and dancing begin about noon, and are kept up until next morning, at three or more different halls, and all are crowded. In spite of the crowd, and the quantities of beer and wine drank—but stronger drinks are scarce, and consequently so are quarrels—the best of humor and hilarity prevail.

The way these dances are managed is a novelty to Americans. Usually there is a committee of three managers at each dancing place, whose business it is to provide the music, keep order, collect the entrance fee from the male dancers; and, above all, supply them with female partners. For this purpose, the best-looking manager is sent with a gay and ribbon-bedecked team, to all places where it is known young ladies live, and politely invite them to take seats in his carriage; and, unless there is a prior engagement, the lasses are always ready to comply. When his carriage is full, he drives to the hall at which he is a manager, unloads, and again sallies forth in another direction until a sufficiency of partners is secured, or the supply of lasses are exhausted. His fellow managers in the meanwhile keep order, arrange the couples, and direct things generally, for the enjoyment and comfort of all.

A good time is had at the homes, as well; the best that can be afforded is cooked and eaten; and among all the cakes and dishes of every kind, honey is accorded a prominent place. Few there are who do not eat bread and butter and honey on Kilbi. The general good time extends into Tuesday, sometimes, but usually Monday night closes the feast, which is not only kept up by the Swiss, but by American youth from a distance, who have learned to share in the celebration.

38

Woods Customs

Veteran woods workers of the old-time lumber camp and log drive era were proud of their occupational skills, memorializing them in song and story. Wisconsin's most widely sung traditional ballad, "The Little Brown Bulls," celebrates an end-of-the-season skidding contest between rival Scots Canadian and New England Yankee crews. The legendary "Whitewater Ole" Horne, an immigrant Norwegian river driver, was reputed to ride the lead log through sluice gates, like a latter-day snowboarder negotiating a half-pipe, before perishing in a log jam.

Wisconsin's woods workers began to engage in public birling or logrolling competitions as early as the 1880s, and by 1898 a logrolling association awarded the first of a string of championships that continues amid Hayward's annual Lumberjack World Championships. The first world champion birler was Tom Fleming of Eau Claire. Since Fleming's victory, eight of the twenty-five champions have been from Wisconsin. Women's birling competitions commenced in 1929, with Agnes Hare Dixon of Ashland emerging as the first of eight Wisconsin women to hold the title. (See *Lumberjack World Championships,* program book [Hayward, Wisc.: Lumberjack World Championships Foundation, 1996].)

The participation of logger athletes in outdoor sports exhibitions and at fairs likewise dates to the early twentieth century. By the 1920s there were several barnstorming birling troupes, the foremost of which were the Eau Claire–based aggregations of Wilbur Marx and Jimmy Murray. Beyond demonstrating birling competitions, the Murray and Marx troupes engaged in "trick and fancy logrolling" involving roller skating, jumping rope, headstands, and other stunts on a log. While Murray had been a river driver, Wilbur Marx never worked in the woods. As a youngster in Eau Claire, the "Sawdust City," Marx hung around mill ponds and became so enamored of birling that he sometimes skipped school to practice. After two years as a challenger, sixteen-year-old Wilbur Marx won his first birling title in 1927 at Bodin's Brownstone Bowl north of Washburn. (Regarding Murray, see "'Jacks' Could Fight as Well as Roll Logs," *The Milwaukee Journal Sunday Magazine,* April 10, 1937; for an overview of Marx's career, see "Babe Ruth of Log Rolling, Wilbur 'Web' Marx," *Sports Minnesota/Wisconsin* 1:7 [1973]:13–17.)

Nearly a century of well-promoted public lumberjack competitions, however, has obscured the most characteristic sporting pastimes of woods workers during the heyday of Wisconsin lumber camps. In actuality, the hard, dangerous work undertaken by men isolated during a long winter from any society but their own was matched by rough and macho play. In their leisure time, Wisconsin's lumberjacks tested greenhorns' mettle with devilish pranks, while enjoying games that involved little more than beating one another with sticks, weighted socks, and overshoes or "rubbers."

The three overlapping accounts offered here begin with that of John Emmett Nelligan, born to Irish parents in New Brunswick, Canada, in 1852. After an apprenticeship in the woods of Maine and Pennsylvania, Nelligan was a timber cruiser and woods boss in the Upper Midwest, chiefly around Wisconsin's Oconto and Florence Counties, from the 1870s through the early decades of the twentieth century. Mary Agnes Starr, born into a French Canadian family in 1901, was raised in Oconto County where many of her neighbors and relatives worked in the woods. Starr also learned traditional songs in French; she performed in the 1930s on Wisconsin Public Radio and for the National Folk Festival, and her songs were recorded for the Library of Congress in 1946. Starr details her lifelong passion for Franco-American and lumber camp folklore in *Pea Soup and Johnny Cake* (Madison: Red Mountain Publishing, 1981). Gregg Montgomery, whose "Characters on the Chippewa Waters" is chapter 7 of this anthology, was a field researcher in the late 1930s for the Wisconsin Folklore Project, directed by Charles E. Brown of the State Historical Society of Wisconsin.

"Lumberjack Games" by John Emmet Nelligan is reprinted from John Emmet Nelligan, *The Life of a Lumberman* (privately printed, 1929), 125–26.

"Lumberjack Games" by Gregg Montgomery is reprinted from the papers of the Wisconsin Folklore Project, under the federal auspices of the Works Progress Administration, ca. 1937—a microfilm copy of which is held by the State Historical Society of Wisconsin, reel P84-2055.

"Wisconsin Pastimes" by Mary Agnes Starr is reprinted by permission of the American Folklore Society from *Journal of American Folklore* 68:264 (1954):184. Not for further reproduction.

Lumberjack Games
John Emmett Nelligan

Wherever and whenever men's work is strenuous, their recreation is the same. Reading the Bible wasn't generally considered the sort of thing with which to prepare one's self for another week of hard labor.

"Shuffle the Brogue" was a typical lumberjack game and was often played in the evenings and on Sundays. It was plain horseplay, but it appealed to the lumberjacks and was always productive of a great deal of merriment. A bunch of the jacks would sit on the floor in a ring. In the center of the ring was another jack who was "It." The men in the ring sat close together and passed a rubber around behind their backs, at the same time yelling "Shove! Shove! Shove!" When it was convenient, one of them would hit the man who was "It" in the back with the rubber and then quickly pass it behind him again and shove it to his neighbor. When "It" caught one of the jacks with the rubber, the caught one had to trade places with "It" and suffer the punishment dealt out by the ring until he caught a man.

Greenhorns in the camp always had to be initiated and this was done in many ways and provided much amusement. One favorite method was the "sheep game." One of the jacks played the part of a farmer who owned a sheep, another posed as a sheep buyer and the greenhorn was rolled up tightly in a heavy blanket and became the "sheep." He was carried by two other jacks. The farmer and the sheep buyer would stage an argument over the weight of the sheep. To determine its real weight they would let it down repeatedly on the "scales." The "scales" was a sharply pointed stick and the "sheep" was always thrown onto the "scales" in such a way that the point of the stick came into violent contact with the tender, rear central portion of his anatomy. This was very uncomfortable for the greenhorn and very laughable for the rest of the crew. Another favorite stunt was to send a greenhorn to the cook shanty to borrow the "bean hole."

Mr. Lumberjack Goes to Washington

A BANGALO, made from a washtub and a lumberjack's peavey, an Irish bull fiddle and a squeeze box will be among the 40 musical instruments dating from the logging camp days which will be taken to Washington, D. C., by four northern Wisconsin men when they leave for the national folk festival Apr. 21. The men, billed as The Lumberjacks, are (left to right) Otto Rindlisbacher, Rice Lake; Frank Uchytil, Haugen, and Earl Schwartztrauber and Ray Calkins, Ladysmith.

38.1. The Wisconsin Lumberjacks, a troupe of musicians and jig dancers organized by Otto and Iva Rindlisbacher of Rice Lake, recreated lumber camp sociability for the National Folk Festival in the late 1930s. This photograph and caption from the *Rice Lake Chronotype* assumes readers' familiarity with Frank Capra's film, *Mr. Smith Goes to Washington.* Wisconsin Folk Museum Collection, courtesy Rice Lake Chronotype.

Lumberjack Games

Gregg Montgomery

Hot Back

In this game "it" sat on the deacon seat with his head in his hat or hands. Someone among those playing struck him (not too gently) with a rubber and he had to guess who did it. If his guess was correct the one who struck him became "it" and the former victim took his place with the other boys.

Shuffle the Brogue

Here the men sat in a circle on the floor as near together as possible. The victim was in the center of the ring. In this case the rubber was handed as fast as possible from one to another along the back of the circle. When "it" was not looking someone would strike him with the rubber, and "it" had to name the one who struck him. If he guessed correctly, the one who administered the stroke would be the next victim.

Rooster

In this game a number of lumberjacks would sit on the floor, each with a stick benind his knees and his hands tied to the stick. The object of the game was to try and tip one another over with their feet. Those who were tipped over and were not able to get up again were counted out of the game.

Broom Game

The jacks would line up with their legs apart and their hands on the shoulders of the one ahead. "It" had a broom with which he would hit the last man with a blow. As soon as he descended the blow he had to drop the broom and crawl through the legs along the line. The boys would attempt to keep him from getting through by squeezing him with their legs. If he got through the line successfully he stood at the head, if not he had to take his place at the end of the line and receive the blow from the fellow he had hit.

Doing the Wash

On Sundays one of the favorite games in camp was for one man to get on a log and another to start it rolling so that one would fall in the river. The challenge was, "Come on, I bet I can do your washing."

Jack-in-the-Dark

In this game a jack is blindfolded and stands in the center of a circle armed with a sock filled with a hard object. The point of the game is for "it" in the circle to hit a man with a sock and name him. If he does the man takes his place in the center of the circle. Another version of the game is for two men to be blindfolded and each given a sock filled with some hard object. A strap was taken from a jacket and each man held onto one end of the strap with one hand and held the sock in the other. One would say, "Where are you Jack?" and the other answered, "Here I am in the dark." Then one would try to hit the other with the sock. If one succeeded in striking the other, then two others would take their places. The jack who was struck was always glad to relinquish his place by that time.

Wisconsin Pastimes

Mary Agnes Starr

Reading "Going to See the Widow"—*Journal of American Folklore* 64 (1951)—reminded me of a relative's experience in the old logging days when he worked on "drives" and in lumber camps from 1897 to 1910 in Oconto County. On the first Saturday night in camp, older fellows who had been in camp would clean up and shave. When asked by a newcomer if they were going somewhere, they would reply, "Oh, we're going to Callahan's Dance." Of course, he would ask to go along. Meanwhile, several men had started out ahead, a few with rifles. By the time the others had come along with the newcomer, they would hear a loud howling like a pack of wolves, and Indian war whoops. Then a shot would ring out and one of the fellows would yell, "They got me," and drop to the ground. Finally, several were lying on the "tote" road that the newcomer and the others were walking on. By this time he was terrified and would usually start back to camp yelling. "Let me in, let me in." On the path to the bunkhouse, those who had remained in camp had placed pots and pans over which he would stumble in his frantic haste to reach the door. As he opened the door he would fall into a tub of water. This completed the initiation. One night, a fellow took off in the wrong direction and got lost. They searched for him all night and most of the day until they found him. The camp boss said, "No more Callahan's Dance around here from now on. Why, that would have been a state's prison offense for sure if that boy would'a died from cold and fright." I have heard other versions of this since from different parts of the state. Last summer I heard a similar version from a former lumberjack in Forest County.

"Snipe Hunt" was known among lumberjacks and hunters in northern Wisconsin. The new recruit would be given a large bag or gunnysack and told to wait at a certain spot while the others drove the snipes in his direction. They would fire a few shots when they were out of sight, just to make it look good. After an hour or two of "holding the bag" he would finally realize that it was all a joke and would start back for camp with murder in his heart! A variant of this from Ladysmith stations the newcomer in the middle of a bridge while the others are to drive the snipes from both sides of the bridge. "You just can't miss 'em that way!"

"Squirrel," "Shove-shove," and many other indoor games or pastimes of the lumberjack also had a practical-joke angle. There were many forms of wrestling too with the old-fashioned roller towel, *Tirer au poigne* (wrist-pulling), and *Jambette*, which I remember seeing many times as a child in a typical lumber town. In this, each man placed his hands on the other fellows' shoulders and had to keep them there. The idea was either to corner him or trip him. As a result, two fellows doing the *Jambette* looked like dancers, as each did his share of fancy footwork while trying to trip up his opponent and yet retain his balance and stay on his feet.

"Seeing stars in the daytime" was popular years ago among Oconto County children. A visitor or new resident in the neighborhood would be asked if he or she would like to see stars in the daytime. The answer was usually, "yes." He would be taken to the woodshed or down in the cellar or other dark place, and the armhole of a coatsleeve would be fitted over his face. He would then be asked, "Do you see the stars yet?" The answer would be, "no." "Then close your eyes and open them real quick." At that, a cup of cold water would descend into the blinking eyes to the utter discomfort of the victim who wouldn't rest until he found someone else who "wanted to see the stars." (I know because I was initiated when I was ten!)

39

Wisconsin Tavern Amusements

James P. Leary

Throughout the state's history, Wisconsin taverns have sustained the legacy of Old World inns, of cultural institutions sharing status with, and often numerically exceeding, churches. In 1944, journalist Fred Holmes described Wisconsin German taverns in a way that characterized many more of the state's ethnic, rural, small-town, and urban-working-class watering holes: ". . . the tavern is a community club house. After church, the whole family, before returning to the farm, is likely to enter to drink beer, while sitting around a table talking with friends and neighbors. These taverns are different in atmosphere from the crowded bar familiar to other communities. They have the attributes of family sociability rather than commercial activity" (*Old World Wisconsin: Around Europe in the Badger State* [Eau Claire, Wisc.: E. M. Hale, 1944], 71). Four decades later, I found much the same features evident but endangered while conducting research for the essay that follows.

At the close of the twentieth century, the prospects for the family-run tavern, the erstwhile "community club house," have worsened. On May 11, 1997, journalist Susan Lampert Smith wrote a special report, "Decline of the Wisconsin Tavern," for the *Wisconsin State Journal*. Citing a marked drop in "ma and pa country taverns," Smith found those still in business beleaguered. Among them Junior Sprecher, proprietor of a "quintessential Wisconsin tavern," in the central Sauk County hamlet of Leland: "Sprecher's has pickled eggs on the back bar, fishing licenses for sale, a friendly pup named Lucy and, behind the bar, Junior Sprecher himself. This 70-year-old charmer in red suspenders comes from the Swiss immigrants who settled this area, the son of a family that has been doing business in this building since 1901. He also knows he's an endangered species, becoming less common than his trophy wild turkey tom that struts in a glass case on the far wall." Sports bars and chain restaurants with liquor licenses may proliferate, but for Junior Sprecher, "Country taverns are a thing of the past."

Modified from an unpublished paper presented to the Society for North American Cultures Survey, Lexington, Kentucky, October 1983.

> If you're moving to Wisconsin,
> And your wife is on the wagon,
> I think it's only fair to warn her
> They've got a bar on every corner.

So begins "Up in Wisconsin," an only partly tongue-in-cheek praise song by Peter and Lou Berryman, natives of Wisconsin's Fox River Valley (Berryman 1980). Home of Berghoff, Blatz, Gartenbrau, Heileman, Hibernia, Huber, Leinenkugel, Miller, Pabst, Schlitz, Sprecher, Point, and Walters breweries, a national leader in beer and brandy consumption, Wisconsin has bars not only on main street thoroughfares, but also in quiet neighborhoods and alongside rural crossroads (Vogeler 1986: 9–15). Indeed, Wisconsin trails only Nevada as the state with the most per capita taverns, and the latter's numbers are swollen by the influx of nightlife-seeking tourists, while the former's patrons are mostly local.

My beginnings as a participant/observer in Wisconsin tavern life came at age fifteen when, having let my beard grow for a few days, I "got served" at Broome's Club 48, Walt's V & M Bar, and Vanderhyde's Tavern. My observations are based on these and subsequent experiences, and as well as on interviews conducted from 1978–1983 with tavernkeepers and their patrons in Barron and Portage Counties.

Situated in northwestern and central Wisconsin, respectively, these counties were settled by non-native peoples in the nineteenth century. WASP capitalists from New England typically financed the region's logging, milling, and railroad industries, but the first generation of workers, farmers, and barroom entrepreneurs were chiefly former peasants and often Catholics or free-thinkers of various ethnicities: "Bohemian" or Czech, German, French, Irish, and Italian in Barron County (Axtell 1980); Polish and German in Portage County.

The proliferation of "foreign" taverns did not please well-to-do Yankees. They attacked the "German Sunday"—practiced with equal enthusiasm by Slavic peoples—wherein whole families spent Sunday afternoons in beer halls enjoying food, music, dancing, cards, conversation, and, of course, beer (Conzen 1976: 156–58). Indeed, as early as the 1870s, Yankee politicians and churchmen, sometimes aligned with pietistic Norwegians, attempted to close beer halls altogether on Sundays (Paul 1979: 302–7; Rippley 1985: 51–52). Albert Sanford's temperance-minded complaints about Portage County Poles, for example, noted that women frequented taverns "as freely as men in the country districts," while in the market center of Stevens Point, taverns were "the only available places of resort for women and children" (Sanford 1901: 287). Wisconsin taverns persisted in this fashion until, with Wisconsin breweries, they were legislated out of existence by America's adoption of prohibition in 1919. Wisconsin was the last state to cease beer production and the first to commence when prohibition ended in 1933 (Rippley 1985: 127–28). Similarly, Wisconsin's taverns, which had been cafés or pool halls or driven out of business altogether, returned with a vengeance.

From the 1930s to the 1980s the most characteristic Barron and Portage County taverns have been, in the local vernacular, "Mom and Pop" establishments. Collectively they share features with places scattered throughout Wisconsin's rural, small town, and urban working class landscape. They are:

1) Family owned, family run, and often family named, as in the case of Portage County's Chet and Ruth's, Hank and Dolly's, Johnny and Elaine's, and Virg 'n' Mary's;

2) Family places, not proverbial dens of iniquity, that are frequently attached to the owners' living quarters, open to women and children, and serve food as well as drink, especially on Friday nights when "fish fries" abound;

39.1. Card players enjoy a game of "tonk" or "whiskey poker" along the bar at Dominic Slusarski's Ritz Tavern on the square, Stevens Point, 1983. Photo: James P. Leary.

3) Patronized by a quasi-extended family of regular patrons whose local residence, ethnicity and/or class backgrounds coincide with the proprietor's;

4) An important source, but rarely the sole source, of family income; and

5) Heirs to the pubs and inns of Old World villages.

In summation, these Mom and Pop or "home territory" taverns, although clearly businesses, are best understood as community institutions: usual places where a regular crowd gathers to engage in traditional sociable activities, to enjoy a range of tavern amusements (see also Cavan 1961: 205–23; Le Masters 1975).

Consider Dominic Slusarksi, born in 1914, who in the early 1940s bought Stevens Point's Ritz Tavern, known more familiarly as "The Polish Nightclub" or simply "Dominic's." Through the 1950s he was an active concertina player and bandleader of The Jolly Seven, which made recordings and played for dances within a hundred mile radius of Stevens Point. Within the barroom Dominic cultivated a genuine and active interest in his patrons: greeting them by name, inquiring about their lives, listening carefully to their talk (be it drunken or sober), offering sympathy and understanding, filling their glasses, then bidding each leave-taker a personal farewell. As he often told me, Dominic wanted the Ritz to be "a friendly place, a family bar." Indeed, after nearly forty years in the business, the tavern seemed like home to Dominic, a place where he presided as a kind of patriarch over those who also found comfort along the bar. He related: "I'm sixty-five now. You know, I could get Social Security and it'd be easy to find a buyer for this place. But then what would I do?

When I'm home I just walk around. In here, though, there are always different people. They come, they have a drink. This is a friendly place. And then there are regular customers who come in every day. Where would they go if I sold out? They've got this place to come to and it makes me feel good" (Slusarski 1979). Dominic did sell out in 1982, but to a proprietor with similar inclinations, Chet Niemczyk, who stressed family and conviviality in calling his place "Uncle Chet's Friendly Bar."

In Dominic's and Chet's establishments, as elsewhere, the physical bar is the locus of tavern sociability. Especially when seated on adjacent stools, and not tucked away at a side booth or table, taverngoers are accessible to one another, and to the publican who patrols the bar's length. Patrons typically acknowledge one another's presence and often move around to stand or sit in shifting groups. At the very least, the roving bartender pays attention to each customer.

Beyond the pleasures of merely sitting amidst fellow human beings, drinking is a fundamental tavern pastime. Whether "mixing" or "chasing," "nursing" or "chugging" their chosen elixir, customers embellish this activity with language and custom. Brand associated and generic nicknames abound: "Leinies," "Old Mill," "Horse Piss," "The Breakfast of Champions," "Ribbon," "Blue Bullets," and "Barley Pop" signify assorted beers. The beer and tomato juice combination favored in Portage County on weekend mornings is called "Red Eye" or the "Polish Martini." Meanwhile such old country names for beer glasses as *stein, shupe,* and *boomba* remain current.

Raising the glass may also be accomplished with a flourish. Those favoring boilermakers might exclaim "Ish that's good!" when swallowing a powerful shot. My dad's favorite was "Here's mud in your eye!" And when foul weather murked fishing holes, Portage Countians like Leo Garski justified tavern refuge with:

> When the wind is from the west,
> The fish bite the best.
> When the wind is from the east,
> The fish bite the least.
> When the wind is from the south,
> They bite from the mouth.
> When the wind is from the nort'
> It's time to go to the tavern for a snort. (Garski 1982)

Non-English toasts also thrive: the Norwegian *skol!*, the German *prosit!*, and the Polish *na zdrowie!* (to your health), the latter sometimes rendered in mock translation as "nice driveway!"

Change from purchased drinks is not pocketed but left in rough piles along the bar. Sometimes cited as a technique for increasing the bartender's ability to claim payment, this practice is also a sign of a customer's openness (Betro, Kezeski, Marchall, Slusarski, all 1983). Indeed those who lay their cash on the bar not only declare that they trust their fellows, but also that they are willing to spend their money—perhaps to buy one another drinks. Companions treat one another through alternate rounds so that, even if everyone spends the same amount, drinkers are

social drinkers favoring reciprocity and community. New or occasional acquaintances likewise solidify friendship with complimentary drafts. Even in hard times,
in the 1930s, celebrating couples or workmen on payday might buy the house a
drink. Pete Trzebiatowski, who ran taverns from the 1930s through the early 1970s,
recalled that "on Friday night or Saturday and Sunday, usually, my wife and I was
behind the bar. Somebody would order a drink: 'Give 'em all a drink.' She'd start on
on end, I'd start on the other. We'd meet in the center. 'How much you got?' That's
the way it would go. We'd add the two together and that would be it" (Trzebiatowski 1983).

Personally, I vividly remember occasions in the late 1960s when Sokup's Tavern, a Bohemian stronghold in Barron County, served "free beer"—generally a keg
or two purchased by a newly married couple for the pleasure of all comers. In parts
of Portage County newlyweds who didn't throw a wedding party for the rural neighborhood, or at least offer free beer at the local tavern, were "shivareed": visited by
a noisy contingent beating pots and pans, demanding drinks or money to buy them
(Trzebiatowski 1978). Nor are tavernkeepers exempt from this give and take. They
too often buy new or regular patrons a drink and are favored in return with "Have
one yourself."

Talking naturally accompanies social drinking. As Sherri Cavan observed, "bar
talk is essentially small talk" (1961: 58). People converse about the weather, sports,
economic conditions, personal situations, local issues, and so on. The exchange of
simple information, opinion, and gossip, however, is frequently enlivened by narrative artistry, including both personal experience stories and jokes.

In the summer of 1978 I recorded more than five hundred humorous jokes and
stories from Portage County raconteurs, many of which were not only told but set
in taverns. Some forty-four jokes featured tavernkeepers (Leary 1982). Sometimes
appearing as bystanders, sometimes as confidants, sometimes as dupes, they were
most often cast as tricksters. A typical example:

This fellow went into this bar. The bartender was playing jokes on him everyday, y'know. He'd
come in there. Bartender'd say, "Where's your buddy Ben?" "Ben who?" He says, "Bend
down and kiss my ass." Next day, same thing'd happen. He'd catch him again. "Oh, your
buddy was just sitting on that stool there." "He was? Who's that?" "Ben." "Ben who?" He'd
say, "Bend over." He'd get him every time. So he went and told his buddy about this. He said,
"Gee, that guy is gettin' me every time on them jokes." He [the buddy] says, "Well, I'll
tell you what you do." He says, "When you go in there, before he has a chance to get you,
you ask him where Ilene is." He says, "And he'll say, 'Ilene who?' And you say, 'Ilene over
and *you* kiss *my* ass.'" "Oh good!" So he goes in there, y'know. Comes up to the bartender,
"You seen Ilene around?" "Yeah," he says, "she just went outa here with Ben." "Ben who?"
(Mason 1978)

More than a few barkeepers cultivated personae that matched fictive tricksters,
among them Pete Trzebiatowski: "One tavern we had, we kept bakery goods, like
bread and that stuff. And, by gol', it was in the fall of the year, on a Sunday afternoon.
This one lady come there about four o'clock. She says, 'My god, we got three or four

cars around there, but when it comes to Sunday one is going hunting, one is going fishing, one is going there, and here I have to walk over here and get bread.' I says, 'Lady don't make nothing of it. There's lots of women come over here and get bred'" (Trzebiatowski 1978). Pete Trzebiatowski's reputation as a wit and raconteur sustained his tavern business for four decades.

The "action" created by clever, often competitive, banter in the barroom is paralleled by a fondness for wagers. While some proprietors like Portage County's Alvina Marchall vigilantly opposed betting (Marchall 1983), others like Dominic Slusarski often held stakes until wagers were decided. Debates regarding athletic contests spurred many to say, "Put your money where your mouth is." Particularly in places with sympathetic owners, betting is "outrageous" and contenders "bet on everything" (Graboski 1983).

Stakes are seldom large, often only a drink or a six pack. This is especially true in the case of riddles and tricks. Widely recognized (Youngman 1974), these traditional questions are known chiefly by, in Pete Trzebiatowski's words, "certain guys." Pete himself had an extensive repertoire of both riddles and tricks. Some of his riddles were what folklorists call "wisdom questions," soluble through logic. For example: "There were three men and they wanted to go across the river in a boat. And they got a boat that would only carry three hundred pounds. And one man weighs three hundred pounds, one man weighs two hundred pounds, and one weighs one hundred pounds. Now, how would they all three get across on that one boat?" (Trzebiatowski 1979).

The descendant of a much earlier riddle-tale about a farmer wanting to cross the river with a fox, a goose, a sack of grain (or a wolf, a goat, and a cabbage), Pete's wisdom question was deciphered as often as not (Tale Type 1579, Thompson 1961). His other riddles, or "catches" based on puns and linguistic ambiguity, were seldom figured out. He might tell some male patron, "I can prove that you did not have a mother." After the listener's rejoinder that, of course, he had a mother, Pete would counter with: "Mother had you. How could you have a mother?" (Trzebiatowski 1978).

In addition to the verbal deception of riddles, bar tricks combined words, actions, and the frequent use of barroom paraphernalia: nickels or matchsticks were arranged in a certain way; glasses of beer were shifted, filled, drained, balanced, or made to float an egg; chairs and tables were brought into play. "Q: You could crawl under that table, and I bet you wouldn't stay there long enough for me to rap three times on that table. A: Well, I could rap maybe once today, once tomorrow, and that last one, maybe next year. You wouldn't want to stay there that long" (Trebiatowski 1979). While some bartenders play these tricks themselves, most, like Dominic Slusarski, are wary of being tricked: "We used to have people come in, they'd have some fancy trick, y'know. 'I'll bet you a dollar' or 'I'll bet you a drink that you can't do this.' I never make this bet with a guy because he knows his bet. I'm beat before I start. I can't win." Sometimes, however, even Dominic took a small bet when particularly intrigued: "if it's just a beer, it's worth it . . . to know the trick" (Slusarski 1983).

Beers and small amounts of money are also won or lost through dice games. Although opposed by a few tavernkeepers as a source of fights or a stimulus to extravagant betting, dice shaking is extraordinarily pervasive. As a rule, five dice are placed in a leather or plastic cylinder dubbed the "dice box" or "dice cup." Dice games are many and varied in both rules and nomenclature. "Poker Dice," in accordance with its status as the most prevalent game, is usually referred to as "Straight Dice" or "Regular Dice." Aces are wild, and players form the best poker hand from three shakes. Sometimes players compete individually against everyone else as part of the "shake of the day" sponsored by the bartender. On other occasions two or more compete. Participants may play only one time through, or they may continue into successive rounds with losers accumulating a "horse" (indicated with a counter or a bottle cap). When a player has an agreed upon number of horses, generally two or three, they lose and, often, must buy a round for participants. The most popular variant—sometimes called "Farmer's Dice," or "Milwaukee," or "No Ace, No Count"—requires that participants have an ace in order that their first shake "qualify." In the case of "Liar's Dice" and the related "Mexican," players use a closed cigar box to hold their shakes. Hidden poker hands are announced and the next player has the option of challenging the hand or believing it and bettering it. Numerous other dice games depart from poker, among them: "Ship Captain, and Crew," a.k.a. "6-5-4" or "3-2-1;" "high/low," or "11/24"; "Threezies"; and "Murder."

Beyond stocking dice, many bartenders keep decks of cards on hand. Dirty Clubs, a variant of Euchre, is the most popular tavern game in Barron County. But old-timers also enjoy *Schafskopf,* or Sheepshead; Smear; and Whiskey Poker. This triad has enthusiasts in Portage County where Whiskey Poker is called "Tonk" in onomatopoeic reference to fists that players pound on the bar to signal a final round of bets. Five Card Stud and "Polish Poker" (Five Card "No Peek") likewise have many adherents; as do "Crazy Eights" and its variant "Screwy Louie," Blackjack, Gin Rummy, Pinochle, and Cribbage.

Constituting the bulk of Wisconsin tavern amusements prevalent at Mom and Pop establishments, social drinking and the buying of drinks, toasts, small talk, storytelling, betting, riddling, tricking, dice shaking, and card games share common features. They each heighten experience, creating a sense of action by demanding participation and fomenting risk and competition. The stakes, however, are small (a word, a few dollars, a drink) and since contests are many, so are the winners: free drinks are sooner or later paid in kind, talkers each get an opportunity to hold forth, dupes learn answers to riddles and tricks, and those who gamble testify that "it all comes out even in the end." In this fashion, reciprocity, a sense of fellowship, and fair exchange are regarded as gaming's outcome. Owners and customers alike acknowledge the value of egalitarian give-and-take in statements like "this place is a second home," or "we're all just one big happy family here." The fact that proprietors and patrons must also coexist in their surrounding rural, small town, and working-class communities provides an added impetus to balance excitement with stability through tavern amusements.

Whether this balance will be maintained in future years remains to be seen.

Wisconsin's local, working-class, ethnic, family-run taverns and the amusements enjoyed within them are currently assailed by, in ascending order, cultural, legal, and economic forces.

The emergence of a "youth culture" in the post–World War II era has led, even in small towns, to the establishment of bars catering to varying ages and tastes. In teenage bars loud jukeboxes, pinball machines, and, recently, video games are in vogue. In such places, pastimes requiring conversation—like storytelling, betting, dice, and cards—are difficult without shouting and considerable effort is devoted, in the words of rocker Bruce Springsteen, to "bangin' those pleasure machines." On the other hand, some contemporary youthful taverngoers do not devote their playful energies completely to solitary competition and exchange with machines. A Barron Countian in his early twenties reckoned "Kohler's Bar has quarter pool. Buckhorn— nothing much there anymore. We go there when we're all snapped up, just to screw around. . . . It's the dirtball bar, or whatever. It's fun to go down there every once in a while and bullshit with 'em. Edelweiss is a kid's bar. The Big O is the spot for dirty clubs. They've got decks of cards, pens, and pads set out there. Midway is a regular bar with older people down to early twenties. We go there to shake dice" (John Leary 1983). Delighting in the new and the old, he patronized them all.

Legal constraints, real and imagined, present a much greater problem. It is against the law for tavernkeepers to derive any "take" from gambling on their premises. It is also rumored that a state law decrees "a bartender can't play cards or shake dice unless there's a backup bartender or only one customer present." For these reasons some bar owners, fearful of losing their license, not only shy away from making wagers but also refuse to let patrons play for even small stakes. Recent stringent drunk-driving laws likewise threaten the tavern's existence. Customers are drinking less, preferring to purchase beverages for home consumption. Supportive of the lifesaving intention of such legislation, many tavernkeepers point out that they have always monitored the intoxication of their customers, sometimes "cutting them off" and even driving them home when they'd had too much. Proposed increases in the "sin tax" on beer and liquor present further worries. Then there is liability insurance to consider.

Family-run operations, Wisconsin's Mom and Pop taverns are caught in the same economic bind as the family farm. Their overhead increases steadily while their market share decreases. In Stevens Point, second-generation publican Chet Niemczyk predicted that places like his "Friendly Bar" would eventually give way to liquor stores and supper clubs (Niemczyk 1983). Ernie Kezeski and Alvina Marchall echoed his fears (both 1983). Meanwhile, in Rice Lake, the Tavernkeepers League battled vainly in opposition to a liquor license for the Pizza Hut chain. As extraregional corporate capital, flexing larger financial muscles, strong-arms into the rural, small town, and neighborhood scene, it is likely to deal a serious blow to Wisconsin's family-run taverns and the amusements practiced within their friendly confines.

Sources

Axtell, Alvah T. 1980. *The First Fifty Years: Rice Lake, Wisconsin, 1875–1925.* Rice Lake, Wisc.: Chronotype Publications.

Berryman, Peter and Lou. 1980. *No Relation.* Madison: Cornbelt Records CB 47.

Betro, Irene. 1983. Tape recorded interview, conducted by J. P. Leary on July 7, Amherst, Wisconsin.

Cavan, Sherri. 1966. *Liquor License: An Ethnography of Bar Behavior.* Chicago: Aldine Press.

Conzen, Kathleen Neils. 1976. *Immigrant Milwaukee: Accomodation and Community in a Frontier City.* Cambridge, Mass.: Harvard University Press.

Garski, Leo. 1982. Tape recorded interview, conducted by J. P. Leary on May 6, Stevens Point, Wisconsin.

Graboski, Ed. 1983. Tape recorded interview, conducted by J. P. Leary on June 1, Stevens Point, Wisconsin.

Kezeski, Ernie. 1983. Tape recorded interview, conducted by J. P. Leary on July 8, Polonia, Wisconsin.

Leary, James P. 1982. "Polish Priests and Tavernkeepers," in *Midwestern Journal of Language and Folklore* 8:1. 34–42.

Leary, John. 1983. Tape recorded interview, conducted by J. P. Leary on July 9, Rice Lake, Wisconsin.

LeMasters, E. E. 1975. *Blue-Collar Aristocrats: Life-Styles at a Working-Class Tavern.* Madison: University of Wisconsin Press.

Marchall, Alvina. 1983. Tape recorded interview, conducted by J. P. Leary on July 7, rural Portage County, Wisconsin.

Mason, Jon. 1978. Tape recorded interview, conducted by J. P. Leary on June 1, Stevens Point, Wisconsin.

Niemcyzk, Chet. 1983. Field notes by J. P. Leary on July 8, Stevens Point, Wisconsin.

Paul, Barbara and Justus. 1979. *The Badger State: A Documentary History of Wisconsin.* Grand Rapids, Mich.: William B. Eerdmans.

Rippley, LaVern J. 1985. *The Immigrant Experience in Wisconsin.* Boston: Twayne.

Sanford, Albert H. 1901. "Polish People of Portage County," *Publications of the State Historical Society of Wisconsin,* Madison. 259–88.

Slusarski, Dominic. 1979. Field notes by J. P. Leary on August 14, Stevens Point, Wisconsin.

Slusarski, Dominic. 1983. Tape recorded interview, conducted by J. P. Leary on July 7, Stevens Point, Wisconsin.

Thompson, Stith. 1961. *The Types of the Folktale.* Helsinki: Suomalainen Tiedakatemia.

Trzebiatowski, Pete. 1978. Tape recorded interview, conducted by J. P. Leary on June 13, Stevens Point, Wisconsin.

Trzebiatowski, Pete. 1979. Tape recorded interview, conducted by J. P. Leary on August 13, Amherst Junction, Wisconsin.

Trzebiatowski, Pete. 1983. Tape recorded interview, conducted by J. P. Leary on June 2, Stevens Point, Wisconsin.

Vogeler, Ingolf. 1986. *Wisconsin: A Geography.* Boulder, Colo.: Westview Press.

Youngman, Henny. 1974. *Henny Youngman's Bar Jokes, Bar Bets, Bar Tricks.* New York: Grammercy Press.

Material Traditions and Folklife

40

Wisconsin Indian Drums and Their Uses

Jordyce A. Kuhm

Museums of "natural history" proliferated in the nineteenth century as a manifestation of western imperialism. "Wild" lands and "savage" people were there to be colonized, developed, and assimilated. European and American settlers, businessmen, bureaucrats, clergy, and even anthropologists typically subscribed to evolutionary theories of culture: it was inevitable, the argument went, that members of "lower" cultures abandon their traditions for the "higher" ways of the conquerors. As advancing civilization obliterated or altered old ways, residual cultural materials might nonetheless be "salvaged": gathered (sometimes pilfered), transported, preserved, and placed on display with dinosaur bones, stuffed passenger pigeons, dried prairie flowers, chunks of sedimentary rock, and other curiosities of lost worlds. Hence the Milwaukee Public Museum organized expeditions, accumulated collections, produced dioramas, and helped establish publications like *The Wisconsin Archeologist*. Hence, Jordyce Kuhm's essay combines minute descriptions of drums on museum shelves with predictions of rapid cultural demise.

Wisconsin's native peoples, however, have disproved evolutionary theories. Their drums still beat, their drummakers still fashion the full range of instruments, and they have even begun to reclaim some sacred drums long institutionalized as "specimens." What Kuhm calls the "washtub drum" remains central to the "drum religion," a pan-Indian spiritual movement with contemporary Menominee and Ojibwe adherents, but it is most evident within the vibrant powwow scene.

In the late 1960s Tom Vennum, eventually the senior ethnomusicologist for the Smithsonian Institution's Office of Folklife Programs, began research on a series of publications, sound recordings, and audiovisual productions that testify to what Wisconsin's Indian peoples have known all along: the resilience of their drums and their uses (see Thomas Vennum, Jr., *The Ojibwa Dance Drum: Its History and Construction* [Washington, D.C.: Smithsonian Folklife Studies, 1982], accompanied by a forty-two minute film, *The Drummaker* [1974] made on Lac Courte Oreilles Reservation, with drummaker Bill Bineshi Baker; *Honor the Earth Powwow: Songs of the Great Lakes Indians*—a sound recording of Ojibwe, Menominee, and Winnebago drum groups performing at Lac Courte Oreilles—on Rykodisk RACD 0199 [1991]; and a two-video cassette set from the Bad River Reservation, *Wisconsin Powwow*/Naamikaaged: *Dancer for the People*, Smithsonian Folkways [1997]).

Reprinted from *The Wisconsin Archeologist* 27:4 (1946): 81–88.

There are three varieties of drums still in use among the Wisconsin Indians; the water drum, the washtub drum, and the tambourine or hand drum. These drums vary in size and structure, and certain ceremonies have their particular types.

The Chippewa word for drum is *dewe igun*, or "throb article," and as rhythm is

40.1. Ken Funmaker, Sr., plays the big drum and sings a Ho-Chunk *Hay Lush Ka* song for spectators
gathered in the Mount Horeb High School gymnasium during the village's Fall Fest, 1992.
Photo: James P. Leary, Wisconsin Folk Museum Collection. (For photographs of
a hand drum and a water drum, see figures 12.1 and 20.1, respectively.)

always associated by Indians with the supernatural, their drums are often used in
religious ceremonies.

The most important drum from the ceremonial point of view is the water drum.
This ancient form of drum is used by all Wisconsin Indian tribes, and it appears
time and again in the mythology of the Menomini tribe, where it is associated with
all of the origin myths of the Medicine Dance ceremony.

The cask-like water drum is made by hollowing out a basswood log about sixteen inches long, the wood being charred and scraped until a cylinder is formed.
The average water drum is sixteen inches high, measuring twelve inches in diameter
at the bottom and nine inches at the top. A small hole fitted with a wooden plug is
drilled part way up on one side of the drum, making it possible to empty the drum
of water without removing the head. The base of the drum is either fitted with a
wooden disc, glued in with pitch to make it water tight, or it is covered by a piece of
rawhide permanently attached across the bottom and secured by a hoop. The head
of the drum is unlike those of other drums in that it is not made of rawhide, but is
composed of a heavy piece of tanned deerskin cut from the neck of a buck, where
the skin attains its greatest thickness. When the drum is used the head is thoroughly
softened by soaking in water, wrung out, tightly stretched over the top of the drum,
and secured by a hoop made of a squared willow branch wound with cloth, which is

pushed over the top and down on the body of the drum. In recent times an iron hoop was often used.

The Indians of the Sauk tribe have lost the art of constructing their own hollow log drums. They now take a two-gallon wooden keg and stretch a piece of deerskin over the top. The corners of the skin are twisted tight with sticks, and knots are tied in them with small sticks thrust through so that they will stay in place.

Decorations on the water drum are symbolic. Chippewa drums are decorated with colored bands indicating the degree held by their owners in the Midewiwin (Grand Medicine Society), and some have on them outlined heads representing the Mide manido (spirits), or an oblong said to represent a bag containing yarrow, which signifies life. The Menomini drums are often decorated by two parallel, horizontal bands of blue or green or red paint near the base. These colors symbolize day and night, summer and winter, joy and sorrow, life and death, and hence eternity, which in turn signifies the lasting character of the Medicine Lodge, whose devotees attain life in the hereafter.

The drumsticks of the water drum have a symbolic meaning pertaining to their ceremonial use. The slender stick used by the Menomini Indians is usually about a foot in length, with the distal or striking end curved downward. The point of percussion is a little larger than the tip of the finger. In many specimens the striking end is carved to represent the head of a loon or some other animal. On some modern drumming sticks the distal end is covered with a cushion of deer hide. The Chippewa attach much importance to the drumsticks used with the water drum in the ceremonies of the Midewiwin. The Mide drumstick is often more valuable than the drum, and it is frequently very old. A water drum is often replaced, while the same drumming stick is used continually. This rather slender stick is thirteen to sixteen inches long and is turned sharply downward at the distal end, which is carved into various forms. Some carved ends represent the owl, but those representing the head and eyes of the loon are regarded more highly, because the loon was the first bird selected to form part of the Mide beliefs.

When it is desired to prepare the water drum for use, from two to four finger's depth of water, into which a little tobacco has been added to please the genius of the drum, is poured into the bottom of the instrument. The Sauk Indians add a little charcoal to the water "to make the drum sound louder." The water in the drum causes the sound to have great vibration and carry long distances, although when close by the sound is a series of dull thuds. On a still night the sound is audible for a mile or so over land, but it has carried for twelve miles across a body of water. The drum is tuned by regulating the depth of the water by means of the plug in the side.

The treatment of the tanned deerskin top determines the quality of the drum's tone. The head of the drum, soft and incapable of resonance when dry, is wet, wrung out, and stretched into place over the top of the drum. If the head becomes too dry it is moistoned by "splashing" the water in the drum or by dipping the hand into water and passing it over the surface of the deerhide. If it is too damp it is held toward the fire or put in the sun for a short time. The warmth tightens the deerhide.

The water drum is never used lightly, as it is considered sacred. It is used primarily in the ceremonies of the Medicine Lodge, although it is not confined to these rites. It is used by Lodge members when they sing songs in private, and it may be used in other ceremonies if a drum requires it.

When traveling, the owner of a water drum carries it in a large bag of white cloth closed by a drawstring with tasseled ends of bright colored yarn. It is probable that similar receptacles of plain, tanned deerskin were formerly made.

The most modern form of Wisconsin Indian drum is the washtub drum. In comparatively recent times the Indians of Wisconsin adopted a form of religion centering around this drum. This Drum or Dream Dance religion was founded on "the brotherhood of man," and was practiced in the upper Mississippi Valley and the Great Lakes region. The Chippewa and Menomini tribes attribute its origin to a Sioux woman who traveled through Wisconsin around 1878. She said that the spirits told her that she must teach a new dance to all the Indian tribes, and that they must put away the small drum that they had always used and make a larger one, for the small drum was no longer large enough to ward off the bad spirits.

The Sioux woman directed the construction of the first drum, and as time passed other drums were made in exact imitation of that one. The drum is made over a foundation composed of a large wooden or galvanized iron washtub from which the bottom has been removed. Wet rawhide heads are stretched over both openings and tightened by means of thongs passed from one head to the other. Upon drying, the heads become very tight and resonant. The upper head is approximately two feet in diameter, the typical measurements for the drum being twenty-five inches across the upper head, twenty-three inches across the lower head, and twelve inches in depth. Before the heads are put on the drum a thong is stretched across the inside and from it is suspended a small bell, usually a sleigh or cow bell, which jingles pleasantly as the drum is being carried about or beaten.

The decorations of the washtub drum are very elaborate. The heads of the drum are painted red, blue, and yellow symbolically, and all are exactly alike. Through the center of the head is painted a yellow band one and one-half inches wide, said to represent the path of the sun. To the south of this line is painted a red stripe about one and one-half inches wide, and next to it a blue stripe of the same width. The remainder of the south side of the drum is painted red to symbolize the brightness of the sun and light towards the south. To the north of the yellow medial line is the same painting, except that the colors are exactly reversed, blue symbolizing the darker sky to the north.

About the head of the drum is fastened a wide band of fur, velvet, or red flannel edged with blue, which forms a sort of skirt reaching from the upper edge down to about an inch below the lower head, covering the sides of the drum completely. The skirt is not tacked along the sides of the drum or at the lower head, and hangs loosely when the drum is suspended from its stakes. Attached to the upper edge of this skirt is a band of beadwork edged with a fringe of bead tassels and metal thimbles. Various pendant articles, some of beadwork, others of metal, often discs of hammered silver or perforated silver coins are also commonly attached to the skirt. Almost anything which will produce a pleasing jingle or add to the good appearance of the drum may be used. The bottom of the skirt frequently ends in a fringe made of buckskin strings provided with small, conical, metal objects that jingle as the drum is being beaten. Usually these objects are thimbles, coins, or conical, metal jinglers from which scarlet-dyed deer hair tufts protrude.

The most important feature of the decorations of the drum is four heavily beaded pieces which hang at the four quarters of its upper edge, equidistant from the adjacent stakes upon which the drum is supported. Two depict a head or bust; the other two depict a hand. These represent the head, or head and body, and hands of the Great Spirit, who gave this ceremony to the people and to whom the invocations during the ceremony are made. The same color symbolism observed in painting the drum heads is found here. The pieces attached to the northwest and northeast are blue, while those attached to the southwest and southeast are red. Very frequently these are provided with jingling fringes like that on the lower skirt of the drum.

Two kinds of drumstick are used with the washtub drum. The four leading drummers use sticks covered with soft brown deerskin and decorated with bands of otter fur or beads and long ribbon streamers. In a certain part of the ceremony the owner of the drum uses a stick which is over three feet long. Over the end of this stick is slipped the skin from the neck of a loon, its glossy black feathers dotted with white.

When the washtub drum is in service it is suspended from four elegantly decorated stakes or supports. The drum is suspended from the stakes by four leather loops, which are very exactly placed in relation to the painting on the head of the drum. A loop appears exactly at each end of the yellow medial line and at each end of the diameter running from north to south. The stakes are placed in holes dug with the greatest of care so that the symbolical coloring will be correct, the yellow medial line exactly delineating the path of the sun at whatever time of year the ceremony is held. When in position, the stakes have a span of about six feet. These curved stakes are usually made of some hardwood and measure about three feet in length. The lower two-thirds of the stakes are plain, while the upper one-third is split by means of a slot one-half inch in length. One of these projections is cut off to a length of two to six inches forming a notch for the leather loop on the drum. On the inner surface of this projection is placed some kind of mark designating the position which that particular stake is to occupy when the drum is set up. This is often done with brass tacks; a single tack indicates one of the cardinal points, two tacks another, and so on. It is essential that the stakes be placed according to the marks. The longer projection is rounded and bent to a greater or lesser degree. This curved horn always projects outward from whatever side of the drum the stake stands on. The projection is ornamented with buckskin, beadwork, or painting. At the extremity of the curve are hung various pendant objects. These may include the tufted end from a cow's tail, several ribbon streamers, short beadwork strips, and always one or more large eagle feathers. The ribbon streamers are blue on the stakes to the west and north and red on those to the east and south. These stakes are kept with the drum between ceremonies.

The Dream Dance ceremony of the Society of Dancing Men (Dreamers) centers around the washtub drum and special calumet (pipe), which form the altar. The ceremony takes place out of doors in a specially prepared dancing ground. Sometimes it is interrupted to reheat the head of the drum, as any rawhide head must be heated in order to tighten it. The tone of the drum is determined by the degree and duration of heat applied.

When not in use the drum is kept in a shrine built in a corner of the wigwam or log cabin of one of the devotees belonging to the local branch of the Dreamers which owns the drum. As the drum is sacred, it is treatest with reverence and at no time is it left without tobacco and an attendant.

The simplest form of Wisconsin Indian drum is the tambourine or hand drum. An early type of this drum consisted of a piece of rawhide stretched over one side of a hoop and laced or tied on the reverse side, forming a handhold. A more common form at the present time is a drum which resembles a tambourine, having two heads with a loop of rawhide as a handhold.

A double-headed hand drum is made by stretching a single hide over both sides of a wooden hoop and sewing it with rawhide thongs on the outer edge of the hoop. These drums are often supplied with cords in the manner of "snare drums." These cords, stretched tightly across the inside of the drum, are provided with several small wooden pegs tied at equal distances. The cord is then twisted to increase the tension, permitting the pegs to vibrate against the deerskin heads.

The tambourine drum is not a sacred instrument and therefore has many uses. Hand drums of a fairly large size, usually eighteen inches to two feet in diameter, are used on the final day of the Drum or Dream Dance ceremony, and they may be used by any individual at any time for accompanying his own songs. In early days Chippewa Indians liked to use several hand drums at once if they could get those that chorded together.

A hand drum of this size is also used to accompany singers at a moccasin game. This game consists of hiding four bullets or other objects under four moccasins. One of the bullets is marked, and the object of the game is to guess the location of the marked bullet. The player hiding the bullet has an assistant who sings and beats on a hand drum while the hiding is in progress, the intention of this being to confuse the player who is trying to guess the location of the marked bullet.

Much smaller specimens of tambourine drums are used as medicine drums. Hand drums of this character contain a small number of beads, seeds, pebbles, or shot, which add a rattling noise. Because of this these instruments are classified as rattles and are commonly called "doctor's rattles," but they are also used as hand drums. Among the Chippewa, if a doctor or juggler is also a member of the Midewiwin he may use these drums when using Mide healing songs. They are also used as hand drums by the shamans (medicine men) of the Wabano and Jesako cults of the Menomini.

The decoration of a tambourine drum depends upon its use, and both heads are frequently decorated. The ornamental paintings on drums of this class used for pleasure are of a purely decorative character, while the drums of the medicine men bear esoteric figures relating to mystic dreams of the users. Many tambourine drums used by medicine men may have attached them to a bunch of woodchuck tails, ribbons, feathers, bells, or short, hollow, bone cylinders which are swallowed by the conjurers to enable them to see through the body of a patient and thus locate the cause of a disease and suck out the sickness. The shamans of the Menomini often attach a small dried snapping turtle, which is one of the mysterious animals from which they derive their power.

Various types of drumming sticks are used with the tambourine drum, the type probably depending upon the choice of the individual using the drum. One stick mentioned is short and knobbed; another stick has a small round hoop at the distal end, the whole stick being wound with cloth.

These purely American drums of the Wisconsin Indians, although still in use, are fast becoming a part of the past. Although these drums may change in time or be replaced by modern ones, specimens of them will be preserved in private and museum collections, and their uses will be recorded in the writings of those who were interested in the study of Indian music.

41

Alex Maulson, Winter Spearer

James P. Leary

On November 20, 1903, the *Rice Lake Chronotype* reported a local fashion trend: "The ladies are wearing Indian beadwork belts quite extensively." The area's Ojibwe people acquired glass beads from French fur traders like August Carot, who established a camp on Rice Lake's southern shore in the eighteenth century. Ladies' beaded belts came later.

By the early nineteenth century, Ojibwe women who harvested wild rice and camped along the northern shore of Rice Lake were substituting glass beads for the seeds, shells, and porcupine quills that once adorned their clothing. Treaties wrested ownership of the lakeshore camp from them by mid-century, and soon after the Knapp-Stout Lumber Company destroyed the rice beds—flooding Rice Lake to form a holding pond for its sawmill. Thrust increasingly into a cash economy, the area's Ojibwe supplemented ancient subsistence patterns of gardening, hunting, and gathering with paid work in lumber camps and sawmills. By 1900, as white settlements grew and resorts succeeded lumber camps, some newcomers of an antiquarian bent sought "authentic Indian artifacts" of the sort Ojibwe might make for their own use, while others hankered after standard items of western apparel adorned with native motifs. Many Ojibwe responded by producing a variety of pieces to suit the tastes and budgets of both collectors and the fashion conscious. Bringing their wares to town, or setting up along the roadside on summer days, they became active participants in the new economy of cultural tourism. With the aid of white sponsors, they even began enacting elements of their traditional way of life at fairs and other public events. In 1906, for example, people from the Lac Courte Oreilles Reservation—the treaty-designated home for Ojibwe who had once lived on Rice Lake—constructed an elaborate camp at the Wisconsin State Fair under the sponsorship of the Wisconsin Archeological Association.

Throughout Wisconsin and indeed the world, peoples viewed by the mainstream as "indigenous" and "folk" have found their material culture similarly admired, coveted, purchased, displayed, and appropriated by outsiders. In keeping with laws of supply and demand, the more their living cultures become endangered and without practical value in a changing world, the more their material productions gain symbolic value by virtue of their scarcity and exoticism. As a consequence, traditional practitioners must often wrestle with the complications and compromises of trying to live some semblance of their culture while making a living. These issues, and the corresponding ethical dilemmas of folklorists, underscore the article reprinted here.

Ojibwe fish decoys took far longer than beadwork to attract outsiders' attention. For decades the decoys—jigged under the ice to attract game fish within a spear thrust's reach—were little known beyond networks of fishing lure collectors. But in the 1980s, as the value of duck decoys soared within antique and folk art markets, fish decoys became "hot" by association. In 1990 New York's Museum of American Folk Art (MAFA) launched the first fish decoy exhibit, "Beneath the Ice: The Art of the Spearfishing Decoy" (see the eponymous catalogue by Ben Apfelbaum, Eli Gottlieb, and Steven J. Michaan [New York: E. P. Dutton, 1990]).

In January 1990, while affiliated with the Wisconsin Folk Museum, I got a call from an old friend and fellow folklorist, Egle Zygas, who, to my surprise, had just become MAFA's education coordinator. Folklorists at the time regarded MAFA warily as an institution less concerned with folk artists than with an elite constituency of connoisseurs, collectors, and dealers in artistic "Americana." Contrary to that approach, Zygas proposed that I join folklorists from Michigan and Minnesota in actually bringing fish decoy carvers to New York City to present their skills and experiences in a series of public programs.

I wasn't sure what to think. Whom would I really be serving, the culture or the collectors? Would my actions contribute to the tradition's conservation as a way of life or its transformation into a cottage industry? What was the greater good? I realized that these questions were best answered by the carvers themselves. My role was not to choose what might be a romantic or, worse yet, paternalistic course, but to inform and support them as best I could.

I contacted several carvers and found they were interested. I offered my view of the MAFA as an institution, and of Zygas's proposed innovations, then outlined the probable logistics, pay, expectations, and implications of the job as carefully as I could. Eventually Alex Maulson and I traveled to New York City. We worked out a presentation combining my slides and his comments. Alex set up a spearing tent, demonstrated his carving, and sold a bag full of decoys, sans middlemen, at a price he liked. He met some other carvers, we wandered around New York City, and then we went home. Eventually Egle Zygas prompted the participating folklorists to write articles for a special issue of *New York Folklore*. When it came out, I sent Alex a copy.

Because of who he is and the choices he made, he still carves decoys more for use than for sale; he remains a winter spearer.

Reprinted from *New York Folklore* 19:3 (1993): 43–58.

Big Crooked Lake, Broken Bow Lake, Cranberry Lake, Crawling Stone Lake, Flambeau Lake, Little Trout Lake, Pokegama Lake, Sugarbush Lake, Wild Rice Lake, and many others dot northern Wisconsin's Lac du Flambeau Ojibwe Reservation. The French named the place for the flaming torches fixed to canoes by Ojibwe who, spears-in-hand, scanned the spring waters for muskellunge and walleye. Months before, however, when lakes were frozen, the spearers had lain in dark tipis peering through holes in the ice and hoping to attract a fish by jigging a wooden decoy.

The "dark house," spear, and fish decoy complex has been found among the Woodland peoples of Michigan and Wisconsin: the Ojibwe, the Potowatomi, the Menominee, the Ottawa, and the Santee and Dakota (who once competed with Ojibwe for the wild rice beds of northern Wisconsin). Shell decoys in the region extend back 1,000 years. And among the Ojibwe, oral traditions concerning spear fishing extend to roughly 1685 when a band from the present-day village of La Pointe on Madeline Island in Lake Superior encountered two starving whites and nourished them with their catch (Warren 1885 as cited by Kimball 1988: 12).

Accounts of Ojibwe spear fishing, written by fur traders, Indian agents, ethnographers, and government bureaucrats, are frequent thereafter, especially regarding fishing on Lake Superior. In 1892 Hugh M. Smith, in the employ of the United States Commission of Fish and Fisheries, observed that "spear fishing for commercial purposes" was practiced by Ojibwe Indians in a channel of Lake Superior's Chequamegon Bay that runs between Bayfield, Wisconsin, on the mainland and the island village of La Pointe.

The Indians go out to fishing grounds in the vicinity of their homes with handsleds or dog teams. On four uprights at the corners of the sleds a canvas house is constructed to protect the fishermen from the wind. A hole is cut in the ice, over which the sled is drawn, and through this the fisherman suspends a decoy fish attached to a line, which is pulled up and down to attract the attention of a passing fish. When a fish is seen the spear is thrown with great force, often to the depth of 30 to 40 feet, the same being withdrawn by means of a line attached to it. This fishing is often carried on with the mercury 40 to 50 degrees below zero, and sometimes lower, the Indians remaining on the ice all day watching and fishing. (Smith 1894: 375)

In the 1990s Ojibwe still ice fish commercially on the same span of Lake Superior, but they set nets beneath the ice instead of jigging decoys and thrusting spears. The Lac du Flambeau Reservation, some 40 miles inland from the "big lake," has become the center of winter spear fishing for Wisconsin's Ojibwe people.

Art and Brad Kimball's *Fish Decoys of the Lac Du Flambeau Ojibway* (1988: 62–72) cites an array of historical sources while listing some seventy spear fishers who have lived on the reservation over the past century. Alex Maulson, Jr., is one of them. Maulson was born in 1939 at the Indian hospital in Hayward and grew up at Lac du Flambeau. His father was a German American from Redgranite, Wisconsin, who had come north during the Depression to work in a CCC [Civilian Conservation Corps] camp. He married a Lac du Flambeau Ojibwe woman and set up a roofing business on the reservation. Young Alex, nowadays a tribal game warden, grew up trapping, hunting, "making rice," and, in winters, spear fishing.

On a mild winter day, January 24, 1990, I met with Alex Maulson at Lac du Flambeau to document his fishing. It was my second trip out on the ice. And, unlike the first time, when veteran decoy carver and spearer Ben Chosa had taken me and folklorist Richard March, I carried along a tape recorder to interview Maulson during slack moments of waiting for a fish to appear.

Alex Maulson has been winter fishing since 1947 when he was eight years old.

A buddy of mine [Louis St. Germaine, Jr.] that I went to school with, he lived on the north end of Pokegama and that's where his dad used to spear and one of his uncles. That's where I started. There was nothing to do on weekends. So that's what we'd do when we were kids.

His fishing has changed very little since then. The "gear is basically the same that we use now"—with a few exceptions.

Nowadays Maulson drives to the shore of a given lake, but years ago "you had to walk anywheres from four to five miles." Nowadays Maulson fills his car trunk with a pair of molded plastic sleds laden with gear. Years ago, "they were homemade sleds . . . they were similar to a wagon only with skis on them instead of wheels." In the 1990s Maulson also hauls the frame for his "dark house" tipi.

Years ago you really didn't have to worry about taking your sticks. You usually used five to seven sticks. But you never had to worry about picking your sticks up or your boughs, because when you got to the lake you could cut them along the shore. There was nobody to bother you, but nowadays people are worried about trespassing and using their property or whatever they consider their property. So nowadays you cut your sticks before you go out to the lake. You've either got a sled or whatever to put them on and you either take them home every night or you take your chances and leave them on the lake at night.

Years ago winter spearing was also entirely on reservation lakes, but Wisconsin's Ojibwe have recently reasserted old treaty rights that allow off-reservation spearing. A minority of resentful local whites have occasionally destroyed the stick frames of untended spearing tipis.

Upon arrival on the shores of Lake Shishebogama, Maulson unloaded his car, ganged two sleds, and began his trek onto the ice. Within two hundred yards he stopped, kicked the snow off a circular area roughly ten feet in diameter, pulled out his chisel, and began to chop a hole (fig. 41.1). Ben Chosa favored "holes" where his grandfather and father had speared. Alex Maulson reckoned spearers chose their hole

from experience . . . you've seen or asked somebody, some of the older Indians, where they've fished. . . . Or if you were on the lake during the summer, you get an idea of how the bottom is, where the bars are, where the weed beds, rock beds are. So you get some knowledge of the lake. Either first hand knowledge or from someone that's been on the lake before. You usually use landmarks.

The hole Maulson fashioned was 18″–20″ in diameter at the top, but flared out to twice that dimension at the bottom "so when you're laying down you can get a little better, little deeper view."

With the hole chiseled and cleared of ice with a dipper, Maulson chopped five small indentations in the ice at equidistant points around his hole. Then he withdrew the "sticks" from his sled that would serve as the frame for his tipi.

I usually use maple because it's a fairly soft wood and easy, and the bark—it's a dark bark so it helps when you make your tipi that it ain't going to be too bright inside.

Placing the butt of each stick in an indentation, Maulson bound the tops with twine, then anchored the butts by inundating them with dippersfull of soon-to-be-frozen water (fig. 41.2).

With the frame in place, Maulson began to cover his snow-cleared circle of ice with a carpet of evergreen boughs. Years ago Maulson might have cut these on the shore, but nowadays he cuts and fills a sled with them in advance. The boughs "keep down the glare, try to make it look natural so that the fish think there's still" snow on the ice. They also provide insulation between the spearer and the ice so that his body heat will not turn the surface ice to slush.

With his "floor" prepared, Maulson swathed the stick frame with an assortment of quilts and blankets that formed an interior covering, added a wind-breaking exterior of canvas and plastic tarpaulins, then weighted down loose ends with the empty plastic sleds. The finished structure was both warm and pitch-dark.

Maulson surveyed his tipi then pulled a cigarette from his jacket. He tore apart its paper casing to let strands of tobacco scatter on the snow.

41.1. Dipping ice from a chiseled hole. The wrist lanyard at the chisel's end prevents it from slipping under the ice. Lac du Flambeau, 1990. Photo: James P. Leary.

41.2. Positioning and lashing the spearing tent or "dark house" frame,
Lac du Flambeau, 1990. Photo: James P. Leary.

Anytime you cut a tree or whatever you offer tobacco to the Great Spirit for giving it to you.
You have to give the earth back something in return . . . it seems like that's how it's been here,
as far as I can remember from the time I started hunting and fishing. You offer tobacco.

With that act, Maulson gathered up his spear, selected a fish decoy, and we
crawled inside.

In contrast to the white daylight glare, the tipi's interior was black. As our eyes
adjusted, however, the ice hole radiated a greenish light. Soon we could clearly see
the bottom twelve feet below and, thanks to the hole's flare, our vision extended ten
feet in all directions. As he readied his equipment and began to fish, Alex Maulson
informed me about his decoys, his jigging stick, his spear, and the act of fishing.

While nowadays small companies make lures for nearly every kind of fishing,
including "hard water" or ice fishing, they have not, at least in Wisconsin, gotten
into the business of manufacturing spearing decoys. Their absence is probably attributable to a severely restricted market. Only native peoples have the right to winter spearing on an annual basis, although there is a season, every other year, for
spearing sturgeon on Lakes Poygan and Winnebago in southeastern Wisconsin.

When Alex Maulson began winter spearing in 1947, "you had to make your
own decoys"—and the same remains true.

Birch, basswood, cedar. It's green wood. Little sapling no more than 2″ in diameter. Nowadays you can buy your cedar from the lumber company or get scrap from the dump. That's what you usually use, or you can go out in the woods and look for an old basswood tree and use that.

There's just basically a chunk of wood and you just start whittling on it [with a jackknife]. Get it in the shape of a fish. It don't have to look identical to a fish, just something that's similar to a fish. A minnow, a whitefish, a little sucker, a perch—whatever you figure the muskie's going to feed on.

[You make them] usually from 6″ to 10″, whatever you feel like. You make them different sizes. . . . They got a little circle [or a curve] at the tail.

You more or less try to put lead in them. You cut out a notch back of their head on the bottom. You just figure out where to cut a notch and after a while you know just about how much lead to use for the weight of the wood. You want them to sink. You don't want them to float, because it don't do no good if they float. You can't get them in the water then.

You usually do it [pour lead] yourself. You either get lead weights from tires—you collect that during the summertime—or little sinkers or whatever chunks of lead you can find. What I usually do is just melt them in a small coffee can over the stove and pour them in the slots that I cut out in the decoy. I do it at home.

[The fins] are made out of old stovepipe. You cut them out. The front ones you fit in the sides where you pour your lead. So when you pour your lead, you put them inside [the notch] so they won't fall out. The tail fins are just small ones that you push into the wood.

A small steel screw eye or "line tie," set just behind the head, completes the basic decoy.

Clearly Maulson's approach to decoy-making, acquired in the 1940s, is evidence of an evolving tradition that may make occasional use of the woods (a basswood tree or saplings), but relies even more on the detritus of mass produced items: scrap lumber, discarded weights, old stovepipe. Similarly Maulson initially used the old-time tactic of charring or smoking his decoys, but with a modern twist. He "baked them in the oven to get them dark."

In later years, when he "could really afford paint," Alex Maulson switched to brushing on color, but his favored hue remained constant. While other Lac du Flambeau decoy carvers might favor "all different colors"—particularly greens, browns, yellows, and blues—Maulson sticks to "mostly black with little white dots or little white stripes." The lighter touches are "to attract the fish. When he sees some flashes, then he comes to investigate. If he likes your fish, well then he tries to get your minnow." A dot of paint serves where others might prefer a glass eye (fig. 41.3).

Maulson attaches his decoys to a jigging stick, roughly 12″ long and ¾″ in diameter, and carved from "any wood that will fit your hand." Of the several sticks Maulson brought out on the ice, one was painted black with a red circle on the handle end for decoration; another had a wider-than-usual handle "so I don't get tired" and was carved from a "left-over sliver of cedar." All of the sticks were notched "at the end where you start the line."

The lines Maulson favored were "anywhere from 20 pound test to 40 pound test" and darkened so as to be nearly invisible in the water. The length of the line is likewise important. Maulson prefers 12′ to 15′, slightly more than the 8′ to 10′ depth he usually spears in.

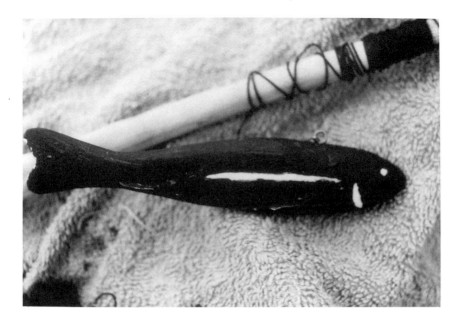

41.3. The characteristic strip and dot profile of a blackened Maulson decoy,
Lac du Flambeau, 1990. Photo: James P. Leary.

It happens that [sometimes] you'll be dozing after fishing, because it gets kind of warm in
these tents . . . you get a tendency to slack off and fall asleep after three or four hours of
leaning on your side and your stomach.

If the jigging stick slips out of his hand, or is knocked loose by a musky, the leaded
decoy will drop to the bottom, but the line will unravel and the jigging stick will
float to the top.

Besides fashioning fish decoys and jigging sticks, Alex Maulson has fabricated
his spear. The shaft is a 3½′ length of ¾″ conduit pipe filled with lead. The spear
itself is "made out of an old pitchfork with the tines straightened out and barbs put
on them. It's welded on, sharpened." (fig. 41.4). The spear's butt end is fitted with
an anchor bolt to which, harpoon-like, 15′ of line is tied. Maulson lashes the end of
the line to the frame of his tent.

The actual fishing by Maulson and spearers like him involves lying prone on
the darkened tipi's floor peering down through the flared hole in the ice. The left
hand works the jigging stick, while the right hand grips the spear. If a decoy has
been well-made, a gentle up-and-down action on the jigging stick will cause it to
"make little looping circles to more or less represent a fish that's wounded." Maulson
generally positions his decoy at a depth of 3–4″ below the ice. If a musky is around,
it will, at least in theory, be drawn by the sight of its prey in trouble.

But each hand-carved fish has its own character, and some seem to "fish" better

41.4. The business end of Alex Maulson's spear, Lac du Flambeau, 1990. Photo: James P. Leary.

than others. After working his first decoy without success, Maulson reckoned he often experimented with decoys, sometimes changing them two or three times in an hour until he found success.

Sometimes I'll be working one like I've been working that one and don't see anything. And then the next one you put in, they'll come right after it. They [the decoys] all got a little different action. Some got long circles that they go, others got little short circles. And the last one I had, the tail was a little straighter and it goes out wider.

An interested musky does not try to devour the decoy with a sudden rush. It investigates, sweeping past the decoy or brushing against it.

Unfortunately no muskies appeared that January day, but Maulson explained that once a fish was in sight

you stop your decoy and you slowly raise it toward the top of the hole. And the musky will follow it up, he'll follow it up anywheres from a foot below the ice. You have to get him so he comes toward the middle of the hole so you can spear him.

With the muskie in the crucial spot, the spearer aims just behind the fish's head. The spear's weight alone provides nearly enough force for smaller muskies, but those weighing more than 30 pounds demand a strong and accurate thrust. "There's fish that guys say took their spear way under the ice and fought until they pulled their spear out."

Once the spear is set, the spearer lets it go. After a bit of thrashing, the muskie generally drops to the bottom. "He'll more or less die or drown." With the fish near death, the spearer pulls in the line on the spear's end and, with a gaff hook, draws the fish through the hole.

Like other Ojibwe, Alex Maulson fishes for subsistence, not sport. His catch is determined by the number of people relying on him for food.

If you only have two or three, well then that one musky's enough. You take him home, you start taking your stuff down and you go home, because that's about all you can eat for one or two meals. That's what I do. There's a certain amount of pleasure in going out and getting a musky. But no one that I know that spears through the ice—they don't go stay right out there from dusk-to-dawn to see how many muskies they can get. They just get enough to feed their family.

Or they spear for relatives or for an elder.

Muskies are a bony fish and not everyone likes to eat them. But Alex Maulson finds them to be "just as good as a walleye," a gamefish that graces the tables of fine restaurants in the Upper Midwest and Canada. While some Ojibwe bake or batter fry their muskellunge, Maulson simply scales them, washes them out in cold water, cuts them into chunks, and deep fries them in grease or lard.

Until very recently the procurement of a musky and its consumption have been the chief reasons for fashioning the paraphernalia of winter spearing. But the economics of winter spearing have begun to change radically.

Like duck decoys, fish decoys have become simultaneously recognized as "folk art" and sought after by collectors. The legal restrictions on spear fishing have likewise narrowed the number of people who can legitimately carve decoys that will subsequently be "worked" or "fished." Interest and scarcity combine to provide a ready market for decoys carved by the Lac du Flambeau Ojibwe. "Purist" collectors prefer working decoys with known pedigrees, but others fancy prettier fish.

Just as carvers of "working" duck decoys have gone on to carve "decorator" versions of ducks and other birds, fish decoy carvers who try to catch collectors as well as fish sometimes add lines, colors, and details that depart from the old tradition. Some of these changes satisfy the individual carver's aesthetic impulse to make something "realistic," some satisfy the need to make money. As Maulson puts it, "it just happened recently that the guys start making them for show instead of for getting food. But I suppose that's a way to get food—by selling them."

Still Alex Maulson has been unwilling to carve anything but working decoys. At another's bidding, he once tried carving a decorative decoy with an extra curve in its body, but he gave up in disgust: "That decoy will never fish, it doesn't move right." Similarly he spurns the glass eyes favored by some carvers as unnecessary: "If I put eyes on them, they're . . . paint—a white dot or a red dot." And he scoffs at the acrylic paint used on decorative decoys because it is water soluble and would be worthless on a working decoy.

Nonetheless, Maulson has sold some of his working decoys to collectors and museums. But only on a small scale. He has no wish to become a production carver, fashioning even working decoys more for sale than for subsistence. To do so would be to wander from the practice of his Ojibwe culture toward merely representing or reenacting that culture for outsiders, toward "playing Indian" for the benefit of whites.

To try to make them look realistic, or store-boughten, I feel we're starting to lose our identity by carving them to represent the real fish when you wouldn't even use that decoy in a lake to spear a fish.

Maulson's stance takes on an important political dimension in the late twentieth century. Wisconsin's Ojibwe or Chippewa peoples have reasserted their rights, granted by nineteenth-century treaties, to spear walleyes in the spring and muskies in the winter on lakes outside the reservations. Although not as controversial as spring spearing, winter spearing is nonetheless a cultural activity that has thrived chiefly as a result of Indian peoples' willingness to take legal action to protect their rights. In the 1980s the state of Wisconsin attempted unsuccessfully to buy off the treaty rights held by several Ojibwe bands, including those of the Lac du Flambeau.

Although clearly less serious, the desire to seek sales over subsistence, to become decoy carvers rather than winter spearers, is nonetheless a subtle threat to the culture of the Lac du Flambeau Ojibwe. Alex Maulson recognizes that threat. He is a winter spearer.

Sources

Apfelbaum, Ben. "Fish Decoys: A Native American Craft." *The Clarion* 15:1 (1990): 46–49.

Davis, Tom. "Lured By Fish Decoys." *Wisconsin Trails* (November 1988): 36–37.

Kimball, Art and Brad. *Fish Decoys of the Lac Du Flambeau Ojibway.* Boulder Junction, Wisconsin: Aardvark Publications, 1988.

Smith, Hugh M. "Fisheries of the Great Lakes." In *Commissioner's Report 1892, United States Commission of Fish and Fisheries.* Washington, D.C.: Government Printing Office, 1894.

Teske, Robert T., Janet C. Gilmore, and James P. Leary. *From Hardanger to Harleys: A Survey of Wisconsin Folk Art.* Sheboygan, Wisconsin: John Michael Kohler Arts Center, 1987.

Warren, William W. *History of the Ojibway People.* St. Paul: Minnesota Historical Society Press, 1984; reprinted from the 1885 edition.

42

Work at Rest

Janet C. Gilmore

Women's handwork retains significance even in an era of ready-made artifacts and machine production. No longer compelled by necessity, many Wisconsin women still find abundant reasons to
wield needles and weave in ways that sustain old traditions. Janet C. Gilmore's "Work at Rest"
provides insights into the varied lives, methods, and motives of eight such women.

Herself a handiworker, Gilmore earned a Ph.D. in Folklore from Indiana University in 1981.
Since then she has worked on numerous public folklore projects, including, from 1986 to 1997,
nineteen surveys of folk arts and traditional culture and as many exhibits. She collaborated in
1986 on the John Michael Kohler Arts Center's pioneering survey of Wisconsin Folk Art, the resulting statewide exhibit *From Hardanger to Harleys: A Survey of Wisconsin Folk Art,* in 1987,
and the significant 1997–1998 exhibit *Wisconsin Folk Art: A Sesquicentennial Celebration.* Affil-
iating with the Wisconsin Folk Museum in 1989, Gilmore annually designed and installed an
exhibit there through 1995, when the museum closed. From 1993 to 1995 she served as the
museum's chief exhibit curator and public programming administrator.

"Work at Rest" is based squarely within the tradition of folk arts exhibits that folklorists began
producing in the 1970s, with support from the Folk Arts Program of the National Endowment for
the Arts. These exhibits combined aspects of, but also departed from, museological models favored
at the time by anthropologists, historians, and art historians, with their respective emphases on the
collective aspects of cultures, on distinctive chronological periods, and on material objects in isolation. Presenting a range of traditional artifacts arranged thematically, folklorists expanded artifact
identifications and often added photographs to convey more fully the context in which a traditional
object is made and used, the creative process and materials involved in making it, and the background and philosophy of the maker. Distinctively, folklorists keyed on the individual as the primary
unit for the sustenance of cultures, on the dynamic, often overlapping, relationship between the
present and the past, and on the ways in which objects communicate their maker's experience
and essence. Based upon extended interview and photography sessions with the traditional artists
featured, "Work at Rest" combines Gilmore's commentary with photographic portraits of the artists, verbatim quotations from some of them, and examples of their work.

Recent exhibits by folklorists, including Gilmore, on Wisconsin's folk arts have also flourished
under the leadership of Robert T. Teske. A Milwaukeean, Teske earned a Ph.D. in Folklore from the
University of Pennsylvania. After teaching stints at Wayne State University and Western Kentucky
University, he served as a grants officer in the Folk Arts Program of the National Endowment for
the Arts before returning to Wisconsin in 1985 as an associate curator of the John Michael Kohler
Arts Center in Sheboygan. Currently the director of the Cedarburg Cultural Center, Teske has cu-
rated four major traveling exhibits of Wisconsin folk arts, while editing their catalogues: *From
Hardanger to Harleys: A Survey of Wisconsin Folk Art* (Sheboygan, Wisc.: John Michael Kohler
Arts Center, 1987); *In Tune With Tradition: Wisconsin Folk Musical Instruments* (Cedarburg, Wisc.:

Cedarburg Cultural Center, 1990); *Passed to the Present: Folk Arts Along Wisconsin's Ethnic Settlement Trail* (Cedarburg, Wisc.: Cedarburg Cultural Center, 1994); and *Wisconsin Folk Art: A Sesquicentennial Celebration* (Cedarburg, Wisc.: Cedarburg Cultural Center, 1998).

Curator's Preface, by Janet C. Gilmore

Like any work of art, the Work at Rest exhibit represented a moment in time, in the development and ideology of the exhibition process at the Wisconsin Folk Museum, and in a particular folklorist's experimentation with exhibit design. The exhibit arose just after three major semipermanent exhibits were in place, altogether occupying three-quarters of the exhibits gallery. The earliest of these, an exhibit of Norwegian American rosemaling in the Upper Midwest, presented thirty-eight rosemaled pieces in three major thematic groups, each of which also reflected an important historical period in the development of the tradition in the region. Generous interpretive text introduced sections and subsections, but artifact labels were minimal, and only a few photos were included. In conjunction with the exhibit, the chief curator, museum founder and director Philip N. Martin, published *Rosemaling in the Upper Midwest: A Story of Region and Revival* (Mount Horeb, Wisc.: Wisconsin Folk Museum, 1989).

Next in the creation sequence, the second semipermanent exhibit displayed the prolific output of three woodcarvers, one "whole log" master who worked in northwoods Wisconsin themes, and two whittlers of "hobo art." Besides interpretive text introducing the major groupings in this exhibit, the signage included a photograph and biography of each carver, more generous artifact identification labels of two or more sentences, and artifacts in progress showing the process by which particular pieces were made.

The third and last semipermanent installation featured introductory exhibits that illuminated the nature of folk art and traditional culture through objects in a variety of media by a range of artists, most obviously expressing ethnic heritage. These displays preponderantly showcased the work of artists represented in the 1987 John Michael Kohler Arts Center's exhibit and catalog, *From Hardanger to Harleys: A Survey of Wisconsin Folk Art*. Here, beyond generous introductory text outlining main concepts and fuller artifact labels describing the artist, context, process, and materials, were a substantial number of photographs of artists, places, the working environment, and even of artifacts themselves interbalanced with the artifacts and text displayed. By the time these three exhibits were installed, discussions had begun to develop complementary exhibits that would speak to the Wisconsin region and emphasize themes that would characterize its people and their folk traditions, and integrate a range of traditions. The stage was set for *Work at Rest*.

The exhibit closely followed upon the curator's involvement in four folk arts surveys—three in Wisconsin and one just over the border in the northwesternmost county of Illinois—and further work with some of the artists to obtain tape-recorded interviews, better photographs, and sometimes artifacts for the museum's growing collection. Recurrent themes and good examples of them emerged spontaneously from this wealth of broad, current documentary evidence: region, community, ethnicity, family, and individual virtuosity—themes that the curators of other exhibits at the museum were also confirming. Interestingly, the themes and good examples emerged particularly from the women's textile art traditions documented, a major area in which women perpetuate their heritage. Past needlework exhibits at the museum had been popular, focusing on quilts, and on the varied fine needlework traditions of one artist. It was time for a textile arts exhibit that presented a range of traditions articulated by different artists.

Since the vast majority of artifacts displayed at the museum were of obvious beauty and intricacy—and most often representative of ethnic heritage—it also seemed important to try to present artifacts that were not necessarily exceptional in terms of first impressions, workmanship, intricacy, rarity of expression, or obvious symbolic significance. While some of the objects chosen for the exhibit were more commonplace, they were nonetheless rich in meaning and interpretive power, both for the artist who created the work and for the folklorist who had visited the artist in the context in which the object served important functions.

By presenting artifacts that might be less immediate draws to the audience, however, it was important to offer other media to explain and support them. Here was an opportunity to elevate contextual matters that were not as easy to present in an exhibit context, particularly in a fairly "low-tech" exhibit context. To emphasize the role of the individual artist in creating an artifact and perpetuating the greater tradition, each artifact was accompanied by a photograph of the respective artist, preferably involved in some way with the work she created. When possible, other photographs were added to give a greater sense of the work, materials and equipment, and the working environment. Each photo and artifact received a label with a caption and succinct sentences identifying it, tying images and artifacts together, and supporting themes developed in the captions and explanatory text. Set on a stand below each artist's display was a sheet with the artist's biography and fairly lengthy interpretive text. Presented in large type face, the text was broken into readily identifiable, readable units. The stands were positioned so that most visitors could read the text easily without bending over. At the same time the stands did not visually interfere too much with the exhibit displays behind them, and they offered protection from curious hands.

While some argued that the biographies and interpretive text were best left to an exhibit catalog—or to a computer-accessed CD-ROM or Web site—the information was right there if someone wanted to read it, but it could be bypassed. It was thus possible for the exhibit to be enjoyed at various levels, by a range of viewers with different interests: visitors could choose to look at the artifacts alone, in combination with other artifacts, or with a selection of photos and brief but enlightening labels; if they wanted to take in more information, they could read the text on the stands. All that was missing in terms of the curator's developing exhibit-text strategy was an extensive quote from each woman. The Allie M. Crumble portion of the following presentation in fact incorporates such a quote, but the display was originally installed in a space adjacent to the Work at Rest area, integrated into another exhibit. On a final note, the Wisconsin Folk Museum collection of artifacts, which included some of the objects in this exhibit, joined the collections of the State Historical Society of Wisconsin in Madison in 1996.

Reprinted, with slight modification, from the text for an exhibit installed in the Wisconsin Folk Museum, Mount Horeb, 1992.

"A woman's work is never done," goes the old adage. The traditional artists presented in this exhibit have proved the rule and led tremendously productive lives. Most have raised three children or more, managed the household, and worked outside jobs as well. To rest, and to take advantage of the rare spare moment, they have generally turned to more work—handiwork—playful but nonetheless purposeful.

Much of women's traditional handiwork serves practical ends, providing economical bedding, clothing, and household ornamentation. Yet most traditional artists find greater motivation in the nature of the work itself, taking pleasure in design, accomplishment, and the transcendent moments that come with rhythmical, repetitive, absorbing activities. They also find inspiration in favorable responses to their handiwork and in contributions they make to others' lives—in the human exchange enabled through artistic expression.

This small exhibit illustrates some of the more social and communicative reasons why women practice and perpetuate these traditional arts.

42.1. Shared Interests, 1986, Madison, Wisconsin. The late Frances Morschauser poses with her daughter, Clara Feuling, the one child of seven who has actively carried on the family quilting tradition. Photo by Janet C. Glimore, courtesy of and © the John Michael Kohler Arts Center.

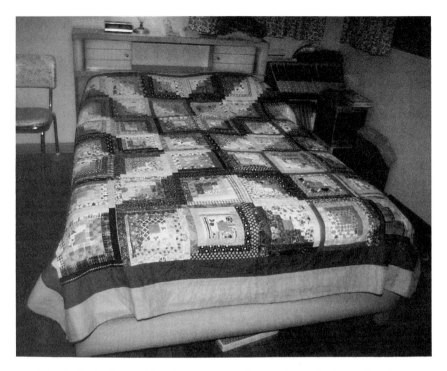

42.2. The Family "Log Cabin" Quilt Pattern, 1986, Madison, Wisconsin. Frances Morschauser produced numerous "Log Cabin" quilts during her lifetime, all featuring this distinctive coordination of light and dark strips in each block to form the resulting pattern of triangles. Morschauser learned the design technique from her grandmother and claimed she never saw another "Log Cabin" quilt like it during her 86 years. Photo by Janet C. Gilmore, courtesy of and © The John Michael Kohler Arts Center.

Family Bond

Quilting is a focal point for family exchange among the Morschausers and Feulings. Physically influencing the household space and thus every inhabitant, the quilting setup is an obstacle to negotiate. A highly visible art work in progress, the quilt is a topic of conversation and a venture to join. Under and after completion, the quilt reinforces family relationships between and across generations, between teacher and learner, between producer and receiver. Several members of the family have used production of a first quilt as a rite of passage into adulthood, signifying proper readiness to start one's own family. Through quilting, the Morschausers and Feulings express the importance of family in their lives and the interest they share in each other.

Frances Morschauser

A third-generation German American, Frances Morschauser (1902–1989) was born and raised on a farm in Roxbury, Wisconsin. With her husband, a neighbor farm boy,

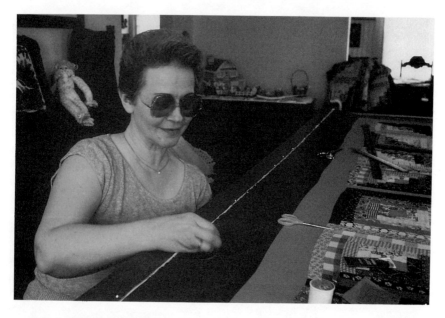

42.3. An Active Bearer of Tradition, 1992, Sun Prairie, Wisconsin. Clara Feuling quilts another of her mother's "Log Cabin" designs, one of the few quilting projects she has pursued since her mother died. When she quilts she typically uses all of her living room space, to her husband's tolerant dismay. Feuling is quilting this one for a sister. Photo by Lewis Koch.

she operated a tourist camp in Middleton and later farmed in Sun Prairie, running a vegetable delivery route in Madison.

Morschauser learned to sew and quilt from her mother and made her first quilt around the time she married. While rearing seven children, she sewed all of their clothing "inside and out" and made quilts for the family each winter. Gardening, harvesting, and preserving produce occupied the rest of her year. After her husband died in 1961, she moved off the farm and threw herself into quilting, producing over six hundred quilts in the ensuing twenty-seven years. She often quilted six to eight hours a day, sometimes until her fingers bled. Uncomfortable with others' quilting, she let only her well-trained daughters help her.

Clara Morschauser Feuling

Born in 1937 in Middleton, Wisconsin, and brought up in Sun Prairie, Clara Morschauser Feuling married an enlisted man in 1957. Her husband's career moved them around the country, but they settled in Sun Prairie in 1972 after he retired. Feuling raised five children, and held a number of clerking and seasonal factory jobs in Sun Prairie.

Feuling and her sisters began helping their mother quilt as soon as they were able, mainly by threading needles. By the time she married, Feuling completed her

42.4 and 42.5. First Quilts: The Next Generation, 1986, Sun Prairie, Wisconsin. Clara Feuling has infected her children with the family enthusiasm for quilting. Several have produced at least one beginning quilt: Lou Anne, *top*, shows off the "Crazy" quilt she completed while still in high school, and Larry, *bottom*, displays the baby quilt he created before the arrival of his first child. Another daughter has fabricated a "Nine Patch" quilt. Photos by Janet C. Gilmore, courtesy of and © The John Michael Kohler Arts Center.

42.6. Doily of Armenian Needlelace, 1930, 8 ½″ in diameter, cotton thread.
Mary Jenanian Arganian, Madison, Wisconsin. On loan from Janet C. Gilmore.
Photo by Janet C. Gilmore.

first quilt, a "Crazy" quilt. After returning to Sun Prairie, she helped her mother quilt and gradually began quilting for her own clientele, a quilt a month at the peak of business. All of her children helped her as she had helped her own mother, and three have gone on to produce at least one quilt. Since Feuling's mother died in 1989, Feuling's interest in quilting has suffered. She misses her mother's companionship, inspiration, and experience, and the act of quilting accentuates the loss.

Domestic Prowess

Armenian girls of Mary Arganian's generation learned sophisticated needlework techniques as part of their schooling. By the time they married, they were expected to produce a trousseau of needlework to decorate their new homes and themselves. Through handiwork they proved their potential for making good wives.

Similarly, Arganian used her needlework to express mastery in the domestic realm. While raising three children and actively volunteering for Racine's St. Hagop's Armenian church and community, she regularly hosted Armenian dignitaries and recent immigrants. She lavishly entertained her guests, taking a week beforehand to clean, shop, and prepare a marvelous spread of Armenian delicacies. For these events, she could showcase her needlework, displayed on furniture and fine

42.7. Ever Hospitable, 1986, Madison, Wisconsin. Mary Arganian puts the finishing coat of sugar syrup on a batch of *mavish*, Armenian rose pastry, a tasty accompaniment to stiff Middle Eastern coffee for special occasions. Mavish is an Arabic word that roughly means "nothing," referring to the fact that you can easily consume quantities of the pastry without feeling that you have had too much.
Photo by Janet C. Gilmore, courtesy of and © The John Michael Kohler Arts Center.

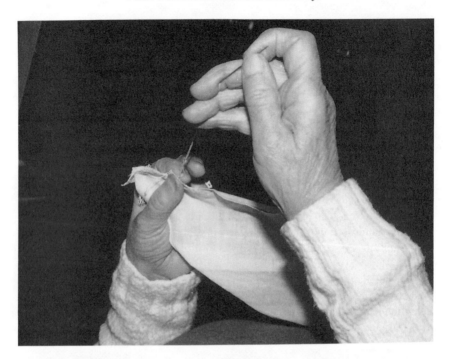

42.8. Armenian Needlelace-Making, 1986, Elizabeth Keosian, Milwaukee, Wisconsin. This ancient
Middle Eastern method of making lace enables exquisitely detailed patterns and requires only a
single sewing needle and a fine twist of thread—plus extraordinary dexterity, improvisational design
skills, and good eyesight. Like the similarly intricate tatting, which generally attracts only the most
devoted needleworkers, Middle Eastern needlelace-making is becoming a rarely practiced art.
Mary Arganian and Elizabeth Keosian largely gave up the work as their eyesight dimmed, and
neither woman was optimistic that young Armenian Americans will continue the tradition.
Photo by Janet C. Gilmore, courtesy of and © The John Michael Kohler Arts Center.

table linens. That she could accomplish such exquisite, intricate handiwork, beyond
adroitly managing the household and orchestrating feasts, proved her domestic
prowess.

Mary Jenanian Arganian

Born in Deört-yol, Adana state, in the Cilician Armenian region of Turkey, in 1904,
Mary Jenanian Arganian moved to Lebanon in her teens. There she completed her
schooling and later helped support her mother by teaching Armenian and French.
She came to Chicago in 1925, then married in 1930 and lived with her husband in
Racine for forty-seven years. After he died, she moved to Madison to be near her
three children, where she resided until her death in 1993.

Arganian learned the basics of Armenian cookery, needlelace-making, and

French cutwork from her mother. She refined her needlework skills in high school, and after she married, she revived her knowledge of Armenian cookery, adding new recipes from friends in the Racine Armenian community. She enthusiastically imparted her knowledge of both needlework and cookery to interested people she had encountered through years of teaching Armenian, English, French, and Turkish while helping Armenian and other immigrants adjust to the United States.

Community Service

Just as an enchanted listener requests another story from a storyteller, people inevitably ask a handiworker to make something special for them, sometimes for money. Traditional artists respond variously. A few find production on demand stressful or inhibiting, and thus decline such work. Most respond sporadically, sometimes completing work before deciding to sell it, sometimes producing to order. For some, the outside interest inspires them to turn an enjoyable activity into a small business. While a few artists can command equitable compensation for their labor, most earn only what local customers can afford—often just enough to cover supplies.

Dorothy Shultz Hess

Dorothy Hess is one who labors more for love than money. Making rag rugs is "just a hobby, I'm not doing it to make money," she says. She likes the activity and the extra cash, but she equally enjoys having something to do, responding to the community's interest in rag rugs. Importantly, she relishes the traditional community loom service she provides and the human interaction it enables.

Born in South Wayne, Wisconsin, in 1918, Dorothy Shultz Hess has lived her life in the Wisconsin-Illinois border area. Her mother's background was upland Southern, while her father's was German. Tenant farmers, her family moved from farm to farm during her childhood. She farmed with her husband after they married in 1938, but due to injury, they sold out and moved to Warren during the 1940s. While raising three children, Dorothy worked at local stores, truck stops, restaurants, dry cleaners, and at Janlin Plastics.

As she was growing up, Hess helped her mother sew "carpet rags" and make quilts during the winter. After she married she continued making carpet rags, taking them to a weaver to loom into rugs for her family. As her children, nieces, and nephews married, she made them gifts of her rugs. Soon she was receiving requests for rugs. When she and her husband retired and their weaver decided to quit rug looming, the two bought an Orco 70 loom to keep up with their burgeoning orders. When her husband died in 1986, Hess began completing the rugs from start to finish herself. She now looms rugs for six church groups, keeps two local craft shops supplied with her rugs, and makes rugs to order for her own customers. She often works five days a week, weaving four to six rugs each morning and tying fringe and preparing rug rags each afternoon.

42.9. Rag Rug, *left*, 1992, 26 ½″ × 44″, excluding 2″ fringes; warp: cotton, weft: cotton-polyester knits. Wisconsin Folk Museum Collection, Dorothy Shultz Hess, Warren, Illinois. Rug Rag Balls, *right*, 1992. To weave a rag rug, first the artist prepares "rug rags," cutting strips from the good cloth left in old clothing. Next she joins the strips together, according to the weaving pattern she designs. Once joined, the strips are rolled into a ball, ready for weaving. Two different women prepared these rug rag balls, and each shows a different method of joining the strips together. Wisconsin Folk Museum Collection. Photo by Janet C. Gilmore.

42.10. At the Loom, 1992, Warren, Illinois. Dorothy Hess weaves another rag rug on her Orco loom. Photo by Lewis Koch.

Quilts and Community

Traditional quilts often express community. Created for one person by another, they define a bond between people. Treated as heirlooms and passed from generation to generation, they prove to be webs of connection through time. Sometimes composed of scraps left over from dressmaking and thus recalling clothes worn by several people, they again reflect a group of people with common bonds. Quilted by several family members, by neighborhood friends, or by a church group, the quilting itself represents a collectivity. Quilt designs of the "Friendship" type actually specify members of a community on the quilt in embroidery, generally the names of the quilter's friends or the quilters who contributed blocks or otherwise to the quilt's creation.

Mrs. Crumble's "Necktie" quilt is a deliberate expression of community. Crumble combined the predictability of neckties becoming outmoded with the friendship quilt idea to represent her church. Rather than embroider a picture of the church building, she chose to designate the church hierarchy, her menfolks' positions within it, and a circle of friends within the membership.

Allie M. Crumble

Born of African American heritage in 1911, Mrs. Crumble grew up on a farm in Sardis, Mississippi. In 1944 she moved to Milwaukee, where she brought up more

42.11. Rag Rugs Ready to Go, 1992, Warren, Illinois. Dorothy Hess uses part of an upstairs bathroom to store the hundreds of rugs she produces each year. The left tier of rugs she wove from "rug rags" provided by local church groups who will then sell the completed rugs at their fall bazaars. The remainder she worked from start to finish herself, to sell to her own customers. Photo by Lewis Koch.

42.12. "Necktie" Quilt, c. 1982, 72″ × 87″; front: cotton-polyesters, ties of various, mostly synthetic fabrics; back: cotton-polyester gingham; batt: polyester; hand-pieced, -appliquéd, and -quilted; machine-edged. Wisconsin Folk Museum Collection. Allie M. Crumble, Milwaukee, Wisconsin. A senior female member of Milwaukee's Metropolitan Baptist Church, Mrs. Crumble is called "Mother Crumble," and she plays an active role in baptisms. To celebrate her involvement in the church community, Mother Crumble got the inspiration to compose a quilt using neckties from fellow church members. She came up with the design and pattern "out of her head": "I just did that myself," she says. She solicited thirty-six ties, starting with the pastors, deacons, and ushers, and then family and friends. She displayed the completed quilt in the church library, to the delight of the membership. Photo by Janet C. Gilmore.

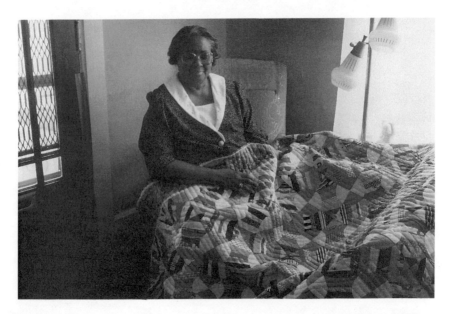

42.13. Fancy Strings by Mother Crumble, 1992, Milwaukee, Wisconsin. Allie M. Crumble holds her "Snowball" quilt that she made from blocks composed of "strings," small leftover strips of cloth that she attached to a paper template backing before trimming to size. Photo by Lewis Koch.

children than she cares to admit. Under her mother's supervision, she began piecing when she was seven and quilting when she was eleven. She has produced quilts ever since, because, she says, "I just love to make them. And they're so good to keep your mind good—keeps you from losing your mind."

What I wanted to do, I wanted to play the piano. . . . But you know I was real little, but I knowed, I knowed, I said, "Lord, I want to do something with my hands." That's what I said. I remember that so good. And then I wanted to play the piano, 'cause my cousin was playing the piano. . . . But my dad, he never did see the place where he could get me one. And I just kept saying, "I want to do something with my hands, that's what I want to do." But you see, the Lord didn't have that for me, he didn't have that for me. He only just said, "Well, wait a minute Allie, I got something else in store for you." And that's these quilts, these quilts, that's what he had for me. And I didn't believe that until I got up pretty good size, you know. Whatever the Lord tell you to do, you better do that. (Allie M. Crumble, Milwaukee, 2 April 1990)

Community Well-Being

Generally concerned with family and community well-being, traditional handiworkers often contribute to activities that benefit their church. They may gather regularly to produce comforters and quilts to give to the less fortunate or to earn money for

42.14. Crocheted Doily, 1991, 15½″ in diameter, cotton thread, starched.
Wisconsin Folk Museum Collection. Pascalena Galle Dahl, Mineral Point, Wisconsin.
Photo by Janet C. Gilmore.

42.15. Work by the Seasons, 1986, Mineral Point, Wisconsin. Pascalena Galle Dahl, with her spring-through-fall work (her vegetable garden) behind her, and her summer-fall work (canning) and fall-winter work (crocheting) before her. Photo by James P. Leary, courtesy of and © The John Michael Kohler Arts Center.

the church. Or they may donate work accomplished alone for the church to sell at fundraisers.

For years Pascalena Dahl has produced more than a dozen large, starched crocheted doilies to sell for twenty dollars apiece at the annual St. Mary's and St. Paul's Church Holly Fair, the first weekend in November. While upcoming weddings of family and friends often motivate her handiwork, the possibility of contributing to the church spurs her productivity. Thus, Dahl's handiwork can be seen largely as an expression of community, of her commitment to her church, family, and friends.

Pascalena Galle Dahl

Pascalena Galle Dahl's father emigrated from the province of Calabria in southern Italy in 1902, and after settling in Mineral Point, he sent for her mother in 1905; unlike most Italian immigrants, they continued to farm in this country. Pascalena, the seventh of fourteen children, was born in Mineral Point in 1918. She grew up helping her father with farming chores and her mother with cooking and tending the large vegetable garden. Dahl has spent her life mostly in Mineral Point, where she lives within a block of three sisters, who all keep up the family vegetable garden tradition. She married in 1944, after working at local stores and at the Oscar Mayer plant in Madison. She raised four children while working at Burgess Battery and then operating a drive-in restaurant with her husband for sixteen years in Mineral Point. Over the years she has continuously managed a large garden, preserved produce, cooked large and savory meals for her family, helped siblings and one son with their farming, and practiced her needlework.

Dahl learned to crochet in her youth from an older sister, since her mother "would go too fast for me to learn from her." She used to stand behind her sister and watch her crochet: "I'd ask her questions and she'd tell me, and then I learned to read directions by myself." Dahl also learned to embroider, sew, and quilt in her youth, and when her children were young, she made their clothes.

Ethnicity

Many Wisconsin traditional artists use their handiwork to express ethnicity. Through the practice of a certain skill, the production of a special artifact, or the manipulation of traditional designs, they identify with a broader community that shares culture and history and embraces the family, friends, and church.

In Wisconsin, where groups of many different national and religious affiliations have settled side by side, there is a heightened sense of ethnicity. Some groups, confronted with the differing customs of neighboring ethnics, have consciously maintained their distinctiveness. Others, like the Latvians, suspecting that their cultural heritage might only survive in the new country, have concertedly cultivated their customs accordingly.

Visually rich with color, pattern, and symbolism, traditional handiwork plays

42.16. Backstrap Loom on Frame, *bottom,* 1991, frame: willow branch, 35″ long; shed roll: 1″ wooden dowel, 5″ long; heddle: ⅜″ wooden dowel, 4 ½″ long; shuttle: wood, 1⅜″ × 7 ½″; beater/pick-up stick: wood, 1⅜″ × 12″; band warp and weft: pearl cotton (not typical, but good for demonstration); band pattern: women's, Piltene district, Latvia. On loan from the artist. Vita V. Kakulis, Milwaukee, Wisconsin. Women's Latvian Belt Patterns, *top,* Lielvarde District, 1991, widths vary from ¾″ to 2″; lengths vary from 4½″ to 8½″ exclusive of fringe; warp: linen; weft: wool. On loan from the artist. Vita V. Kakulis, Milwaukee, Wisconsin. Photo by Janet C. Gilmore.

42.17. Backstrap-Woven Latvian Belt in Place, 1992, Milwaukee, Wisconsin.
Vita V. Kakulis wears her costume representing the Lielvarde district of central Latvia, where she
was born. From 1976 to 1978, she wove the wool and linen belt, sewed and embroidered the all-linen
blouse, and sewed the wool jumper from cloth she did not weave. From 1981 to 1983, she finished the
wool-embroidered linen married woman's cap. She wove the required wool
twill shawl in 1992, after acquiring a larger loom. Photo by Lewis Koch.

42.18. Back-Strap Weaving, Demonstration Style, 1986, Milwaukee, Wisconsin.
Vita V. Kakulis weaves a belt using the demonstration back-strap loom. Here she uses the pick-up stick and beater to separate upper from lower warp threads before sending through the shuttle with weft thread. This procedure ensures a tight and even weave. Photo by Janet C. Gilmore, courtesy of and © The John Michael Kohler Arts Center.

42.19. Early Work and Inspirations, 1992, Milwaukee, Wisconsin.
While in the displaced persons camps in Germany after World War II, Vita V. Kakulis wove her first belt, shown here. The red wool thread she unraveled from an old sweater. The belt rests on a notebook of patterns that Kakulis drew from the belt of a fellow Milwaukee Latvian— one that inspired the one she now wears with her costume. Photo by Lewis Koch.

42.20. Miniature Wool Comforter, *right*, 1990, 26½″ × 43″, front: wools and
wool blends, back: cotton flannel, batt: wool quilted in cheesecloth, hand-edged, -tied,
machine-pieced. Wisconsin Folk Museum Collection. Ethel Wetterling Soviak, Ladysmith,
Wisconsin. Work-in-the-Cold Socks, *left*, 1992, men's size 9; heel to toe, 9″; heel to top of cuff, 12″;
yarn: 4-ply 100% virgin wool, 4 oz. skeins; needles: 4 double-pointed, size 4. Wisconsin Folk
Museum Collection. Ethel Wetterling Soviak, Ladysmith, Wisconsin. Photo by Janet C. Gilmore.

an important role in conveying and reinforcing ethnicity through costumery and decoration of public and private spaces and events.

Vita V. Kakulis

Born in 1936 in Valmiera, Latvia, in the Lielvarde district of the central Vidzeme region, an agricultural area, Vita V. Kakulis fled with her family as the Russians advanced into Latvia during World War II. The family then spent several years in displaced persons camps before migrating to the United States in 1949. After graduating from college and working a number of administrative jobs, Kakulis met her Latvian American husband in Milwaukee and married in 1961. Except for a brief spell in Madison, she has lived there since.

As a child, Kakulis learned the basics of embroidery and knitting in the home. In the displaced persons camp she first learned backstrap belt-weaving to complete the costume needed to join a choral group. As she stayed home with her two preschool sons to teach them Latvian, she reacquainted herself with Latvian handiwork skills. As her sons grew, participated in Latvian community youth activities, and needed costumes, Kakulis produced several sets for her sons and herself. In the process she researched Latvian folk arts and acquired additional Latvian belt- and

42.21. Knitting Those Wool Socks, 1992, Ladysmith, Wisconsin. Ethel Soviak races through another pair of the wool socks that her family loves so dearly. Photo by Janet C. Gilmore.

loom-weaving training. As she has gained expertise and participated in regular regional, national, and international gatherings of Latvians, she has exhibited and sold
work to fellow Latvians, and gained a reputation for her artistry.

Region

The production of warm wool comforters and knitted wool socks for life and work in
cold-weather climates survives especially well in the northern reaches of the Upper
Midwest, often among people of northern European heritage. Wool continues to
make sense for protection against the cold and damp among people who have customarily used and manipulated the material for generations. In a region where it is
hard to make a living, home production of bedding, socks, gloves, mittens, and even
the yarn makes good economic sense.

While not intentionally expressing region, Soviak's work in wool reflects the
cultural and physical environment and the greater regional community in which
she lives.

Ethel Wetterling Soviak

A "duke's mixture" of Swedish-German, French, Dutch, and English, Ethel Wetterling Soviak was born in Ladysmith, Wisconsin, in 1923. Except for a year in
Milwaukee in the 1940s, she lived in the area until her death in 1992. Her parents
farmed, but since marrying in 1945 she always held a housekeeping, restaurant, or
factory job while raising her six children.

In her youth, Soviak learned to sew and crochet from her mother. After she
learned to weave in school, her mother said, "If you can weave, you can darn socks."
In her teens, darning the large family's socks became her "evening's entertainment."
Every year she also helped her mother produce one to three wool comforters from
worn clothes and leftover cloth for family use. Soviak continued the practice with
her own family.

She taught herself to knit when her fourth son was born in December 1950, her
husband was out of work, and they had no money for booties. She knitted booties,
mittens, and sweaters for family members until her death, and in recent years began
knitting wool socks for them. A brother-in-law and nephew, both well-drillers, spend
the year with wet feet, so Soviak kept them supplied with the socks. A grandson-in-
law wore no others in his barn boots, and his wife had trouble getting them off him
for washing.

43

Meet a Wooden Shoe Hewer

Gladys Fossum

Before the mass production of rubber boots and the availability of treated leather, many Wisconsin farmers relied on wooden shoes, as had their old country ancestors, when trodding through barnyard mud, or when milking cows or cleaning the barn. The late Sigvart Terland of Frederic, born in 1907 in the Norwegian village of Helleland, grew up on a farm where he learned to make wooden shoes as his father and grandfather had done. "They'd have long nights in the winter," he told me in 1986, "and I'd sit in the dark and carve." From ages nine to nineteen he made shoes for his parents, two grandparents, himself, and five siblings (see also *From Hardanger to Harleys: A Survey of Wisconsin Folk Art* [Sheboygan, Wisc.: John Michael Kohler Arts Center, 1987], 57, 61, 103).

Terland continued to make wooden shoes in Wisconsin, as did many others. North Germans, or *Plattdeutschers,* farming Dodge County bottomlands found wooden shoes as useful as they had been along the Baltic Sea. Near Lake Michigan's shore, J. F. Wojta of Two Creeks reported that "John Last, August Kraase, Fred Messman, and others, who came from Germany, brought with them the art of making *Pantoffeln,* a kind of wooden slipper. The bottoms were carved out of basswood or pine blocks . . . and leather vamps were attached to these bottoms" (Wojta, "Town of Two Creeks, from Forest to Dairy Farms," *Wisconsin Magazine of History* 1:3 [1944]: 422).

Belgians to the north likewise favored a type of wooden clog:

> When plowing, they wore them without socks, for the *sabots* soon filled up with loose soil. Being warm and dry they were also worn in winter when logging or working around the sawmills. . . . In those days there were many wooden shoemakers, and they often produced very artistic *sabots* beautifully carved and colored. (Hjalmer Rued Holand, *Wisconsin's Belgian Community* [Sturgeon Bay: Door County Historical Society, 1933]. 52–53)

Wisconsin's center of wooden shoe production, however, has been in the Sheboygan County communities of Cedar Grove, Gibbsville, and Oostburg, an area settled in the 1840s by the Dutch, or "Hollanders."

Traveling through this district a century later, journalist Fred Holmes discovered pairs of well-worn wooden shoes on the back porches of farm homes. Gibbsville's William Ros, described as "the only cobbler of wood left in the community," touted the virtues of wooden shoes over their leather counterparts: "They are fine to wear while doing chores in winter. If a cow steps on your toe it doesn't hurt. Afterward, when you come in from the barn, it's easy to kick them off and go about the house in stocking feet" (Holmes, *Old World Wisconsin: Around Europe in the Badger State* [Eau Claire, Wisc.: E. M. Hale, 1944], 121).

Fifteen years later Gladys Fossum profiled another "last wooden shoemaker," William Klompenhauwer, proprietor of Oostburg's "Klomp Shop."

By the time Klompenhauwer put away his tools in the mid-1960s, nearby Cedar Grove had established its annual "Holland Days" celebration, featuring the youthful "Klompen Dancers" who continue to perform street dances in wooden shoes. In Klompenhauwer's absence the community

43.1. William Klompenhauwer works on a wooden shoe
in his Oostburg shop, 1950s. Cedarburg Cultural Center.

imported Fred Oldemulders, a wooden shoemaker from Holland, Michigan. And by the mid-
1970s, Bob "Sieg" Siegel, a retired insurance agent and woodworker from Mequon, had suc-
ceeded Oldemulders as southeastern Wisconsin's "last wooden shoemaker." (See *Passed to the
Present: Folk Arts Along Wisconsin's Ethnic Settlement Trail*, ed. Robert T. Teske [Cedarburg, Wisc.:
Cedarburg Cultural Center, 1994], 44–45; and Anne Siegel, "Klompen: Shoes from Trees," *Fine
Woodworking* [September/October 1985]: 55–57.)

Gladys Fossum's article below, from the *Wisconsin Agriculturalist*, is representative of many
informative features journalists have published on Wisconsin's practitioners of folk cultural traditions. The defunct *Ocooch Mountain News* and a pair of current periodicals—the Eau Claire–
based farm newspaper, *The Country Today*, and Madison's tourist-oriented *Wisconsin Trails*—are
consistently rewarding sources. So are local newspapers. Since the early 1970s I have kept a
clipping file from the *Rice Lake Chronotype* that bulges with accounts and photographs of carvers
of miniature farms and lumber camps, farm sign painters, gunsmiths, pack-basket makers, quilters,
and rag rug weavers.

Journalist Gladys Fossum was raised on a North Dakota farm prior to attending North Da-
kota Agricultural College, and the Pratt Institute in Brooklyn, New York. She was a home agent in
Nebraska and Maryland before becoming the "Home Editor" of the *Wisconsin Agriculturalist* in
1957. Her columns and features over the next two decades frequently concerned practitioners of
Wisconsin's folk traditions, including Danish cooks, German quilters, Ojibwe wild rice harvesters,
Swiss yodelers, Welsh hymn singers, and Winnebago basketmakers. In keeping with her own
Norwegian background, she wrote the first of several columns on *rosemaling* on November 11,
1959, profiling the work of Mount Horeb artist Oljanna Venden Cunneen. Eventually Fossum pub-

lished *Rosemaling Picture Book* (Racine: Wisconsin Agriculturalist, 1968), a significant forerunner to Philip Martin's definitive *Rosemaling in the Upper Midwest: A Story of Region and Revival* (Mount Horeb, Wisc.: Wisconsin Folk Museum, 1989).
Reprinted from the *Wisconsin Agriculturalist,* January 11, 1963, 30.

Across the street on the north side of Village Park in Oostburg is a small yard with a modest home and two bright colored windmills. Near the house and garage is a little shop.

The little shop is a shoe factory. There is no name on it, and it's different than any other shoe factory in Wisconsin. It is in this little shop that William Klompenhauwer makes wooden shoes.

"My name means 'wooden shoe maker,'" says Klompenhauwer. "*Klompen* means wooden shoe, and *hauwer* means hewer. As far back as I know my family name was Klompenhauwer. I don't know if my grandfather got the name before or after he made wooden shoes."

Several rows of wooden shoes lined one side of the shop the day I visited Klompenhauwer. There were little shoes with curled up toes, and larger shoes to fit men and women. Some shoes were in the process of being finished.

"I work all winter except in very cold weather," Klompenhauwer explains. "I've got a stove in the shop. Making shoes gives me something to do."

He uses his grandfather's carving tools which his father brought over from Holland. They are over a hundred years old but shiny and sharp for carving. They have long curved blades, and some have T-shaped handles for carving inside.

When Klompenhauwer was a little boy, his father made wooden shoes for 25 cents a pair. He was able to make four pairs a day. Sometimes young Klompenhauwer helped his father.

"It takes quite a bit of practice to make good shoes," says Klompenhauwer. "I spent about two years learning how to do it. Once in a while I spoil a pair. But who doesn't? Look at the big factories. They spoil some too."

Basswood is used for making the shoes. Klompenhauwer gets his wood from trees about five miles from where he lives in Sheboygan County.

"I need clear wood," he says. "Trees should be at least 16 inches in diameter to be big enough to make shoes."

He starts with a rough wooden block a little larger than a finished shoe. It takes about four hours to make a medium size pair.

Most of them are made to order. When tourists visit him in summertime, he takes footprints to make shoes to fit each individual. Sometimes he makes them to order by mail.

"There always has to be a left shoe and a right shoe," Klompenhauwer points out. "Sometimes they are different for people whose feet are a different size. It's best to have people try them on if they want to wear them."

When Klompenhauwer first made wooden shoes there were a dozen or more shoemakers around Gibbsville and Cedar Grove. As far as he knows, he is the only remaining wooden shoemaker in Wisconsin.

44

Feast of Folklore: The St. James Church Pork Hocks and Sauerkraut Supper

Terese Allen

In 1996, Gary Legwold published *The Last Word on Lutefisk: True Tales of Cod and Tradition* (Minneapolis: Conrad Henry Press), a handbook on what the author aptly called the fish noted for its "lye bath and legendary odor." Legwold offered factual and facetious information on this Scandinavian American culinary mainstay before concluding with "The Lutefisk Dinner Directory," thirty-plus pages in small print that included forty-three Wisconsin entries, many of them Lutheran churches. The Directory did miss a few. Our Savior's Lutheran Church, east of Rice Lake, for example, hosts its annual "Ole and Lena Lutefisk and Meatball Supper" on the first Saturday in December. Yet I can imagine Wisconsin's hardcore lutefisk fanciers will find it as, garbed in Nordic sweaters, they roam late autumn highways in search of the perfect Lutheran church dinner.

Janet Gilmore, who is after all part Norwegian, and I have attended more than a few lutefisk dinners with our two kids. She and I always eat plenty of lutefisk, but Bella and Finn prefer the *lefse:* a thin sort of potato bread that has been rolled flat like a tortilla and cooked on a griddle. Lefse is especially delicious with butter, brown sugar, and cinnamon.

Like most church dinners, the feeds we've attended at the Burke, Vermont, and West Blue Mounds Lutheran Churches have been served family style. You can eat all you want at the table, but, as in bygone lumber camps, it's against the rules to carry food away. That doesn't stop some from trying. I've heard several accounts of elderly women caught in the act of leaving dinners with purses full of purloined lefse. I've heard the same story told about would-be thieves of Czech *kolacky* at Haugen's Holy Trinity Catholic Church in northern Barron County, and it wouldn't surprise me to hear it in connection with the German *pfeffernuesse* hand rolled in the kitchen of Madison's St. James Catholic Church. You can't buy such delicacies in a store.

Far more than fund-raisers, church dinners are expressions of ethnic heritage and identity, revelations of heirloom food traditions practiced in local families, and unmatched good eating. Terese Allen richly conveys all these elements in her study of the "St. James Church Pork Hocks and Sauerkraut Supper." A native of Green Bay, Allen credits her Belgian and Polish background with inspiring her lifelong interest in Wisconsin foodways, and the development of her career as a professional chef, caterer, and cooking teacher. Terese Allen is also an accomplished writer, contributing frequent articles to *Wisconsin Trails*, including one on church dinners, "Goodness Gracious," that combines sketches of the St. James Supper, Our Savior's Lutheran Lutefisk Dinner in Westby, the Ashton area's St. Peter's Catholic Church Fish Fry, and St. Hagop's Armenian Church Picnic in Racine (*Wisconsin Trails* 38:1 [February 1997]: 42–45). Allen's *Wisconsin Food Festivals* (Amherst, Wisc.: Amherst Press, 1995) is an excellent survey of the state's local "food and folk events."

Apart from Allen's work, Harva Hachten's *The Flavor of Wisconsin* (Madison: State Historical Society of Wisconsin, 1981) offers a fine historical survey of Wisconsin foodways, including those practiced by ethnic groups and church congregations. Likewise, many of the state's churches have published cookbooks that reveal their members' treasured recipes. Favorites from my home territory include: *Holy Trinity Church Cook Book* (Haugen, Wisc.: Walter's Publishing, 1982), with six recipes for kolacky and as many for their fillings; and *Bethany Lutheran Bazaar Centennial Cookbook, 1883–1983* (Rice Lake, Wisc.: Morris Press, 1983), that includes this recipe for lefse:

> Yew tak yust ten big potatoes
> Den yew boil dem til dar don.
> Yew add to dis some sveet cream
> And by cups it measures vun.
>
> Den yew steal t'ree ounces of butter
> And vit two fingers pench some salt,
> Yew beat dis wery lightly.
> If it ain't gude it is your fault.
>
> Den yew roll dis tin vit flour
> An' light brown on stove yew bake,
> Now call in all Scandihuvians
> Tew try da fine lefse yew make!

Reprinted from a paper written for a course, Folklore of Wisconsin, at the University of Wisconsin–Madison, fall 1995.

Heartland cooking is *in*. Midwestern foodstuffs and heritage dishes, like their once-fashionable Cajun and Californian counterparts, are now touted in culinary magazines and cookbooks, on cooking videos, and at upscale restaurants and trendy urban farmers' markets. But for those in search of a truly genuine taste of the region, it won't be found in a glossy magazine. For the real thing, the place to go is a church supper.

The Wisconsin calendar is filled with Lutheran lutefisk dinners, Catholic fish fries, and Greek Orthodox banquets, and with meals like pancake breakfasts and chicken booyah picnics sponsored by fire departments and community centers. Such events offer a feast of home-cooked regional specialties as well as large helpings of history, sociability, education, and community support. Rarely advertised outside church bulletins, these repasts are low-key, low-priced affairs fueled by word-of-mouth and repeat business. Volunteers do the work; the monies they raise fund community projects and the traditions they carry on communicate a range of cultural expressions that reflect and perpetuate enduring values—something one is not likely to get from a cooking video.

Church suppers have provided culinary cultural expression—called foodways by folklorists—from early on in Wisconsin's history. Harva Hachten, in *The Flavor of Wisconsin* (Madison: State Historical Society of Wisconsin, 1981), suggested that the first church fair in the state was held in 1835 or 1836 when the Green Bay land sales office was selling the newly platted communities of Milwaukee and Navarino. Wanting to mark the occasion, "women of all denominations got together to raise money. . . . There was a church supper of great quantity and much variety," wrote Hachten. Whether or not this was the first, churches have certainly been producing such meals ever since, contributing a wealth of material, customary and verbal lore

44.1. Lutefisk consumers at the Burke Lutheran Church's
annual dinner, Dane County, 1996. Photo: Andrew Lubansky.

that has been relatively unexplored in academic and popular writings.[1] Here I concentrate on one such event—the annual St. James Catholic Church Pork Hocks and Sauerkraut Supper in Madison—to explore the context, performance, function and meaning of church suppers, as well as the relation between their "folk" (people) and "lore" (cultural expressions).

When it comes to the pork hocks and sauerkraut supper, Emmett Schuchardt (pronounced shoo-kart) is the man behind the meal. Born in Madison to German parents, Schuchardt has lived all but two of his seventy-three years in the near west side neighborhood that surrounds St. James, the parish to which he also has belonged throughout his life. One of eight siblings and a graduate of Central High School, he married and with his wife Tillie raised three children. His father owned and operated Carl's Lunch, a small Park Street eatery that, according to Emmett, catered to the kind of appetites that prevailed when "people worked with wheelbarrows and shovels, when people had to eat."[2] From his father, Emmett inherited the restaurant (and operated it until 1970) as well as the pork hock recipe that later became a focal point of the church's annual fund-raiser. Although he's now retired from food service, the restaurant blood in Schuchardt's veins must still be pumping strong, for he spends most of his time as the volunteer manager of St. James's kitchen, doing everything from "cooking funeral meals to keeping the [dining] hall clean."

One task he has performed for "at least twenty, twenty-five years" is organizing the pork hocks and sauerkraut dinner. Schuchardt is a neatly dressed man who looks and sounds comfortable with his role as the one in charge. His rare, brief smiles open his face like a door and reflect a considerable generosity. He is modest about the contribution he makes to an event that raises three to four thousand dollars for church and school maintenance and programs. Schuchardt explains that the Kraut Feed, as it is often called, is sponsored by the Fellowship, a volunteer group that supports parish social events and fund-raisers. In compact phrases and a low, matter-of-fact voice, he describes how the German-style meal had its origins in a neighborly impulse:

> It started with the spaghetti dinner, at least 30 years ago. St. Joe's had closed.[3] We wanted to do something for the Italians. They came here when their parish closed down. Yes, it was a fund-raiser, but mostly we wanted to involve the Italians. Well, this is was a German church. We had to have our dinner, too.
>
> I was thinking of things that went good [at the restaurant]. Franz Haas made homemade sauerkraut.[4] Along with the sauerkraut we did the pork hocks.
>
> My sister [Phyllis Schuchardt] was the one who would make it all German. A German day and the whole deal. She had flags, posters, place settings. She died about five years ago. For years a high school band would play German music. All they took for it was food to eat. But now it's getting away from the German thing.

These days, whimsical handcrafted pink pig centerpieces adorn the dinner tables instead of German flags, and the only truly German American particulars at the event are its menu items and a number of the older diners and dinner volunteers.

What was once primarily a celebration of heritage is now a coming together of a widely diverse community. Contrasting with the parish's earliest families, whose European heritage was so pervasive that sermons were given in both German and English,[5] St. James' multicultural churchgoers now include families, senior citizens, single people, and University of Wisconsin students.

The parish office estimates that St. James currently has between seven and eight hundred members (a membership can mean a family or an individual). Like the surrounding neighborhood, the parish has changed significantly since the church incorporated in 1905. University of Wisconsin students dominate the area; those who attend services and make donations may or may not register as members of the parish. According to Emmett Schuchardt, half the grade school students aren't Catholic. What is not so different from the past are the many and varied parish activities: a choir, the Fellowship, senior citizen programs, weekly services, religious education, and school programs like the Cub Scouts.

Parishioners make up about half of the four hundred to six hundred diners who attend the event each year and the rest "come from all over," estimates Schuchardt. No wonder, for it is a feed one is unlikely to find elsewhere. The menu includes boiled potatoes, cream-style corn, rye bread, sauerkraut, and pork hocks. For those to whom pigs' ankles sound unappetizing, there's Polish (or smoked) sausage or wieners.

"You got to have wieners for the kids," says Schuchardt, but the choice of meats is offered not just for the children. Pork hocks may seem exotic to diners who have had little or no contact with ethnic German fare. Offering a choice of meats maintains the ethnic image yet keeps the meal "safe" and welcoming for the unaccustomed. This may be particularly important in a culturally diverse congregation like St. James's.

Coffee or milk is included in the six dollar meal price (three dollars for children); tap beer and homemade desserts are available for an extra charge. The all-you-can-eat spread takes place from 11 A.M. to 6 P.M. on a Sunday in February or March. "We always had the spaghetti dinner in March on St. Joseph's [feast day], that was the Italian one," says Schuchardt. "But they had those all over the city, so we moved it to January because of the competition, and now we have hocks in late February or March."

Organizing the event is at once casual and complex. Long-standing cooperation and familiarity among the core workers characterize the planning; still, the number of details and volunteer hours required is astonishing.

For dinner chef Emmett Schuchardt, things really get cooking the Tuesday before the meal, when the pork hocks arrive. "We get them frozen from UW Provisions.[6] They know just what I want. I like the big Canadian hock, at least a pound a piece, very meaty. Not a knuckle, where you don't get as much meat. Canadians are tender, they won't fall apart if you cook them right." The hocks are cooked on Wednesday: "You boil them with salt, peppercorns, and bay leaves. Simmer two, two-and-a-half hours, then cool them in the stock. And keep 'em covered with the stock." As the rich stock cools and gels around the hocks, the dish develops flavor.

Giant, heavy duty kettles are used to cook the hocks; they're refrigerated until early Sunday morning, when "you pop them in the oven, jelly and all, and bake until the broth is dissolved and hot. But you gotta keep [the hocks] covered with the broth, or they'll turn dark and get hard."

At 7 A.M. on Sunday morning it is also time to start the sauerkraut. Or rather, finish it, for the cabbage has already been fermenting in parishioner John Haas's basement for several weeks. Son of Franz Haas, who produced the dinner's sauerkraut for years, John contributes thirty-five gallons of homemade kraut to the meal. "It comes fresh in big crocks," says Schuchardt. "You could eat it just like that, but it's important to cook it, to break down the cabbage, so it's limp. That's the way it should be. People eat sauerkraut fresh, but the thing to do is cook it." For flavor, Schuchardt adds caraway seeds, brown sugar and some of the broth from the pork hock kettles ("you need the juice") and simmers the kraut in a forty-five-gallon steam kettle for four hours.

Meanwhile, the potatoes are boiled with salt until "just soft, not overcooked" in more huge pots. Schuchardt uses Wisconsin russets and has a group come in on Saturday to "run them through the peeler" (that is, have them peeled in a commercial vegetable peeling machine, then remove potato eye holes and other blemishes by hand.) The cream-style corn comes from cans. "We serve it separate, but the way to eat it is pile your corn on top of the sauerkraut. That's really the way to do it." Sausages are cooked ("sometimes grilled") and kept hot in steam tables with some of the sauerkraut. The rye bread usually comes from a Madison bakery, but "it's hard to get good rye now," so, time permitting, Schuchardt bakes it himself.

Throughout the day Schuchardt manages six or seven kitchen helpers at a time; they work two or three hour shifts. "It used to be I had a bunch of old fogies who know their jobs, but now I'm losing them. I tell the Fellowship how many workers I need—they get them for me. Every year I tell [each one] what to do." With a wry smile, Schuchardt describes experiences with his trainees:

I show them how to slice the bread; I tell them just so. Then pretty soon you can read a newspaper through [the bread they've cut]. Oh, everybody's gotta stir: if there's a spoon in their hand, they gotta be stirring and making a mess out of a good looking thing. I've got to watch things. I tell them: only one [piece of meat] at a time, to avoid waste. I'm all over. I really watch things. I watch the garbage cans religiously, that's where the money is made.

At the serving line, the food is placed and served in a particular order: first the sauerkraut, next the pork hock or other meat, then potatoes. Corn is served family style (in bowls on the table), as are bread and butter.

A staff of about twenty servers waits on customers, who are seated by a greeter at eight-foot tables lined up in the church basement dining room. Each year, my friend Venita Plazewski (pronounced pwah-shefs-skee) is one of those servers. Plazewski attended St. James Grade School until 1951, when her German and Polish American family moved farther west in Madison; she rejoined the parish in 1984. At fifty-eight she is a physical therapist with the Veteran's Administration Hospital. Her volunteer commitment to St. James includes being the president of the Elderly and Shut-In Committee for the last ten years. She once spent three years traveling the globe on a bicycle, and is as open-minded, observant and curious about life as taking such a trip might indicate.

Plazewski says she "does very little" for the pork hock dinner, but as one of the servers who races from serving line to tables during a two-hour shift, she is partly responsible for the friendly, attentive service that is a mark of the meal. Plazewski takes her cues from Betty Schuchardt (Emmett's sister), who organizes the servers and "gives us the run-down."

"We're assigned an apron," says Plazewski.

Each server gets two long tables. The tables are numbered and when we go up to [the diners] we take their ticket and ask, "Do you want pork hocks, Polish sausage or wieners?" You tell them "It's all you want, but one meat at a time," then you indicate on the back of the ticket the type of meat. Then it's up to the [serving] window where they take the ticket and call off the order. You stand to one side and await the tray. We also get coffee and ask about beer or milk. The beer is extra; you can have it by the glass or the pitcher. We stick a pencil behind the ear to keep track. Oh, we gotta have that pencil!

We bring them extra of anything as they desire. When they're finished, we ask about dessert. The kids run the dessert cart; we signal them to bring it. That costs extra, too: fifty cents.

The desserts have been cut into serving pieces and are wheeled to diners by eighth graders who, perhaps with their parents, have supplied the sweets from home. Dessert money is used by the students for programs like class trips.

It should be noted that St. James Church organizes a number of other food-related public events each year, as well as many meals for meetings, weddings, funerals, and other church functions. The annual spaghetti dinner is still going strong and there's a chicken and ham feast that is offered during the parish's annual fall festival. Perhaps the most celebrated of St. James food events, however, is the *pfefferneusse* sale, which also occurs during the fall fest. (Pfefferneusse, spelled Pfeffernusse in some culinary dictionaries, is a spicy cookie of German origin; the St. James version is a tiny, crunchy cookie sold by the bagful and often given as a holiday treat.)[7] Despite competition with a great many area restaurants and community happenings, St. James' culinary efforts, including the church suppers, are well-attended and favorably-received. With good reason.

Meinrud Diederich, who grew up in Waunakee where his father operated Diederich's Meat Market, is an elderly gentlemen who frequents church suppers. "That's where you get your home-cooked meals," says Diederich about the weekly jaunts he and his wife Jeanette take around the Madison area. "You get to see people you wouldn't normally. It gets you out there." Nourished by the "comfort food" and friends he finds at church suppers, Diederich is also enthusiastic about the particular pleasures of various events:

Everyone of them has their own specialty. St. John's in Waunakee has the homegrown lettuce. St. Bernard's in Middleton does different salads—everybody brings their favorite salads. Pine Bluff has their cucumber salad. St. Albert's in Sun Prairie has tomatoes and lettuce. At Lodi it's Swiss steak. Have you been to the fish fry at Ashton? They have that homemade bread. Dane has a fish fry with, what do they call those? Fritters. And Ashton has that homemade bread.[8]

Traditional ethnic dishes and "from-scratch" specialties offer nostalgic pleasures for many diners. When I attended the St. James supper, it was the first time I
had tasted pork hocks in years. I was reminded of "boiled dinner," a dish my Polish
and Belgian American family relished when I was young, and was subsequently
motivated to prepare homemade sauerkraut myself.[9]

Unlike restaurants, where cooks and servers are clearly separate from customers, church suppers are characterized by a feeling of unity among workers and eaters. The kraut feed is no exception to this. While I felt well attended to by the servers
at St. James, it was no surprise when one of them stopped in the midst of his work
to chat with my group, nor when another sat down and joined us for a beer. Such
friendly banter among diners and volunteers illustrates the feeling of fellowship that
is at the core of the meal.[10]

Good cooking and social contact are not the only draws to community meals.
Venita Plazewski mentions the "festive spirit, the music, the camaraderie" that
make such events so entertaining for her. "They're a bargain. They're casual and
fun. You don't have to get all dressed up." According to Schuchardt, dinnergoers at
St. James are also motivated to support their parish: "They know they *should* go."
With a sense of obligation comes the knowledge that one is doing his part—true for
diners, but particularly important to volunteers for whom community service is an
intentional as well as heartfelt value. This and other values are passed on to parish youth who operate the dessert carts at the kraut feed, raising money for school
programs, developing a sense of responsibility and teamwork, and gaining a sense
of the history of their parish. Most volunteers also like the recognition that comes
with the job. It's an identifying and unifying event, one that, as Schuchardt puts it,
"keeps the parish on the map."

Furthermore, those who make unique or specialized contributions also gain a
sense of personal fulfillment. By putting his professional cooking and organizational
skills to good use, Schuchardt gets to do what he knows, needs, and enjoys: "This is
the way I can help out. I like to be active. I get to do things my way. And I want to
do my share."

It's no surprise that many of the dinner volunteers are older parishioners. (Indeed, senior citizens are the most active of St. James volunteers.) Perhaps this
speaks to another kind of meaning to be found in an ongoing participation in events
such as the kraut feed. In *We Gather Together: Food and Festival in American Life*
(Logan: Utah State University Press, 1991), editors Theodore C. Humphrey and Lin
T. Humphrey and contributor Sue Samuelson note that "all rituals function to mediate our progress through life towards death, informing us of the inevitability of it,
and preparing us emotionally and intellectually for it. . . . When we participate in
celebratory exchange and consumption of food, [our] behaviors become ritualized
over time and function to mediate our passage." As time goes by, supper participants
watch how their lives, their community, and their world changes—as well as how
they stay the same.[11]

One question longtime volunteers and church supper fans might ask is, "What's
going to happen to parish events when the older volunteers are gone?" Emmett Schu-

chardt's response is, "I haven't figured out how it's going to work. People today would rather put their hand in their pocket and give you twenty dollars [than volunteer]. They don't have the time, and there's so many other things going on." But if Schuchardt is concerned, he is not pessimistic: "Right now things are done my way [at the kraut feed]. When I'm gone, they'll be done somebody else's way. They'll still have the events.[12] It's the people that make the parish. If you look at the whole picture, things are pretty good all in all."

Things are good indeed, at St. James and in other communities, for those who crave the local flavor and fellowship of a neighborhood gathering, who prefer living traditions to trendy restaurants, and who appreciate a little meaning with their meal.

Notes

1. In researching this paper, it was notably difficult to locate books, articles or essays specifically about the folklore of church suppers. I did find some mention and/or coverage in several books about American foodways.

2. Schuchardt noted that the house specials at Carl's Lunch included dishes like ribs, liver and onions, baked beans, and pork hocks with sauerkraut.

3. St. Joseph's was a nearby Catholic parish that closed in the 1960s when urban renewal razed Greenbush, a neighborhood largely populated by Italian families. For more on St. Joseph's, the "Bush" and the neighborhood's culinary customs, see Catherine Murray, *A Taste of Memories from the Old "Bush"* (Madison: The Italian-American Women's Mutual Society, 1988.)

4. According to Emmett Schuchardt, St. James parishioner Franz Haas ran a service station and was a local politician during the early years of the kraut feed. Franz's son John now provides the homemade sauerkraut and manages beer sales for the meal, among other tasks. Schuchardt and other dinner regulars often refer to the meal as "Haas's Kraut Feed."

5. On October 8, 1905, solemn services were held when St. James Congregation's first church's corner stone was laid. "The Reverend John M. Naughton of St. Raphael's Church preached the English sermon and the Reverend Joseph Heyde the German sermon." This and other occasions of sermons offered in both languages were recorded in *St. James Congregation Golden Jubilee, 1905–1955*, a booklet published by the parish in 1955.

6. UW Provision Company, a wholesale meat processing company and food distributor located in Middleton, near Madison.

7. Another of Emmett Schuchardt's culinary responsibilities at St. James is the preparation of pfefferneusse. The parish still uses the recipe from Mrs. German—who first baked the cookies for the sale—with a few changes made by Schuchardt in the years after he was chosen to learn her secrets. Schuchardt purchases fifteen hundred pounds of flour, six hundred pounds of sugar, and six hundred pounds of lard, among other ingredients, to make enough cookies. The dough is mixed in a giant Hobart Mixer, pushed through a makeshift cutter unearthed by Schuchardt at a warehouse, and hand-rolled into dime-size balls. "There's something about the hand-rolling, I don't know what it is," says Schuchardt. "Maybe it's the oil in your hands. Maybe it works the anise oil into the dough. But it makes a difference in texture and flavor." For nine weeks beginning in August, on Monday and Wednesday evenings and Thursday afternoons, volunteers meet in the church kitchen to roll and bake the minuscule cookies. St. James pfefferneusse is the best I have ever tasted.

8. For more about church community events and specifically the chicken and ham dinners at St. John's Church in Waunakee and St. Peter's in Ashton (Middleton), see Therese Allen, *Wisconsin Food Festivals* (Amherst, Wisc.: Amherst Press, 1995).

9. My family's boiled dinner consisted of pork hocks, cabbage, onions, carrots, and potatoes cooked in a pressure cooker. I wasn't crazy about the cabbage or the carrots, but coveted the rest of the blandly-named but delicious concoction.

10. For more about the relationship between servers and eaters at church suppers, see Charles Camp, *American Foodways: What, When, Why and How We Eat in America* (Little Rock: August House, 1989), 70–72.

11. I might also mention here that spiritual exchange and/or comfort was not mentioned or implied as a motivator by those I interviewed for this paper, and it was rarely mentioned in other resources I researched. Still, I would venture to say that at church-sponsored meals, spirituality is an unstated element for at least some participants.

12. Schuchardt might be pleased to see such confidence augmented by a June 1994 article in the *Milwaukee Journal*. Newspaper writer Nick Carter reported a rise in the number of church-sponsored festivals in the Milwaukee area.

Appendix: Recipe for Pork Hocks and Sauerkraut

There are no written-down recipes for the St. James Catholic Church Pork Hocks and Sauerkraut Supper. "I got it all here," says chief cook and organizer Emmett Schuchardt as he taps his head and smiles. The following recipe comes from *The Minnesota Ethnic Food Book* by Anne R. Kaplan, Marjorie A. Hoover, and Willard B. Moore (St. Paul: Minnesota Historical Society Press, 1986).

6 fresh pork hocks
1 teaspoon poultry seasoning
½ cup finely chopped onion
½ teaspoon caraway seed
1 can or package (1 pound, 11 ounces to 2 pounds) sauerkraut, undrained
2 tablespoons sugar
2 tablespoons vinegar, preferably white
1 teaspoon salt
1 cup peeled and grated apple

Wash pork hocks and pat dry. Place in 6-quart kettle or Dutch oven. Add poultry seasoning, onion, caraway seed, and 1 quart water. Bring to a boil, reduce heat, and simmer for 2½ to 3 hours or until meat is tender. Combine undrained sauerkraut, sugar, vinegar, salt, and grated apple in a bowl and mix. Pour off cooking water. Add sauerkraut mixture to pork hocks. Cover kettle and simmer for at least 30 minutes. Can be cooked longer. Can be prepared the day before, refrigerated and then reheated the next day over moderate heat. Makes 6 to 8 servings.

45

Shrines and Crosses in Rural Central Wisconsin

Dennis L. Kolinski

Wisconsin's Catholic communities are alive with folk religious expressions. Encouraged by but not officially bound up with the institutional church, these ancient folk expressions range from personal prayers, to elaborately braided and significantly placed palm fronds, to home altars, to outdoor shrines. Shrines in particular animate the landscape.

Statues of the Virgin Mary—encased in stone grottos, under wooden arches, or against the curved and sky-blue painted porcelain of upended, partially buried recycled bathtubs—sanctify yards in and around the German village of Roxbury in northwestern Dane County. Chapels built in the Belgian settlements around Green Bay for family prayer hold kneelers, votive candles, and images of the Sacred Heart of Jesus, the Virgin Mary, and Saints Hubertus, Francis of Assisi, Joseph, Roch, and Teresa of Avila. Likewise, Poles in Armstrong Creek, in Pulaski, and especially in central Wisconsin—America's largest rural Polish settlement—have erected wayside shrines and crosses.

Just as many old Catholic prayers draw upon elements of so-called pagan charms, just as woven strands of palms assume the protective magic of wheat woven into harvest blessings, so do outdoor shrines represent what Dennis Kolinski describes as the Church's attempt to "sacrilize" pre-Christian associations between significant places and the supernatural. Predictably, old, super-natural folk beliefs in spirits inhabiting the household, crossroads, and woodlands may not only persist in tandem with Christian religious faith, but also fuse with it.

Malcolm Rosholt, central Wisconsin's foremost local historian, was well aware of the old Norwegian folk beliefs in otherwordly beings held to some degree by his immigrant ancestors (see chapter 15, "Ghost Stories (As Told by Old Settlers)," pp. 149–58). His research among Portage County ethnic groups likewise included evidence of Irish fairies and Polish water spirits:

> Like the first Norwegians who brought along their trolls to plague them in the new land, the early Polish immigrants brought along their respect for the *boginki,* or water spirits with invisible human bodies who could be heard washing their clothes at night or at midday and who could bear children and even exchange their own for human ones, particularly if they had not been baptized. Instead of the bear, although there were enough of them in Portage County, the Polish mother was apt to scare her children with the threat of calling *jezda,* the horrid old witch. . . . .Occasionally the loneliness and frustration of the early years of life in America brought on tensions which the immigrant was unable to cope with and he went to all kinds of lengths to defeat the power of the *boginki.* At such times, lacking psychiatric treatment, the local priest was brought in, and, by performing certain rites, he attempted to cast out the evil spirits which allegedly inhabited the house. Often it had the right effect. (Rosholt, *Our County, Our Story: Portage County, Wisconsin* [Stevens Point, Wisc.: Portage County Board of Supervisors, 1959], 130–31)

However skeptical, priests who wished to keep parishioners' respect took their beliefs in boginki seriously.

Dennis Kolinski, a program officer at the Illinois Humanities Council, was raised, like Malcolm Rosholt, in central Wisconsin where he took courses in Polish American Studies and also received a B.A. in German at the University of Wisconsin–Stevens Point. In the early 1980s, Kolinski studied in Poland where, in 1984, he earned an M.A. in Slavic ethnography from the Jagiellonian University in Krakow. At the same time he began intensive fieldwork on the wedding customs, music, and religious expressions of Wisconsin's rural Polish Americans. His writings are exemplary for their rich understanding of both Polish and Polish American folklore (see his "The Evolution of Polish American Wedding Customs in Central Wisconsin," in *The Polish Diaspora, Volume II: Selected Essays from the Fiftieth Anniversary International Congress of the Polish Institute of Arts and Sciences of America,* ed. James S. Pula and M. B. Biskupski [Washington, D.C.: East European Monographs, 1993], 35–46; and "Music and Social Life in Early 20th Century Rural Polonia," in *Ethnicity. Culture. City: Polish Americans in the U.S.A., 1870–1950,* ed. Thomas Gladsky, Adam Walaszek, and Malgorzata M. Wawry Kiewicz [Warsaw: Biblioteka Polonijna, Polska Akademia Nauk, Komitet Badamia Polonii, Ofieyna Naukowa, 1998], 62–84).

Reprinted from *Polish-American Studies* (1995): 33–47.

In America of the 1990s, proponents of the separation between Church and State are striving increasingly to restrict religion and spiritually to church buildings and homes. In contrast to this, traditional Slavic consciousness saw the realm of the sacred in the whole world around us. It permeated the entire landscape, finding expression in a multitude of sacred sites, which were frequently marked by shrines and crosses of almost every conceivable type. Polish ethnographer, Tadeusz Seweryn, described them as "the exultation of pious hearts expressed in physical form" (Seweryn 1958: 8) and they were so characteristic of the Polish landscape (Kuncyzn- ska-Irack 1988: 178) that romantic poets liked to call Poland "the land of graves and crosses" (Seweryn 1958: 11).

This tradition, so integral to Polish village culture, also found expression here in the midst of a predominantly secular American countryside. Polish immigrants, who began settling central Wisconsin in 1857 felt a need to similarly sacrilize their surroundings with scores of wayside shrines and crosses, many of which today continue to dot the land. Few people outside of the region are aware of their existence and little is written about them.[1]

Most puzzling, however, is the fact that outside of a relatively small section of central Wisconsin, they are almost nonexistent in most other Polish, or even Catholic settlements. By this, I exclude the numerous examples of grottos and sacred sculptural environments associated with many church and monastery complexes throughout the country. Similar sacral objects can also be found in central Wisconsin, but what differentiates them from sites such as Dickeyville, Wisconsin, is their derivation.[2] Those objects strictly associated with religious institutions were generally conceived by educated clerics who specifically wished to create a spiritual environment for the faithful. The phenomenon of country shrines in central Wisconsin, on the other hand, is a true form of folk art—conceived and created by simple Polish farmers who themselves yearned to give physical expression to their own spiritual feelings, as if to satiate an inner hunger to see the same reflection of the supernatural in their American landscapes as they remembered in the Old Country.

However, any attempt to understand this phenomenon in central Wisconsin must begin with a look at their origin. Poland has been covered for centuries with countless numbers of these devotional monuments. In any given village it was not unusual to find tens, if not scores of them bordering fields, forests, and roads (Kunczynska-Iracka 1988: 178). In them, one could conjure up miniature churches, altars, cyboria, and reliquaries (Kryzysztofowicz 1972: 27), extraordinarily varied in their function, form, and manner of construction (Roczek 1980: 143–44). Most frequently they were erected at crossroads, at the entrance or edge of a village as a border post, on hills, as well as in front of churches and in cemeteries. They were also located at the site of suicides, murders, witch burnings, or heavenly apparitions, near "miraculous" springs, and at gravesites of persons buried in fields or forests (Jackowski 1981: 197; Seweryn 1958: 25).

Just as the form of wayside shrines was extremely varied, so too were they connected with untold numbers of customs and practices, which were still very much alive in the second half of the nineteenth century. They often fulfilled several functions: landmarks or border posts among unmarked fields, spiritual protection against evil forces, as well as objects of unofficial devotion during life's difficult periods (Piwocki 1981: 36). They functioned as places where one prayed, gathered during important moments in the life of the village, bid farewell to army recruits and the dead, sentenced criminals, and took oaths of loyalty (Jackowski 1981: 197).

The origins of Polish shrines and crosses is hidden in the mists of the distant past. It is generally assumed that this tradition had its beginning over a millenium ago before the conversion of the Slavs. A highly probably hypothesis claims that wayside shrines were a Christian sacrilization of pagan rituals and sites. Many elements related to their cultural role and spacial placement can be connected with pre-Christian traditions. Among them was their location near roads and crossings, or in fields and forests, all of which belonged either to ancient categories of sacred space or the magical significance of borders and the center of spaces—beliefs that persisted long into modern times.

Because of the malevolent spirits that supposedly lived there, borders were unsafe. Common belief held that devils and demons had an affinity for crossroads. In addition, the location of shrines next to water and on trees possibly reflected a survival of certain pagan practices and beliefs connected with sacred cults. After the introduction of Christianity, the Church quickly attempted to sacrilize these places (Kunczynska-Iracka 1988: 179; Byston 1980: 244–326).

Nestor also told us in his eleventh-century chronicle that, after cremating their dead, pagan Slavs placed the ashes (and sometimes the bones) in "roofed" ceramic containers that were placed on top of posts to honor the dead (Seweryn 1958: 13). Some present-day shrines are very reminiscent of this, leading ethnographers to speculate strongly that certain Slavic shrines could have had their origin in this pre-Christian custom.

During the sixteenth century, shrines and crosses in Poland were not numerous, but that changed drastically during the seventeenth century, when during the Count-erreformation, following the Council of Trent, they were the most important vehicle for reinforcing Catholicism among the peasantry. From the eighteenth into the nine-teenth century, many more appeared on the village landscape, when alongside their traditional votive role, they also began to assume a secular function as family monu-ments (Kunczynska-Iracka 1988: 179–80).

The physical form of Polish shrines originated from several sources: traditional native architecture, classical forms disseminated by the Church, historical styles, and creativity of anonymous craftsmen (Seweryn 1958: 13). Vertical height was a prominent feature and among the five basic types found in Poland, variants abound. Wooden crosses, standing alone or in groupings are the most numerous. Small roofed boxes, open on one side can be found on trees or buildings. "Column shrines"— round, square, or rectangular columns made from wood, stone, or masonry with a niche open to one or more sides at their summit and capped by a roof—constitute a highly developed form of wayside shrines. Found widely throughout Poland, carved figures of saints placed on a column or base are the simplest and very likely the oldest form. The last type consists of larger shrines, which look like small structures with regular sloped or onion-top roofs (Kunczynska-Iracka 1958: 178; Jackowski 1981: 199–200; Reinfuss 1989: 21, 135–37, 143; Tloczek 1980: 144).

Wayside shrines and crosses played an important devotional role in Polish vil-lage culture as votive offerings in thanksgiving for answered prayers, requests for favors, memorials of important events in the lives of funders, parishes or the country, in addition to many other reasons (Jackowski 1981: 197). They were erected to help in the salvation of the dead, and to protect the living against wandering lost souls or bad spirits (Kunczynska-Iracka 1988: 180). Some drove away spirits, but others were "haunted" themselves (Krzysztowicz 1972: 180).

They provided a place for individual prayer, and in villages without their own church, shrines were often sites for communal prayer. Some of them were used as sites for altars in processions for Corpus Christi and Rogation Days.

Despite the enormous distance separating the two countries, many pre–World War II shrines and crosses in central Wisconsin bear an uncanny resemblance to those in Poland. The origins of those built prior to World War I are particularly difficult to ascertain because few people are still alive who can recall their history with any detail.

Over fifty are still standing today and evidence indicates that there were prob-ably many more in the past. Despite their relatively short history in this country, the shrines and crosses found in central Wisconsin exhibit almost the same degree of variety in function and form as their precursors from the Polish village. They can most frequently be found at crossroads, in addition to sites along the roadside, near churches, in cemeteries, and in later years, next to homes.

We know little about specific reasons for erecting many of the older shrines and crosses. Often a family member today replies that an earlier relative simply wanted to "have it look like he remembered his village in Poland." Most of the funders were considered to be deeply religious.

That the motivations for erecting shrines and crosses, in addition to the beliefs connected with them, must have survived the trip from Polish villages to central Wisconsin is attested to by an account that could have easily been a description from nineteenth century rural Poland. It seems as if a certain crossroad in the rural community of Polonia was haunted—a common belief in Slavic folklore. People in the area still recall hearing of how strange creatures or "devils" would appear and disappear on that corner years ago. Therefore, custom dictated that they erect a cross in order to ward off malevolent spirits. (Shrines are not seen now as a protection against evil spirits, but some people see shrines—such as the one at "Konkol Corner"—as a protection against car accidents.)

Considering that central Wisconsin constitutes a relatively small region its shrines and crosses nonetheless exhibit a broad diversity of form. Those built prior to World War II maintained traditional patterns, virtually identical to those found in Poland. After the war, however, local creativity developed several new forms in favor of the old.

All five basic types of shrines found in Poland are also found in central Wisconsin: crosses, "column shrines," statues placed on a base, forms related to minor sacral architecture, and shrines hung on trees (the only example of this type known to me is one made by my grandmother, that she placed in a pine grove on her farm). In time, regional variants of these types developed, along with the introduction of a new form which appeared around World War II—the grotto.

Of the older types, wooden crosses are the most numerous. Sixteen in relatively good condition remain standing in the region—most located at a crossroads but several also found alongside roads and in cemeteries. Their number must have been much greater at one time because an elderly Polish American gentleman recently related to me that "years ago, there was a cross on every corner." Although this was undoubtedly an exaggeration, there nonetheless must have been many more at one time in order to evoke such a recollection.

Existing crosses have been almost impossible to date—only two have inscribed dates, 1911 and 1939—and estimates of their age have gone back as far as 1875. As a rule, they were quite tall (early crosses may have been considerably taller), but with the passage of time, wood at the base began to rot from the ground moisture around it, and people usually cut them down and sunk them once again in the ground. Some are surrounded by a small fence and they often stand out prominently against the rolling fields as landmarks for the local community.

All of them are based on the Latin cross. The simplest of them consists of squared logs, cut off straight at the ends. On some, ends of the beams are cut off diagonally to form a pyramid shape. In others, the ends are first tapered slightly inward and then rounded off into a circle. Still another variation has ends that are cut in the shape of three perpendicular half-circles to form a type of clover leaf. Usually, a disproportionately small metal figure of the crucified Christ is hung at the

45.1. Wayside cross on the farm of Stanley and Arlene Brezinski. The metal corpus and small cross on the top were brought over by the present owner's grandfather when he emigrated from the Kaszuby region of Poland. Originally much taller, this cross was shortened after the lower portion began to rot. Bevent Township, Marathon County, 1993. Photo: Dennis Kolinski.

point where the beams cross and almost all of them also have a small semi-circular metal roof over the figure.

A few of the crosses were sheathed in sheet metal—either entirely or along the edges—apparently in an effort to protect the wood from the effects of the weather. The primary maintenance of crosses consisted of occasional repaintings, most frequently white, but there are also black crosses and one uniquely done in red and white [the Polish national colors]. As a rule, caretakers decorated shrines and crosses with flowers—artificial on the inside of shrines and real flowers around the base in the summer. In the past, people made the sign of the cross as they passed by and men tipped their hats, but that is rarely seen today.

A very unusual type of cross, which appears to have Orthodox influence, once stood in the cemetery of St. John the Baptist in Heffron, a small isolated Polish community on the southern edge of Portage Country. Instead of a metal figure of Christ, a thin board cut in smooth grooves was attached to the crossing, on which was painted the figure of Christ Crucified, vaguely similar to crucifixes characteristic among the Orthodox. The reason for this may be that Poles who settled in Heffron probably came from a part of Poland different from the "Prussian Poles" in other parts of the county. The point of origin of these Heffron Poles may be Galicja, which was also populated by Orthodox Christians (Rosholt 1959: 129).

The best known type of shrine found in central Wisconsin is the "column shrine" constructed from red brick and capped with a tin roof—in the past they were probably covered with wooden shingles. It has been equally difficult to date most of them with any certainty. Indeed only two can be dated: 1917 and 1934. In the earlier one, the date is engraved in a cement slab surrounding the base of the shrine and the other was ascertained because of its construction from brick that remained following the construction of St. Adalbert's Church in Alban, the date of which is known. The brick used in column shrines is identical to that used to construct Polish farmhouses in the area and therefore they probably appeared about the same time. An expert on historical houses in Portage County states that the earliest Polish red-brick home dates from 1899, therefore the earliest shrine of this type could potentially have appeared shortly after that (Nelson 1993).

Their form is relatively simple—a square column built from red brick, ornamented with modest cornices. Gothic arched openings on three sides open to an interior space in the upper portion of the column. The openings are framed and fitted with glass panes. Access to the interior is gained either through the front window or a rectangular door on the backside of the shrine. They are almost identical to some shrines seen in the Kaszuby region where many central Wisconsin Polish immigrants were born and raised. For example, Adeline Sopa, descendant of the founder of the "Konkol Corner" shrine, saw just such a red-brick shrine in the Kaszubian village of Podjazy, from where her grandparents immigrated.

Although erection of crosses ceased after World War II, shrines continued to be built. Creativity abounded and several new forms appeared. Most were variations of the column shrine, but during the 1940s an entirely new form appeared—the grotto, in which builders attempted to simulate with natural rough-hewn stone and mortar their conception of the grotto at Lourdes, France. With time, stylized variants of this form also appeared.

The custom of erecting shrines remained very much alive, and in addition to individual piety of the builders, a new motivation appeared. In several cases since the early 1970s, the decision to build a shrine reflected dissatisfaction with the late-

45.2. Wayside shrine on the farm of Bernice Jakubek. Constructed of red brick with sheet metal covering the roof, it was probably erected in 1917. This particular shrine east of the village of Polonia is a well-known landmark for the people of that area. It contains statues of the Sacred Heart (patron of the local parish), the Blessed Virgin, and St. Joseph. Corner of highways I and Z, Sharon Township, Portage County, 1993. Photo: Dennis Kolinski.

twentieth-century trends in the American Catholic Church, which have led to the unconscionable gutting of beautiful old churches. People have explicity stated that they wanted to "make up for those things missing these days in churches" by displaying religious figures themselves. Some of them even incorporated statues that were "saved" from modernized churches.

Around 1970 a variation of the column shrine appeared, based on the ingenuity of one rural builder. After placing an old refrigerator with its door and shelves removed on the desired site, he encased it in small round fieldstones mortared together to form a low, rectangular column with a hinged glass door opening at the front. The refrigerator provided a clean white interior for the shrine, while its outside created a convenient form upon which to provide illumination of the interior.

Shrines and crosses in central Wisconsin also played a vital role in the community's religious life. When they were erected, the parish priest usually came to bless them—in some instances, several miles in procession from the church with other parishoners. In days when the church was a long drive away by horse cart, they served as a site where people prayed and sang religious songs. Some crosses located near churches provided the three sites where altars were built for Corpus Christi and Rogation Day processions.

Shrines related to minor sacral architecture are also found in central Wisconsin. One is a small wooden chapel that was originally used for Corpus Christi processions and to store coffins of those who died during the winter. It was built by Jan and Wiktoria Trzebiatowski (Sopa 1993). The other was a red-brick chapel built in the Polonia convent garden by a local farmer in 1911. In time, a special devotion to Mary—known under the name "Our Lady of the Sacred Heart"—developed at the shrine. After news spread of several extraordinary favors through her intercession, many people began to visit the chapel. Their numbers increased such that it was necessary to enlarge the shrine twice and in time, a complex of shrines, built by local farmers, grew around it in the convent garden.

That the existence of wayside shrines and crosses, in addition to their unusual proliferation, in Polish central Wisconsin is unique cannot be denied when compared to the predominantly secular landscape of Protestant America. They are a characteristically Catholic phenomenon which many other ethnic enclaves in rural America, however, did not develop for some reason. Their occurence is so rare in the United States, that I venture to say that most Americans live out their entire life without the slightest realization that such things exist within our borders.[3]

After considerable investigation (as well as a certain degree of luck), I did discover other sites which had wayside shrines or crosses but they were few and not as prolific as in central Wisconsin. Examples can be found in Polish settlements near Pulaski, Wisconsin, and Warsaw, North Dakota, as well as the Czech settlement near Stangelville, Wisconsin, and the Belgian settlement northeast of Green Bay, Wisconsin.[4] It may be that they are unknown to us and can be found in other Polish locales, but if others exist, I venture to state that they are not numerous.

We are left then with the quandary of why shrines and crosses appeared in certain locales and not in others. With little hesitation one can claim, that with one

45.3. This yard shrine, belonging to Florian and Dolores Gorecki, is a post–World War II variant of the column shrine constructed from local fieldstone mortared around an old refrigerator, which provided an interior space lit for statues. Peter Trzebiatowski, the creator of this new style of shrine, seen at work here, has constructed numerous such shrines throughout the region. Grand Avenue (Highway 66) Rosholt, Portage County, 1987. Photo: Dennis Kolinski.

exception, their existence in America is closely linked with Slavic settlements—particularly Polish. This, however, still does not answer all of our questions related to their origin, because when looking solely at Polish sites, there are exceptionally few. Even within the boundaries of central Wisconsin's extensive Polish settlement, shrines and crosses are not equally distributed.

The one common thread that appears to link all of these sites is an unusually strong and prominent religious factor in the history of all of them. In central Wisconsin it was Father Józef Dabrowski, whose untiring and deep faith triumphed over a violent local church conflict and nurtured a significant rural center of Polish Catholicism at Polonia. In Pulaski, the Polish Franciscans established a monastery, which flourished for years, and the Belgians established a shrine on the site where the Blessed Virgin appeared to a young Belgian farm girl in the mid-1850s. In all of these cases, the tradition of erecting wayside shrines and crosses was pre-existing deep within the heritage of the early settlers. What they needed was a stimulus—something that would reawaken an internal need to erect these "exultation[s] of pious hearts expressed in physical form" like the ones they left back home. Starting a new life in the wilderness was difficult and nonessentials were easily put off. Apparently, many Catholic immigrant communities did not receive an adequate degree of personal religious development during the early years of settlement in order to stimulate an internal need to build shrines, and a custom that originally played an integral role in their culture eventually withered and died forever.

This article is a revised version of a paper delivered at the annual meeting of the Polish American Historical Association in San Francisco, California, January 7, 1994.

Notes

1. The only reference to them can be found in newspaper articles written by local reporters: John Anderson, "Konkol Corners," *Stevens Point Journal* (September 24, 1988); Bonnie Bressers, "Three farms south of the shrine . . . ," *Stevens Point Journal* (date missing). This essay, therefore, is the first comprehensive study ever made of them. Information which forms the basis of this article was collected from field research in central Wisconsin in 1987, 1988, and 1993.

2. The major examples in the Upper Midwest are large grotto complexes in West Bend, Iowa, Dickeyville, Wisconsin, and Rudolph, Wisconsin. All three of these were the work of a local parish priest. An excellent book which outlines the history of grotto building, as well as many examples of similar folk art throughout the region, was prepared as a catalogue for an exhibit at the School of the Art Institute of Chicago. Lisa Stone and Jim Zanzi, *Sacred Spaces and Other Places: A Guide to Grottos and Sculptural Environments in the Upper Midwest* (Chicago: The School of the Art Institute of Chicago Press, 1993).

3. The "Mary in a bathtub" shrine is another manifestation of the shrine phenomenon, which deserves further consideration. Although it is less unique than the other types of shrines discussed here, it belongs to the same category of religious expression. Usually, little creativity is displayed with these types of yard shrines, but in essence they fall within the category of traditional Polish shrines in which figures are placed on columns or raised bases.

They can be found widely in Polish American communities, but also in other Catholic communities.

4. I personally conducted research on Pulaski shrines in 1988 and read an undated article about them from the *Pulaski News,* which was shown to me by a local resident. These shrines are also built from brick but differ considerably in shape and treatment from those in central Wisconsin. A few cemetery crosses can also be seen. A number of Polish wooden crosses can be found in North Dakota; see Theodore B. Pedeliski, "Slavic Peoples," in *Plains Folk: North Dakota's Ethnic History,* ed. William Sherman and Playford Thorson (Fargo: North Dakota State University, 1986), p. 298. This information was also corroborated by a conversation in December 1993 with Ed Gudajtes of Minto, North Dakota. A sole survivor of several stone Czech wayside crosses used for Rogation Day processions stands near Stangelville in eastern Wisconsin. See *A Visitor's Guide to Wisconsin's Ethnic Settlement Trail* (Sheboygan: Wisconsin's Ethnic Settlement Trail, Inc., 1993), p. 45. Additional information was obtained by letter from Denmark, Wisconsin, resident Raymond Selner. About nineteen Belgian wayside shrines, in addition to stone and mortar grottos, can still be seen in Door, Kewaunee, and Brown Counties of northeastern Wisconsin. They are the only non-Slavic examples that have surfaced and vary significantly in appearance from those in central Wisconsin and Pulaski—striking one more as unassuming small white wooden sheds near the roadside. See Betty Althaus, "Belgium's Chapels Experience Rebirth and Remodeling," *Compass* (date missing); and *A Visitor's Guide to Wisconsin's Ethnic Settlement Trail* [ibid.], pp. 46–47.

Sources

Byston, Jan Stanislaw. 1980. "Tajemnice drog i granic," *Tematy, które mi odradzano.* Warsaw: Panstwowy Instytut Wydawniczy.

Jackowski, Aleksander. 1981. "Sztuka ludowa," *Etnografia Polski: Przemiany kultury ludowej,* vol. II. Wroclaw: Zakłady Narodowy imienia Ossolinskich Wydawnictwo.

Krzysztofowicz, Stefania. 1972. *O sztuce ludowej w Polsce.* Warsaw: Wiedza Powszechna.

Kunczynska-Iracka. 1988. *Sztuka ludowa w Polsce.* Warsaw: Wydawnictwo Arkady.

Nelson, Wendell. November, 1993. Conversation with the author. Nelsonville, Wisconsin.

Piwocki, Ksawery. 1981. "Drewno w ludowej rzezbie figuarlnej," *Drewno w polskiej architekturze i rzezbie ludowej.* Wrocław: Zakłady Narodowy imienia Ossolinskich Wydawnictwo.

Reinfuss, Roman. 1989. *Ludowa rzezba kamienna w Polsce.* Warsaw: Zakłady Narodowy imienia Ossolinskich Wydawnictwo.

Rosholt, Malcolm. 1959. *Our County, Our Story: Portage County, Wisconsin.* Stevens Point, Wisconsin.

Seweryn, Tadeusz. 1958. *Kapliczki i krzyze w Polsce.* Warsaw: Instytut Wdydawniczy PAX.

Sopa, Adeline (grandchild of Jan and Wiktoria Trzebiatowski). November, 1993. Interview with the author.

Tloczek, Ignacy. 1980. *Polskie budownictwo drewniane.* Wrocław: Zakłady Narodowy imienia Ossolinksich Wydawnictwo.

46

"We Made 'Em to Fit Our Purpose": The Northern Lake Michigan Fishing Skiff Tradition

Janet C. Gilmore

The proverbial "cultural baggage" of immigrants to Wisconsin sometimes literally included such handmade folk artifacts as items of clothing, specialized tools, and esoteric musical instruments. More often newcomers arrived with little more than know-how. This was certainly true when it came to the design, construction, and use of houses, barns, and boats.

Wisconsin's cultural landscape testifies to the rich folk knowledge of assorted ethnic builders, and their work has attracted a succession of architectural historians, landscape architects, cultural geographers, and folklorists. In the 1930s, Robert M. Neal of Mineral Point began efforts to research and preserve the homes of Cornish immigrants that replicate their old-country dwellings. (See Neal, "Pendarvis, Trelawny, and Polperro: Shake Rag's Cornish Houses," *Wisconsin Magazine of History* 30 [1946]: 391–401.) Soon after, Richard W. E. Perrin, an architectural historian, called attention to the state's ethnic folk structures in a series of articles culminating in *Historic Wisconsin Architecture: A Survey of Pioneer Architecture, 1835–1870* (Milwaukee: Milwaukee Public Museum, 1962).

In the 1960s William H. Tishler, a landscape architect at the University of Wisconsin, led students in a project to design an outdoor museum of Wisconsin's ethnic folk architecture. The eventual result was the State Historical Society's Old World Wisconsin, the nation's finest outdoor museum of European American folk architecture. Tishler continues to study folk architecture throughout the state (for a succinct introduction, see his "Built From Tradition: Wisconsin's Rural Ethnic Folk Architecture," *Wisconsin Academy Review* 30:2 [March 1984]:14–18). He has also, especially in collaboration with cultural geographer Arnold Alanen, extended the consideration of discrete folk architectural forms to include the traditional ways in which they contribute to Wisconsin's larger cultural landscape of farmsteads, communities, and regions. (See, for example, Alanen and Tishler's study of Oulu Township in Bayfield County, "Finnish Farmstead Organization in Old and New World Settings," *Journal of Cultural Geography* 1:2 [1980]: 66–81; also *Historic Preservation and the Cultural Landscape: An Emerging Land Use Planning Concern,* ed. William H. Tishler [Madison: University of Wisconsin, 1977].)

The well-deserved attention given Wisconsin's ethnic folk buildings, farmsteads, and landscapes, however, has been paralleled by a general neglect of the state's maritime material folk culture. Part of the nation's "north coast," Wisconsin has a longstanding fishery not only on Lakes Michigan and Superior, but also on the Mississippi River. The region's commercial fishers are overwhelmingly descendants of prior seasonal fishers, "jacks-of-all-trades" who typically also logged and farmed. Learning from one another, they have also combined elements from the maritime traditions of their ethnic ancestors, whether Belgian, Finnish, French, German, New England Yankee, Norwegian, Ojibwe, Polish, or Swedish.

Janet C. Gilmore's pioneering study of skiffs made on the Wisconsin and Michigan sides of Green Bay draws upon extensive field research with the commercial fishers who build and use them. A descendant of Norwegian American shipbuilders, Gilmore currently works out of Mount

Horeb, Wisconsin, as an independent folklorist. Since the mid-1970s she has conducted research among commercial fishers on the Great Lakes, the Mississippi River, the Oregon Coast, and Puget Sound. Beyond examining their work skills, artifacts, and foodways, Gilmore has also illuminated the ways in which image affects the "social standing and political clout" of commercial fishers in her "Fisherman Stereotypes: Sources and Symbols," in "Maritime Identity," ed. Laurier Turgeon, a special issue of *Canadian Folklore* 12:2 (1990):17–38.

Reprinted from *The Old Traditional Way of Life: Essays in Honor of Warren E. Roberts*, ed. Robert E. Walls and George H. Schoemaker (Bloomington, Ind.: Trickster Press, 1989), 58–78.

Commercial fishing is an occupation fraught with change. Experienced fishers know that the abundance of fish ebbs and flows cyclically, but they cannot predict the exact amounts they will be able to catch each year. Likewise they know that fish do not return at precisely the same times nor to exactly the same fishing spots year after year. When the fish are plentiful, they may not be worth much on a glutted market; when scarcer but more valuable, the weather can unexpectedly undo that rare good day of fishing by swamping the boat, dumping the catch, and perhaps destroying the fishing boat and gear as well.

Because of the unpredictability of the business, most commercial fishers follow several kinds of fish and employ different varieties of equipment. If one kind of fish is not plentiful, perhaps another will be; if one kind of gear is not working, perhaps another will, and if one location is not productive at the moment, perhaps another is. Before the days of state-mandated fishing districts, Great Lakes fishermen, like nomads, went where the fish were, over the lakes and across state lines. Louis Ruleau of Cedar River, Michigan, recalls Lake Erie pound-netters coming to the northern Lake Michigan shore in the 1940s to try their luck (Interview 1988). Northern Lake Michigan fishermen like the late "Pep" Nylund fished out of Oscoda on Lake Huron, as well as along the Wisconsin, Illinois, and lower Michigan shores of Lake Michigan (Interview 1986) (fig. 46.1.). Tom Ruleau of Bark River, Michigan, formerly migrated over the Upper Peninsula in the fall with his father and uncles to fish herring and whitefish at Big Bay on Lake Superior (Interview 1988). His cousins, Louis and Bob Ruleau of Cedar River, built their first steel pound-net skiff in 1958 in order to pack a boat in their semi and bounce it down the highway to Two Rivers, Wisconsin, where they could take good advantage of the earlier arrival and higher prices of smelt in that area; their wooden skiff would not have endured the trip (Louis Ruleau interview 1988).

Wherever they went, fishers encountered other fishers from other Great Lakes locations, observed their equipment and working methods, and picked up ideas. Because of the questing nature of commercial fishermen, pound nets and accompanying pound-net boats spread with and among fishermen from New England to Lake Erie, and by the 1850s, to upper Lake Michigan (Smith and Snell 1891: 26, 72). At one time they were one of the most prevalent types of fishing gear used throughout the Great Lakes, and Green Bay was "the center of the pound-net fishery" on Lake Michigan during the late 1800s (Smith and Snell 1891: 72–73). Subsequently the gill net and the more complicated but less labor-intensive trap net have overshad-

46.1. The western Great Lakes region.

owed the pound net in popularity for capturing whitefish, the commercial fisher's chief quarry. Yet over the years, fishers in the Green Bay area of Lake Michigan have persisted in making and employing pound nets, most often to capture prolific and low-valued species such as alewives, smelt, and suckers. Some few Wisconsin Lake Superior and Lake Michigan fishers, like Dennis Hickey of Bailey's Harbor, Wisconsin, remain dedicated to using the gear to entrap whitefish, claiming that it injures the fish less and thus produces a better quality catch than the other types of nets do (Hickey interview 1986).

In spite of the flux and experimentation traditional in the fishing business, and despite radical changes in equipment and the character of the fisheries wrought by machines, materials of the industrial era, and legislation during the past century,

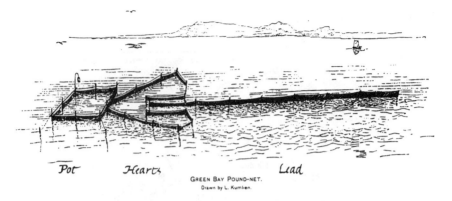

Fig. 46.2. Pound net typical in the Green Bay area of Lake Michigan in the 1880s.
Drawing by L. Kumlien reprinted from Smith and Snell 1891: plate XXI.

pound-net fishing equipment has remained remarkably constant. A semi-permanent fish-impounding device, the northern Lake Michigan pound net (pronounced "pond net") consists of three main components—"pot," "hearts," and "lead"—staked in place by wooden poles imbedded in the lake bottom (fig. 46.2).[1] The vertical sections of the net are positioned additionally by floats on the top lines and lead weights on the bottom lines. Composed of netting on the bottom and all four sides, the giant rectangular "pot" is open at the top. It measures ten to sixty feet deep, twenty to forty feet wide, and thirty to forty feet long. A long 1,000- to 1,200-foot fence-like "lead" of netting stretches from the pot shoreward to lead the fish to the pot and into it through a tunnel. In case the fish turn away from the pot, additional fences of netting, called "hearts," extend from the tunnel opening to confuse the fish and send them back toward the pot. Fishers tailor the dimensions and mesh-sizes of the nets according to the type of fish they seek, the depth and character of the fishing location, and the lengths of their boats.

The related trap net operates on the same principle and is similar in configuration and size. However, the tunnel and hearts are more intricately fashioned; the "trap," the equivalent of the pound-net pot, is entirely enclosed in mesh, top, bottom, and sides; the hearts are also covered and floored with netting; and the entire construction is held taut with lines and anchors instead of wooden stakes. While trickier in design, the trap net has several advantages over the pound net: it can be set on rocky lake bottom where stakes cannot be implanted; it can be pulled up by machine instead of by hand; the prey is protected from predators (birds); and the gear is hidden better in the water from competitors and poachers. As its use has expanded in the past two decades for catching the major commercial species of fish, fishers and specialized net-builders have rapidly refined its design.[2]

For both kinds of net, fishermen employ two boats, generally a larger one with greater power and carrying capacity to get to the nets and carry the catch, and a smaller one with much less power, which can be paddled or rowed, to tend the lines.

To work the pound net, fishers generally place the smaller boat, but sometimes the larger one instead,[3] inside the pot; they lift the bottom of the pot up by hand as they move the boat along, "bag" the fish in one end, and scoop the fish out of the net into the larger boat (cf. Hornell 1950: 86; von Brandt 1984: 190). With the trap net, fishers use the larger boat to lift the trap up over the boat deck so they can open up the trap and scoop or dump out the fish into the big boat.

A hundred years ago, the two pound-net boats were built of wood, simply and economically (Chapelle 1951: 50), "by both boat-builders and fishermen, without plans or models" (Chapelle 1951: 128). In the Green Bay area, according to pound-netter Richard Grabowski of Menominee, Michigan:

Most of the fishermen made their own boats, years ago. Most all the old timers, they always made their own boats. . . . The ones that had money had the carpenters come in and help them. . . . just plain carpenters. . . . anybody that fished could get a hold of any carpenter that would. . . . A carpenter, he can cut better fits, you know, if he's used to it, and do a lot nicer work, than a guy that isn't used to it. (Interview 1988)

Both the larger "pound boat" and the smaller pound-net dinghy were constructed in roughly the same shape as their New England sharpie relatives (Collins 1891: 25–26; Chapelle 1951: 104–33, 352–54). They were open boats with a sharp bow, slight flare to the sides, a square stern with a raked transom which was quite wide in the larger boat and proportionately narrower in the dinghy, and a flat bottom which had "a good deal of camber to the after part" (Collins 1891: 26) (see figs. 46.3 and 46.4). The larger boat was built to sail, and averaged twenty to thirty-four feet in length, seven to twelve feet in beam, and two-and-a-half to four feet in depth on Lakes Erie, Michigan, and Superior (Collins 1891: 26; cf. Chapelle 1951: 126–31, 354; and Chapelle 1976: 302–3). Fish Commission field worker Mr. L. Kumlien reported in 1880 that the pound boats along the northern Lake Michigan shore from the Peshtigo River to the Cedar River (Menominee area) averaged twenty-two feet by seven feet and were steered by a long oar (Collins 1891: 26). The dinghy averaged sixteen to eighteen feet long and five feet wide at the fullest part (Collins 1891: 28); it was built to be rowed or, according to Richard Grabowski, sculled with one oar that passed through the transom (Interview 1988) (fig. 46.5).

Contemporary Menominee-area fishermen, David Behrend, Richard Grabowski, and Louis Ruleau, then in their fifties, recall working with the smaller wooden boats into the 1950s and '60s (Interviews 1988). Independently, each described a procedure for building the "skiffs" that is virtually identical to the one Howard Chapelle outlined for the sailing sharpie/flat-bottomed skiff class of the American bateau model (Chapelle 1951: 46–48). They were built upside down around a jig-like frame. First the side planking was bent around the frame and nailed to the bow stem and stern transom; softwood planking would not be steamed first, whereas hardwood planking would. Each side and the stern consisted of two or three wide (12"), usually pine or cedar planks placed edge to edge lengthwise (cf. Chapelle 1951: 128). Side planking was generally ⅝ " to 1" thick (1 ⅛ " planed down to 1" according to Grabowski), while the stern was composed of thicker 1½ " to 2" boards.

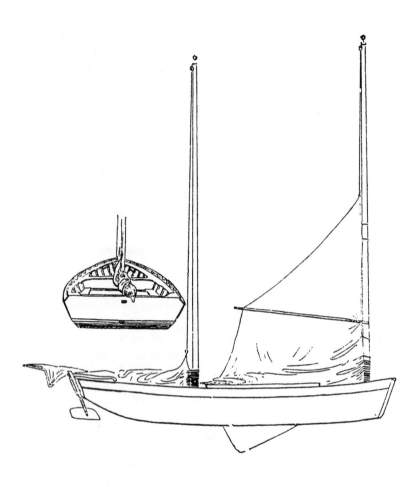

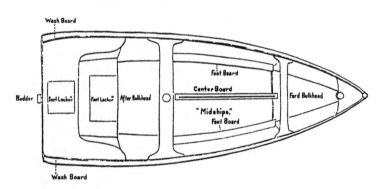

46.3. Plans of an 1880s pound-net boat probably more typical of the lower lakes than of northern Lake Michigan. Drawing by Henry W. Elliott reprinted from Smith and Snell 1891: plate VI.

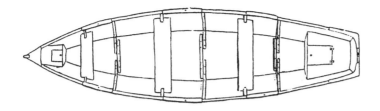

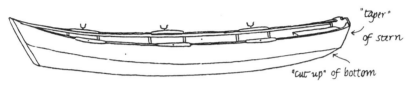

46.4. Plans of an 1880s pound-net dinghy drawn by Henry W. Elliott and reprinted from Smith and Snell 1891: plate VIII. The Green Bay area dinghies were roughly the same shape, but the positioning of the thwarts (seats) appears to have been somewhat different and the interior framing substantially different, more like that in the pound boat shown in figure 46.3.

The straight, raked bow stem, carved of a single piece of white oak, was rabbeted so that the butt-ends of the side planks fit into the grooves on each side.[4] Louis Ruleau recalls that:

. . . they whittled the bow stems out, you know, they were a vee-shaped piece of wood, and notched. They cut in there, I remember them chiseling that out. And then they fit the boards in that so that was a smooth piece. . . . so that this here bow stem took the, if you hit anything, you know I mean that was the whole bow, that was one solid chunk of usually oak. (Interview 1988)

After the side and stern planking had been installed, white oak ribs were inserted every twelve inches to hold the planks together. A strip of white oak was steamed, fitted, and nailed lengthwise to the ribs inside the "gunnels" (gunwales), the uppermost part of each side (fig. 46.5). Another strip, which Grabowski called the "bilge keelson" and Chapelle terms the "chine log," was similarly installed along the ribs inside the bottom of each side. The bottom planking, also of pine or cedar but sometimes 2″ thick (and usually no more than 6″ wide), was laid crosswise, not lengthwise, and nailed to the sides, the two "bilge keelsons," and additional blocks of oak that had been inserted between the ribs and keelsons at the bottom. The bottom planking was sometimes further secured lengthwise, down the center, with a 4″ wide, 1″ thick plank inside, and a 4″ × 1″ to 2″ plank outside, which was sometimes rabbeted to the bow stem.[5] According to Louis Ruleau, the outer "center board" additionally acted as a keel and kept the caulking in the bottom seams. Seats placed

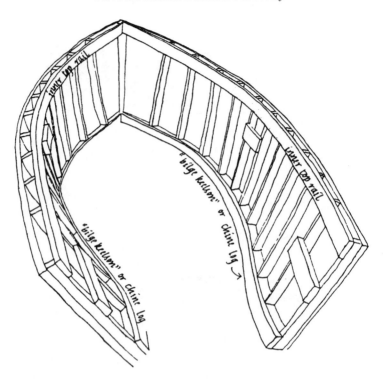

inner gun rail

bilge keelson" or chine log

inner gun rail

"bilge keelson" or chine log

46.5. Interior framework of wooden pound-net skiff built and used in the Menominee, Michigan, area. The illustration was drawn from a slide of a skiff deteriorating on the shore of Lake Michigan's Green Bay. The stern transom had disappeared, leaving the side planking and attached frames to open out; the bottom was covered inside with a dense mat of leaves; and the bow framework was obscured inside with a heavy piece of driftwood. In other words, some drawing details are conjectural, and the illustration does not represent the boat as it once was, when fit for fishing.

at the stern, in the bow, and across the center for rowing, supplied additional stiffen-ing; Grabowski called the seats "thwarts," pronouncing the term like "thoughts." All seams were generally caulked except sometimes not between the bottom planks where the swelling of the wood as it soaked up water often sufficed to close up the gaps. Louis Ruleau remembers forged iron square nails as the earliest fastenings, and in later years builders switched to galvanized steel—galvanized screw nails according to Behrend, galvanized eight-penny nails according to Grabowski.

As engines became available, fishermen abandoned sail power and installed inboards in the pound boats and, eventually, outboards in the skiffs. The inboard took up space, added weight, and strained the flat-bottomed build, but it provided the opportunity to fish deeper waters farther from shore more safely. Fishermen be-gan preferring features more characteristic of the bigger, sturdier gill-net tugs; they installed decking and cabins and adopted hulls with slight vee-bottoms and longer, beamier, deeper dimensions. Few pound-net fishermen continued to fish with the open pound boat, but all retained the open skiff. When non-tribal Michigan fishermen were required to switch from gill-netting to trap-netting gear during the 1970s (Kuchenberg 1978: 88–94), many purchased existing pound-netting, trap-netting, and gill-netting "rigs"—mostly steel vessels built after World War II, often obtained from the lower lakes—and subsequently modified them. Many of today's trap-net boats are modified pound-net rigs, and the same kind of big boat is often used for both kinds of fishing. As in current pound-netting, an open skiff remains an integral part of the rig.

Fisherman embraced steel construction and began replacing first the larger wooden boats after World War II, and later the smaller wooden skiffs, with steel versions. Compared to wood, the steel was "much more durable, didn't need all this maintenance," exclaimed Louis Ruleau (Interview 1988). The non-specialized builders and self-taught welders found the material more forgiving to work, and the "shell" construction even easier to execute in steel.[6] Welder and occasional boatbuilder Curtis Folstad of Menominee explained:

I could cut these pieces out and put them together and shape it up, and if I didn't like it I could change it real easy, you know, taper a little bit more here. . . . If I didn't like it, then I'd just cut a few tacks of weld and lay it down and cut it out a little different. It was easy to change the shape if you didn't like it, or if you didn't have what you wanted. I could change it easy. (Interview 1988)

Whereas the wooden boats "had to be absolutely perfect," according to Richard Grabowski, in order to resist the abuses of work and water, the steel ones would work well even when their shapes and joinery were not true (Interview 1988). Concluded Louis Ruleau, "they weren't real sharp-looking, but they were usable" (Interview 1988).

In order to repair, modify, and build the steel vessels, most northern Lake Michigan fishermen began to acquire "electric" or "stick" welding equipment and skills, often in that order, during the 1940s and 1950s—shortly after electrical service was extended into the area (Louis Ruleau interviews 1986 and 1988). In recent years a few have graduated to more modern "wire-feed" equipment. Richard Grabowski, who picked up the rudiments of welding from a co-worker while temporarily working at the local shipyard, Marinette Marine, in 1950, justifies his acquisition of the equipment this way:

I bought that welder and that acetylene torch. . . . in the fishing business you pr't' near got to have, you got to have that stuff, because you couldn't afford to have it hired all the time. And if you break down right on the job, you got your own stuff to do it with, you know. So you couldn't think of calling a welder out here to weld a patch on a boat, you know, it'd cost you too much. (Interview 1988)

And farther up the shore at Fairport, "Junior" Vetter echoes this sentiment:

You just buy a machine. You have to. You can't afford to go to town every time you want something welded or something breaks, you know. (Interview 1988)

For the same reasons of economy, speed, and self-sufficiency that they had often built their own wooden skiffs, many fishermen in turn began building their own steel skiffs, basing them directly on wooden forerunners. Similarly today, fishermen base new steel skiffs on existing ones. As in building the wooden skiffs and in acquiring welding skills and equipment, they continue to build steel skiffs because it is cheaper to do the work themselves than to hire someone else to do it. Richard Grabowski reused two sheets of steel formerly engaged in making pressboard at a local plant to build his skiff for well under $100 (Interview 1988). Bob and Louis Ruleau built their first skiff of two new 8' × 4' sheets of steel for a total of $130 (Interview 1988). The same amount of steel purchased new today would cost around $500, but a custom-built steel skiff might run well over $1,000, and there are few custom welders in the region who will readily take on a boatbuilding project for just any commercial fisherman.

The procedure is also perceived to be relatively simple, as Fairport trap-netter Wayne Seaman says, "Nothing to build a boat, 'cause all you got to do is get some idea what you want, then with welding and a steel torch, you can do anything . . ." (Interview 1988). Armed with basic welding skills and equipment, and steel plates easily obtained and custom cut at a local steel supply house, machine shop, or boilerworks, a fisherman—usually with a helper to lift and position the steel plates— takes about three to five days to build a skiff from scratch. Working alone at a less intense pace, some spread the job over ten days to two weeks.

Fishermen also build the small boats because each wants something a little different, and accordingly, they do not make the best clients. Menominee-area pound-netter David Behrend reasoned:

. . . each individual fisherman will have his own idea what he wants, and if you built it for him it would be nothing but a giant headache because he'd be standing over your shoulder telling you, "I want this, I want that, I don't want what you're doing." Best thing to do is to let him build his own boat. (Interview 1988)

They know what they want in a skiff from their own experiences, observations, and trial and error. Trap-netter Ben Peterson of Fairport states his capability to design and build the skiffs this way:

I kept watching and looking around, and I watched other guys's boats and I seen how they were holding up, and then we got in their boats and seen how tippy they were and whatnot, and finally, one day, I said, "Well, I think I can build a boat." (Interview 1988)

Pound- and trap-netter Tom Ruleau of Bark River, " . . . more or less went by the ones my uncle had and that stuff there, we kind of got an idea from them there and kind of made them similar to them" (Interview 1988). Basically, says Richard Grabowski, "If you know what a boat looks like, and you've done any welding at all, you just got to, you got to shape it like you got in your mind, whatever you want, the way you want it. You cut it accordingly" (Interview 1988).

With all the differences in opinion and experiences among their builders, natu-

46.6. "Bill" Seaman's steel trap-net skiff which he built from a pattern he made of a Folstad skiff, Fairport, Michigan, 1988. Photo: Janet C. Gilmore.

rally modern-day skiffs vary quite a bit in construction details—materials, building method, exact dimensions and shapes—just as the wooden ones of days past did.[7] Fishermen have variously tried ten- , twelve- , fourteen- , and sixteen-gauge steel, but most are leaning toward the heavier gauges, ten-gauge especially.[8] As with the wooden skiffs, some have used heavier gauge material for the stern piece and bottom (ten-gauge, for example) than for the sides (twelve-gauge, for example).

Fishermen also do not follow the same methods of replicating existing skiffs. David Behrend simply encased his wooden pound boat in steel, later extracting the wooden planks when he decided to enlarge the vessel (Interview 1988). Some make a full-scale pattern from an existing boat, placing cardboard against each plate (side, stern, [bow], bottom) and trimming it to the proper shape. In Fairport, Bill Seaman built his skiff (fig. 46.6) from a pattern he made in this manner from a Folstad skiff owned by fellow fisherman Peter Hermess (Interview 1988); in turn Jeff Harvey and "Junior" Vetter made a pattern from Seaman's skiff in order to build theirs (Interview 1988). Richard Grabowski (fig. 46.7), however, took key dimensions off a wooden pound boat by placing steel rods on the boat at appropriate intervals along the bottom and sides, and cutting each rod a few inches longer; he first lofted the rods into a skeleton of the boat before cutting the steel plates according to the shapes he had defined (Interview 1988).[9] Still others, like Ben Peterson, figure measurements from internalized models:

46.7. Richard Grabowski's steel pound-net skiff, which he fashioned directly
after a wooden pound boat, Menominee, Michigan, 1988. Photo: Janet C. Gilmore.

I bought all the steel that I figured I needed. I just kind of drew a plan up in my head and
decided what I needed and wrote down dimensions. And I got the steel home and I drew up
a pattern on the floor of my dad's garage, on what I had wanted. . . . I had the measurements
in my mind, what I wanted, how I wanted it. (Interview 1988)

Most commonly, as in the wooden skiff building tradition, fishermen build the
boat upside down, shaping the sides around a jig-like wooden frame. Welder and
occasional boat-builder Lyle Thill of the Fairport area explains:

First of all you make a form out of wood, you know, especially for the center of it and for the
stern so you will know that when you get your two sides made, how to pull it into shape, what
shape you want. (Interview 1988)

Says Tom Ruleau of the process:

. . . the shape it more or less falls right into place when you kind of bend it and that stuff
there, and bring it in, they pretty much shape theirself. . . . You got an idea what it's going to
be like, you know, and you pretty much know. (Interview 1988)

As in the wooden skiff building tradition, they install ribbing or stiffening after
the side plates have been shaped and tacked together. Thill continues:

. . . then you put in the framework afterwards, for your ribs inside and your vee-bottom. You
build these upside down, you know. Tack-weld it all together first, get the whole boat tack-
welded, and then you start your welding. . . . (Interview 1988)

Richard Grabowski, however, invoked the larger gill-net tug-building tradition by
first shaping a skeleton of steel rods, upside down, and then welding the side, stern,
and bottom plates onto this framework (Interview 1988). Similarly Ben Peterson
reports that he set up his steel ribbing first, upside down, then put on the bottom,
sides, stern and bow pieces (Interview 1988). And Jeff Harvey and "Junior" Vetter

built their vee-bottom skiff upright, tacking the four bottom plates together and bending the entire structure with a hand-operated winch called a "come-along" (a cinched chain) "until it shapes how you want it." They then added on the sides and inserted the ribbing later (Interview 1988).

The actual dimensions and shapes of the skiffs vary widely according to the individual's preferences and work habits, just as Richard Grabowski explained of the wooden boats:

Everybody had a little different idea, they maybe, Williams wanted his built this way, a little longer, a little narrower. See, these boats were all built for what you wanted to use them for, you know. (Interview 1988)

Indeed, increasingly the variations fall into one of two categories of use: pound-netting or trap-netting.

Skiffs built for pound-netting (fig. 46.7) bear the strongest resemblance in size and shape to the earlier wooden pound dinghies. Some pound-netters have even kept to the sixteen-by-five-foot average recorded for Green Bay skiffs in the 1880s. Most, however, have modified or built the boats wider, as wide as six to seven feet, proportionately increasing their beam slightly. As Louis Ruleau explains:

We made 'em to fit our purpose, for lifting these pound nets in. It was a lot nicer lifting in a larger—sixteen foot they were by six foot—and they were real stable, you know, you could get three, four guys on one side and they didn't lean down very much. . . . (Interview 1988)

With changes in licensing procedures for tenders, most Michigan pound-netters have also lengthened the skiffs beyond the former sixteen-foot limit to as long as nineteen to twenty feet;[10] the greater lengths ease the use of wider pots that can capture more fish (cf. Taylor 1982: 67).

The flat bottom has remained particularly well-suited for the typical pound-net operation, which is worked just off the beach for smelt or in the mouths of shallow rivers for redhorse suckers. The shape rides high even when loaded and thus allows working in the shallow shoal waters; it also gives the vessel good carrying capacity for the typically large loads of fish (cf. Taylor 1982: 67). "It carries a big load, and for smelts, that's what we need," confirms Louis Ruleau (Interview 1988). Coupled with adequate beam, the flat bottom additionally affords a measure of stability for working from the boat (cf. Taylor 1982: 67).

While pound-netters have also retained the sharp—"peak-ed" they say—bow of the wooden boats, some have curved the forefoot of the bow stem so that the boat will tow more easily (ride up instead of dive) and move more effortlessly over the lines into the pound-net pot. Also to improve the shape's towing performance, some have added one to three keels to the bottom. Finally, in addition to enlarging the boat, widening it proportionately, and making small adjustments for improved performance, most pound-net fishermen have omitted all or most ribbing. They have found that a top rail of 1″ diameter steel pipe provides the necessary stiffening; an inner rail that some position for pinning netting while working the net gives additional support.

At the same time in the 1950s, '60s, and '70s that fishermen were building their own steel skiffs, some preferred to purchase them custom-made. In particular, Curtis Folstad of Menominee and his chief welder, Bernie Barker, turned out dozens—some custom built, some stock built—for fishermen all over the Great Lakes (Interview 1988). As a youngster, Folstad had also built wooden skiffs of roughly the pound-net dinghy shape and size, but he applied the bottom planking lengthwise and fitted the boat with ribs that extended across the bottom from side to side—a construction that some area fishermen disliked because the planks tended to splinter when they hit the beach, and their replacement took more work (Louis Ruleau 1988). Later, similarly, Folstad built full ribs across the bottoms of his steel skiffs, applied a keel, and eventually gave the bottom a slight "V" toward the bow, mimicking features of both sportfishing boats and the bigger wooden vee- and round-bottomed fishing tugs used in the area. Partly in response to his customers, many of whom were trap-netters, he also created more work space in the bow, lessening its sharpness.

When non-tribal Michigan gill-netters suddenly needed trap-netting skiffs in the 1970s, they employed existing ones, the flat-bottomed pound-net variety or Folstad's slight-vee and ribbed type. Over the past decade or two, they have used, modified, and worn out these skiffs, and built new ones incorporating features that work best for their purposes. Elements of the Folstad design have proven particularly workable.

Trap-netters have retained roughly the same length to beam ratio for their boats (figs. 46.6 and 46.8) as in the pound-net skiffs, but they prefer slightly shorter lengths, twelve to sixteen feet, with a four- to five-foot beam. With the heavy-gauge steel, the smaller shape guarantees a sturdy build that can take more abuse than the pound-net skiff, but that remains comparatively light enough for two men to lift on board the bigger boat when necessary. Lyle Thill reasons:

. . . these boats got to be pretty seaworthy out there . . . they use them for setting anchors all the time, for the trap net anchors, and there's two guys in the boat all the time, they use them in the fall of the year for pulling trap net anchors. And if they're not sturdy little boats—and they got to be built light—you know, it could mean somebody's life, if they weren't built sufficient. (Interview 1988)

Because the trap-net skiffs are towed behind the bigger boat for greater distances and at much higher speeds than the pound-net skiffs are, they take a real beating, pounding in the waves from the big boat's wake. Trap-netters insist on plenty of well-braced ribbing, that extends down the sides and across the bottom, to keep the bottom well secured. To keep the boat from pounding and darting back and forth over the waves, they also favor a keel and a slight vee-bottom. Explains "Junior" Vetter, "it breaks the sea, you don't bam all the time with it, throws the waves off to the side. When you're towing it, it follows you straight down the line" (Interview 1988). Finally, because trap-netters often work out of the bow of the boat instead of the side as in pound-netting, they have lessened the sharpness of the bow, and some have built skiffs with pram-like square noses narrower than the stern (fig. 46.8).[11] Ben Peterson explains:

46.8. Wayne Seaman's square-nosed vee-bottomed steel trap-net skiff,
Fairport, Michigan, 1988. Photo: Janet C. Gilmore.

. . . I decided that I'd put a pug nose on it, because we do a lot of the work right in the bow of the boat, and I figured if it was a pug nose, then it would have a little bit more room up there, you know, sometimes two of us have to get in the bow, like when you check over a net. . . . (Interview 1988)

Today, northern Lake Michigan fishermen are building two different kinds of steel fishing skiff depending on "what you wanted to use them for." Fishers mainly in the Menominee area—the "ancient" seat of the pound-net fishery, where pound-netting remains active—articulate a broad, flat-bottomed, "peaked" boat (fig. 46.7) for working in shallow, calm waters and bearing large loads of fish, mirroring the wooden pound boats of days past. Fairporters, "converts" from gill-netting to trap-netting, are rapidly evolving a smaller, sturdier, boxier, vee-bottomed skiff (figs. 46.6 and 46.8) for traveling at higher speeds in turbulent offshore water, integrating ideas from pound-net and Folstad skiffs especially.

While the differences between these two builds appear to be increasing, both still share the most basic characteristics and bear the kernel of the older wooden pound-net boat idea. In building either style, fisher-builders adhere roughly to the rule that "one-third the length would be the width" (Folstad interview 1988). They keep within a fairly narrow range of lengths (12′ to 20′), widths (4′ to 7′), and depths (of the sides; 2′ to 2 ½′). They flare the bow—even a square-nosed one—and the sides to turn water away from the boat. They keep the transom flat and "taper" it (rake it outward), nowadays mostly to accommodate the outboard instead of to row the boat (see fig. 46.4).

There still are a few fishermen who like rowing capability, so in addition to retaining the taper of the stern, they "cut up" the bottom (fig. 46.4) and place a seat usually just back of the center and fullest beam so that when rowing the bow will not dive and the stern will ride the water properly. Most fishermen do not care to row the skiffs, however, so they flatten out the after part of the bottom and omit the center rowing seat. Indeed, since the steel build does not require thwarts and because the open work space is most desirable, there is a tendency to eliminate all seats. But many retain some seats anyway: in the stern for convenience while operating the outboard, and in the bow and stern for safety, to double as flotation chambers. Relieved of the need for rowing capability or rowing-seat stiffening, but perhaps frustrated by the resistance of heavy-gauge steel to produce the fairest of lines, builders rarely articulate the graceful continuous curve of the sides from the stem around a midships bulge to the stern. Now they usually make a boxier boat, placing the fullest beam at the stern or keeping the beam constant from the stern to well forward of amidships (at the point where the bow begins to taper into a peak or pug).

For northern Lake Michigan's fisher-builders, the pound-net skiff remains a powerful idea. They see its essence confirmed in the existing pound-net and trap-net tenders of their peers; they recall it in past generations of skiffs logged now only in memory; and when they begin to build a new skiff, they use it as their point of departure. Conceivably there are other boat shapes with different proportions that might serve as well (cf. Taylor 1982: 66–67). But until there is a major upheaval in their fishing methods, these fisher-builders will maintain their legacy, perhaps because the familiar shape and the easy build lend themselves so well to an attitude that appears to have been as current among fishermen a century ago as it is today. David Behrend articulates this stance:

Most of these boats were built just to serve a purpose, and they weren't supposed to be beautiful or anything else, they just did a job and that was it. I mean it wasn't something you went riding in on Sunday, it was to use. . . . And generally you didn't monkey around with it too much because you needed a boat and you needed it just as quickly and cheaply as you could get it, and hurry up. Get at it and build it, because it's going to have to go in the water. (Interview 1988)

Now over a century old, the fishing skiff building tradition on the northern Lake Michigan shore will likely remain healthy as long as commercial fishermen see a reason for "making them to fit their purpose."

Notes

I dedicate this very descriptive first step in the analysis of Lake Michigan fishing skiffs to Warren E. Roberts in recognition of his love for the fit of form to function and the legacy of "the old traditional way of life." A shorter, even rougher version of this paper, and the fieldwork upon which it was based, were commissioned by the Michigan Traditional Arts Program of the Michigan State University Museum in East Lansing. The first paper, published in the 1988 Festival of Michigan Folklife program booklet, benefited from readings by Yvonne H.

Lockwood, James P. Leary, and especially David A. Taylor. The opportunity to rework the paper allowed me to act upon many of Taylor's "boatological" suggestions, to improve the accuracy of the description, and most importantly, to bring to the public more of the fisher-builders's wonderful observations about their skiffs, in their own words. I thank all of the victims of my quick fieldwork forays into the U. P. for their graciousness and help in taking me in and answering my peculiar questions. Particularly I am grateful to Richard Grabowski, Louis Ruleau, and David and Eileen Behrend for their patience, kindliness, and helpfulness in talking about those common little skiffs. Hopefully the dialogues will continue and the data will take yet more and better shapes.

1. Cf. Hornell 1950: 153–57 and von Brandt 1984: 191–92; also Smith and Snell 1891: 108–9 for descriptions and measurements of the nets as used in the area during the 1880s. The description of this type of net and its operation, as well as of the trap net, are based especially on interviews conducted in August 1986 with pound-netter Richard Grabowski, pound- and trap-netter Louis Ruleau, trap-netter Ben Peterson (and his crew, Rod Gierke and Rich Lynts), and net-builders Alvin Champion and Otis Smith. Richard Grabowski and Charlie Nylund additionally instructed me in the workings and set-up of the nets at the Festival of American Folklife in Washington, D.C., in June–July 1987.

2. According to the testimony of contemporary fishermen, the trap net appears to have as long, but not as wide, a use as the pound net on the Great Lakes and adjacent smaller, primarily sportfishing lakes such as Lake Winnebago in eastern Wisconsin.

3. Richard Grabowski's larger boat, for example, is a boxy 18′ × 35′ powerless "scow" which he uses inside his pound-net pots.

4. In contrast, Chapelle (1951: 48) claims that the stem was usually not rabbeted but "built up" of an inner and outer piece instead. The side planks were thus nailed to the inner piece and sawn off flush with its outer edge, and the outer piece then covered the inner piece and sawn edges of the planks.

5. Louis Ruleau claims that the inner "center board" was sometimes used in the early stages of construction as part of the initial framework of bow stem, transom, and "form."

6. Shell construction, where the ribbing is inserted after the skin of the boat has been shaped, is distinguished from skeleton construction where the ribbing is set up first to define the skin. See Greenhill 1976: 287–92.

7. Chapelle (1951: 128) noted the concomitance of variation in skiff construction details with the variety of specialized and non-specialized builders who used neither plans nor models in building the boats.

8. The gauge of a sheet of steel pertains to its thickness; a ten-gauge sheet is one-tenth of an inch thick, twelve-gauge one-twelfth of an inch, and so on. The higher the gauge number, the thinner the steel.

9. He thus bypassed the step of translating the measure into a numerical equivalent and using the numbers in turn to mark the proper measure on each rod.

10. With the massive changes in Michigan's fisheries legislation enacted in the late 1960s and mostly in the 1970s, came changes in the registration of boats. Fishers could no longer avoid a registration fee on their smaller boat by claiming it on the larger boat's registration as a powerless tender under sixteen feet.

11. The square nose is not an anomaly in the area. Peterson's fellow Fairporter, Wayne Seaman, also decided to try out a square nose in his latest skiff, recalling that when he was around eight years old (c. 1942), his father built the family a twelve-foot square-nosed flat-bottomed wooden row boat. Seaman referred to the boat as having a "scow-type" shape, and

Peterson calls his skiff a "scow," a name that locals usually apply to large, boxy vessels that some area fishermen, like Richard Grabowski and his partner Curt Williams, use in pound-netting to carry the large catches. Over the past one hundred years, scows appear to have been used to complement other pound-netting boats in one capacity or another. The pile-driving equipment used through the 1940s to hammer pound-net stakes into the lake bottom was generally borne on a scow; Collins describes such a "stake-boat" in Smith and Snell's 1885 fisheries report (1891: 29).

Sources

Brandt, Anders von. 1984. *Fish Catching Methods of the World.* Third edition. Surrey, England: Fishing News (Books) Ltd.

Chapelle, Howard I. 1951. *American Small Sailing Craft: Their Design, Development, and Construction.* New York: W. W. Norton and Company.

Chapelle, Howard I. 1976. *The National Watercraft Collection.* Second edition. Washington, D. C., and Camden, Me.: Smithsonian Institution and International Marine Publishing Co.

Coberly, Catherine E., and Ross M. Horrall. 1980. *Fish Spawning Grounds in Wisconsin Waters of the Great Lakes.* Madison: University of Wisconsin Sea Grant Institute.

Collins, J. W. 1891. "Vessels and Boats Employed in the Fisheries of the Great Lakes." In "Review of the Fisheries of the Great Lakes in 1885." Edited by Hugh M. Smith and Merwin-Marie Snell, 19–29. In "Report of the Commissioner for 1887." *U.S. Fish Commission Report,* Vol. 15, Appendix I. Washington, D.C.: Government Printing Office.

Gilmore, Janet C. 1987. "Fishing for a Living on the Great Lakes." In *1987 Festival of American Folklife,* pp. 60–64. Washington, D.C.: Smithsonian Institution.

Gilmore, Janet C. 1988. "We Made 'em to Fit Our Purpose: The Upper Lake Michigan Fishing Skiff Tradition." In *1988 Festival of Michigan Folklife,* pp. 32–39. East Lansing: Michigan State University Press.

Greenhill, Basil. 1976. *Archaeology of the Boat: A New Introductory Study.* Middletown, Conn.: Wesleyan University Press.

Halverson, Lynn H. 1955. "The Commercial Fisheries of the Michigan Waters of Lake Superior." *Michigan History* 39: 1–17.

Hornell, James. 1950. *Fishing in Many Waters.* Cambridge: The University Press.

Kuchenberg, Tom. 1978. *Reflections in a Tarnished Mirror: The Use and Abuse of the Great Lakes.* Sturgeon Bay, Wisc.: Golden Glow Publishing.

Smith, Hugh M., and Merwin-Marie Snell. 1891. "Review of the Fisheries of the Great Lakes in 1885." In "Report of the Commissioner for 1887." *U.S. Fish Commission Report,* Vol. 15, Appendix I. Washington, D.C.: Government Printing Office.

Taylor, David A. 1982. *Boatbuilding in Winterton, Trinity Bay, Newfoundland.* Canadian Center for Folk Culture Studies Paper, No. 41. Ottawa: National Museums of Canada.

Author's Interviews

Behrend, David, and Eileen (Kleinke). 1988 (March 29). Menominee, Mich. For the Michigan Traditional Arts Program, MSU Museum, East Lansing.

Champion, Alvin, and Steven. 1986 (August 24). Marinette, Wisc. For the Office of Folklife Programs, Smithsonian Institution, Washington, D.C.

Folstad, Curtis. 1988 (March 28). Menominee, Mich. For the Michigan Traditional Arts Program, MSU Museum, East Lansing.

Grabowski, Richard. 1988 (March 28). Menominee, Mich. For the Michigan Traditional Arts Program, MSU Museum, East Lansing.

Grabowski, Richard. 1986 (August 26). Menominee, Mich. For the Office of Folklife Programs, Smithsonian Institution, Washington, D.C.

Hermess, Peter. 1986 (August 25). Garden, Mich. For the Office of Folklife Programs, Smithsonian Institution, Washington, D.C.

Hickey, Dennis. 1986 (August 16). Bailey's Harbor, Wisc. For the John Michael Kohler Arts Center, Sheboygan, Wisc.

Nylund, Charlie. 1988 (March 27). Menominee, Mich. For the Michigan Traditional Arts Program, MSU Museum, East Lansing.

Nylund, Charlie. 1986 (August 26). Marinette, Wisc. For the Office of Folklife Programs, Smithsonian Institution, Washington, D.C.

Nylund, Wilbert "Pep." 1986 (August 26). Marinette, Wisc. For the Office of Folklife Programs, Smithsonian Institution, Washington, D.C.

Peterson, Benjamin. 1988 (March 31). Fairport, Mich. For the Michigan Traditional Arts Program, MSU Museum, East Lansing.

Peterson, Benjamin. 1986 (August 25). Fairport, Mich. For the Office of Folklife Programs, Smithsonian Institution, Washington, D.C.

Ruleau, Louis. 1988 (March 29). Cedar River, Mich. For the Michigan Traditional Arts Program, MSU Museum, East Lansing.

Ruleau, Louis. 1986. (August 24). Cedar River, Mich. For the Office of Folklife Programs, Smithsonian Institution, Washington, D.C.

Ruleau, Tom. 1988 (April 1). Bark River, Mich. For the Michigan Traditional Arts Program, MSU Museum, East Lansing.

Seaman, "Bill." 1988 (March 31). Fairport, Mich. For the Michigan Traditional Arts Program, MSU Museum, East Lansing.

Seaman, Wayne. 1988 (March 31). Fairport, Mich. For the Michigan Traditional Arts Program, MSU Museum, East Lansing.

Smith, Otis. 1986 (August 25). Fayette, Mich. For the Office of Folklife Programs, Smithsonian Institution, Washington, D.C.

Thill, Lyle L. 1988 (March 31). Garden, Mich. For the Michigan Traditional Arts Program, MSU Museum, East Lansing.

Vetter, Emil "Junior" and Jeffrey P. Harvey. 1988 (March 30). Fairport, Mich. For the Michigan Traditional Arts Program, MSU Museum, East Lansing.

Weborg, Jeff. 1986 (August 16). Gill's Rock, Wisc. For the John Michael Kohler Arts Center, Sheboygan, Wisc.

47

Tobacco Growing In Southwestern Wisconsin: Ethnicity In a Traditional Labor Practice

Thomas E. Barden

Wisconsin's commercial fishers, loggers, farmers, and participants in other ongoing rural, outdoor occupations generally learn their fundamental skills traditionally—by watching, listening, and doing. The more specialized their work, the more they rely on special techniques and tools. Beyond its universally recognized status as "America's Dairyland," Wisconsin also ranks among the nation's leaders in the production and/or processing of cranberries, ginseng, horseradish, maple syrup, pickled cucumbers, sauerkraut, and sphagnum moss—each of which demands specific skills and equipment. (See *Agricultural Diversity in Wisconsin,* ed. Tom McKay and Deborah E. Kmetz [Madison: State Historical Society of Wisconsin, 1987].)

Less significant nationally, tobacco production is nonetheless a mainstay of Wisconsin's rural economy. Commercial tobacco farming began in the Wisconsin Territory in the 1830s, and the crop's cultivation has been confined for most of the twentieth century to southern and western districts. The former is based in Dane County, overlapping into Rock, Jefferson, Dodge, and Columbia Counties; the latter centers around the the Vernon County villages of Viroqua and Westby, and extends into parts of Grant, Richland, Crawford, La Crosse, Monroe, and Trempealeau Counties.

Norwegians have been involved with tobacco production since the mid-nineteenth century and Wisconsin's tobacco bastions coincide with heavy areas of Norwegian settlement. Here old-time Norwegian fiddle tunes carry names like the Bergerson Family's "Tobacco Waltz," or the "Tobacco Setter's Waltz" from the repertoire of the Goose Island Ramblers (included on the sound recordings *Across the Fields* [Folklore Village Farm FV201] and *Midwest Ramblin'* [Wisconsin Folk Museum 9001]). Here distinctive tobacco barns, with their gable-ended openings and louvred sides, dot the landscape (see Karl B. Raitz, "The Wisconsin Tobacco Shed: A Key to Ethnic Settlement and Diffusion," *Landscape* 20:1 [1975]: 32–37). And here craftsmen like Alvin Stockstad of Stoughton fashion tobacco axes and spears in the way he learned from his father, Oscar, in the late 1920s (see Janet C. Gilmore, *From Hardanger to Harleys: A Survey of Wisconsin Folk Art* [Sheboygan, Wisc.: John Michael Kohler Arts Center, 1987], 69–70, 103).

In the early 1980s folklorist Tom Barden, a fieldworker in the dual sense of being both hired hand and researcher, documented additional tobacco tools and techniques that locals deemed "Norwegian." Indeed the everyday, informal, private, and continuous traditional labor practices Barden encountered in Wisconsin's tobacco belt, although subtle and nearly invisible to outsiders, are perhaps more powerful indicators of ongoing "Norwegianness" than the self-conscious, formally organized, public, and sometimes invented cultural displays that anthropologist Robert Ibarra found to characterize Westby's annual Norwegian Syttende Mai festival a decade earlier. (See Ibarra's "Ethnicity Genuine and Spurious: A Study of a Norwegian Community in Rural Wisconsin," Ph.D. dissertation, University of Wisconsin–Madison, 1976.)

Biographical information on Tom Barden precedes his article on the Czech Masopust festival, in chapter 34, p. 352.

Reprinted from *Midwestern Journal of Language and Folklore* 12:1 (1986): 24–37.

The driftless region of southwest Wisconsin is a scenic area of high rolling prairies and stream-laced valleys. It is called driftless, or unglaciated, because it was not touched by the ice age glaciers that flattened most of the Upper Midwest. Its hilly, rocky terrain is unsuitable to large monocrop farm operations and agribusiness, so it has remained a preserve of the small family farm. There are several active ethnic communities in the area, predominantly Bohemians, Amish, and Norwegians. Its economic marginality and ethnic component make the region particularly rich in folklore and traditional culture. I have been conducting an ongoing study of the folklife of a portion of this area since 1979 when I coordinated a field survey of the Pine River Valley sponsored by the Wisconsin Humanities Council. My focus is on an area called the Ocooch Mountains. It is bounded by the Wisconsin River to the south, the Baraboo Mountain Range to the north, the Mississippi River to the west, and the eastern valley of the Pine River to the east.

I have included in my study several occupations and labor practices which rely on traditional methods under the assumption that these constitute a significant dimension of the folklife of the area and also because I am interested in social strategies for getting a living in an economically marginal region. Further, following the concepts of Wendell Berry in *The Unsettling of America: Culture and Agriculture* (1977), I have assumed that there is a direct connection between agricultural labor practice and cultural forms and values. The major forms of traditional labor in the Ocooch Mountains are apple growing, which is centered in the Gays Mills area of Crawford County; small-to-medium-scale cheese making, which is an integral part of the grade-B dairy farming conducted throughout the area; and the cash crop production of leaf tobacco, which is centered in Vernon County in the Kickapoo River watershed.

My purpose in this paper is to describe the practice of tobacco growing in the Ocooch Mountains and to look at the importance of the strong Norwegian presence to its practice and social context. The data derive from fieldwork conducted during the 1982 tobacco year, beginning in April with seed bed preparation and ending in January 1983 with a "tobacco expo," which is held to celebrate the sale of the 1982 crop. Supplementary data come from *Wisconsin and Tobacco* (1963). A few statistics will help set the scene. There were approximately 12,000,000 pounds of tobacco grown in southwest Wisconsin in 1982 on 6,200 acres of land. The crop was valued at approximately $28 million. The average size of each grower's crop was three acres. Most growers in the area (over 90%) grow tobacco in conjunction with some other agricultural enterprise, such as dairying, hog and corn farming, or raising beef cattle. No other cash crop in Wisconsin entails as much work as tobacco; it requires 189 hours of labor per acre annually, as compared with 76.5 hours of labor per cow for a dairy herd.

It is illegal to grow tobacco commercially in the United States without federal approval. Authorization is granted only if a farm has had a history of growing the crop for a certain period and is granted only for a specific acreage, which is measured to the nearest hundredth of an acre. The penalties for exceeding this allotment are severe, and there are frequent field checks by the Agricultural Stabilization and Conservation Service. A farm's allotment transfers with ownership of the farm.

This fact was the basis of my principal informant's introduction to tobacco growing. Before John and Margaret Duncan bought their farm between Viroqua and Westy in central Vernon County, they had never grown tobacco. John told me that when he used to pass tobacco fields while driving from his old farm in Sterling, Illinois, to relatives in Minnesota, he thought the plant was cabbage. But when he bought his Wisconsin farm in 1966, an allocation of seven acres of tobacco came with it. John's closest neighbor was Henry Linrud, a farmer of Norwegian descent who had raised 22 seasons of tobacco with horses before switching to a tractor in 1950. In effect, Duncan served an apprenticeship with Linrud, and two other of Duncan's neighbors, Maynard Ostrem and Clarence Mellem. Their descriptions are augmented by personal observations I made while working the 1982 harvest for Duncan. The descriptions of remembered early techniques come mainly from Linrud and Mellem, both of whom are 72. (Since these techniques vary greatly from those conducted in the warmer regions of the country, which are the principal areas of American tobacco production, these data, in addition to the purpose of description, will provide a basis for comparing regional tobacco practice.)

The first phase of the work is the production of sprouts from seeds. Originally done by each grower on his own acreage, this part of the job is now carried out by a few specialists in seed preparation. In the previous season several plants are stripped of leaves so that extra nutrition goes directly to the seeds. These stripped plants produce the seeds for the next year's crop. In 1982 my informants knew of only two growers who made new seeds. Both of these individuals sent samples to the University of Wisconsin in Madison for germination and disease checks. These growers' seeds were enough to produce the entire crop for the Ocooch area. An interim step in the specialization of seed preparation involved certain Norwegian women in the town of Westby, who took on the task for the growers as a specialty. The seeds had to be kept warm and moist, and Henry Linrud recalled that they were traditionally hung off the back of wood cooking stoves in an old brown sock; the women made sure the sock was moistened daily throughout the winter. This practice ended by the mid-1950s.

The seeds eventually produce small sprouts, somewhat like alfalfa sprouts. By the end of April or the beginning of May they are ready for bedding. The sprouted seeds are placed in a watering can with enlarged holes and sprinkled into seedling beds, which have been processed to be completely free of weeds. There are several methods of accomplishing this step. The newest is the use of methyl-bromide gas, which is released from tanks into a plastic tent placed over the bedded dirt. An older traditional technique, carried over from the days when steam engines were common on the agricultural scene, is steaming the beds. In this process a large metal pan is placed over a section of the bed, and steam is applied for approximately fifteen minutes (fig. 47.1). The bed steamer I interviewed, Ira Melsna of La Farge, is one of five steam operators who provide this service in the Ocooch area. He said the steam is applied, "until it can cook an egg at 12 inches down." Another method,

47.1. Ira Melsna and assistant lift the pan after steaming a bed section
for fifteen minutes, Vernon County, 1982. Photo: Thomas E. Barden.

said to be even earlier than steaming, was the burning of brush and trash over the
bed area. The earliest method of all was simply hand weeding.

What Mellem called the Norwegian method of fertilizing the plants in the beds
was to hang chicken or cow manure in a bag in the water barrel that was used to
water the beds; it was either poured through the white muslin covers or applied
when they were pulled back. This provided organic nitrogen. Nowadays, the beds
are fertilized for the most part with manufactured nitrogen. The muslin covers provide protection from direct sunlight until the plants are strong enough to withstand
it. For the last few weeks of the seedling phase the muslin is folded back.

A saying in circulation about tobacco is that it is a holiday crop—pulled on the
Fourth of July, harvested on Labor Day, and stripped on Thanksgiving. This proved
true for the Duncans' seedlings in 1982; they pulled on Independence Day weekend.
There were enough plants for Duncan's fields, and he sold about twenty acres worth
to neighbors who didn't bed their own. The rule of thumb is that a plant is ready to
pull from the bed if it has four leaves.

Planting the seedling plants is one phase of the work which has been somewhat
mechanized. The oldest method described to me involved rolling a spiked wheel
through the field to mark distances and then hand-planting the seedlings in the
spike holes and giving them a shot of water. The mechanization of planting began
with a rolling two-seat chaise with a water barrel and a box for plants fixed on it. In
this process two planters sit about four inches off the ground and are slowly pulled

through the field, planting one row. A recent innovation is the two-row, high-riding planter, which grasps the plants roots-side up and turns them on a wheel into the row and injects a shot of water. Less than a third of the Ocooch tobacco is planted by high-riders.

The growing period after the seedlings are planted is 60 days. During this period there is relatively little to do. Two or three cultivations between the rows and a walk-through for pulling tobacco worms (unless insecticides are used) are all that is needed until it is time to pull the suckers, the small leaves that grow between the plant's main leaves. Then, in the middle of August, the plants must be topped; the pale lavender flowers of the *Nicotiana tabacum* are cut off to keep the plants from going to seed. Linrud notes that a better leaf is produced by topping before the plant flowers, but it is hard to see the shoots then and so the work is harder.

I should point out that throughout my informants' discussions I detected a clear tension between labor-saving techniques and those which produce the best leaf. The high-riding planter, for example, was denounced by both Linrud and Mellem as making for bent stems. Linrud said, "It takes long plants and it don't put 'em in straight either. Did you notice a lot of John's plants was crooked and had lots of suckers? Well, that's because of the new planters."

The harvest begins approximately 18 days after topping. This stage of the tobacco raising process involves intensive group hand labor. Up to this point, although much of the work is done by hand, it can be done by one or two people, usually the farmer and members of the family. At harvest a crew of at least ten people is needed, even for a small plot. The crew is divided into a field group and a shed group. The steps in the harvest are cutting, piling, spearing, and hauling. In the shed the work is the hanging of laths of speared plants.

Cutting is done with a tomahawk-like cutting ax. The field crew moves along rows, cutting the plants just above the roots. Cut plants are left in the sun to wilt before they are piled—that is, stacked in piles of twenty to twenty-five plants along the pile rows. (These two steps vary markedly from the southern harvesting method in which leaves are stripped from the plants in the field and the stalks left standing.)

Spearing is done from these piles. There are two methods of spearing, the process of placing five or six plants on a piece of lath four feet long. The old method uses a spearing horse (or spearing jack, or spudding horse or jack), which holds the lath in a horizontal position as the plants are slipped onto it over a steel spear point (fig. 47.2). The new method is simply to hold the lath vertically and spear the plant down over the spear-point onto the lath (fig. 47.3). If the rare, hand-carved, hardwood lath is used, a spear-point is not needed, since one end of the lath is sharpened to a point. At the Duncans' farm only two or three of these pieces of lath were found during the harvest.

The laths of speared plants are left in piles until a hauling wagon is driven down the row; they are loaded onto the hauling wagon and taken to the shed. There are two methods used here, too. The older one involves a wagon with two parallel bars from which the lath is hung. The newer method simply uses a flatbed wagon on which the speared laths are laid.

47.2. Clarence Mellem spears tobacco with a spearing jack,
Vernon County, 1982. Photo: Thomas E. Barden.

47.3. John Duncan displays a hand-carved hardwood
spearing lath, Vernon County, 1982. Photo: Thomas E. Barden.

47.4. Tobacco barn with louvers on Vernon County
Highway S near Viroqua, 1982. Photo: Thomas E. Barden.

Once the plants are in the shed they must be hung on spacers, called bents, where they get air circulation as they cure. This step involves a separate crew, which is usually formed on the second day of the harvest after enough plants have been speared to keep the hangers busy. Hanging begins at the peak and descends to the ground level; so the required size of this crew, which must hand the speared lath up to the hanger, becomes smaller as the shed fills (fig. 47.4).

Although there is no stated sexual division of labor, I was told the shed crew is almost always male, while the field crew is always mixed and often includes older children. Mellem's grandson, beginning at age eight, has been a watercarrier for the field crew for several years. The harvest creates a social grouping, which shares one large mid-day meal and a half-hour rest period as well as two fifteen minute breaks, called lunches, one at mid-morning (10:00 A.M.), and one at mid-afternoon (3:00 P.M.). These breaks, which are strictly adhered to, are the occasion for fruit juices, cookies, and coffee.

At the Duncans' harvest in 1982 Irene Mellem, Clarence's wife, helped Margaret Duncan with the preparation of meals and lunches, adding a Norwegian ethnic foodways component to Margaret's standard midwest farm menu of meat, vegetables, potatoes, bread, jello, etc. The Norwegian food Irene and Margie made included *lefse, römmögrot,* and the almond sugar cookies called "scrolls."

I will describe the rest of the tobacco year before returning to the harvest setting for further comments. Once the tobacco is hung, curing continues until "case" weather occurs sometime in late November or early December. "Case" is a period of morning fog weather, which adds moisture to the dried tobacco. The moisture allows it to be taken down without cracking or breaking. "Too high a case," as the term goes, will make the tobacco damp and create a danger of rot. "Too low a case" makes the leaves crumble.

Once the correct case is determined and the tobacco is taken down, another group activity, stripping the plants, takes place. This task demands skilled labor, which must be learned through experience and on-the-job training. It is competitive as to speed. Pride in the skill is enhanced by the stripping contests held at the yearly tobacco expo. As witnessed by the children's categories in these contests, it is also a skill that is learned at an early age. As the leaves are stripped from the stalks, the tobacco is baled, compressed, and tied. The bales are taken to warehouses where the crop is sold, either privately by the grower or through the tobacco co-operatives. In early January the tobacco expo is held. It is a large festival, at which prize tobacco is displayed, a polka band is featured, food abounds, and tobacco spitting contests, as well as the above-mentioned stripping contests, are held. Over 400 people attended the 1982 season expo held in Westby, Wisconsin, on January 15, 1983.

The tobacco year entails an involved set of manual processes and weather judgments, which must be learned by word of mouth and imitation. The bearers of this traditional knowledge and these traditional skills in southwest Wisconsin are the Norwegians; tobacco culture here is a Norwegian domain. I reached this conclusion through my interviews and observations in 1982, but the fact had already been determined precisely by two cultural geographers in 1971 when they conducted a survey to find the correlation between tobacco growers and Norwegian ethnicity in southwest Wisconsin. They found that 72% of the area growers were themselves Norwegian; when they included growers with spouses of Norwegian descent, the figure increased to over 80% (Raitz and Mather 1971). The statistic is corroborated by much anecdotal information I have gathered. One statement by Dr. Neil Bard, a physician who recently moved into the area, is indicative: he said his attempt to grow tobacco on his small allotment put him in touch with "every Norwegian within a ten-mile radius." The connection is there, both in fact and in the mental landscape of the region. A locally published Norwegian joke book shows a lanky Norwegian on its cover. He is standing in front of his tobacco field, chewing a large wad of tobacco and saying "ooff-da," a Norwegian expletive which conveys a large range of emotions, from danger to dismay.

A paper, "Ethnicity and Entrepreneurship in Rural Wisconsin," published by Arnold Strickon in 1979, traces the historical origins of the Norwegian-tobacco connection. A Norwegian businessman and entrepreneur, Martin Bekkedahl, developed a large trade in tobacco by buying exclusively from the Norwegian community in the late nineteenth century. A shrewd businessman, Bekkedahl grew wealthy through this tactic and by 1910 had established his own links with eastern tobacco firms and was producing record sales and packing record crops. He was an intermediary between the Norwegian community and the Yankee businessmen and institutions in the Vernon County area, and this fact strongly prompted local Norwegians to enter the tobacco growing enterprise. Strickon wrote, "Bekkedahl's strategy of positioning himself between community and ambient system, between Yankee and Norwegian, paid off well indeed" (Strickon 1979). Bekkedahl's presence, combined with the Norwegians' willingness to work the labor-intensive crop, gave the Norwegian ethnic community a virtual corner on the southwest Wisconsin tobacco market by the turn of the century. This dominance continued to the time of the Raitz and Mather survey in 1971 and was clearly still operating in the fall in 1982.

Going back to the group work described earlier, we see this ethnic dominance functioning in the maintenance and transmission of the farming techniques and attitudes that accompany them. One other factor in the overall dynamic needs to be pointed out. This is the tobacco grading system. Until the 1940s, all the tobacco grown in southwest Wisconsin was "type 55 leaf," which was used for cigar wrapper. Leaf was graded during stripping as either first grade, stemming, or filler. The buyers also graded the leaf in these categories and paid premium prices for the first grade, which had to be free of holes, rips, and cracks for use as cigar wrappers. The effect of this grading on the work practice was to put an economic premium on taking extreme care of the leaves. The importance of this care is reflected in several specific steps in the tobacco process, the two most conspicuous ones being the use of the spearing jack and the parallel bar hauling wagon. Another practice involving extreme care of the leaves is that of opening and shutting the hinged doors on the during sheds daily. Linrud and Mellem called this strictly a Norwegian trait and noted that new pole sheds built for tobacco do not even have the curing doors. Also recall Linrud's and Mellem's disdain for the high-riding planters.

All tobacco grown in southwest Wisconsin today goes for chewing tobacco or snuff. It is processed by being shredded into fine, cigarette-tobacco–sized strips before being pressed for chew or ground for snuff. It is no longer graded by growers or buyers. There is no practical reason for the process to place any value on leaf care. But this value is still very much alive. And it is much associated with Norwegian-ness. At the tobacco expo it is a point of great pride that the hands of tobacco (which are judged in the old way) taking first, second, and third prize are always from Norwegian fields.

The disappearance of the rationale for the older, time-consuming, economically non-functional steps of the tobacco growing process has of course given rise to newer, economically efficient methods. But they have not prevailed entirely, and the disappearance of the rationale has not caused the disappearance of the old methods themselves. They exist in tension with the newer ones and are strongly asserted by tradition. Even those old techniques that are economically equal with the newer ones divide along ethnic lines. Ira Melsna, who steams tobacco beds, stated that, to the last one, his customers are the Norwegians, who "don't want to get involved with that poison gas" (the methyl bromide). The cost of the two techniques is the same.

Of all the steps in the tobacco process, the use of the spearing jack is the most highly visible old-labor practice. A spearing jack can be found in almost any southwest Wisconsin tobacco field, and it serves as a badge of ethnic identity to use it. It is clearly no longer functional economically; growers pay field crews between four and five dollars an hour, and Duncan and Mellem estimated that using the spearing jack takes approximately 30% more time than other spearing techniques. The fact that the spearing jack produces a first-grade leaf is completely irrelevant economically.

But the tenaciously persistent use of the spearing jack in the labor practice of southwest Wisconsin tobacco growers shows its complete relevance socially, connecting the Norwegian ethnic community with its tradition of highest quality and reminding the region's overall tobacco culture of the Norwegian community's historically predominant position in this traditional labor practice.

Sources

Berry, Wendell. 1977. *The Unsettling of America: Culture and Agriculture.* New York: Avon Books.

Raitz, Karl, and Cotton Mather. 1971. "Norwegians and Tobacco in Wisconsin," in *Annals of the Association of American Geographers* 61:4.

Strickon, Arnold. 1979. "Ethnicity and Entrepreneurship in Rural Wisconsin," in *Entrepreneurs in Cultural Context,* ed. Sidney Greenfield. Albuquerque: University of New Mexico Press.

Wisconsin and Tobacco, Tobacco History Series, 2nd ed. 1963. Washington, D.C.: The Tobacco Institute.

48

The Pickle Factory

Michael Clark

As a high school student in the mid-1960s I began a series of part-time minimum wage jobs that included stuffing and addressing newspapers for the local weekly, loading trucks and sorting empty bottles on a conveyor in a soft-drink plant, and building molds before carrying and pouring ladles of molten iron at a small-scale foundry. I soon learned that each job had its complication and its rhythm. And you had to learn a trade's tricks and pace quickly or face interminable drudgery and frustration. I also learned that each worksite was more than a place where labor was performed. It was a cultural scene, a way of life set off from but overlapping with the surrounding world.

There are many such work sites and scenes in Wisconsin. In the courses I now teach at the University of Wisconsin–Madison, I expect students to discover folklore in their present as well as their past. The undergraduates who take American Folklore are required to "ponder and make notes on a particular workplace as a cultural scene," and to

> Record, photograph, sketch, diagram, write down or otherwise document instances of . . . jargon, nicknames, phrases and expressions, instances of joking relationships, jokes, personal experience stories, pranks and initiations, games and competitions, techniques/"tricks of the trade," gestures, customs, job-related clothing, foodways, and specialized or modified tools and equipment.

Students must also analyze the meaning and use of the folklore they encounter. Does it foster community or conflict? pride or alienation?

The papers are almost always very good, and Michael Clark's effort was exceptional. Clark grew up in an Irish Catholic family in northeastern Wisconsin. In May 1997, he graduated from the University of Wisconsin–Madison with a degree in pharmacy, but he didn't always wear a white collar. Clark's vivid account of evolving from a callow rookie to a wily veteran; of the clamor, stench, danger, and dexterity of line work in an old-fashioned factory; of the everyday implications of class and gender; of memorable characters and incidents; and of after work parties not only registered with my own experience but must have been lived with only slight variation thousands of times by thousands of workers throughout Wisconsin. Their rich but virtually unrecorded occupational folklore deserves chroniclers with Mike Clark's insight and eloquence.

From a paper for the course American Folklore at the University of Wisconsin–Madison, October 1996.

The City Foods Company of northeastern Wisconsin is better known in the local community as the "pickle factory." It was founded in the late 1800s and has become one of the nation's largest processors of pickles. The diverse background of the em-

48.1.   Pea-canning line, Columbus, ca. 1939. Photo: Melvin E. Diemer,
State Historical Society of Wisconsin, WHi (D479) 12198.

ployees in a traditional, old-style industrial setting makes for a work environment rich in occupational folklore.

The pickle season begins in mid-June and ends in late September or early October, depending on when the crop is planted, as well as on how the weather cooperates. To meet the demands of the season, the company will hire about four hundred seasonal employees to help in the canning process. Among those hired were my sisters Kathy and Mary, and myself, from the summers of 1981 through 1984. During this time each of us was preparing to enter college or using this as a summer job while in college. At the time we ranged in age from seventeen to our early twenties. My memories recall that period.

In the early 1980s, the best way for a seasonal employee to get hired was to walk into the personnel office and ask for a job. This was how many people got hired, including my sisters and me. During the peak of the season the need for workers was so great that they would hire just about anyone off the streets in summer. One thing all these people had in common was that they were in need of money and were willing to work for minimum wage.

There were also a few hundred nonseasonal employees who worked year round at the factory. When the pickle season was done there was a cranberry season that lasted a few months, and after this there were also pickles that would get repasteurized and relabeled. The regular employees ranged in age from their mid-twenties to mid-eighties. This latter age range was estimated based on a seniority listing the company posted, which showed that the oldest person still working in 1984 had started in 1906!

My sister Kathy was working next to a woman once, and she began a conversation by asking how long the woman had worked there. The woman replied, "I have been working here for forty-four years and will die here." Kathy said the lady did not look to be older than mid-fifties. I believe that many of these people became comfortable with their job and did not have enough confidence or sufficient skills to seek employment elsewhere—so they stayed. However, there was no adequate retirement system for these people so they worked well beyond a normal retirement age.

The pickle factory is located in the middle of a residential neighborhood. In the early 1980s many of the permanent employees lived in the old houses near the factory and walked to work. This was a similar setting to those found in other traditional industrial areas, where the houses are two-story, spaced about fifteen feet apart, and have only a few feet of front yard space. The houses themselves were almost all in need of repairs, from the roof to the foundation. If the wind was coming from the right direction you could smell the pickle brine used in the canning process from six to seven blocks away.

The pickle fields were located outside the city and the cucumbers to be pickled were heaped onto dump trucks that made multiple trips to the factory each day in caravans of eight to fifteen trucks. Along the way cucumbers would fall from trucks and land on the roads to be squashed by passing cars, leaving a trail to mark the route from the fields to the factory. The pickle trail was joked about by the employees.

Before the evening shift, employees would gather at picnic tables outside the building to await the start of work. It was common for someone to joke, "Here comes Mike. Hey Mike, you found the trail again today." When it was time for the shift to begin, a supervisor would come out and yell, "Time to punch in!" To the supervisor's comment someone would occasionally reply, "The wicked witch is calling us into the oven."

The factory was not physically separated into two parts but functioned this way in the minds of the employees. The "front" of the building was where the pickles got put into jars for pasteurization. The "back" of the factory was where the jars were labeled and put into cases. The cases were then stacked onto pallets for storage.

The work in general was physical, demanding, and repetitive. Gender also had a large influence on the roles assumed in the work setting. Men filled jobs historically considered "men's work," such as heavy lifting and driving machinery. Women comprised the majority of workers at the factory, but their work was limited to putting the pickles into jars and putting the jars into cases.

The first shift in front began at 6:30 in the morning and ended at 3:00 in the afternoon. The second shift began at 3:00 and ended at 11:00 at night. Outside the building it was the men who drove the trucks from the fields to the factory. Men also drove front-end loaders called "cats" (for the manufacturer, the Caterpillar company) that took the pickles from piles and placed them on a conveyor belt so they could enter the factory.

Inside the factory there was little ventilation and the temperature rose as high as 105 to 115 degrees, with nearly 100 percent humidity on an average summer day. As the pickles entered the factory there were women standing near the conveyor belt to pull off any dead rodents or birds that were collected with the pickles while they were in the fields. The quality pickles were sprayed with water to clean them. Next the pickles were collected by a front-end loader and dumped into a large metal trough that was filled with water for a final rinse. They were then scooped out of the trough by a man using a large net, similar in construction to a fishing net, and placed onto conveyor belts where women started putting them in jars.

The conveyor belts were referred to as the "lines" because they were long, winding lines where women stood elbow-to-elbow to fill jars. The role of women filling jars changed as one went further down the line. At the start of the line pickles were placed into the empty jars, and toward the end of a line the last pickle was placed into the jar with the aid of a rubber mallet.

To make sure the lines operated efficiently there were female supervisors, women of seniority who walked along the lines to ensure the pickle packers did not talk and kept a steady pace. This style of supervision seemed more typical of what would be expected for prison inmates. This form of interaction resulted in a relationship where the women who were seasonal employees distanced themselves from the supervisors and would not associate with them at lunch or any other time. The women who worked year round on the lines were not supervised during the off season and their work was not criticized as much as that of the seasonal help. For example, the permanent employees could talk and the supervisor would not yell at them if their pace slowed down. This inequity was interpreted by the seasonal help as unfair and set up a division between the two types of workers. Because of this the seasonal and regular employees did not associate with each other very often.

The seasonal help was also given the more disgusting work. Seasonal women were the ones placed near the conveyor belts, where pickles entered the factory, to remove the dead rodents and birds. Another favorite job to give the seasonal help involved having them soak and peel labels off jars from cases that had a broken jar in them. When a jar broke inside a case, the brine damaged other labels, so they had to be removed and the jars repasteurized. The jars sat in a case for long periods of time, long enough so that maggots sometimes covered the jars—and this was why the job was given to seasonal help. Select groups of the seasonal help were also favorite targets for such jobs: anyone who dressed too femininely, college students, or those who tended to talk, or to work too slowly.

The regular help liked to test the seasonal employees to see how tough they were. My sister Mary said the regular employees would sometimes walk by and say things like, "Now you know what I've done year round for thirty years." Being thrown into the disgusting jobs could be too much for some women, and they often quit within days. This gave the regulars a feeling of superiority in their environment. Some may have felt that some of the seasonal help might be smarter or more beautiful than they were, but that they themselves were superior pickle factory workers. The regulars knew that the next day there would be someone else left to fill the spot left by a seasonal employee who quit—someone who would go through this testing process just as the others before them.

Not only did some women find the work too demanding or disgusting, but some, including my sister Mary, got motion sickness as they watched the endless lines of jars go by hour after hour. Many of the women, when they started on the line, soon began to sway and had to leave to throw up. This also gave the regulars pleasure to see, as it reinforced their feeling of superiority in the work setting. Mary said that many of the women who got sick would quit because they felt they could find an easier job somewhere else, and getting motion sickness was just not worth the money. Other women found out from the veterans that Dramamine, a pill used for motion sickness, could help, and so they were able to continue working.

The supervisors sometimes interacted with the women on the lines by communicating in a cocky, joking way; my sisters, however, could not remember any specific things that were said. They *did* say that the dialogue was short because it was hard to hear well with the noise of the machines. In fact, everyone in the factory was required to wear ear plugs. My sister Mary said that the cocky attitude held by her supervisor on the night shift, a woman named Sadie, often intimidated women working on the lines.

Mary said she began to joke back to Sadie and, because of this, developed a better relationship with her. Mary felt that if you could tough out whatever they gave you to do, without complaining, then you earned their respect and they would joke with you. If you understood this and joked back with them, you broke the invisible barrier and were better accepted. Mary found the relationship with Sadie beneficial. She was eventually pulled off the lines and given a much better position—she became a "capper."

The capper was the person who watched the brine fill the jars, which then got capped before they went into the pasteurizer. If there were any problems the capper had a switch to stop the process. This job was considered a promotion because the person no longer had to stand and do physical work, instead she sat and watched jars in case a problem arose.

Once the jars were capped, they entered a large pasteurizer, also called a "cooker," where the contents were sterilized to increase the shelf life of the product. On the way through the pasteurizer the jars heated up, which weakened the glass, and when they bumped against each other some of the jars broke and had to be removed from the line. My first job at the factory was pulling the broken jars from the lines. From each cooker there were about twenty jars that left every few seconds to go on separate conveyor belts. Each pasteurizer had two conveyor belts that swept the jars away, and each conveyor belt moved at a different speed—so one had to train her gaze to avoid motion sickness.

The end of the pasteurizer line was where the "front" of the factory ended and the "back" began. The back differed from the front in several ways. First, the crew in the back started work about one hour later than the crew in the front, since it took about forty-five minutes to run the pickles through the pasteurizers. The workers in the back did not interact with those in front, and this is what made such a separation between the two areas. Another notable difference was that the managers, called "white hats," rarely made it to the back of the factory, but instead called in information to this area by telephone.

White hats, named for the white hard hats they wore, had offices in the business area of the factory and wore their hats when they went into the plant itself. White hats were routinely present in the front of the factory and communicated information to the line supervisors directly. Because the white hats did not get to the back very often, there was a much more relaxed atmosphere there. There were also no white hats on the night shift, resulting in a management style that was much different from that of the day. Managers on the night shift were regular employees during the off season who volunteered to become supervisors at night, and many of these supervisors handled their responsibility in a unique way. The best example of this concerns my first boss.

During my first night working behind the pasteurizers pulling jars off the lines, I was politely introduced to a man named Wayne who was to be my boss for the next few summers. As soon as the manager introducing us left, Wayne got very cold in demeanor and said that the person who had done the job before me was a girl and she learned to do a series of jobs—all of which were his responsibility. One job was learning to read and record pickle temperatures, as the jars were going through the cooker, to make sure they were being pasteurized. Another was climbing a ladder to get to a precarious catwalk that had to be navigated to unclog boxes that traveled on conveyor belts, near the ceiling above the cooker, on their way to the labeling room. Wayne also expected me to read and manipulate a large panel of dials and buttons that controlled the pasteurizers. The panel had buttons to push if a pasteurizer overheated, and other buttons for shutting a pasteurizer down if the need arose.

Wayne's comment expressing his expectation that I perform the additional responsibilities was offered as a challenge: a *girl* was able to do all these things before me. In the factory setting, where men's and women's roles were well-defined, I had to meet this challenge and perform all the tasks, or I would have been viewed as less competent than a "girl" and would never have gained his respect. Without his respect I risked developing a distant relationship with him, one that could make my pickle factory experience more difficult.

As I pulled broken jars from the lines I would place them into fifty-gallon drums. The drums were quite heavy when full, and Wayne offered no assistance in getting rid of full drums or in getting an empty replacement drum. He would sit in his chair, doing nothing but watching. The only way to move a full drum was to tip it carefully onto its bottom edge and roll it to its destination. I quickly became more efficient at performing the tasks Wayne would show me, and as I gained his respect he began to help me with my job. He would get a forklift and bring a new drum for broken jars and transport the full drums away. In time, Wayne began to joke with me and our relationship grew. I became so proficient at doing his jobs that, in my second year working nights behind the cookers, he would leave and go to a bar down the street to get drunk. He told me to tell anyone asking where he was that he had gone to a shed outside and was helping some guys with an emergency problem. Sometimes everything would go wrong and I would be running everywhere to keep up. When Wayne would show up again, he would tell me to punch his time card out at the end of the night and he would stagger across the street to his house.

I was promoted to the "palletizer" in the middle of my second season, after someone quit. A palletizer was one who placed the cases full of labeled jars onto wooden pallets so they could be transported by a fork lift to a storage area. The cases of pickles came from the labeling room down a track of rollers to an area where the pallets were. As the cases came to the end of the roller, the palletizer used his hip to prevent the cases from running off the end of the track. All too often a case with broken jars would hit the palletizer's hip and the brine would gush all over his pants. By the end of the night a palletizer was soaked with brine from the waist down. Taking a shower did not eliminate the smell of brine from the skin, so I smelled like a pickle the rest of the summer—which lead to many comments when I would be out in a public place or with friends.

The longer I stayed at the factory, the more I was promoted. In my final year, they created a new position for me in the labeling room. I later found out that Wayne had a lot to do with making sure I got the job. This was because he had developed a respect for me by the time I left his area, and he wanted to repay me for all that I had done for him. The new job transferred me from the night shift to working days. I arrived at 6 A.M. and usually left around 4:00 to 4:30 P.M. My responsibilities in this area were to attend to any problems that arose and do what I could to keep things running. It was imperative to do whatever could be done to keep the cookers running so the rest of the factory did not stop working. Sometimes this meant that most of the day I would pull cases of full pickles off the line and stack them up, only to place them back on the line. This was done when the labeler broke, or the palletizing machines broke.

There were women who would place the labeled jars into cases. The process was known as "jumping jars." The "jar jumpers" would grab four to six jars, depending on their size, and put them into a case all at once. The sizes of the jars ranged from eight ounces to forty-eight ounces. There was quite a technique to jumping jars, and I learned it the hard way.

When the women would need a break, I would rotate around and jump jars into the boxes. At first I tried to do it their way and wound up breaking many jars—so I resorted to putting one in each hand, and this slowed everyone up. The women found much amusement in my breaking jars, especially since I would have to clean up the mess. In time I could jump jars as well as the women and became proficient in all the tasks in the labeling room. When I gained the respect of the women, they began to joke with me by making lewd comments and grabbing my butt. One of the women would repeatedly say she wanted to have sex with me at a public swimming pool at night when it was closed. When she would say this all the other women on the line would laugh and add further comments, trying to embarrass me. One of the reasons they expressed themselves this way was that I was the only male in the labeling room, other than the foreman, so I was a gender minority for them to pick on.

The pickle factory, like many industrial settings, had its tales of danger and injury. I found out about the danger of pulling broken jars from the lines my first night on the job. One of the ladies in back took me to a lady in the labeling room who had two fingers missing from one hand. I was told that the edges of a broken jar are so sharp they can cut off your fingers before you feel it. As a safety measure I was given cotton gloves that were double-dipped in rubber to protect me from sharp jars. The gloves helped some, but I still managed to get cut, and when this happened the salty brine would make the cut sting a great deal. The cuts also bled a lot and the rubber gloves would hold the blood so that, when I raised my hand, the blood poured down my arm.

My sister Kathy told me a story about a college student from Oshkosh who was working on a machine that cut the pickles into spears. One night the machine clogged and she thought she had shut it down. When she went to unclog the machine it cut her hand off at the wrist. The women picked up her hand and brought it to the supervisor Sadie, who threw up at the sight. The girl calmly said that she thought she needed some help. She was rushed to a hospital where the hand was reattached.

Other stories related to injuries were told at parties held at the house of one of the employees who worked on the night shift. There I was warned about a man called "Crash." Proud of his nickname, Crash was a forklift driver who had many accidents with his machine. He once took the time clock off the wall. I was told you could tell Crash by the doll he strapped to the front of his forklift: a baby with no head.

Another story was about a man cleaning a pickle cutter who forgot to remove the blade. When he used his finger to clean out the area where the blade was, it cut the finger off. There was also a story about a man on the cleaning crew who stepped backwards into a pail of very hot oil that melted his rubber boot to his foot. When they removed the rubber from his foot, the skin came off with it.

The parties held after the night shift were not only a place to hear stories, they were also opportunities to learn the ins and outs of the factory, and to get to know some of the regular employees. The parties were held on Saturday nights after work and would last until about 7 A.M. Sunday morning. A lot of people would not go to the parties, as they did not get started until about 12:30 A.M., many employees opted to go home and sleep. I found the parties to be a way to break the tension between the regular employees and myself—because the regular employees viewed those who went to the parties as more down-to-earth and approachable—and this made it much better when I was at work. When I bonded with them at the parties, they would not only ride me less at work, but also make a point to come over and talk to me and find out if things were going okay. I also noticed that I was spared from getting many of the more unpleasant jobs reserved for seasonal help.

The pickle factory job taught me a lot about people and how they relate to each other. It was more than just a job. By looking beyond the surface of the events that happened around me, I was able to gain a richer understanding of the work environment—one that enabled me to make the best of what could have been a bad situation.

The City Foods Company may have changed since I worked there, but I will always remember it as I knew it years ago.

This list is indeed selective and, beyond a few general references, I have confined inclusions to works primarily concerned with the folklore of Wisconsin's diverse peoples—that is, to works that make verbal, musical, customary, and material folklore their focus, rather than considering it along the way or confining it to the background. The entries below are also, for the most part, substantive and accessible. Additional treatments of Wisconsin's folklore—some rich, others scant—lurk in local histories, reminiscences, novels, periodicals, newspapers, and the occasional media production. My notes preceding essays in this anthology cite many such sources. Yet there are many more, and I wish the curious good hunting.

General Works
Historical and Cultural Overviews

For humanistic considerations of Wisconsin peoples, life, and culture that parallel, complement, and intersect with a folklorist's perspective, see:

Bourdeau, Richard. 1986. *The Literary Heritage of Wisconsin*, 2 volumes. La Crosse, Wisc.: Juniper Press.
Nesbit, Robert C. 1973. *Wisconsin: A History.* Madison: University of Wisconsin Press.
Ostergren, Robert C. and Thomas R. Vale. 1997. *Wisconsin Land and Life.* Madison: University of Wisconsin Press.
Rippley, LaVern J. 1985. *The Immigrant Experience in Wisconsin.* Boston: Twayne Publishers.
Stephens, Jim. 1989. *The Journey Home: The Literature of Wisconsin Through Four Centuries*, 3 volumes. Madison: North Country Press.
Trigger, Bruce. 1978. *Handbook of North American Indians, Volume 15: Northeast.* Washington, D.C.: Smithsonian Institution. With essays on the Southwestern Chippewa by Robert E. Ritzenthaler, the Menominee by Louise S. Spindler, the Oneida by Jack Campisi, the Potawatomi by James A. Clifton, and the Winnebago by Nancy Oestreich Lurie.
Woodward, David, et al. 1996. *Cultural Map of Wisconsin: A Cartographic Portrait of the State.* Madison: University of Wisconsin Press.

American Folklore

Parties wishing to contemplate the folklore of Wisconsin's peoples within larger contexts might begin with this trio:

Brunvand, Jan H. 1996. *American Folklore: An Encyclopedia.* NYC and London: Garland Publishing.
Brunvand, Jan H. 1998. *The Study of American Folklore,* 4th edition. New York: Norton.
Dorson, Richard M. 1983. *American Folklore: A Handbook.* Bloomington: Indiana University Press.

Overviews of Wisconsin Folklore

Regarding Wisconsin's folklore specifically, Fred Holmes' *Old World Wisconsin: Around Europe in the Badger State* (Eau Claire, Wisc.: E. M. Hale, 1944) offers an affectionate and remarkable detailed—albeit sometimes romantic—overview of settlement history and folk cultural practices within the state's Belgian, Cornish, Czech, Danish, Dutch, Finnish, French, German, Hungarian, Icelandic, Irish, Italian, Luxembourger, Norwegian, Polish, Russian, Slovak, Swedish, Swiss, and Welsh ethnic enclaves. *Old World Wisconsin* has been reprinted several times, but some later editions lack the evocative sketches and photographs of the original.

Robert E. Gard and L. G. Sorden compiled a miscellany of the state's folklore, *Wisconsin Lore* (New York: Duell, Sloan, and Pearce, 1962). Emphasizing verbal folklore, Gard and Sorden drew heavily on Fidelia Van Antwerp's collection of Wisconsin folklore, solicited under the auspices of the Wisconsin Regional Writers' Association, to offer sections on ghost stories, lumberjack lore, folk medicine, Indian place name legends, circus lore, buried treasure, local characters, folk belief, and proverbs. The original Van Antwerp collection resides in the archives of the State Historical Society of Wisconsin.

Walker D. Wyman, a historian at the University of Wisconsin-River Falls, relied upon historical sources, local field research, and his students' folklore collections to produce *Wisconsin Folklore* (Madison: University of Wisconsin Extension, 1979). Chapters concern lore of the discovery and exploration era, mythical creatures, place names, folk medicine, weather, dowsing, beliefs about birth and death, legends, and the folklore of immigrants, animals, and students.

My own "An Annotated Bibliography of Wisconsin Folklore," *Midwestern Journal of Language and Folklore* 8:1 (1982): 52–81, cited many of the earlier sources mentioned here, while casting its net more broadly to include otherwise historical reminiscences that mention folklore significantly. Herbert Halpert offers bibliographical additions in: "Wisconsin Folklore Bibliography: A Supplement," *Midwestern Journal of Language and Folklore* 11:1 (1985): 50–53. Charles Brown offered an early sketch on organizations of folklorists in Wisconsin: "Wisconsin Folklore Society," *Journal of American Folklore* 56:221 (1943): 190–91; see also Richard M. Dorson, "Badger State Folklore Society," *Journal of American Folklore* 60:237 (1947): 303; and Anonymous, "Badger Folklore Society," *Journal of American Folklore* 61:240 (1948): 213.

For a folklorist's historical perspective on the state's pioneering folklorist, see Herbert Halpert, "A Note on Charles E. Brown and Wisconsin Folklore," *Midwestern Journal of Language and Folklore* 11:1 (1985): 54–59.

Numerous additional brief articles, both frothy and solid, present aspects of Wisconsin's folklore in bygone and current periodicals. The best appear in the *Ocooch Mountain News* (1974–1981), edited by Emily Osborn, a monthly publication on politics and culture in rural southwestern Wisconsin. Earlier in this century *The Wisconsin Magazine* (1923–1932) offered historical and cultural essays, in a popular vein, to tourists and interested locals, an approach sustained by Howard and Nancy Mead's *Wisconsin Tales and Trails* (1960–1970) and its successor, *Wisconsin Trails* (1971–the present).

Ethnographies and Histories Incorporating Folklore

The following works—concerned, respectively, with ethnic, occupational, and microregional cultures—include rich considerations of a range of folklore forms and practices:

Dunn, James Taylor. 1965. *The St. Croix: Midwest Border River.* New York: Holt, Reinhart, and Winston.

Gard, Robert E. and Maryo Gard. 1978. *My Land, My Home, My Wisconsin: The Epic Story of the Wisconsin Farm and Farm Family from Settlement Days to the Present.* Milwaukee: The Milwaukee Journal.

Koltyk, JoAnn. 1997. *New Pioneers in the Heartland: Hmong Life in Wisconsin.* New York: Allyn and Bacon.

Pfaff, Tim. 1995. *Hmong in America: Journey from a Secret War.* Eau Claire, Wisc.: Chippewa Valley Museum Press.

Radin, Paul. 1923. "The Winnebago Tribe." *Thirty-Seventh Annual Report of the Bureau of American Ethnology.* Washington, D.C.: Smithsonian Institution; reprinted in 1990 (Lincoln: University of Nebraska Press).

Ritzenthaler, Robert E. and Pat Ritzenthaler. 1970. *The Woodland Indians of the Western Great Lakes.* Garden City N.J.: Natural History Press.

Skinner, Alanson and J. V. Satterlee. 1915. "Folklore of the Menomini Indians." *Anthropological Papers of the American Museum of Natural History* 12:3. 217–546.

Life Histories of Wisconsin Folk

These life histories—in which individuals variously sustain, modify, invent, abandon, and acquire traditions—provide vivid, poignant, and personal accounts of the ways in which folklore is carried on or cast aside as individuals make choices amid the relentless cultural change that has characterized life in Wisconsin:

Blanchard, Louis, as told to Walker D. Wyman. 1969. *The Lumberjack Frontier: The Life of a Logger in the Early Days on the Chippewa.* River Falls: University of Wisconsin-River Falls Press.

Corrigan, George. 1976. *Calked Boots and Canthooks: One Man's Story of Logging the North.* Ashland, Wisc.: NorthWord, 1976.

Lurie, Nancy Oestreich. 1961. *Mountain Wolf Woman: The Autobiography of a Winnebago Indian.* Ann Arbor: University of Michigan Press.

Mattison, Wendy, Laotou Lo, and Thomas Scarseth. 1994. *Hmong Lives: From Laos to La Crosse.* La Crosse, Wisc.: The Pump House Regional Center for the Arts.

Mitchell, Roger. 1984. "From Fathers to Sons: A Wisconsin Family Farm." In Norwegian Americans in Marathon County, special issue of *Midwestern Journal of Language and Folklore* 10:1–2.

Nelligan, John Emmett. 1929. *The Life of a Lumberman.* Self-published, reprinted as *A White Pine Empire: The Life of a Lumberman* (St. Cloud, Minn.: North Star Press, 1969).

Peters, Robert. 1988. *Crunching Gravel.* Madison: University of Wisconsin Press. Depression-era farming near Eagle River, Wisconsin.

Radin, Paul. 1919–1920. "The Autobiography of a Winnebago Indian." *University of California Publications in Archeology and Ethnology* 16. 381–473.

Rolland, Barbara J. and Houa Vue Moua. 1994. *Trail Through the Mists.* Eau Claire, Wisc.: self-published. A Hmong woman's story of life in Southeast Asia and Wisconsin.

Starr, Mary Agnes. 1981. *Pea Soup and Johnny Cake.* Madison: Red Mountain. A life amid Wisconsin's French traditions.

Xan, Erna Oleson. 1950. *Wisconsin: My Home.* Madison: University of Wisconsin Press. Norwegians in central Wisconsin.

Terms and Talk

Names

The earliest and most prolific studies of Wisconsin's folk speech concern personal and place naming practices, especially but not exclusively those of native peoples. They include:

Ashton, J. W. 1944. "Some Folk Etymologies for Place Names." *Journal of American Folklore* 57:224. 139–40.

Bicha, Karel D. 1992–1993. "From Where Come the Badgers?," *Wisconsin Magazine of History* 76:2. 121–31.

Calkins, Hiram. 1855. "Indian Nomenclature, and the Chippewas of Northern Wisconsin, with a Sketch of the Manners and Customs of the Chippewas." *Annual Reports and Collections of the State Historical Society of Wisconsin* 1. 119–26.

Cassidy, Frederic G. 1947. *The Place Names of Dane County, Wisconsin.* Greensboro, N.C.: American Dialect Society.

Cassidy, Frederic G. 1948. "Folklore in Place Names," *Badger Folklore* 1:1. 21–24.

Cassidy, Frederic G. 1973. "The Names of Green Bay, Wisconsin," *Names* 21:3. 168–71.

Cassidy, Frederic G. 1985. "From Indian to French to English: Some Wisconsin Place Names," *Names* 33:1–2. 51–57.

Cassidy, Frederic G. 1986. "Some French Place Names in Wisconsin." In *From Oz to the Onion Patch,* ed. Edward Callary. DeKalb, Ill.: North Central Name Society. 27–36.

Cole, Harry Ellsworth. 1912. *Baraboo and Other Place Names in Sauk County, Wisconsin.* Baraboo: The Baraboo News Publishing Co.

Gard, Robert and L. G. Sorden. 1968. *The Romance of Wisconsin Place Names.* New York: October House.

Hathaway, Joshua. 1854. "Indian Names," *First Annual Report and Collections.* Madison: State Historical Society of Wisconsin (reprinted 1903). 116–118.

Kuhm, Herbert W. 1952. "Indian Place-Names in Wisconsin." *The Wisconsin Archeologist* 33:1–2. 1–157.

Legler, Henry E. 1902. "Origin and Meaning of Wisconsin Place Names, with Special Reference to Indian Nomenclature." *Transactions of the Wisconsin Academy of Sciences, Arts and Letters,* part 1, 14. 16–39.

Martin, Lawrence T. 1992. "Reflections of Ojibwa Mythology in Place-Names of the Upper

Midwest." In *Old English and New: Studies in Language and Linguistics in Honor of Frederic G. Cassidy*, ed. Nick Doane and Dick Ringler. New York: Garland Press. 370–83.

Ritzenthaler, Robert. 1944. "Acquisitions of Surnames by the Chippewa Indians." *American Anthropologist* 47. 175–77.

Savage, Howard J. 1923. "Word List from Southwestern Wisconsin." *Dialect Notes* 5:6. 233–40.

Skinner, Alanson. 1919. "Some Menomini Indian Place Names in Wisconsin." *The Wisconsin Archeologist* 18:3. 97–102.

Smith, Huron H. 1930. "Indian Place Names in Wisconsin." *Yearbook of the Milwaukee Public Museum* 10. 252–66.

Vogel, Virgil J. 1991. *Indian Names on Wisconsin's Map*. Madison: University of Wisconsin Press.

Verwyst, Chrysostom. 1892 "Geographical Names in Wisconsin, Minnesota and Michigan Having a Chippewa Origin." *Collections of the State Historical Society of Wisconsin* 12. 390–98.

Dialect and Jargon

Beyond a few highly technical studies, the literature on Wisconsin's overlapping regional, ethnic, and class dialects is scant. Yet the folk speech of the state's citizens is well represented in the magisterial works of Frederic G. Cassidy and Einar Haugen, both of whom undertook their studies while faculty members at the University of Wisconsin. Loggers, meanwhile, are the state's only occupational group whose workaday jargon has been documented in print.

Buckman, Albert. 1952. "Logging Language." *Badger Folklore*. 13–20.

Cassidy, Frederic G., et al. 1985, 1991, 1996. *Dictionary of American Regional English*, volumes 1–3. Cambridge, Mass.: Harvard University Press.

Eichhoff, Jurgen. 1971. "German in Wisconsin." In *The German Language in America*, ed. Glenn C. Gilbert. Austin: University of Texas Press.

Flom, George T. 1926. "English Loanwords in American-Norwegian—as Spoken in the Koshkonong Settlement, Wisconsin." *American Speech* 1. 541–48.

Flom, George T. 1929. "On the Phonology of English Loanwords in the Norwegian Dialect of Koshkonong, Wisconsin." In *Studier Tillägrade Axel Kock*. Lund, Sweden: C. W. K. Gleerup. 178–89.

Flom, George T. 1934. "English Elements in Norse Dialects of Utica, Wisconsin." *Dialect Notes* 2. 257–68.

Haugen, Einar. 1969. *The Norwegian Language in America: A Study in Bilingual Behavior*. Bloomington: Indiana University Press.

Sorden, L. G. 1969. *Lumberjack Lingo*. Spring Green, Wisc.: Wisconsin House.

Taunts and Insults

Taunts and insults—so abundant in folk speech, and often cast in verse and metaphor—have been little noted by any scholars, anywhere. And while that has certainly been the case in Wisconsin, Reinhold Aman, formerly of Waukesha, includes occasional instances of such genres from Wisconsin in *Maledicta*, the journal of the society he founded in the late 1970s for the study of verbal aggression.

Allen, Harold B. 1958. "Pejorative Terms for Midwestern Farmers." *American Speech* 33. 260–65.

Aman, Reinhold. 1981. "Menomini Maledicta: A Glossary of Terms of Deprecation, Sexuality, Body Parts & Functions, and Related Matters," *Maledicta* 5:1–2. 177–90. Derived from Leonard Bloomfield, *Menomini Lexicon* (Milwaukee: Milwaukee Public Museum Publications in Anthropology and History 3, 1975).

Ritzenthaler, Robert. 1945. "Totemic Insult Among the Chippewa." *American Anthropologist* 47. 322–24.

Ture, Sue [a pseudonym]. 1984–1985. "Milwaukee Medical Maledicta." *Maledicta* 8. 117–18.

Ture, Sue [a pseudonym]. 1988–1989. "More Milwaukee Medical Maledicta." *Maledicta* 10. 36.

Proverbs

The enormous compilation of proverbs from Wisconsin speakers, undertaken by Lee Burress while on the faculty of the University of Wisconsin-Stevens Point, sadly remains unpublished.

Burress, Lee. 1967. "Folklore Collecting in Wisconsin." *Journal of the Ohio Folklore Society* 2:3. 125–33.

Leary, James P. "'The Land Won't Burn': An Esoteric American Proverb and Its Significance." 1975. *Midwestern Journal of Language and Folklore* 1:1. 27–32. Reprinted in *Folk Groups and Folklore Genres: A Reader,* ed. Elliott Oring (Logan: Utah State University Press, 1989), 302–07.

Storytelling

The entries below are subdivided with regard to their status as sacred narratives (myths), fictitious narratives (tales), and narratives that are "supposed to be true" whether or not they are actually regarded as true (legends), this latter category including stories concerning local people that are regarded as true and are usually—but not always—true. Some entries, however, defy such easy categorization by presenting narratives from several genres. In such cases I have placed them in sections indicative of their overall emphasis, but I have also tried to point out [in brackets] their inclusion of other genres.

Myths

In the late nineteenth and early twentieth century anthropologists were especially active documenters of sacred narratives performed among Wisconsin's Ho-Chunk (Winnebago), Menominee, and Ojibwe (Chippewa) peoples. I indicate cultural affiliation whenever it is not clear from a publication's title.

Barnouw, Victor. 1977. *Wisconsin Chippewa Myths and Tales: And Their Relation to Chippewa Life.* Madison: University of Wisconsin Press.

Behncke, Nile. 1939. "Winnebagoland Legends." *The Wisconsin Archeologist* 34:2. 31–34.

Bloomfield, Leonard. 1929. "Menomini Texts." *Publications of the American Ethnological Society* 12. 1–607.

Brown, Charles E. 1930. *Wigwam Tales: Thunder Birds, Water Spirits, Horned Serpents, Tie Snakes, Wind Bird, Windigos, Little Indians, Spider Men and Witches, Creation Myths, Star Lore, Animal Lore, and Other Indian Folktales.* Madison: self-published.

Brown, Charles E. 1931. *The Waupaca Chain O'Lakes Indian History Survey: The Lakes, Indian Archeology and History, Myths and Legends.* Waupaca, Wisc.: Chain o' Lakes Protective Association.

Brown, Charles E. 1935. *Moccasin Tales: Indian Short Stories of the Chippewa, Winnebago, Dakota, Potawatomi, Menomini, Sauk, Fox, and Other Tribes, for Story Telling at the Campfire and Fireside.* Madison: State Historical Society of Wisconsin.

Hoffman, Walter J. 1890. "The Mythology of the Menomini Indians." *American Anthropologist* 3. 243–58.

Jenks, Albert E. 1902. "The Bear Maiden: An Ojibway Folk-Tale from Lac Court Oreilles Reservation, Wisconsin." *Journal of American Folklore* 15. 33–35.

McKern, W. C. 1929. "A Winnebago Myth." *Yearbook of the Public Museum of the City of Milwaukee* 9. 215–30.

McKern, W. C. 1930. "Winnebago Dog Myths." *Yearbook of the Public Museum of the City of Milwaukee* 10. 317–22.

Michelson, Truman. 1911. "Menominee Tales." *American Anthropologist* 13:1. 68–88.

Michelson, Truman. "Ojibwa Tales." *Journal of American Folklore* 24. 249–50.

Peet, Stephen D. 1909. "Mythology of the Menominees." *American Antiquarian and Oriental Journal* 31. 1–14.

Radin, Paul. 1909. "Winnebago Tales." *Journal of American Folklore* 22:85. 288–313.

Radin, Paul. 1948. "Winnebago Hero Cycles: A Study in Aboriginal Literature." *Memoir No. 1, International Journal of American Linguistics,* Indiana University Publications in Anthropology and Linguistics 14:3. 1–168.

Radin, Paul. 1950. "The Origin Myth of the Medicine Rite: Three Versions/The Historical Origins of the Medicine Rite." *Memoir No. 3, International Journal of American Linguistics,* Indiana University Publications in Anthropology and Linguistics 16:1. 1–78. [Ho-Chunk (Winnebago)].

Radin, Paul. 1956. *The Trickster: A Study in American Indian Mythology,* with commentaries by Carl Kerenyi and C. G. Jung. New York: Philosophical Society. [Ho-Chunk (Winnebago)].

Tales

The fictitious traditional narratives or folktales documented among Wisconsin tellers have been chiefly brief and humorous: tall tales associated with the woods, ethnic jokes, and floating anecdotes told "for true" on local characters. Victor Barnouw's *Wisconsin Chippewa Myths and Tales,* cited in the prior section, provides a rare glimpse of lengthy Eurasian *marchen* or magic tales from métis, or French Indian, raconteurs like Prosper Guibord. Richard Dorson also recorded such tales from Joe Woods, a Polish immigrant who lived for a time in Wisconsin before settling just across the border in the Upper Peninsula of Michigan. Betty Carriveau Sherman's *Stories Papa Told* offers an equally rare sense of the lengthy trickster tales passed down within her French American family. The "Liar's Club" and Bunyan stories owe as much to popular culture and the chapbook as to oral tradition.

Bartlett, William W. 1923. "Some Odds and Ends of Logging Camp Humor," *American Forestry* 29 (October). 589–91.

Brown, Charles E. 1922. *American Folklore: Paul Bunyan Tales.* Madison: State Historical Museum; second edition, 1927.

Brown, Charles E. 1935. *Paul Bunyan Natural History: Describing the Wild Animals, Birds, Reptiles and Fish of Big Woods About Paul Bunyan's Old Logging Camp.* Madison: self-published.

Brown, Charles E. 1935. *Shanty Boy: Bard of Paul Bunyan's Wisconsin and Michigan Logging Camps: Tales of the Great Singer, Storyteller, and Dancer, The Blue Hills, Paul's Farm, Camp Evangelist, and Old Abe's Visit.* Madison: Wisconsin Folklore Society.

Brown, Charles E. 1940. *"Cousin Jack" Stories: Short Stories of the Cornish Lead Miners of Southwestern Wisconsin, for the Campfire and Fireside.* Madison: Wisconsin Folklore Society.

Brown, Charles E. 1940. *Whiskey Jack Yarns: Short Tales of the Old Time Lumber Raftsmen of the Wisconsin River and Their Mythical Hero: Raft and River Bank Tales.* Madison: Wisconsin Folklore Society.

Brown, Charles E. 1941. *Flapjacks from Paul Bunyan's Cook Shanty.* Madison: Wisconsin Folklore Society.

Brown, Charles E. 1942. *Brimstone Bill: Famous Boss Bullwhacker of Paul Bunyan's Camps: Tall Tales and Exploits.* Madison: Wisconsin Folklore Society.

Brown, Charles E. 1943. *Bluenose Brainard Stories: Log Cabin Tales from the Chippewa Valley in the Wisconsin North Woods.* Madison: Wisconsin Folklore Society.

Brown, Charles E. 1943. "A Wisconsin Endless Tale," *Hoosier Folklore Bulletin* 2. 20–21.

Brown, Charles E. 1943. "Wisconsin Versions of 'Scissors!,'" *Hoosier Folklore Bulletin* 2. 46–47.

Brown, Charles E. 1943. "Wisconsin Parallels to Indiana Folktales," *Hoosier Folklore Bulletin* 2. 100–101.

Brown, Charles E. 1945. *Bunyan Backhouse Yarns.* Madison: Wisconsin Folklore Society.

Brown, Charles E. 1945. *Ole Olson: Tales of the Mighty Swede Blacksmith of Paul Bunyan's Wisconsin and Other Lumbercamps.* Madison: Wisconsin Folklore Society.

Brown, Charles E. 1945. *Paul Bunyan Classics: Authentic Original Stories Told in the Old Time Logging Camps of the Wisconsin Pineries.* Madison: Wisconsin Folklore Society.

Brown, Charles E. 1945. *Sourdough Sam, Paul Bunyan's Illustrious Chief Cook, and Other Famous Culinary Artists of the Great Pinery Logging Camps: Old Time Tales of Kitchen Wizards, the Big Cook Shanty, the Camp Fare, the Dinner Horn and Sam's Cook Book.* Madison: Wisconsin Folklore Society.

Curvin, Jonathan W. 1951. *Early Wisconsin Through the Comic Looking Glass.* Madison: The Wisconsin Idea Theater and the Badger Folklore Society.

Deindorfer, Robert G., ed. 1980. *America's 101 Most High Falutin', Big Talkin', Knee Slappin' Golly Whoppers and Tall Tales: The Best of the Burlington Liar's Club.* New York: Workman.

Dorson, Richard M. 1946. "Two City Yarnfests," *California Folklore Quarterly* 6:1. 72–82.

Dorson, Richard M. 1949. "Polish Wonder Tales of Joe Woods," *Western Folklore* 8:1. 25–52.

Dorson, Richard M. 1949. "Polish Tales from Joe Woods," *Western Folklore* 8:2. 131–45.

Dorson, Richard M. 1952. *Bloodstoppers and Bearwalkers: Folktales of Canadians, Lumberjacks, and Indians.* Cambridge: Harvard University Press.

Halpert, Herbert. 1942. "The Mosquitoes and the Kettle," *Hoosier Folklore Bulletin* 1:2. 49.

Hulett, O. C. 1935. *Now I'll Tell One.* Chicago: Reilly and Lee [Burlington Liars Club].

Krotzman, James Michael. 1973. "Folktales Found in the St. Croix Valley." Eau Claire: University of Wisconsin-Eau Claire, M.A.T. thesis.

Leary, James P. 1980. "The 'Polack Joke' in a Polish-American Community," *Midwestern Journal of Language and Folklore* 6:2. 26–33.

Leary, James P. 1982. "Polish Priests and Tavern Keepers," *Midwestern Journal of Language and Folklore* 8:1. 34–42.

Leary, James P. 1984. "The Favorite Jokes of Max Trzebiatowski," *Western Folklore* 43:1. 1–17.

Leary, James P. 1984. "Style in Jocular Communication," *Journal of Folklore Research* 21:1. 29–46.

Leary, James P. 1991. *Midwestern Folk Humor.* Little Rock: August House.

Poppe, Roger Louis. 1968. "Narrative Folklore and Its Transmission in a Northern Wisconsin [Potawatomi] Indian Family." Madison: University of Wisconsin, M.A. thesis in anthropology.

Sherman, Betty Carriveau. 1981. *Stories Papa Told.* New York: Vantage Press.

Watrous, James. 1997–1998. "The Paul Bunyan Murals at Memorial Union," *Wisconsin Academy Review* 44:1. 22–29.

Yates, Norris. 1949. "Some 'Whoppers' from the Armed Forces," *Journal of American Folklore* 62:244. 176–77.

Legends

The entries here attest to the abundance of true or supposedly true stories that have circulated in Wisconsin. Derived from Woodland Indian and European immigrant cultures and from ongoing events, they typically concern accounts of supernatural occurences and anecdotes of local characters. Although the chroniclers of Wisconsin's legendry sometimes opt for a text-oriented quasi-literary presentation, many also provide useful information about the identities and experiences of the legend tellers, their communities, and the ways in which legends are told in every day life.

Boyer, Dennis. 1993. *Ghosts of Iowa County (Except for Ridgeway's).* Dodgeville, Wisc.: Eagle Tree Press.

Boyer, Dennis. 1994. *Tall Tales and Odd Characters in Grant County.* Dodgeville, Wisc.: Eagle Tree Press.

Boyer, Dennis. 1995. *Hilltales from Vernon County.* Dodgeville, Wisc.: Eagle Tree Press.

Boyer, Dennis. 1996. *Driftless Spirits: Ghosts of Southwest Wisconsin.* Madison: Prairie Oak Press.

Brown, Charles E. 1927. *Lake Mendota Indian Legends.* Madison: State Historical Society of Wisconsin.

Brown, Charles E. 1931. *Ghost Tales: Ghosts, Spooks, Phantoms, Spirits, Skulls, Skeletons, Ghouls, Hexes, Undertakers and Burying Grounds: Short Stories for Use at the Fireside and Campfire.* Madison: Self-published.

Brown, Charles E. 1933. *Lake Mendota: Prehistory, History, and Legends.* Madison: Democrat Printing Company.

Brown, Charles E. 1934. *Prairie Stories.* Madison: Self-published.

Brown, Charles E. 1940. *Old Man River.* Madison: Wisconsin Folklore Society.

Brown, Charles E. 1942. *Sea Serpents.* Madison: Wisconsin Folklore Society.

Brown, Charles E. 1944. *Bear Tales.* Madison: Wisconsin Folklore Society.

Brown, Charles E. 1944. *Ben Hooper Tales: Settler's Yarns from Green and Lafayette Counties.* Madison: Wisconsin Folklore Society.

Brown, Charles E. 1945. *Hermits: Tales of Some Wisconsin Hermits and Misers.* Madison: Wisconsin Folklore Society.

Brown, Charles E. 1945. *Lost Treasure Tales.* Madison: Wisconsin Folklore Society.

Cowley, Mert. 1996. *A Hundred Hunts Ago: Seasons of the Past.* Chetek, Wisc.: Banksiana Publishing Company. Deer hunting.

Cox, William T. 1910. *Fearsome Creatures of the Lumberwoods.* Washington, D.C.: Judd and Detweiler; reprinted in Wyman 1978. 27–65.

Gard, Robert and Dale O'Brien. 1971. *Down in the Valleys: Wisconsin Back Country Lore and Humor.* Madison: Wisconsin House.

Gard, Robert E. and Elaine Reetz. 1973. *The Trail of the Serpent: The Fox River Valley Lore and Legend.* Madison: Wisconsin House.

Hatch, K. L. 1950. "Richland County Eccentrics," *Badger Folklore* 2:1. 7–9.

Ivey, Zida C. 1952. "Fort Atkinson Tales," *Badger Folklore* 3. 21–22.

Kearney, Luke Sylvester "Lakeshore." 1928. *The Hodag.* Wausau, Wisc.: Democrat Printing Company. A miscellany of lumbercamp legends and tall tales, along with logger poetry by William N. Allen ("Shan T. Boy").

Kortenhof, Kurt Daniel. 1996. *Long Live the Hodag! The Life and Legacy of Eugene Simeon Shepard: 1854–1923.* Rhinelander, Wisc.: Hodag Press.

Leary, James P. 1976. "Fists and Foul Mouths: Fights and Fight Stories in Contemporary Rural American Bars." *Journal of American Folklore* 89:351. 27–39.

Lewis, Jeanie. 1975. *Ridgeway: Host to the Ghost.* Dodgeville, Wisc.: Dodgeville Chronicle.

Matson, Elizabeth and Stuart Stotts. 1996. *The Bookcase Ghost: A Storyteller's Collection of Wisconsin Ghost Stories.* Mount Horeb, Wisc.: Midwest Traditions.

Miller, Dorothy Moulding. 1937. "Indian Lover's Leaps in Wisconsin," *The Wisconsin Archeologist* 17:4. 84–87.

Miller, Dorothy Moulding. 1937. "Legends of the Wisconsin Hills," *The Wisconsin Archeologist* 18:1. 17–24.

Miller, Dorothy Moulding. 1938. "Wisconsin Indian Cave Legends," *The Wisconsin Archeologist* 18:2. 59–62.

Miller, Dorothy Moulding. 1938. "Legends of Wisconsin Springs," *The Wisconsin Archeologist* 18:3. 79–86.

Miller, Dorothy Moulding. 1938. "Myths and Legends of Wisconsin Waterfalls," *The Wisconsin Archeologist* 18:4. 110–20.

Miller, Dorothy Moulding. 1938. "Legends of Wisconsin Rocks," *The Wisconsin Archeologist* 19:1. 7–13.

Miller, Dorothy Moulding. 1938. "Indian Tree Myths and Legends," *The Wisconsin Archeologist* 19:2. 30–36.

Miller, Dorothy Moulding. 1940. "Fire Myths and Legends," *The Wisconsin Archeologist* 20:4. 84–90.

Miller, Dorothy Moulding. 1940. "Wisconsin Indian Corn Origin Myths," *The Wisconsin Archeologist* 21:1. 19–27.

Miller, Dorothy Moulding. 1941. "Indian Winter Legends," *The Wisconsin Archeologist* 22:4. 49–53.

Miller, Dorothy Moulding. 1943. "Rain Legends and Beliefs," *The Wisconsin Archeologist* 24:2. 27–31.

Mitchell, Roger. 1979. "The Press, Rumor, and Legend Formation," *Midwestern Journal of Language and Folklore* 5:2. 5–41. Regarding the murderer Ed Gein.

Mitchell, Roger. 1986. "The Will To Believe and Anti-Refugee Rumors," *Midwestern Journal of Language and Folklore* 10. 5–15. Hmong refugees in Eau Claire.

Scott, Beth and Michael Norman. 1980. *Haunted Wisconsin.* Madison: Stanton and Lee.

Tithecott, Richard. 1996. *Of Men and Monsters: Jeffrey Dahmer and the Construction of the Serial Killer.* Madison: University of Wisconsin Press.

Webber, Peter L. 1977. *Collected Writings of a Wisconsin, Michigan Logger.* Porterfield, Wisc.: self-published. Also includes "logger poetry".

Wyman, Walker D. 1978. *Mythical Creatures of the U.S.A. and Canada.* River Falls: University of Wisconsin-River Falls Press. Includes and expands upon Cox 1910.

Wyman, Walker D. 1984. *Wisconsin and North Country Wolf and Bear Stories.* River Falls: University of Wisconsin-River Falls Press.

Wyman, Walker D. 1986. *Stories About Domestic Animals and Other Creatures in Wisconsin and the Upper Midwest.* River Falls: University of Wisconsin-River Falls Press.

Wyman, Walker D. 1986. *Wisconsin and North Country Stories About Fish and Fishermen.* River Falls: University of Wisconsin-River Falls Press.

Wyman, Walker D. 1987. *Stories About Hunters and Hunting in Wisconsin and the North Country.* River Falls: University of Wisconsin-River Falls Press.

Music, Song, and Dance
Surveys of Wisconsin's Folk Music, Song, and Dance

Andresen, Robert. 1978. "Traditional Music: The Real Story of Ethnic Music and How It Evolved in Minnesota and Wisconsin," *Minnesota Monthly* (October). 9–13.

Baader, Mary Lenore. 1967. "The Music of Early Wisconsin." Washington, D.C.: Catholic University of America, M.A. thesis in music education.

LaRonge, Philip V. S. 1979. "The Folksong and Folkmusic Traditions of the Chippewa-Flambeau Region in Northwestern Wisconsin: A Historical Approach." Detroit: Wayne State University, M.A. thesis in folklore.

Leary, James P. 1987. *The Wisconsin Patchwork: A Commentary on Recordings from the Helene Stratman-Thomas Collection of Wisconsin Folk Music.* Madison: University of Wisconsin Department of Continuing Education in the Arts.

Leary, James P., and Richard March. 1996. *Down Home Dairyland: A Listener's Guide.* Madison: University of Wisconsin Extension.

March, Richard. 1993. "The Down Home Dairyland Saga," in *Celebrating America's Cultural Diversity,* ed. Laura Costello. Washington, D.C.: National Assembly of State Arts Agencies. 24–29.

Stratman-Thomas, Helene. 1948. "Folk Music in Wisconsin," *Badger Folklore* 1:1.

Stratman-Thomas, Helene. 1977. "Field Journal," in *Folksongs Out of Wisconsin,* ed. Harry Peters. Madison: State Historical Society of Wisconsin. 23–41. Journal entries and photographs from folk musical fieldwork in 1940, 1941, and 1946.

Sundell, Steven L. 1994. "Folk and Ethnic Music," in *Wisconsin Music: An Annotated Bibliography.* Madison: Woodrow Press. 71–80.

Woodland Indians: General Works

Gray, Judith A., and Dorothy Sara Lee. 1985. *The Federal Cylinder Project: A Guide to Field Cylinder Recordings in Federal Agencies*, volume 2. Washington, D.C.: American Folklife Center, Library of Congress. Part 1 of this volume constitutes the "Northeastern Indian Catalog" and, with regard to Wisconsin's peoples, lists recordings of "Chippewa Indian Music" by Frances Densmore and by Laura Miller Taylor; of "Menominee Indian Music" by Densmore and by Alanson Skinner; and of "Winnebago Indian Music" by Densmore, Alice C. Fletcher, Paul Radin, and Huron H. Smith.

Leary, James P. 1992. "Sawdust and Devils," in *Medicine Fiddle: A Humanities Discussion Guide*, ed. James P. Leary. Bismarck: North Dakota Humanities Council. 30–35.

Lee, Dorothy Sara. 1979. *Native American Music and Oral Data: A Catalogue of Sound Recordings, 1893–1976*. Bloomington: Indiana University Press. An index of collections at the Indiana University Archives of Traditional Music, including recordings by members of such Wisconsin Woodland Indian nations as the Menominee, Ojibwe (listed as Chippewa and Ojibwa), Oneida (listed as Iroquois—Oneida), Potawatomi, and Winnebago (i.e. Ho-Chunk).

Woodland Indians: Ho-Chunk (Winnebago)

Densmore, Frances. 1928. "Music of the Winnebago Indians." *Explorations and Fieldwork of the Smithsonian Institution in 1927*. Washington, D.C.: Smithsonian Institution. 183–88.

Densmore, Frances. 1929. "Music of the Winnebago and Menominee Indians of Wisconsin," *Explorations and Field-Work of the Smithsonian Institution in 1928*. Washington, D.C.: Smithsonian Institution. 189–98.

Densmore, Frances. 1930. "Music of the Winnebago, Chippewa, and Pueblo Indians," *Explorations and Field-Work of the Smithsonian Institution in 1930*. Washington, D.C.: Smithsonian Institution. 217–24.

Densmore, Frances. 1940. "Winnebago Music." Washington, D.C.: Smithsonian Institution, unpublished manuscript.

Hoffmann, Charles. 1947. "American Indian Music in Wisconsin, Summer 1946," *Journal of American Folklore* 60:237. 289–93.

Radin, Paul. 1911. "The Ritual and Significance of the Winnebago Medicine Dance," *Journal of American Folklore* 24:92. 149–208.

Woodland Indians: Menominee

Densmore, Frances. 1932. "Menominee Music," *Bureau of American Ethnology Bulletin* 102. 1–230; reprinted in 1972 (New York: De Capo Press). See also Densmore 1929 in the Ho-Chunk section above.

Skinner, Alanson. 1925. "Songs of the Menomini Medicine Ceremony," *American Anthropologist* 25. 290–314.

Slotkin, J. S. 1957. "The Menominee Powwow," *Milwaukee Public Museum Publications in Anthropology* 4. 1–166.

Woodland Indians: Ojibwe (Chippewa)

Barnouw, Victor. 1960. "A Chippewa Mide Priest's Description of the Medicine Dance," *The Wisconsin Archeologist* 41:4. 77–97.

Barrett, S. A. 1911. "The Dream Dance of the Chippewa and Menominee Indians," *Bulletin of the Milwaukee Public Museum* 1:4. 251–406.

Densmore, Frances. 1910, 1913. "Chippewa Music," parts 1 & 2, *Bureau of American Ethnology Bulletin*, vols. 45 and 53. 1–216, 1–341, respectively; reprinted in 1973 (Minneapolis: Ross and Haines) with an introduction by Thomas Vennum, Jr. See also Densmore 1930 in the Ho-Chunk section above.

McNally, Michael David. 1996. "Ojibwa Singers: Evangelical Hymns and a Native Culture in Motion." Cambridge, Mass.: Harvard University, Ph.D. dissertation in ethnomusicology.

Sturtevant, Gene. 1934. "The Dream Dance Drum," *The Wisconsin Archeologist* 13:4. 86–90.

Vennum, Thomas, Jr. 1978. "Ojibwa Origin-Migration Songs of the *Mitewiwin*," *Journal of American Folklore* 91:361. 753–91.

Vennum, Thomas, Jr. 1982. *The Ojibwa Dance Drum: Its History and Construction.* Washington, D.C.: Smithsonian Institution Press, Smithsonian Folklife Studies No. 2.

Vennum, Thomas, Jr. 1985. "The Ojibwa Begging Dance," in *Music and Context: Essays for John M. Ward,* ed. Anne D. Shapiro. Cambridge, Mass.: Harvard University Press. 54–78.

Woodland Indians: Oneida

Cornelius, Richard and Terence J. O'Grady. 1987. "Reclaiming a Tradition: The Soaring Eagles of Oneida," *Ethnomusicology* 31. 261–72.

O'Grady, Terence J. 1991. "The Singing Societies of Oneida," *American Music* 9:1. 67–91.

European Americans: Surveys

Greene, Victor. 1992. *A Passion for Polkas: Old Time Ethnic Music in America.* Berkeley: University of California Press.

Leary, James P. 1981. *A Beginning Fieldworker's Guide to European Ethnic Music in Northern Wisconsin.* Ironwood, Mich.: North Country Press.

Leary, James P. 1983. "Ethnic Country Music on Superior's South Shore," *John Edwards Memorial Foundation Quarterly* 19. 219–30.

Leary, James P. 1984. "Old Time Music in Northern Wisconsin," *American Music* 2:1. 71–88.

March, Richard. 1991. "Polkas in Wisconsin Music," in *The Illustrated History of Wisconsin Music, 1840–1990,* ed. Michael Corenthal. Milwaukee: Yesterday's Memories. 385–97.

European Americans: Occupational Traditions

Greene, Daniel W. 1968. "'Fiddle and I': The Story of Franz Rickaby," *Journal of American Folklore* 81:322. 316–36.

Leary, James P., and Richard March. 1993. "Farm, Forest, and Factory: Songs of Midwestern Labor," in *Songs About Work: Essays in Occupational Culture,* ed. Archie Green. Bloomington: Indiana University Folklore Institute. 253–286.

Mueller, Theodore. 1948. "Folklore and Great Lakes Lore," *Badger Folklore* 1:1. 3–7.

Mueller, Theodore. 1951. "More Sailor's Lore," *Badger Folklore* 3:1. 5–7.

Plummer, Beverly. 1969. "Ray Calkins and his Wisconsin Lumberjack Band," *Wisconsin*

Tales and Trails 10 (Summer). 10–12.

Rickaby, Franz. 1926. *Ballads and Songs of the Shanty-Boy.* Cambridge, Massachusetts: Harvard University Press; reprinted by the Clearfield Company (Baltimore: 1993), with an introduction by W. K. McNeil.

Rickaby, Franz. 1977. "Field Journal," in *Folksongs Out of Wisconsin*, ed. Harry Peters. Madison: State Historical Society of Wisconsin. 17–22. Journals from Rickaby's northern Wisconsin fieldwork in 1919.

Topping, Brett. 1980. "The Sydney Robertson Cowell Collection," *Folklife Center News* 3:3. 4–5, 8. Includes accounts of the Ford-Walker family, lumber camp and Anglo-Celtic singers from northern Wisconsin.

European Americans: British and Irish

Beatty, Arthur. 1907. "Some New Ballad Variants," *Journal of American Folklore* 20:77. 154–56.

Beatty, Arthur. 1909. "Some Ballad Variants and Songs," *Journal of American Folklore* 22:83. 63–71.

Bohlman, Philip V. 1980. "The Folksongs of Charles Bannen: The Interaction of Music and History in Southwestern Wisconsin," *Transactions of the Wisconsin Academy of Sciences, Arts and Letters* 68. 167–87.

Corcoran, Erin. 1998. "'Come Back to Erin': The Revival of Irish Traditional Music and Dance in Milwaukee." Madison: University of Wisconsin, M.A. thesis in Music.

Hendricks, Cecilia Hennel. 1944. "Robin Tamson's Smiddy," *Hoosier Folklore Bulletin* 2:2. 55–57.

Peters, Harry. 1977. *Folksongs Out of Wisconsin.* Madison: State Historical Society of Wisconsin.

Stuttgen, Joanne Raetz. 1991. "Kentucky Folksong in Northern Wisconsin: Evolution of the Folksong Tradition in Four Generations of Jacobs Women," *Southern Folklore* 48. 275–89.

European Americans: Czechs (Bohemians)

Janda, Robert. 1976. *Entertainment Tonight: An Account of Bands in Manitowoc County Since 1910.* Manitowoc Wisc.: Manitowoc County Historical Society, Monograph No. 28.

Leary, James P. 1981. "The Peasant Songs of Jerry Novak," *North Country Folk* 1:3. 4–7, 30.

Leary, James P. 1997. "Czech Polka Music in Wisconsin," in *New Perspectives in American Music*, ed. Kip Lornell and Anne Rasmussen. New York: Schirmer Books. 25–47.

European Americans: French

Starr, Mary Agnes. 1957. "Traditions et Folklore Francais du Wisconsin," *French Folklore Bulletin* 56 (Winter). 1–8.

European Americans: Germans

Bohlman, Philip V. 1979. "Music in the Culture of German-Americans in North-Central Wisconsin." Champaign: University of Illinois, M.A. thesis in ethnomusicology.

Bohlman, Philip V. 1984. "Hymnody in the Culture of German-Americans in North Central Wisconsin," *The Hymn* 35. 158–164.

Bohlman, Philip V. 1985. "Prolegomena to the Classification of German-American Music," *Yearbook of German-American Studies* 20. 33–48.

Leary, James P., and Richard March. 1991. "Dutchman Bands: Genre, Ethnicity, and Pluralism in the Upper Midwest," in *Creative Ethnicity: Symbols and Strategies of Contemporary Ethnic Life*, ed. Stephen Stern and John Allan Cicala. Logan: Utah State University Press. 21–43.

Werth, Charles E. 1980. "Fiddle-Playing Teacher," *Concordia Historical Institute Quarterly* 53:3. 126–28.

Norwegians

Blegen, Theodore. 1936. *Norwegian Immigrant Ballads and Songs.* Minneapolis: University of Minnesota Press.

Haugen, Einar. 1959. "A Norwegian-American Pioneer Ballad," *Norwegian-American Studies and Records* 15. 1–19.

Hoeschen, Kevin. 1989. "The Norwegian Hardanger Violin in the Upper Midwest: Documentation and Interpretation of an Immigrant Tradition." Minneapolis: University of Minnesota, M.A. thesis in music.

Kirk, William F. 1905. *The Norsk Nightingale: Being the Lyrics of a "Lumberyack."* Boston: Small, Maynard.

Martin, Philip. 1979. "The Hardanger Fiddle in Wisconsin," *Ocooch Mountain News* 5 (August). 10–11.

Martin, Philip. 1980. "Hardanger Fiddlers," *Ocooch Mountain News* 6 (January/February). 10–11.

Martin, Philip. 1982. "The Lively Art of Old Time Fiddling," *The Sons of Norway Viking* 79 (May). 148–49, 161.

Martin, Philip. 1985. "The Tunes of Yesteryear," *The Sons of Norway Viking* 82 (July). 232–35.

Martin, Philip. 1994. *Farmhouse Fiddlers: Music and Dance Traditions in the Rural Midwest.* Mount Horeb, Wisc.: Midwest Traditions.

Minahan, P. R. 1950. "John Hopper's Mill," *Badger Folklore* 2. 3–6.

Poles

Keil, Charles, Angeliki V. Keil, and Dick Blau. 1992. *Polka Happiness.* Philadelphia: Temple University Press.

European Americans: Slovaks

Leary, James P. 1981. "The Musical Traditions of Moquah's Slovaks," *North Country Folk* 1 (September). 4–7.

Slovenians

Keil, Charles. 1982. "Slovenian Style in Milwaukee," In *Folk Music and Modern Sound*, ed. William Ferris and Mary L. Hunt. Jackson: University of Mississippi Press. 32–59.

March, Richard. 1985. "Slovenian Polka Music: Tradition and Transition," *John Edwards Memorial Foundation Quarterly* 21:75–76. 47–50.

Further Reading: A Selected List

Swedes

Martin, Philip. 1976. "Ed Johnson, Heavenly Sounds from the Devil's Instrument," *Wisconsin Trails* 17:4. 10–11.

Melloh, Ardith K. 1981. "Grandfather's Songbooks, or the *Psalmodikon* in America." *The Swedish Pioneer Historical Quarterly* (October). 265–88.

European Americans: Swiss

Leary, James P. 1991. *Yodeling in Dairyland: A History of Swiss Music in Wisconsin.* Mount Horeb, Wisc.: Wisconsin Folk Museum.

Beliefs and Customs
Traditional Beliefs and Practices

Baker, Fred T. 1948. "Farming By the Moon," *Badger Folklore* 1:1. 27–28.

Bergen, F. D. 1896. "Some Customs and Beliefs of the Winnebago Indians," *Journal of American Folklore* 9:32. 51–54.

Blakeslee, Allen D. 1910. *The Religious Customs of the Ojibway Indians.* Hayward, Wisconsin: Journal-News Print.

Cassidy, Frederic G. 1951. "Folk Cures and Weather Lore," *Badger Folklore* 2:4. 3–4.

Curtis, Martha E. 1952. "The Black Bear and White-Tailed Deer as Potent Factors in the Folklore of the Menomini Indians," *Midwest Folklore* 2:3. 177–90.

Dorson, Richard M. 1947. "Folklore at a Milwaukee Wedding," *Hoosier Folklore Bulletin* 6:1. 1–13.

Fletcher, J. E. 1854. "Manners and Customs of the Winnebagoes," in *Information Respecting the History, Condition, and Prospects of the Indian Tribes in the United States,* Vol. 4, ed. Henry R. Schoolcraft. Philadelphia: Lippincott, Grumbo, and Co.

Forrest, George T. 1950. "Folk Cures," *Badger Folklore* 2:4. 4–6.

Grant, Bruce Herman. 1995. "Spirituality and Sobriety: The Experience of Alcohol Use and Abuse among Menominee Indians of Wisconsin." Washington, D.C.: Catholic University of America, Ph.D. dissertation in anthropology.

Harsted, Peter T. 1959–1960. "Disease and Sickness on the Wisconsin Frontier," *Wisconsin Magazine of History* 43. 253–63.

Hoffman, Walter J. 1891. "The Midewiwin or 'Grand Medicine Society' of the Ojibwe," *7th Annual Report of the Bureau of American Ethnology, 1885–1886.* Washington, D.C.: Smithsonian Institution. 143–300.

Kolinski, Dennis L. 1991. "The Evolution of Polish American Wedding Customs in Central Wisconsin," in *The Polish Diaspora, Volume II: Selected Essays from the Fiftieth Anniversary International Congress of the Polish Institute of Arts and Sciences in America,* ed. James S. Pula and M. B. Biskupski. Washington, D.C.: East European Monographs. 35–46.

McKern, W. C. 1928. "A Winnebago War-Bundle Ceremony," *Yearbook of the Milwaukee Public Museum of the City of Milwaukee* 8. 146–55.

Olson, Ruth. 1995. "A Community Gathering: Selecting the Symbols of Stewardship in the Ojibwe and Farming Communities of Northern Wisconsin." Philadelphia: University of Pennsylvania, Ph.D. dissertation in folklore.

Radin, Paul, and O. Lamere. 1911. "Description of a Winnebago Funeral," *American Anthropologist* 13:3. 437–44.

Radin, Paul. 1914. "Religion of the North American Indians [Winnebago]," *Journal of American Folklore* 27:106. 344–51.

Radin, Paul. 1914. "A Sketch of the Peyote Cult of the Winnebago," *Journal of Religious Psychology* 7. 1–22.

Radin, Paul. 1922. "Thunder-Cloud, a Winnebago Shaman, Relates and Prays," in *American Indian Life*, ed. Elsie Clews Parsons. New York: B.W. Huebsch. 75–80.

Ritzenthaler, Robert. 1945. "Ceremonial Destruction of Sickness by the Wisconsin Chippewa," *American Anthropologist* 47. 320–22.

Ritzenthaler, Robert. 1954. "Reminiscences of a Chippewa Mide Priest," *The Wisconsin Archeologist* 35:4. 83–112.

Sieber, George W. 1966. "A 1964 Winnebago Funeral," *Journal of the Wisconsin Indians Research Institute* 2:1. 102–105.

Skinner, Alanson. 1911. "War Customs of the Menomini," *American Anthropologist* 13:2. 299–312.

Skinner, Alanson. 1913. "Social Life and Ceremonial Bundles of the Menomini Indians," *Anthropological Papers of the American Museum of Natural History* 13:1. 1–165.

Skinner, Alanson. 1922. "Little-Wolf Joins the Medicine Lodge," in *American Indian Life*, ed. Elsie Clews Parsons. New York: B.W. Huebsch. 63–73.

Spindler, Louise S. 1952. "Witchcraft in Menomini Acculturation," *American Anthropologist* 54. 593–602.

Folk Games, Drama, and Festivals

Alexander, Martha. 1986. "Stoughton, Wisconsin's Syttende Mai Celebration: The Dynamic of a Small-Town American Festival." Bloomington: Indiana University, Ph.D. dissertation in folklore.

Brown, T. T. 1930. "Plant Games and Toys of Chippewa Children," *The Wisconsin Archeologist* 9. 185–86.

Bubbert, Walter. 1948. "Seven Pig Fairs in Manitowoc County," *Badger Folklore*. 18–20.

Caldwell, James R. 1945. "A Tale Actualized in a Game," *Journal of American Folklore* 58:227. 50.

Culin, Stewart. 1907. "Games of the North American Indians," *Twenty-fourth Annual Report of the Bureau of American Ethnology*. Washington, D.C.; reprinted in two volumes, "Games of Chance" and "Games of Skill," (Lincoln: University of Nebraska Press, 1992). Includes details on the dice, stick, ball and other games of the Chippewa (Ojibwe), Menominee, and Ho-Chunk (Winnebago).

Dundore, Walter M. 1954. "The Saga of Pennsylvania Germans in Wisconsin," *The Pennsylvania German Folklore Society* 19. 142–145, section on "Folklore and Social Customs".

Enderis, Dorothy C. 1951. "Milwaukee's Holiday Folk Fair," *Wisconsin Magazine of History* 35:2. 119–122.

Hoelscher, Steven D. 1998. *Heritage on Stage: The Invention of Ethnic Place in America's Little Switzerland*. Madison: University of Wisconsin Press.

Hoelscher, Steven D., and Robert C. Ostergern. 1993. "Old European Homelands in the American Middle West," *Journal of Cultural Geography* 13:2. 87–106.

Hoffman, Walter J. 1890. "Remarks on Ojibwa Ball Play," *American Anthropologist* 3. 133–35.

Ibarra, Robert Antonio. 1976. "Ethnicity Genuine and Spurious: A Study of a Norwegian

Community in Rural Wisconsin." Madison: University of Wisconsin, Ph.D. dissertation in anthropology.

Kronewiter, Uwe. 1997. "*Ethnische Folk Festivals in Wisconsin* [Ethnic Folk Festivals in Wisconsin]." Munich: University of Munich, M.A. thesis in American studies and sociology.

Krueger, Lillian. 1938–1939. "Social Life in Wisconsin: Pre-Territorial through the Mid-Sixties," *Wisconsin Magazine of History* 22. 156–75, 312–28, 396–426.

Neff, Deborah and Phillip B. Zarrilli. 1987. *Wilhelm Tell in America's 'Little Switzerland,' New Glarus, Wisconsin.* Onalaska, Wisc: New Glarus Wilhelm Tell Community Guild.

Prosterman, Leslie. 1995. *Ordinary Life, Festival Days: Aesthetics in the Midwestern County Fair.* Washington, D.C.: Smithsonian Institution Press.

Skinner, Alanson. 1911. "The Menomini Game of Lacrosse," *American Museum Journal* 11. 139–41.

Thiel, Mark G. 1982. "The Powwow: A Celebration of Tradition," *Wisconsin Academy Review* 28. 20–30.

Vennum, Thomas, Jr. 1994. *American Indian Lacrosse: Little Brother of War.* Washington, D.C.: Smithsonian Institution Press.

Material Traditions and Folklife
Folk Architecture: Woodland Indians

Nabokov, Peter and Robert Easton. 1989. *Native American Architecture.* New York: Oxford University Press. 52–91.

Folk Architecture: European American Landscapes and Farmsteads

Alanen, Arnold. 1995. "Back to the Land: Immigrants and Image-Makers in the Lake Superior Region, 1865–1930," in *Landscapes in America,* ed. George F. Thompson and Charles E. Little. Austin: University of Texas Press. 111–140.

Brandt, Lawrence R. and Ned E. Braatz. 1972. "Log Buildings in Portage County, Wisconsin," *Pioneer America* 4:1. 29–39.

Durand, Loyal, Jr. 1942. "Dairy Barns of Southeastern Wisconsin: Relation to Dairy Industry and to Regions of 'Yankee' and 'German' Settlement," *Annals of the Association of American Geographers* 32:1. 112–31.

Grant, David P. 1971. "Early Folk Architecture in Crawford County, Wisconsin." Madison: University of Wisconsin, M.A. thesis in landscape architecture.

Perret, Maurice E. 1973. "Cultural Diversity in Central Wisconsin," *Transactions of the Wisconsin Academy of Sciences, Arts and Letters* 61. 45–57.

Perrin, Richard W. E. 1962. *Historic Wisconsin Architecture, 1835–1870.* Milwaukee: Milwaukee Public Museum.

Perrin, Richard W. E. 1966. "Log Houses in Wisconsin," *Antiques* 89:6. 867–71.

Perrin, Richard W. E. 1967. *The Architecture of Wisconsin.* Madison: State Historical Society of Wisconsin.

Tishler, William H. 1977. "The Site Arrangement of Rural Farmsteads." *Association for Preservation Technology Bulletin* 10 (February). 63–79.

Tishler, William H. 1984. "Built From Tradition: Wisconsin's Rural Ethnic Folk Architecture," *Wisconsin Academy Review* 30 (March). 14–18.

Tishler, William H. 1985. "Sign, Symbols and Gable Cutouts on Early Wisconsin Barns." *Lore* 35 (Summer). 25–29.

Tishler, William H. 1986. "Wisconsin's European Architectural Heritage: A National Cultural Resource." *Wisconsin International Trade Magazine* (March/April). 7–9.

Tishler, William H. 1987. "The Study of Ethnic Vernacular Landscapes: A Summer Field Course Approach." *Proceedings of the 1987 Meeting of the Council of Educators in Landscape Architecture.* Providence: The Rhode Island School of Design. Pamphlet, 4 pages.

Tishler, William H. 1987. "European Folk Architecture in Wisconsin: The Transfer of Old World Building Traditions To A New World Setting," in *Proceedings of the 8th International Council on Monuments and Sites.* Washington: United States Committee, International Council on Monuments and Sites. 792–99.

Tishler, William H. 1989. "The Homestead Farm and Dwelling: A Political Statement of Form on the Wisconsin Landscape." *Abstracts, Third International and Interdisciplinary Conference on Built Form and Culture Research, Intercultural Processes.* 73.

Tishler, William H. 1992. "Imprints of Cultural Diversity in Wisconsin's Rural Landscape," *PAST: Pioneer America Society Transactions* 15. 67.

Folk Architecture: Belgians

Calkins, Charles F., and William G. Laatsch. 1979. "The Belgian Outdoor Ovens of Northeastern Wisconsin," *PAST: Pioneer America Society Transactions* 2. 1–12.

Laatsch, William G., and Charles F. Calkins. 1986. "The Belgian Roadside Chapels of Wisconsin's Door Peninsula." *Journal of Cultural Geography* 7:1. 116–28.

Laatsch, William G., and Charles F. Calkins. 1992. "Belgians in Wisconsin," in *To Build a New Land: Ethnic Landscapes in North America,* ed. Allen G. Noble. Baltimore: Johns Hopkins University Press. 195–210.

Pansaerts, Carl. 1993. "Red Brick Houses and White Roadside Chapels: Belgian Immigrant Architecture in Door County, Wisconsin, and Lyon County, Minnesota," in *Re-Discoveries of America: The Meaning of Cultures,* ed. Johan Callens. Brussels, Belgium: Vubpresse. 103–19.

Tishler, William H., and Erik Brynildson. 1986. "The Architecture and Landscape Characteristics of Rural Belgian Settlement in Northeastern Wisconsin." Madison: Department of Landscape Architecture, University of Wisconsin. Pamphlet, 108 pages.

Tishler, William H., and Erik Brynildson. 1992. "The Namur Rural Historic District," in *Guidelines for Evaluating and Documenting Rural Historic Landscapes,* ed. L. McClelland, et al. Washington, D.C.: U.S. Department of the Interior, National Register Bulletin 30. 29–30.

Tishler, William H., and Erik Brynildson. 1992. "The Namur Belgian-American Rural Historic District," *The Alliance for Historic Preservation Newsletter* (Spring). 4.

Tishler, William H., and Erik Brynildson. 1992. "A Landmark Decision: Belgian Settlement in Door County Gains National Recognition," *Voyageur* 9:1. 50–55.

Folk Architecture: Czechs (Bohemians)

Tishler, William H. 1997. "The Vernacular Architecture of Bohemian Immigrants in East-Central Wisconsin," in *Encyclopedia of Vernacular Architecture of the World,* ed. Paul Oliver. Oxford: Blackwell. 1857–58.

Folk Architecture: Finns

Alanen, Arnold, and William H. Tishler. 1980. "Finnish Farmstead Organization in Old and New World Settings," *Journal of Cultural Geography* 1. 66–81.

Kaups, Matti and Cotton Mather. 1963. "The Finnish Sauna: A Cultural Index to Settlement," *Annals of the Association of American Geographers* 53:4. 494–504.

Perrin, Richard W. E. 1961. "Log Sauna and the Finnish Farmstead: Transplanted Architectural Idioms in Northern Wisconsin," *Wisconsin Magazine of History* 44. 284–86.

Roescher, Oscar. 1941–1942. "The Davidson Mill," *Wisconsin Magazine of History* 25. 329–30.

Tishler, William H. 1979. "The Finnish Farmsteads at Old World Wisconsin," *Architectural Digest* (May). 78–85.

Folk Architecture: Germans

Bastian, Robert. 1975. "Southeastern Pennsylvania and Central Wisconsin Barns: Examples of Independent Parallel Development," *Professional Geographer* 27. 200–204.

Calkins, Charles F., and Marty Perkins. 1980. "The Pomeranian Stable of Southeastern Wisconsin," *Concordia Historical Institute Quarterly* 53:3. 121–25.

Perrin, Richard W. E. 1959. "Fachwerkbau Houses in Wisconsin," *Journal of the Society of Architectural Historians* 18:1. 29–33.

Perrin, Richard W. E. 1959. "A Fachwerk Church in Wisconsin," *Wisconsin Magazine of History* 43. 29–33.

Perrin, Richard W. E. 1960–1961. "German Timber Farmhouses in Wisconsin: Terminal Examples of a Thousand Year Old Tradition," *Wisconsin Magazine of History* 44. 199–202.

Tishler, William H. 1986. "Fachwerk Construction in the German Settlements of Wisconsin," *Winterthur Portfolio* 21. 275–292.

Tishler, William H. 1986. "German Immigrants Brought Old World to Midwest," *Preservation News* (October). 12–13.

Tishler, William H. 1986. "Fachwerk Vernacular Houses," *Old House Journal* (August). 314.

Tishler, William H. 1986. "Midwest Germans," in *America's Architectural Roots*, ed. Dell Upton. Washington, D.C.: The Preservation Press, 1986. 142–47.

Tishler, William H. 1989. "The North German Fachwerk House in Wisconsin: A Profile of Artifact Shelter Transfer and Adaptation," in *Perspectives in Vernacular Architecture III*, ed. Thomas Carter and Bernard Herman. Columbia: University of Missouri Press. 238.

Tishler, William H., and C. Witmer. 1986. "The House Barns of East-Central Wisconsin," in *Perspectives in Vernacular Architecture II*, ed. Camille Wells. Annapolis: Vernacular Architecture Forum. 102–10.

Folk Architecture: Norwegians

Bakken, Reidar. 1994. "Acculturation in Buildings and Farmsteads in Coon Valley, Wisconsin, from 1850–1930," in *Material Culture and People's Art Among the Norwegians in America*, ed. Marion John Nelson. Northfield, Minnesota: Norwegian-American Historical Association. 73–91.

Lee, Charles R. 1984. "The Engum House at Norskedalen," *Wisconsin Academy Review* 30:2. 22–23.

Perrin, Richard W. E. 1960–1961. "An Architectural Remnant of Old Muskego: John Bergen's Log House," *Wisconsin Magazine of History* 44. 12–14.

Raitz, Karl B. 1975. "The Wisconsin Tobacco Shed: A Key to Ethnic Settlement and Diffusion," *Landscape* 20:1. 32–37.

Selkurt, Claire. 1985. "The Domestic Architecture and Cabinetry of Luther Valley," *Norwegian-American Studies and Records* 30. 247–72.

Tishler, William H. 1986. "Early Buildings, Farmsteads and Landscapes in the Coon Valley Norwegian Settlement of Wisconsin: A Research Report With Recommendations for Historic Preservation." Madison: Department of Landscape Architecture, University of Wisconsin. Pamphlet, 64 pages.

Tishler, William H. 1992. "Norwegian Folk Architecture and Settlement in Wisconsin," in *To Build a New Land: Studies in Ethnic Landscapes of North America*, ed. Allen G. Noble. Baltimore: Johns Hopkins University Press. 226–41.

Folk Architecture: Swiss

Tishler, William H. 1997. "Swiss Vernacular Architecture of South-Central Wisconsin," in *Encyclopedia of Vernacular Architecture of the World*, ed. Paul Oliver. Oxford: Blackwell. 1871–72.

Tishler, William H., and J. Eisely. 1989. "The Honey Creek Swiss Settlement in Sauk County: An Expression of Cultural Norms in the Rural Wisconsin Landscape," *Wisconsin Magazine of History* 73:1. 3–20.

Folk Architecture: Construction Techniques

Jenkins, Paul B. 1923–1924. "A 'Stove-Wood' House," *Wisconsin Magazine of History* 7. 189–95.

Perkins, Martin C. 1987. "Cobblestone Architecture: A Southeastern Wisconsin Example of Western New York's Masonry Building Tradition," *Pioneer America Society Transactions* 10. 1–8.

Perrin, Richard W. E. 1974. "Wisconsin's Stovewood Architecture," *Wisconsin Academy Review* 20:3. 2–8.

Tishler, William H. 1979. "Stovewood Architecture." *Landscape* 23. 28–32.

Tishler, William H. 1982. "Stovewood Construction in the Upper Midwest and Canada: A Regional Vernacular Architectural Tradition," in *Perspectives in Vernacular Architecture*, ed. Camille Wells. Annapolis: Vernacular Architecture Forum. 125–36.

Folk Architecture: Outdoor Museums

Bigler, Brian, and Lynn Mudrey. 1992. *The Norway Building at the 1893 Chicago World's Fair*. Blue Mounds, Wisc.: Little Norway.

Brown, Charles E. 1943. "Log Building Museums of Wisconsin," *The Wisconsin Archeologist* 25:3. 46–48.

Perrin, Richard W. E. 1975. *Outdoor Museums*. Milwaukee: Milwaukee Public Museum.

Smedal, Elaine, and Anne Tressler. 1948. "Little Norway." *School Arts* 47:7. 221–22.

Tishler, William H. 1989. "Ein Freilichtmuseum nach deatschem vorbild: Old World Wisconsin," *Globus* (January–February). 20–21.

Tishler, William H., et al. 1973. *Old World Wisconsin: An Outdoor Ethnic Museum.* Madison: State Historical Society of Wisconsin.

Folk Art: Sacred Sites and Visionary Environments

Calkins, Charles F. 1992. "Cobblestone Tombstones in Door County, Wisconsin," *PAST: Pioneer America Society Transactions* 15. 49–58.

Cole, Wanda G. 1978. *Grass Roots Art: Wisconsin.* Oshkosh, Wisc.: Office of University Publications, University of Wisconsin-Oshkosh.

Niles, Susan A. 1997. *The Dickeyville Grotto: The Vision of Father Mathias Wernerus.* Jackson: University Press of Mississippi.

Perret, Maurice E. 1975. "Cemeteries: A Source of Geographic Information," *Transactions of the Wisconsin Academy of Sciences, Arts and Letters* 63. 139–61.

Perret, Maurice E. 1975. "Tombstones and Epitaphs: Journeying Through Wisconsin Cemeteries," *Wisconsin Academy Review* 21:2. 2–6.

Stone, Lisa. 1991. *The Art of Fred Smith: The Wisconsin Concrete Park.* Park Falls, Wisc.: Self-Published.

Stone, Lisa, and Jim Zanzi. 1993. *Sacred Spaces and Other Places: A Guide to Grottos and Sculptural Environments in the Upper Midwest.* Chicago: The School of the Art Institute of Chicago Press.

Stuttgen, Joanne Raetz. 1992. "Enlarging Life Through Miniatures: Bill Austin's Roadside Carnival," *Western Folklore* 5:3–4. 303–15.

Folk Arts and Crafts: Overviews

Foote, Anne, and Elaine Smedal. 1948. *Decorative Art in Wisconsin: A Portfolio of Serigraphs.* Madison: Screen Art Company.

Gilmore, Janet C. 1998. "Marking Time, Honoring Connections, Recording Meaning," in Teske 1998. 28–47.

Leary, James P. 1983. "Wisconsin Crafts: A Report from the Field," in *Traditional Craftsmanship in America,* ed. Charles Camp. Washington, D.C.: National Council for the Traditional Arts. 39.

Leary, James P. 1990. "Wisconsin Folk Musical Instruments: Objects, Sounds, and Symbols," in Teske 1990. 11–28.

Leary, James P. 1994. "Ethnic Crafts and Rural Life: Subsistence, Ceremony, Symbolism," in Teske, 1994. 15–19.

Leary, James P. 1997. "Leaving Skibbereen: Exile and Ethnicity in Wisconsin Folklore," in Teske, 1998. 48–63.

Leary, James P., and Janet C. Gilmore. 1987. "Cultural Forms, Personal Visions," in Teske, 1987. 13–22.

Leeds-Hurwitz, Wendy. 1984. "Folk Toys in the Milwaukee Public Museum," *Wisconsin Academy Review* 30:2. 19–21.

Olson, Ruth. 1997. " 'Up North': Regionalism, Resources, and Self-Reliance," in Teske 1998. 64–78.

Schereck, William C. 1956. "Collecting Wisconsin Ethnic Material," *Wisconsin Magazine of History* 39:4. 263–65.

Teske, Robert T. 1987. *From Hardanger to Harleys: A Survey of Wisconsin Folk Art.* Sheboygan, Wisc.: John Michael Kohler Arts Center.

Teske, Robert T. 1990. *In Tune With Tradition: Wisconsin Folk Musical Instruments.* Cedarburg, Wisc.: Cedarburg Cultural Center.

Teske, Robert T. 1994. *Passed to the Present: Folk Arts Along Wisconsin's Ethnic Settlement Trail.* Cedarburg, Wisc.: Cedarburg Cultural Center.

Teske, Robert T. 1998. *Wisconsin Folk Art: A Sesquicentennial Celebration.* Cedarburg, Wisc.: Cedarburg Cultural Center.

Whyte, Bertha Kitchell. 1961. *Wisconsin Heritage.* Newton, Mass.: Charles T. Branford.

Whyte, Bertha Kitchell. 1971. *Craftsmen of Wisconsin.* Racine, Wisc.: Western Publishing.

Zwolinski, Mary A. 1994. "Ethnic Identity and Urban Life in Southeastern Wisconsin," in Teske 1994. 21–26.

Folk Arts and Crafts: Woodland Indians

Apfelbaum, Ben. 1990. "Fish Decoys: A Native American Craft," *Clarion* 15:1. 46–49.

Carter, B. F. 1933. "The Weaving Technic of Winnebago Bags," *The Wisconsin Archeologist* 12. 33–47.

Densmore, Frances. 1929. "Chippewa Customs," *Bureau of American Ethnology* 86. 1–204; reprinted in 1979 (St. Paul: Minnesota Historical Society Press), with an introduction by Nina Marchetti Archabal.

Hall, Robert L. 1989. "The Material Symbols of Winnebago Sky and Earth Moieties," in *The Meanings of Things: Material Culture and Symbolic Expression,* ed. Ian Hodder. Boston: Unwin Hyman. 178–84.

Kimball, Art, and Brad Kimball. 1988. *Fish Decoys of the Lac Du Flambeau Ojibway.* Boulder Junction, Wisc.: Aardvark Publications.

Kuhm, Herbert W. 1961. "Use of Native Herbs by Wisconsin Indians," *The Wisconsin Archeologist* 42:3. 97–132.

Olson, Gordon L. 1977. *Beads: Their Use By Upper Great Lakes Indians.* Grand Rapids, Mich.: Grand Rapids Public Museum.

Ritzenthaler, Robert. 1950. "The Chippewa Indian Method of Securing and Tanning Deerskin," *The Wisconsin Archeologist* 28:1. 6–13.

Ritzenthaler, Robert. 1950. "Building a Chippewa Indian Birchbark Canoe," *Bulletin of the Public Museum of the City of Milwaukee* 19:2. 1–47.

Schoewe, Charles G. 1932. "Uses of Wood and Bark Among Wisconsin Indians," *The Wisconsin Archeologist* 11:4. 148–52.

Skinner, Alanson. 1921. "Material Culture of the Menomini," *Indian Notes and Monographs* 20. 1–478.

Whiteford, Andrew Hunter. 1977. "Fiber Bags of the Great Lakes Indians." *American Indian Art Magazine* 2:3. 52–64.

Whiteford, Andrew Hunter, and Nora Rogers. 1994. "Woven Mats of the Western Great Lakes." *American Indian Art Magazine* 19:3. 58–65.

Folk Arts and Crafts: Finns

Abell, Alma. 1948. "Finns in Douglas County." *School Arts* 47:7. 244–45. Birchbark baskets, carding and spinning.

Renken, Arlene. 1986. "Symbolic Ethnicity in the Rag Rug Weaving Craft of Finnish-Americans." Madison: University of Wisconsin, Ph.D. dissertation in curriculum and instruction.

Folk Arts and Crafts: Hmong

Cubbs, Joanne. 1986. *Hmong Art: Tradition and Change.* Sheboygan, Wisc.: John Michael Kohler Arts Center.

Folk Arts and Crafts: Norwegians

Alexander, Martha. 1984. "Norwegian Nineteenth Century Material Heritage in Stoughton, Wisconsin," *Wisconsin Academy Review* 30:2. 31–33.

Anderson, Kristin M. 1985. "Per Lysne, Immigrant Rosemaler." Minneapolis: University of Minnesota, Ph.D. thesis in art history.

Anderson, Kristin M. 1994. "Altars in the Norwegian-American Church: An Opportunity for Folk Expression," in Nelson 1994. 199–226.

Bohn, Tora. 1956. "Norwegian Folk Art in America," *Norwegian American Studies and Records* 9. 62–88.

Colburn, Carol. 1990. "Immigrant Handweaving in the Upper Midwest," in *Norwegian Immigrant Clothing and Textiles,* ed. Catherine Cole. Edmonton, Alberta: Prairie Costume Society. 43–64.

Colburn, Carol. 1994. "Well, I Wondered When I Saw You, What All These New Clothes Meant," in Nelson 1994. 118–55.

Colburn, Carol. 1995. "Norwegian Folk Dress in America," in Nelson 1995. 157–69.

Ellingsgard, Nils. 1993. *Norwegian Rose Painting in America.* Decorah, Iowa: Vesterheim.

Ellingsgard, Nils. 1995. "Rosemaling: a Folk Art in Migration," in Nelson 1995. 190–94.

Gilbertson, Donald E., and James F. Richards, Jr. 1975. *A Treasury of Norwegian Folk Art in America.* Osseo, Wisc.: Tin Chicken Antiques.

Haugen, Einar. 1947–1948. "A Norwegian Calendar Stick in Wisconsin," *Wisconsin Magazine of History* 31. 145–67.

Henning, Darrell, Marion John Nelson, and Roger L. Welsch, eds. 1978. *Norwegian-American Wood Carving of the Upper Midwest.* Decorah, Iowa: Vesterheim.

Hibbard, Carlin. 1994. "S. O. Lund, A Community Artist from Norway," in Nelson 1994. 176–98.

Lovoll, Odd S. 1995. "Emigration and Settlement Patterns as They Relate to the Migration of Norwegian Folk Art," in Nelson 1995. 125–32.

Martin, Philip. 1989. *Rosemaling in the Upper Midwest.* Mount Horeb, Wisc.: Wisconsin Folk Museum.

Nelson, Marion John. 1976. "Folk Art among the Norwegians in America," in *Norwegian Influence on the Upper Midwest,* ed. Harald S. Naess. Duluth: Continuing Education and Extension, University of Minnesota-Duluth. 71–92.

Nelson, Marion John. 1978. "Norwegian-American Woodcarving in Historic and Aesthetic Context," in Henning, et al., eds., 1978. 12–20.

Nelson, Marion John. 1989. *Norway in America.* Decorah, Iowa: Vesterheim.

Nelson, Marion John. 1994. *Material Culture and People's Art Among the Norwegians in America.* Northfield, Minnesota: Norwegian-American Historical Association.

Nelson, Marion John. 1995. *Norwegian Folk Art: The Migration of a Tradition.* New York: Abbeville Press.

Smedal, Elaine, and Anne Tressler. 1948. *Norwegian Design in Wisconsin: A Portfolio of Serigraphs.* Madison: Campus Publications, University of Wisconsin.

Folk Arts and Crafts: Occupational and Domestic Traditions

Garthwaite, Chester. 1990. *Threshing Days: The Farm Paintings of Lavern Kammerude*, with an introduction by James P. Leary Mount Horeb, Wisc.: Wisconsin Folk Museum.

Nickels, Pat L. 1991. "Mary McElwain: Quilter and Quilt Businesswoman," *Uncoverings* 12 98–117.

Shackelford, Sandra. 1996. "Grand Duke of the Hobos," *Voyageur: Northeast Wisconsin Historical Review* 13:1. 4–13. Adolph Vandertie, Green Bay whittler.

Vandertie, Adolph and Patrick Spielman. 1995. *Hobo and Tramp Art Carving: An Authentic American Folk Tradition*. New York: Sterling.

Foodways

Allen, Terese. 1995. *Wisconsin Food Festivals*. Amherst, Wisc.: Amherst Press.

Conlin, Joseph R. 1979. "Old Boy, Did You Get Enough Pie?: A Social History of Food in Logging Camps." *Journal of Forest History* 23:4. 164–85.

Hachten, Harva. 1981. *The Flavor of Wisconsin*. Madison: State Historical Society of Wisconsin.

Jenks, Albert E. 1902. "The Wild-Rice Gatherers of the Upper Lakes: A Study in American Primitive Economics," *19th Annual Report of the Bureau of American Ethnology, 1900*. Washington, D.C.: Smithsonian Institution. 1013–37.

Schuette, H. A., and Sybil C. Schuette. 1935. "Maple Sugar: A Bibliography of Early Records," *Transactions of the Wisconsin Academy of Science* 29. 209–36.

Stuttgen, Joanne Raetz. 1993. *Cafe Wisconsin: a Guide to Wisconsin's Down Home Cafes*. Minocqua, Wisc.: Heartland Press.

Vennum, Thomas, Jr. 1988. *Wild Rice and the Ojibway People*. St. Paul: Minnesota Historical Society Press.

Documentary Sound Recordings

Accordions in the Cutover: Field Recordings From Lake Superior's South Shore, produced by James P. Leary (Ashland and Mount Horeb, Wisc.: Northland College and Wisconsin Folklife Center), double LP with booklet. Includes performances from the late 1970s and early 1980s by Croatian, Czech, Finnish, Norwegian, Polish, Slovak, and Swedish instrumentalists and singers from northern Wisconsin and the western Upper Peninsula of Michigan.

Ach Ya! Traditional German-American Music from Wisconsin, co-produced by Philip Martin and James P. Leary (Mount Horeb, Wisc.: Wisconsin Folklife Center), double LP FVF 301, with liner notes. Field recordings from the mid-1980s, and reissues of earlier commercial and field recordings by a broad range of the state's German-American performers.

Across the Fields: Traditional Norwegian-American Music from Wisconsin, produced by Philip Martin (Mount Horeb; Wisc.: Wisconsin Folklife Center), LP and cassette FVF 201, with liner/insert notes. Field and studio recordings from the late 1970s and early 1980s, with an emphasis on instrumental dance tunes performed on fiddle and button accordion.

American Warriors: Songs for Indian Veterans, coproduced by Thomas Vennum, Jr. and Mickey Hart (Salem, Mass.: Rykodisk), compact disk RCD 10370, with booklet insert. Field recordings of honor songs, most from the mid-1990s, commemorating the participation of American Indians in America's wars; includes performances by Ho-Chunk (Winnebago), Menominee, and Ojibwe singers from Wisconsin.

Deep Polka: Dance Music from the Midwest, produced by Richard March (Washington, D.C.: Smithsonian Folkways), compact disc SFCD 40088, with booklet insert. Studio recordings from the 1990s by Wisconsin bands in Croatian, Czech, Finnish, German, Norwegian, Polish, and Slovenian polka traditions.

Down Home Dairyland, coproduced by James P. Leary and Richard March (Madison: University of Wisconsin Extension), forty half-hour radio programs on twenty cassettes, with accompanying 230-page book by Leary and March. Each program combines commentary, interviews with performers, and commercial and field recordings of Wisconsin and Upper Midwestern traditional and ethnic music. Programs include: "The Many Forms of Wisconsin Indian Music," "Woodland Indian Fiddles and Jigs," "The Tunes of String and Bow,"

"Couderay Jig in the Buckhorn," "Wendy Whitford: The Soul of Wisconsin's Country Music," "The Goose Island Ramblers," "Wisconsin's Ethnic Country Music," "Snow Country Hillbillies:" "Northern Country Music," "German-American Music in Wisconsin," "*Ach Ja!* The Syl Groeschl Story," "Music Before Milking: The Very Musical Brueggen Family," "The Minnesota Dutchmen," "Humorous Scandinavian Dialect Songs," "Ole in Dairyland:" "Scandinavian Ethnic Humor," "Finnish-American Music in Superiorland," "Green Fields of Wisconsin: Irish Music in the Badger State," "From *Masopust* to *Cesky Den:*" Czech and Slovak Music in Wisconsin, "The Manitowoc Bohemian Sound," *Wallonie en Porte:* Door County Belgians," "The Polish Fiddlers of Posen," "Old Time Music in Stevens Point," "Pulaski is a Polka Town," "The Tamburitza," "*Sjajno More* ("Shining Sea"): Tamburitza from Gary to Sheboygan," "Echoes of Slovenia," "The Milwaukee Polka," "The Hartmann-Meisner Polka Dynasty," "Old-Time Dance Music in Madison," "Swissconsin," "Women Polka Band Leaders," "Midwestern Ethnic Radio," "In Tune With Tradition: Wisconsin Instrument Builders," "The Accordions," "The Concertina," "Crying Holy Unto the Lord: Midwestern Sacred Musical Traditions," "Gospel in Wisconsin," "*Borinquen Suelo Querido:* Puerto Rican Music in Wisconsin," "The East in the North: Southeast Asian Music in Wisconsin," "Small Labels, Big Music," and "Saving the Sounds of Tradition."

Finseth, Leonard. *Scandinavian-American Old Time*, produced by LeRoy Larson and Robert Andresen (Minneapolis: Banjar Records), LP BR-1834, with liner notes. Studio recordings from the late 1970s by a Norwegian old-time fiddler from Mondovi.

Folk Music from Wisconsin, produced by Helene Stratman-Thomas (Washington, D.C.: Library of Congress), LP AFS L55, with booklet. Field recordings from the 1940s of ballad and folksong singers and lumber camp instrumentalists, with an emphasis on Anglo-American traditions.

The Goose Island Ramblers, *Midwest Ramblin*, produced by James P. Leary (Mount Horeb, Wisc.: Wisconsin Folk Museum), cassette 9001, with insert notes. Studio recording from 1990 by an eclectic "Norwegian polkabilly band" from the Madison area whose distinct regional repertoire includes old time country ballads, fiddle tunes, polkas, dialect songs, and comic novelty performances.

Honor the Earth Powwow: Songs of the Great Lakes Indians, coproduced by Thomas Vennum, Jr. and Mickey Hart (Salem, Mass.: Rykodisc), cassette and compact disk RACS 0199 or RCD 10199, with booklet insert. Field recordings from the 1990 Honor the Earth Powwow held by Wisconsin's Lac Courte Oreilles Ojibwe, includes performances by Ho-Chunk (Winnebago), Menominee, and Ojibwe drum groups.

Johnson, Bernard. *It's a Mighty Pretty Waltz*, produced by Thomas E. Barden (Gillingham, Wisc.: Ocooch Mountain Records), LP with booklet. Studio recordings from 1983 by a Richland County Anglo-American old time fiddler whose repertoire also includes Czech and Norwegian tunes.

Les Wallons d'Amerique (Wisconsin), produced by Françoise Lempereur (Belgium: Centre d'Action Culturelle de la Coummunauté d'Expression Francaise), LP FM 33010, with booklet in French and English. Field recordings from the 1980s of Walloon Belgian musicians and singers from northeastern Wisconsin.

Polkaland Records, run by Greg Leider of Fredonia, Wisconsin, offers a broad array of performers from Wisconsin's various polka traditions. Polkaland's liner notes generally lack historical and contextual information, although the numerous reissues of Bohemian polka music by the Romy Gosz Band are commendable exceptions.

Scandinavian-American Folk Dance Music, Vol. 2, produced by LeRoy Larson (Minneapolis:

Banjar Records), LP BR-1830, with liner notes. Diverse performances of Wisconsin Norwegian music from the late 1970s, including the tunes of Leonard Finseth and Otto
Rindlisbacher.

Songs of the Chippewa, produced by Frances Densmore (Washington, D.C.: Library of Congress), LP AFS L22, with booklet. Field recordings from the 1920s made among Minnesota's Ojibwe and at Wisconsin's Lac du Flambeau reservation.

Songs of the Menominee, Mandan and Hidatsa, produced by Frances Densmore (Washington,
D.C.: Library of Congress)., LP AFS L33, with booklet. Field recordings of Menominee
singers from the 1920s and 1930s that include an array of hunting, medicine, and war
songs.

Swissconsin My Homeland, produced by Philip Martin (Mount Horeb, Wisc.: Wisconsin Folk
Museum), cassette 8801, with insert notes. Recordings of Wisconsin Swiss musicians and
singers from the late 1980s, along with reissues of commercial recordings from the 1920s
through the early 1960s.

Tunes from the Amerika Trunk, produced by Philip Martin (Mount Horeb, Wisc.: Wisconsin
Folklife Center), LP and cassette FVF 202, with liner/insert notes. Mid-1980s studio recordings of Wisconsin Norwegian-American dance musicians.

The Wisconsin Patchwork, produced by Judy Rose (Madison: University of Wisconsin, Department of Continuing Education in the Arts), thirteen half-hour programs on seven cassettes,
with accompanying sixty-nine-page book by James P. Leary. Based upon the 1940s field
recordings of Wisconsin folk music by Helene Stratman-Thomas for the Library of
Congress, the programs include: "Introduction," "Fiddlers," "Songs of the Homeland,"
"Putting Down Roots," "Other Instruments," "Some Lovely Old Songs," "Lumbercamps
and Rivers," "Work Songs," "The Recording Process," "Ensembles," "A Mixed Bag,"
"Hymnody," and "A Final Program."

Wolf River Songs, produced by Sidney Robertson Cowell (New York: Folkways), LP FE 4001,
with booklet. Field recordings from the early 1950s of northern Wisconsin's Ford-Walker
family, whose extensive repertoire favored Anglo-Celtic and lumber camp songs.

Films and Videos

The Drummaker, produced by Thomas Vennum, Jr. 1974 (Washington, D.C.: Smithsonian Institution, Office of Folklife Programs). Regarding the making of a dance drum by Lac
Courte Oreilles Ojibwe drummaker Bill Bineshi Baker. The film, also available in video
format, complements Vennum's monograph, *The Ojibwa Dance Drum*, which includes a
transcription of comments made in the film by drummaker Baker.

Ethel Kvalheim, Rosemaler, produced by Jocelyn Riley. 1992 (Madison: Her Own Words). A
profile of Stoughton's Ethel Kvalheim, whose Norwegian folk paintings have won acco-
lades from the King of Norway and the National Endowment for the Arts.

Her Mother Before Her: Winnebago Women's Stories of Their Mothers and Grandmothers, produced by Jocelyn Riley, 1992 (Madison: Her Own Words).

Medicine Fiddle, produced by Michael Loukinen. 1991 (Marquette, Mich.: Up North Films).
Menominee and Ojibwe fiddlers and step dancers from the late 1980s whose eclectic métis
traditions are linked to the fur trade and the lumber camps.

Mountain Wolf Woman: 1884–1960, produced by Jocelyn Riley. 1990 (Madison: Her Own

Words). Profile of a Ho-Chunk (Winnebago) woman, based on Nancy O. Lurie's biography, *Mountain Wolf Woman.*

Naamikaaged: Dancer for the People, produced by Thomas Vennum, Jr. 1997 (Washington, D.C.: Smithsonian Institution Office of Folklife Programs and Cultural Studies). Follows a young Ojibwe, Richard LaFernier, as he sets up his tent, honors his ancestors, dresses and paints himself, and sings at northern Wisconsin powwows at Bad River and Lac Courte Oreilles.

Polka from Cuca, produced by Dave Erickson. 1994 (Spring Green, Wisc.: Ootek Productions). Combines interviews, performances, and dance footage of German, Norwegian, Polish, Slovenian, and Swiss polka musicians in action in 1994 at the River View Ballroom in Sauk City and at Cheese Days in Monroe. the video also features Cuca Records, founded by Jim Kirchstein in Sauk City, for whom all the musicians recorded.

Winnebago Women: Songs and Stories, produced by Jocelyn Riley. 1992 (Madison: Her Own Words).

Wisconsin Powwow, produced by Thomas Vennum, Jr. 1997 (Washington, D.C.: Smithsonian Institution Office of Folklife Programs and Cultural Studies). A documentary of an early 1990s powwow held by Wisconsin's Bad River Ojibwe. This production, emphasizing the participants' perspective, forms a two video package with *Naamikaaged* (above) and is accompanied by a 40-page booklet.

Yodel: Straight from the Soul, produced by Lori Maass Vidlak. 1996. (Bennet, Neb.: Good Earth Production). Beyond western and blue yodelers, this video offers interviews and performances by Austrian and Swiss yodelers from Wisconsin.

All place names are in Wisconsin unless otherwise indicated.